FAMILY THERAPY

FAMILY THERAPY

MODELS AND TECHNIQUES

Janice M. Rasheed
Loyola University Chicago

Mikal N. Rasheed
Chicago State University

James A. Marley
Loyola University Chicago

Los Angeles | London | New Delhi
Singapore | Washington DC

For information:

SAGE Publications, Inc.
2455 Teller Road
Thousand Oaks, California 91320
E-mail: order@sagepub.com

SAGE Publications Ltd.
1 Oliver's Yard
55 City Road
London EC1Y 1SP
United Kingdom

SAGE Publications India Pvt. Ltd.
B 1/I 1 Mohan Cooperative Industrial Area
Mathura Road, New Delhi 110 044
India

SAGE Publications Asia-Pacific Pte. Ltd.
33 Pekin Street #02-01
Far East Square
Singapore 048763

Printed in the United States of America

Library of Congress Cataloging-in-Publication Data

Rasheed, Janice M. (Janice Matthews)
Family therapy : models and techniques / Janice M. Rasheed, Mikal N. Rasheed, James A Marley.
    p. ; cm.
Includes bibliographical references and index.
ISBN 978-1-4129-0574-9 (cloth : alk. paper)
   1. Family psychotherapy. I. Rasheed, Mikal N. (Mikal Nazir) II. Marley, James A. III. Title.
   [DNLM: 1. Family Therapy—methods. 2. Family—psychology. 3. Models, Psychological.
4. Psychological Theory. WM 430.5.F2 R224f 2011]

RC488.5.R355 2011
616.89′156—dc22   2010020637

This book is printed on acid-free paper.

10   11   12   13   14   10 9 8 7 6 5 4 3 2 1

Acquisitions Editor:	Kassie Graves
Editorial Assistant:	Veronica K. Novak
Production Editor:	Libby Larson
Copy Editor:	Melinda Masson
Typesetter:	C&M Digitals (P) Ltd.
Proofreader:	Charlotte J. Waisner
Indexer:	Sheila Bodell
Cover Designer:	Gail Buschman
Marketing Manager:	Stephanie Adams

CONTENTS

PREFACE

There was one driving purpose that inspired the writing of this book, and that was to write a family therapy text that would prepare students to actually begin the practice of family therapy. We wanted students to have a comprehensive and working knowledge of the field that would prepare them to become family therapists with the supervision of a professionally trained family therapist. Our goal in the formulation of the outline and content of this textbook was to go beyond a general overview of models and present a step-by-step description of theories, concepts, skills, and techniques of each family therapy model that is extensive and complete in its presentation and discussion. In addition, in order to facilitate a depth of understanding of each model, the authors have also provided a history of each model (background, origin, and leading figures), as well as a description of the conceptual and theoretical underpinnings.

In essence, this is a student-driven and student-oriented book written for students, trainees, and practitioners who seek to become family therapists (and/or to enhance their understanding of the practice of family therapy). Every aspect of this text considers the content that is needed to provide training for practice in this field. Our philosophy is that instructors (educators, trainers, and supervisors) should seek to develop their students and trainees as family therapists to whom they would actually go for their own family therapy. This should be the litmus test in preparing students for family therapy, and this book seeks to facilitate that goal.

This textbook is written in a user-friendly manner and is easy to understand in its straightforward presentation of content. In addition, the language used in this book is not overly technical and convoluted, and the text was written for students and trainees of family therapy. Hence, the reader is not overwhelmed and/or distracted by excessive jargon that does not contribute to the understanding and comprehensiveness of the material. This book is also practical while including key content that is needed for a comprehensive coverage of the material. Researchers, theorists, and academicians will appreciate the comprehensiveness of the content; however, this text was written for students and trainees of family therapy.

This comprehensive text presents the history of family therapy, a systems/ developmental perspective on families, a description of families in transition and alternative family patterns, a discussion of ethnicity and family life, the impact of stress and trauma on families, clinical issues that are unique to family therapy practice, major models of family therapy (with each model presenting extensive case illustrations of a family interview; more on this feature is discussed below), and the implications of family therapy research on family therapy practice.

This book on family therapy is unique in several respects in that we address gaps in family therapy literature. The first of these gaps is that our text covers (in detail) generic clinical issues that are specific to family therapy practice but are not addressed in models of family therapy. There is a significant amount of literature on general clinical issues and the implication for individual therapy (engagement, goal setting, resistance and termination, etc.). However, the literature on general clinical issues and their implication for family therapy is sparse and scattered. In Chapter 11 our book provides an expanded coverage of these issues: pre-session planning (planning for the initial interview, etc.), initial phase issues (engagement, therapist's use of self, goal setting, etc.), middle phase issues (managing conflict and resistance, etc.), and end phase issues (termination, relapse prevention, the follow-up plan, etc.)—to name a few. These clinical skills and techniques are not specially addressed and/or not addressed in sufficient detail but are common across models of family therapy. This chapter outlines these skills to assist the family therapist in managing the complexities of family interaction and intervention.

Virginia Satir is considered to be one of the pioneer family therapists. Her communications/humanistic family therapy model is intrinsic and speaks to the heart of interventions with families—their communication. To some extent, other models of family therapy address the fundamental issue of communication between and among family members; however, their focus and philosophies may be different. That being said, this book presents a complete description of Satir's family therapy model. Her philosophy (key to understanding Satir's model), along with her concepts, theories, and techniques, is presented in full. This endeavor was a labor of love in that the authors are excited about the possibility of bringing Satir's family therapy model back to "center stage."

Case illustrations are an important part of family therapy training. The student trainee will especially enjoy the format in which we chose to illuminate aspects of each model of family therapy. At the end of each chapter on models of family therapy (Chapters 4–10) there is a clinical interview of a family therapy session that also includes highlights of specific stages, issues, concepts, theories, and techniques. This approach, providing the reader with an example of a family interview, is intended to facilitate the reader's understanding of key features of each model and how they are applied to the case vignette. This format illustrates and reinforces the understanding of each family therapy model.

One of the challenges for instructors and trainers of family therapy is locating relevant articles that highlight various issues in family therapy that are not typically covered in basic textbooks on family therapy. There is a *Reader* that accompanies this textbook, which is a compilation of articles addressing issues that are intended to extend and deepen the student trainee's understanding of the content in a given chapter. Each article has editorial comments that highlight the utility and relevance of the content to the particular chapter. This *Reader* contributes to the comprehensiveness and uniqueness of this text on family therapy and facilitates the overall education and training of future family therapists.

In summary, the writing of this textbook on family therapy has been a joyous occasion for the authors—all of whom currently teach, train in, and practice family therapy. As family therapy practitioners and instructors we have become acutely aware of the training needs of family therapists. We sought to write a book that embodies all the features of a textbook that we have needed over the years. We are excited about the opportunity to share with you the collective culmination of our knowledge that we believe is important to the family therapy training process.

Janice Rasheed

Mikal Rasheed

James Marley

ACKNOWLEDGMENTS

The authors are deeply grateful to the Marley and Rasheed families for their ongoing and unconditional support in the writing of this book. A special thank-you goes to Leslie and Eliza Marley for all their support and patience during this writing project. We would also like to thank Professor and Dean Jack Wall of the Loyola University Chicago School of Social Work for his encouragement.

The authors are very grateful for the support and assistance received from the SAGE family in the final production of this book (Kassie Graves, Veronica Novak, Aja Baker, Libby Larson, and Melinda Masson). A very special thank-you goes to Kassie Graves for the belief, patience, and guidance that she gave to us, which was critical from start to finish. Kassie, we couldn't have done this without you.

Many thanks to the following reviewers for their insight and suggestions:

Michael Axelman
Santa Clara University

Judith F. Esposito
Elon University

Rosalyn V. Green
Bowie State University

Geoffrey L. Greif
School of Social Work University of Maryland

Margherite Matteis
Regis College

John W. Seymour
Minnesota State University, Mankato

Part I

INTRODUCTION AND BACKGROUND

Chapter 1

THE HISTORY OF FAMILY THERAPY
Conceptual and Clinical Influences

Family therapy as a distinct method of psychotherapy practice did not actually emerge until the early 1960s. However, the conceptual and clinical influences that informed the development of family therapy can be traced to a much earlier period. The task in this chapter is to identify some of the major social factors as well as those conceptual, research, and clinical efforts that nourished the soil for the growth of family therapy as a treatment modality. Whereas the seeds of contemporary family therapy were planted by those engaged in family-centered research on the etiology of schizophrenia in the 1950s, the tillers of this soil were from a much earlier historical period. Beginning with the development of professional social work in the Progressive Era of the late 19th and early 20th centuries, along with the early group work, marriage counseling, and child guidance movements in the early 20th century, the soil from which family therapy was to spring forth was duly cultivated (Becvar & Becvar, 2000; Nichols & Schwartz, 2008; Sayger, Homrich, & Horne, 2000).

This soil was to be enriched in the late 1940s and early 1950s by the development of cybernetics, systems, and communication theory. These theories, informed by concepts from multiple disciplines including sociology, anthropology, and biology, provided powerful theoretical frameworks for a more in-depth understanding of the complexities of family interaction. These theories provided the conceptual framework for much of the early family-centered research on schizophrenia. These research initiatives challenged the dominant psychoanalytic understanding that emotional disorders were of intrapsychic origin by postulating the rather innovative and then novel hypothesis that these disorders were symptomatic of troubled family relationships. It was then up to a group of innovative clinicians in the 1960s who applied this research to psychotherapeutic work with families. Based on their creative and groundbreaking work with families, family therapy truly emerged in the 1970s as a clinical method to address issues of emotional suffering in families.

The history of family therapy also reveals profound paradigm shifts in understanding the causative factors that contribute to emotional disorders. In the following discussion, these paradigm shifts will become evident as we examine the many theoretical and clinical influences on the formation of the varied family therapy models. As we will see in this discussion, the historical development of family therapy reveals initially a challenge to the notion of the *autonomous self* with the systems-based concepts of the *relational self*. We will also see how some contemporary family therapy models are now grounded in the notion of the *narrative self*.

It is without saying that one of the earliest and enduring paradigms for understanding the human self is based on the notion of individualism, self-reliance, or what can be labeled as the autonomous self. This notion of the autonomous self as containing the psychological and structural property of self-agency coupled with the belief in the self's ability to stand independently over and against other selves and its environment has been the foundational assumption of much of the psychology treatment models especially in the first half of the 20th century. Based on the paradigm of the autonomous self, emotional disorders were viewed as symptomatic of a disordered (inner) self. Even though the family unit has always been valued as a basic social institution in society, the family was seen as a collection of individuals or an institution that could either support or impede the development of the *autonomous self*.

There were two significant sociological theories, symbolic interactionism and later structural functional theories that challenged the notion of the autonomous self with the understanding that the human self was embedded in a system of human relationships. With the emergence of systems and communication theories, those theorists and researchers who were giving attention to understanding mental disorders such as schizophrenia confirmed that the human self was indeed a relational and communicating being. And this self is embedded in a system of relational networks, the primary one being the family. This concept of the human self as embedded or as the *relational self* was to be the guiding paradigm for early family therapy. For early family therapists, the source of human emotional suffering was seen as symptomatic of disordered family relationships and/or disordered family communication patterns.

The third paradigm, which reflects a more contemporary and postmodern perspective of the self, is the *narrative self*. This postmodern understanding of the self provides a unique insight into understanding families by giving attention to how family members construct their intrafamilial experiences through language. Language is the means of organizing and structuring life experiences. It is the narrative that individuals construct about their lives that provides them with a sense of personal identity. Narratives further reveal the significance of individuals' lived experience within the context of their social worlds (Gergen, 1999; Polkinghorne, 1988). Here the focus shifts from examining relational interactions and communication patterns to examining the meaning embedded in narrative forms of expression. Human actions and relationships as expressed through narratives or stories are seen as efforts to create meaning out of personal experiences. These efforts at meaning construction are reflected in narratives or stories that give organization and structure to a person or family (Kilpatrick & Holland, 2009). Thus family problems are located within narrative constructions of meaning. The narrative emphasis on "meaning" is further supplemented by a focus on ways in which broader sociopolitical influences impact family and individual narratives.

As the history of family therapy unfolds in this chapter it will be apparent that the following account will be both chronological and thematic. The chronological account will attempt to locate key events and movements in the history of family therapy in terms of a timeline. Yet, as will be seen, there were research efforts, social movements, and clinical initiatives that occurred at the same point in time and were independent of each other. These efforts, movements, and initiatives are joined together by a thematic connection as they were addressing the same clinical, research, or conceptual issues often without mutual awareness. It is the confluence of these events and themes that forms the historical narrative of family therapy.

THE PROGRESSIVE ERA AND EMERGING CONCERNS ABOUT THE FAMILY

The opening chapters of the history of family therapy were written in the late 19th century. Beginning in 1890 and ending at the start of the Great Depression, this era in American history known as the Progressive Era was a time marked by the appearance of a wide range of social and political reform movements. It was during this period that the United States witnessed a dramatic shift from an agrarian-based society to an industrialized urban society. Because of this transition many urban families found themselves coping with an array of issues stemming from rapid social change resulting from the impact of the industrial revolution and rapid urbanization. Social problems such as poverty, increasing social dislocation, immigration, illiteracy, disease, exploited labor, and slum housing adversely impacted the lives of increasing numbers of individuals and families.

Many of these families often found themselves living in crowded tenements with more than one family living in small and rodent-infested quarters. Many individuals, including children, also found themselves working in the highly dangerous, unsafe, and exploitative conditions in the emerging factory system. Living in such marginally economic and otherwise vulnerable conditions these individuals were without the benefit of health protection and coverage for themselves and their families.

These conditions along with the increasing number of European and Asian immigrants generated concern among many Americans about the seeming deterioration of the social and moral fabric of American society. There were those individuals who viewed these changing social conditions with a sense of moral concern and social responsibility. These individuals, later to be labeled as "Progressives," engaged in an array of efforts to bring about social reform in such areas as child labor, worker compensation, health care services, and the responsiveness of local governments to the needs of urban residents.

Photo 1.1 Many families at the turn of the 20th century were beginning to experience the impact of the industrial revolution and rapid urbanization

Source: ©Brand X Pictures//Thinkstock

These reformers, influenced if not inspired by an ideological commitment to the ideas of the potential for social progress, believed that through their reform efforts and initiatives the ills of urban society could be ameliorated. Their efforts were a further expression of a *modernist* view of society. Modernism was descriptive of a period in European culture from the late 19th to the mid 20th century. As an expression of 18th-century European Enlightenment philosophy, modernist thought emphasized a faith in reason, freedom, and social progress. Imbued with an optimistic spirit there was this sense during the Progressive Era that through human reason, science, technology, and political initiatives the ills of society could be understood and ameliorated.

The Emergence of Professional Social Work

The Progressive Era witnessed the emergence of two organizations or movements that herald the beginnings of organized efforts to respond to the needs of those troubled families who became victims of the effects of those rapid social changes borne by urbanization and industrialization. Through the efforts of the Charity Organization Society (COS) and the Settlement House Movement, the concerns about the disruptive influences of urban life on family living became the focus of public interest and social intervention. Each of these movements gave recognition that on some level families required some form of organized and sustained intervention to help them cope with the vicissitudes of urban living. Though both movements were still held captive by the dominant social value placed on individualism and "self-reliance," both the Charity Organization Society and the Settlement House movement began to indirectly challenge this individualistic perspective by their belief that individuals experiencing problems in living might be best understood and helped by being viewed within the context of their family, community, and social, political, and economic environments (Davis, 1973; Janzen, Harris, Jordan, & Franklin, 2006).

Charity Organization Society

Armed with the belief in the Progressive ideology, these early Charity Organization Society staff, called "friendly visitors," attempted to build helping relationships with poor urban families. Their goal was to help these families cope with the stresses of urban living. The focus of help provided by the early friendly visitors was through the provision of in-home charity support and concrete assistance. While such services were obviously needed, these helpers were guided by the belief that a family's failure to cope with the problems of living was as much due to individual character defects and moral failures as to environmental or societal factors.

As the initial work of the friendly visitors was marked by goodwill informed by a parochial and moralistic understanding of human behavior, Mary Richmond, a director of the COS, sought a more systematic method for assessing and understanding family and individual needs. In giving attention to a more in-depth assessment or "social diagnosis" of individual or family needs (Richmond, 1917), she also emphasized the need for supportive counseling of the individuals within their family context. Though Richmond brought the family to the foreground of attention for early social casework diagnosis, her writings did not suggest involving family members as a group in the intervention activities. Still the focus of change remained on the individual though acknowledging that understanding the individual within the context of his or her family was important in developing a social diagnosis.

Settlement House Movement

Whereas the focus of the Charity Organization Society was on the individual within the family, the Settlement House Movement gave attention to the family within the broader environment. The Hull House founded by Jane Addams and Ellen Gates Starr in 1889 viewed family problems as resulting from debilitating environmental conditions. Contrary to the "moral treatment" orientation of the friendly visitors, those within the Settlement House Movement sought to change those societal, city, and neighborhood conditions that had a deleterious impact on family life. As such, this movement shifted the intervention orientation from a sense of "moral responsibility" to one of "social responsibility" (Hull & Mather, 2006). In other words, the concern of the Settlement House workers emphasized increased social and public responsiveness to family and human need rather than addressing defective individual moral character.

Settlement Houses were often set up in immigrant neighborhoods. These community-based settings provided a venue for both individuals and families to learn those life skills that would enable the participants to support their families. These life skills were taught through educational programs, recreation activities, and other forms of social and community involvement. In these various activities the Settlement Houses provided the opportunity for individuals and families to come together for mutual support and assistance. It is important to note that the focus of these activities was more on providing the participants with those life skills that would enable them to better assimilate into a dominant culture that reflected White middle-class values and cultural habits (Hull & Mather, 2006).

THE EARLY RESEARCH ON GROUP DYNAMICS

The activities within the Settlement Houses were often conducted within small informal groups. As such, the use of groups in the Settlement House Movement was a major impetus for the later development of group work as a major modality of helping within professional social work. Concurrent with the use of groups in the early years of professional social work there were a number of social scientists who began to turn their attention to studying group dynamics. For example, in the late 19th century there were studies on the impact of groups on individual behavior (Triplett, 1898). Additional studies on the impact of groups on individual task performance were conducted in the early 1900s (Allport, 1924; Moede, 1920).

In addition to the above studies, there were other social scientists in the 1930s who further examined the influence of groups on individuals. One example is the seminal research conducted by Lewin, Lippett, and White (1939). This work, which examined the influence of groups and group members on different leadership patterns, prompted additional research on such group dynamics including issues such as leadership styles, group productivity, and group decision making. In Lewin's (1946) later research on group dynamics he introduced several key concepts such as roles, norms, and group cohesion that would contribute to understanding the family as a group. Another key insight that emerged from his research was the impact of group dynamics on promoting group members' self-awareness and insight.

One of the major contributions to family therapy that can be gleaned from the early research on group dynamics was the awareness that in order to be effective in working with groups one must have both an understanding of group dynamics and a particular set of skills in conducting small groups. The implication of this awareness was obvious for the field of family therapy. And some early family therapists turned to group therapy and group dynamics as a model for conducting therapy with families.

THE MARRIAGE COUNSELING MOVEMENT

Another precursor to the family therapy movement was the marriage counseling movement in the 1920s. During this period, greater social attention was being given to providing troubled couples with information, support, counseling, and guidance. Though there were no individuals specifically trained as marriage counselors, such counseling was provided by a number of professionals who interfaced with couples as a part of their professional work (Broderick & Schrader, 1981). This diverse group of marriage counselors composed of clergy, lawyers, gynecologists, social workers, and college professors often presented itself to the public as a group of family life specialists. It was not unlikely that these professionals were perceived as specialists in family life, for it was often these professions that couples turned to at significant times in the life of a family—times that included birth, marriage, illness, and death. Many of the couples who sought the services of these counselors were primarily seeking guidance about the everyday facts of marriage and family life rather than help in resolving relationship issues. These counseling efforts included premarital counseling, guidance to newlywed and married couples who were seeking it, and support and information on the legal and social obligations pertaining to marriage (Barker, Kessler, & Lehn, 1984). Much of this "marital counseling" utilized a range of psycho-educational approaches rather than focusing on an exploration of individual psychological dynamics (Broderick & Schrader, 1981).

As marriage counseling began to gain more public recognition and professional status, two physicians, Abraham and Hannah Stone, opened up a marriage consultation center in 1929 and offered professional marriage counseling at the Community Church in New York City. The next efforts at institutionalizing marriage counseling occurred in the 1930s with the formation of the American Institute of Family Relations, the Marriage Counsel of Philadelphia, the Groves Conference on Marriage and Family, and the National Council on Family Relations. Leaders from these two latter organizations formed the American Association for Marriage and Family Therapy in 1942. While the profession of marriage counseling underwent its own professional development into what is now referred to as marriage or couples therapy, this treatment modality shares some of the same history with family therapy.

THE CHILD GUIDANCE MOVEMENT

As with the marriage counseling movement the child guidance movement had its origin in the Progressive Era and the efforts of Clifford Beers, who sought to improve the care and treatment of people in mental hospitals. Beers emerged as a national advocate for mental health reform after 5 years of psychiatric hospitalization in three different mental hospitals. His exposé of the range of abusive and inhumane treatment of patients in mental hospitals began a movement that, fueled by his vision, brought about major changes in legislation and funding for mental health services. One of the outcomes of this movement was a more enlightened understanding of mental illness. This movement challenged the impression that mental illness was an intractable condition while promoting the understanding that mental illness might reflect a range of troubling human behaviors other than those associated with "insanity." These insights were the source for the development of the psychiatric hospitals that provided short-term inpatient care and child guidance clinics that emphasized community-based prevention and treatment of children within the context of their parental relationships (Friedman, 2002). Viewing the parent-child relationship as the nexus for mental health intervention was indeed a clinical precursor for examining relational dynamics within the family system.

The initial goal of the child guidance movement was to address juvenile delinquency through teaching parents how to understand their children and respond to them with the appropriate use of love and discipline. Based on the child development theory of Alfred Adler and later the Adlerian psychiatrist Rudolf Dreikurs, early child guidance practitioners viewed the concept of the inferiority complex as one of the determinate factors in childhood psychological disturbances. Thus early psychological intervention with a child focused on helping the child overcome feelings of inferiority and inadequacy that could in turn deter the child from manifesting behavioral problems. The most important outcome of such interventions was that the child would therefore become a productive and successful adult.

One of the significant outcomes of this movement as it relates to the future development of family therapy was as child guidance practitioners began to understand the child they began to examine the ways in which both social and family dynamics might influence the child's psychological difficulties. For example, these practitioners began to recognize the importance of intervening with the entire family units around child-focused issues. In addition there was a shift in understanding the causative factors in childhood psychological disorders. The child's emotional stability was increasingly being understood as reflective of parental, especially maternal, child-rearing behaviors. While much of this understanding was informed by psychoanalytic theory there was an increased focus on the relational dynamics within the family.

FROM THE *AUTONOMOUS SELF* TO THE *RELATIONAL SELF*: CHANGING PERSPECTIVES IN PSYCHODYNAMIC THEORY

Freud and Psychoanalytic Theory

Even though the child guidance movement represented in part a movement away from traditional orthodox Freudian psychoanalytic theory, this perspective had a dominant influence on ways of understanding human behavior. Freud (1956) took the position that much of human behavior is motivated by unconscious sexual and aggressive instincts and that the expressions of these instincts are shaped by early childhood relationships between children and their parents.

Freudian psychoanalytic theory was based on the concept of the embodied and autonomous self. Attention given to family dynamics was only in terms of exploring the extent to which family members, primarily the parents, had an impact on the development of the patient's inner life. In fact it was the belief by those influenced by traditional psychoanalytic theory that the involvement of family members as a part of analysis or analytically informed psychotherapy would impede the development of the transference relationship between the analyst and the patient. Such an influence would thereby sabotage treatment. Thus there was a strong taboo against seeing family members of the patient while allowing the family to be symbolically represented within the context of the therapy hour. Here the patient was given the opportunity to relive the family drama or key family relationships through the projection of those relationships onto the therapist via transference.

Alfred Adler and Individual Psychology

Alfred Adler (1870–1937), though an early collaborator with Sigmund Freud, was one of the first major figures to break away from Freudian psychoanalysis to establish an independent school of personality and psychotherapy. Adler's formulations challenged Freudian theory, which understood human motivation as being biologically and instinctually driven. For Adler, individuals were social beings and were motivated by the drive to overcome feelings of inferiority and to achieve a sense of self-esteem, adequacy, and power within their social and relational worlds. A person's character and personality including behaviors, perceptions, feelings, and thoughts illuminate how he or she fits into the social milieu (Sherman & Dinkmeyer, 1987). Alder and later Adlerians viewed the family as the primary social matrix that exerts an influence on the formation of personality. A person's sense of self-esteem, self-worth, and ability to establish healthy human relations emerges from observing and interacting with parental models. With a focus on relationships and parenting strategies, Adlerian psychology clearly formed the basis for the child guidance movement. Most important, Alder with his emphasis on understanding the self within the social context provided a conceptual framework for understanding human motivation as relational and social rather than individualistic and autonomous.

Harry Stack Sullivan, Frieda Fromm-Reichmann, and Interpersonal Analysis

Another, though lesser known, psychiatrist whose work in psychoanalysis challenged the intrapsychic orientation of Freudian psychoanalysis was Herbert

"Harry" Stack Sullivan (1892–1949). Influenced by Adler, Sullivan's (1953) theory of psychiatry, *interpersonal analysis,* was based on the theory that both interpersonal relationships and social forces play a critical role in the formation of the self. In his study of the social sciences, especially the sociological theories of George Herbert Mead, Sullivan understood that human behavior was motivated not only by the desire for physical satisfaction but more important by a drive to attain a sense of security in relationships. This sense of security, which is key to Sullivan's understanding of the self, develops and is reinforced by the nature of the interpersonal relationship with the caregiver, primarily the mother. The child's sense of security is shaped by those aspects of his or her behavior that the caregiver responds to either positively or negatively. According to Sullivan, maternal anger or disapproval can contribute to childhood insecurities and anxiety and perhaps future emotional disturbances such as schizophrenia. Thus for Sullivan, parental disapproval and approval within the network of family relationships was key to understanding psychopathology.

Beginning in 1935 Frieda Fromm-Reichmann, a student and colleague of Sullivan, worked in a hospital for mentally disturbed patients. Through her work she began to give attention to the etiology of schizophrenia from an interpersonal orientation. As she states in 1948:

> The schizophrenic is painfully distrustful and resentful of other people due to the severe early warp and rejection he encountered in important people of his infancy and childhood, as a rule, mainly in a schizophrenic mother. (p. 265)

In her research Fromm-Reichmann concluded that schizophrenia, especially male schizophrenia, was the result of a cold, domineering, and rejecting yet overprotective mother. She introduced the term *schizophrenogenic mother* to describe this type of maternal behavior. This mother in combination with a passive, detached, and ineffectual father can cause the male child to feel confused, inadequate, and ultimately schizophrenic (Schultz, 1984).

Both Sullivan's interpersonal approach to personality development and Fromm-Reichmann's research on schizophrenia heavily influenced the thinking and work of some of the early family therapists. Both Sullivan and Fromm-Reichmann contributed to the shift in thinking about the self as autonomous to the self that was intractably embedded in a network of relationships. For Sullivan and Fromm-Reichmann an understanding of interactions between people rather than the intrapsychic domain was critical to understanding the etiology of emotional disorders. Finally their work, especially the work of Fromm-Reichmann, gave rise to a number of family pathology studies, which extended into the 1950s. These studies gave attention to the relationships between the dysfunctional behavior of individuals and their family's interpersonal patterns. It was the outcome of these studies that formed the conceptual framework for early family therapy treatment models (Atwood, 1992).

THE IMPACT OF SOCIOLOGICAL
THEORY IN THE HISTORY OF FAMILY THERAPY

As stated earlier, Sullivan was influenced by sociology. Though the impact of sociological thinking on the development of family therapy is evident in some of the family therapy approaches (Minuchin, 1974), many of the historians of family therapy do not give much attention to the role of sociological inquiry in the development of models of family therapy. Virginia Goldner (1985) states that all family therapy is influenced by the structural/functional theories of the sociologist Talcott Parsons. Ho, Rasheed, and Rasheed (2004) make similar claims when they describe how the early models of family therapy are informed by either of two sociological theories, symbolic interactionism or structural/functionalism. A discussion of these theories is important as they represent the broader conceptual context that impacted some of the basic theoretical formulations of family development theory, psychosocial theories about the family, and family therapy.

Structural/Functional Theory

Structural/functionalism, one of the dominant sociological theories in the 1950s, had a tremendous impact on family studies during that period. The leading thinker of the structural/functionalist school was Talcott Parsons (1951). This sociological perspective holds that societies and social units are held together by cooperation and orderliness. These social units work best when they function smoothly as an organism with all parts working toward the natural or smooth working of the system. Cooperation and orderliness are maintained through adherence to consensually agreed-upon social norms and roles.

As natural social units dynamically interact with external or natural environments, such interaction requires ongoing adaptation. In order for balance to be maintained within a social unit there must be a division of labor within that unit to enable each interrelated part to work with the others to create efficiency and harmony. Structural strain caused by disturbance within the social unit must be restored; otherwise it can lead to social disorganization. Likewise if significant conflict emerges between social units then there is the necessity for some form of adaptation to maintain equilibrium between these units (Ingoldsby, Smith, & Miller, 2004).

For a structural/functionalist the function of the family is to socialize children to fit into overall society. A structural description of the family would refer to the composition of the family as a social institution and its role within the social order. A functional description of the family would detail the services that the family provides to society as well as the tasks and roles required within the family structure to provide for the physical welfare and emotional and psychological needs of the family. For a structural/functionalist, viewing the family as a mediating system within the larger society, the concern would center on understanding ways in which the family maintains both internal harmony and equilibrium Additionally a structural/functionalist would be as concerned about how well a family maintains its structural role of instilling and socializing children with social values and norms. As family therapy models incorporated the language of "family dysfunction" they were drawing upon a structural/functional base analysis of families. Families that needed therapeutic intervention were in need of change to correct the interrupted function of the family and thereby restore a form of balance, harmony, and equilibrium.

Symbolic Interactionism

More of a microsociological perspective that emerged around the time of structural/functional theory, the core principles of symbolic interactionism revolve around the concepts of social interaction, language, and the formation of self. Grounded in the pragmatic philosophy of the early 1900s, the sociological theories of George Herbert Mead (1863–1931) and Herbert Blumer (1969), symbolic interactionist theory presents human beings as meaning-generating creatures embedded in social interactions. These interactions are shaped by the meaning people assign to those interactions as meaning is not inherent in the interactions. In the ability to use language to name and generate symbols that have meaning and value, humans have the capacity to assign meaning to people, things, and events. Thus humans do not act toward things as they are but based on the meaning they ascribe to these things. This meaning is not generated based on inward reflection but is based on the social interaction one has with others within his or her interactional field. These meanings are further modified not only by inner reflection but by outward interaction and discourse.

One of the key concepts of symbolic interaction that is important for family therapy is the concept of the self. The self is not found solely through the process of inner reflection (*the "I"*). Rather it is discovered by taking on the role of the "other" and imagining how one's sense of self is perceived from another's perspective (the *looking glass self* or the *"me"*). Thus the self has both inner and outer dimensions, but most important the self is subject to the socializing influences of a community (the *generalized other*) of other selves, in terms of its expectations and responses to the individual self. From this sociological perspective the family is the interactional, communicative, and meaning-generating network that is critical in the formation of self.

SYSTEMS, CYBERNETICS, COMMUNICATIONS, AND ECOLOGICAL THEORIES: THEIR IMPACT ON FAMILY THERAPY

While the sociological perspectives of structural/functionalism and symbolic interactionism shaped in part the conceptual milieu for family therapy, the development of family therapy was influenced in the 1950s by four powerful theories—general systems theory, cybernetics, communications theory, and ecological theory. These four theories formed the theoretical foundations for the development of family therapy models. Furthermore, cybernetics, systems, and communications theories allowed researchers and later clinicians to free themselves from psychoanalytic formulations for understanding emotional disorders such as schizophrenia and to expand their understanding of these disorders as a function of disturbed relational and communication patterns within families. Ecological theories provide a conceptual framework for understanding the impact of the transactions between a family and its broader environment.

Systems, cybernetics, communications, and ecological theories challenged the influences of psychoanalytic thinking, which was the dominant perspective from the early 1920s well into the late 1950s. With the exception of theorists such as Alfred Alder and Harry Sullivan, psychoanalytic theory focused on the individual and intrapsychic conflicts emanating from the experiences of childhood and the fantasy life emanating from the inner psychological world. External family members were only important to the extent that they were symbolic players in the inner drama of the individual's internal psychological world.

These new theories acknowledged that a person's behavior is not determined solely by one's internal world but that the social context is a powerful determinant in shaping behavior. Furthermore individual psychopathology cannot be understood without a detailed appreciation of the psychosocial and ecological context of the individual and his or her family. In terms of a direct impact on the historical development of family therapy, systems, cybernetics, and communication theories informed early research studies on families with schizophrenia. The findings from this research sparked many initiatives to translate such findings into therapeutic interventions with families. Ecological theories though not having a profound impact in the early history of family therapy became more influential as family therapists began to gain a greater appreciation of the impact of the social, economic, cultural, and political environments on family life. An overview of ecological theory will be presented later in this chapter as the discussion turns to more contemporary conceptual and clinical influences on family.

Systems and Cybernetics Theory

During the 1940s and 1950s an interdisciplinary group including mathematicians, physicists, biologists, engineers, psychologists, cultural anthropologists, and sociologists began to look at inanimate, organic, and human organizations and structures as a complex arrangement of component parts and interacting elements. These interacting elements together form interdependent entities that these theorists labeled as "systems." It was primarily through the works of biologist Ludwig von Bertalanffy (1969), who is considered the father of general systems theory, and Norbert Wiener (1948), who coined the term *cybernetics,* that these interdependent entities were understood as sharing certain characteristics that allowed them to function as systems, regardless of their type or level or organization. As general systems theory describes the structural aspects of systems, cybernetics addresses the functioning of systems. Structurally these interdependent entities or "systems" are composed of interrelated parts (subsystems) that constitute an ordered whole with each part of the system impacting all other parts as well as the system as a whole. Functionally, systems have a quality of self-organizing, self-directing, and self-governance behaviors through the process of establishing feedback mechanisms by which they can maintain a sense of equilibrium or homeostasis. This process allows for a system, through its own information processing system, to reinsert into its structure the results of its past performance or output in order to alter or correct its functioning.

The impact that systems theory had on the historical development of family therapy is that it provided a conceptual framework in which one could understand the complexities of family dynamics. More profoundly, systems theory represented a challenge to the Newtonian view of analysis and causality in the natural sciences and later in the social sciences. The prevailing Newtonian view of phenomena was from the perspective that physical reality could be reduced to matter consisting of substance, mass, and energy. An analysis of any observable and complex phenomena could be best understood by breaking down or reducing the whole into its parts. Only by analyzing the parts as distinct entities could one make inferences about the whole. Furthermore this understanding is grounded on how the parts impact or act upon other parts. Implicit in this approach is a particular understanding of causality or the causal relationship between the parts, components, or events. In this simple Newtonian view of physical science it made sense to think in terms of linear causality: A causes B, which acts upon C, causing D to occur.

Translated to the arena of human relationships, a linear causal model would involve seeking the causal connection between thought, behavior, and emotions. The goal would be to uncover the primary cause for the expressed thoughts, behaviors, or emotions. From a psychodynamic perspective the primary cause of emotional disturbance resides within the inner world of the psyche. And even these inner-world dynamics are impacted by early childhood experiences.

The systems view by contrast called for a different perspective on analysis and causality. Entities could be understood not in reductionist isolation from other entities in the observational field but in their relationship and interactions with other elements in the observational field. Causality is nonlinear and more circular. Here it is understood that forces do not simply move in one direction in which each event is caused by a previous event. Rather, seemingly discrete events become part of a causal chain with each event both influencing and being influenced by other events in a nonlinear manner. From this perspective the focus of analysis is shifted to a broader field of observation to understand the dynamic interaction of events rather than seek the linear causal relationship between events.

As systems thinking was a new way to think about relationships between entities it provided a conceptual framework that allowed the observer of families to view individuals within families as existing in a web of complex, interacting, and interdependent relationships. Systems thinking further freed the observer from psychoanalytic thinking, which tended to isolate the patient from his or her relational network in order to render a diagnosis. Families could no longer be seen as a collection of autonomous individuals. A systems perspective gave the observer the lens to examine and explore how the individual both influences and is influenced by the dynamics within the interior of a family system. Following in Table 1.1 are some selected concepts from systems theory that have relevance for understanding families from a systems perspective.

Mental Research Institute and Communication Systems Theory

Whereas the systems perspective gives attention to the relationship and interaction between parts of a given phenomenon, interpersonal communication systems theory addresses the interactional *patterns* reflected in the processing of information within the system. From a communication systems perspective the communication patterns within the larger system such as a family shape the operation and function of the system (see Table 1.2). Beginning in the early 1950s research on the role and impact of communication on systems emerged. Drawing on the ideas from systems theory, cybernetics, and the work of anthropologist Gregory Bateson, a group of researchers including Don Jackson and Paul Watzlawick joined with several scholars and researchers to study the communication patterns

Table 1.1	Key Characteristics of Systems

System

A set of orderly and interrelated elements that form a functional whole.

Boundaries

Repeatedly occurring patterns that characterize the relationship within a system and give that system a particular identity. A boundary is like a membrane surrounding and enclosing a living cell.

Subsystem

A secondary or subordinate system within a larger system.

Homeostasis

The tendency for a system to remain relatively stable and in a constant state of balance. If something disturbs the system it will strive "to adapt" and "restore the stability previously achieved." Homeostasis is the status quo—whether that condition is positive or negative.

Role

A socially expected behavior pattern usually determined by an individual's status in a particular society.

Relationship

The mutual emotional exchange; dynamic interaction; and affective, cognitive, and behavioral connection that exists between two or more persons or systems.

Source: Adapted from Ingoldsby, Smith, & Miller (2004). Used with permission.

and interpersonal interaction patterns within the families of schizophrenics. Their work at the Mental Research Institute (MRI) in Palo Alto, California, challenged the assumption that communication within families is motivated by individual motives and personality characteristics. Out of this work on communication and systems came a model of human communication that incorporated a systems perspective (Watzlawick, Beavin, & Jackson, 1967).

In 1952 while affiliated with the Mental Research Institute, Gregory Bateson recruited Jay Haley who was a graduate student in communications. Along with John Weakland, a former chemical engineer trained in cultural anthropology, they became aware of double-bind communication patterns, which represented a contradiction between levels of messages in that what might be communication on one level by one person may be contradicted on another level by the same person. As they observed families with schizophrenic members they found such pathogenic communication patterns. This pathogenic or double-bind element in this communication reflected the parental invitation for closeness along with an injunction to stay away. This led to the speculation that schizophrenia was the result of disturbed interpersonal communication rather than an intrapsychic disorder. These researchers concluded that contradictory communication patterns and injunctions within a family contributed to the etiology of schizophrenia.

The contributions of those affiliated with the Mental Research Institute extend well beyond the early research on the relationship between communication patterns and family schizophrenia. Many of the early practitioners in family therapy,

Table 1.2	Principles of Interpersonal Communication Systems Theory

1. **One Cannot Not Communicate**: Interpersonal communication occurs on multiple levels including both verbal and nonverbal. An attempt to avoid communication, for example through silence, nonetheless communicates the sender's intent and feelings to the receiver.

2. **Human Beings Communicate Both Digitally and Analogically**: Language is digital communication in that words have no similarity to the things or ideas they describe yet they refer to these things or ideas by name. Analogical communication on the other hand represents things and ideas by likeness. For example, nonverbal communication through tone of voice, facial expression, and touch mirrors gradations of feeling. For example, problems in communication occur when one uses digital communication to label nonverbal communication such as facial expressions, thus leading to difficulties in understanding the range, scope, and depth of the feeling conveyed by the facial expression.

3. **Communication Equals Both Content and the Relationship**: Communication involves the content of what is said, but the relationship shapes and provides the context that virtually surrounds the content and impacts the interpretation of the content. The tone of voice, an emphasis on certain words, and other nonverbal forms such as facial clues direct how the message is to be interpreted. The relationship level influences metacommunication, which is communication about communication.

4. **The Nature of the Relationship Depends on How Both Parties Punctuate the Communication Sequence**: Though communication patterns appear to be sequential, these patterns occur within the context of dynamic and interactive relationships. Drawing upon the systems concept of circular causality one party in a given communication sequence may punctuate the sequence and view him- or herself as either the cause or the reactor to a perceived sequence of interpersonal interactions.

5. **All Communication Is Either Symmetrical or Complementary**: While an understanding of relationships speaks to issues of belongingness, intimacy, and trust, communication theory addresses issues of control, status, and power as each relationship contains elements of control, status, and power. Symmetrical communication is based on equal power; complementary communication is based on a differential in power.

Source: Adapted from Griffin (1997).

including Virginia Satir, Jay Haley, and Don Jackson, were affiliated with the MRI during its early years. It is without saying that the work at MRI has been profoundly influential in the historical development of family therapy. It is also important to note that many of the contemporary models of family therapy including the MRI brief therapy model, solution-focused therapy, and the Milan systemic therapy orientation trace their heritage to the early work at the MRI. Some of these models will be discussed in more detail later in this text.

SCHIZOPHRENIA AND THE FAMILY SYSTEM: AREAS OF RESEARCH

In the early to mid 1950s there were major research initiatives in the area of schizophrenia within the family. Informed by the early work in systems and communication systems theory there were different centers in which there was research on schizophrenia and the family. Many of these researchers were working independently and were not aware of each other's research until much later in the 1950s. As discussed earlier it was during this period that researchers at the Mental Research Institute were conducting family research in the area of schizophrenia and communication. During this period Theodore Lidz at Yale and Murray Bowen and Lyman Wynne at the National Institute of Mental Health were also exploring the relationship between schizophrenia and family dynamics. What is significant is that many of those who were involved in this early research later translated their findings and observations into clinical models of family therapy.

Theodore Lidz: Schizophrenia and Disturbed Marital Relationships

Theodore Lidz and his wife Ruth Lidz (1949) began their study of schizophrenia at Yale's John Hopkins Hospital. The hospital population included a small group of schizophrenics who had a history of being deprived of one parental figure. These families were further marked by emotional instability and turmoil. Rather than accepting the assumption that schizophrenia reflected a disturbance in the mother-child relationship Lidz expanded his observation to include the marital relationship. As he examined the marital relationship of those families of hospitalized schizophrenics he observed the existence of marital conflict in which each marital partner, being so preoccupied with his or her own problem, failed to create a compatible and reciprocal relationship with the other spouse. Furthermore he observed the partners competing for loyalty, affection, sympathy, and support of the children. These parents also displayed fear that one of the children may grow up like the other parent. The other marital pattern that Lidz observed were those marriages that, while not threatened with possible dissolution, were nonetheless reflective of a mutual destructive pattern within the relationship wherein the psychological disturbance of one partner dominates the emotional climate of the house. In those situations he found the dependent spouse accepting and normalizing the situation and not being sensitive to the impact of these destructive behaviors on the children. Such parental attitudes created a sense of distortion and denial on the part of the children.

One of contributions that Lidz made to the study of schizophrenia was the attention given to the father's role in the etiology of schizophrenia. Lidz, Cornelison, Fleck, and Terry (1957) identified patterns of pathological fathering of schizophrenics. These patterns involved fathers who, when in constant and severe conflict with their wives, ally themselves with their daughters; fathers of sons who turn their hostility toward their sons rather than their wives; fathers with grandiose and paranoid thinking who create a pathological atmosphere within the family; fathers who have failed in life while becoming nonentities in their home; and passive fathers who demand little for themselves and act like siblings (Schultz, 1984).

Murray Bowen: Schizophrenia as a Family Process

During the period in which Lidz was conducting his study on the impact of the marital relationship on schizophrenia, Murray Bowen, trained as a psychoanalyst, was at the National Institute of Mental Health near Washington, DC. There Bowen arranged for mothers to move into cottages near the hospitalized schizophrenic children for several months. What Bowen observed were periods in which the parents moved between being overly close and being overly distant. This vacillating movement enabled the parents to maintain a degree of emotional balance while keeping the schizophrenic child helpless and needy. Based on further observations, Bowen concluded that schizophrenia is embedded in a family process that spans at least three generations. As parents of schizophrenics experienced emotional conflict with their own parents they subject their children to the same conflict. Consequently these children as adults may in turn seek out marital partners with a compatible upbringing and corresponding psychological difficulties. They in turn pass on the emotional vulnerability to another generation (Goldenberg & Goldenberg, 2008). Bowen (1976) viewed families as open natural systems whose members enter and exit over time and thereby alter the boundaries of the family. Therefore most families are understood from an intergenerational perspective of interlocking, reciprocal, and repetitive relationships.

Bowen, who was one of the pioneers of family therapy, based his theory of family therapy on his early clinical study of schizophrenia. Bowen was impressed with the "emotional stuck-togetherness" (fusion) of family members with schizophrenia. His theory, later to be called Bowenian family therapy, incorporates important intergenerational processes, allowing family therapists to explore critical historical events and intergenerational patterns affecting current family functioning. Problems related to unresolved family issues of past generations are conceptualized as having a potential emotional impact in subsequent generations.

Lyman Wynne at the National Institute of Mental Health

Lyman Wynne was at the National Institute of Mental Health in 1952, 2 years before Bowen came in 1954. Wynne was trained in both psychiatry and the social sciences. In one of his classic papers on schizophrenia, he and his colleagues stated that the purpose of that paper was to "develop a psychodynamic interpretation of schizophrenia that takes into conceptual account the social organization of the family as a whole" (Wynne, Ryckoff, Day, & Hirsch, 1958, p. 205). Wynne focused his work on two areas. One area was examining how individuals could develop relationships with others while at the same time maintaining a sense of personal identity (Schultz, 1984). The other area of research was on the blurred, ambiguous, and confused communication patterns in families with schizophrenic members.

He identified that some individuals within families display a sense of relatedness and family togetherness even though the family members in fact are emotionally disengaged or distant. In these *pseudomutual* relationships any attempt of the individuals within the family to establish a separate identity is perceived as a threat to the family's relationship system. Wynne presented the hypothesis in 1958 that intense and enduring pseudomutuality characterizes the family relationship of schizophrenics. On the other hand Wynne contended that in some families one might observe individuals who would use expressions of anger or pseudohostility to mask a need for intimacy.

As individuals attempt to establish their sense of self in those families marked by pseudomutuality, they may encounter patterns of family behavior that counter those efforts at establishing identity. These patterns of family behavior were described by Wynne as a *rubber fence* in which the family is like an elastic boundary that shifts and changes to obviate any attempts at establishing individual identity or autonomy. Through communication patterns within the family the emotional, structural, and role boundaries move to blur differences while keeping the person contained within the unthreatening pseudomutual relationship. In such families individuals develop ways of perceiving, thinking, and communicating that reflect a distortion in their interpretation of their internal states and external events leading to chronic schizophrenia. Such distortions in thinking and feelings can lead to panic. Though schizophrenia was viewed as a thought disorder, Wynne saw communication patterns within the family as a vehicle for transmitting thought disorders (Nichols & Schwartz, 2008).

RESEARCH TO PRACTICE: CLINICAL APPLICATIONS

Motivated by such powerful insights on the relationship between family dynamics and mental disorders the researchers in these family studies began to explore the implications of their findings for clinical practice with families in the 1960s. The 1960s were a rich period in the history of family therapy. One might even suggest that in the social and political climate of social activism of the 1960s there emerged a group of sometimes iconoclastic and innovative therapists who were staging their own social revolution within the fields of psychiatry, psychology, and social work. It was during this time that as family research studies on schizophrenia moved into family therapy there was also a proliferation of family therapy approaches.

As there were theorists from different theoretical perspectives there was perhaps some ideological tension between those who were influenced by their previous psychoanalytic training and those who were more systematic in their perspective. Yet these therapists did not remain in isolated ideological camps as their ideas began to influence each other. There were different venues and publications, and there were collaborations. A good example of this was when psychodynamically oriented Nathan Ackerman joined with Don Jackson who was influenced by communications and systems theories to collaborate together to publish one of the leading journals in the field of family therapy, *Family Process*.

Moving Through the Generational History of Family Therapy Approaches

As family therapy continues to transition from the 1960s into the early 21st century a shift in perspective is occurring. The first generation of family therapy models was clearly influenced by systems theory. As the early family therapy practitioners embraced systems theory, they positioned themselves as observers outside the family system. The therapist became the "expert" with a toolbox of therapeutic interventions grounded in clearly articulated and conceptually sound theoretical frameworks. Their theories of change were also guided by their understanding of what constituted optimal family functioning. Operating within the assumptive framework of a modernist perspective, these practitioners implicitly believed that the right theories and models could guide them in uncovering and manipulating salient aspects of a family's systemic interactions in order to bring about change and problem resolution (Becvar & Becvar, 2000). These first-generation clinicians in fact subscribed to either a structural/functional or a communicative/interactive perspective. This latter perspective was clearly influenced by symbolic interactionist theory. In many respects the first-generation therapists, by adhering to the rather conservative and status quo theories of structural/functionalism and symbolic interactionism, only gave minimal recognition to factors of gender, race, and culture in their theories or intervention strategies. This lack of attention to issues of gender, race, and ethnicity generated much critique regarding the applicability of family therapy to diverse populations. Ironically the only possible exceptions to this critique were those approaches influenced by Minuchin's (1974) structural family therapy model and ecological theory.

The second-generation clinicians have provided a postmodern critique of the first-generation system-based approaches (Nichols & Schwartz, 2008). The nature of the critique is that the systems approach represents a mechanist view of families to be manipulated and changed by the "expert" therapist. Such an approach ignores the impact of the therapist's presence on the family system, the dynamics of gender and power, and the larger ecological, historical, and cultural context in which the family is embedded (Nichols & Schwartz, 2008). From this second-generation perspective the families, not the family therapist, are the experts of their own lives. The second-generation clinician sees the family as constituting a language system or narrative with family difficulties constructive in language. In the development of a new language, the clinician is a participant-manager of the conversation about the "problem." In the second-generation approaches, the individual identity is

Photo 1.2 The marriage counseling movement emerged in the 1920s to provide couples with guidance and support in coping with the demands of married life

Source: © Thinkstock/Comstock/Thinkstock

embodied in a personal narrative about self. Additionally these self-narratives are context dependent, thus allowing for different versions of the self. As a person moves through the different arenas of her or his life, a different narrative presentation of self may emerge.

In the reality of practice many therapists may move between first- and second-generation approaches. As a corrective measure to systems theories the postmodern critiques do address some of the major limitations of family systems theories. Yet these critiques do not necessitate a rejection of systems-based theories. The focus of the structural/functional practice and communicative/interactive models can provide a framework for understanding the actual structure of the family, and the postmodern language and narrative-based approaches can allow for the therapist to understand the meaning and interpretation of that structure by family members as impacted by ethnic, cultural, historical, economic, and sociopolitical factors.

Whether a family therapist's theoretical perspective falls within a first- or a second-generation framework the level of change sought by family therapists is a fundamental revision of the family's structure, function, interaction patterns, or language system (Goldenberg & Goldenberg, 2008). This level of change, described by Watzlawick, Weakland, and Fisch (1974) as second-order change, is focused on helping the family reach a different level of functioning rather than engage in superficial behavioral or first-order changes. Such first-order changes, while bringing about the possible cessation of the presenting family problem, will fail to address the underlying systemic rules that sustain the presence of the presenting problem. For Watzlawick (1978) family therapy should focus on second-order changes. Given this focus of intervention the family can engage in reconstituting itself in a different way (Goldenberg & Goldenberg, 2008).

FIRST-GENERATION FAMILY THERAPIES: STRUCTURAL/FUNCTIONAL PRACTICE MODELS

As presented earlier in this chapter, the structural/functional framework for family therapy was based on the anthropological and sociological work of Talcott Parsons (1951). Strongly committed to the systems outlook, the structural/functionalist position emphasizes the active, organized wholeness of the family unit. Structural/functionalists are interested in the components of the family system and observe the activities and functions of the family to provide a clue to how the family is organized or structured. Within a structural/functional framework are several systemic orientations. One is the psychodynamic orientations in which family is defined as a group made up of the interlocking dynamics of its members who are at various developmental stages. Another family systems paradigm defines a family as a system that operates independently and from which individual psychodynamics, including those that created symptoms, emerge. Another orientation is when family is defined as a system that shares isomorphic characteristics with all natural systems in a hierarchy according to classes—from quarks to universes—with higher systems containing those lower in the hierarchy.

The relevance of these approaches from a structural/functionalist orientation lies with their emphasis on the family as a *boundary-maintaining* social system in constant transaction with the environment or other systems. The internal family system is composed of individual members who define both the family as a whole and the various subsystems within the whole—that is, the marital, parent-child, and sibling units. In transacting with the environment, individual members are viewed primarily as reactors who are subject to influences and impingement from the greater social system. The healthy functioning of a family system can be measured by its adaptive boundary-maintenance ability following stressful situations caused by pressures from transactions with other environmental systems or with society as a whole. Hence, therapy as guided by this conceptualization suggests interventions that strengthen the boundary-maintaining ability of the family for adaptive purposes and that serve stability or equilibrium needs.

The following group of clinicians and their therapeutic approaches represents a structural/functionalist orientation to family therapy practice. Bowen's model of family therapy as discussed earlier and whose approach will be represented in more detail later saw the family as an emotional system that shares similar characteristics with other natural systems. Other earlier clinicians who were psychodynamically influenced were Nathan Ackerman and Ivan Boszormenyi-Nagy. John Elderkin Bell viewed families from the position of social groups while Salvador Minuchin, whose approach will be discussed in more detail in a later chapter, articulated a clearly structural model of treatment.

Nathan Ackerman and Psychodynamic Family Therapy

In the early 1950s in New York, child psychoanalyst Nathan Ackerman began to use family interviews in his analytic work with families. Ackerman (1958) was one who theorized that family problems reflected both the individual psyche and environmental issues. Furthermore, not only was a symptomatic family member reflecting an underlying family disturbance in the family system, but that intrapsychic conflict was being manifested in the family system. In many ways Ackerman's work challenged what he felt was the undue emphasis on the research on schizophrenia and its causes. He thought that researchers and clinicians needed to look at the nonpsychiatric disorders in children as they relate to the family interactions (Ackerman, 1966). Ackerman could not fully move beyond his psychoanalytic orientation, which caused him to maintain his attention on the individual within the family. Yet his work demonstrated that he gave attention to the recursive interaction between a patient's intrapsychic world and the family's interactional and relationship patterns. As such, Ackerman considered that interpersonal conflicts might be a manifestation of unconscious elements operating within the family system.

Ivan Boszormenyi-Nagy and Contextual Family Therapy

Psychiatrist and trained psychoanalyst Ivan Boszormenyi-Nagy's "contextual therapy" approach represented an integration of four dimensions of family life: (a) the factual context of the relationships, (b) the internal dynamics of the individual, (c) the observable patterns in the relationship, and (d) the dimension of relational ethics (Boszormenyi-Nagy & Spark, 1973). While these dimensions were interwoven, they were not reducible to each other. It was the last dimension of relational ethics that spoke to the uniqueness of Nagy's contextual approach. By integrating object-relational psychodynamic therapy, a systems perspective, with the existential and relational philosophy of the Jewish theologian Martin Buber, Boszormenyi-Nagy addresses the ethical dimension of family relationships. Not only do family relationships reflect certain interactional patterns, but these patterns can create transgenerational entitlements and indebtedness within the family. Additionally unconscious or "invisible" loyalties or emotional obligations across generations influence present behaviors. These loyalties create a ledger of what one gives out of obligation and what one is owed based on current or past actions within the family. These ledgers reflect the relational entitlement and indebtedness for each individual within the family system.

John Elderkin Bell and Group Family Therapy

John Bell, a psychologist, was one of the first clinicians to see families conjointly. He integrated group dynamics and group psychotherapy as the conceptual foundations for family therapy. In one of the classics in the field of family therapy, *Family Group Therapy* (1961), Bell described families as small groups. In doing so, he gave attention to the structure, process, and function of families in terms of those roles that allow them to handle intrafamilial issues. Though he borrowed from group therapy and small group theory Bell did recognize the difference between stranger groups and family groups. As groups have a temporary life together, families have a level of emotional bonding that has a history. In using group theory as his conceptual frame of reference, Bell did view family members as individual group members rather than a part of an interactional relationship system.

Salvador Minuchin and Structural Family Therapy

In the late 1960s there was increased attention to the issue of welfare reform with much attention given to those families that seemed to be entrapped in welfare systems and faced not only poverty but issues of delinquency, neglect, and severe health problems. These multiproblem families became the focus of family therapists. The one therapist and clinical model that attempted to address this population is Salvador Minuchin and his structural family therapy model, which will be discussed in more detail in a later chapter. The structural model, while incorporating a generational view, focuses on balancing the structure of the family using a direct, concrete, here-and-now approach to problem solving (Nichols & Schwartz, 2008). Relying somewhat on an ecological systemic perspective, Minuchin's approach emphasizes how stressful contact of the whole family with extrafamilial forces can produce role confusion and power conflict within a family. The major subsystems within the family (spousal, parental, sibling) may need restructuring to restore healthy boundaries and functional roles. Anticipating the critique of postmodern therapists, the structural approach is sensitive to the political, social, and cross-cultural processes of poverty and discrimination that culturally diverse and sociopolitically oppressed families may experience over time.

FIRST-GENERATION FAMILY THERAPIES: COMMUNICATIVE/INTERACTIVE PRACTICE MODELS

Still considered a first-generation approach the communicative/interactive practice models developed and advanced by Carl Whitaker, Jay Haley, Virginia Satir, and the Milan Group are based on George Herbert Mead's (1934) symbolic interactionism. These practice models all place to varying degrees an emphasis on the communicative and interactive process taking place between individual family members and subsystems within the family. While contemporary family theorists may view these practice models as being eclipsed by postmodern constructionist and narrative theories, there is great compatibility with communicative/interactive models and social construction theory in that both practice models give attention to humans' need to make meaning out of everything they experience (Cheung, 1997; Satir, 1988) and the importance of language in creating meaning. One of the assumptions of the communicative/interactive model is that family culture is sustained and maintained through communication and, more important, through the subjective and everyday interpretations of behavior.

The contributions of the interactional framework center primarily on changes within the family unit that are a result of interactions between members. From this framework, an analysis can be made in which individual family members act and react to the actions of others and the interpersonal meanings attached to these actions. Interactive processes that are of particular importance to therapy include communication, conflict, role relations, and decision making. Because the communicative/interactive framework is concerned primarily with change rather than with stability, the concepts of family *equilibrium* and family transaction with the outside world are less important. The framework, when applied singularly, can easily shift from one that concentrates on interactive processes between system members to one that emphasizes intervention methods that focus primarily on individual actions or behaviors. With the exception of Carl Whitaker, other communicative/interactive clinicians such as Virginia Satir, Jay Haley, and the Milan Group represent the work done at the Mental Research Institute.

Carl Whitaker and the Symbolic Experiential Approach

Whitaker, who was originally trained in obstetrics before moving to psychiatry and psychoanalysis, worked with schizophrenic patients and families, children, and child guidance clinics. Whitaker is considered by many as being quite atheoretical, but he was known for his symbolic/experiential approach. His approach is described as existential (Luepnitz, 1988) in that he was not focused on symptoms as such but he viewed symptoms as symbolic of some of the existential contingences of life, the processes of life and death. Not being psychoanalytical in his overall theoretical orientation, though he studied under Melanie Klein and Carl Jung, Whitaker viewed family symptoms as symbolic expressions of often-unconscious elements operating within family life. These elements reflected the struggle for individual autonomy and family cohesion. In many ways, Whitaker saw therapy as a growth process. Forsaking the rather disciplined and methodical approach of psychoanalysis Whitaker was much more spontaneous and intuitive and a provocateur in terms of technique. His approach was highly interactional, flexible, engaging, and creative.

Virginia Satir and Humanistic Family Therapy

As one of the original members of the MRI, Virginia Satir merged communication theory with a human growth perspective. As will be discussed in a later chapter, Satir focused her systems-oriented approach on the communications patterns within families. Her assumption was that there is a unique pattern of communication within troubled families, as well as a correlation between self-esteem and communications. Satir's approach was to enhance the self-esteem among family members, as well as increase communication and problem-solving skills. Her focus also emphasized the growth potential of all individuals. She further reinforced, through her therapeutic interventions, the family's central and critical function of enhancing the self-esteem of its members. As will be elaborated later, her therapeutic goal was the facilitation of clear, direct, and honest communication within the family system.

Jay Haley and Strategic Family Therapy

Another original member of the MRI who made profound contributions to family therapy is Jay Haley. With an MA in communications he was one of the early researchers in the studies on schizophrenia and family communication patterns. He was one of the founders of the strategic family therapy model, which is a brief approach of observing and altering the interactional sequences in which the specific family problem is embedded. Influenced by the work of Milton Erickson and hypnotherapy, Haley challenged notions of patient-therapist transference therapy and emphasized the role of relational power within the family system. With his direct therapeutic approach, his strategic methods focused on the sequences of behaviors and communication patterns as revealed within the "here and now" of a therapeutic session. By developing directive and action plans to change behaviors to alter power relationships and hierarchy, the family's patterns of interaction could be altered. Some of the therapeutic techniques unique to the strategic approach are the use of paradoxical directives or prescribing the symptoms of resistance, metaphoric tasks given to family members to symbolize a problem or issue not discussed by family, or giving the client a task greater than the distress of the symptom. The types of directives given to families to change interpersonal interactions may be straightforward, paradoxical, metaphorical, or playful (Madanes, 1984, 1991). A strategic approach searches for the interpersonal meanings of symptomatic behaviors. For example, illnesses such as alcoholism may mean exerting control over relationships.

The Milan Group

In the mid 1970s Italian psychoanalyst Mara Selvini Palazzoli, along with Luigi Boscolo, Gianfranco Cecchin, and Giuliana Prata, developed an approach to family therapy that initially drew many of its concepts from the strategic family therapy model and the work at the Mental Research Institute. Though this approach has been modified over the years the earlier view of families having difficulties was that though families wanted to address their symptoms there was a paradoxical resistance to change. The goal of therapy was to address those resistant behaviors or games with strategies that would undercut those resistance behaviors. This undermining was not direct as with the strategic approach, but the Milan strategy would be to engage the family through the systematic use of questions that would have an impact on family dynamics. Through the use of circular questions these researchers were able to uncover a family's history and family interactional patterns. The later-modified

Milan approach called for seeking positive connotation for problematic behaviors and how these behaviors may (or may not) be useful for the individual and others in the family. In addition therapists would use positive connotations on how or why family members may be cooperating with the problem (Boscolo, Cecchin, Hoffman, & Penn, 1987). As the Milan approach evolved they supported a more collaborative nonblaming approach to the family. This newer approach marked a shift in therapists' "expert" role in their relationship to the family.

GENDER AND MULTICULTURAL ISSUES: A CRITIQUE OF FIRST-GENERATION FAMILY THERAPIES

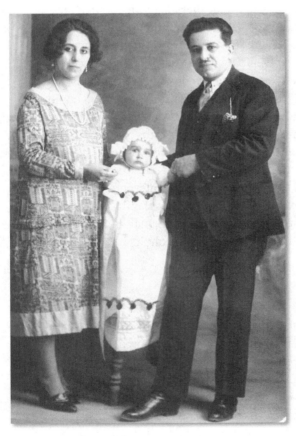

Photo 1.3 A child's emotional stability was viewed by the Child Guidance movement as reflective of parent-child relationship

Source: ©iStockphoto.com/hakinci

The first-generation family therapy models implicitly held certain assumptions regarding what constituted family normality as well as those family structures, interactional patterns, and value orientations that were indicators of family emotional health. In many respects these assumptions were based on middle-class or work-class notions of the ideal family. Yet there was the undeniable fact that families do differ in how they structure their family lives. Due to variables of race, gender, and class, there were alternative family forms that deviated from the generally accepted assumptions about "ideal" families. There was also the increasing acceptance that many of the first-generation family therapy practice theories were apolitical in that they ignored the broader sociopolitical context structuring the lives of families. According to Fish (1993), although many family therapy models understood the dynamics of power in the helping relationship, the client's or family therapist's gender, class, ethnic, or racial location within the larger social order was not considered as having an impact on the therapeutic process. Without this understanding of the possible power differential association with a client's or therapist's social location, a salient aspect of a client's experience was felt to be ignored.

Gender and Family Therapy

With regard to the issue of gender, first-generation therapy models were challenged for failing to consider the larger social, political, and ideological context when looking at family dysfunction (Hare-Mustin, 1978; Laird, 1989; Luepnitz, 1988). In terms of gender, first-order family therapies were viewed as biased in that they adhered to the notion that all family participants, regardless of gender, contribute equally and have shared responsibility for family problems. And as a consequence of such biases therapists assumed a neutral stance toward those inherent sexist and patriarchal practices that were unquestionably seen as a part of "normal" family life. Those who challenged these sexist assumptions in family therapy theories felt those therapists were continuing to see mothers as the source of pathology in family. Furthermore by not looking at the differential power relationships as structured by traditional gender roles and expectations, these therapists were contributing to maintaining the sexist and patriarchal sexist status quo. As a consequence they could not interrogate the role of women as being exploited, devalued, and oppressed especially within families structured by more traditional and structural/functionalist ideas of gender roles and expectations.

Multiculturalism and Family Therapy

Along with concern about gender biases, there was a greater recognition within the discipline of family therapy of the disparity in the social status of ethnic minorities. Furthermore there was greater awareness that these disparities often reflected the realities of racism, poverty, and oppression. As family therapy practitioners became engaged with racial and ethnic minority families, questions emerged as to what extent these practice models take into account the following stressors that these families encounter (Ho et al., 2004). In addition to coping with racism, oppression, poverty, and societal constraints, there was the recognition that ethnic minority families encounter the following stressors that impact their engagement in family therapy.

1. Concern about immigration status: Aside from the immigrant's possible concerns about legal status, factors such as geographical relocation and intergenerational family emotional disconnection can have adverse implications for family structure and functioning.

2. Language concerns: Ethnicity is often experienced and persists through language. Although many ethnic minority clients are bilingual, problems of miscommunication may still occur.

3. Ethnicity and class status: The intersection of ethnicity and class may be a salient factor for families as they navigate the social terrain of ethnic group membership and social class location. Gordon (1965) uses the term *ethclass* to describe the point at which social class and ethnic group membership intersect.

4. Fluid ethnic identities: Ethnic identity generally refers to attributes of a group of people who view themselves as being bound together by a common history, traditions, language, and geographic origin. Yet for many individuals ethnic identities are experienced as fluid and socially and historically constructed. An example of fluid identities can be found within immigrant, biracial, and bicultural families. Within such families individual members may define their ethnic identities based on a variety of considerations, one being their level of acculturation or their wish to be accepted within a particular sociopolitical context (Cornell, 2000).

For many ethnic minority families, how they are viewed by society may constrain their ability to construct more empowering and potentiating solutions to family problems. Thus as ethnic minority families present themselves for family therapy, family therapists are to acknowledge that they must be culturally attuned to how the family's experience is shaped by its unique ethnic, racial, and/or cultural experiences. Finally there is the increasing acceptance that a family therapist cannot understand the significance of a family's problem without recognition of the material, power-laden, and affectively charged elements of living within certain discriminatory and disempowering environments.

THE ECOLOGICAL SYSTEMS PERSPECTIVE: BROADENING THE VIEW OF THE FAMILY

The concerns about the limitations of first-generation therapies to attend to issues of gender, race, and ethnicity presented a significant challenge to the relevancy of family therapy for diverse families. Remaining within the epistemological framework of systems theory, the ecological or ecosystemic perspective emerged in response to this challenge by broadening the context for understanding families. In an ecological framework families are understood in terms of their location within their environment or habitat (Ho et al., 2004). As the concept of environment is described within an ecological systems framework it becomes much broader than one's habitat. The environment includes not only the family's physical or geographical location or habitat but the sociopolitical, cultural, and economic context that surrounds one's living space. It is the broader context of culture, economics, and politics that determines if one's habitat is supportive of the mental, physical, and social functioning of the individual and family.

The sustaining and nurturing resources within a family's environment are further determined by one's niche—that is, one's social position, class location, ethnic and racial identity, and economic status within the overall social structure. A good or *enabling niche* is one that avails the occupant the rights of equal opportunity to educational and economic resources (Kilpatrick & Holland, 2009; Taylor, 1997). There are, however, individuals and families with devalued personal or cultural characteristics, such as color, ethnicity, gender, sexual orientation, age, poverty, or other types of bias and oppression, who are entrapped in niches that are incongruent with fulfilling their human needs and well-being (Kilpatrick & Holland, 2009; Taylor, 1997).

The ecological or ecosystem perspective provided a framework for addressing issues of diversity, marginalization, and oppression. From this perspective the therapists could ground their intervention strategies on the following practice principles (Ho et al., 2004).

1. Individual or family problems are not conceived as pathology; instead, problems or difficulties are understood as a lack or deficit in the environment (as in the case of migration of immigration) or a result of interrupted growth and development (role conflict and resource deficits in the environment).

2. Intervention efforts are directed at multivariable systems, and a single effect can be produced by a variety of means. The principle of *equifinality,* which means that a number of different interventions may, owing to the complexity of systems, produce similar effects or outcomes, encourages flexibility and creativity in seeking alternative routes to change. While a therapist may try to relate intervention strategies to existing theories that are Western middle-class American oriented, innovative strategies of change based on the client's cultural background are encouraged.

3. Intervention strategies should make use of natural systems and life experiences and take place within the life space of the client. The family itself is a natural helping system and an instrument of change.

4. Emphasis on the client's life space and family as a natural helping system places the therapist in a role of *cultural broker* instead of intruder, manipulator, or cultural expert.

An ecological systems framework was viewed as providing a lens in which the family and family members could be understood within the context of transactions with a variety of biological, psychological, cultural, and historical environments. By adopting an ecosystem perspective, a family therapist could focus on adaptive (and maladaptive) transactions between persons and between the person and various environments—that is, the interface between them.

POSTMODERN THOUGHT AND SECOND-GENERATION FAMILY THERAPIES

Newer formulations of family therapy that have been influenced by postmodern, constructivist, and social constructionist ideas, however, have provided a critique of all systems-based models of family therapy. The nature of the critique is that the systems approach represents a mechanist view of the family as an entity to be manipulated and changed by the "expert" therapist. Postmodern theorists are also concerned that systems approaches ignore the impact of the therapist's presence on the family system; the dynamics of gender and power; and the larger historical and cultural context in which the family is embedded (Nichols & Schwartz, 2008).

Described as second-generation approaches, those practice models informed by postmodern thought challenge what can be "known" about the external world. Whereas the first-generation therapies are based on conceptual models that attempt to objectively describe the structure, function, communication, and interactional patterns within a family, the second-generation models question this very effort. For the second-generation therapist the issue is not "what is known" but "how do we know." In other words, second-generation therapies are concerned about *epistemology,* a philosophical term referring to the study of knowledge.

From a constructivist perspective what is known about the external world is shaped by our innate mental and sensory structures (Maturana & Varela, 1984). From a social constructionist perspective, ideas, beliefs, customs, subjective experiences, values, and myths (and all those things that make up our psychological reality) are socially constructed within the context of human interactions and expressed through the medium of language (Ariel, 1999; Freeman & Combs, 1996). Thus from both a constructivist and a social constructionist worldview, the observable objective world cannot be known as it is or independent from the knower. Rather the objective world is constructed and shaped by the knower. The world is either a product of our mental or sensory makeup or a product of social discourse.

The major postmodern family therapies are based on a social constructionist epistemology. Language as expressed through narrative form is the means of organizing and structuring life experiences. It is the narrative that individuals construct about their lives that provides them with a sense of personal identity. Narratives further reveal the significance of an individual's lived experience within the context of his or her social world (Gergen, 1999; Polkinghorne, 1988; Semmler & Williams, 2000). Thus family problems are located within narrative descriptions. And as with narrative descriptions, the focus is not on what is described but on the *interpretation* of what is described. Reality is thus a matter of interpretation rather than a description of an objective or external given. Thus a family problem may gain its saliency and potency not on its factual presence and existence but on its effects, interpretive description, and meanings for family members. The therapist's task is to create a therapeutic space for the emergence of alternative and more empowering interpretations of the "problem." Facilitating, in a collaborative manner, a change in the family's language from a problem-oriented discourse to a solution-focused discourse creates a space for increased individual or family competency. In this collaborative relationship the therapist moves from the hierarchical expert position to a collaborative relationship with the family.

One of the important contributions of this perspective is that it can contextualize the meaning of both the family therapist's and the family members' *lived experience* in therapy by locating that experience within a specific ecological, historical, economic, and political context. To say that the "personal is political" underscores one of the basic assumptions of a postmodern orientation. Any understanding of an individual or family system or family narrative must include an inquiry into the family's social, political, economic, and cultural position within the social order. The therapist must view her or his narrative (and the family's narrative) with a critical eye to uncover the extent to which the unique reality of both the therapist's and the family members' lived experience is shaped by the dominant social and political ideology.

The postmodern-oriented practitioner can view liberation from oppressive ideologies and structure as an indispensable condition of the quest for human potential and authenticity (Stevens, 1989). Liberation is attained by first developing a state of "critical consciousness," which is achieving an awareness of how the social, political, and economic ideology constrain a family member's *sense of agency* and identity (Freire, 1973). Informed by this new awareness, the therapist and family members can take action against those oppressive structures and articulate in their own "voice" a *narrative of self* that represents their *unique lived experience*.

One of the interesting implications of the postmodern perspective is that the "self" is no longer viewed as a stable, enduring, embodied, and autonomous object in which the task of the clinical observer is to discover what is within the self. This is the position taken by the psychodynamic and other individual nonsystems approaches to therapy. The postmodern perspective also raises questions about the relational self or the self that is defined within the context of systems or interactional patterns. While postmodern thought acknowledges that the self is embedded, the embedment is found more in the narrative text of one's own or others' narrative renditions rather than relationships.

Two approaches that speak to this perspective are the solution focus and the narrative approach. As these two approaches will be elaborated later, a brief summary of these perspectives is presented here.

Solution-Focused Approach

The solution approach is marked by a more collaborative stance between the therapist and the family. Family problems are not seen as a sign of failure. In fact problem-saturated narrations of the problem are deliberately ignored (de Shazer, 1985). The focus of the therapist-family collaboration is on discussing patterns for previously attempted solutions. Focusing on the times when the problem or symptom is less or not present allows the therapist with the client to design interventions around the exceptions. It is these "exceptions" that form the basis for a solution. As the solution patterns are amplified the problem patterns can recede into the background.

Narrative Approach

In accordance with the above description of the role of narrative in constructing reality the narrative approach as developed by White and Epston (1990) gives attention to how language shapes problem perceptions and definitions. As the family "stories" its experiences around the problem, a narrative orientation focuses on themes of oppression and liberation and how the family members may be "oppressed" by the problem(s). By externalizing the problem, the problem—not the persons involved—becomes the problem. A narrative therapist helps families notice their own expert knowledge and, through the use of literary metaphors, acknowledge their ability to reauthor their own lives with more empowering narratives.

THE EMERGING THIRD-GENERATION PERSPECTIVE: EVIDENCE-BASED APPROACHES

With the postmodern emphasis on meaning, there was a shift in thinking about family dynamics. The major shift was from observing behavior and communication patterns to how one thinks about and interprets communication and behavior. There is another major shift occurring as family therapy moves into the 21st century. This shift is predicted as reflecting an increased focus on the effectiveness of family therapy approaches (Hanna & Brown, 2004). Influenced by such societal changes as the emergence of managed care, the major concern in medicine, psychology, and social work is the integration of clinical judgments with research evidence. Thus the third generation of family therapy may not be grounded in theoretical models or concerned with issues of epistemology but rather may be grounded in empirically supported interventions. This emphasis on evidence-based practice is also generating more integrative models and approaches in family therapy. As there is the movement toward integrative models there may be fewer adherences to specific models. The focus is beginning to shift to examining the efficacy of specific interventions as they demonstrate effectiveness with specific client populations. Giving attention to matching interventions to specific client populations is creating a therapeutic climate that calls for deliberate and careful decision making regarding intervention. It is interesting to note that as postmodernism challenged the epistemological basis for theory and model construction, the evidence-based orientation by being "anti-model" is moving family therapy into another, perhaps more viable, era.

One model representing this new generation of family therapy is cognitive-behavioral family therapy. This approach expands traditional cognitive and behavioral family therapy to an approach that is research based and problem focused and addresses multiple levels of the change process. As an integrative model it gives attention to internal processes (thoughts, expectations, images, and affect) and how they influence behavior. The intervention techniques share commonalities with the Milan, structural, and strategic approaches (Hanna & Brown, 2004). This approach has also provided the theoretical foundation for psycho-educational and parent training protocols.

SUMMARY

As we end this chapter on the history of family therapy we can summarize some of the distinguishing features of family therapy as a treatment modality (Collins, Jordan, & Coleman, 2007). As we describe family therapy we can say that the framework for family therapy is directed by thinking of "family as context" informed by the belief systems wherein the family is a special social environment conceptualized as consisting of multiple systems. A family is more than the sum of its individual parts; it is a unique system with particular responsibilities and functions, and changes within the family system affect all family members.

By approaching a complicated family situation from a systems theory perspective, the practitioner is able to be somewhat more objective about family issues. Utilizing a multiple systemic perspective for family assessment and intervention addresses many important aspects in helping families and the systems interacting and supporting the individuals in families. Practitioners who see the family context as interactions of multiple systems, the family, and its social environment will be better able to build on strengths and resilience in families and promote family self—a notion critical to practice.

The ecosystem perspective, because of its "person-in-environment" focus, provides a lens through which the family and family members can be understood within the context of transactions with a variety of biological, psychological, life cycle, cultural, and historical environments. Families from different cultural, racial, ethnic, and religious groups and representing alternative lifestyles may experience the impact of legal, social, and economic biases and discrimination that may impact family functioning. Finally, families have their own unique narrative or story that defines their identity, their place in the world, and how they interpret significant events and intrafamilial relationships (White, 2007; White & Epston, 1990).

While we have reviewed some of the clinical and conceptual influences on the history of family therapy, we have not included all the major theorists who have made and continue to make a significant contribution to the field of family therapy. But we have given an overview of some of the significant theorists, researchers, and clinicians who have made family therapy what it is. We have further presented some of the conceptual and theoretical influences on family therapy as a psychotherapeutic modality. We have presented some of the issues and critiques that continue to inform the theoretical development of family therapy models.

Let us say in summary that as a corrective measure to systems theories, the postmodern critiques do address some of the major limitations of family systems theories. Yet these critiques do not necessitate a rejection of systems-based theories. The focus of the structural-functional and communicative-interactive practice models, within the context of ecological theories, can provide a framework for understanding the actual structure of the family along with the narrative meaning and interpretation of that structure by family members as they are impacted by ethnic, cultural, historical, economic, and sociopolitical factors. This orientation informed by research can provide the clinician with sound judgments in providing the most effective help to families in need.

RECOMMENDED READINGS

Becvar, D. S., & Becvar, R. J. (2000). *Family therapy: A systemic integration.* Needham Heights, MA: Pearson Education.

Broderick, C. B., & Schrader, S. S. (1981). The history of professional marriage and family counseling. In A. S. Gurman & D. P. Kniskern (Eds.), *Handbook of family therapy* (Vol. II, pp. 5–38). New York, NY: Brunner/Mazel.

Hull, G. H., & Mather, J. (2006). *Understanding generalist practice with families.* Belmont, CA: Thomson Brooks/Cole.

Sayger, T. A., Homrich, A. M., & Horne, A. M. (2000). Working from a family focus: The historical context of family development and family systems. In A. Horne (Ed.), *Family counseling and therapy* (pp. 12–38). Itasca, IL: F. E. Peacock.

DISCUSSION QUESTIONS

1. The Progressive Era, which began in the late 1890s and ended at the start of the Great Depression, was marked by a wide range of social and political reform movements. How might these reform movements be seen as historical precursors to family therapy?

2. What impact did systems, cybernetics, communications, and ecological theories have on the development of models of family therapy?

3. It is suggested that during the social and political climate of social activism of the 1960s a group of iconoclastic and innovative therapists who were staging their own social revolution within the fields of psychiatry, psychology, and social work emerged. Who were these therapists, and what were their contributions to the development of family therapy?

4. As the field of family therapy has moved into the 21st century, what have been the key paradigm and generational shifts in theoretical perspectives?

REFERENCES

Ackerman, N. W. (1958). *The psychodynamics of family life.* New York, NY: Basic Books.

Ackerman, N. W. (1966). *Treating the troubled family.* New York, NY: Basic Books.

Allport, F. (1924). *Social psychology.* Boston, MA: Houghton Mifflin.

Ariel, S. (1999). *Culturally competent family therapy.* Westport, CT: Greenwood.

Atwood, J. D. (1992). *Family therapy: A systematic behavioral approach.* Chicago, IL: Nelson-Hall.

Barker, R. L., Kessler, H., & Lehn, J. M. (1984). *Treating couples in crisis.* New York, NY: Free Press.

Becvar, D. S., & Becvar, R. J. (2000). *Family therapy: A systemic integration.* Needham Heights, MA: Pearson Education.

Bell, J. (1961). Family group therapy [*Public Health Monograph* No. 64]. Washington, DC: U.S. Government Printing Office.

Blumer, H. (1969). *Symbolic interactionism: Perspective and method.* Englewood Cliffs, NJ: Prentice-Hall.

Boscolo, L., Cecchin, G., Hoffman, L., & Penn, P. (1987). *Milan systemic family therapy: Conversations in theory and practice.* New York, NY: Basic Books.

Boszormenyi-Nagy, I., & Spark, G. (1973). *Invisible loyalties: Reciprocity in intergenerational family therapy.* New York, NY: Harper and Row.

Bowen, M. (1976). Theory and practice of psychotherapy. In P. J. Guerin (Ed.), *Family therapy: Theory and practice* (pp. 42–50). New York, NY: Gardner Press.

Broderick, C. B., & Schrader, S. S. (1981). The history of professional marriage and family counseling. In A. S. Gurman & D. P. Kniskern (Eds.), *Handbook of family therapy* (Vol. II, pp. 5–38). New York, NY: Brunner/Mazel.

Cheung, M. (1997). Social construction theory and the Satir model: Toward a synthesis. *American Journal of Family Therapy, 25*(4), 331–342.

Collins, D., Jordan, C., & Coleman, H. (2007). *An introduction to family social work.* Belmont, CA: Thomson Higher Education.

Cornell, S. (2000). That's the story of our lives. In P. Spickard & W. J. Burroughs (Eds.), *Narrative and multiplicity in constructing ethnic identity* (pp. 41–51). Philadelphia, PA: Temple University Press.

Davis, A. (1973). *American heroine: The life and legend of Jane Addams.* New York, NY: Oxford University Press.

de Shazer, S. (1985). *Keys to solution in brief therapy.* New York, NY: Norton.

Fish, V. (1993). Poststructuralism in family therapy: Interrogating the narrative/conversational mode. *Journal of Marital and Family Therapy, 19*(3), 221–232.

Freeman J., & Combs, G. (1996). *Narrative therapy.* New York: Norton.

Freire, P. (1973). *Education for a critical consciousness.* New York, NY: Beacon.

Freud, S. (1956). On psychotherapy. In *Collected papers* (Vol I., pp. 256–268). London, England: Hogarth.

Friedman, M. B. (2002). Clifford Beers: The origins of modern mental health policy. *The Mental Health News.* Retrieved from http://www.mhawestchester.org/advocates/beers802.asp

Fromm-Reichmann, F. (1948). Notes on the development of treatment of schizophrenics by psychoanalytic psychotherapy. *Psychiatry, 11,* 253–273.

Gergen, K. J. (1999). *An invitation to social construction.* Thousand Oaks, CA: Sage.

Goldenberg, H., & Goldenberg, I. (2008). *Family therapy: An overview.* Belmont, CA: Thomson.

Goldner, V. (1985). Feminism and family therapy. In *Family Process, 24,* 31–47.

Gordon, W. E. (1965). Basic constructs for an integrative and generative conception of social work. In G. Hearn (Ed.), *The general systems approach: Contributions toward a holistic conception of social work.* New York, NY: Council on Social Work Education.

Griffin, E. (1997). *A first look at communication theory.* New York, NY: McGraw-Hill.

Hanna, S. M., & Brown, J. H. (2004). *The practice of family therapy: Key elements across models.* Belmont, CA: Thomson Brooks/Cole.

Hare-Mustin, R. T. (1978). A feminist approach to family therapy. *Family Process, 17,* 181–194.

Ho, M. K., Rasheed, J. M., & Rasheed, M. N. (2004). *Family therapy with ethnic minorities* (2nd ed.). Thousand Oaks, CA: Sage.

Hull, G. H., & Mather, J. (2006). *Understanding generalist practice with families.* Belmont, CA: Thomson Brooks/Cole.

Ingoldsby, B. B., Smith, S. R. & Miller, J. E. (2004). *Exploring family theories.* Los Angeles, CA: Roxbury.

Janzen, C., Harris, O., Jordan, C., & Franklin, C. (2006). *Family treatment: Evidence-based practice with populations at risk.* Belmont, CA: Thomson.

Kilpatrick, A. C., & Holland, T. P. (2009). *Working with families: An integrative model by level of need.* Boston, MA: Pearson.

Laird, J. (1989). Women and stories: Restorying women's self construction. In M. McGoldrick, C. H. Anderson, & F. Walsh (Eds.), *Women in families* (pp. 427–450). New York, NY: Norton.

Lewin, K. (1946). Behavior as a function of the total situation. In L. Carmichael (Ed.), *Manual of child psychology* (pp. 791–844). New York, NY: John Wiley & Sons.

Lewin, K., Lippett, R., & White, R. (1939). Patterns of aggressive behavior in experimentally created "social climates." *Journal of Social Psychology, 10,* 271–299.

Lidz, R., & Lidz, T. (1949). The family environment of schizophrenic patients. *The American Journal of Psychiatry, 14,* 241–248.

Lidz, T., Cornelison, A., Fleck, S., & Terry, D. (1957). Intrafamilial environment of the schizophrenic patient: I. The father. *Psychiatry, 20,* 329–342.

Luepnitz, D. A. (1988). *The family interpreted: Feminist theory in clinical practice.* New York, NY: Basic Books.

Madanes, C. (1984). *Behind the one-way mirror: Advances in the practice of strategic therapy.* San Francisco, CA: Jossey-Bass.

Madanes, C. (1991). Strategic family therapy. In A. S. Gurman & D. P. Kniskern (Eds.), *Handbook of family therapy* (Vol. VII, pp. 396–416). New York, NY: Brunner/Mazel.

Maturana, H., & Varela, F. (1984). *The tree of knowledge: Biological roots of human understanding.* London, England: Shambhala.

Mead, G. (1934). *Mind, self, and society from the standpoint of a social behavioralist.* Chicago, IL: University of Chicago Press.

Minuchin, S. (1974). *Families and family therapy.* Cambridge, MA: Harvard University Press.

Moede, W. (1920). *Experimentelle massenpsychologie.* Leipzig, Germany: S. Hirzel.

Nichols, M. P., & Schwartz, R. C. (2008). *Family therapy: Concepts and methods* (7th ed.). Boston, MA: Pearson.

Parsons, T. (1951). *The social system.* New York, NY: Free Press.

Polkinghorne, D. E. (1988). *Narrative knowing and the human sciences.* Albany: State University of New York.

Richmond, M. (1917). *Social diagnosis.* New York, NY: Sage.

Satir, V. (1988). *The new peoplemaking.* Palo Alto, CA: Science and Behavior.

Sayger, T. A., Homrich, A. M., & Horne, A. M. (2000). Working from a family focus: The historical context of family development and family systems. In A. Horne (Ed.), *Family counseling and therapy* (pp. 12–38). Itasca, IL: F. E. Peacock.

Schultz, S. J. (1984). *Family systems therapy*. New York, NY: Jason Aronson.

Semmler, P., & Williams, C. B. (2000). Narrative therapy: A storied context for multicultural counseling. *Journal of Multicultural Counseling and Development, 28*(1), 51–62.

Sherman, R., & Dinkmeyer, D. (1987). *Systems of family therapy: An Adlerian integration*. New York, NY: Brunner/Mazel.

Stevens, P. E. (1989). A critical social reconceptualization of environment in nursing: Implications for methodology. *Advances in Nursing Science, 11*(4), 56–68.

Sullivan, H. (1953). *The interpersonal theory of psychiatry*. New York, NY: Norton.

Taylor, J. B. (1997). Niche practices: Extending the ecological perspective. In D. Saleeby (Ed.), *The strengths perspective in social work practice* (pp. 217–227). New York, NY: Longman.

Triplett, N. (1898). The dynamogenic factors in peacemaking and competition. *American Journal of Psychology, 9,* 507–533.

von Bertalanffy, L. (1969). *General systems theory*. New York, NY: George Brazziller.

Watzlawick, P., Beavin, J., & Jackson, D. (1967). *Pragmatics of human communication: A study of interactional patterns pathologies and paradoxes*. New York, NY: Norton.

Watzlawick, P., (1978). *The language of change: Elements of effective communication*. New York, NY: Basic Books.

Watzlawick, P., Weakland, J. H., & Fisch, R. (1974). *Change: Principles of problem formation and problem resolution*. New York, NY: Norton.

Weakland, J. H. (1976). Communication theory and clinical change. In P. J. Guerin Jr. (Ed.), *Family therapy: Theory and practice* (pp. 111–128). New York, NY: Gardner Press.

White, M. (2007). *Maps of narrative practice*. Adelaide, Australia: Dulwich Centre.

White, M., & Epston, D. (1990). *Narrative means to therapeutic ends*. New York, NY: Norton.

Wiener, N. (1948). Cybernetics. *Scientific American, 179,* 14–18.

Wynne, L., Ryckoff, I., Day, J., & Hirsch, S. (1958). Pseudomutuality in the family relations of schizophrenics. *Psychiatry, 21,* 205–220.

Chapter 2

THE ECOLOGY OF FAMILIES
A Systems/Developmental Perspective

The 19th-century philosopher and psychologist William James (1890/1981) described the infant's perceptual world as "a great blooming, buzzing confusion." This particular metaphor is often used to describe one's initial encounter with the immediacy of a rather complex, daunting, and variegated experiential world. Such encounters can be overwhelming, thus compelling one to strive to attain some perceptual, descriptive, and explanatory clarity of that world. Describing a family therapist's work with a family as an encounter with the "blooming, buzzing confusion" of family life may represent a rather exaggerated application of this metaphor. Nonetheless it speaks to the therapist's sometimes frustrating efforts to understand the complex dynamics of family interactions. More important, it is often the family members' inability to understand and cope with the confusing complexities of their family life that brings them to the family therapist.

While this book presents a range of clinical models that render coherence and guidance to clinical interventions with families, this chapter will focus on a broader and more generic view of the family. In this chapter we will begin our discussion by posing the question "What is a family?" We will see that this question defies a simple answer, as there is great variation among contemporary families in terms of their structure, composition, and cultural and ideological lifestyles.

Though the focus of family therapy interventions is on the relational dynamics within a particular family, a family therapist cannot ignore the expectations society places on families as a social institution. In addition to fulfilling a variety of functions for individual family members, the family, as a social institution, fulfills a variety of functions for society. As a family therapist understands societal expectations for families then, she or he can better understand the possible stress experienced by the family as it attempts to fulfill those functions. The therapist can better understand and even witness the consequences when the family fails to perform those social expectations. These "consequences" may appear in the form of "presenting problems" requiring family therapy intervention. We shall discuss later in this chapter that, when a family therapist sees families in trouble, the therapist must also give attention to the family's ecological context. By viewing the family from this broader perspective the therapist will be able to assess the extent to which there are sufficient social resources and supports needed by that family to fulfill its societal obligations.

We will then turn our attention to discussing the characteristics of families in terms of how they are structured and how they function. The family is not just a collection of individuals. Families are interactional systems involving a network of interrelated and interdependent relationships. This interactional system has a level of complexity that gives the family a particular organizational structure. It is this unique characteristic of families that shapes how families function in performing their tasks.

The family as an interactional system is not a static entity. Families exist within the context of space and time and are impacted by the existential realities of birth, growth, and death. In addition, families can be profoundly impacted by other contingencies of life including political, social, and economic events as well as natural disasters. Understanding the complexities of family life involves confronting the developmental and nondevelopmental changes that families experience as they navigate through their unique life cycle. It is these changes that can produce varying amounts of stress affecting both the family as an entity and all members. These stressors require that the family rely on an array of psychosocial resources to cope with and adapt to these developmental and nondevelopmental life events, while maintaining its responsibilities to its members and fulfilling its role and function as a social institution.

As we examine the above topics we will draw upon concepts derived from ecological, systems, and life cycle theories. These theoretical perspectives represent key generic domains (Falicov, 1998) in which we can gain an understanding of the realities of family life. Many postmodern and feminist family therapy theorists question the adequacy of an ecological and systems perspective for addressing issues of social justice, sexism, and racism in family therapy practice (Franklin, Hopson, & Ten Barge, 2003). The empirical basis for systems-based theories has also been questioned (Wakefield, 1996a, 1996b, 1996c). We maintain the position that despite these critiques, ecological and systems theories remain as powerful theoretical frameworks for understanding the structure and functioning of the family and families' interaction with their broader social environment. Our stance is not to reject systems-based perspectives. We suggest that in practice, many family therapists use a combination of theories including traditional as well as postmodern. We would agree with Franklin and Jordan (2002) that a systems-informed integrative and technical eclectic perspective is the preferred approach in practicing family therapy. The application of a systems perspective can inform and guide assessment and intervention with families regardless of theoretical perspective.

From a broader ecological perspective the family as a system is nested in larger social, economic, and political systems. These systems may or may not support the family's efforts to discharge its social role as well as meet the needs of its members. These systems or environments may pose limitations and constraints as well as possibilities and opportunities for families (Bubotz & Sontag, 1993). It may be those limitations or constraints that bring a family to therapy, and it may be those possibilities that can be mobilized to support the family in its problem-solving efforts.

An ecological, systems, and developmental perspective enables us to understand that families as systems are challenged to attend to several key tasks. In the first task the family must establish a clear identity for itself as a whole and for each individual member. Second, a family must develop strategies for the execution of its social responsibilities. The third task is that a family must develop clearly defined boundaries between the family and the outside world and between individual members within the family. The fourth task is that a family must manage the family household (allocate chores, handle finances, solve problems, etc.). In the final task a family must create a warm and nurturing emotional environment, while responding to the developmental and nondevelopmental stresses encountered over time (Anderson & Sabatelli, 2003). The extent to which a family is systemically capable in addressing these tasks indicates the family's level of functioning as a system.

THE CHANGING FAMILY

It is generally a well-accepted premise that the family is the most basic and enduring of human institutions. Families are found in some form or another in every culture and/or society, and most people begin their lives within families. The significance of the family is profound in its impact on human behavior. It is also generally accepted that our personality is profoundly shaped by our experiences in our family of origin (parents, siblings, and extended family). In our most formative experiences as humans, the family is the most unique of human groupings. Families give initial shape to our identity and place in the world.

Though we can agree on the general importance of families and its endurance as a social institution, the family as an institution has taken on different permutations throughout human history. For example, the large family of the early American

Western frontier is different from the family in today's urban and suburban communities. The Western frontier family was likely a self-sufficient economic unit with each member contributing to production. By comparison the economic viability of the contemporary (urban and suburban) family unit is more than likely supported by family members working outside the family unit. Even families in today's rural America differ from the (typically) large family of the early American Western frontier, in that today's rural American families may have members of the household working outside of the home. Another important difference in today's urban family (more so than rural and/or suburban families) is (especially in large metropolitan areas) a diversity of cultural family life that is encased in rich and enduring ethnic and cultural traditions.

As we attempt to define what a family is we may likely find ourselves confronted with different images, different structures, and different cultural and ethnic practices. We might initially be prone to rely on the definition of a family given by the U.S. Census Bureau (2008): "A family is a group of two people or more (one of whom is the householder) related by birth, marriage, or adoption and residing together; all such persons (including related subfamily members) are considered as members of one family." In spite of the "apparent" inclusiveness of this definition, a specific image or concept comes to mind. This image is that of the nuclear family in which a married heterosexual couple resides with its biological children. For many who grapple with the task of defining the family, one wonders if this definition of family life truly represents today's family structure. That is, do these definitions and images of the (nuclear) family capture the increasing complexities of contemporary American family life? Crawford (1999) gives us an answer to this question:

> Society's definition of "family" is rapidly expanding and has come to include single parents, biracial couples, blended families, unrelated individuals living cooperatively, and homosexual couples, among others. Unfortunately, family policy has been slow to catch up to changing trends in modern lifestyles. (p. 271)

Crawford's statement speaks to emerging trends in family life that challenge the notion of the traditional and/or nuclear family. There are increasing variations in contemporary family structures including single-parent families, stepfamilies, blended families, gay and lesbian families, foster and adoptive families, biracial families, reconstituted families, fictive kinship families, and nonlegal (cohabitation) relationships, all of which function as families. Data supporting these trends are reflected in the U.S. Census Bureau report *America's Families and Living Arrangement* (Fields & Casper, 2000):

- In 2000 there was a decline in the proportion of households with biological children under the age of 18. This fact represents an overall decline in these types of households and family size from 1970.
- Households with biological children dropped from 45% in 1970 to 35% in 1990 and then to 33% in 2000. Such decline was attributed to changes in fertility, marriage and divorce rates, and mortality.
- Other findings revealed that single mothers increased from 3 million in 1970 to 10 million in 2000.
- The number of single fathers grew from 393,000 to 2 million in the same period.
- In 2000 there were 3.8 million households classified as unmarried-partner households. This number, representing 3.7% of all households, may actually underrepresent the true number of cohabiting couples, primarily because of possible reluctance to identify themselves as such to interviewers. Rather than classifying a cohabitation relationship, terms such as *roommates*, *housemates*, or *friends not related to each other* might be used.

Photo 2.1   As the contemporary family has changed from the traditional nuclear family structure, single fathers have assumed greater child-rearing responsibilities

Source: ©Jochen Sand/Digital Vision/Thinkstock

Such data might suggest that there are possible changes in social attitudes toward what is considered to be a family. It may appear that what was once thought of as a deviant and controversial family form such as single parenthood is more acceptable and "tolerated" in today's society.

The diversity of family structures is presented by Goldenberg and Goldenberg (2002) as they describe a contemporary scenario of a person after leaving his family of origin. As we follow this person thorough the trajectory of his future relationships we might witness the following. This person may live alone or with a roommate of the same sex. Later he may cohabit with an adult of the opposite sex, perhaps marry, have children (in or out of wedlock), get divorced, live alone again or with a lover of the same or opposite sex, become a stepparent, perhaps become widowed or divorced a second time, marry for a third time, and so forth. Though this example is not the norm, it is not necessarily an exception for individuals in contemporary society. The fluidity of relationship arrangements represents a significant number of individuals who may move through different family forms and structures during their adult years.

Even considering these emerging and increasingly socially acceptable (or at least "tolerated") family forms and structures, it is not uncommon to hear statements about the status of contemporary family life and the seeming "decline of the family." Furthermore, some view this "decline" as a contributing factor (if not causally linked) to an array of social problems. Social concerns such as poverty, drug abuse, teenage pregnancy, and juvenile delinquency are often laid at the threshold of these emerging family forms.

These social problems are seen as indicators of contemporary social and moral decline and are attributed to the erosion and decline of the traditional family. What is often not stated, yet implicit in these concerns, is that the family as an institution is not declining but the traditional and/or nuclear family is not the prominent or the dominant family structure. Without question the traditional family is considered as the family structure in which there is clarity of purpose, values, and role expectations along gender and age. The traditional family structure is further viewed as congruent with prevailing social norms. Finally, and most important, to those who raise concerns about the status of contemporary family, the stable "traditional" family contributes to social cohesion, social stability, and social well-being.

The increase in single-parent families, the increase in divorce rates, and the call for the legalization of gay marriage are considered (by those who are ringing the death knell of the traditional family) as being the cause of the moral and social decline. Those who decry the disappearance of the traditional or nuclear family and those who cry for the emergence of family values as a basis for public policy and national politics tend to speak in one voice. According to them, the family is under a death watch, if not already buried.

The Myth of the Declining Family

Do we have reason to be concerned about the so-called demise of the family? Skolnick and Skolnick (2003) challenge the notion of the singular family structure. In other words, to speak of the demise of the family conceals the assumption that there is only one singular family form. Therefore if that particular family form is on the decline then all families are on the decline. This logic is called into question in that the family as a social unit as found throughout human society varies in organization, membership, life cycles, emotional environments, ideologies, social and kinship networks, and economic and other functions. There is no one singular family structure to be found in human society.

Skolnick and Skolnick (2003) also point out that there are other assumptions about the history of the family. These assumptions imply that the family structure, in this case the traditional or nuclear image, of the past was more functional than contemporary families. As the family historian Demos (1976) points out in his studies, there is no historical "Golden Age" of the family and clearly no reason to justify that current trends indicate a decline or possible extinction of the family. For example, in previous historical periods people might have either stayed in loveless marriages or just left ("deserted") because divorce was highly stigmatized. Such desertions might have preserved the existence of a traditional family as a legal entity but rendered a family unable to give attention to the emotional well-being of its members. Stephanie Coontz (1991), another family historian, points out we may be victims of a nostalgic and idealistic image of family in which there is a clear definition of gender roles and responsibilities.

Our sense of nostalgia is further shattered as Skolnick (1991) questions whether the image of the traditional or nuclear family or the breadwinner-and-housewife form of family life is really a historical, viable, and realistic portrayal of the model family structure. This form, which emerged in the late 19th century and reproduced through the public media in the 1950s through such television programs as *The Adventures of Ozzie and Harriet*, *The Donna Reed Show*, *Father Knows Best*, and *Leave It to Beaver*, was far from traditional according to Heiner (2002) and Skolnick (1991). These television families usually consisted of a married couple with a clear division of roles and responsibilities based on gender. The father worked from 9 to 5, and the mother worked inside the home as the homemaker and nurturer. When the father came home he took charge of the family. It was this family structure that was projected as the normative family form.

According to Coontz (2003) this traditional family of the 1950s was a qualitatively new phenomenon as prior to the 1950s the historic trend had been rising divorce rates, falling birthrates, and a later age for marriage. To a great extent the stock market crash of 1929 and the Great Depression of the 1930s resulted in increased incidents of domestic violence. Divorce rates fell, but informal separations soared, along with families that were being uprooted or torn apart. The immediate post–World War II years, in many ways, further contributed to increased domestic strife as many women resented being fired from their wartime jobs when the soldiers returned. Men who in many cases had been away from their families for extended periods due to military duty found themselves on the margins of family life when they returned. Reintegration into their families was not always an easy task. With the beginning of economic recovery following World War II, people were eager to create a family life that could truly be a haven from the tumultuous period of the Depression and World War II. The 1950s images of family life became this haven. What occurred was that this image of family of the 1950s represented in the minds of many a picture of how families were supposed to be rather than what families really were (Coontz, 2003). This image of family life became entrenched in the public consciousness as the normative family structure.

While the 1950s construction of the family represented the ideal, the reality was that this family model represented middle- and upper-middle-class White families who could afford such lifestyles. Working-class White, Native, African American, Latino, and Asian families were rendered invisible in the media. Families from Central and Eastern Europe were also ignored as representative images of family life. Furthermore, issues of social inequality based on race, gender, and sexual orientation, along with family issues including marital strife, domestic violence, and child physical and sexual abuse, though present, had not emerged in the public consciousness as social and family problems. Yet many still wax nostalgically for the families of the '50s, even though it was an idealized family form that was brought about by a unique set of historical conditions. It was a model that ignored the realities of the life of many families, and was a model inaccessible to millions of poor families (Heiner, 2002). From this discussion we might conclude that part of the problem in trying to prognosticate the future of the family is how we construct or define a family.

A Working Definition of the Family

What general understanding of family life might be important to a family therapist? Returning to our earlier discussion on the definition of the family, Fitzpatrick and Wamboldt (1990) suggest that a family can be defined using three different criteria either in combination or as singular definitions. For instance, when family membership is determined by a biological and legal kinship relationship the criterion is physical. When a family is defined by the tasks it is to perform for its members the criterion is functional. The third criterion is relational or more specifically the quality of the relationships within a particular unit called a "family."

Both the physical and functional criteria can be contested due to their inadequacy in capturing what can be considered by some as constituting family and family relationships. For example, in certain ethnic communities, such as the African American community, nonbiologically related persons may be considered as part of a given family system. Though the term *fictive kin* is used to describe this form of family relationship, the sociological origin of this term fails to describe the sense of emotional bonding that may characterize kinship based on "fictive" family relationships. The functional criterion does address the fact that families have an array of social and intrafamilial expectations and obligations regarding care of members. Yet there are indicators that in some families these functions cannot be discharged because of a lack of resources and/or social supports. Can this family still be a family? Relying on this "functional" criterion alone then becomes problematic for determining whether a particular "family" unit is functioning as a family.

The relational criterion is what makes families distinct from other groups (Yerby, Buerkel-Rothfuss, & Bochner, 1995). Whereas other groups are based to some extent on voluntary associations, family membership is nonvolitional and cannot be dissolved regardless of the quality of interactions. The level of commitment and intimacy further distinguishes family groups from other groups. It is this criterion that is important for family therapists. It is this relational criterion that is the basis for understanding the family as an interactional system that covers a variety of relationships within families. Such relationships include meaningful sexual relationships, the parent-child relationship, permanent and long-lasting relationships, intimate relationships, and legal and nonlegal relationships (Longress, 2000).

Anderson and Sabatelli (2003) offer a compelling definition of the family for an ecological and systems-oriented family therapist. They understand a family as a complex structure consisting of an interdependent group of individuals who have a shared sense of history, who have experienced some degree of emotional bonding, and who have devised strategies for meeting the needs of the individual members and the group as a whole. This definition makes it clear that there is no monolithic or essentialist definition of a family as there is an array of structural variations. The family is structurally complex and is more than a singular legal definition or a given family composition, structure, or kinship relationship. From a clinical and what might be considered a pragmatic perspective, the focus for therapy is what a family *does in terms of fulfilling its tasks* and how the family is systemically organized to accomplish its tasks. Searching for definitional clarity for "What is a family?" will be a challenge as the family continues to morph into different and diverse structures. It is these diverse family structures that present themselves to the family therapist. It is these diverse family structures that struggle to attain problem-free interactions among family members.

THE SOCIAL ECOLOGY OF FAMILIES

Regardless of the variety of family structures, the family is viewed as having the primary functions of socialization and the protection of the health and well-being of the child, if children are a part of the family composition. As the transmitter of culture, traditions, values, and language the family also assumes a mediating role between the individual family member and society. In carrying out these roles the family is seen as having the following four central functions: establishing family membership and family formation; providing economic resources for the family members; providing for the nurturance, education, and socialization of the dependent family members; and protecting its vulnerable members. In this mediating role the family fulfills these important functions for the individual members and society (see Table 2.1). If families are successful in fulfilling these functions

Table 2.1 Primary Function of the Family for Individual Members and for Society

Family Function	Individual Family Members	Society
Membership and family formation	Provides a sense of belonging Provides personal and social identity Provides meaning and direction for life	Controls reproductive functions Ensures continuance of the species
Economic	Provides for basic needs of food, shelter, and clothing and other resources to enhance human development	Contributes to healthy development of members who are becoming contributing members of society (and who need fewer public resources)
Nurturance, education, and socialization	Provides for the physical, psychological, social, and spiritual development of children and adults Instills social values and norms	Prepares and socializes children for protective adult roles Supports adults in being productive members of society Controls antisocial behavior and protects society from harm
Protection of vulnerable members	Provides protective care and support for young, ill, disabled, or otherwise vulnerable members	Minimizes public responsibility for care of vulnerable, dependent individuals

Source: Adapted from Patterson (2002).

society benefits. When families fail then society bears the cost of the family's failure. Conversely when society fails the family becomes the cause. Families have an awesome responsibility, and society gives these responsibilities to the family. The issue becomes whether there is societal support for the family in carrying out these responsibilities.

We can see that as families carry out a broader social mandate, they are embedded in a much broader social context and are inextricably interconnected with these larger, more expansive social systems. Families are not islands unto themselves but are involved in multiple transactions with other systems within their environment or niche (Auerswald, 1968; Bronfenbrenner, 1979; Germain & Gitterman, 1996). As we discussed how the emergence of family therapy represented a paradigm shift from the autonomous self to the relational self, the ecological perspective shifts our understanding of families as being isolated, autonomous, and independent social units to being a relational system that is dynamically interconnected with other social systems. These systems constitute the social ecological context in which the family is embedded. Within this context are institutions that specifically assist the family in performing its function. For example, medical services, day care centers, parent training programs, schools, law enforcement agencies, governmental income maintenance policies, and other institutions important to family functioning are located within the ecological space of families.

A family's social ecology includes four levels or systems, each of which is nested in a larger system. These four levels are known as the *microsystem, mesosystem, exosystem, and macrosystem* (Bronfenbrenner, 1977, 1979, 1986). The first system level or *microsystem* is the individual and those within his or her immediate life space. For children the microsystem includes family, peers, school, and neighborhood. The adult's microsystem context might include the significant other, the immediate family (of origin and of procreation), work, and the neighborhood. The *mesosystem* represents the relationships between the members within an individual's microsystem. The primary mesosystem relationship for children may include their parents' interaction with the school, and for adults a mesosystem relationship may be between the individual's significant other and his or her parents or siblings. The *exosystem* includes those systems that the individual may never deal with directly but that can influence the individual's well-being. The exosystem includes institutional structures such as the local government and voluntary associations such as the Chamber of Commerce. Finally there are macrosystems, which include the cultural context of family life. This includes values, traditions, laws, cultural factors, and larger social institutions that impact the well-being of families. A basic social ecological premise is that the environment for a family includes the sociopolitical, cultural, and economic context that surrounds the lived experiences of the family and family members. It is the

Photo 2.2 Uries Bronfenbrenner's social ecology theory provided a framework for understanding families in the context of larger social systems

Source: © AP Photo

broader context of culture, economics, and politics that can significantly determine if the family's social ecological context is supportive of the mental, physical, and social functioning of the individual and his or her family.

Yet it is within the realm of a family's mesosystem and exosystem context that a more direct impact on families may be had. As Connard and Novick (1996) point out there may or may not be the resources and relationships within a community that a family needs to carry out its family and social responsibilities. As a result each family may have to actively develop its own network of support from the formal and informal resources available. Garnering those resources may be particularly challenging in certain communities. For example, rural families have few employment opportunities, lower economic well-being, fewer educational opportunities, and less access to health care and social services. In many inner-city urban communities, parents must cope with the threat of violent crime in their neighborhood, more impersonal ties, and an unresponsive and/or uncoordinated network of formal support services and resources. A family's response to demands and challenges from these urban environments may promote or hinder family functioning. In many instances a family's informal social network provides services that are more accessible, culturally appropriate, and acceptable than the services that may be offered by formal support systems (Unger & Sussman, 1990).

These multicontextual and multilayered systems are not static but are dynamic and evolving in reciprocal relationships with each other. This dynamic interplay of influence between individuals, their families, and the larger environments have "cascading" and cross-system effects (Robbins, Mayorga, & Szapocznik, 2003; Szapocznik & Coatsworth, 1999) that impact the structure, function, and course of family development. Along with transacting with the larger ecological influences, individuals and families are constantly changing as they move through life cycle issues. From an *ecodevelopmental* perspective (Szapocznik & Coatsworth, 1999) attention must be given to the reciprocal interactions between and within the family's ecological context that emerge during the developmental life. As families change during their life cycle the ecological context may also change within the context of *a chronosystem*. This refers to the changes in one's social ecological context over time (Gardiner & Komitzki, 2002). The confluence of these multiple factors can create stressor events for the family. These stressors present challenges for families to adapt a systemic response.

The transactional relationships between families and their social ecological environments support the idea that "as the family goes so goes society." But as the interactions between the family and society form a complex circular feedback loop one could say that "as society goes so goes the family."

A SYSTEMS APPROACH TO UNDERSTANDING FAMILIES

As we discussed in the previous chapter, the field of family therapy emerged out of the efforts of family researchers and family therapy practitioners to understand the impact of family life on the mental health of individuals. It was discovered by these researchers that there was something unique and potent about the relational dynamics within families that could support and reinforce emotional difficulties. These researchers and practitioners began to speculate that even if gains were made in individual psychotherapy, the relational dynamics within the family, if unchanged, could reverse those therapeutic gains causing the patient to revert back to his or her original emotional difficulties. These observations supported the conclusion that there were systemic properties of the family unit that contributed to the etiology of emotional difficulties.

From these observations it was concluded that the problematic behaviors of family members were interconnected with the behaviors of other family members. These behaviors not only were viewed as possibly serving a function or purpose for a family but also may be unintentionally maintained and reinforced by the interactional systems within the family. Even as behavioral and emotional problems were viewed as symptoms of current family relationship patterns there was some evidence to support that these patterns of behavior had been transmitted across generations. These research discoveries and clinical insights further supported the development of a systems approach to families. Utilizing a systems perspective is supported by the issues that families bring to the family therapy practitioner. These issues are multiple and varied and reflect difficulties in managing family relationships. Janzen and Harris (1997) present a classification of family problems that therapists might encounter (see Table 2.2). This list, adapted from Hill (1958), is not exhaustive, but

Table 2.2	A Classification of Family Crises

1. Accession to Marriage
   - Marriage or remarriage
   - Pregnancy (wanted or unwanted) and parenthood
   - Deserter or runaway returns
   - Stepparent addition or remarried family combination
   - War reunions
   - Foster child addition, adoption, or other adult additions
   - Restoration to health (e.g., terminated alcoholism)

2. Loss of Membership
   - Death
   - Hospitalization
   - War or employment separation
   - Child starting school, leaving home
   - Wife starting employment

3. Demoralization
   - Abuse, battering, violence
   - Chronic illness or handicap
   - Job problems, including job loss
   - School problems
   - Parent-child, sibling conflict
   - Nonsupport or other income loss
   - Infidelity or other marital conflict
   - Alcoholism or other addiction
   - Delinquency
   - Community and neighborhood conditions

4. Demoralization Plus Accession or Loss
   - Illegitimate or unwanted pregnancy
   - Runaway or desertion
   - Separation or divorce
   - Imprisonment
   - Suicide or homicide
   - Hospitalization for mental illness

5. Change of Status
   - Sudden shift to poverty or wealth
   - Move to new housing or neighborhood
   - Maturation due to growth (e.g., adolescence, aging, therapy, or other sources of individual change)

Each event has consequences for:

   - Individual adjustment both psychologically and behaviorally
   - Family group adjustment, role relationship, tasks
   - Family group relationship to the outside world

Source: Janzen & Harris (1997), adapted from Hill (1958).

it does suggest that families experience emotional changes, emotional tensions, and problems in their various roles as parents, grandparents, couples, stepparents, children, and teenagers (Herbert & Harper-Dorton, 2002). These roles are performed within the systemic context of family life.

Principles of Systems Theory

Systems theory has a set of guiding principles that helps us think dynamically about how families are structured and how they function. As each family is organized differently it is important to gain an understanding of the distinctive properties of systems as they apply to families. In the following section we will explore seven selected characteristics of the family system.

- The Whole Is Greater Than the Sum of Its Parts
- The Interdependence of Family Relationships
- Circular Causality
- Family Homeostasis
- Family Boundaries and Subsystems
- Family Roles
- Family Rules

The Whole Is Greater Than the Sum of Its Parts

Families are much more than a collection of individuals who live together and are related to each other. It is the *relationship* between family members rather than the family members themselves that defines this systems characteristic of families. To say that the "whole is greater than the sum of its parts" is to describe the interactional and relationship patterns that constitute the family as an entity. From a systems perspective it is the process, the relationship, or the dynamic interactions that give character and characteristics to a family system. Collins, Jordan, and Coleman (2007) liken a family system to music. In a music composition a singular note does not constitute the musical piece. But several notes arranged together according to certain rules of music composition and interacting with each other in a particular manner yield a composed arrangement. It is the interaction and relational dynamics and patterns between the members of a family that constitute the family "melody."

This "melody" or interactive pattern is the substance of a family's identity. This identity represents the structural wholeness of the family with its unique relational and interactive characteristics. Each family has its own rules, its own communication patterns, and its own way of managing both its internal organization and its relationship to the external environment. The structural organization of the family, as maintained by certain recursive interactional patterns and family rules and roles, is subject to shifts and changes as family members move through their own life cycle. Even as families shift and change, they still remain as systemic entities whose systemic properties are "greater" than the aggregate of the individual family members.

The Interdependence of Family Relationships

Implicit in the above discussion on the systemic wholeness of families is that one part of the family system cannot be understood in isolation from other parts. This state of interdependence further amplifies the concept of wholeness. As family relationships are interdependent the locus of family problems can be located not within an individual family member but within the relational interactions of the family members. For example, a child's problem behaviors cannot be understood outside of the context of his or her family's interactional patterns. Any description of a child has to consider the circular patterns of interaction within the child's family system. A family is like a mobile or objects connected by a string. When one of the objects is hit the others move. As with a mobile, the behavior of one family member is related to and dependent on the behavior of another family member. The interdependence of family members has been confirmed in many psychotherapeutic settings where it was observed that improvement or a regression in one family member impacts either positively or negatively other family members (Goldenberg & Goldenberg, 2008; Nichols & Schwartz, 2008; Watzlawick, Beavin, & Jackson, 1967).

Circular Causality

From a systems perspective one cannot simply discern a simple linear cause-and-effect relationship between emotional and behavioral responses within families. As family relationships are interdependent these relationships are embedded in reciprocal and mutually reinforcing interaction patterns. The concept of circularity describes how every member within a family system influences every other member in a circular chain reaction. In this complex causal chain, family members are engaged in a continuous series of feedback loops in which every member of a system influences every other member.

Take for example a parent-child conflict. Rather than a child's acting-out behavior causing a particular parental response, that very same parental response may continue to activate or reinforce the child's behavior. Within the context of this network of circular feedback loops, the parent's behavior while reactive does influence, within the context of mutual reciprocal interactions, the child's behavior. Families do act in predictable ways with repetitive patterns of behavior. Due to the systemic nature of families these patterns become ingrained over time. Within these repetitive patterns a family therapist can locate circular patterns of interactions.

Family Homeostasis

The family as an organizational entity attempts to maintain equilibrium, stability, and order in its overall functioning. This stability is maintained through the enforcement of family norms, rules, and mutually reinforcing feedback loops. Family rules are like a thermostat or baseline norms that regulate family interaction within a range of acceptable behaviors. This acceptable range represents the balance. When the interactions deviate from this setting (family rules) homeostasis is impacted. Homeostasis is affected as families adapt and cope with the developing and emerging needs of family members. Yet in responding to and adapting to these changes, the family must retain a state of stability.

An example of efforts to maintain family homeostasis can be seen in a blended family as it attempts to establish a stable family system after experiencing the disruption of a previous family arrangement. This family is faced with the tasks of (a) attempting to find a balance between perhaps different styles of parenting, (b) examining what tasks must be undertaken to achieve and maintain stability within a new family arrangement, and (c) supporting the different developmental concerns of family members while attending to change and adapting to a new family environment. Several questions can be asked about this family. Are there family members who resist change? Are they dealing with reorganization issues? Are they able to attain what may appear to be the elusive goal of equilibrium while trying to respond to change? It is inevitable that these questions will emerge as the family moves toward establishing stability, order, and structure.

Families will encounter pressures to respond to external environments and the internal and developmental needs of family members. These pressures have the potential of destabilizing a family. Divorce may threaten homeostasis. Having an elderly parent or and adult child move back into the home can affect the equilibrium of a family, with a reverberating impact throughout the family. The ability to adapt and change is a marker of a family's ability to maintain homeostasis. If the family cannot change its rules and role functioning and "get back on track" then problems may ensue. In these instances the question for the family is whether it has the capacity to achieve homeostatic balance though the balance might be precarious and delicate.

Family Boundaries and Subsystems

Family boundaries are a way of demarcating who is in and who is out of the family. Those who are given access to the family and those who are not define the family's boundaries. Family boundaries also represent the point of contact between the family system and other larger systems within its social ecology. As boundaries separate a family from the larger systems, boundaries also delineate subsystems within the family system. Family subsystems include spousal subsystems, parent-child subsystems, and sibling subsystems. There may be other subsystems within a family, for example subsystems based on a mutual interest in particular activities. These subsystem boundaries must be sufficiently well defined and flexible in order to allow those within the subsystem to perform their tasks while remaining open to permit contact with other subsystems within the family (Rosenblatt, 1994). This allows for both autonomy and interdependence between the subsystems. In families there are system hierarchies and boundaries that demarcate one subsystem from another—according to the subsystems hierarchal position within the family system.

Family systems and subsystems have boundaries that can be relatively open (permeable) or closed (rigid) allowing for information to be included in or excluded from the system. The "filtering" function of boundaries allows a system to exclude any external element that may seem threatening to the family's rules, norms, and sense of who its members are. At the same time, this function incorporates those elements that seem beneficial and supportive to the family. It is possible then to classify family boundaries on a continuum from open to closed, depending on how permeable or flexible the boundaries are (Ingoldsby, Smith, & Miller, 2004).

Family Roles

Family roles are recurrent patterns of behavior by which family members fulfill family functions and needs (Epstein, Bishop, Ryan, Miller, & Keitner, 1993). Each subsystem has certain tasks or functions within the systems. Each member of a subsystem may have a prescribed role and function that is defined both by his or her position in the family and by his or her location in the subsystem. Roles reflect a family member's status within the family and differential and behavioral expectations that family members have of each other. Roles can be consciously assigned reflecting who performs what set of tasks in the family. Roles may also originate from specific interactional patterns between family members. An example of a role that emerges from specific interactions is the role of being the family "scapegoat." The family member occupying that role serves the function of being the family's "symptom bearer." Roles may also be based on gender role expectations. Traditional gender role assignments generally associate instrumental tasks with men and expressive tasks with women. Roles may reflect and be supported by social sanctions, and role expectations may be influenced by culture and ethnic background, family of origin, and lifestyle.

Family Rules

Family rules are unspoken guidelines that inform and structure family interactions. Family rules emerge from repetitive interactional patterns and serve as norms to organize family interactions (Ingoldsby et al., 2004). Even as families change and these changes impact the interactional patterns within the family, the family will attempt to maintain its identity within the context of change. This may be done through the enactment of family rules. Again referring to the previous example of a blended family, this family can be understood by examining the unique rules that structure and regulate the interaction among the family members. In this new family structure the initial rules that organize this family may represent remnants of rules from its previous family experience. The task for newly constituted families is to negotiate rules that will structure interactions in this new family structure. These rules will determine what is permitted and what is prohibited— "the dos and don'ts," the prescriptions and injunctions. These rules, in identifying the new expectations for interaction among family members, will have to be flexible enough to allow for stability, cohesiveness, and the establishment of a new family identity.

Strategies for Maintaining the Family System

A family must design certain strategies and tasks to maintain the viability of the family system. These tasks or strategies are those unwritten policies and procedures a family adapts to maintain its optimal functioning. These policies and procedures influence the unique patterns of interaction that each family establishes to execute these tasks. Anderson and Sabatelli (2003) describe these strategies as first- and second-order tasks that are common to all families regardless of the particular composition, socioeconomic status, and cultural and ethnic or racial heritage of a family. The first-order tasks include (a) identity formation, (b) socialization of family members, (c) maintenance of family boundaries, and (d) promoting the health and welfare of family members. The second-order tasks are those strategies that families employ to adapt to first-order tasks in order to manage change and stress. We will address the second-order tasks following our discussion of the family life cycle. The performance of these tasks is of course shaped by the family's ecological context. The ecological context may offer support, guidance, and resources to the family as it implements these strategies.

Identity Formation

The formation of the family identity includes developing those family themes or organizing narratives that define the unique identity of that family. This family narrative has both conscious and unconscious elements and is woven into the relational life of the family. In many respects it is a framework for establishing the family's place in the social order and the core values that define a particular family. Family identity formation through the narrative involves the family establishing its unique identity in terms of how its members may want others to view them in terms of their own distinctiveness. This family narrative is also the framework around which family members attain both self-identity and identity as a member of their family. This narrative also incorporates multigenerational, ethnic, and cultural themes.

Socialization Tasks

The socialization task is the process in which the family provides the family members with experiences and information that form and inform their identity. This identity is not just an extension of the family narrative but also includes issues of gender, personal qualities, and how to view and relate to others in the family. Socialization tasks also include preparing family members for the external society; this task is one of the primary responsibilities of a family—the process involved in developing those skills that navigate the broader social environment. This task also calls for the enlistment of external resources and other institutions to assist the family in these socialization tasks. Within the domain of a particular family, there may also be mutigenerational support that can be mobilized in this effort as well.

Boundary Maintenance Tasks

As discussed earlier the systemic properties of boundaries refer to those activities that the family must undertake in defining who is in the family and how they regulate the flow of information. The ability to manage information relates to whether family boundaries are open or closed and how permeable these boundaries need to be. The issue of boundary permeability applies to both a family's external boundaries and boundaries with subsystems within the family. As we approach these boundary issues the question becomes to what extent boundaries can change according to the developmental needs of the family and within the family over time. Hence, the question is how these boundaries become regulated while maintaining balance within the family.

Promoting the Health and Welfare Task

The final task involves promoting the health and welfare of family members. This task involves the family establishing priorities regarding resource allocation to ensure the health and well-being of family members. This strategy focuses on basic survival needs of the family including the acquisition of food, clothing, and shelter for the family. Hence, the family must be organized to allocate time and resources to accomplish this task, in that there must be a decision-making system in place. The family must have some system in place (i.e., a decision-making hierarchy as to who is in control of the allocation of resources).

This particular task also involves developing ways to define and enforce the authority, power, control, and structure within the family, as well as developing a method to support the emotional climate within families. Managing the emotional climate involves a variety of efforts within the family to communicate effectively in a problem-solving capacity, in that managing the emotional climate of a family involves allowing members to be nurtured, supported, and valued. The family must develop a structure within the family to allow family members to work cooperatively to accomplish common family goals. As families have conflict, families must have the structure necessary to manage the inevitable conflict that will occur.

THE FAMILY LIFE CYCLE

Family systems change over time. As families change they move through what might be considered predictable developmental states. For example, changes in family size are usually due to additions or losses of family members through birth or death. There are also changes in the ages of family members with corresponding changes in role relationships. There may be changes in work status. There are changes in the household composition. There may be changes due to relocation issues due to employment-related factors.

Photo 2.3 The birth of the first child is a significant event in the life of a couple causing a major realignment in their relationship in order to integrate a child into their expanding family

Source: Copyright © Can Stock Photo Inc./Graytown

Families must also respond to the demands and expectations from work, social groups, community institutions, and the society as a whole, as they are impacted by changes within their exosystem and macrosystem environments. All these changes impact the family system in an untold number of ways and do not occur without a degree of stress. Stress builds when the resources and coping skills of a family are inadequate to meet the demands and expectations of the multiple systems within the family's ecological environment. If stress increases beyond a certain point, for whatever reason, a family's ability to function might be impacted (Schorr, 1989).

There are several changes that could possibly impact the family system during the life of a family (Ragg, 2006).

1. The interactive system may change as the family grows and adds new members.

2. Hierarchal systems may change over time as family members (parents and children) negotiate issues of power and autonomy and the extent and limit of parental authority.

3. Support functions may change, as members move from dependence to independence.

4. Boundaries and subsystem boundaries change as family members move in and out of the family household due to their developmental stage.

5. The meaning of relationships changes as family members shift and change role relationships and role obligations with each other.

6. Role functions change as new roles are assumed, adding to the possibility of role renegotiation.

Life cycle theories attempt to capture the impact of these changes on family life by identifying predicable stages and developmental tasks that families experience over time. Key to the life cycle perspective are not only the stages families go through but also challenges they face in each stage, how they resolve these challenges, and their ability to transition to the next stage. One of the key assumptions in life cycle theory is that the success or difficulties in mastering the tasks in one stage may impact the readiness for the next stage. From a life cycle perspective, family problems are seen as (a) a developmental arrest at one stage of development or (b) being unable to move on because of the failure to achieve certain competencies at particular stages (Ragg, 2006).

In many stage theories of human development there are some basic critiques of the family life cycle perspective (Becvar, 2007; Ragg, 2006). A major critique of family stage theories is that they may tend to convey the notion that each developmental stage is an isolated and static event in the life of families. As family life is ongoing and interactive, these theories may not be able to truly capture the rich dynamic process of family life as it is impacted by time. These theories may also lead to the assumption that each family progresses through these life cycle stages in a linear, orderly fashion, which is seldom the way family life actually occurs. The other critique is that life cycle models fit only a small percentage of American families. As previously discussed the issue of the diversity of family structures would also suggest that there may be varied modifications of the life cycle of different family structures. For example, single-parent families, step and blended families, and gay and lesbian families will experience unique developmental challenges quite different from the "traditional" nuclear family. We will examine family therapy practice with different family structures in later chapters; we will also describe some of these life cycle variations.

Finally as the life cycle speaks to the movement of families through time, we have to acknowledge that there are different qualities of time (Ingoldsby et al., 2004). *Ontogenetic* time refers to one's personal awareness of time as one is going through one's unique life cycle. From an existential perspective ontogenetic time is lived time or one's subjective experience of time. The other dimension of time is *generational* or how one experiences time within one's social group in one's family or cohort. This is the experience of time related to being a member of a group and the collective experience of time. *Historical* time refers to how time is experienced in a greater historical period and how this period shapes and influences one's experience and identity in a larger panoramic and historical context. These dimensions of time may differentially shape one's experiences as one move through the family life cycle.

Stages of Family Development

A life cycle model, even with its shortcomings, provides a framework for capturing some of the key developmental tasks for families. The model presented in Table 2.3 (Collins et al., 2007) is an adaptation from three life cycle models: Becvar and Becvar (1993), Carter and McGoldrick (1988), and Duvall (1957). This model, which is primarily descriptive of the stages and tasks that families encounter over time, is useful in identifying some of the stressors that families might experience as they move through life.

Table 2.3   Stages of the Family Life Cycle

Stage	Family Task
1. Marriage/couple/ pair bonding	• Committing to the relationship • Formulating roles and rules • Becoming a couple while separating from the family of origin • Making compromises and negotiating around concrete and personal needs
2. Families with young children	• Restabilizing the couple unit with a triangle • Bonding with the child and integrating that child into the family • Realigning relationships with one another, deciding on work or career and domestic chores
3. Families with school-aged children	• Allowing greater independence of children • Opening family boundaries to accommodate new social institutions and new people • Understanding and accepting role changes
4. Families with teenagers	• Dealing with teen demands for independence through appropriate boundary adjustments • Adjusting to a new definition of personal autonomy • Rule changes, limit setting, and role negotiation
5. Families with young people leaving home	• Preparing young persons for independent living through schooling and job skills • Accepting and promoting these youths' self-sufficiency
6. Boomerang stage	• Readjusting families to accommodate children returning home as young adult children • Dealing with couple issues • Renegotiating personal and physical space • Renegotiating role responsibilities
7. Middle-aged parents	• Adjusting to new roles and relationships not centered on children
8. Aging family members	• Involvement with grandchildren and partners of the children • Dealing with issues and difficulties of aging • Striving to maintain dignity, meaning, and independence

Source: Collins et al. adapted from Becvar & Becvar (1993), Carter & McGoldrick (1988), and Duvall (1957).

Marriage/Couple/Pair Bonding

Making a decision to live together in a committed relationship is a major life decision. This decision may or may not include marriage, but it does involve two people forming their own unique couple system. If this is the first such relationship after leaving one's family of origin, one may find him- or herself realigning his or her relationships with his or her family of origin and friends to now include the "significant other." The event prior to this decision might have included a period of courtship or engagement or a period in which the individuals are engaged in exploring their images of the ideal mate and the ideal couple relationship. A comparison between the "ideal" and the "real" is made with an evaluation as to whether this particular partner is the "right" one. What may be considered as "right" may be based not solely on romance but on other factors including personality, social and cultural expectations, family history, and economics (Collins et al., 2007).

As couples come together they bring to the relationship two distinct narratives about couple relationships. These narratives are informed by their family of origin experiences and/or their prior relationship experiences. In this new relationship the couple begins to embark on creating its own new and unique couple narrative. The creation of this new couple narrative involves some negotiating and adjustment in key areas. For instance how to manage finances; combining the nuances of lifestyle differences; allocation of household duties; developing relationships with in-laws; if no prior sexual relationships, adjusting in the areas of sexuality and sexual intimacy; and decisions about when or if to have children all become themes to consider in the new couple story. The couple is also challenged to establish a degree of psychological intimacy that supports a sense of interdependency. Here the couple is formulating new roles and rules to govern the family and make compromises and negotiate around concrete and personal needs.

Families With Young Children

In this stage there is the accepting of new members into the couple's relationship. The birth of a child is an option for some couples, and having children may occur prior to the actual

Photo 2.4   Monica McGoldrick along with Betty Carter develop the family life cycle model, which outlined the major developmental tasks for families

Source: © Ascender Graphic Arts Corporation

commitment to the couple's relationship. The question for the couple at this juncture is what is the agreement about having children? Did the initial pregnancy occur within the context of a committed relationship, or did the commitment occur during or after the pregnancy or birth? These factors may have a significant impact on how the couple manages the tasks in this stage. The major task and/or stressor is adjusting the relationship system to make the space to integrate the new family member (child) into the system. The needs of this new dependent member of the family prompt the basic role transition from a partner relationship to a parenting relationship, which includes accepting and adjusting to a dependent personality while maintaining a functional and satisfying partner relationship.

The child, who is totally dependent on the parents, needs a safe and comfortable relationship environment to ensure that both psychological and physiological needs are met. To meet the child's needs while maintaining a functional partner relationship requires the couple to reevaluate roles, rules, and responsibilities (McGoldrick, 1999). Such issues for consideration include negotiating child-rearing responsibilities, financial matters, work and career decisions, domestic chores, and how to integrate extended family members into a new role from in-laws to grandparents. This developmental stage becomes more complex because of the six types of life cycles it encompasses: the family life cycle, the couple's life cycle, the individual life cycle of each adult, the child's life cycle, the cycle of each partner's family of origin, and the extended family life cycle.

Families With School-Aged Children

In this stage the first dependent child transitions from the protective "womb" of the family into the larger world (school and other environments). The parents now become concerned about a variety of issues as the child moves toward greater independence. Such concerns evoke a greater sense of protectiveness and safety. If the child comes from an ethnic minority family or a family of color the parents may be concerned about the child's encounters with discrimination and individual prejudice. The parents may be concerned about increased exposure of the child (and his or her family) to external parental images or different ideologies and sharing the external care of the child with other institutions.

In this stage the parents have to abdicate some of their parental authority and share it with other institutions. In sharing parental authority, the parents also have to allow for greater independence of the child. In this transition the child's behaviors in public and institutional spaces become reflective of the parents' parenting skills, and the parents are now under public scrutiny. In addition the parents have to enter into these public spaces as they support and/or protect their child as he or she enters into new domains. The parents have to instill the skills in the child that will enable him or her to manage and adapt in the broader world. If there are younger children in the home, the parents are further challenged to attend to the different developmental needs of their children.

Families With Teenagers

Adolescence is a period of rapid developmental changes. Great biological, psychological, and cognitive changes occur as the adolescent moves toward exploring different identities. During this period, the challenge for the parent is to provide the space for the adolescent to establish his or her own identity, which may be experienced as oppositional to the values of the parents and family. In the movement to define a self, the adolescent may test the family boundaries and rules. As the parent deals with the teen's demands for autonomy, the parent is challenged to adjust to the teen's new definitions of personal autonomy.

During this period the adolescent is working through life cycle issues such as forming and solidifying an identity while establishing some autonomy and differentiation of self from the family. Along with this identity struggle the adolescent may be attempting to examine his or her own sexual roles by comparing with those of his or her parents and/or differentiating from them his or her ideas about appropriate sexual behaviors. The issue of sexuality may be fraught with some anxiety for the parents, and they will have to become more comfortable with their own sexuality to permit discussion with their adolescents.

As the adolescent is challenged by the parents in terms of becoming more responsible for decision making, the family is faced with the task of reevaluating and developing flexible authority to permit increased independence on the part of the adolescent. The adolescent may further be encouraged to participate in decision making while the parents maintain their executive authority.

Families With Young People Leaving Home

As a young adult leaves home he or she is now moving outside of the family support network to establish both emotional and financial independence and responsibility. This stage involves the young adult establishing his or her own identity separate from the family of origin. The young adult also may be engaged in developing his or her own independent household and establishing him- or herself in a career or vocation. Making choices of whether to marry or remain single may be another consideration. When the last child leaves the home, the couple will have to rework the couple narrative to include living with an "empty nest." The couple may be involved in accepting multiple exits from the family system and coping with the task of "letting go." This can be a period of new stress with the parents having to renegotiate their relationship with their now adult children. When the final exit of a dependent member comes, the family copes with issues of becoming smaller and/or of extended family (grandparents, in-laws), if the young single adult becomes involved in a bonding relationship.

Boomerang Stage

Collins et al. (2007) recognized that this is a significant stage that is not included in other life cycle theories. Though a child may leave home as a young adult there are situations where the young adult may return home. This return may be due to a variety of factors including illness, relationship problems, or financial setbacks. The challenge for the family is avoiding reverting back to former parent-child roles by maintaining an adult-to-adult relationship. Yet in the adult relationship, the family has to negotiate the level of household and financial contributions to the family.

Middle-Aged Parents

This is a period in which the parents may be involved in reviewing and reappraising where they are in terms of their earlier goals, dreams, and life aspirations. It may be the period of the proverbial midlife crisis. One may be looking at areas of fulfillment and disappointments in his or her individual life and couple relationship. There may be a change in the relationship with the parents of the couple that might involve care for aging parents. If this couple is experiencing the boomerang period along with carrying for elderly parents, the stress on the couple's relationship could be extremely intense. There may be a reflective time in which the couple may begin to develop a spiritual foundation that will sustain each or both members through declining physical health and loss of loved ones. This may be the point at which there is contemplation of retirement.

Aging Family Members

At this stage the aging family members are coping with the vicissitudes of the aging process and retirement. This may include declining health and increased dependency on their children. Social activities may change along with the adjustment to changing physical abilities. The aging person may also have to consider different living arrangements that may limit mobility and independence. The aging family member may be dealing with issues of finding one's place in life despite the aging process. If death of one's partner has occurred, then the individual may be focused on issues of loneliness while maintaining his or her own functioning and interest in the face of physiological decline. In the face of declining physical ability the aged person may still strive to maintain dignity, meaning, and independence. He or she may still be involved in the exploration of new familial and social role options. This exploration may occur while he or she is dealing with the aging process, illness, and death and achieving serenity, spirituality, and isolation and dependency.

FAMILY STRESS: AN INTEGRATION OF SYSTEMS AND DEVELOPMENTAL THEORY

Thus far in this chapter we have described the social function and social ecology of the family. We further discussed the family as a system that embraces change as family members as well as the family move through a series of life transitions. The major tasks of the family system are to adapt the family's interactional system to manage its social responsibilities, to maintain the adequate functioning of the family system, and to adapt to transitional and life cycle transitions. According to Anderson and Sabatelli (2003) families must develop what they describe as second-order tasks. These tasks are the family's ability to adapt its interactional system to cope and to adapt to change and stressful events while maintaining the adequate functioning of the family as a system.

Families encounter generally two kinds of stress, normative and non-normative (Anderson & Sabatelli, 2003). There are those changes, or normative stressor events, that come from ordinary transitions affecting the family. These include developmental changes such as puberty, aging, role changes, loss, and other crisis events faced by families. Carter and McGoldrick (1988) describe these as *horizontal stressors* or those developmental stressors that reflect life cycle transitions. How the families manage horizontal stress is reflective of what is described as *vertical stressors*, which include multigenerational family patterns resulting from family secrets and unresolved issues. The level of stress within a family is determined by both horizontal and vertical factors. Figure 2.1 describes both horizontal and vertical stressors.

There are other occurrences or non-normative stressor events that may be events that create unanticipated hardships on the family. These hardships or situational events require adaptations or alteration in those strategies used by the family to maintain functioning of the family system. These situational events may include such disasters as hurricanes, fires, economic changes, and other calamities. There are those instances when families are called to cope with both normative and non-normative stressors. For example, there are families who find they are dealing with a natural calamity, the death of a loved one, and historical economic pressures—all of which can have a significant and profound impact. Such cumulative stressor

Figure 2.1 Flow of Stress Through the Family

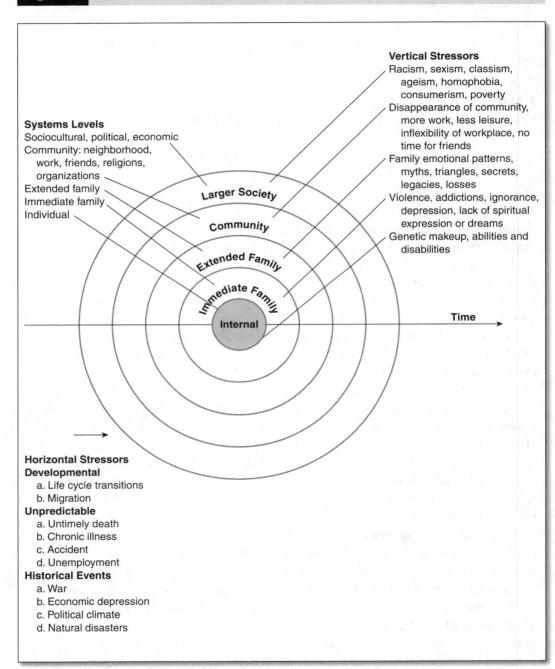

Vertical Stressors
Racism, sexism, classism, ageism, homophobia, consumerism, poverty
Disappearance of community, more work, less leisure, inflexibility of workplace, no time for friends
Family emotional patterns, myths, triangles, secrets, legacies, losses
Violence, addictions, ignorance, depression, lack of spiritual expression or dreams
Genetic makeup, abilities and disabilities

Systems Levels
Sociocultural, political, economic
Community: neighborhood, work, friends, religions, organizations
Extended family
Immediate family
Individual

Larger Society

Community

Extended Family

Immediate Family

Internal

Time

Horizontal Stressors
Developmental
  a. Life cycle transitions
  b. Migration
Unpredictable
  a. Untimely death
  b. Chronic illness
  c. Accident
  d. Unemployment
Historical Events
  a. War
  b. Economic depression
  c. Political climate
  d. Natural disasters

events can create a *pile-up stressor event* situation (Anderson & Sabatelli, 2003; McCubbin & Patterson, 1983).

What is being suggested is that stressors both normative (developmental) and non-normative (situational) can impact a family to the extent that the family system will have to adapt to these stressor events. These stressors may call the family to bond together emotionally to realign boundary maintenance tasks. In addition, these stressors may call on the family to be flexible in its role relationships and relationships ruled to adapt to new developmental and situational challenges. The family may reassess its communication patterns to be able to respond to change more readily.

The Circumplex Model

Olson, Russell, and Sprenkle (1989) provide a framework for examining how family systems cope with developmental and situational stress. This framework identifies three dimensions that speak to the family's capacity to respond to change. These dimensions refer to the family's ability to establish a sense of cohesion as it encounters those changes, its flexibility in adapting to changes, and its patterns of communication as it encounters change.

Family Cohesion

A family's ability to cope with change depends on family members' ability to work together in time of stress (Janzen & Harris, 1997). Cohesion refers to the extent of togetherness in the family and the amount of individual autonomy granted to family members. It is also an indication of the extent to which a family's relationship system is addressing change. Cohesion is the balancing of individual and family needs. The level of cohesion is indicated by the degree of emotional bonding; mutual inclusiveness; exclusion of nonfamily members; and shared time, space, friends, and interest. The degree of cohesion may vary over the course of a family life cycle with the emphasis on connection being more apparent earlier in the family's life cycle. *Disengaged* families have low cohesion; members are afforded maximum autonomy and have limited attachment to their family. *Separated* families value individual autonomy, but they have a sense of family unity and identity. *Connected* families value closeness and may prefer it. However, connected families also recognize and support development of autonomy in their members. *Enmeshed* families value family closeness above all. In enmeshed families, to sacrifice togetherness for independence is seen as a violation of family values.

Enmeshed families and disengaged families tend to be the most problematic for individuals and families. These families are unable to respond appropriately and supportively to individual family members as they move through the life cycle. Either role relationships and relationship rules are rigidly enforced to disallow for flexibility or authority, or they are nonexistent. When there are little to no rules, the family compromises its function to provide guidance and support for younger family members as they move into broader social environments.

Family Flexibility

Flexibility refers to a family's ability to modify its rules, roles, and structure in response to the pressures and conflicts of family life. The focus on flexibility is on how family systems balance the conflicting tension between balance and change. *Chaotic* families have little structure for dealing with the problems of family life. Rules are unclear and frequently not enforced. *Flexible* families are receptive to change and have the ability to resolve problems through appropriate changes in rules and roles. *Structured* families are less able than flexible families to modify rules and roles; however, these families are able to adapt and change when necessary. *Rigid* families are reluctant to change rules and roles and tend to maintain the status quo at all cost.

Family Communication

Communication is a facilitation dimension and is critical in facilitating movement between the dimension of family cohesion and family flexibility. This dimension addresses the family as a group's empathic and active listening skills. This dimension also addresses speaking skills, self-disclosure (or the ability to share feelings about self), and regard and respect for other family members. Families that have balanced communication tend to have enhanced problem-solving abilities and are able to achieve a better balance between family cohesion and family flexibility. These families are able to share thoughts and feelings in a clear and forthright manner. Such clarity of communication provides the family with a tool to mobilize the family structure to cope with the ambiguities of developmental and situational stressors.

CHARACTERISTICS OF HEALTHY AND DYSFUNCTIONAL FAMILIES

As we examine these three dimensions of cohesion, flexibility, and communication in the context of our understanding of systems theory we can see some of the characteristics of healthy and dysfunctional families (see Table 2.4). Families that function at an optimal level have subsystem boundaries and family rules that are clear and flexible. As these families encounter the many challenges throughout their life cycle they have

Table 2.4 Characteristics of Healthy and Dysfunctional Families

Family Health	*Family Dysfunction*
Subsystem boundaries are clear and may be altered as family requires.	Subsystem boundaries are rigid and diffuse and are not subject to change.
Family rules are clear and fairly enforced. Rules may change as family conditions change.	Rules are unchanging and rigidly enforced, or family has no rules or methods or organizing behavior.
Family members have a clear understanding of their role as conditions change.	Roles are rigid and may not be modified, or roles are not clearly defined and members are unsure what is required to meet expectations.
Individual autonomy is encouraged, and a sense of family unity and identity is maintained.	Individual autonomy is sacrificed for family togetherness, or autonomy is required because of lack of family unity.
Communication is clear and direct without being coercive.	Communication is vague and indirect or coercive and authoritarian.

Source: Adapted from Fenell & Weinhold (2003).

the internal systemic flexibility to meet these new demands. Under these changing conditions family cohesion is not shattered, family rules are not compromised, clarity of internal communication is maintained, and individual autonomy is respected.

There are fragile and dysfunctional families that have difficulties in managing change and adapting to the normative or non-normative stressors that families encounter. These families are marked by inflexibility and rigidity in the areas of subsystem boundaries, family rules, and family roles. Though these families may appear to be cohesive, individual autonomy is sacrificed for this appearance of cohesiveness. These families further have a communication style that is vague and indirect or coercive and authoritarian.

As family therapists encounter families in trouble, families may function somewhere on the continuum of health and dysfunction. Families that come to therapy may be in varying stages of crisis, and what is presented may not be an indicator of a family's primary level of functioning. As in crisis theory, the goal of the intervention is to enable the family to regain a level of optimal functioning.

SUMMARY

In this chapter we have discussed the generic dimensions of family life. We have presented some of the key concepts of family systems and family lifestyle theories. We have presented these concepts within the framework of a social ecological perspective. One of the key concepts for social ecological theory is "goodness of fit." As Connard and Novick (1996) point out, healthy family development and functioning depend on the match between the needs and resources of a family and the demands, supports, and resources offered by the surrounding environment. The family responds to the "environmental fit" through developmental processes associated with stress management, coping, and adaptation.

From an ecological perspective we recognize that some environments are supportive of development and some are threatening. Many vulnerable families encounter impoverished environments that may compromise the healthy development of families. These families may need targeted interventions within other domains in their social ecology. For an at-risk-family, the focus may be not on strengthening the family as a unit but on strengthening environmental supports.

As we indicated earlier, families as systems are in transactions with a broader social ecology. Family therapists have moved from viewing the individual as an autonomous self to understanding the individual as embedded in a network of relationships. Likewise family therapists must continue to move from viewing the family in isolation to viewing the family in transaction with a social ecological network. From this perspective family therapists must be cautious of locating the problem of family dysfunction within the family system. The assessment lens must also focus on the family's transaction with its ecological context.

RECOMMENDED READINGS

Becvar, D. S. (2007). *Families that flourish.* New York, NY: Norton.

Coontz, S. (1991). *The way we never were: American families and the nostalgia trap.* New York, NY: Basic Books.

Coontz, S. (2003). What we really miss about the 1950's. In A. S. Skolnick & J. H. Skolnick (Eds.), *Family in transition* (12th ed., pp. 31–40). Boston, MA: Pearson Education.

Franklin, C., & Jordan, C. (2002). Effective family therapy: Guidelines for practice. In A. R. Roberts & G. J. Greene (Eds.), *Social workers desk reference* (pp. 256–262). New York, NY: Oxford University Press.

Robbins, M., Mayorga, C. C., & Szapocznik, J. (2003). The ecosystemic "lens" to understanding family functioning. In T. L. Sexton, G. R. Weeks, & M. S. Robbins (Eds.), *Handbook of family therapy* (pp. 21–36). New York, NY: Brunner-Routledge.

DISCUSSION QUESTIONS

1. Though families as a social institution are found throughout human societies, what are the factors that contribute to the variety of family structures?

2. What are the various criteria by which one can define a family?

3. What are the primary functions of the family?

4. Describe how systems theory helps a family therapist understand the relational dynamics within a family.

REFERENCES

Anderson, S. A., & Sabatelli, R. M. (2003). *Family interaction: A multigenerational developmental perspective* (3rd ed.). Boston, MA: Pearson Education.

Auerswald, E. H. (1968). Interdisciplinary versus ecological approach. *Family Process, 7,* 202–215.

Becvar, D. S. (2007). *Families that flourish.* New York, NY: Norton.

Becvar, D. S., & Becvar, R. (1993). *Family therapy: A systematic integration* (2nd ed.). Boston, MA: Allyn & Bacon.

Bronfenbrenner, U. (1977). Toward an experimental ecology of human development. *American Psychologist, 32*(7), 513–531.

Bronfenbrenner, U. (1979). *The ecology of human development.* Cambridge, MA: Harvard University Press.

Bronfenbrenner, U. (1986). Ecology of the family as a context for human development. *American Psychologist, 32*, 513–531.

Bubotz, M. M., & Sontag, M. S. (1993). Human ecology theory. In P. G. Boss, W. J. Doherty, R. LaRossa, W. R. Schumm, & S. K. Steinmetz (Eds.), *Sourcebook of family theories and methods: A conceptual approach* (pp. 419–448). New York, NY: Plenum Press.

Carter, B., & McGoldrick, M. (1988). *The changing family life cycle: A framework for family therapy.* New York, NY: Gardner Press.

Collins, D., Jordan, C., & Coleman, H. (2007). *An introduction to family social work* (2nd ed.). Belmont, CA: Thomson.

Connard, C., & Novick, R. (1996). *The ecology of the family.* Retrieved from http://www.nwrel.org/cfc/publications/ecology2.html

Coontz, S. (1991). *The way we never were: American families and the nostalgia trap.* New York, NY: Basic Books.

Coontz, S. (2003). What we really miss about the 1950's. In A. S. Skolnick & J. H. Skolnick (Eds.), *Family in transition* (12th ed., pp. 31–40). Boston, MA: Pearson Education.

Crawford, J. M. (1999). Co-parent adoptions by same-sex couples: From loophole to law. *Families in Society: The Journal of Contemporary Human Services, 80*, 271–278.

Demos, J. (1976). Myths and realities in the history of American family life. In H. Grunebaum & J. Christ (Ed.), *Contemporary marriage: Structure, dynamics and therapy* (pp. 9–31). Boston, MA: Little, Brown.

Duvall, F. (1957). *Family transitions.* Philadelphia, PA: Lippincott.

Epstein, N. B., Bishop, D., Ryan, C., Miller, I., & Keitner, G. (1993). The McMaster Model: View of healthy family functioning. In F. Walsh (Ed.), *Normal family process* (pp. 138–160). New York, NY: Guilford.

Falicov, C. J. (1998). *Latino families in therapy: A guide to multicultural practice.* New York, NY: Guilford.

Fenell, D. L., & Weinhold, B. K. (2003). *Counseling families: An introduction to marriage and family therapy.* Denver, CO: Love.

Fields, J., & Casper, L. M. (2000). *America's families and living arrangement: March 2000* [Current populations reports, P20–537]. Washington, DC: U.S. Census Bureau.

Fitzpatrick, M. A., & Wamboldt, F. S. (1990). Where is all said and done. *Communications Research, 17*(4), 421–430.

Franklin, C., Hopson, L., & Ten Barge, C. (2003). Family systems. In C. Jordan & C. Franklin (Eds.), *Clinical assessment for social workers* (pp. 255–313). Chicago, IL: Lyceum.

Franklin, C., & Jordan, C. (2002). Effective family therapy: Guidelines for practice. In A. R. Roberts & G. J. Greene (Eds.), *Social workers desk reference* (pp. 256–262). New York, NY: Oxford University Press.

Gardiner, H., & Komitzki, C. (2002). *Lives across cultures: Cross-cultural human development.* Boston, MA: Allyn & Bacon.

Germain, C. B., & Gitterman, A. (1996). *The life model of social work practice* (2nd ed.). New York, NY: Columbia University Press.

Goldenberg, H., & Goldenberg, I. (2002). *Counseling today's families.* Pacific Grove, CA: Brooks/Cole.

Goldenberg, H., & Goldenberg, I. (2008). *Family therapy: An overview.* Belmont, CA: Thomson.

Heiner, R. (2002). *Social problems: An introduction to critical constructionism.* New York, NY: Oxford University Press.

Herbert, M., & Harper-Dorton, K. V. (2002). *Working with children, adolescents and their families* (3rd ed.). Chicago, IL: Lyceum.

Hill, R. (1958). Generic features of families under stress. *Social Casework, 49,* 139–150.

Ingoldsby, B. B., Smith, S. R., & Miller, J. E. (2004). *Exploring family theories.* Los Angeles, CA: Roxbury.

James, W. (1981). *Principles of psychology.* Cambridge, MA: Harvard University Press. (Original work published 1890)

Janzen, C., & Harris, O. (1997). *Family treatment in social work practice* (3rd ed.). Itasca, IL: Peacock.

Longress, J. F. (2000). *Human behavior in the social environment.* Itasca, IL: Peacock.

McCubbin, H., & Patterson, J. (1983). The family stress process: The double ABCX model of family adjustment and adaptation. *Marriage & Family Review, 6*(7), 7–37.

McGoldrick, M. (1999). Becoming a couple. In B. Carter & M. McGoldrick (Eds.), *The expanded life cycle: Individual, family and social perspectives.* Boston, MA: Allyn & Bacon.

Olson, D., Russell, C., & Sprenkle, D. (1989). *Circumplex model: Systemic assessment and treatment of families.* New York, NY: Haworth.

Patterson, J. M. (2002). Understanding family resilience. *Journal of Clinical Psychology, 53*(3), 233–246.

Ragg, D. M. (2006). *Building family practice skills: Methods, strategies, and tools.* Belmont, CA: Thomson.

Robbins, M., Mayorga, C. C., & Szapocznik, J. (2003). The ecosystemic "lens" to understanding family functioning. In T. L. Sexton, G. R. Weeks, & M. S. Robbins (Eds.), *Handbook of family therapy* (pp. 21–36). New York, NY: Brunner-Routledge.

Rosenblatt, P. C. (1994). *Metaphors of family systems theory.* New York, NY: Guilford.

Schorr, L. B. (1989). *Within our reach: Breaking the cycle of disadvantage.* New York, NY: Doubleday.

Skolnick, A. S. (1991). *Embattled paradise: The American family in an age of uncertainty.* New York, NY: Basic Books.

Skolnick, A. S., & Skolnick, J. H. (2003). *Family in transition* (12th ed.). Boston, MA: Pearson Education.

Szapocznik, J., & Coatsworth, D. (1999). An ecodevelopment framework for organizing the influences on drug abuse: A developmental model of risk and protection. In M. D. Glantz & C. R. Hartel (Eds.), *Drug abuse: Origins & interventions* (pp. 331–366). Washington, DC: American Psychological Association.

Unger, D., & Sussman, M. (Eds.). (1990). *Families in community settings: Interdisciplinary perspectives.* New York, NY: Haworth.

U.S. Census Bureau. (2008). *Current population survey: Definitions and explanations.* Retrieved from www.census.gov/population/www/cps/cpsdef.html

Wakefield, J. C. (1996a). Does social work need the ecosystems perspective? Part I. Is the perspective clinically useful? *Social Service Review, 70*(1), 1–32.

Wakefield, J. C. (1996b). Does social work need the ecosystems perspective? Part 2. Does the perspective save social work from incoherence? *Social Service Review, 70*(2), 183–213.

Wakefield, J. C. (1996c). Does social work need the ecosystems perspective: Reply to Alex Gitterman. *Social Service Review, 70*(3), 476–481.

Watzlawick, P., Beavin, J., & Jackson, D. (1967). *Pragmatics of human communication: A study of interactional patterns pathologies and paradoxes.* New York, NY: Norton.

Yerby, J., Buerkel-Rothfuss, N., & Bochner, A. P. (1995). *Understanding family communication.* Scottsdale, AZ: Gorsuch Scarisbrick.

Chapter 3

ETHNICITY AND FAMILY LIFE

American society is undergoing a dramatic change in its ethnic and racial landscape as ethnic minority families represent a growing population. The number of individuals and families who identify themselves as being members of racial or ethnic minority groups has grown in the United States over the last 30 years. Such growth has increased the possibility that family therapists will find themselves providing clinical services to a range of ethnic families (see Table 3.1). Billingsley (1976),

Table 3.1	Ethnic Minorities

- From 1990 to 2000 the total population in the United States increased from 248.7 million to 281.4 million, with an increase in the ethnic minority population from 60.0 million to 86.9 million (a 44.83% increase).
- In 2000 the overall population was represented by approximately 81% Caucasians, but this figure is estimated to fall to 72% by the year 2050.
- The Latino population is expected to grow exponentially faster than any other subpopulation, with a representation of 12.6% of the total population in 2000 and a projected representation of 24% in 2050.
- The Asian and Pacific Islanders population is expected to grow from 4% in 2000 to 8% in 2050.
- African Americans constituted 12.7% in 2000 and are expected to comprise 14.6% by 2050.
- Based on the 2000 Census data, the most rapidly growing ethnic groups in the United States are Hispanics and Asians. In 2000, the population of Hispanics was 35,305,818—a 52% increase from the 1990 Census. The population count of Asians was 11,898,828, up from 6,908,632 in 1990—a 72% increase.
- The immigrant population is composed of 28,910,800 (foreign-born population) in the United States. Within this population, 46.4% are Hispanic or Latino, 25.9% are Asian, 22.1% are White, and 5.5% are Black.

Source: U.S. Census Bureau (2004), in Cheung & Leung (2008).

a noted researcher on African American family life, observed that for these ethnic minority families the concepts of ethnicity and family life are so intricately entwined that it would be difficult to observe either without seriously considering the other. Yet as we examine the current and historical experiences of these families not only must we examine issues of culture, race, ethnicity, and ethnic identity, but we must also examine experiences of discrimination and racism, for these social forces have had a powerful impact on the lives of ethnic minority families.

The major objective of this chapter is to highlight the significance of culture, race, and ethnicity for these ethnic minority families along with those experiences of discrimination and racism. We will also consider how these factors might impact family therapy interventions. In this discussion we will focus on four ethnic groups: Asians, Native Americans or First Nations Peoples, Latinos, and African Americans.

CULTURE, RACE, AND ETHNICITY

In the previous chapter we discussed how a systems and ecological perspective allows us to understand each family as a unique system embedded within broader social systems. We further described how families as a system must develop a range of strategies for managing a range of family system maintenance tasks, one of which is constructing a family identity (Anderson & Sabatelli, 2003). This family identity includes those family themes or organizing narratives that define the unique identity of that family. This identity is the framework for establishing the family's place in the social order and the core values that define a particular family. This identity further enables the family to establish its unique identity in terms of how its members may want others to view them in terms of their own distinctiveness. This family identity is also the framework around which family members attain both self-identity and identity as a member of their particular family.

For some families this identity is strongly influenced by ethnic, racial, cultural, or subcultural values that influence the organizational structure of the family. A family whose identity is strongly influenced by racial or ethnic identifications may experience transactions within its ecological network as affirming and supportive of the family. Yet other families, because of their racial or ethnic identification and subsequent experiences of discrimination or oppression, may find themselves in multisystem transactions that not only rob them of those self-affirming powers but also block them from those resources needed to acquire that power. This state of vulnerability and this status of powerlessness may reflect a relationship between that family and its broader environment that is unequivocally negative, thus creating a power imbalance between the family and those broader ecological networks. The experiences of powerlessness and oppression can become one of the primary themes in the family identity narrative as well as informing the family's racial and ethnic identification.

For many ethnic minority families, disempowering sociopolitical metanarratives about their particular ethnic group may constrain the family's ability to construct more empowering and potentiating solutions to family problems. As ethnic minority families present themselves for family therapy, a culturally attuned therapist must have the clinical skills that allow the therapist to enter into the family's narrative world to uncover with the family the interplay of those ethnic themes and broader sociocultural metanarratives. Ethnic identities are socially and historically constructed within the context of "evolving products of material and social circumstances and the actions of groups themselves, wrestling with, interpreting and responding to those circumstances, building or transforming (ethnic) identities in the process" (Cornell, 2000, p. 42). A family therapist cannot understand the significance of an ethnic minority family's problem without understanding the material, power-laden, and affectively charged elements of the prevailing sociocultural metanarratives about the family's ethnic group (Ho, Rasheed, & Rasheed, 2004). A family therapist, assuming a narrative stance (Laird, 1998) in working with families, can create a space where more empowering narratives can be coauthored.

Understanding Culture

Though the term *ethnic minority* is used in this discussion, it is not without recognition that discussions of such terms as *cultural diversity*, *multicultural*, *ethnicity*, *culture*, and *race* involve conflicting, ambiguous, and imprecise definition of these terms. Terms such as *cultural diversity* may refer to social reference groups including ethnicity, gender, social class, sexual orientation, age, and disability. Others may alternate the use of the terms *race* and *ethnicity* in referring to the same population without clearly making a distinction as to what is meant by either term. In attempting to bring some clarity to these discussions Carter (2005) presents five assumptions that are embedded in the various meanings used to describe cultural differences: universal, ubiquitous, traditional, race-based, and pan-national. The following descriptions highlight the basic assumptions of each perspective:

> *Universal*—Culture is equated with individual differences. Humans are alike and differ only in terms of their unique characteristics. Social and reference group membership (e.g., ethnicity, race, gender, culture), though noted, is only secondary

in terms of having an impact on experience and personal identity. This approach takes a color-blind view of cultural, ethnic, and racial differences.

Ubiquitous—All differences associated with group membership(s) are salient. All forms of social or group identity are considered cultural. From this perspective culture can be a function of geography, income, gender, age, race, religion, ethnicity, and sexual orientation. Thus one can have membership in multiple cultural groups, and one's cultural identity can be multilayered and multicontextual. This perspective is quite prevalent in the literature on therapy with culturally diverse individuals and families.

Traditional—This anthropological perspective defines cultural difference as deriving from a country with a common language, values, beliefs, and rituals. One is a member of a cultural group by birth and country influences.

Race-based—In this perspective cultural groups are identified on the basis of race especially in North America. Though races are classified by factors such as skin color and other physical features, definitive aspects of culture such as values are psychologically grounded in socially race-based categories. As race is the most visible of "cultural differences," experiences associated with race including racism, social exclusion and inclusion, and belonging to a racial group supersede all other experiences in the United States.

Pan-national—Race as definitive of culture is viewed in a global context. Examining the legacy of colonialism and the attending experiences of oppression, violence, and slavery, the cultural identity of people of color is based on denial, denigration, and exploitation (Wallace & Carter, 2003).

After reviewing these basic assumptions, Carter (2005) concludes that race as culture or a race-based assumptive perspective is a more viable approach to understanding cultural differences because it is a historically and sociopolitically based construct.

Race Versus Ethnicity

For some sociological theorists, the concepts of race and ethnicity overlap. Coles (2006) uses the terms *racial* and *ethnic* interchangeably, acknowledging that individuals may have differing racial opinions as to how to label their identity. For example, some individuals may define themselves as African American whereas others may describe themselves as Black Americans. The U.S. Census defines *Hispanic* as an ethnicity, not a race, though there are those individuals who define themselves as Hispanic but whose phenotype may resemble various racial groups. In our culturally heterogeneous society the shifting dominance of race or racial identity and ethnicity or ethnic identity is a function of the salience of visible racial characteristics (primarily skin color) that continue to be used to label and categorize people in the United States (Kwan, 2005). Yet racial group membership does not necessarily characterize racial or ethnic group identity. Furthermore one's sense of ethnic identity does not necessarily characterize one's racial identity. In the case of individuals with parents of different "racial" groups, they may find that as they present their biracial identity, they may choose (depending on skin color and other phenotype characteristics) to identify with one or the other parent's racial group. The choice may be contextual or influenced by their immediate social or racial environment. Rather than identify with either racial group, other biracial individuals may remain comfortable and secure with their biracial identity.

Though the construct of race continues to be used as a means to classify human beings into distinct social groups, modern biological science rejects the existence of distinct groupings based on the concept of race. In reality race is not a genetic or biological concept but a socially constructed concept used to identify large groups of human species that share a more or less distinctive combination of hereditary and physical characteristics. Race as a construct refers to any people who distinguish themselves or consider themselves distinguished in social relations with other people by their physical characteristics such as skin color (Cox, 1948). Race as such has no self-evident meaning; rather it has primarily social meaning. In other words race is real in its social consequences, and the concept of race has a real impact on the social organization of society. The social and political discourse about race continues to be based on the assumption that race is a biological certainty (Coles, 2006). Helms (1995) further supports the salience of race as a political construct when he notes that societal power and social resources have been distributed according to the visible attributes of skin color or race.

Contrary to the concept of race, the term *ethnicity* is generally used to define a group in which members share unique social, national, and cultural characteristics and heritage. There is a sense of commonality and connectedness where specific aspects of cultural patterns are shared and where transmission of these patterns over time creates a common history. This common history reflects cultural heritage, possible religious affiliation, language and/or dialect, and/or tribal affiliation. Furthermore the term *ethnicity* is generally related to a specific geographical location (a homeland).

Yet the conceptual relationship between the construct of race and ethnicity becomes ambiguous as one examines Census data. For example, in the 2000 Census the attempt was to gather ethnicity-specific data to get a clearer picture of the racial and ethnic diversity in the United States. The taxonomic categories used by the Census were race based in terms of distinguishing Whites from non-Whites.

After determining these "racial" differences, the Census questions were oriented toward identifying ancestry or ethnic identification only for those in the non-White category. What was clear is that while Whites were not distinguished by separate ethnic categories, non-White ethnic groups were differentiated, thus implicitly subsuming ethnicity under race while acknowledging an interdependence between the two constructs (Kwan, 2005). As the 2000 Census provided the opportunity for individuals to list multiple racial identifications in response to the demands of multiracial populations, racial identification became a matter of choice rather than societal mandated designation (Cornell & Hartman, 2007).

This newer understanding of ethnicity as reflected in the 2000 Census challenged the concept that ethnic identification is a fixed and categorical identity that is ascribed at birth (Geertz, 1963: Isaacs, 1975; Stack, 1974). This categorical understanding of ethnicity is understood to be quite limited in that it does not address the personal dimensions of ethnicity or how one identifies oneself as an ethnic being. At the same time this conceptualization of ethnicity does not acknowledge the similarity and differences within ethnic minority groups and within ethnic minority families.

The ethnic behaviors and practices found within and between racially and ethnically diverse families result from a constellation of factors. While there may be cultural tendencies that result in certain family themes, system maintenance strategies, and cultural practices being more common than others within each ethnic minority family, it is important to realize that each family is unique. Ethnic minority families as with all families are products of not only their ethnic heritage but intergenerational themes and legacies, level of educational and socioeconomic status, present living conditions, and level of assimilation into the dominant cultural and current social context. But most important we cannot ignore that for ethnic minority families their ethnic affiliation can serve as an important filter influencing family themes and images, boundary process, resources, priorities, and predominant orientation to the management of emotional issues (Anderson & Sabatelli, 2003).

THE COMPLEXITY OF ETHNIC IDENTITY

One formulation of ethnicity that has significance for our discussion of ethnicity and family therapy is proposed by Phinney (1996). Phinney's definition of ethnic identity refers both to an identity that centers around race as it might be concretely defined (e.g., skin color or facial features) and to aspects of identity that focus on heritage, culture, behavioral rituals, attitudes, and awareness. As the concept of race is subsumed under the rubric of ethnicity, Phinney contends that the term *ethnic group* be used when referring to members of nondominant groups of color from non-European origins. Over the last 25 years, Phinney and her colleagues have developed a theoretical framework of ethnic identity development based on the results of extensive research on ethnic minority and White adolescents (e.g., Phinney, 1992; Phinney, Cantu, & Kurtz, 1997; Phinney & Devich-Navarro, 1997). She describes ethnicity as having three independent and overlapping aspects that may vary within and across ethnic groups: (a) the cultural values, attitudes, and behaviors that distinguish ethnic groups and in our discussion ethnic minority families; (b) the subjective sense of ethnic group identity held by group (family) members; and (c) individual and family experiences associated with minority status including powerlessness, discrimination, and prejudice (Juby & Concepcion, 2005).

Ethnicity as Culture

Ethnicity as culture refers to the cultural characteristics of a group such as typical values, norms, attitudes, and behaviors that are specific to a common culture and are transmitted across generations. Additionally culture can refer to the meaning that people give to events that directly impinge upon their day-to-day lives. For family members culture can play an important role in determining how various family tasks will be managed, how family boundaries will be structured, and how resources will be spent.

According to Kluckhohn (1951), culture can be distinguished by the value orientation of specific cultural and/or ethnic populations. These values represent generalized and organized conceptions regarding time orientation, the natural world and man's place in it, interhuman transactions, and man's ethical nature. Ethnic minority families may be distinguished by the particular values that inform their perspectives in these areas. With certain ethnic minority families they must adjust to tensions created by conflicting value systems of the White society (Ho et al., 2004). In contrast with the middle-class White American cultural values, which emphasize man's *control of nature and the environment*, many ethnic minority groups emphasize man's *harmony with the environment*. While the mainstream societal ideal is future oriented, worshipping youthfulness and making sacrifices for a "better" tomorrow, some ethnic groups reminisce about the past and take pleasure in the present. In the relational dimension, while the middle-class American cultural ideal is individual autonomy, an ethnic minority cultural value may reflect a preference for *collectivity*. Because the *doing orientation* is basic to the middle-class White American lifestyle, *competitiveness* and upward mobility will characterize this mode of activity. The Asian cultural ideal reflects self-discipline. Many African Americans exhibit resiliency in the midst of suffering, and both Native Americans and Latinos may prefer a *being-in-becoming* mode of activity. Finally, the sociological structure of the mainstream society addresses itself basically to the nuclear family, which contrasts with the extended family common to many ethnic minority families.

Ethnicity as Identity

Ethnicity as identity involves an enduring fundamental aspect of the self that include a sense of membership in an ethnic group and the attitudes and feeling associated with that membership (Phinney, 1990). Phinney's work has identified three components of ethnic identity that can be applied to any ethnic group while acknowledging each group's individual experiences: (a) self-identification, (b) sense of belonging, and (c) behavioral practices.

Phinney (1990) pointed out that in many research studies on ethnic identity researchers assigned racial or ethnic group labels to their participants that did not necessarily match the person's own evaluation of his or her racial or ethnic identity. This observation confirmed that ethnic designations may be imposed on ethnic minorities by the dominant culture based on an assessment of superficial traits, such as skin color or a person's name. Phinney (1990) pointed out that using only one label for American ethnic minorities is inaccurate, as these individuals must constantly gravitate between their minority culture and the dominant culture. Threats to survival and self-esteem require adaptation from ethnic minorities that causes "a split in the acculturative process resulting in the development in the duality of culture" (Dreyfuss & Lawrence, 1979, p. 78). Biculturalism demands the bilateral bringing together of items, values, and behaviors. It signifies participation in two cultural systems and often requires two sets of behaviors (Ho et al., 2004). For example, a Latino (male) may behave according to a hierarchical and vertical structure at home with his family and friends, as his culture demands, but he can behave competitively in the workplace as the White American culture requires.

A sense of belonging is the emotional component of Phinney's conceptualization of ethnic identity. Some individuals or families may internalize negative characterizations made by the dominant culture regarding their ethnic group, which then may cause them to feel anger or resentment toward their ethnic group. Consequently, these individuals could feel detached from their ethnic group and have a weak sense of belonging. In contrast, some individuals might have positive feelings about their ethnic group due to the strong support system provided by the group, which promotes a deep sense of belonging. Finally, there is a behavioral component of ethnic identity—behavioral practices and system maintenance strategies within families—that takes into account the degree to which a person engages in cultural practices and rituals that are specific to his or her ethnic group.

Ethnicity as Minority Status

For Phinney (1996) ethnicity as minority status denotes experiences of oppression, discrimination and powerlessness. Ho et al. (2004) point to several factors that affect the status and adjustment of ethnic minorities in this country. The status of each ethnic group or subgroup experience, along with their historical and governmental relationships affects social adjustment of ethnic minority families. A history of slavery for African Americans and their struggle to maintain African cultural roots in a society that challenges and oppresses them make African Americans feel precarious at best and demoralized at worse. Racism and colonialism have made Native Americans "emigrants" in their own homeland. In contrast to any other ethnic minority group in the United States, a person is not indigenous or an authentic Native American unless he or she fits into categories defined by the federal government, including blood degree and tribal status. In order to be eligible for federal Native programs, a person must be able to prove he or she has at least one-quarter Indigenous "blood" as recognized by the federal government.

Immigration status also plays a vital role in the living experiences of many ethnic minority individuals and their families. Some Southeast Asians and refugees realize they may never be able to return to their homeland. They often experience an emotional cutoff from their country of origin and wonder if and when there will be any reunion with relatives. Such geographical disconnection and intergenerational family emotional cutoff have adverse implications for family structure and functioning. Conversely, minority groups such as Puerto Ricans can consider their stay on the mainland transitory and know that they can easily visit their families again. Whether the ethnic minority individual is a legal resident or an undocumented resident is also significant. Incredible abuses toward undocumented residents are well known. Many live in fear of being reported.

An ethnic minority family's socioeconomic class location may impact its ethnic identification. Individuals may act in accordance with their perceived class interest in some situations and in accordance with their cultural preferences or ethnic minority identity in others. Gordon (1969) uses the term *ethclass* to describe the point at which social class and ethnic group membership intersect. A limited number of ethnic minority families may have more income and be in the upper or middle classes, work in more highly valued and rewarding occupations, and have more prestige than others. This in turn affects the extent of their well-being, including health, help-seeking patterns, real and perceived power to achieve desired goals, self-respect, and the degree of dignity conferred by others. For those who are in the lower social class, their ethnic reality may reflect continual and persistent discrimination in jobs, housing, education, and the responsiveness of health care and welfare institutions (Ho et al., 2004).

Members of ethnic minority groups who have achieved material goals continue to be frequently reminded of the oppression that plagues their kindred and of their identification with the specific ethnic group. Although economically and materially successful, some ethnic minority group members still experience difficulty in being accepted by the White middle-class society. At the same time, they may feel alienated from their own ethnic group (Combs, 1978). There is established evidence that socioeconomic location for ethnic minority individuals is positively correlated to a member's English efficiency, educational level, and acculturation rate (DeAnda, 1984). However, ethnic minority group members' higher social class status does not imply that their ethnic identity plays a less important role in their life. As Mass (1976) indicates, the influence exerted by the value patterns that were acquired throughout childhood is often considerable even among those whose behavior is highly Westernized. Other studies (McAdoo, 1978; Native American Research Group, 1979; Staples, 2004) have also indicated that "successful" or "acculturated" ethnic minority families show a strong interest and need in keeping alive the folkways, arts and crafts, language, and values associated with their heritage.

Finally, skin color is an important factor in determining the experiences of an ethnic minority person or family. Because color is one of the most pervasive reasons for discrimination, some ethnic minority individuals may attempt to "pass" as White. Puerto Ricans (or any ethnic minority person from a mixed heritage) can easily be traumatized by societal pressure to define themselves as "Black" or "White," complicated further when other family members are labeled differently. That the 2000 Census allowed biracial individuals to classify themselves as such may mitigate against such felt tension of being biracial.

In spite of the growth of ethnic minorities, the pervasive presence of racism, poverty, and oppression shapes their life experiences. African Americans continue to live with the legacy of slavery, while Native Americans live with the historical experience of genocide. Racism and oppression for many ethnic families are the causes of generational poverty and a diminished self-esteem that produces community violence, self-medicating with drugs and alcohol, and disproportional involvement with the criminal justice system (Thomas, 2000). While current demographic data indicate that ethnic minorities have made considerable gain in the areas of family income, education, and other indicators of social, economic, and political status (Karger & Stoesz, 2002), almost any set of data that is examined continues to show the subordinate position of many ethnic families within the social order. In reviewing the continued disparity in wages, incomes, poverty levels, education, home ownership, job promotion rates, and middle management and top management positions, data reflect that ethnic minorities continue to bear a disproportionate share of social problems (Axinn & Levin, 1997; Jansson, 2001).

The disparity in the social status of ethnic minorities clearly documents the realities of racism, poverty, and oppression as potent factors that continue to have a negative effect on the lives of ethnic minority individuals and families. These factors also affect the minorities' help-seeking behaviors that include underutilization of family therapists who generally are White, monolinguistic, middle class, and ethnocentric in their family problem assessments and interventions (Acosta, Yamamoto, & Evans, 1982).

ENCULTURATION, ACCULTURATION, AND FAMILY ETHNIC IDENTITY

Enculturation is the process in which a person learns how to live with his or her primary cultural identity. This process involves learning the values, attitudes, and beliefs and corresponding behavioral patterns of his or her reference ethnic group. Acculturation on the other hand refers to the meeting of at least two different cultures with the subsequent socialization into other cultural or ethnic groups' cultural practices (McAuliffe, 2008). For ethnic minority groups, acculturation can be stressful in that they have to continually negotiate how to adapt to and move within the dominant culture while retaining the norms of their culture of origin. As pointed out by Berry, Trimble, and Olmeda (1986) and emphasized by McAuliffe (2008), enculturation and acculturation are not unitary experiences. Individuals and families may experience any of four levels of acculturation: integration, assimilation, separation, or marginalization.

Integration is the process in which the individual becomes proficient in the culture of the dominant groups while retaining proficiency in his or her indigenous culture. This person has developed the ability to navigate in both worlds without compromising a sense of ethnic identification. With this capacity comes the tension of living in two worlds—in two ethnic and cultural contexts. This bicultural existence may call for a constant assessment of the appropriateness of one's behaviors in these multiple contexts.

Assimilation on the other hand involves the individual rejecting his or her ethnic identifications as he or she absorbs the cultural practices and norms of the dominant culture. Assimilation as a strategy for adaptation is not without a price. As we will see later in this chapter in our discussion of Native Americans, assimilation was forced due to the hegemonic practices of the dominant culture. In this instance assimilation was the mask for cultural genocide.

Separation occurs when the individual and family are interested in retaining and maintaining their cultural and ethnic identity and doing so by resisting any form of acculturation with the dominant culture. These individuals and families may reside in ethnic enclaves that can provide sufficient cultural and social resources, connections, and relationships that allow them to maintain their cultural integrity without the need for assimilation.

Finally the *marginalized* status is the most problematic for ethnic minority individuals and families. These individuals and/or families have no interest in maintaining or acquiring proficiency in either their visible ethnic or cultural reference group or the dominant society. They are in essence "persons without a country" (McAuliffe, 2008). Such individuals may be ashamed of their ethnic identity yet, because of their historical experiences of oppression, powerlessness, and vulnerability in their interactions with the dominant culture, feel a sense of cultural alienation.

It is suggested that the ethnic minority family plays a critical role in both the enculturation and the acculturation process. In the previous chapter we discussed the first-order tasks for families and the strategies that families use to accomplish these tasks, which involve the formation of family themes, the regulation of family boundaries, and the management of family households. The family strategies represent those policies, procedures, and unique patterns of interaction that each family establishes to execute its task. One of the tasks that ethnic minority families have is negotiating, managing, and coping with the enculturation and acculturation processes as they attempt to maintain optimal family system functioning and identity integrity as an ethnic minority family. It is not without saying that within a particular ethnic minority family, individual family members may have a different sense of their ethnic identification due to mixed acculturation patterns in one family. Such mixed patterns may be due to generational differences, immigration experiences, socioeconomic locations, and the educational level of different family members.

In the remainder of this chapter we will focus on the predominant beliefs, customs, and practices of particular ethnic groups. We must add a cautionary note that the following discussion must balance the tendency to overgeneralize about ethnic groups with an appreciation for the variations found within and between cultural groups.

THE EXPERIENCE OF ETHNIC MINORITY FAMILIES

Asian Americans

Demographics

The U.S. Census reported that in March 2002, 12.5 million Asians were living in the United States representing 4.4% of the civilian noninstitutionalized population (Reeves & Bennett, 2003). After passage of the Immigration and Nationality Act of 1965, immigration contributed greatly to the growth of the Asian population (Chang, 2003). The majority of Asian households are less likely to divorce and more likely to have large families (Cheung & Leung, 2008). Asian Americans are more likely than Caucasians to have earned at least a college degree but at the same time more likely to have less than a ninth-grade education. Asian Americans are concentrated in managerial and professional specialty occupations, and in 2003 11.8% of Asians (1.4 million) lived below the poverty level (U.S. Census Bureau, 2004).

In this discussion the term *Asian American* includes Chinese, Japanese, Korean, Filipino, Samoan, Guamanian, and Hawaiian Americans and other Pacific Islanders. This category also includes immigrants from Vietnam, Thailand, Cambodia, Laos, and Indonesia and persons from India, Pakistan, Bangladesh, Bhutan, Maldives, Nepal, and Sri Lanka. Children of mixed marriages where one parent is Asian American are also included.

For Westerners, the differences among the Asian American populations may seem minimal, yet in addition to obvious language differences the historical, social, and economic differences among these nations should not be overlooked. Within the context of living in the United States, there are within-group distinctions among individuals based on immigrant, refugee, and transnational status (Ishii-Kuntz, 2000; Lott, 1998).

While vastly different with respect to ethnic, historical, language, and social factors, Asian American families may share some common features in cultural values and family structure. Yet in understanding Asian Americans one of the fundamental

Photo 3.1   Ethnic minority families represent a growing population within American society

Source: © Jupiterimages/Goodshoot/Thinkstock

differences between Asian and U.S. culture is that while religious traditions vary among the various Asian ethnic groups, the cultural traditions of this population are founded on non-Judeo-Christian beliefs (Appleby, Colon, & Hamilton, 2007).

The Model Minority

Due to the economic and educational achievements of Asian Americans, this diverse ethnic group has come to be considered the "model minority." As a model minority the Asian American is portrayed as hardworking, industrious, and, most important, compliant, as he or she strives to fully assimilate into mainstream American culture (Cooper, 1995; Ishii-Kuntz, 2000). Yet this perception of Asian Americans ignores the many ways in which Asian and Pacific Islander Americans have been discriminated against and stigmatized throughout U.S. history. Two of the most shameful eras of racism, discrimination, and stigmatization in this country's history are the internment of Japanese Americans in detention camps during World War II and the hate crimes committed against Southeast Asian refugees in the 1970s and 1980s during and immediately following the Vietnam War.

Economic discrimination is a harsh reality confronting Asian Americans. For example, Southeast Asians currently are at a higher risk of poverty than White Americans. There are many recent Asian immigrants working in low-wage "sweatshops" in urban Chinatowns. Asians are underrepresented in the higher-salaried public and private career positions (despite impressive academic achievements). Though many Asian Americans have become successful small business owners, for some this role is forced on them as a last-resort employment endeavor, given the consequences of racism and discrimination (Karger & Stoesz, 2002). Many of the recent immigrants from South Asian countries may be less educated and lack basic English skills. Thus they may find employment as taxi and truck drivers, convenience store clerks, small hotel owners, or small business owners (Inman & Tewari, 2003; Sandhu & Malik, 2001). There are also those immigrants from South Asian countries who might have held a professional status in their country of origin (medical doctors, engineers, scientists) yet who have difficulty finding equivalent positions in the United States (McAuliffe, 2008).

The economic, occupational, and political realities of Asian American life clearly do not support the notion of the successful and well-integrated model minority. It is ironic and unfortunate that the resentment toward Asian Americans' success, work ethic, and emphasis on education plays a role in the racism and discrimination displayed against Asian and Pacific Islander Americans. It is also significant that not only are they a model minority but possibly an invisible minority as well. One of the authors of this book recently encountered an Asian woman who shared her childhood abuse experiences. In her account she discussed how visible and psychological signs of her abuse were ignored by public school officials because she was seen as a member of a "problem-free" minority group. Given the fact of her high academic achievement, her plight was further rendered "invisible."

Traditional Cultural Values

Traditional Asian values governing family life have been heavily influenced by the religious and ethical codes emanating from Confucianism, Taoism, Buddhism, Hinduism, and Islam. These ethical and religious traditions may be reflected in the family's actual religious and cultural practices, family values, and the family's identity narrative (Hong, 1993; Hong & Friedman, 1998; Hong & Ham, 2001). Such values support the concept that qualities essential to harmonious family living involve moderation in behavior, self-discipline, patience, maintaining a harmonious family life, and submission and devotion to group interests and purposes. The importance of these cultural values has a direct bearing on the relationship subsystems, structure, and interactive patterns of Asian American families. Table 3.2 outlines some of the major values undergirding Asian family life.

Table 3.2 Asian Cultural Values

Avoidance of family shame. Family reputation is a primary social concern. The worst thing an individual can do is to disgrace her or his family.

Collectivism. Individuals should feel a strong sense of attachment to the group to which they belong and should think about the welfare of the group before their own welfare. Group interest and goals should be promoted over individual interest and goals.

Conformity to family and social norms and expectations. Conforming to familial and societal norms is important; one should not deviate from these norms. It is important to follow and conform to the expectations that one's family and the society have for one.

Deference to authority figures. Authority figures are deserving of respect. Individuals should not question a person who is in a position of authority.

Filial piety. Children are expected to manifest unquestioning obedience to their parents. Children should never talk back to their parents, go against their parents' wishes, or question the authority of their parents.

Importance of family. Individual family members feel a strong sense of obligation to the family as a whole and a commitment to maintaining family well-being. Honor and duty to one's family are very important, more important than one's own fame and power; personal accomplishment is interpreted as a family achievement.

(Continued)

Table 3.2	(Continued)

Maintenance of interpersonal harmony. One should always try to be accommodating and conciliatory and never directly confrontational. One should not say things that may offend another person or that would cause the other person to lose face.

Placing others' needs ahead of one's own. An individual should consider the needs of others before considering her or his own. One should anticipate and be aware of the needs of others and not inconvenience them. Overasserting one's own needs is a sign of immaturity.

Reciprocity. An individual should repay another person's favor—that is, repay those people who have helped or provided assistance to the individual. When one does favors for others, she or he should accept favors in return.

Respect for elders and ancestors. Ancestors and elders should be viewed with reverence and respect; children should honor their elders and ancestors. Elders have more wisdom and deserve more respect than young people.

Self-control and restraint. One should exercise restraint when experiencing strong emotions. The ability to control emotions is a sign of strength.

Self-effacement. It is important to minimize or depreciate one's own achievements. One should be humble, modest, and not boastful. It is inappropriate to draw attention to oneself.

Educational and occupational achievement. Educational and occupational achievement should be an individual's top priority. Success in life is defined in terms of one's academic and career accomplishments.

Ability to resolve psychological problems. One should overcome distress by oneself. Asking others for psychological help is a sign of weakness. One should use one's inner resources and willpower to resolve psychological problems.

Source: McAuliffe (2008, p. 199). Used with permission.

Immigration and Acculturation

There are two interrelated levels of adaptive cultural transitions that every immigrating Asian family must face: (a) the physical or material, economic, educational, and language transitions and (b) the cognitive, affective, and psychological (individual members and family as a unit) transitions. The transformation from these two levels of cultural transition can cause enduring family problems for Asian families.

In the midst of coping with those normative and non-normative stressor events as described in the previous chapter, the primary strength of a traditional Asian family structure is in providing an environment for mutual support and interdependence. The process of immigration dramatically represents a stressor event. In such instances, relatives and close friends are often no longer available to provide material and emotional support to the immigrating family. The absence of interpersonal interaction outside of the immigrating family, in turn, forces greater demands and intense interaction within the nuclear family, leaving members with a high degree of vulnerability and unresolved conflicts (Ho et al., 2004).

After the family immigrates it may experience differing acculturation patterns between husband and wife and between parents and children. These mixed acculturation experiences can have negative effects on the decision making and functioning of a family. Asian American youth may be more receptive to Western culture and value orientation as they may desire to be accepted by the larger society, especially in a school setting. Individual family members' acceptance and incorporation into the Western orientation of individualism, independence, and assertiveness, especially in attitudes related to authority, sexuality, and freedom of individual choice, make the cultural values of traditional Asian families an extremely uncomfortable fit for them.

Inherent in the immigration experience is a cognitive response that each family member goes through. Shon and Ja (1982) listed these responses as follows: (a) cultural shock and disbelief at the disparity between what was expected and what actually exists, (b) disappointment at what exists, (c) grief at the separation from and loss of what was left behind, (d) anger and resentment, (e) depression because of the current family situation, (f) some form of acceptance of the situation, and (g) mobilization of family resources and energy. There are many variations to this generalized scheme of responses, and each family member may experience these responses in a different order. These seven factors contributing to the cultural transitional difficulties have also drastically altered the structure and content (relationship) of current Asian and Pacific Islander American families (Ho et al., 2004).

Immigration can seriously impact the support network provided by the extended family. Those individuals who have immigrated as single individuals may experience being cut off from emotional and social support provided by their network of relatives who still may reside in their country of origin (Hong & Ham, 2001; Lee, 1996). For example, couples experiencing marital conflict are unable to turn to their families for consultation and support. Additionally, support for life and family development issues such as marriage and childbirth or other life events that may have culturally prescribed means of handling may be absent. Such social isolation may create various forms of individual, family and marital discord (Hong & Ham, 2001). The erosion of the extended family thus can be attributed to factors of migration and uprooting from the homeland.

Family Help-Seeking Patterns and Behaviors

The cultural values presented here are highly applicable to first-generation immigrants, recent arrivals, and, to a less but important extent, the American-born.

As Mass (1976) indicates, the influences exerted by value patterns that are acquired throughout childhood are often considerable, even among those whose behavior is highly integrated.

Very traditional Asian Americans do not typically consider dysfunctional family dynamics and psychological theories in attempts to account for behavioral difficulties (Green, 1999; Sue & Sue, 2008). Instead, social, moral, and organic explanations are used. When an individual behaves in a dysfunctional manner, external events such as physical illness, death of a loved one, or the loss of a job are viewed as the cause of his or her problems. The individual is always the victim of unfortunate social circumstances over which the individual has no control, and therefore is not to blame (Ho et al., 2004).

Moral explanation also may be used to explain family problems. Such explanation describes the violation of interpersonal duties and loyalties held sacred by a specific cultural group. Dysfunction is seen as a punishment or a direct result of immoral behavior. Hence the dysfunction or suffering of an Asian individual may be attributed to his or her violation of filial piety. Community elders or family members may be expected to exhort the individual to improve his or her dysfunctional behavior. Organic explanations for personal dysfunction are most common in some Asian ethnic groups (Kleinman & Lin, 1981). For example, the Chinese model of yin and yang, suggesting the imbalance between two basic life forces, has long been accepted as the source of difficulty in physical and emotional functioning. The social, moral, and organic explanations to account for behavioral dysfunction not only maintain the individual's dignity but also help safeguard the honorable family name.

While an Asian family undergoes several stages in its attempt to help its members, different families may have different help-seeking patterns. Generally, there are three types of Asian American families in the United States, based on their level of enculturation and acculturation to American society.

1. *Recently arrived immigrant or refugee families.* For a considerable period of time after their arrival in the United States, new immigrant families must direct most of their energy simply to adjusting to a completely new environment (Lee, 1997; Ngo, Tran, Gibbons, & Oliver, 2001). Due to cultural differences and language barriers, these families seldom seek personal and psychological help. These families have a strong ethnic identity and pride.

2. *Immigrant American families.* Such families are characterized by foreign-born parents and their American-born children and the great degree of cultural conflict between them. Younger members are usually more integrated or assimilated in accepting the values of the dominant culture; they are Americanized—assertive, individualistic, and independent. Some children may not know or speak their

parents' native language, making communication and negotiation among family members nearly impossible. These families usually require help in resolving generational conflicts, communication problems, role clarification, and renegotiation. Though they may encounter acculturative pressures to establish a hyphenated identity, family members may try to hold on to dominant cultural practices, dress, and manner in the workplace, while maintaining ethnic-based cultural practices, values, and family relationship patterns in their private lives. Yet the degree to which they are able to maintain ethnic integrity is determined not solely by their adherence to cultural practices or level of acculturation but by their experiences of and encounters with racial discrimination, the culture of their community area, the presence of other immigrant ethnic communities, and the success in preserving their cultural practices within the home environment (Bhatia & Ram, 2004).

3. Immigrant-descendent families. Such families usually consist of second-, third-, or fourth-generation American-born parents and their children. They are acculturated to the Western value orientation and speak English at home. They usually reside outside the Asian and Pacific Islander American neighborhood and can seek help from traditional human service agencies or private practitioners with some degree of comfort and little stigma.

Native Americans

Demographics

There are multiple designations for the ethnic or racial group originally labeled as *Indians* or *American Indians* and *Alaska Natives*. Though the term *American Indian* is no longer considered appropriate by many, one or more of the following generic designations—*Native Americans*, *Native People*, *First Nations Peoples*, and *Indigenous Peoples*—are currently used to replace it (Weaver, 2003; Yellow Bird, 2001). Each of these labels attempts to encompass a diversity of languages, lifestyles, kinship systems, and organizations (McGoldrick, Giordano, & Pearce, 1996; Polacca, 1995). Yet each label has significant sociopolitical implications. As Yellow Bird (2001) points out in discussing the significance of these terms,

Many Indigenous Peoples are mistakenly called *Indians, American Indians,* or *Native Americans.* They are not Indians or American Indians because they are not from India. They are not Native Americans because Indigenous Peoples did not refer to their lands as America until Europeans arrived and imposed this name on the land. Indians, American Indians, and Native Americans are "colonized" and "inaccurate" names that oppress the identities of First Nations Peoples. (p. 61)

Though we will alternately use the terms, "First Nations Peoples" or "Native Peoples," it is important to note that each of these terms, while representing the diversity of a group of people, is still generic. To honor their own unique culture and traditions, First Nations Peoples would rather self-identify and hence be referred to by the specific indigenous sociopolitical and cultural group or nation—for example, Navajo, Apache, or Chippewa. The implication of Yellow Bird's words speaks to the tumultuous and tragic history of a group of people who have struggled to maintain a cultural and ethnic identity and the integrity of their heritage. Furthermore, these struggles have provided the cultural and historical context for the families of Native People, for their family life has dramatically been shaped and altered by historical and contemporary experiences and events.

In the continental United States and Alaska there are over 550 distinct indigenous tribes. Historically, the term *tribe* has been used in an ethnological sense and in an official "political sense." Prior to the official federal definition of a Native tribe, this term specifically referred to a "group of indigenous people bound together by blood ties, who were socially, politically, and religiously organized to the tenet of their own culture, who lived together, occupied a definite territory, and who spoke a common language or dialect" (Utter, 2001, p. 57).

Native "tribes" are as ethnically differentiated as Europeans and are far more diverse culturally and linguistically (Lum, 2003). Some of the tribes are small with fewer than 100 members, while the Cherokee, Choctaw, Sioux, Navajo or Diné, Chippewa or Ojibwa, and Latin American Indians have populations over 100,000 (U.S. Census Bureau, 2000). According to the 2000 Census, 43% of First Nations Peoples live in the Western United States. About half of the total number of Native Peoples live in urban areas (Sutton & Broken Nose, 1996). For example, in New York City and Los Angeles there are approximately 100,000 Indigenous Peoples. Other nonurban Indigenous Peoples are very traditional, live in isolated rural areas on reservations, and may know very little English. Many others have been raised in urban areas and have had little or no contact with their Native

Photo 3.2   Cultural diversity may refer to a variety of social reference groups including ethnicity, gender, social class, sexual orientation, age, or disability

Source: Copyright © Can Stock Photo Inc./tobkatrina

heritage. Regardless of their location, many First Nations Peoples experience a continual struggle and conflict in attempting to achieve a balance between their Native values and those of the dominant society.

One hundred years ago the population of U.S. Native People was about 250,000. In the 1990 Census there were approximately 2 million Native People. The 2000 U.S. Census data revealed that of the total U.S. population of 281.4 million, 4.1 million or 1.5% reported "American Indian" or "Alaska Native" as their ethnic identity. This figure includes the 2.5 million people or 0.9% who reported only "American Indian" or "Alaska Native" as their racial or ethnic identity. As the 2000 Census allowed persons to indicate one or more racial or ethnic identities, an additional 1.6 million reported their racial identity as "American Indian" and reported at least one or more other racial identities. Given the fact that the 2000 U.S. Census for the first time permitted respondents to report one or more races if they considered themselves as such, the data from 2000 are not directly comparable to those of earlier censuses. In the 1990 Census, using the population who identified only as "American Indian," there were only 2 million Native People. The increase between 1990 and 2000 is 26%. If one were to combine the number of "American Indians" who reported only one race with the "American Indian" individuals who reported more than one race, the population increase would be 110%.

In contrast to any other ethnic minority group in the United States, a person is not a "real" or "authentic" Native unless he or she fits into categories defined by the federal government, including blood degree and tribal status. In order to be eligible for federal Native programs, a person must be able to prove he or she has at least one quarter Native "blood," as recognized by the federal government. The fact is that over 60% of First Nations Peoples are of mixed heritage, having Black, White, and Hispanic backgrounds (Sue & Sue, 2008).

First Nations Peoples are generally perceived as a homogeneous group, a composite of certain physical and personality characteristics that have become stereotypes reinforced by the media. Obviously, the idea that there is an "Indian" stereotype that could fit all or even most First Nations Peoples today is naïve and simplistic. Like other clients, the Native client wishes to be recognized as a person, a human being, and not as a category. To recognize the Native client as a person, a family therapist must understand and respect his or her unique cultural family background and rich heritage (Ho et al., 2004).

History of Oppression

Over the course of U.S. history the United States government determined which Indigenous groups were tribal "political entities." Such designation allowed federal officials to negotiate peace treaties, grant land acquisitions, regulate Native affairs, permit claims by First Nations Peoples against the government, and determine which Indigenous groups were affected by particular statutes (Cohen, 1982). Many First Nations Peoples were relegated to reservations, and there were situations in which culturally and ethnically distinct groups were bound together on one reservation or split up and spread over two or more reservations to be absorbed into a socially constructed "tribe" for governmental political designations. Though a definition for the term *tribe* does not exist in the U.S. Constitution, this term is specifically found in numerous treaties, legislative agreements, statutes, and even presidential executive orders (Cohen, 1982).

The breakdown of First Nations cultural traditions and family customs began in the early 1800s. In 1815, the U.S. government coerced tribal leaders into signing treaties they could not read and thus could not understand (Costa & Henry, 1977). These treaties opened the door for a greater influx of European homesteaders and miners. As the influx of Whites continued, and they eventually became a political dominant group, Native People became restricted to reservation areas. By 1849, the Bureau of Indian Affairs was given full authority to oversee the activities of First Nations Peoples. The sacred Black Hills were taken by an illegal treaty, the buffalo were destroyed, and the language and religious practices were forbidden by the missionary schools (Kelly, 1990). It was during this period that First Nations children were taken away from their parents with the intention of educating them in the White man's mold. These placements later included boarding schools, religious institutions, foster care, and adoption. These practices severed the links of the support system that centered on children and thus encouraged the destruction of the basic tenets of tribal life. Fortunately, these practices were corrected in 1978 with the federal Indian Child Welfare Act. This act was created to resolve the large number of Native children placed in foster care by ensuring jurisdictional control of child welfare cases with tribal courts if the child is domiciled and resides on a reservation and to ensure that Native children remain with their parents whenever possible. The intent of this act was to preserve First Nations culture. Before the Indian Child Welfare Act one in four Native children was being removed from his or her home and placed into a boarding school, residential home, or non-Native foster home.

The Dawes Act of 1887 (Kelly, 1990), which divided the reservation land into allotments and individual ownership, forced Native men and women to become farmers and ranchers. With the shift of occupational skills and requirements, Native men were no longer recognized as brave warriors or hunters. Native women were also traumatized as they painfully watched their children be taken away and as they witnessed the gradual psychological deterioration of their husbands.

Following World War II, the unemployment rate for First Nations Peoples returning to their reservation soared. In 1952, the Bureau of Indian Affairs sought to relieve the high unemployment problem by finding jobs for them in urban areas (Stuart, 1977). This program was considered as yet another attempt by the government to destroy the Native culture and family structure by encouraging assimilation into the urban environment rather than attempting to strengthen First Nations ways of life by developing more work opportunities on reservations (Farris, 1973). Between 1952 and 1968 some 67,522 First Nations Peoples who were heads of households were relocated through this direct employment program (Bureau of Indian Affairs, 1971).

From the above historical overview it can be seen that though Native Peoples are diverse, they in fact share a common history of oppression and colonialization (Yellow Bird, 2001). This history of struggle and oppression and the experiences of colonialization and cultural genocide have a multigenerational impact on the contemporary experiences of Native People and their families (Yellow Bird, 2001). The grief, trauma, and oppression experienced by the ancestors are ever present in the lives of Native People and within the historical and emotional matrix of the family (Brave Heart-Jordan & DeBruyn, 1995). The grief and unresolved trauma resulting from these historical events in turn contribute to the array of current social difficulties faced by First Nations Peoples.

The statistics for income, education, and mental health among Native People present a bleak picture. In discussing the array of social and economic problems facing First Nations Peoples, Karger and Stoesz (2002) presented the following data:

- In 1990 more than 16 percent of Native males living on reservations were unemployed compared to 6.4 percent of the total population.
- In 1990, 33 percent of the Native population lived below the poverty line compared to 14.5 percent of Whites.
- Sixty-five percent of Native people on reservations are high school graduates.
- Sixteen percent of Native homes are without electricity; the U.S. average is 0.1.
- Roughly 43 percent of Native people who live beyond infancy die before age 55; compared to slightly more than 16 percent for the general population.
- Native people have a maternal death rate 20 percent higher than the national average.
- The death rate for tuberculosis is six times higher than that for the population as a whole; [the rate for] chronic liver disease is four times the norm; [the rates for] diabetes, influenza, and pneumonia are two times the norm.
- Suicide rates are twice the national average, with rates highest among young people.
- Native people have the highest rate of alcoholism of any ethnic group in the United States. (pp. 67–68)

Living against such ecological stress and daily survival threats continues to threaten the cultural and ethnic integrity of First Nations families. Additionally, children of urban Native families are being raised with fewer contacts with traditional life. Their peers are often non-Natives, and they increasingly grow up to marry non-Natives, diluting further their indigenous heritage (Price, 1981). Yet, despite a multitude of adversities, First Nations families have a long history of durability and persistence in survival.

Family Help-Seeking Patterns and Behaviors

The First Nations culture emphasizes harmony with nature, endurance of suffering, respect and noninterference toward others, a strong belief that man is inherently good and that he should be respected for his decisions, and so on. Such traits make a family in difficulty very reluctant to seek help. The family's fear and mistrust toward non-Natives caused by past oppressions and discrimination make it almost impossible for a non-Native family therapist to gain entry into the family system. While a Native family experiences several stages in its attempt to assist its members, different families may have different service needs and help-seeking patterns. Judging by family lifestyle patterns, contemporary Native families can be classified into three types: the traditional family, the nontraditional or bicultural family, and the pantraditional family (Red Horse, 1980).

1. The *traditional family* overtly adheres to culturally defined styles of living. The parents and grandparents speak the native language. The family practices tribal religion, customs, and mores and has an extended family network.

2. The *nontraditional or bicultural family* appears to have adopted many aspects of nontraditional styles of living. Although the parents or grandparents are bilingual, English constitutes conversational language at home. The family adopts the dominant cultural belief system and actively takes part in social activities with groups and individuals from the dominant culture. The structure of the family is extended and lies with kin from reservations and across states.

3. The *pantraditional family* overtly struggles to redefine and reconfirm previously lost cultural lifestyles. Both English and the native language are spoken in the pantraditional family. These families practice a modified tribal belief system and struggle to maintain their traditional extended family network as well as cultural activities. As may be expected, traditional families generally will not seek help or receive help from a family therapist. In their attempt to recapture

and redefine cultural lifestyles, pantraditional families also may not be receptive to the idea of family therapy. The bicultural families are the ones most likely to be receptive to family therapy for they have adopted the dominant culture and its mores.

The different family lifestyle patterns among First Nations Peoples do not imply an ongoing erosion of cultural values. Studies suggest, however, that Native core values are retained and remain as a constant, regardless of family lifestyle patterns (Weaver, 2001; Yellow Bird, 2001). The extended family network maintained by all three family lifestyle patterns is one good example reflecting the Native family's resistance to cultural assimilation. When a family needs help, the extended family network is the first source to be contacted. Second, a religious leader may be consulted to resolve problems plaguing the family. Third, if the problem is unresolved, the family will contact the tribal community elders. Last, when all these fail, the family *may* seek help from the mainstream family and health care system. Yet when the family has contact with the therapist, the family is not psychologically or emotionally ready for help. Some families see a therapist only when ordered to do so by a court. Such contacts usually result in failure of service delivery, and they further reinforce the Native family's distrust of family service providers (Ho et al., 2004).

Latino Americans

Demographics

In 2004 there were 20.4 million Latinos in the civilian noninstitutional population in the United States representing 14% of the total population (U.S. Census Bureau, 2004). In the Latino population, two thirds (65.9%) were of Mexican origin and 40.3% were foreign born. Latinos represent a population that is increasingly heterogeneous. They are very diverse in terms of national origin, level of acculturation, length of U.S. residency, social class, and other demographic factors. The three largest Latino groups are Mexican, Puerto Rican, and Cuban. Mexican Americans represent approximately 59% of the Latino population, Puerto Ricans make up approximately 10% of this population, and Cubans constitute only 3% of the total Latino population in the United States. Latinos from the Dominican Republic (one of the newer Latino immigrant groups) are the fastest-growing Latino group in the United States, constituting about 2% of the Latino population. Latinos from Central America (whose countries of origin are Belize, Guatemala, El Salvador, Honduras, Nicaragua, Panama, and Costa Rica) and South America (whose countries of origin are Argentina, Bolivia, Chile, Colombia, Ecuador, Paraguay, Peru, Uruguay, and

Venezuela) combined make up about 9% of the total Latino population. Several factors are said to have contributed to this rapid increase in the Latino population. One notable factor is the increased influx of immigrants especially from Mexico. The other factor includes the relatively high fertility rates of Latinas. Finally, another contributing factor to this increase in the Latino population reflects the initiative and mandate of the U.S. Census Bureau to count undocumented immigrants (Ho et al., 2004).

Such an aggressive effort to "count" undocumented Latinos in the United States has at least two ramifications. One ramification is evident in the increased number of Latinos in America and the possible social, economic, and political presence they can garner due to the increased population numbers. The most ominous ramification is whether the increased number of Latinos will also increase the potential for confrontations between Latinos and other ethnic groups around limited and/or shared social, economic, and political resources. Without a doubt such a formidable presence with the United States will likely gain Latinos increased visibility within American society.

Photo 3.3 Latino families are very diverse in terms of national origin, level of acculturation, length of U.S. residency, social class, as well as other demographic factors

Source: Copyright © Can Stock Photo Inc./Feverpitched

The Latino population in the United States is heterogeneous in its ethnicity, physical appearance, cultural practices, traditions, and Spanish language dialects. These populations represent a diverse group of multigenerational immigrants from different Spanish-speaking countries as well as long-term residents in the southwestern United States (Santiago-Rivera, Arredondo, & Gallardo-Cooper, 2002). Mexican Americans have continued to make up by far the largest segment of the U.S. Latino population (59%), so it should come as no surprise that a significant portion of the research on Latino populations includes only Mexican-origin groups (Demo, Allen, & Fine, 2000; Massey, Zambrana, & Bell, 1995). Unfortunately, as is the case with other racially oppressed ethnic minority groups, the outcomes of studies on Mexican-origin groups have been generalized to other Latino populations. The homogenization of ethnic minority groups is not a new phenomenon. The authors of this text challenge family therapists working with Latino families to strive to "culturally tailor" their interventions within this population and take time to better understand important differences between and among Latino families.

Ethnic Identity: Hispanic or Latino?

Ethnic identity is a narrative identity that is often reflective of an ethnic group's sociopolitical struggle for self-determination. A group's right to establish its own identity is based on how the group interprets its collective history and the efforts of the group to create and maintain sociopolitical consciousness and ethnic pride. In this context the use of the term *Hispanic* has been challenged as to whether it represents the ethnic and cultural identity of a people. The term *Hispanic*, which has been used to define Spanish-speaking immigrants, was introduced by the U.S. government Office of Management and Budget in 1978. The rationale for using this term was to aid census takers who needed a term for Whites (and others) who claimed some degree of Spanish language or cultural affiliation. As a result, the Federal Register defined a "Hispanic" as a person of Mexican, Puerto Rican, Cuban, Central or South American, or other Spanish origin, regardless of race (Green, 1999).

Given the origin of this term the designation *Hispanic* has increasingly come under criticism. Some do consider the word *Hispanic* offensive, whereas others merely see it as a bureaucratic term with very little personal significance. Falicov (1998) states that the term *Latino* more accurately describes the sense of linguistic and cultural connectedness of those persons of Mexican, Puerto Rican, Cuban, Central or South American, or other Spanish origin in that it

affirms their native pre-Hispanic identity . . . "Latino" is a more democratic alternative to "Hispanic" because *Hispanic* is a term strongly supported by politically conservative groups that regard their Spanish heritage as superior to the "conquered" indigenous groups of the Americas. *Latino* is also geographically more accurate, since it refers to people from Latin America rather than to people from Spain. (p. 34)

Even the term *Latino*, though progressive, should not be used as a personal cultural or ethnic descriptor for those with Spanish cultural and linguistic affiliation. A person of this origin may more likely describe him- or herself in terms of country of origin. Thus one may describe her- or himself as Cuban, Mexican, Puerto Rican, Dominican, Nicaraguan, or another nationality that resides within Central or South America (Garcia-Preto, 1996). In spite of the preference to use one's country of origin as the basis for ethnic identification, the term *Latino* is viewed as reflective of a proud yet general sense of cultural and linguistic connection between persons from various Spanish-speaking countries in the Americas (Ho et al., 2004).

Language as a Shared Identity

The Spanish language binds Latinos into a sense of cultural connectedness and "anchors" their shared identity (Falicov, 1998). Though the Spanish language may represent this sense of cultural affinity, each group or nationality may speak Spanish with a cultural style that highlights group differences by using idioms and metaphors that are unique to that group (Arredondo & Perez, 2003; Zuniga, 2003) in that the same word or term may vary in meaning between Cubans and Puerto Ricans.

In spite of the shared identity through the Spanish language, Arredondo and Perez (2003) point out that the use of the Spanish language in the United States is shaped by its sociopolitical context. The use of Spanish in the English-speaking United States has clear social, cultural, and political ramifications causing some Latinos to prefer to speak English rather than Spanish. Arredondo and Perez (2003) state the following reasons for this preference.

- Language can be associated with the time of immigration in the United States, with recent immigrants possibly being more monolingual Spanish speakers who have English as a second language. As one becomes more assimilated one may prefer the use of English over Spanish.
- Many Latinos, particularly Mexican Americans, do not speak Spanish at all, as they may have been taught by their parents that in order to assimilate and to avoid "punishment" for speaking Spanish, as their parents experienced, they (the children) should not learn Spanish.
- While being bilingual or speaking Spanish whenever possible could be an indication of comfort for the Latino immigrant, speaking Spanish in the workplace is often discouraged in order not to make people feel "uncomfortable."

- "Code-switching" or using Spanish and English in the same sentence may be used to emphasize a point with a particular English or Spanish word, yet the primary and accepted language for discourse remains English.
- Being bilingual is an academic, psychological, social, and economic asset for those in bicultural and bilingual settings (Arredondo & Perez, 2003, p. 121). Yet English remains the accepted language for discourse.

The preference for English over Spanish can more fully be understood within the context of an "antibilingual" movement within the United States culminating in "antibilingual" legislation in Arizona in 2000 and in California in 1995 (Arredondo & Perez, 2003). This type of public reaction to an integral part of one's cultural identity such as one's language has implications for the sociopolitical realities and reactions to Latinos in the United States. These negative reactions can further create a sense of conflicted cultural and linguistic loyalty for Spanish-speaking immigrants. The linguistic dilemma as to what extent they can or should refrain from speaking their language of origin or to what extent they compromise their language in the act of assimilation into an English-speaking culture certainly has psychological implications for one's sense of self-esteem.

Latinos: A Racially Mixed Ethnic Group

As stated earlier, the construct of race has no defined biological meaning, yet the movement of people across territorial borders is described as a history of racial interactions, if not warfare and strife. The significance of race for the Latino population is that Latinos may be considered a racially mixed group. From this historical and cultural blending of African, Indigenous, and European heritage in countries such as Mexico, Puerto Rico, Cuba, and other Central and South American countries, one finds within the heterogeneous Latino cultures the presence of *mestizos*—persons of Indian and European heritage—and *criollos* or *mulattos*—persons of Indian, African, and European heritage. Not only are there different national groups; there are issues of racial phenotype, for example color, which may range from White to Black within one family. Those darker-color Latinos may find themselves subjected to stereotypes and color-based discrimination within the United States. Those with a lighter skin complexion may become an "invisible minority" (Montalvo, 1991) by blending into the White melting pot (Flores, 2000). These factors contribute to the degree of biracial and bicultural experiences within the Latino population in the United States.

Cultural Values in Relation to Family Structure

The traditional Latino family unit has changed; recent data show that the percentage of children living in intact families in the United States has declined from

74% in 1980 to 64% in 1995 (Estrada, 2000). This statistic is very significant in that the Latino family structure plays a very vital role in the lives of this large ethnic group. The following discussion is an overview of the cultural values and family structure of Latinos. The heritage of Latinos is rich and diverse. The cultural concepts that form the foundation for the Latino American family structure and relationships include *familismo*, *dignidad*, *respeto*, *personalismo*, *machismo*, *spiritualism*, and *fatalism*. These common cultural Latino values significantly influence Latino family life, organization, and structure. Each of these cultural values is described below, and a discussion of how these values affect family subsystems and overall family interaction follows.

Familismo. Familismo is manifested in a shared sense of responsibility to care for children, provide financial and emotional supports, and participate in decision-making efforts that involve one or more members of the family (Falicov, 1998; Santiago-Rivera et al., 2002). An individual's self-confidence, worth, security, and identity are determined by his or her relationship to other family members. The importance of family is evident in the cultural use of family names (Fitzpatrick, 1981). The man generally uses both his father's and his mother's name together with his given name, for example *Jose Garcia Rivera*. Garcia is his father's family name, and Rivera is his mother's family name. If the man is to be addressed by only one name, the father's family name is used. This reflects the patriarchal pattern of the Latino family. *Familismo* is one of the strengths of Latino culture.

Dignidad, Respeto, and Personalismo. Along with the concept of *familismo,* a Latino defines his self-worth in terms of those inner qualities that give him self-respect and earn him the respect of others. He feels an inner dignity (*dignidad*) and expects others to show respect (*respeto*) for that "*dignidad.*" *Personalismo* is also a cultural trait that reflects a collectivistic worldview (Levine & Padilla, 1980) where there is a great deal of emotional investment in the family and positive interpersonal interaction will help maintain mutual dependency and closeness for a lifetime. Hence, great importance is given to those positive interpersonal and social skills to facilitate warm, close relationships.

Machismo. Closely related to the concept of *personalismo* is the quality of *machismo,* literally, maleness. *Machismo* is referred to as a quality of personal magnetism that impresses and influences others. It is a style of personal daring by which one faces challenges, danger, and threats with calmness and self-possession. More centrally, *machismo* encompasses a man's responsibility to be a good provider, protector, and defender for his family (Morales, 1996). Loyalty and responsibility to family and community are what makes a man a good man.

The Latino meaning of *machismo* has been confused with the Anglo definition of *macho* that describes sexist, male chauvinist behavior (Morales, 1996). The Latino meaning of *machismo* should not be pathologized and erroneously equated with what Americans have come to (more negatively) understand as one who is "macho" (insensitive, domineering, and certainly not manifesting a protective family function). The Latino meaning of *machismo* conveys the notions of an "honorable and responsible man" (Morales, 1996).

White middle-class Americans stress individualism and emphasize the individual's ability to compete for higher social and economic status. The Latino culture values those inner qualities that constitute the uniqueness of the person and his goodness. A Latino believes that every individual has some sense of personal dignity and will be sensitive about showing proper respect (*respeto*) to others while demanding self-respect as well. This expectation is intensified when a Latino first encounters a non-Latino and interprets the latter's insensitivity as personal insult or disdain. Contrarily, if *personalismo* is reciprocated in a social or professional interaction, trust is developed and so is a sense of obligation. Hence a Latino family may seek and perhaps benefit from family therapy not because of agency affiliation or the professional reputation of the therapist but simply because of the therapist's skill and ability to convey *personalismo* when dealing with the family.

Spirituality and Spiritualism

In the Latino cultural orientation there is the clear interrelationship between faith, religion, spirituality, and spiritualism (Flores & Carey, 2000; Santiago-Rivera et al., 2002). Latinos emphasize spiritual values and are willing to sacrifice material satisfaction for spiritual goals. Catholicism is the predominant religion for Latinos (Santiago-Rivera et al., 2002). Their Roman Catholic ways of worship, however, differ from those of other ethnic groups, such as the Irish. In the Latino culture there is the belief that one can make direct contact with God and the supernatural, without the assistance of intervention of the clergy. A significant part of the Latino population, especially the Puerto Rican, believes in spiritualism. The belief is that the visible world is surrounded by an invisible world inhabited by "good" and "evil" spirits who influence human behavior (Falicov, 1998). Thus spirits can either protect or harm and prevent or cause illness. In order to be protected by good spirits, an individual is expected to produce good and charitable deeds in the secular world.

The Latino culture values the spirit and soul as much as it values the body and perhaps less than it values worldly materialism. The Latino culture emphasizes transcendent qualities such as justice, loyalty, and love. This worldview teaches that one should not be preoccupied with mastering the world. There is a keen sense of destiny (partly related to fundamental fears of the sacred) and a sense of divine providence governing the world. The once popular song, "Que Sera, Sera" ("Whatever Will Be, Will Be"), reflects the Latino cultural expression of *fatalism*. According to Falicov (1998), therapists working with Latinos must distinguish between a "deficit-oriented" fatalism and a "resource-oriented" one. A "deficit" understanding may disempower an individual. On the other hand the fatalistic attitude can serve as a functional quality leading to the acceptance of many tragic and unfortunate events as beyond one's control. Furthermore, it softens the sense of despair or personal failure that is the common by-product of the middle-class American value system. American family therapists are strongly cautioned not to pathologize the concept of Latino fatalism or view this as a negativistic, fatalistic, "doomsday" perspective. This interpretation is a gross misunderstanding of the true essence of this very functional, adaptive cultural concept and should not be confused with the American notion of "fatalism."

Help-Seeking Patterns in Latino Families

Studies indicate that Latinos do not consider mental health services a solution to their emotional and family problems. Latinos consider the family their primary source of support. It is difficult for a husband-father who is the head of the family to admit that he is not fulfilling his leadership role of providing for the family. Before outside help is solicited, godparents or *compadres* may be consulted. If the family problem involves marital discord, the *compadre* of the marriage may function as mediator for the couple (Sue & Sue, 2008). In a Puerto Rican family, the *padrino* also is used to mediate intrafamily conflict and act as an advocate for the family (Fitzpatrick, 1981). The *padrino* is an individual, in a higher position of the family structure, who has a personal relationship with the family for whom he provides material needs and emotional guidance. Because Catholicism plays a vital role in the life of Latino Americans, in times of stress and illness, priests, folk healers, and religious leaders can be strong family resources. It is not unusual for a Latino to equate the role of the family therapist with that of a priest and to expect some immediate help from the therapist. At other times, the Latino family member may see the family therapist as a physician from whom he or she traditionally seeks help for emotional and psychological problems (Padilla, Carlos, & Keefe, 1976).

In terms of family therapy needs, Latino families can be categorized into three types (Casas & Keefe, 1980; Padilla et al., 1976): (a) newly arrived immigrant families, (b) immigrant American families, and (c) immigrant-descent families. Newly arrived immigrant families need information, referral, advocacy, and such concrete services as English-language instruction. Due to cultural and language barriers, they seldom seek personal or family therapy. Immigrant American families are characterized by cultural conflict between foreign-born parents and American-born children. They need help in resolving generational conflicts, communication problems, role clarification, and renegotiation. Native or immigrant-descent families usually are integrated, speak both languages at home, and can seek help from mainstream social services, including private practice family therapists.

African American Families

Defining the African American Family

The African American family is far more complex than has been recognized. The complexities of the African American family are reflected in Billingsley's (1992) definition of the African American family as an

intimate association of persons of African descent who are related to one another by a variety of means, including blood, marriage, formal adoption, informal adoption or by appropriation; sustained by a history of common residence in America; and deeply embedded in a network of social structures both internal to and external to itself. Numerous interlocking elements came together, forming an extraordinarily resilient institution. (p. 28)

Billingsley's definition suggests that the African American family, as a social system interacting with a number of other systems, must be understood within a historical perspective in order to comprehend its structure and function (Goldenberg & Goldenberg, 2002). His definition further suggests that the African American family structure should be perceived as an adaptation to a set of social-political conditions existing in the family's wider social and ecological environment.

Taylor (2003) takes the stance that to understand the African American family one must take a holistic perspective that emphasizes the influence of historical, cultural, social, economic, and political forces in shaping contemporary African American family life. The confluence of these multiple forces contributes not only to the complexity of the African American family but also to its diversity, as there is no such entity as the singular "African American family." The African American family is in fact a social reality determined by a complicated interplay of factors making African American families less than homogeneous (Devore, 2001). The African American family while "forming an extraordinarily resilient institution" (Billingsley, 1992, p. 28) represents a collection of individual families with different religious and spiritual backgrounds, socioeconomic statuses, educational levels, skin colors, family structures, levels of acculturation, diverse values, and lifestyles (Boyd-Franklin, 1995).

Photo 3.4 The African American family has been described by many family theorists as egalitarian and characterized by complimentary and flexible family roles

Source: © Jupiterimages/Creatas/Thinkstock

What Is in a Name?

Ethnic identities are embedded in those collective narratives that ethnic groups recount as their distinctive "connectedness." In that sense, ethnic identities are socially constructed. How an ethnic minority group "labels" itself or the term used to identify the collective ethnic identity serves many purposes. The self-designated term or identity label may

- represent the fact that the designated identity serves as a buffer against racism and oppression;
- serve as an experience of bonding that helps individuals form attachments with others who share similar cultural practices and worldviews;
- allow the group to adapt to a particular environment that may be more or less supportive of its cultural identity; or
- serve as the basis for pride and achievement (Parham & Brown, 2003).

The social and cultural history of African Americans speaks to their struggle for self-designation and self-definition. As with the First Nations Peoples and

Latinos, the issue of ethnic "name" has been the issue of achieving a state of self-determination and a sense of personal and collective empowerment. Pejorative terms such as *Negro, Colored,* and even *Black* have been labels imposed upon a group of people of African descent in the Americas. These labels signify the operation of the "victim system," which places those of African descent in a marginalized, disempowered, and "invisible" position within the existing social order. The issue of "what is in a name" is also significant for many who come from other ethnic and cultural backgrounds and who are uncertain as to the appropriate term to "label" those of African descent. In this chapter, the term *African American* refers to descendents of enslaved Africans brought to the United States. *Black* refers to all people of color and African descendents in the Diaspora including those from the West Indies, Africa, and the Americas (Grace, 1992; McRoy, 2003).

The other significance of "what is in a name" is reflected in the history of those of African descent who also have within their genealogy the presence of other ethnic, racial, or cultural groups. While this group has historically been designated by the existing term used for those of African descent, there is an emerging group of individuals of bicultural and biracial descent who do not want to be referred to by any ethnic label (McRoy, 2003). The social and cultural ramifications of this emerging group on African American family life are only now beginning to be documented (Moran, 2001). The increasing number of interracial marriages and children resulting from such unions is only part of the story. We will discuss interracial marriages later in this chapter.

The presence of this "multiracial" group is reflected in part in the 2000 U.S. Census. In the 2000 U.S. Census, between 34.7 million and 36.4 million U.S. citizens reported being Black or African American. The reason for the range is that in the 2000 U.S. Census individuals were able to check off more than one race and 34.7 million identified as Black or African American only while the remaining number indicated being both African American and "another race." It is those from this latter group who are raising concern about where they fit in the existing social schema of racial classification. For many in this "multiracial" group, there are conflicted and divided loyalties. For others, they have achieved a sense of personal identity that is either inclusive of their multiple ethnic identities or transcends their multiple identities through use of the term *multicultural*.

Cultural Values in Relation to Family Structure

As we begin to examine the African American family from the perspective of resiliency and strength, we see specific Africentric cultural themes that speak to the uniqueness of African American families. These themes are (a) strong kinship bonds, (b) strong education and work achievement orientation, (c) flexibility in family roles, (d) commitment to religious values and church participation, (e) humanistic orientation, and (f) endurance in a hostile environment.

Strong Kinship Bonds. Strong kinship bonds and the extended family are heavily influenced by a traditional African cultural orientation that values collectivity above individualism. It is generally acknowledged that the African American kinship network is more cohesive and extensive than kinship relationships among the White population. For example, in 1992 approximately 1 in 5 African American families were extended compared to 1 in 10 White families (Glick, 1997). Herskovits (1958), Sudarkasa (1997), and Taylor (2003) report that in comparative research on West African, Caribbean, and African American family patterns they found evidence of cultural continuities in the significance attached to coresidence, formal kinship relations, and nuclear families among Black populations in these areas. In contrast to European extended families where primacy is given to the conjugal unit, the African and African American extended family is centered primarily on extended blood ties (Taylor, 2003).

Strong kinship bonds can provide valuable functions and needed services to African American families. In an earlier work on African American extended families, Stack (1974) describes how problems occurring within an individual's life may reverberate within the extended kinship network. Other studies have revealed that the kinship network may assist extended family members with financial aid, child care, household chores, and other forms of mutual support (Martin & Martin, 1978; Shimkin, Shimkin, & Frate, 1978).

Many extended family members become a part of an individual African American family through informal adoption or informal foster parenting (Hatchett, Cochran, & Jackson, 1991). This form of child care, which has been practiced since slavery, involves an adult relative in an extended family taking care of children whose parents are unable to care for them. Extended African American families may also include "nonblood" significant others who are considered relatives or "fictive kin" (Manns, 1988). These individuals may be given such designations as *play brother and sister* and are granted the same rights and responsibilities within the extended family as blood relatives. In summary, strong kinship bonds enhance the emotional relationships within the extended family network and beyond. They help the family deal with environmental threats in such a way as to ensure the survival, security, and self-esteem of its members (Chestang, 1976).

Strong Education and Work Achievement Orientation. Parents in African American families have a dearth of experience with the harsh social reality of racism and oppression. Yet many African American parents still believe that the essential path to success in life is through higher education, work security, and social mobility (Billingsley, 1992; Boyd-Franklin, 1995). Many parents who are without a college education strongly desire a college education for their children, as these parents expect their children to surpass them. As a result of their efforts an overwhelming majority of African American college students are first-generation college students.

In the context of the extended family network, relatives along with parents or older siblings may make self-sacrifices to enable the younger members of the family to secure a good education. The extended family network may be involved in collective support of an individual family member to help him or her achieve a higher education, make a transition into work, or establish independent residence (Hines & Boyd-Franklin, 2005). This "reciprocal obligation" (McAdoo, 1978) process explains why some older children drop out of school. They enter the labor force as a means to support their younger siblings' education. Additionally, following the adage that "to whom much is given much is expected," many successful African American family members often feel that they have the responsibility to "give back" to needy family members and to support their education.

Flexibility in Family Roles. The African American family has been described as egalitarian and characterized by complementary and flexible family roles (Billingsley, 1992; Hill, 1972; Taylor, 2003). The widely accepted standard (of the dominant society) that the husband-father performs the instrumental (i.e., economic) functions while the wife-mother carries out the expressive (i.e., domestic and emotional) functions does not necessarily apply to a large number of African American families. According to Billingsley (1968) such a framework for examining the functioning of African American families is too simplistic, for it fails to take into consideration the historical and political perspectives of African Americans.

Many African American husband-fathers perform expressive functions while wives-mothers perform instrumental functions. In data gleaned from the National Survey of Black Americans (NSBA) on household composition and family structure Hatchett et al. (1991) conclude there is strong support among African American men for an egalitarian division of labor regardless of their educational or socioeconomic status. This finding is not true among college-educated African American women. This latter group was more likely than women with less education to support the flexibility and interchangeability of family roles and tasks. This gender difference in attitude toward the flexibility of family roles may be related to the fact that historically the African American female had greater access to the economic opportunity structure of society than the African American male.

The fluid interchanging of roles within the African American nuclear family is assumed to have emerged out of the economic imperatives of African American life. Yet this greater acceptance of role flexibility and power sharing in African American families may figure prominently in marital instability (Taylor, 2003). Gender role flexibility may present contradictory messages to young African American men in terms of encouraging them to embrace an androgynous gender role within the African American family, while being expected to perform according to the White male gender role paradigm in other nonfamily contexts. The African American woman on the other hand may be socialized into a message of "be independent because it is hard to find an African American man to care for you," while hearing the contradictory message of "find a man so he will care for you" (Franklin, 1986).

African American husbands in the early stages of marriage are found to have greater anxiety over their ability to function in the role of provider if they feel their wives have equal power in the family and if the wives feel there is not enough sharing of family tasks and responsibilities (Hatchett et al., 1991). The tension while possibly reflecting changing attitudes and definitions of family roles among young African Americans may more significantly reflect the African American male's anxiety over his economic viability and potential. It is important to note that because the wife-mother may assume instrumental functions, therapists should not assume that African American families are matriarchal. The fact of African American women assuming instrumental functions within the family may be more reflective of a socioeconomic structure that creates employment barriers for African American men.

Commitment to Religious Values and Church Participation. The African American church has historically served a nurturing function for African Americans. A committed religious orientation was a major aspect of the lives of Black people in Africa and during the era of slavery. The church played a vital role in the escape of African Americans from the oppression of slavery and continues to serve as an advocate for social and political action against racism and discrimination. Today, in times of crisis, the church and other African American faith communities such as Islam have been the supportive element in revitalizing hope for African Americans in the midst of the hopelessness and despair of racism and oppression. For some African Americans, church attendance and participation may not solely reflect a profound religious or spiritual orientation. Rather the church may serve primarily as a social institution for social and communal affiliation. In this sense the church provides a venue for the expression of the Africentric value of collectivity and communalism.

The church is a source of psychosocial support and can have an impact on every aspect of life (McAdoo & Crawford, 1990). In addition to providing African

American families with social services such as senior citizen activities, child care, educational groups, parenting groups, and housing development, the church also provides latent functions such as helping maintain family solidarity, conferring of social status, leadership development, release of emotional tensions, social or political activity, and recreation (Staples, 2004). Because the African American church has been ever present in the provision of human services, it has become an alternative social service delivery system for many African American families.

Humanistic Orientation. In the midst of their daily struggle for survival in a racist society, African American families have not lost sight of the value and the importance of concern for each other. Solomon (1976) has referred to this value dimension of the African American family as "more humanistic and [African Americans] have greater validity than the hollow values of middle-class American society" (p. 169). This humanistic attitude is connected to the Africentric value of viewing the spiritual or nonmaterial component of the human being as coequal with this "material" aspect. This is in contrast to the materialistic and capitalist-driven characteristics of White American values, which are predominately task oriented and motivated by economic achievement to the exclusion of other values. The Africentric humanistic orientation stresses person-to-person relationships and their cultivation. African American expression through music, dance, and literature is suggestive of this humanistic aspect of African American culture. The humanistic orientation of African American culture can have strong implications during various therapeutic phases. It is the working alliance or relationship that is most significant or preferred over the accomplishment of a specific task according to a specific time frame.

Endurance in a Hostile Environment. In view of the adversity African Americans face, they have developed a great capacity for coping with conflict, stress, ambiguity, and ambivalence. Further, they have developed a "healthy cultural paranoia" (Grier & Cobbs, 1968) that makes them hyper-vigilant against acts of racism and oppression. Religion and spirituality have further provided a refuge from racism while providing the spiritual power to support the political and economic battles against racism and oppression. Yet in spite of the capacity for coping with racism and oppression, many African Americans have had acute psychological and physiological reactions to racism (Utsey, Bolden, & Brown, 2001). Many of these reactions are the consequences of failed attempts to successfully manage bicultural or acculturative tensions and bicultural or acculturative stress.

These reactions while impacting an individual's psychological state and ability to cope with racism and oppression can reverberate through a family system and create disruptions in the family's ability to cope with internal and external family stressors. Yet in spite of these reactions the African American family has continued to survive. African American families' efforts at coping with racism-related conflict, stress, ambiguity, and ambivalence and the psychological and physiological toll such coping exacts may partly explain their underutilization of social services and high dropout rate in therapy. African American families may exhibit a cultural paranoia in light of their prior experiences with racism and oppression (Grier & Cobbs, 1968; Rasheed & Rasheed, 1999). This unwillingness to engage in a helping relationship may also reflect a reaction to the existing power differential between therapist and client. The therapy relationship becomes a reproduction of the power differential in society. This power differential, for many African Americans, can produce a sense of mistrust and distrust.

The African American cultural values of strong kinship bonds; education and work achievement orientation; flexibility in family roles; religiosity and church participation; humanistic orientation; and endurance in hostile, oppressive, and racist environments significantly influence African American family organization and structure. A discussion of how these values affect subunits and overall family interactions follows.

Family Help-Seeking Patterns and Behaviors

African American families often hesitate in seeking mental health services. In addition to their general mistrust toward mainstream institutions, African Americans rely heavily on extended family ties and church organizations during times of crisis. Such patterns of help seeking are present among all African American families regardless of socioeconomic class (McAdoo, 1977). Reliance on natural support systems produces fewer feelings of defeat, humiliation, and powerlessness. Martin and Martin (1978) label such practice the "mutual aid system." It operates on the twin premises that families should seek security and independence, and when family integrity is threatened, sharing resources and exchanging services across households become even more crucial.

Many African Americans still view therapy as "strange" and think of it as a process for "strange or crazy people" only. Their contact with family therapy is usually precipitated by crises and happens when other sources of help have been depleted. African Americans' underutilization of psychological help and family therapy is also related to their general mistrust of the therapist, especially the White therapist. African Americans' negative attitudes toward therapists may explain to some extent why they have been found to drop out of therapy earlier and more frequently than Whites (Sue & Sue, 2008).

While African Americans do prefer African American therapists over White therapists, they also prefer competent therapists over less competent African American therapists. Competent skills and techniques in work with African Americans must take into consideration, from an African American perspective, the complexities of life, particularly family and community life.

There are several factors that characterize the use of individual and family psychotherapy among American Americans:

- African American women are more likely than men to seek both informal and professional help.
- Persons with physical health problems are more likely than people with other types of problems to seek both professional and informal help.
- Respondents with emotional problems are less likely than those with other types of problems to seek both informal and professional help.
- People with physical problems are less likely than those with other types of problems to seek only informal help.
- Respondents with emotional problems are more likely than persons with other types of problems to seek no help at all.
- Gender, age, and problem types influence help-seeking behavior.

Dana (1993) and McRoy (2003) indicate that African Americans do become involved in the helping process but they initially may be guarded and reserved. They may later try to equalize the power differential between them and the therapist by challenging the therapist and questioning the background and experience of the therapist in understanding their situation as an African American. The next stage may involve partial identification with the practitioner, and they may begin to engage in the helping relationship. The work stage is then marked by a greater sense of comfort on the part of the African American client and by less defensiveness toward the therapist.

SUMMARY

As these groups represent a larger percentage of the population, there will be a corresponding increased demand for mental health services to ethnically diverse families (Aponte & Wohl, 2000; Cheung & Snowden, 1990). One of the significant factors for family therapists working with racially and ethnically diverse families different from their own is that it is necessary to understand the ethnically informed themes that construct the family's identity. Green (1999) states, "The discrepancy between the proportion of people of color in the general population and in the profession of family therapy means that racial minority families are usually treated by white majority family therapists and that the caseloads of white family therapists will increasingly be composed of families of color" (p. 94). The challenge for the family therapy field is the need to reformulate and adapt existing models of family therapy and to develop new ones that are attuned to the ethnic identity of these populations. A competent and multicultural perspective challenges what might be considered as universal traits but takes into consideration the possible biases of theories and does not confuse cultural ways of being as being dysfunctional. The philosophical orientations and techniques employed by some of the theoretical approaches may diametrically oppose the indigenous cultural values and family structures of ethnic minority families (Sue & Sue, 2008). A culturally competent family therapist must accept the legitimacy of their worldviews and culturally unique practices. Further, the family's orientation to the process of help seeking and the "fit" between traditional paradigms and those utilized by providers may be critical to successful clinical process and treatment outcomes (Green, 1999).

RECOMMENDED READINGS

Appleby, G. A., Colon, E., & Hamilton, J. (2007). *Diversity, oppression and social functioning.* Boston, MA: Pearson.

Arredondo, P., & Perez, P. (2003). Counseling paradigms and Latino/a Americans: Contemporary perspectives. In F. D. Harper & J. McFadden (Eds.), *Culture and counseling* (pp. 115–132). Boston, MA: Allyn & Bacon.

Boyd-Franklin, N. (2003). *Black families in therapy.* New York, NY: Guilford.

Flores, M. T. (2000). La familia Latina. In M. T. Flores & G. Carey (Eds.), *Family therapy with Hispanics: Toward appreciating diversity* (pp. 2–28). Boston, MA: Allyn & Bacon.

Ho, M. K., Rasheed, J. M., & Rasheed, M. N. (2004). *Family therapy with ethnic minorities.* Thousand Oaks, CA: Sage.

Ishii-Kuntz, M. (2000). Diversity with Asian American families. In D. Demo, K. R. Allen, & M. Fine (Eds.), *Handbook of family diversity* (pp. 274–293). New York, NY: Oxford University Press.

Ngo, D., Tran, T., Gibbons, J., & Oliver, J. (2001). Acculturation, pre-migration, traumatic experiences, and depression among Vietnamese Americans. In N. Choi (Ed.), *Psychological aspects of the Asian American experience: Diversity within diversity* (pp. 225–242). New York, NY: Haworth.

Phinney, J. S., Cantu, C. L., & Kurtz, D. A. (1997). Ethnic and American identity as predictors of self-esteem among African American, Latino, and White adolescents. *Journal of Youth and Adolescence, 9,* 34–49.

Utsey, S. O., Bolden, M. A., & Brown, A. L. (2001). Visions of revolution from the spirit of Franz Fanon: A psychology of liberation for counseling African American confronting societal racism and oppression. In J. G. Panteroto, J. M. Casus, L. A. Suzuki, & C. M. Alexander (Eds.), *Handbook of multicultural counseling* (pp. 311–336). Thousand Oaks, CA: Sage.

Utter, J. (2001). *American Indians.* Norman: University of Oklahoma Press.

Yellow Bird, M. J. (2001). Critical values and First Nations peoples. In R. Fong & S. Furuto (Eds.), *Culturally competent practice: Skills, intervention and evaluations* (pp. 61–74). Needham Heights, MA: Allyn & Bacon.

DISCUSSION QUESTIONS

1. The family as a system develops a range of strategies for managing a range of family system maintenance tasks, one of which is constructing a family identity (Anderson & Sabatelli, 2003). What function does a family's identity serve as a system maintenance task? In what ways might a family's ethnic identification impact its multisystem transactions?

2. What are the various dimensions of ethnicity?

3. Why is understanding the dimensions of ethnic identity important for a family therapist?

REFERENCES

Acosta, F. X., Yamamoto, J., & Evans, L. A. (Eds.). (1982). *Effective psychotherapy for low-income and minority patients.* New York, NY: Plenum.

Anderson, S. A., & Sabatelli, R. M. (2003). *Family interaction: A multigenerational developmental perspective* (3rd ed.). Boston, MA: Pearson Education.

Aponte, J. E., & Wohl, J. (2000). *Psychological intervention and cultural diversity.* Des Moines, IA: Allyn & Bacon.

Appleby, G. A., Colon, E., & Hamilton, J. (2007). *Diversity, oppression and social functioning.* Boston MA: Pearson.

Arredondo, P., & Perez, P. (2003). Counseling paradigms and Latino/a Americans: Contemporary perspectives. In F. D. Harper & J. McFadden (Eds.), *Culture and counseling* (pp. 115–132). Boston, MA: Allyn & Bacon.

Axinn, J., & Levin, H. (1997). *Social welfare: A history of American response to need.* New York, NY: Longman.

Berry, J. W., Trimble, J., & Olmeda, E. (1986). The assessment of acculturation. In W. J. Lonner & J. W. Berry (Eds.), *Field methods in cross-cultural research* (pp. 291–324). London, England: Sage.

Bhatia, S., & Ram, A. (2004). Culture, hybridity and the dialogical self: Cases for South Asian diaspora. *Mind, Culture and Activity, 11,* 224–240.

Billingsley, A. (1968). *Black families in White America.* Englewood Cliffs, NJ: Prentice-Hall.

Billingsley, A. (1976). *The evolution of the Black family.* New York, NY: National Urban League.

Billingsley, A. (1992). *Climbing Jacob's ladder: The enduring legacy of African American families.* New York, NY: Simon & Schuster.

Boyd-Franklin, N. (1995). Therapy with African American inner city families. In R. H. Mikesell, D. Lusterman, & S. H. McDaniel (Eds.), *Integrating family therapy: Handbook of family psychology and systems theory* (pp. 357–371). Washington, DC: American Psychological Association.

Boyd-Franklin, N. (2003). *Black families in therapy.* New York, NY: Guilford.

Brave Heart-Jordan, M. Y. H., & DeBruyn, L. (1995). *So she may walk in balance: Integrating the impact of historical trauma and historical unresolved grief among the Lakota.* Unpublished doctoral dissertation, Smith College School for Social Work, Northampton, MA.

Bureau of Indian Affairs. (1971). *Information office statistics.* Washington, DC: Author.

Carter, R. T. (2005). Uprooting inequity and disparities in counseling and psychology: An introduction. In R. Carter (Ed.), *Racial-cultural psychology and counseling* (pp. 115–132). Hoboken, NJ: Wiley.

Casas, S., & Keefe, S. (1980). *Family and mental health in Mexican American community.* Los Angeles, CA: Spanish Speaking Mental Health Research Center.

Chang, C. Y. (2003). Counseling Asian Americans. In N. A. Vacc, S. B. DeVancy, & J. Brendel (Eds.), *Counseling multicultural and diverse populations: Strategies for practitioners* (pp. 73–92). New York, NY: Brunner-Routledge.

Chestang, L. (1976). The Black family and Black culture: A study in coping. In M. Satomayer (Ed.), *Cross cultural perspectives in social work practice and education.* Houston, TX: The University of Houston Graduate School of Social Work.

Cheung, M., & Leung, P. (2008). *Multicultural practice & evaluation.* Denver, CO: Love.

Cheung, F. K., & Snowden, L. R. (1990). *Community mental health and ethnic minority population, 26,* 277–291.

Cohen, F. S. (1982). *Felix S. Cohen handbook of federal Indian law.* Charlottesville, VA: Michie.

Coles, R. A. (2006). *Race & family: A structural approach.* Thousand Oaks, CA: Sage.

Combs, D. (1978). *Crossing culture in therapy.* Monterey, CA: Brooks/Cole.

Cooper, R. L. (1995). *We stand together.* Chicago, IL: Moody.

Cornell, S., & Hartman, D. (2007). *Ethnicity and race.* Thousand Oaks, CA: Pine Forge Press.

Cornell, S. (2000). That's the story of our lives. In P. Spickard & W. J. Burroughs (Eds.), *Narrative and multiplicity in constructing ethnic identity* (pp. 41–51). Philadelphia, PA: Temple University Press.

Costa, R., & Henry, J. (1977). *Indian treaties: Two centuries of dishonor.* San Francisco, CA: Indian Heritage.

Cox, O. C. (1948). *Caste, class, and race.* Garden City, NY: Doubleday.

Dana, R. H. (1993). *Multicultural assessment perspective for professional psychology.* Boston, MA: Allyn & Bacon.

DeAnda, D. (1984). Bicultural socialization: Factors affecting the minority experience. *Social Work, 29,* 101–107.

Demo, D. H., Allen, K. R., & Fine, M. A. (Eds.). (2000). *Handbook of family diversity.* New York, NY: Oxford University Press.

Devore, W. (2001). Whence came these people? An exploration of the values and ethics of African American individuals, families and communities. In R. Fong & S. Furuto (Eds.), *Culturally competent practice: Skills, intervention and evaluations* (pp. 33–36). Needham Heights, MA: Allyn & Bacon.

Dreyfuss, B., & Lawrence, D. (1979). *Handbook for anti-racism.* Norman: University of Oklahoma Press.

Estrada, L. F. (2000). *Children: A demographic profile.* Unpublished manuscript, University of California, Los Angeles, School of Public Policy and Social Research.

Falicov, C. J. (1998). Latino life cycle. In B. Carter & M. McGoldrick (Eds.), *The expanded life cycle: Individual, family, and social perspectives* (pp. 141–152). Boston, MA: Allyn & Bacon.

Farris, C. (1973). A White House conference on the American Indian. *Social Work, 18,* 80–86.

Fitzpatrick, J. (1981). The Puerto Rican family. In C. Mindel & R. Habenstein (Eds.), *Ethnic families in America.* New York, NY: Elsevier.

Flores, M. T. (2000). La familia Latina. In M. T. Flores & G. Carey (Eds.), *Family therapy with Hispanics: Toward appreciating diversity* (pp. 2–28). Boston, MA: Allyn & Bacon.

Flores, M. T., & Carey, G. (2000). *Family therapy with Hispanics: Toward appreciating diversity.* Boston, MA: Allyn & Bacon.

Franklin, C. (1986). Black male-black female conflict: Individually caused and culturally nurtured. In R. Staples (Ed.), *The Black family: Essays and studies* (pp. 106–113). Belmont, CA: Wadsworth.

Garcia-Preto, N. (1996). Latino families: An overview. In M. McGoldrick, J. Giordano, & J. K. Pearce (Eds.), *Ethnicity and family therapy* (pp. 141–154). New York, NY: Guilford.

Geertz, C. (Ed). (1963). *Old societies and new states: The quest for modernity in Asia and Africa.* New York, NY: Free Press.

Glick, P. (1997). Demographic picture of African American families. In H. McAdoo (Ed.), *Black families* (pp. 118–139). Thousand Oaks, CA: Sage.

Goldenberg, H., & Goldenberg, I. (2002). *Counseling today's families.* Pacific Grove, CA: Brooks/Cole.

Gordon, W. E. (1969). Basic constructs for an integrative and generative conception of social work. In G. Hearn (Ed.), *The general systems approach: Contributions toward a holistic conception of social work* New York, NY: Council on Social Work Education.

Grace, C. A. (1992). Practical considerations for program professionals and evaluators working with African-American communities. In M. A. Orlandi (Ed.), *Cultural competence for evaluators: A guide for alcohol and other drug abuse prevention practitioners working with ethnic/racial communities* (pp. 55–74). Rockville, MD: U.S. Department of Health and Human Services, Office of Substance Abuse Prevention.

Green, J. W. (1999). *Cultural awareness in the human services.* Boston, MA: Allyn & Bacon.

Grier, W., & Cobbs, P. (1968). *Black rage.* New York, NY: Basic Books.

Hatchett, S., Cochran, D., & Jackson, J. (1991). Family life. In J. Jackson (Ed.), *Life in Black America* (pp. 46–83). Newbury Park, CA: Sage.

Helms, J. E. (1995). An update on Helm's White and people of color racial identity models. In J. G. Ponterotto, J. M. Casas, L. A. Suzuki, & C. M. Alexander (Eds.), *Handbook of multicultural counseling* (pp. 181–191). Thousand Oaks, CA: Sage.

Herskovits, M. J. (1958). *The myth of the Negro past.* Boston, MA: Beacon.

Hill, R. (1972). *The strength of Black families.* New York, NY: Emerson-Hall.

Hines, P. M., & Boyd-Franklin, N. (2005). African American families. In M. McGoldrick, J. Giordano, & N. Garcia-Preto (Eds.), *Ethnicity and family therapy* (pp. 87–101). New York, NY: Guilford.

Ho, M. K., Rasheed, J. M., & Rasheed, M. N. (2004). *Family therapy with ethnic minorities.* Thousand Oaks, CA: Sage.

Hong, G. K. (1993). Contextual factors in psychotherapy with Asian Americans. In J. L. Chin, J. L. Leim, & M. D. Hong (Eds.), *Transference and empathy in Asian American psychotherapy: Clinical values and treatment needs* (pp. 3–13). Westport, CT: Praeger.

Hong, G. K., & Friedman, M. M. (1998). The Asian American family. In M. M. Friedman (Ed.), *Family nursing: Theory and practice* (pp. 547–566). Norwalk, CT: Appleton & Lange.

Hong, G. K., & Ham, M. D. (2001). *Psychology and counseling with Asian American clients.* Thousand Oaks, CA: Sage.

Inman, A. G., & Tewari, N. (2003). The power of context: Counseling South Asians within a family context. In G. Roysircar, D. S. Sandhu, & V. E. Bibbins, Sr. (Eds.), *Multicultural competencies: A guidebook of practices* (pp. 41–107). Alexandria, VA: Association for Multicultural Counseling and Development.

Isaacs, H. R. (1975). *Idols of the tribe: Group identity and political change.* Cambridge, MA: Harvard University Press.

Ishii-Kuntz, M. (2000). Diversity with Asian American families. In D. Demo, K. R. Allen, & M. Fine (Eds.), *Handbook of family diversity* (pp. 274–293). New York, NY: Oxford University Press.

Jansson, B. S. (2001). *The reluctant welfare state.* Belmont, CA: Books/Cole.

Juby, H. L., & Concepcion, W. R. (2005). Ethnicity: The term and its meaning. In R. Carter (Ed.), *Handbook of racial-cultural psychology and counseling* (pp. 26–40). Hoboken, NJ: Wiley.

Karger, H. J., & Stoesz, D. (2002). *American welfare policy.* Boston, MA: Allyn & Bacon.

Kelly, L. (1990). *Federal Indian policy.* New York, NY: Chelsea House.

Kleinman, A., & Lin, T. (Eds.). (1981). *Normal and deviant behavior in Chinese culture.* Hingham, MA: Reidel.

Kluckhohn, F. (1951). Values and value orientation. In T. Parsons & E. Shiles (Eds.), *Toward a general theory of actions* (pp. 388–433). Cambridge, MA: Harvard University Press.

Kwan, K. L. K (2005). Racial salience: Conceptual dimensions and implications for racial and ethnic identity formation. In R. Carter (Ed.), *Racial-cultural psychology and counseling* (pp. 115–132). Hoboken, NJ: Wiley.

Laird, J. (1998). Theorizing culture: Narrative ideas and practice principles. In M. McGoldrick (Ed.), *Revisioning family therapy* (pp. 20–36). New York, NY: Guilford.

Lee, E. (1996). Chinese families. In M. McGoldrick, J. Giordano, & J. Pierce (Eds.), *Ethnicity and family therapy* (pp. 249–267). New York, NY: Guilford.

Lee, E. (Ed.). (1997). *Working with Asian Americans: A guide for clinicians.* New York, NY: Guilford.

Levine, E., & Padilla, A. (1980). *Crossing cultures in therapy: Pluralistic counseling for the Hispanic.* Monterey, CA: Brooks/Cole.

Lott, J. (1998). *Asian Americans: From racial category to multiple identities.* Walnut Creek, CA: Altamira.

Lum, D. (Ed.). (2003). *Culturally competent practice.* Pacific Grove, CA: Brooks/Cole.

Manns, W. (1988). Supportive roles of significant others in black families. In H. R. McAdoo (Ed.), *Black families* (pp. 198–213). Newbury Park, CA: Sage.

Martin, E., & Martin, J. (1978). *The Black extended family.* Chicago, IL: University of Chicago Press.

Mass, A. I. (1976). Asians as individuals: The Japanese community. *Social Casework, 57,* 160–174.

Massey, D. S., Zambrana, R. E., & Bell, S. A. (1995). Contemporary issues for Latino families: Future directions for research, policy, and practice. In R. E. Zambrana (Ed.), *Understanding Latino families* (pp. 190–204). Thousand Oaks, CA: Sage.

McAdoo, H. (1977). Family therapy in the Black community. *Journal of the American Orthopsychiatric Association, 47,* 74–79.

McAdoo, H. (1978). The impact of upward mobility on kin-help pattern and the reciprocal obligations in Black families. *Journal of Marriage and the Family, 4,* 761–776.

McAdoo, H., & Crawford, V. (1990). The Black church and family support programs. *Prevention and Human Services, 9,* 193–203.

McAuliffe, G. (2008). *Culturally alert counseling.* Thousand Oaks, CA: Sage.

McGoldrick, M., Giordano, J., & Pearce, J. K. (Eds.). (1996). *Ethnicity and family therapy.* New York, NY: Guilford.

McRoy, R. (2003). Cultural competence with African Americans. In D. Lum (Ed.), *Culturally competent practice* (pp. 217–237). Pacific Grove, CA: Brooks/Cole.

Montalvo, F. (1991). *Phenotyping, acculturation, and biracial assimilation of Mexican Americans: Empowering Hispanic families, a critical issue for the 90's.* Milwaukee, WI: Family Service America.

Morales, E. (1996). Gender roles among Latin gay and bisexual men: Implications for family and couple relationships. In J. Laird & R. Green (Eds.), *Lesbians and gays in couples and families: A handbook for therapists* (pp. 272–297). San Francisco, CA: Jossey-Bass.

Moran, R. F. (2001). *Interracial intimacy.* Chicago, IL: University of Chicago Press.

Native American Research Group. (1979). *American Indian socialization to urban life.* San Francisco, CA: Scientific Analysis.

Ngo, D., Tran, T., Gibbons, J., & Oliver, J. (2001). Acculturation, pre-migration, traumatic experiences, and depression among Vietnamese Americans. In N. Choi (Ed.), *Psychological aspects of the Asian American experience: Diversity within diversity* (pp. 225–242). New York, NY: Haworth.

Padilla, A., Carlos, M., & Keefe, S. (1976). Mental health service utilization by Mexican Americans. In M. R. Miranda (Ed.), *Psychotherapy with the Spanish-speaking: Issues in research and service delivery* (Monograph Series 3, pp. 9–20). Los Angeles: Mental Health Research Center.

Parham, T. A., & Brown, S. (2003). Therapeutic approaches with African American populations. In F. Harper & J. McFadden (Eds.), *Culture and counseling* (pp. 81–98). Boston, MA: Allyn & Bacon.

Phinney, J. S. (1990). Ethnic identity in adolescents and adults: Review of research. *Psychological Bulletin, 108*, 499–514.

Phinney, J. S. (1992). The multigroup Ethnic Identity Measure: A new scale for use with diverse groups. *Journal of Adolescence Research, 7*(2), 156–176.

Phinney, J. S. (1996). When we talk about American ethnic groups what do we mean? *American Psychologist, 51*, 918–947.

Phinney, J. S., Cantu, C. L., & Kurtz, D. A. (1997). Ethnic and American identity as predictors of self-esteem among African American, Latino, and White adolescents. *Journal of Youth and Adolescence, 9*, 34–49.

Phinney, J. S., & Devich-Navarro, M. (1997). Variations in bicultural identification among African American and Mexican adolescents. *Journal of Research on Adolescence, 7*(1), 3–32.

Polacca, M. (1995). *Cross-cultural variation in mental health treatment of aging Native Americans.* Unpublished manuscript, School of Social Work, Arizona State University.

Price, J. (1981). North American Indian families. In C. Mindel & R. Habenstein (Eds.), *Ethnic families in America.* New York, NY: Elsevier.

Rasheed, J. M., & Rasheed, M. N. (1999). *Social work practice with African American men: The invisible presence.* Thousand Oaks, CA: Sage.

Red Horse, J. G. (1980). Family structure and value orientation in American Indians. *Social Casework, 61*, 462–467.

Red Horse, J. G. (1982). Clinical strategies for American Indian families in crisis. *Urban and Social Change Review, 15*(2), 17–20.

Reeves, T., & Bennett, C. (2003). The Asian and Pacific Islander population in the United States: March 2002. In *Current population reports.* Washington, DC: U.S. Census Bureau. Retrieved from http://www.census.gov/prod/2003pubs/p20-540.pdf

Sandhu, D. S., & Malik, R. (2001). Ethnocultural background and substance abuse treatment of Asian Indian Americans. In S. L. A. Straussner (Ed.), *Ethnocultural factors in substance abuse treatment* (pp. 368–392). New York, NY: Guilford.

Santiago-Rivera, A. L., Arredondo, P. A., & Gallardo-Cooper, M. (2002). *Counseling Latino and la familia: A practical guide.* Thousand Oaks, CA: Sage.

Shimkin, D., Shimkin, E., & Frate, D. (1978). *The extended family in Black societies.* The Hague, The Netherlands: Mouton.

Shon, S., & Ja, D. (1982). Asian families. In M. McGoldrick, J. Giordano, J. K. Pearce, & J. Giordano (Eds.), *Ethnicity and family therapy* (pp. 208–228). New York, NY: Guilford.

Solomon, B. (1976). *Black empowerment.* New York, NY: Columbia University Press.

Stack, C. (1974). *All our kin.* New York: Harper & Row.

Staples, R. (2004). *Black families at the crossroad: Challenges and prospects.* San Francisco, CA: Jossey-Bass.

Stuart, P. (1977). United States Indian policy. *Social Service Review, 47*, 56–62.

Sudarkasa, N. (1997). African American families and family values. In H. P. McAdoo (Ed.), *Black families* (pp. 9–40). Thousand Oaks, CA: Sage.

Sue, D. W., & Sue, D. (2008). *Counseling the culturally different* (5th ed.). New York, NY: Wiley.

Sutton, C. T., & Broken Nose, M. A. (1996). American Indian families: An overview. In M. McGoldrick, J. Giordano, & J. K. Pearce (Eds.), *Ethnicity and family therapy* (pp. 31–44). New York, NY: Guilford.

Taylor, R. L. (2003). Diversity within African American families. In A. S. Skolnick & J. Skolnick (Eds.), *Family in transition* (pp. 365–388). New York, NY: Allyn & Bacon.

Thomas, N. D. (2000). Generalist practice with people of color. In J. Poulin (Ed.), *Collaborative social work* (pp. 265–325). Itasca, IL: Peacock.

U.S. Census Bureau. (1993). 1990 *census of the population: Persons of Hispanic origin in the United States.* Washington, DC: U.S. Government Printing Office.

U.S. Census Bureau. (2000). *Current population survey.* Washington, DC: U.S. Government Printing Office.

U.S. Census Bureau. (2004). *U.S. interim projections by age, sex, race, and Hispanic origin 2000–2050.* Retrieved from http://www.census.gov/population/www/projections/usinterimproj/

Utsey, S. O., Bolden, M. A., & Brown, A. L. (2001). Visions of revolution from the spirit of Franz Fanon: A psychology of liberation for counseling African Americans confronting societal racism and oppression. In J. G. Panteroto, J. M. Casus, L. A. Suzuki, & C. M. Alexander (Eds.), *Handbook of multicultural counseling* (pp. 311–336). Thousand Oaks, CA: Sage.

Utter, J. (2001). *American Indians.* Norman: University of Oklahoma Press.

Wallace, B. C., & Carter, R. T. (Eds.). (2003). *Understanding and dealing with violence: A multicultural approach.* Thousand Oaks, CA: Sage.

Weaver, H. N. (2001). Organizing and community assessment with First Nations people. In R. Fong & S. Furuto (Eds.), *Culturally competent practice: Skills, intervention and evaluations* (pp. 178–195). Needham Heights, MA: Allyn & Bacon.

Weaver, H. N. (2003). Cultural competence with First Nations peoples. In D. Lum (Ed.), *Culturally competent practice* (pp. 197–217). Pacific Grove, CA: Brooks/Cole.

Yellow Bird, M. J. (1999). What we want to be called: Indigenous people's perspective on racial and ethnic identity labels. *American Indian Quarterly, 23*(3), 1–21.

Yellow Bird, M. J. (2001). Critical values and First Nations peoples. In R. Fong & S. Furuto (Eds.), *Culturally competent practice: Skills, intervention and evaluations* (pp. 61–74). Needham Heights, MA: Allyn & Bacon.

Zuniga, M. E. (2003). Cultural competence with Latino Americans. In D. Lum (Ed.), *Culturally competent practice* (pp. 238–260). Pacific Grove, CA: Brooks/Cole.

Part II

MODELS OF FAMILY THERAPY

Chapter 4

COMMUNICATIONS/ HUMANISTIC FAMILY THERAPY

BACKGROUND AND LEADING FIGURE

Virginia Satir is considered to be one of the founders of the field of family therapy. Satir is also the leading figure in the development of a communications family therapy model. Hence, it is befitting that we begin Part II on family therapy models and this chapter with a focus on the works of Virginia Satir, specifically her contribution of the development of her communications/humanistic model of family therapy.

Satir's family therapy model is identified primarily with the communication approach and secondarily with the experiential. It is accurate to state that her work defies a rigid categorization. To this end we will be focusing our primary attention on an articulation of Satir's communications/humanistic model.

Virginia Satir was a social worker by training and began her clinical career in Chicago—initially seeing families in private practice in 1951 and then in 1955 joining the staff at the Illinois State Psychiatric Institute where she set up training programs for resident students of family therapy. In 1959 Satir joined the Palo Alto, California, group of the Mental Research Institute (MRI). There she served as director of training and remained until 1966, when she joined the Esalen Institute in California as director.

In her later years Satir conducted many workshops and lectures. Eventually, Satir's focus on the individual and the family system expanded to community and ultimately turned her attention to world peace (the congruence between people and the global context). She formed and/or was involved with several organizations. The two most notable were the Beautiful People in 1969 (which later registered as

Photo 4.1 Virginia Satir became an international ambassador whose mission was to empower people to transform conflicts, develop possibilities, and enable them to take responsibility for their lives, health, work, and relationships

Source: © William Meyer

the International Human Learning Resources Network) and the Avanta Network in 1978. These organizations advanced Satir's philosophy of humanism in which people who were committed to her vision gathered together for training experiences and workshops. Satir died in 1988 of pancreatic cancer.

Satir left an important legacy to the field of family therapy, one of a fluid integration of artistry and theory in family therapy practice. In fact Satir so (seemingly) effortlessly understood and attended to the pulse of people's affective emotional experience (both in their family dynamics and processes and in their emotional experience in therapy) that in her early years as a family therapy theorist she was viewed by some as being atheoretical and too intuitive to immolate.

In the following years Satir finally garnered well-deserved respect as a gifted clinician and brilliant theorist. Later in this chapter we will illustrate the theoretical preciseness of her approach in understanding and in addressing family dysfunction that will allay the notion of her approach being too idiosyncratic to learn. This is not to deny Satir's warm, nurturing, and charismatic personality and the influence of her own style in her approach. However, the authors assert that the values, beliefs, and personalities of other family therapy architects similarly impact the unique family therapy process. It is the task of the beginning therapist to find and develop his or her own therapeutic style while adopting various family therapy models of practice.

Satir's flagship works are embodied in the books *Conjoint Family Therapy* (1964, 1967, 1983) and *Peoplemaking* (1972; see also *The New Peoplemaking* [1988]). These books remain as classics in the field of family therapy. Virginia Satir's family therapy model has been known by several names throughout its development: conjoint family therapy, process therapy, and the Human Validation Process Model. Satir's Human Validation Process Model (Satir & Baldwin, 1983) is the result of an evolution of sorts from her earlier focus on communication processes to an emphasis on humanistic values.

PHILOSOPHICAL, CONCEPTUAL, AND THEORETICAL UNDERPINNINGS

Although primarily identified with the communications approach and then the experiential, it is nevertheless accurate to state that Satir's therapy defies categorization.

Her approach embodies major tenets of all the schools of family therapy. Her work with triads and subsystems dealing with boundary and hierarchical issues in the family touches on work central to the systems approach. Her attention to intergenerational and multigenerational issues in parental styles of communication and family rules and roles gives her work a family of origin perspective as well as embodies role theory. Her use of bodily proximity and touch, sculpting, and psychodrama incorporates aspects of an experiential approach.

To understand Satir one must begin by appreciating her respect for the individual. Satir viewed self-esteem and its enhancement as one of the most important family functions, if not the most important one. Satir believed in the inherent goodness and growth potential of the individual. She felt that individuals are not always in touch with their (growth) potential, in that all human beings carry within them resources they need to grow. Satir saw her approach as helping people gain a sense of their wholeness and potential and a commitment to individual awareness and expression, self-fulfillment, and individual growth. In essence Satir believed in self-help ability and self-discovery—given a nurturing environment.

From the above discussion we can see some of the (philosophical) seeds of Satir's approach. Her conceptual framework can be summarized in the following five major tenets.

1. Our family of origin, including past generations, has a significant influence on our attitudes and behaviors.

2. Families are systems and as such seek balance; when that balance is maintained through inappropriate roles, restrictive rules, and/or unrealistic expectations, the members' needs will not be met, and dysfunction will occur.

3. The result of dysfunctional family systems is low self-esteem and defensive behavior, as the basic drive of human beings is to enhance self-esteem and defend against threats to it.

4. Each person contains all the resources one needs for growth and healthy functioning.

5. The therapist and his or her beliefs are the most important tools at his or her command.

We will now revisit each of these concepts in turn.

Concept 1: The Family of Origin's Influence

In *Conjoint Family Therapy* (1983), Satir describes her concept regarding the influence of the family.

I see the parents as architects of their present family. They bring together what they have learned in their own families, blending it both consciously and unconsciously to form the context of their current family. (p. 145)

Satir saw the family as a hierarchy in which there are inequalities, power imbalances, disharmony, conformity, and the loss of a sense of uniqueness and personhood. Someone dominates and believes that there is a "right way" to which everyone must conform. When this is the case, there is loss of self, as all the members—including the dominant ones—must give up some of their true selves to accommodate to the system. Hence, Satir viewed the present family (of procreation) as being unduly influenced by past generations and as having significant influence on the present family's attitude, behaviors, family structure, hierarchy, power, and balance.

Concept 2: Families as Systems

Satir wrote extensively about unrealistic expectations within families (e.g., unrealistic marital expectations, unrealistic expectations of children—ignoring or not understanding development needs, etc.). Marital partners may expect the other partner to be a parent to them to meet unmet needs or be a vehicle through which undesirable attitudes or behaviors can be projected or acted out (Satir, 1964, 1967, 1983). Parents may expect a child to make them feel worthy by achieving or performing, to be grateful for getting what they did not get as children, or to parent them.

Parents may have unrealistic expectations of their children because they are not aware of children's developmental needs. For example, expecting a child to perform beyond his or her developmental capacity or to remain at a developmental stage longer than is appropriate is one of the many ways in which unrealistic expectations and restrictive rules may cause dysfunction in families.

Concept 3: Low Self-Esteem/Self-Worth

At the core of Satir's philosophy and central to her approach is the notion that families must respond to each other in ways that enhance each other's self-esteem. (Later in the chapter we will discuss dysfunctional communication stances that contribute to low self-esteem in family members.) Low self-esteem can cause a person to respond to family members in unhealthy, maladaptive ways. How we choose to cope often relates to our level of self-esteem. Satir, Banmen, Gerber, and Gomori (1991) add that with low self esteem, we tend to think some "cause" determines our reaction. We believe that events make us angry, when, in fact, our choices of reacting range from extremely dysfunctional behavior to optimally functional behavior and a very positive growth-oriented state of mind. Causes do not determine our reactions. We can take charge of meanings we make of ourselves, others, and our context. We can also take charge of our feelings about those feelings. This capacity enables us to make the major shift from being victims of circumstances, others, or ourselves, to being empowered and taking personal, emotional responsibility. (p. 28)

Low self-worth is different from feeling low. One may feel discouraged, sad, or despairing without having low self-worth. Feeling low, however, becomes low self-worth when a person experiences feelings of unworthiness but is unable or is afraid to acknowledge these feelings. In other words, low self-worth has to do with what the individual communicates to him- or herself about such feelings and the need to conceal rather than acknowledge them.

Satir et al. (1991) contrast the feelings of persons with low self-esteem with those of persons with high self-esteem in terms of the coping stances that may be taken. For example, the coping stance derived from one of Satir's dysfunctional communication roles is that of the *placator* (to be described in more detail later in the chapter). This coping stance is an example of how a person with low self-esteem communicates. That is, his or her communication renders the message of "I'll do anything to please you as long as you don't reject me (emotionally)." However, a person with high self-esteem copes with interpersonal conflict by taking the communication stance of "I do what fits as my (emotional) survival will not be compromised at the expense of *self*." One might expect that since the level of self-worth or self-esteem impacts communication of the individual it will also play a significant role in family communication and hence family behavior.

Finally, Satir theorized that persons with low self-esteem tend to marry each other and create an environment wherein their children also experience feelings of low self-esteem. She believed that low self-esteem is the foundation of individual and family mental health and that many of the problems brought in to family therapy are ultimately connected with low self-esteem. Hence raising the self-esteem of individual family members is one of the essential foci for intervention within this approach.

Concept 4: Resources of the Whole Person

Satir held a positive view of the nature of man and one's relationship to one's environment. Satir operated from the assumption that each person has all the resources she or he needs to function in a healthy manner. These resources include the capacity for learning, changing, awareness, compassion, rationality, wisdom, hope, self-acceptance and the acceptance of others, esteem, making good choices, being cooperative, admitting and correcting mistakes, asking for what one needs, and having courage to take action (Loeschen, 1998). Satir's philosophy regarding connecting with "inner resources" is reflected in her statement: "I am convinced that all people can grow. It is a matter of connecting them with their inner resources. This is the therapeutic task" (Satir, 1983, p. 264). This belief is very important in terms of helping people who are stuck and do not feel any hope. In essence Satir believed that change—especially internal change—is possible for everyone, regardless of age or other circumstances.

Concept 5: The Therapist and His or Her Beliefs

To help people change, Satir believed that therapists must serve as a model for family members. The therapist's ability to respond to the underlying messages of what is being communicated and the nonjudgmental qualities of the therapist's responses are essential; they provide new models of communication to the family (Satir & Baldwin, 1983). Furthermore, Satir believed that the humanness of the therapist is more important than therapist expertise.

THEORIES AND CONCEPTS

Early critics of Satir saw her model as lacking sufficient theory. What these critics did not acknowledge is that Satir's approach not only gracefully adds new and important concepts and theory but also successfully utilizes existing concepts and theories from other family therapy perspectives. Furthermore, Satir's approach intrinsically interweaves her philosophy, value assumptions, and conceptual framework with specific theory. Hence, as one acknowledges all aspects that constitute Satir's approach, one can appreciate the richness and fluidity of its theoretical base. This chapter will outline the major concepts and theories used by Satir in her communications/humanistic family therapy approach.

Dysfunctional Communication

Families with poor communication are families in which the communication is indirect, unclear, vague, dishonest, distorted, and incomplete. These same families are not as adept at nurturing each other, due to inability to communicate. Given that these families are low on the nurturing scale, low self-esteem is often a result. In essence, poor communication results in low self-esteem, which can trigger individual or familial maladaptive responses, especially in times of high stress. Satir theorized that families with poor communication skills are more vulnerable in times of stress and are not as adept in dealing with developmental or environmental changes.

Satir viewed functional families as having clear, complete, congruent communication in which there are clear roles and rules to govern family processes. These family rules are few in number, relevant, flexible, developmentally appropriate, and consistently applied. A functional family is compatible with Satir's notion of an "open system"—a clear interchange of information and resources within and without the system that is adaptive and dynamic. A functional family will be able to effectively operate within the context of larger (social and cultural) systems.

A dysfunctional family is a "closed system" in which there is a poor exchange of information and resources within and without the system that is rigid and maladaptive. The presence of dysfunction in one family member is symptomatic of dysfunction in other family members and/or the larger family system. Dysfunctional family systems are unable to cope effectively because their rules are fixed, rigid, arbitrary, and inconsistently applied. These rules may tend to maintain the status quo or a *dysfunctional homeostasis* and may serve to bolster the self-esteem of the parents over that of the children and/or one spouse's self-esteem over the other's. Ultimately a dysfunctional family system is unable to cope and can become chaotic. Satir viewed family problems as in effect an inability to cope. Family presenting problems are not the problem; she viewed coping as the problem, and coping is the outcome of self-worth, rules of family systems, and links to the outside world. In essence symptom relief is secondary to personal integrity.

At the heart of Satir's communications/humanistic model is the constellation of concepts described in her book *Peoplemaking* (1972). These four dysfunctional communication stances are different ways to hide the reality of one's real feelings from oneself and from others. Real feelings of low self-esteem and low self-worth are communicated to other family members as they take on various incongruent communication roles.

1. The *placator* hides his or her feelings of low self-worth and vulnerability by attempting to please others, not because he or she really feels it but because his or her emotional survival depends on it. The placator engages in apologetic, tentative, and self-effacing communication that is designed to please others. In attempting to please others the placator tries to avoid rejection. This person also expends enormous emotional energy in serving as a mediator between family members in

family disputes. The placator's primary interest in his or her mediation attempts is to assuage his or her own feelings of low self-esteem and self-worth by gaining the acceptance of other family members—resolving family disputes is only secondary to the placator's goal of pleasing other family members. To this end the placator may, in fact, serve to block important communication attempts between members and thus serve to inhibit open communication. Consider the example of a mother who constantly intercedes in ensuing conflict between her husband and teenage son. While on the surface it may appear that her intentions are to resolve family conflict between two warring parties, in fact the outcome is that father and son are not allowed to work through their own dyadic issues. The mother's constant interception or interference has effectively blocked communication between father and son and impeded potential problem solving between the two parties.

2. The *blamer* hides his or her feelings of low self-worth and vulnerability by attempting to control others and by disagreeing indiscriminately, thus giving him- or herself a sense of importance despite his or her inner feelings of loneliness and failure. The blamer engages in fault finding, name calling, and criticism. It is as if the blamer cannot feel good or secure about him- or herself without placing other family members in the "one down" position. The result is often establishing dishonest communication in which the metacommunication is "I am better than you, and my opinion is more important than yours. I am always right." A father rules a family (and his wife) with an iron fist, seldom yielding (or even considering) the opinions or feelings of other family members. A significant portion of his communication with other family members is criticism, and he is never wrong. Even the wife is subject to his dictatorial style of relating, and at times he even criticizes her in front of the children.

3. One who takes the *super-reasonable* stance hides his or her own feelings by attempting to anesthetize and insulate him- or herself from his or her true feelings. His or her response to family communication, especially family conflict, is often an intellectual or overly rational one—bypassing the (emotional) inner self. This posture conveys noninvolvement and control—but the reality of the super-reasonable's inner feelings is one of (emotional) vulnerability. The impact on family communication is one in which inner feelings are downplayed or avoided altogether, encouraging other family members to do the same, hence impeding open and honest communication between family members. In a family wherein there is not much positive communication and considerable open conflict, an adolescent male attempts to hide his feelings of low self-worth and contempt for his parents—even from his siblings. His responses to their attempts to create a stronger affiliation is to ignore their complaints (of which he shares the same sentiment) and to attempt to justify the dysfunctional communication and open family conflict.

4. One who takes the *irrelevant* stance handles family conflict and stress by pretending it is not there. Internally the irrelevant stance taker feels uncared for and alienated from the family. Hence he or she attempts to refocus family communication elsewhere from the present context or topic under discussion and away from inner feelings. The irrelevant stance taker will engage in tangential or even totally irrelevant verbalizations that serve to refocus attention away from the topic at hand. The impact on family communication can be one of incomplete communication, wherein important dialogue is not fully explored. Consider this example: A young teenage girl is a member of a very male-oriented family in which females are not very highly valued. She feels like an outsider in this family, not even aligning herself with her mother (who spends her time trying to downplay family conflict and assuage hurt feelings, never confronting or affirming the children's feelings and opinions). The teenager responds to family conflict and tension by making jokes and being sarcastic in the heat of family disputes.

Virginia Satir did not view the above communication stances as rigid and unchangeable (Satir & Baldwin, 1983). Rather any family member can take on one or all of the dysfunctional communication stances under different circumstances or contexts.

It is important to note here that Satir was not naïve in her understanding of environmental factors and the role that they can play in family problems. Rather, as a social worker, Satir was very well aware of the socio-politico-economic and cultural systems and how these systems can and do have a major bearing on family distress. Her position was more one of how one reacts to external stimuli and not one's ability to necessarily control one's environment.

Incongruent Communication Messages

Essential to Satir's notion that family dynamics and family processes should serve to enhance the individual self-esteem of family members is congruence with family communicative messages. Congruency not only is obtained by the matching of the verbal (overt) message with the nonverbal (covert) message; it also entails using words that accurately reflect and match one's feelings and experiences. A congruent person is in touch with his or her feelings, and a family with congruent communication is a family in which "anything can be talked about, anything can be commented on; there is nothing to hold back" (Satir, Stachowiak, & Taschman, 1975, p. 49). Incongruence, on the other hand, implies the opposite of congruence. Incongruence is a type of communication in which (overt) verbal and (covert) nonverbal messages do not match. Intended messages are distorted. Family members are often confused, conflicted, and even hurt by incongruent messages.

Satir (1967) further describes incongruent communication messages

as a discrepancy between the verbal and the nonverbal message. Incongruent messages can also be exhibited by subtle external discrepancies and changes in voice tone, posture, facial expression, skin coloration, respiration and gesture. Contradictory messages are sent via different levels (e.g., verbal versus nonverbal) wherein these messages contradict each other. The listener does not know which level message to respond to—verbal or nonverbal, especially if the context of the communication and nonverbal signals contradict each other. If any of these levels of messages seem misaligned, the family therapist should ask for clarification, thus helping the person to get in touch with feelings that they may not be aware of—furthering the therapeutic process. (p. 84)

Metacommunication

Intrinsic to understanding the above defined concepts of dysfunctional communication stances and incongruent communication messages is the concept of *metacommunication* (message about the message). Metacommunication conveys the sender's attitude, feelings, and intentions. There should be congruence between the communication and the metacommunication so that there are no conflicting messages. That is, metacommunication punctuates and explains the real and possibly hidden message to the receiver. Metacommunication serves to ensure that the sender's full and intended message is accurately received—regardless of whether the message is functional or dysfunctional, or congruent or incongruent. One "cannot NOT metacommunicate" (Satir, 1967, p. 82) in that a message can be totally nonverbal (i.e., relayed by facial expression, body posture, and/or gesture). Verbal messages are always accompanied by and punctuated with nonverbal messages. As described above, congruent messages are ones in which the verbal and nonverbal components relay the same message. The metacommunication of a message may be affirmed and punctuated by congruent nonverbal messages. The context of a message (family situation) may also serve to either affirm or disaffirm the verbal message. Consider the example of a mother who never says what she means; rather her mixed messages are often confusing. That is, her nonverbal message is not congruent with her verbal message; in addition her metacommunication is expressed by facial grimacing, body posture, and lack of eye contact. For example, a college-bound daughter notices that her mother has a sad look on her face with downcast eyes as the daughter excitedly gives the news of her admission to her chosen college. The metacommunication of this response is "I am too sad for myself (that I didn't get to go to college) to be happy for you." The metacommunication of her verbal response (see the next paragraph) is "Why don't you get a job instead of going to college so that you can help out with the family's finances?"

Double-Bind Message

Another key concept of Satir's is that of the *double-bind message*. In a double bind the message itself is paradoxical. The messages (statements or commands) are mutually exclusive, in that the receiver feels punished (or is punished) no matter which way he or she responds. To revisit our previous example of the daughter who is accepted to the college of her choice, when she asks one of her parents if she can go, the parent responds, "I didn't get to go to college; I had to work to support my brothers and sisters." In this exchange, not only does the child not receive an answer to her question, but she is made to feel guilty (and/or punished) no matter which way she responds. Double-bind messages (also referred to as double-level messages) can be considered a catch-22: damned if you do and damned if you don't. In another example one spouse feels that spontaneity is lacking in the physical relationship with his partner, so he looks to his partner and requests that she "be more spontaneous." The problem with this request is that no matter how the receiver responds, she is not being spontaneous if she complies with the request. However, if she does not attempt to be more spontaneous (at least immediately), then she as the receiver of the message may be criticized for complying with the request—that is, for being spontaneous by not doing what she was asked.

In double-bind exchanges Satir (1967) specifies that there must be certain conditions present for a child or spouse to experience the pressures associated with a double bind:

(a) First, the child (or spouse) must be exposed to double-level messages repeatedly and over a period of time.

(b) Second, these (double-level) messages must come from persons who have survival significance.

(c) Third, perhaps most important of all, he must be conditioned from an early age not to ask [clarifying questions such as] "Did you mean that or that?" but must accept conflicting messages in all their impossibility. He must be faced with the hopeless task of translating them into a single way of behaving. (p. 36)

In summary, families in which there are incongruent messages may contribute to family dysfunction—especially under times of stress. Conversely, families who communicate congruently are better able to cope with problems as they arise. If they need help around a specific issue they are able to obtain it without needing a major overhaul (Satir & Baldwin, 1983).

Family Rules and Roles

Central to understanding family pathology and dysfunction are Satir's concepts of *family rules and roles*. Satir saw family rules and roles as a transgenerational issue; that is, rules from one's family of origin are passed down through one or several generations to the family of procreation—either consciously or unconsciously. Family rules and family roles are an important communication factor in family pathology, in that family rules are expected behaviors that get woven in the "family fabric."

Family rules encompass all the behaviors that family members believe should or should not be performed in a given situation. Satir also described family rules as being overt, but more often it is the covert messages that are accepted among family members. Family rules and roles can influence an infinite number of family and individual behaviors, such as communication patterns and styles, sharing of information, family rituals and routines, career choices, emotional rules, family myths and secrets, how to respond to family problems and dysfunction, and behaviors for various systems and subsystems (conjugal, parent-child, and sibling).

Satir describes the concept of inappropriate and unhealthy roles in *Conjoint Family Therapy* (1983). Healthy, functional, and adaptive family rules and roles are those that are clear, flexible, and adaptive to the environment and changing developmental needs of the family and its individual members. On the other hand, dysfunctional family rules are rigidly enforced, autocratically developed, and everlasting. Satir believed that rules restricting freedom of expression are especially instrumental in decreasing self-esteem and functionality. Satir sometimes referred to family rules and family roles as "shoulds" and "survival beliefs" that operate as benchmarks by which one can gain approval from one's family.

Family Myths and Secrets

Family secrets are typically erected to protect some family members—usually the children—from the reality of their environment. Satir and Baldwin (1983) go on to state that

> family members do not comment about these areas openly and often justify their secrecy with statements such as "You are too young to understand" or "what you don't know won't hurt you." These secrets are often intended to keep a good parental image, so that children will not know that mother had an abortion before she married, or that father has a drinking problem. (p. 204)

Family myths are also typically erected to protect some family members from some reality of their existence. For example, the father is not an alcoholic, nor is he verbally abusive with the mother. The father is always right, even in the face of the opposite reality. The mother can protect the children from the father's wrath.

Satir theorized that some family myths and secrets are traceable back through three or more generations. This helps us recognize the circumstances that give rise to and perpetuate some enduring family myths and secrets.

GOALS OF THERAPY

Virginia Satir eventually came to refer to her therapeutic approach as the Human Validation Process Model (Satir & Baldwin, 1983).

> At this time, I see my therapeutic task lies in reshaping and transforming into useful purposes the energy bottled up in a person's or a family's demonstrated pathology. This is in contrast to my earlier belief that my task was limited to exterminating the pathology. I refer to my present approach as a health-oriented approach, although it is really more than that. I call it the Human Validation Process Model. (p. 207)

Satir's model is a natural extension of her philosophical beliefs about the process of change and her belief that all individuals have within them all the resources that they need to grow, change, and of course solve problems. Satir viewed family problems as being a symptom of an indication of impaired communication. Impaired communication blocks the freedom of family members to grow and denies them an opportunity to thrive in a family environment that promotes health, well-being, and good self-esteem. Helping individual family members feel good about themselves is the family's first priority and the major focus of the Satir approach to family therapy.

Satir's primary goal was to enhance the growth potential of the individual (self-actualization). Her goal in therapy was to integrate the needs of each individual family member for independent growth with the integrity of the family system (Satir & Baldwin, 1983). This process also entails the installation of hope, helping the family and its individual members enter therapy with (and/or develop) a positive feeling. Helping refocus the family off of the presenting problem or symptom (negative energy) and on to the strengths within the family (positive energy) is one of Satir's initial therapeutic moves. Hence, her model is a growth-oriented approach that focuses on the transformation of the individual (an additive process) rather than an attempt to eliminate or extinguish behaviors.

Another goal of therapy is to strengthen and enhance the coping skills of individual family members, teaching them new problem-solving skills. In a lecture Satir elaborated that "problems are not the problem; coping is the problem. Coping is the outcome of self-worth, rules of family systems, and links to the outside world" (Golden Triad Films, 1984). Satir sought to help families develop new ways of viewing their family problems, as well as new ways of handling the problems.

Central to Satir's approach is the therapeutic task of improving communication. Her approach also seeks to help family members become more aware of dysfunctional communication roles and patterns, especially as dysfunctional communication contributes to the low self-esteem and sense of low self-worth of individual family members. To this end Satir sought to model healthy (clear, honest, open) communication. She did not hesitate to explore how an individual family may be experiencing a negative reaction to a specific interchange. To this end, the Satir approach also helps family members explore new ways of relating to each other.

Helping families become aware that they have the ability to make choices and to feel competent and better able to cope with situations is another way that Satir approached the therapeutic task of developing better coping and problem-solving skills. In this growth-oriented approach, Satir sought to help the family develop health rather than to eradicate symptoms. To quote her (Satir & Baldwin, 1983),

> My hope is that every interview will result in a new window for each person to look through with the result of feeling better about himself or herself and gaining the ability to do things more creatively with other members of his or her family. This is really what I mean by saying that I am dealing with a coping process rather than a problem solving process. . . . I am not trying to solve a specific problem such as should they get a divorce or should they have a baby. I am working to help people find a different kind of coping process. I do not see myself as wise enough to know what is the best thing for a person to do. Should the wife ask her mother-in-law to leave? Should she *demand* that she leave? Should the wife leave her husband if the mother-in-law doesn't leave? These kinds of questions are not mine to answer. My task is to help each person with his or her own coping so that he or she can decide to do the things that work for him or her. (p. 186)

In summary, the goals of Satir's (1983) therapy approach are stated as follows:

Treatment is completed:

- When family members can complete transactions, check, and ask for feedback
- When they can interpret hostility
- When they can see how others see them
- When one member can tell another how he/she manifests him/herself
- When one member can tell another what he/she hopes, fears, and expects from him/her
- When they can disagree
- When they can make choices
- When they can learn through practice

- When they can free themselves from harmful effects of past models
- When they can give a clear message, that is, be congruent in their behavior, with a minimum of difference between feelings and communication, and with a minimum of hidden messages. (p. 176)

ROLE OF THE THERAPIST

Satir felt that a therapist must share in her underlying beliefs and philosophical assumptions about families, family processes, and human growth and potential in order to effectively immolate her therapy approach. In Satir's family approach, the role of the therapist is not one of a neutral party standing on the sidelines casually intervening from time to time. Satir's presence in family therapy sessions is legendary. Her warm, charismatic, and (seemingly) intuitive style was an important part of the therapeutic process. However, it is important not to make the mistake of misconstruing what usually is referred to as intuition; Satir's innate ability was actually the result of many years of learning and appreciating human and family processes.

In spite of Satir's obvious gift for nurturing and healthy communication, it is important that one does not regard her interactions with families as casual, off-the-cuff exchanges. Michele Baldwin (Satir & Baldwin, 1983) eloquently explores this issue:

When watching Virginia work, one is confronted with an overwhelming amount of information: the way she moves, her voice tone, the way she touches, who she turns to next, the sensory cues she uses to orient herself to different members of the family, etc. It is easy to lose the forest for the trees and difficult to see her very systematic approach and organization. The process usually flows smoothly, without any apparent transitions, and hides the fact that Virginia is highly structured about her process. (p. 209)

Satir believed that the therapist's role is to help people realize their own potential. To this end, she also believed that the therapist him- or herself is the therapist's main intervention tool. In essence, the therapist is the center point around which successful therapy revolves. To have this effect the therapist must obviously be in touch with his or her own feelings, attitudes, and thoughts. Satir encouraged therapists to become aware of their beliefs so that they could make conscious choices regarding their actions as therapists.

In summary, Satir's therapeutic roles are that of a *facilitator* (of healthy communication within the family), a *role model* to the family (for good communication), a *mediator* (to help families with communication impasses), and a *teacher* and *educator* (to help the family see new solutions for old problems and view new ways of coping with problems).

PROCESS OF THERAPY

Overview of Satir's Therapeutic Process

The Human Validation Process Model (Satir & Baldwin, 1983) can be divided into three stages. Like many other approaches, these stages overlap and are not always easy to distinguish from each other. However, they do have distinct characteristics, and different phases may vary in length.

The first stage consists of establishing contact and making an informal working contract (agreement). The second stage is characterized by chaos, during which the therapist intervenes in the family system and disturbs the status quo. The third stage consists of integration of new skills learned in the therapeutic process. An overview of the stages is illustrated in Figure 4.1.

Figure 4.1   Three Stages of Therapy

Stage 1: Making Contact

- Reach out to every family member and affirm each one's individual worth
- Establish trust with and gain acceptance of the family
- Ask questions and observe family process and dynamics
- Offer hypotheses based on therapist observations (in a nonjudgmental manner) and check out observations with the family
- Create an aura of hope and encourage positive energy within the family
- Create a readiness for change
- Develop an assessment plan early to gain the confidence of the family
- Make an informal working contract (agreement) with the family

Stage 2: Disturbing the Status Quo

- Develop awareness of communication roles and patterns through experience
- Create new understanding in family members through new or increased awareness
- Disturb the status quo and challenge the family's homeostasis
- Move the family to reveal protected or defended areas

Stage 3: Integration of New Skills

- Re-create an aura of hope and a willingness to do things in a different or new way
- Have family members express and apply these new understandings through experiences within the session
- Have family members use the new behaviors outside the therapy session
- Help the family understand what happened in the "chaos stage" for enhanced learning

We will now discuss each of these stages in turn.

Stage 1: Making Contact

As the assessment process began with the first introductions, Satir strove to make families feel comfortable and to decrease anxiety. It may appear that she was engaging in nonproductive chitchat; however, to the contrary, Satir was craftily going about her process of human validation—affirming the individual worth and identity of each family member (by taking care to learn the names of all members), while gaining the trust of the family, making important observations, and creating a comfortable therapeutic environment.

Satir did not have a standard procedure for assessment; however, she did utilize some of her interventions to further the assessment process (e.g., family life chronology, family map, and family sculpture—we will describe some of these interventions later in this chapter, in the section on tools and techniques). The first step in the assessment process is to gather information about the family by asking questions and by observing family dynamics and processes. Questions and observations should seek to uncover information about major triadic relationships in the system—that is, to uncover the roles, rules, and communication processes in the family; to examine relational messages (especially those messages communicated nonverbally); and to examine the content of communication with the family.

Satir started her interventions in the family system before she completed her assessment. As she asked clarifying questions of the family about what she was seeing, Satir was careful to be nonjudgmental—not only in how she phrased the questions but also in making more explicit what she was learning about the family. Therapists who take this nonjudgmental approach effectively model for the family as they teach family members to report their own observations in a nonjudgmental way as well. In this safe and informal atmosphere in which individuals do not feel intimidated, family members begin to realize that they can begin to behave in a more natural way—which certainly benefits the assessment process.

As Satir began to make more explicit what she had learned about the family (always being careful to check out her newly gained knowledge with the family), she took time to affirm the strengths of the family—creating feelings of hope and trust.

By focusing on emerging communication patterns and self-esteem issues, Satir gained an understanding of the survival skills or defenses used by family members to protect their self-esteem. In fact, in the Satir approach the content of the communication, as well as the presenting problem itself, takes a backseat and is seen only as a consequence of a dysfunction in the family system.

Satir sometimes asked every family member in turn what brought the family into therapy. This slow assessment process paid off as Satir began to better understand family conflict by virtue of how various family members viewed their problems. Satir brought to life these variant perceptions and attitudes with the skillful use of her experiential techniques. However, Satir did not probe beyond defenses in this initial stage; people expressed only those feelings that were already in the family's public domain. It is important to differentiate that although Satir did not (initially) make a particular family problem the focus of the therapy, she did help family members find a more creative way to handle the issue.

As Satir began to explore expectations for change among family members, she did not begin to negotiate a working contract with the family until she deemed it appropriate. She took her cues from the family in determining how much direction and structure was needed toward negotiating such a contract.

Stage 2: Disturbing the Status Quo

The second stage of Satir's therapy model is characterized by general confusion and disorder. Satir began this stage by upsetting the equilibrium and (dysfunctional) homeostasis of the family. Satir allowed (and even encouraged) family members to express angry feelings and underlying feelings of hurt and vulnerability via her revealing experiential exercises (to be outlined later in this chapter).

In this stage one or more family members are encouraged to move beyond protected and defended areas, in contrast to Stage 1 wherein the status quo is maintained. Satir theorized that family members are able to begin to associate these intense feelings of anger and hurt (exposed in this stage) with a sense of mastery and growth in these new areas as fundamental changes are made.

In observing Satir one would have viewed her ability to be tough with the family while retaining her trademark gentle and caring therapeutic style. As stated in Satir and Baldwin (1983),

> The toughness in Virginia is always present when needed, although sometimes hard to detect. . . . She manifests toughness in relation to the person's obstructive part only after she has established a therapeutic alliance with him. In other words, she has allied herself with the individual's growth goal and has teamed up with the parts of that person desiring growth. If this therapeutic alliance is not present, Virginia will not push because she would then be violating the person's defended territory and trust. Until the person is willing to take the risk, growth cannot occur. (p. 217)

Satir so skillfully obtained the cooperation of family members that resistance was not likely to be a major factor in the therapy process. Satir's charisma was oft misconstrued to be the reason when, in fact, families' lack of resistance was more likely attributed to her attention to system boundaries—as she probed for flexibility (willingness to change) within the system. That is, Satir was aware of the changes that families were willing to make (their positive energy and growth potential) but gave them the support that they needed to overcome impasses.

While supporting a particular family member, Satir was careful to attend to the needs of other family members, never losing contact with what was happening with the rest of the family—this allowed her to shift her attention to another family member when necessary.

In the chaos stage, Satir also kept the family focused on the present. She elaborates:

> People in this phase are in touch with their inner turmoil more than with the reality around them, and their fears are reinforced by memories of the past or uncertainties about the future. The task of the therapist is to bring them into the present, helping them use their senses and forcing them to pay attention to what is real rather than what is imagined. (Satir & Baldwin, 1983, p. 218)

Satir's artistry is apparent not only in her ability to apply her humanistic philosophy to her therapy but also in the balance she was able to achieve between toughness and empathy (Satir & Baldwin, 1983). The second stage is critical to her overall approach and must be handled skillfully, in that one must be careful not to rush Stage 2 in challenging the (dysfunctional) homeostasis of the family. However, one must also take care not to avoid the chaos stage, as this stage is essential for overall change to occur.

Stage 3: Integration of New Skills

The three stages of therapy are not as clearly defined in actual practice as described here. There is often overlap of these three stages, and family members are not always in the same stage at the same time. In addition, whereas Stage 2 is characterized by feelings of "stuckness" and hopelessness and an inability to move forward, the third stage is characterized by the feeling of hopefulness and a willingness to do things in a different way (Satir & Baldwin, 1983). It is important for the therapist to know which stage of therapy he or she is in; Satir also emphasized that as the stage of integrating new skills begins, it is essential for the family to understand what happened in the chaos stage.

Satir viewed herself as only the facilitator of the process; that is, she did not make decisions for people but rather helped families make decisions about their own lives. This distinction is important, as Satir believed that the distinction between making decisions for people and empowering them to do so was more likely to garner her the family's trust and hence its willingness to take risks in therapy.

Satir also saw herself as an educator. She guided family members to explore new communication patterns and healthier ways of coping within and outside of the session (via various homework assignments). Within the session Satir supplied cognitive information for the family to assimilate, as she made little distinction between teaching and therapy. Satir viewed some problems as resulting from a lack of (educational) information more than as emotional problems.

Satir paid special attention to internal messages and metacommunication, in an attempt to help family members figure out what happened in the chaos stage as new behaviors were learned. She helped family members make the connection between verbal and nonverbal messages, as well as pay special attention to the congruence between communication and metacommunication, so that there were no conflicting messages.

To summarize the essence of Satir's Human Validation Process Model (Satir & Baldwin, 1983),

> The art of therapy is in maintaining a balance between the overall direction of the therapy and new issues that emerge along the way. The process can be compared to threading a needle: if one ignores the small knot that has formed by the eye of the needle, the threading gets blocked. Similarly, the therapist who neglects to deal with a frown or other seemingly unimportant detail runs the risk of creating a blockage in the process. (Virginia checks her interventions every step of the way to make sure that no knot has formed. Virginia often compares her therapy to the process of weaving.) The process of weaving consists of picking up strands that often appear unrelated and connecting them until they eventually form a coherent design. Similarly, one thought, or strand, expressed by a family member is expanded by using other family members' input. Then another strand is picked up and developed. A strand that had been dropped is later picked up again. Eventually, the seemingly disconnected strands combine to form a design. (p. 222)

TOOLS AND TECHNIQUES

In the previous sections of this chapter we highlighted and emphasized Virginia Satir's sheer artistry. To this end, we also discussed how her uncanny talent and wisdom have led to an undervaluing of the theoretical richness of her approach. However, Satir has been credited as being the architect of some of the most defining and expansively applied techniques in the field of family therapy (e.g., family sculpting and use of the metaphor). Despite this fact, one would still not accurately think of her as a technician—even though her approach encompasses many rich and wonderful tools and techniques.

Michele Baldwin (Satir & Baldwin, 1983) captures Satir's essence and intent (in regard to the use of her tools and techniques) as she warns the reader not to go about using Satir's techniques in a cookbook or cookie-cutter fashion. Rather, she suggests that the *context* in which her techniques are used and what they try to accomplish with each technique are of more importance. In their book, *Satir Step by Step* (1983; unfortunately for the field, it is now out of print), Baldwin and Satir begin their chapter on tools and techniques with a story reported by John O. Stevens in the foreword of *Frogs Into Princes* (1979). The moral of this story is that a highly paid boilermaker's expertise does not lie in the elaborateness of his tools and techniques; rather it lies in the skill and wisdom of his knowing *how* to use these simple tools. It is in this spirit that the authors attempt to describe Satir's major tools and techniques, and the foreword of this story is recounted here:

> There is an old story of a boilermaker who was hired to fix a huge steamship boiler system that was not working well. After listening to the engineer's description of the problems and asking a few questions, he went to the boiler room. He looked at the maze of twisting pipes, listened to the thump of the boiler and the hiss of escaping steam for a few minutes, and felt some pipes with his hands. Then he hummed softly to himself, reached into his overalls and took out a small hammer, and tapped a bright red valve, once. Immediately the entire system began working perfectly, and the boilermaker went home. When the steamship owner received a bill for $1,000 he complained that the boiler-maker had only been in the engine room for fifteen minutes, and requested an itemized bill. This is what the boilermaker sent to him:

> For tapping with hammer $ .50

> **For knowing where to tap**   999.50
> $1,000.00

> (Satir & Baldwin, 1983, pp. 239–240)

Using Techniques in Context: Knowing Where to Tap

"For Virginia, knowing where and how to tap is more important than the tapping itself" (Satir & Baldwin, 1983, p. 240). Satir conceptualizes techniques as a means of engaging family members around a specific exercise for a particular purpose. Hence there is an amorphous quality to her techniques in that they should always be adapted to fit the particular needs and specific situation of the family (that is to say that her techniques are [and should be] constantly changing in some way or another in order to help families see themselves, their interactions, and their situations in new ways). "The implicit can be made explicit, the unfamiliar can be made familiar, the verbally inexpressible can be expressed, and new awareness can be developed" (Satir & Baldwin, 1983, p. 241).

Satir's approach is so replete with wonderful tools and techniques that it may be easy to become overwhelmed with so many choices. Suffice it to say that given the concept of *equifinality* (more than one means to an end), there are also many good choices that can be made. Hence it is of utmost importance for the therapist to have a solid assessment and a strong therapeutic alliance as a foundation upon which to make choices in the use of various tools and techniques in this approach.

Satir and Baldwin (1983) outline eight key questions that can help a therapist decide how to begin, questions that can facilitate the therapist's thinking process:

1. What is going on right now, with this person, family, or group?

2. What is present but not manifest?

3. What needs to be changed?

4. What would I like to accomplish?

5. What would be a good way to accomplish the immediate goal I see right at this moment?

6. What resources do I have at my disposal in terms of time, people, and context?

7. Are individual family members ready for the experience that is developing in my mind?

8. Will this experience achieve the expected outcome, or would another one fit better?

The authors contend that Satir's approach as a model of family therapy is one that the beginning therapist can and should attempt (with competent supervision, of course). The therapy process is carefully delineated and the role of the therapist clearly defined, and as you will read in the remainder of this chapter, the techniques are simple and straightforward.

The Human Validation Process Model includes 12 basic techniques, developed by Virginia Satir. We will now briefly describe each of these techniques in turn.[1]

Family Sculpture[2]

Family sculpture portrays the nature of the family's relationship system in space. It is the physical arrangement of family members as determined by an individual family member's perception of the family. Family members are asked to sculpt or design their relationships with each other using bodily posture, facial and other gestures, and components of distance and closeness to each other—aimed at portraying family dynamics and processes (i.e., communication roles, relationship patterns, and family rules and roles. The therapist may choose to select several family members to successively do a sculpture, depending on the assessment issue or therapeutic task at hand).

The person doing the sculpting acts as the artist or director of the family sculpture. Verbal instructions may be given to family members to strike a particular pose or position. A family member may also "finish" his sculpture by positioning family members himself.

In addition to using sculpting to portray family relationships and dynamics, the sculptor may also rearrange the sculpture of his family to show how he would like for the family relational system to be. In addition, other members of the family may be asked to rearrange the sculpture to match their own inner (emotional) picture of family relationships and/or portrayal of how to remedy a particular family problem. At times (when there was an adequate therapeutic alliance), Satir would also sculpt a family to illustrate how she viewed the family.

Family Metaphor

A metaphor is a figure of speech in which a word or phrase denotes a likeness or an analogy between an object and an idea, which can also be used in place of one another. In Satir's approach a metaphor is used to help people see the similarities of their interpersonal relationships to other events, objects, or situations. Metaphors help people gain increased awareness (or a new awareness) especially in highly threatening situations. "The use of the metaphors can develop new awarenesses by connecting or linking two events, ideas, characteristics, or meanings and transforming experiences from one mode to another" (Satir & Baldwin, 1983, p. 244).

In 1987 Peggy Papp conducted a live demonstration with a young married couple wherein there was intense ongoing open conflict and hostility between them. Papp made several valiant attempts to get the wife to understand how her husband feels when she berates and criticizes him (especially in public). Nothing worked! (The wife's retort was that because her statements about her husband are true, he should have "thicker skin" and use her observations as an opportunity to change for the better.) Papp then gave instructions to the husband to *show* the wife how he feels when he perceives that he is being berated by his wife in public. The husband recounted the most recent episode from a cocktail party and then asked his spouse to take off one of her shoes. She complied, and he then proceeded to lie down on the floor next to her. He then instructed her to place her foot on his neck. At that point he began to writhe violently on the floor mimicking a snake with the wife's foot on his throat. The wife broke down and started to cry vehemently and profusely apologized to her husband; she did not fully realize the extent of the (negative) emotional impact that her "observations" had on him.

Satir (1983) contends that because metaphors allow for the creation of imagery, they reinforce learning. We can see from the above case vignette how the use of family metaphor when applied to a highly toxic interpersonal situation can be key in resolving a long-standing source of hostility and conflict.

Family Drama

Much like the use of the metaphor, family drama allows for the metaphorical expression of interpersonal relationships that may be otherwise difficult (or too threatening) to verbalize. In family drama the entire family is asked to act out a scene from its family life. Also like the family sculpture, family drama allows for family members to reenact troubling family scenarios, perhaps in a less threatening environment. Pantomime and sculpting are used in the family drama, which likely helps diffuse highly volatile situations. The goal of family drama is to assist family members with achieving new insights and possibly develop new coping skills to use in dysfunctional situations.

Reframing/Relabeling

Reframing (also referred to as relabeling by structuralists and strategic family therapists) is an attempt to get the family to view a family problem in a new light. The problem or dysfunction is redefined so that the problem behavior may be handled more constructively. The purpose of a reframe is to create a change in the perceptions of family members so that new solutions to old problems may occur. "The therapist decreases threat of blame by accentuating the idea of puzzlement and the idea of good intentions" (Satir, 1983, p. 142).

Humor

Humor is used in the Satir approach to make contact with family members. Humor adds a light touch in intense moments in therapy. The Satir approach also uses humor to clarify or exaggerate a dynamic, as well as to encourage movement away from defensive reactions. "Laughter is a powerful therapeutic tool which can transform the way in which a family looks at itself" (Satir & Baldwin, 1983, p. 247). Satir felt that laughter can be a useful therapeutic tool that has the power to change how a family views itself.

Touch

One of the most misunderstood and (needlessly) controversial of Satir's techniques is that of touch. In our graduate classes on family therapy (and in our agency training, as well) hardly a semester will go by when we won't have a family therapy student to remark how uncomfortable he or she would be to physically touch a client. These students also wonder as to the client's reactions to the trademark "Satir touch." Our response to them is that the technique of touch is not a requirement for conducting Satir's communications/humanistic approach. In fact, therapists and clients are better off if the technique of touch is avoided when discomfort is present. In all likelihood if the family therapist is uncomfortable, then the client will likely pick up on that anxiety and become uncomfortable as well.

It is important to point out that Satir's touch is not an automatic, mechanistic "technique" that she used indiscriminately (Satir & Baldwin, 1983). Although Satir typically would shake the hands of each family member in the introductions, she was very cognizant of and sensitive to how powerful physical contact could be and took her cues from the client—and only used touch after she had established a rapport with individual members.

Photo 4.2   It is important for therapists to model nurturing behavior that affirms the importance and value of the individual

Source: ©iStockphoto.com/Chris Schmidt

Satir elaborates on her philosophy of touch, which informs the use of this technique:

> My hands are my most valuable treatment asset. Also my body and my skin, in sensing what is going on; and my eyes seeing; and the connections that all of these make. Hands are so important! This is one of the reasons I try to help people educate their hands. Something else I do in affectional relationships with people is to help them to educate their bodies and also to be aware of space and boundaries. I am quite convinced that that's what this business of making connections really means. What I have just said helps me make a definition of intimacy. It is simply the freedom to respect the spaces between people—to go in when there is an invitation, and not to invade when there isn't one. That is real intimacy. (Satir & Baldwin, 1983, pp. 247–248)

Communication Stances

The communication stances are often integrated and combined with other techniques (i.e., family sculpting). Communication stances are re-creations of the four dysfunctional communication stances—placator, blamer, super-reasonable, and irrelevant—as outlined and described earlier in this chapter. Persons are asked to take on (a caricature of) each posture to represent these communication stances. "By adopting these positions in sequence, participants become aware of their preferred interactional pattern, its meaning for themselves, and its meaning in relation to others" (Satir & Baldwin, 1983, p. 249). Family members may also benefit by better understanding the emotional impact of these dysfunctional and incongruent communication positions on another family member.

Family Stress Ballet

The family stress ballet is an extension of the communication stances, where participants are asked to shift (incongruent) positions in rapid succession, as they might in real life (Satir & Baldwin, 1983). This exercise adds a fluid (more three-dimensional) aspect to the communication stances, which are more static. The purpose here is to help family members experience the negative emotional impact of multiple and successive incongruent communications on the family system.

Simulated Family

The simulated family (which can be a teaching tool in workshops as well) is a form of reverse role play, if you will, in that family members are asked to take on the role of another family member (or rather their perception of that family member's interactions with others). This is done to "simulate" a dysfunctional interaction and to help family members experience for themselves how others experience them as a result of their interactions.

Ropes as a Therapeutic Tool

Ropes as a therapeutic tool can be seen as a metaphor for family relationships, to demonstrate how one part of the family system affects the rest of the family.

Each family member receives a short rope, the "self" rope, to attach around his or her waist. In addition, each receives as many ropes as there are other family members. He ties these ropes, which represent his relationships to every other family member, around his own waistline rope. Then, each family member hands the appropriate relations rope to the family member to whom it belongs.

Each member is thus encumbered by all the ropes representing his relationship to other family members as well as by all the ropes representing their relationships to him. (Satir & Baldwin, 1983, p. 251)

The ropes concept is likened to the systems concept of *reverberation* (throughout the system). Reverberation refers to the general systems notion that one part of the system is impacted by all. (A stone thrown in a pond will have a ripple effect, depending on the size of the stone, that could reach the shoreline. The closer one is to the point at which the stone hits the water, the greater the ripples will be.) Hence, we emphasize three points: first the interconnectedness of all family members; second the fact that one cannot be attentive to *every* family member at the same time—thus one must be judicious in how one attends to family relationships; and third how tension and stress can be transferred to other close family members. Finally ropes can be a useful therapeutic tool for large families (extended, augmented, step, and blended), in that one has many relationships to juggle and special attention needs to be paid to maintaining these important relationships.

Anatomy of a Relationship

Anatomy of a relationship is an extension of the family sculpting technique. Family members are asked first to sculpt the way they see themselves in the relationship and then to sculpt the way they would like the relationship to be (Satir & Baldwin, 1983). This too can be very diagnostic for the parties involved, as well as for the family therapist. Members can become more aware of their hidden agendas, unconscious desires, and unspoken expectations.

Family Reconstruction[3]

Satir saw family reconstruction as being the most representative of her theories on how people evolve and change (Satir & Baldwin, 1983). This technique aims to guide family members to unlock dysfunctional patterns stemming from their families of origin. This technique is a rich blend of general systems theory, Gestalt therapy, group dynamics and group processes, role theory, communications theory, and psychodrama and psychoanalytic theory. The goal of this technique is to move beyond old notions of family rules and roles that the family of procreation has outgrown by reenacting multigenerational family drama from the family of origin from past generations.

There are three general goals: The first is to reveal the source of old learning, the second is to develop an awareness of the personhood of one's parents (separating fact from fantasy and expectations and desires from reality), and the third is to challenge distortions of how one views one's parents and to use "adult eyes" so that the gaps that exist between adult child and parent can be filled in.

CASE ILLUSTRATION

IP (identified patient).	Mr. and Mrs. Richardson were referred to therapy for help with their 15-year-old son, Charles, Jr. (The family calls him Chuck and the father Charles. The family also includes 12-year-old Felicia, an honor student and an excellent athlete—both children run track.) The school's social worker has received numerous complaints about Chuck's outrageous behavior in school (e.g., getting the school's track team—of which Chuck is a member—disqualified from a meet due to his unsportsmanlike behavior; eating sandwiches in the classroom). It appears that this behavior is a pattern; Chuck has been kicked out of two other (private) high schools, and his parents now reluctantly enroll him in the local public suburban high school. (In fact Chuck was also expelled from his initial elementary school—he transferred to a private elementary school from which he graduated with honors, but he also graduated while on probation for similar acting-out behaviors.)
Possible **self-esteem issues**: That the family lives in a fairly affluent neighborhood and expresses extreme reluctance (almost a defeatist resignation) to send its son to the local high school—which enjoys a wonderful reputation for being college preparatory—is quite puzzling.	
Touch.	I shook everyone's hand and asked their names again. In the initial session it was very apparent who was in charge. The mother took the lead on every question posed to the family, as well as interrupted the father and son. Mr. Richardson seemed to be more resigned to Mrs. Richardson running things, more so than any agreement that this is best for the family.
Poor communication: People are not allowed to speak for themselves.	
Family rule: Mother gets to speak other people's minds.	I stated to the family that it was important for me to understand how everyone viewed the problem of Chuck's trouble with school officials, and it took a lot of effort for me to get the mother to give other family members a chance to speak. In turn they began to give their story (I also asked Felicia for her view—she was there in the waiting room, as they had just picked her up from school, so I asked her to come in as well.).
Human validation.	
	This part of the session was very revealing. Mrs. Richardson, who volunteered first, stated that she felt the father was at fault in that Mr. Richardson had been downsized from his corporate position and had showed "very little initiative" in finding new employment. Mrs. Richardson further stated that Mr. Richardson spends most of the day sleeping and doesn't pick up the slack in helping with household chores. Mrs. Richardson believes that sons take after their fathers and "like father, like son."
Blaming stance.	
Family myth.	

Low self-worth.

Dysfunctional communication pattern: boundary intrusion of conjugal subsystem.

Irrelevant stance.

Family myth.

Conflict around **gender roles**.

Double-bind communication (Mrs. Richardson: "I want you to work, but not that job.").

Mediator stance (especially dysfunctional when a child is placed in the role of mediating parental disputes).

Multigenerational message.

Family theme and **family myth**.

Mr. Richardson had (what I thought was) a weak response to his being attacked and maligned by Mrs. Richardson—especially in that she made these statements in front of the children, without any apparent regret or hesitation.

Upon asking Mr. Richardson his thoughts about his son's problems at school, Mr. Richardson implicitly seemed to agree with his wife's hypothesis, in that he was apologetic for his employment status and began to give a very long and technical explanation of the world of high finance and how difficult it is to start over again. (Although Mr. Richardson has not worked in several months, he received a handsome severance package that the family lives on. Mrs. Richardson is also employed in the corporate sector but now feels that she is supporting the family. Apparently Mrs. Richardson does not make nearly as much as Mr. Richardson did when he was employed; in fact it is apparent that Mrs. Richardson resents working at all and feels "put upon" having to work. In a later session it came up that Mrs. Richardson has very extravagant taste, which Mr. Richardson resents [he seems to be the more thrifty type].)

Mr. Richardson did point out that he has attempted to find work, but Mrs. Richardson was critical of the starting salaries—so much so that he did not pursue these employment leads. Mrs. Richardson stated that the jobs he was considering taking were "barely above minimum wage; and that apparently you aren't looking hard enough." Felicia interrupted her parents and asked them to stop arguing all the time, in that Chuck was to blame for his own behavior.

It is important to mention here that at the mother's insistence, the family follows a strict vegetarian diet. Her own mother died of cancer at the age of 45, and Mrs. Richardson is now convinced that she can avoid the same fate if she makes changes in her diet and lifestyle. However, the daughter and mother are the only ones that strictly follow this regimen, as both father and son eat meat when they are away from home—to the mother's strong disapproval. (She refuses to cook meat or fish or allow it to enter the home.)

It became apparent that the daughter had adopted the role of the "good child"—obedient, star pupil, and athlete. Even though the mother is very strict (perhaps inappropriately so—for example, the daughter's curfew on the weekend is 8:00 p.m., and she is not allowed to go to games held at school if they are at night—even on the weekends), Felicia never complains about her mother's strict rules.

(Continued)

(Continued)

Mediator stance. **Irrelevant role**. There is obviously **poor communication** in this family, characterized by **incomplete, distorted, vague, and dishonest communication**. **Negative (energy) communication** to the son further undermines his low self-esteem. **Positive (energy) communication** to the daughter, but only on the condition of strict obedience and loyalty to the mother, also puts the daughter in the **placator role**. This also creates feelings of low self-worth in the daughter, whose "worth" is based on her mother's acceptance. Career choices influenced by **family of origin**. **Family rule** (Mrs. Richardson: "I get to decide with whom we stay in contact."). Likely source for Mrs. Richardson's **sense of low self-worth** and reasoning for her affluent taste and need for status (e.g., private schools for the children).	Chuck, on the other hand, had adopted the role of the "bad child." His grades fluctuate tremendously; although he demonstrates apparently well-above-average intelligence and his standardized test scores are always in the 90th percentile, he gets Cs and some Ds in his classes—regardless of whether he is placed in the regular or honors tract at school. Chuck is somewhat of a class clown and takes this role in family dynamics as well. When questioned in the initial session about his behavior, he mostly digresses to how he is misunderstood and that the rules "are stupid." No one complains about anything in this family for fear that they will be ridiculed even further by the mother. I received a call from the mother to reschedule an appointment, and she was interrupted twice by the children—both apparently wanting to know what was for dinner and such things. I asked the mother which child was which as I felt that I could tell from her response to them, her tone of voice, and her manner which child she was talking to at which time. In subsequent sessions I learned a great deal about both parents' background. The father came from a working-class background and the mother from a middle-class background (her mother was a teacher). Mrs. Richardson in fact had also become a teacher but soon opted for the corporate world to increase her income. The dynamics between these two families are even more of a contrast. Mr. Richardson's family of five (he has three brothers—all of whom live in the general area) seems to be close knit with strong ties among members. Although Mr. Richardson's family does not see or socialize with the family of origin due to the wife's disapproval of them (she considers them too blue collar and "country") for her taste, Mr. Richardson stays in close phone contact with occasional visits. Mrs. Richardson's family, on the other hand, appears to be not as functional as her husband's (her mother is deceased, there is no mention of the father, and she is not in close contact with either of her siblings). Apparently there was domestic violence in the home, wherein the mother was physically abused. Although Mrs. Richardson did not say, I gather that she was also the occasional target of the abuse.

Also **family of origin** is the likely source of **communication roles and patterns** as set by Mrs. Richardson (i.e., her obvious need to be in charge and take control of everything so she won't be a victim again).

Stage 1 interventions: reaching out to every family member—affirming their individual worth.

Establishing trust with the family/**gaining acceptance** of the family—especially in the case of the most powerful member of the family, Mrs. Richardson.

Sculpting; family metaphor; family drama, and communication stances.

Also in **Stage 1** I was very careful about not **offering hypotheses in a nonjudgmental manner** so as not to alienate the most powerful member of this family (I wanted the family to return).

Create readiness for change.

After two sessions in which I asked a lot of questions and observed family processes and dynamics, we began to **work out a contract**.

Create an aura of hope—encourage positive energy within the family.

Develop awareness of dysfunctional communication patterns through experience and **disturb the status quo**.

In **Stage 2** I purposefully allowed the family's communication **to move into unprotected areas**.

Challenge the family's homeostasis.

In terms of the interventions I made sure that all members got to speak and were heard by all.

Also in initial sessions, I did not move too quickly and wanted to be sure not to reprimand Mrs. Richardson's controlling style.

Early on I began to ask family members to engage in various experiential exercises to better communicate how each felt (especially in times of heated discussions).

It was through these exercises that I was able to really get Mrs. Richardson to "hear" what family members were essentially unable to tell her verbally. These experiential exercises also allowed family members to experiment with other more congruent and less dysfunctional styles of communication.

We agreed on eight family sessions and two couple sessions. Our goal was for all family members to put their heads together and help Chuck figure out how to better navigate his way around school.

I pointed out the strengths in this family; it had an adequate source of income, and everyone loved one another—although some members had more problems showing it than others.

I purposefully increased the amount of discussion after various experiential exercises. Mr. Richardson began to express some of his concerns about Chuck's relationship with his mother—she is extremely critical of him. Both parents began to "correct" Felicia when she began to referee their disagreements. Even Chuck began to express some of the pain and hurt he feels under the constant barrage of criticism from his mother.

In this stage of family therapy I began to comment on how the family communicates differently than it did when it first came to therapy. I was careful again not to be judgmental but to allow the family members to cast their prior communications as negative. I merely pointed out for them how these patterns of communication did not seem to work for them.

(Continued)

(Continued)

In Stage 3, I re-created an aura of hope and a willingness to do things in a different way.	Mr. Richardson, toward the end of therapy, was much better at expressing himself and seemed to become more engaged with the children—especially his son.
Have family members express and apply these new understandings through experiences in the session. Use **simulated family** and **anatomy of a relationship**.	Seeing this, Mrs. Richardson became much more pleased with Mr. Richardson and was much less critical of him, in general. Chuck seemed to respond well to the closeness that he was beginning to experience with his father, as well as responded well to much less criticism from his mother—he, in turn, seemed much more positive toward his mother. His behaviors at school were beginning to become minor infractions versus those behaviors that lead to expulsion.
Use new behaviors outside the therapy session.	

SUMMARY

Virginia Satir left the field of family therapy an important legacy. Her family therapy model of the human validation process stands alone in its humanistic orientation emphasis. Satir became well known around the world for her demonstrations and her approach to families that combined her interest in clarifying communication discrepancies between family members with her humanistic orientation toward enhancing the self-esteem and feelings of self-worth in the entire family. Satir's respect for the individual, her belief in the inherent goodness of people and their potential for growth, and her commitment to individual awareness and expression are unparalleled.

Critics of Satir's approach are skeptical that her intuitive artistic style may be difficult for others to emulate—as her therapeutic techniques are so much of a reflection of her values and philosophy. Unfortunately, her untimely death in 1988 has left a void in the field of communications family therapy. It is also unfortunate that her apparent popularity in the field has waned.

It is the intention of these authors to revitalize that interest (with the writing of this chapter exclusively devoted to the works of Virginia Satir) and to help others see that Satir's approach has a clear conceptual framework, clearly defined stages with many useful skills and techniques. Hence, the Satir approach not only is teachable and can be learned but also is potentially powerful in its ability to attend to basic human processes—those of human communication and attention to the self-worth and self-esteem of individuals.

NOTES

1. The reader is directed to the original works of Virginia Satir for a comprehensive description of each of these techniques: *Conjoint Family Therapy* (Satir, 1964, 1967, 1983), *Peoplemaking* (Satir, 1972), and *Satir Step by Step* (Satir & Baldwin, 1983).

2. Virginia Satir developed the sculpturing technique in 1965. It has been greatly expanded since that time.

3. For a more comprehensive presentation of family reconstruction see *Satir Step by Step* (Satir & Baldwin, 1983).

RECOMMENDED READINGS

Loeschen, S. (1998). *Systematic training in the skills of Virginia Satir.* Pacific Grove, CA: Brooks/Cole.

Satir, V. (1983). *Conjoint family therapy* (3rd ed.). Palo Alto, CA: Science and Behavior Books.

Satir, V. (1988). *The new peoplemaking.* Palo Alto, CA: Science and Behavior Books.

Satir, V., & Baldwin, M. (1983). *Satir step by step: A guide to creating change in families.* Palo Alto, CA: Science and Behavior Books.

Satir, V., Banmen, J., Gerber, J., & Gomori, M. (1991). *The Satir model.* Palo Alto, CA: Science and Behavior Books.

DISCUSSION QUESTIONS

1. What are the principal tenets essential to understanding Satir's communications/humanistic family therapy approach? Discuss.

2. Why is it important for therapists to embrace and clients to accept these tenets in order to facilitate therapeutic success?

3. Discuss the theoretical and philosophical shifts that influenced Satir to change the name of her approach to working with families from communications family therapy to the human validation process model.

REFERENCES

Golden Triad Films. (Producer). (1984). *The essence of change* [Video]. Available from http://www.goldentriadfilms.com/films/satir.htm

Loeschen, S. (1998). *Systematic training in the skills of Virginia Satir.* Pacific Grove, CA: Brooks/Cole.

Papp, P. (1987). *Lecture.* Tulane University, School of Social Work, New Orleans, LA.

Satir, V. (1964). *Conjoint family therapy*. Palo Alto, CA: Science and Behavior Books.

Satir, V. (1967). *Conjoint family therapy* (2nd ed.). Palo Alto, CA: Science and Behavior Books.

Satir, V. (1972). *Peoplemaking*. Palo Alto, CA: Science and Behavior Books.

Satir, V. (1983). *Conjoint family therapy* (3rd ed.). Palo Alto, CA: Science and Behavior Books.

Satir, V. (1988). *The new peoplemaking*. Palo Alto, CA: Science and Behavior Books.

Satir, V., & Baldwin, M. (1983). *Satir step by step: A guide to creating change in families*. Palo Alto, CA: Science and Behavior Books.

Satir, V., Banmen, J., Gerber, J., & Gomori, M. (1991). *The Satir model*. Palo Alto, CA: Science and Behavior Books.

Satir, V., Stachowiak, L., & Taschman, H. A. (1975). *Helping families to change*. New York, NY: Tiffany.

Schwab, J. (1990). *A resource handbook for Satir concepts*. Palo Alto, CA: Science and Behavior Books.

Stevens, J. O. (1979). Foreword. In R. Bandler & J. Grinder (Eds.), *Frogs into princes: Neuro linguistic programming*. Moab, UT: Real People Press.

Walsh, W. W., & McGraw, J. A. (1996). *Essentials of family therapy: A guide to eight approaches*. Denver, CO: Love.

Chapter 5

FAMILY OF ORIGIN FAMILY THERAPY

BACKGROUND AND LEADING FIGURES

Murray Bowen is the founder of intergenerational family systems theory and therapy. Family of origin family therapy is known by several different names: intergenerational family therapy, family systems therapy, Bowen family therapy, and

Photo 5.1   Murray Bowen is the architect of the theoretically rich family of origin model. He felt that therapists should be guided by theory (rather than by technique), which would help the family therapist maintain emotional neutrality with the family.

Source: The Bowen Center

Bowen family systems therapy. There were other pioneering family therapists who incorporated generational issues in their work with families. They are Ivan Boszormenyi-Nagy and James Framo.

Bowen was trained as a physician and elected to specialize in psychiatry. One of the early pioneers in family therapy, Bowen first worked with families at the Menninger Clinic in Topeka, Kansas, in the early 1950s.

Bowen was but one of the small group of clinical researchers who began to study the family in the late '40s and early '50s. Bowen's approach grew out of his clinical study of schizophrenia. Bowen became impressed, as were other family researchers (Jackson, 1957; Lidz, Cornelison, Fleck, & Terry, 1957; Wynne, Ryckoff, & Hersch, 1958), with the "emotional stuck-togetherness" of families (Bowen, 1978, p. 207). His initial studies focused on mother-child symbiosis. Later he continued his interest and research at the National Institute of Mental Health (NIMH) from 1954 to 1959, and then he moved to Georgetown University School of Medicine in Washington, DC, and began to include the entire family. There he built the largest, and now oldest, family center and training program housed within a traditional medical setting.

During Bowen's years at NIMH his research was on families with schizophrenic offspring. Bowen admitted entire families to the psychiatric research wards. There Bowen's theory evolved from his original focus on the symbiotic relationship between mothers and their children to include the entire family. Bowen (1978) states:

> Since that time the effort has been extended to the theoretical orientation from a family concept of schizophrenia to a family theory of emotional illness and to adapt the family psychotherapy to the entire range of emotional illness. (p. 105)

During Bowen's early period at the Menninger Clinic he was deeply interested in psychoanalysis. He originally had hoped that his family research would lead him to a contribution to psychoanalytic theory. However, Bowen's family studies at NIMH led him away from a psychoanalytic orientation and from the medical/disease model as a means of understanding and helping people with emotional dysfunction.

Bowen (1978) describes his thinking at this time:

> I had no idea the research would take the direction it did. The big changes began soon after the research began. The early family researchers of the 1954–1956 period were describing a completely new order of observations never previously described in the literature. I think it was related to the ability to finally shift thinking from an individual to a family frame of reference. . . . In my research, the change came as a sudden insight shortly after schizophrenic patients and their entire families were living together on the research ward.

Then it was possible to really see the family phenomenon for the first time. After it was possible to see this phenomenon in schizophrenia, it was then automatic to see varying degrees of the same thing in all people. (p. 394)

Bowen died in 1990, and the family therapy field lost not only one of its pioneers but one of its greatest theoreticians. Bowen pursued theory development more diligently than other pioneers in the family movement. Bowen wrote with considerable passion about the importance of theory and its power. Bowen felt that family therapists should focus on theory rather than technique (Wylie, 1991). He believed that theory should guide therapeutic action and hence the therapist would be much less likely to get caught up in the emotional field of the family. Bowen's family therapy model is very theoretically rich as you will read in the remainder of this chapter. Bowenian theory continues today with such figures as Philip Guerin, Michael Kerr, Daniel Papero, and Thomas Fogarty (all longtime students of Bowen and major contributors to intergenerational family systems theory and therapy) and Monica McGoldrick and Betty Carter (who are proponents of integrating life cycle and feminism to family therapy).

PHILOSOPHICAL, CONCEPTUAL, AND THEORETICAL UNDERPINNINGS

The cornerstone of Bowen's approach is the concept of the family as a system and the importance of that system in the development and life of all human beings. Central to Bowen's theory is his belief in the influence of one's family of origin on present-day functioning. How we form attachments, deal with anxiety, manage intimacy, deal with and resolve conflict, and so on reflect more or less earlier patterns of family functioning. Bowen believed that unresolved emotional issues with our parents continue to impact how we operate in our everyday lives and within our own families of procreation. Symptoms among family members reflect unresolved issues in the family of origin and may continue to appear in later generations.

Bowen family theory grew out of clinical research, including thousands of hours observing families in action, which resulted in a shift to a family focus. Bowen sought a different framework or theoretical context. Bowen believed that psychiatrists had used discrepant models in organizing their perception of the family—models taken not only from medicine but also from literature (for example the Oedipus complex).

Bowen believed that human beings and human families are a part of the natural world, and hence it was the study of biology, ethology, phylogenesis, and other natural sciences that Bowen relied upon for his theory building. Bowen's interest in linking the understanding of families with analogues in other systems, for example

Photo 5.2   Family themes, patterns and issues can be passed down through generations and impact family functioning in future generations

Source: ©Jack Hollingsworth/Photodisc/Thinkstock

cell biology, immunology, and virology, and with other societal processes is similar to general systems theory. Bowen had hoped that through this route, the study and treatment of both the family and emotional problems could share the language of the sciences, one day becoming a science in a relationship of complementarity with other sciences.

It is important to clarify the relationship between Bowen's work and general systems theory (GST). Bowen had little or no knowledge of GST as he worked on family theory. Although there is a theoretical congruence between Bowen's theory and GST, which has been noted, this congruence has likely led people to assume that Bowen's thinking grew out of GST. The development of systems thinking and Bowen's systemic approach is an example of the parallel emergence of systems thinking in many fields.

Bowen believed that human beings are composed of two (sometimes conflicting) systems—the intellectual system and the emotional system. He also believed there should be a balance between the two systems and that there should be harmony between the two systems. That is, individuals have the choice between reacting emotionally to a situation or decision and reacting in an intellectual (logical) fashion. Hence when there is anxiety, the emotional system can take over, or a person's reaction can be tempered with intellect (reasoning). Bowen believed that a balance between the two is the preferred mode of operating.

Bowen also hypothesized that the family is an emotional system and that change (or emotion) in one part of the system will effect changes in another part of the system; that is, the family is an (emotionally) interdependent unit. Bowen believed in *isomorphs* or family patterns that can be repeated over time and throughout several generations of family members. Furthermore, Bowen believed that families exert a strong influence over family members to maintain the family's status quo (*steady state*) as well as exert pressure to promote conformity of family members' behavior (*homeostasis*). Hence, families are systems that engage in predictable patterns of behavior that will pressure their members to maintain the status quo—even if the status quo is a dysfunctional state. These same (predictable) family systems also operate to repeat these behaviors over several generations within the family.

Several key observations inform Bowen's theory of families. First is the ability to see the family as an emotional unit or system and the symptoms as an element in the emotional functioning of that unit. (Everyone in the family plays a role in symptom functioning.)

Another important observation is the role of anxiety in family functioning. Family relationships can produce and alleviate anxiety, and the effects can be observed in fluid patterns of involvement. As anxiety spreads throughout the family, Bowen observed that this family anxiety can result in turmoil among mental health staff and hence result in a loss of objectivity with the family. Bowen also noted the degree to which such staff can become involved in the emotional processes of the family. Bowen (1966) observed that when the researcher was relatively free of emotional attachment to a research family, the family made better progress toward therapeutic goals. Finally Bowen (1971) observed that once patterns of emotional process could be seen in the research families, it was then possible to see them in other less impaired families as well. Bowen saw the difference between psychosis and neurosis as quantitative rather than qualitative. He observed that the emotional processes were essentially similar; the major differentiating factor between psychosis and neurosis was the degree of impairment. Hence, human functioning could be placed on a continuum from the poorest to the highest, a major factor being the intensity or pressures that propel the process. This continuum led to the concept of *differentiation,* which we will define further later in the chapter.

THEORIES AND CONCEPTS

Bowen family systems theory consists of eight interlocking concepts. All eight concepts are interlocking in that none is fully understandable without some understanding of the others. The original six concepts—triangles, nuclear family emotional process, family projection process, multigenerational transmission process, differentiation of self, and sibling position—were formally presented in 1966. In 1974

Bowen added two additional concepts, emotional cutoff and emotional processes in society. These concepts are the result of years of clinical research with families experiencing a broad range of problems. These eight concepts represent the cornerstone of Bowen's theoretical approach to families. The first six concepts describe emotional processes that take place in the nuclear and extended family, and the later two concepts describe emotional processes across generations in a family and in society.

All eight of these concepts are tied together by the hypothesis that chronic anxiety is ever present in families and that feeling states can pass between and among family members with great speed. The mode of transmission is often subtle and may not involve language. Much like Satir's work is that visual cues are important as are other more subtle sensory processes. When intensity is used in reference to an interaction, it denotes a feeling state produced in one or more family members that may move those individuals toward the strong end of the continuum. Hence anxiety can serve to override the cognitive (rational and logical) system of the individual, and behavior can become increasingly and automatically emotional. Bowen used the term *emotional reactivity* to refer to such strong automatic responses. Furthermore, when anxiety pervades a family there is more of a tendency toward togetherness; family members begin to think and act as if they are responsible for the happiness, comfort (or discomfort), and overall well-being of others. However, some family members may rebel and define themselves in a manner opposite to the others, and the family may be blamed for their personal failures.

Chronic anxiety thus represents the underlying basis of all symptomatology, and its only resolution is for the individual to find his own way, rather than following the directive of the family. We will now define and discuss each of these eight forces that shape family functioning.

Triangles

Triangles are a systematic theoretical approach to understanding emotional function and dysfunction within families. Triangles exist in all families, to one degree or another. According to Bowen, triangles are the basic building block in a family's emotional or relational system. The dyad or two-person emotional system may enjoy a comfortable back-and-forth exchange of feelings in times of low stress and minimum anxiety. However, during times of high stress, which generates higher anxiety within the family (whether this stress emanates from within or outside of the family), this same two-person dyad will become unstable. In order for this dyadic relationship to become stable again, the dyad will involve a vulnerable third person to achieve stability in this relational system. Hence this triangulation helps diffuse the anxiety and tension between the two parties in the dyad, and the tension and anxiety are more tolerable. A clear example is in the case of a conflict-ridden marital relationship wherein one spouse reaches out to a third party to have an affair. On the surface this affair may appear to have a calming effect on the marriage. In actuality the result is the avoidance of conflict, which then causes a reduction of tension between the couple. However, if the affair is discovered tension will return and may escalate beyond the point of the former level of tension and anxiety between the couple.

Bowen described triangles as attempts to regulate distance and stabilize fusion in relationships. Generally speaking, the higher the fusion in a family, the greater the efforts to triangulate to relieve tension. Bowen observed that a lot of energy goes into regulating distance in dyadic relationships, and hence how triangles (e.g., a child, a hobby, a job, an affair, religion) come into play helps regulate the distance in the dyad. There are times when this regulation is healthy and adaptive, and there are times when regulation attempts are unhealthy and thus form triangles.

Bowen observed that a two-person system is stable as long as it is calm. However, when anxiety increases, the relational dyad immediately involves the most vulnerable other person—often the most undifferentiated person in the family—to become a triangle. (The triangulated child is the main focus of the *family projection process*—to be discussed later in the chapter.) The function of a triangle is to manage anxiety, conflict, and tension and to stabilize and regulate emotional distance in the dyad. Bowen further theorized that when the tension in a triangle is too great, then others are involved to become a *series of interlocking triangles: especially those members with a low level of differentiation.* Bowen further hypothesized that when available family triangles are exhausted, the family system will then triangle in people from the outside; this is the externalization of tension within the family.

There can be many triangles within a family, and these triangles tend to interlock (i.e., they unite or join closely with one another to form *interlocking generational triangles*). These interlocking generational triangles may spread across generations or may go back into a generation that is "unknown" to a family. Hence, unresolved difficulties pass onto the next generation until they reach the apex of the funnel; at this point symptoms develop due to the fact of an overloaded generation of a series of triangles.

Triangles are always a closed system, in that movement within the triangle is always reciprocal in order to regulate fusion. The original idea of a "scapegoat" has been replaced by the concept of the triangle—as there are no victims or victimizers. (This is not to say that the consequence of a triangle does not cause some parties more discomfort than others—or may not pressure the triangulated person into symptomatology.) However, the theory behind triangles is that all members of a triangle participate equally in this closed system. Unfortunately for the third party, emotions (problems and conflicts) of the original dyad may overflow onto the triangulated person and impact his or her functioning in some way.

Triangles also refer to the nature of the relationship (e.g., the under- or overinvolvement) among the people involved in the triangle. The concept of the *inverted triangle* is the notion of one parent's overinvolvement (or fusion) with another generation versus the underinvolvement of the other parent with that child. Some family structures are more vulnerable to inverted triangles than others—specifically families in transition (separating, divorcing, step-, or blended families) wherein family conflict (around divorce issues or step-/blended family issues) may manifest itself in the formation of a perverse triangle.

There are times when triangulation does not reduce the tension and anxiety within the original dyad. In these instances, Kerr and Bowen (1988) outline four possible outcomes: (a) A stable twosome can be destabilized by the addition of a third person (e.g., the remarriage of a parent may bring conflict into the relationship of a parent and child); (b) a stable twosome can be destabilized by the removal of a third person (the separation or divorce of that remarried parent); (c) an unstable twosome can be stabilized by the addition of a third person (a conflict-ridden parent-child relationship may become less so with the remarriage of that same parent—as it may operate to diffuse some of the tension and anxiety in that dyadic relationship, and possibly transfer that tension to the new marriage); and (d) an unstable twosome can be stabilized by the removal of a third person (change in custody arrangements wherein the child then spends less time in that home, or the divorce of the remarried couple).

Nuclear Family Emotional Process

Nuclear family emotional process describes another mechanism by which family members manage anxiety when it becomes too intense in the nuclear family. (The concepts of differentiation and fusion are important in understanding Bowen's concept of the nuclear family emotional process.) Bowen theorized that people marry persons with similar levels of differentiation. Hence the lower the level of differentiation, the more intense the emotional fusion within the marriage. Both partners attempt to deal with the intensity of this fusion by using mechanisms similar to those used in their relationship to their parents. Efforts to survive the intensity of the relationship result in four patterns or mechanisms that operate in the nuclear family (parents and children). The greater the level of fusion or "we-ness" of the conjugal unit, the greater the likelihood that these mechanisms will be used frequently (Papero, 1990).

Bowen described four mechanisms of the nuclear family emotional process that attempt to absorb the level of undifferentiation between spouses: emotional distance, spousal conflict, transmission of the problem onto one or more children, and/or sickness or dysfunction in one spouse. All four mechanisms may be employed, but the family may predominantly use one or more of these mechanisms. It is also important to note that the greater the chronic level of anxiety, the greater the likelihood that these mechanisms will be employed; this is an important clinical distinction in working with families experiencing chronic anxiety— whether anxiety originates internally or externally. Likewise, a family with a lower level of chronic anxiety may reveal its mechanisms only in the presence of acute anxiety. Each of these four mechanisms, generally played out in the conjugal relationship, is described in more detail below.

Emotional Distance

In a fused family system with high levels of anxiety, a family member may increase interpersonal distance when he or she is unable to manage emotional reactivity (Bowen, 1978). The result can be more (emotional) distance than the individual actually wants. For example, one spouse will find reasons to spend more time away from the home (work, hobby, volunteer community work, religious activities, etc.). The result is that the couple will actually spend very little time together, and whenever the spouses are together it may be in the presence of others (children, friends, relatives). If the involvement with a significant other is great enough, a triangle may result.

Marital Conflict

Marital conflict may be overt or covert and range from mild to severe. It is widely acknowledged as a symptom of tension in a relationship or in the family. The degree of conflict in a marriage is generally a function of the degree of fusion in the relationship and the intensity of the underlying anxiety (Papero, 1990). There may be a cyclical aspect to the conjugal conflict in which conflict is followed by emotional distance, then a period of warm togetherness, and then an increase in tension that precipitates another conflict and so on. For instance, Dr. Tom Fogarty (1976), a well-known psychiatrist in intergenerational family systems theory and therapy, describes the concept of the *pursuer-distancer*. This dynamic involves the emotional involvement or tendency of one spouse to attempt closeness in the relationship (purser) versus the reaction of the other spouse to detach from the relationship (distancer). This dynamic can be cyclical in nature in order to meet the individual and relational needs of both partners in terms of anxiety about relational proximity.

Within moderate to severe marital conflict there is a high emotional reactivity wherein age-old conflicts can resurface with the slightest provocation. Cognitive processes are skewed in which each partner is more focused on the negative aspects of the other and the relationship. Papero (1990) aptly describes these processes:

> It is not uncommon for years-old grievances to be brought forward yet again. The effect is usually similar to pouring gasoline on smoldering coals. If the intensity of the conflict exceeds the capacity of the relationship to manage it, the automatic movement to bring in a significant third occurs. In extreme examples, outside agencies intervene in the form of the police and various crisis intervention services. (p. 53)

There has always been a great deal of concern as far as the well-being of children reared in a family where there is moderate to severe marital conflict (be that conflict overt or covert). The assumption is that marital conflict (especially prolonged and intense conflict) inevitably has a negative impact on the child's development. Clinical observation suggests that children run a greater risk when the parent becomes anxious about the effects of the marital interaction upon the child (Papero, 1990). When this anxiety shapes the interaction of the parent with the child the result is an involvement of the child in the emotional process of the marriage. It is this anxious involvement of a parent with a child that is the basis for the third major mechanism of nuclear family emotional process.

Transmission of the Problem to a Child

Kerr and Bowen (1988) believed that the development of physical, emotional, and social symptoms in one or more children of a nuclear family is influenced by their basic level of differentiation and level of chronic anxiety—the same two factors that influence symptom development in adults. The most poorly differentiated child is the most vulnerable to increases in family anxiety.

The problems and anxiety within a marriage can be avoided by parental focus on one or more children. The literature notes that a common pattern is for the mother to focus much of her emotional energy on a child while the father responds by distancing himself (perhaps triangulating work or hobbies; Walsh & McGraw, 2002). The child to whom the emotional energy is directed is more likely to suffer from increased (emotional) reactivity and the fusion of intellect and emotion and is the most vulnerable to the development of problems (Walsh & McGraw, 2002).

The degree to which children become involved in the emotional process of the parents is the basis of the concept of *multigenerational transmission* (to be discussed later in this chapter). Bowen believed that when this process becomes so intense that it results in the impairment of the child's ability to function in life, it plays a part in the development of schizophrenia and other severe and difficult symptoms.

Dysfunction in a Spouse

The fourth mechanism of nuclear family emotional process involves the reaction of the spouses to one another. In a healthy marriage there is compromise in which one spouse yields to the other alternately. However, in dysfunctional marriages this pattern becomes fixed wherein one spouse is more often than not the yielding spouse. The result can be a decreased functioning in one spouse and an apparent overfunctioning in the other. The overfunctioning spouse may have been trained to make decisions for others. The underfunctioning spouse likewise may have become accustomed to allow others to make decisions for him or her. In some conjugal situations alternating reciprocal roles may develop in the couple wherein one spouse is the inadequate or dysfunctional one and the other is overly adequate and vice versa.

The overfunctioning-underfunctioning reciprocity pattern in a conjugal relationship may exacerbate the extent to which an individual develops a chronic mental and/or physical malady. Kerr and Bowen (1988) elaborate:

> While a dominant-subordinate or overfunctioning-underfunctioning reciprocity in a relationship is an important mechanism for binding anxiety and stabilizing the functioning of both people, an increase in the levels of chronic anxiety can exaggerate this pattern to the point that one person's functioning is so impaired that symptoms develop. The person most prone to becoming symptomatic is the one who makes the most adjustments in his or her thoughts, feelings and behavior to preserve relationship harmony. The one making the most adjustments may be an overfunctioning person who, feeling an exaggerated sense of responsibility about making things "right" for others, is trying to do too much, or it may be an underfunctioning person who, feeling little confidence in his ability to make decisions, is depending on others too much. In both instances the person generates and absorbs more anxiety than he can manage without developing symptoms. (p. 172)

Family Projection Process

Bowen theorized that the *family projection process* is the passing on of the parents' level of differentiation to one or more of their children. This concept describes the process by which parental problems are projected onto the child. Generally one child in a family will have increased emotional involvement with the parents. Papero (1995) further describes this process as being uneven—in that some of the children emerge with a higher level of differentiation than their parents, some with a lower level of differentiation, and others with a similar level of differentiation. Bowen (1976) believed that poorly differentiated parents tend to

select as objects of their attention the most immature or physically or mentally vulnerable of the children—regardless of birth order.

This overinvolvement can range from the parent being especially solicitous to
the child to the parent being extremely hostile to the child. This relational dynamic
impairs the child's ability to function in other social settings. As is the case within
Bowen's other concepts, the degree of the level of differentiation of the parents and
the level of anxiety in the family can operate to intensify the family projection
process. That is, the greater the level of undifferentiation of the parents, the more
they will rely upon the family projection process to stabilize their conjugal system.
Hence it becomes more likely that one child will be emotionally impaired.

This process is thought to begin at birth when one or both parents respond to
the child as if their anxiety is in the child, rather than residing within them.
Anxiety heightens the parent's feelings for that child. The parent's feelings can
become intense and range from an overly positive and overly protective posture to
revulsion (Papero, 1990). The child gains a heightened sensitivity to the anxiety of
the parent, and it is often the case that the other parent supports this overinvolvement with the child and/or withdraws from the child. Bowen theorized this process
as being multigenerational, going back in time two or more generations. There is
said to be a cumulative effect of what has happened in preceding generations,
which is the basis for Bowen's concept of *multigenerational transmission* (to be
discussed next in this chapter).

The dysfunction of the parental unit lays the groundwork for inclusion of the
child within the mother-father-child triangle, whereas the parents may manage
their anxiety in other ways and only occasionally involve the child in their emotional process. This process may also shift to other children in the family at times;
especially if the anxiety is intense enough it may "spill over" to involve other siblings (Papero, 1990).

Bowen noted that parents often have some awareness of the intensity of the
relationship and that neither parent nor child is at fault in this process. He also
theorized that parents may not want this type of emotional involvement with their
child but may not be able to react differently.

Multigenerational Transmission Process

The *multigenerational transmission process* is a process in which severe mental and/or physical impairment is the result of a repetitive pattern of successively
lower levels of differentiation being transmitted over several subsequent generations. Bowen proposed that individuals marry persons with similar levels of differentiation. Hence, two persons with low levels of differentiation will marry each
other and produce children with even lower levels of differentiation than themselves. This process continues wherein each successive generation of offspring

goes on to marry persons with similar low levels of differentiation, and hence this process culminates with a level of differentiation that is so low as to contribute to the development of serious dysfunction and symptomatology such as schizophrenia, chronic alcoholism, bipolar disorder, and possibly even chronic physical illnesses (Papero, 1990). It may take as many as eight to ten generations to produce persons with this level of impairment (Papero, 1990).

In any particular generation favorable circumstances (e.g., less stress and anxiety within the family) can slow this process down, and unfavorable circumstances (e.g., lack of needed resources) and severe stress can speed it up. The ability of mechanisms other than the projection process to absorb anxiety in a relationship is also an important variable.

Differentiation of Self

Differentiation of self refers to the variable degree of emotional separation that people achieve from their families of origin and accounts for their operating at different levels of functioning independent from (or dependent on) the family. Bowen developed a *scale of differentiation* wherein there is a continuum ranging from low to high levels of differentiation. The scale is primarily of theoretical importance and was not designed as an instrument that could be used to assign people an exact level. Nor does the scale define clinical diagnostic categories. Rather it describes a person's *adaptiveness* to stress. Dr. Philip Guerin, a psychiatrist and major contributor to intergenerational family systems theory and therapy, developed the concept of *adaptive level of functioning*. Guerin, Fay, Burden, and Kautto (1987) define the adaptive level of functioning as the ability of the person to function in the face of stress and emotional pressures from family members. Note that one can change his or her adaptive functioning, but one can change his or her level of differentiation only by a few points on Bowen's scale of differentiation.

Most people fall somewhere on the continuum of self-differentiation—being neither completely differentiated nor completely undifferentiated. Complete differentiation exists in a person who has fully resolved the emotional attachment to his family and has attained complete emotional maturity in the sense that his self is developed sufficiently that, whenever it is important to do so, he can be an individual in a family or in a group (Kerr & Bowen, 1988). Complete undifferentiation exists in a person who has achieved no emotional separation from his family; he has no "self" and is incapable of being an individual in a family or a group.

The characteristic that best describes the difference between being differentiated (or *individuated*) and being undifferentiated is *the degree to which a person is able to distinguish between the feeling process and the intellectual process*. Another defining characteristic is the ability *to choose between having one's functioning guided by feelings and having it guided by thoughts*. The more anxiety ridden and intense the emotional atmosphere a person grows up in, the more likely that person's life will be governed by (his own and other people's) feeling responses.

The undifferentiated self is a very "feeling-dominated" individual wherein one is fused emotionally and intellectually; that is, such individuals have difficulty distinguishing feeling from fact (their intellect is flooded or dominated by emotionality). So much energy is put into seeking love and approval and the maintenance of relationships that there is little energy left for "life-directed" goals. They are less flexible, less adaptable, and more emotionally dependent on others, and they are more easily stressed into dysfunction. Their lives are relationship oriented, and their self-esteem is very dependent on others. They find it difficult to make decisions based on logic, thinking, and reasoning (they tend to make decisions based on feelings).

Two related concepts are that of the *solid self* and the *pseudo self*. The solid self operates on the basis of clearly defined beliefs, opinions, and principles developed through a process of intellectual reasoning and the consideration of alternatives. The basic "self" is not negotiable in the relational system. The pseudo self, on the other hand, makes choices based on emotional pressures rather than on the basis of reasoned principles—choices vary depending on whom the person is emotionally involved with at the time. There is a pretend self that, when pressured by the emotional system, may make choices that are inconsistent from time to time.

Bowen theorized that the more the core self is regulated by a pseudo self, the more likely that person will respond emotionally and display greater undifferentiation to the family unit. With increased autonomy the person whose core self functions more from a solid self has a greater awareness of self, is less likely to respond to times of high stress and anxiety from a purely emotional stance, and will be able to find more of a balance and give a more logical or rational (intellectual) response that is tempered with emotion. In essence, the difference between an individuated person and an undifferentiated one is their varying ability to preserve a degree of autonomy in the face of pressures for togetherness (within the family, conjugal dyad, or group) and display more of a solid self than a pseudo self.

In the context of an emotional (or relational) system the differentiated person or person with a solid self can act with a degree of autonomy as that individual remains in meaningful relationships with others. The highly differentiated individual has a more fully integrated, solid self (i.e., a concept of self that is nonnegotiable with others), and that behavior is guided primarily by intellect. Conversely, individuals with low levels of differentiation are guided primarily by their pseudo self, and their behaviors are more often than not guided by their emotions.

Consider the following example. A very competitive father instructs his son to act in an unsportsmanlike manner in the son's high school basketball game in order to win the game. The son is then faced with a moral crisis. Does he operate with autonomy and play to his own conscience, or does he follow his father's edict and commit the foul in order to preserve "togetherness" within the family? The more highly differentiated (individuated) person would be true to self (assuming that the core self ideally wishes to take the high road) and thus operate from a solid self and play in a sportsmanlike manner, but the pseudo self (the less individuated or undifferentiated person) would then betray his own morals and values "for the sake of family togetherness."

Bowen (1971) observed the human tendency to group together and called it the "togetherness force." When anxiety pervades a family, the tendency toward togetherness is most observable. That is, family members think, feel, and behave alike and act as if they are responsible for each other's comfort, happiness, and well-being. Hence as tension mounts, the family manifests more togetherness, and a loss of individuality increases.

Conversely, as tension and anxiety mount, the less individuated or undifferentiated person may act in the complete opposite manner—depending on whether the feeling climate is positive or negative. In a negative feeling climate the undifferentiated person may act in a rebellious manner (betraying one's true or solid self), still denying the family's role in this behavior. Each of these postures relates to the pressures for group cohesion and sameness in the family. However, the more autonomous (more highly differentiated) person has a greater awareness of self as a responding element in a relational network. The higher the level of chronic anxiety in the family, the more each individual life course comes to be determined by various reactive mechanisms.

Bowen observed that people vary greatly in their ability to manage (emotional) reactivity. As anxiety increases, so does the tendency to react from a purely emotional stance. Some people operate with continued emotional reactivity; life for them is primarily about pleasing others and being accepted by others. Major life decisions (e.g., career choice, spousal selection) are heavily influenced (if not primarily determined) by their relational systems, and not from a standpoint of being true to the core self. Conversely, people who operate from a solid self and who are more differentiated (or individuated) can enter into intimate relationships with other people and not have their life choices governed solely by those relationships. This is not to say that their (life) choices are not influenced at all by others (especially in the case of varying cultural values in which the family takes on more importance than individual wishes). Rather, they are aware of their choices and do not deny the importance of others in their lives but reason that they do have a degree of choice in the matter and may elect to place the family's needs and wishes before their own at times. They are then responding to a situation in a less emotional and more thoughtful manner, and with less reactivity to anxiety.

A related construct is that of the *undifferentiated family ego mass* or *fusion*. (Bowen eventually began to prefer the term *fusion* over *undifferentiated family ego mass*.) Bowen described these related constructs as similar to a "glooey blob," or the emotional oneness between family members—that is to say the degree of "emotional stuck-togetherness" of a family. Emotional fusion essentially represents a loss of boundaries; it is a concept that describes relational proximity and its lack of functionality. Clinically speaking it can be thought of as "mind reading" (between family members), wherein the pronoun *we* is used interchangeably with the pronoun *I*. Family members take responsibility for each other; they may interrupt and answer for each other. There is a mass of self, with no one taking a clear "I" position.

Sibling Position

Walter Toman published *Family Constellation: A Psychological Game* in 1961, and Bowen incorporated Toman's research into family systems theory in the early 1960s. Toman's theoretical premise is that certain fixed personality characteristics are determined by a number of factors within one's sibling composition: birth order, gender composition, and the size of the sibling composition. For instance the oldest sibling may tend to emerge as a leader and better able to endure the hardships that come with responsibility. The youngest sibling does best when others look out for him or her, and it is not as natural for him or her to assume leadership or to accept responsibility as it is for the eldest sibling. The only girl of the family, especially if she is the youngest, may be more accustomed to being taken care of and not as accustomed to sharing. Persons from large families may be more adept at managing multiple relationships while only children may value their privacy and alone time. Spacing of the sibship is also important, in that 5 or more years' difference between siblings usually reduces the predictability of the characteristics associated with each position.

Toman's work presented profiles of the characteristics of people who occupy any of 10 sibling positions (e.g., older brother, older sister, younger brother, younger sister, middle child, only child, twins). Toman's profiles are so detailed and precise that his own writings should be reviewed to appreciate the full extent of his contributions.

Bowen added an important dimension, differentiation of self, to Toman's "normal" sibling profiles. Toman's research described characteristics of functioning but not levels of functioning. That is, all eldest siblings are not the same; a mature eldest sibling accepts responsibility easily but does not attempt to control or to intrude on others (Kerr & Bowen, 1988). He or she can allow others to be responsible for him- or herself. However, an immature eldest sibling may be overbearing and disrespectful of the rights of others. On the other hand, a mature younger sibling can take responsibility for him- or herself and may possess valuable qualities, but an immature younger sibling, while not accepting responsibility for him- or herself, may be demanding and rebel against authority.

The concept of sibling positions was also adapted to predict aspects of the personality fit between marriage partners. According to Toman, marriage partners have complementary, partially complementary, or noncomplementary sibling positions. Toman suggested that marital partners with noncomplementary sibling positions have greater difficulty in marriage than partners with complementary or partially complementary sibling positions. For example, two eldest children marrying could lead to competition between the two to see who is in charge. Conversely, two youngest children marrying may cause the couple to experience a lack of direction on important tasks and decisions as no one is taking the lead. However, an oldest child would do well to marry a youngest child in that their accustomed sibling roles complement each other.

While Toman's research found that the predicted relationship between personality development and functioning exists, we know that there are a number of mitigating factors that go to shape personality development (e.g., cultural background, social class factors, and different levels of differentiation). However, these descriptions are not meant to be precise for a particular person; they indicate trends and patterns of behavior that generally characterize persons occupying a given sibling position (Papero, 1990). In addition, we also know that there is no such thing as the best sibling position; each position has its positive and negative aspects. Kerr and Bowen (1988) elaborate:

> An oldest son and a youngest son can make an excellent team, each contributing unique attitudes and methods of approach to a task. Under stress, however, they may have difficulty cooperating. The person who is an oldest child may feel he is doing all the work and that he is "over used" and under appreciated." The person who is a youngest child may feel pushed aside and that he is being "dominated" or "negated." (p. 316)

Emotional Cutoff

Emotional cutoff describes the manner in which people deal with the emotional intensity that exists between generations and the way some people handle their unresolved emotional attachment to their parental family. This is a process of separation, withdrawal, running away, and denying the importance of the family of origin when the degree of fusion and the level of undifferentiation is high. Bowen (1978) described this process wherein unresolved attachment (to the family of origin) is handled by the intrapsychic processes of denial and isolation of self while living close to the parents, by physically running away, or by a combination of emotional isolation and physical distance. It is the way people separate themselves from their past in order to start their lives in the present generation.

Bowen hypothesized that the lower the level of differentiation and the higher the degree of fusion, the more intense the unresolved attachment and the greater the likelihood the generations will cut off from one another. The individuated or differentiated person does not have to "cut off" in order to resolve conflict (with the family of origin). People who are sufficiently differentiated can be close to their families without becoming lost in the emotional system and can be away from their families without cutting themselves off. That is, they can be different from their families and risk taking "I" positions without fearing rejection. Conversely, they can be *like* their families without losing their sense of self. Hence, they are free to love without fusing and can maintain a person-to-person relationship with each member of their family system without triangulating or achieving closeness at the risk of self.

Such a person can then manage his or her life through planful, intellectual decision making and have the energy and interest available for living a productive, goal-directed life. Bowen (1978) writes:

> The over-all goal is to help individual family members to rise up out of the emotional togetherness that binds us all. . . . The goal is to help the motivated family member to take a microscopic step toward a better level of differentiation, in spite of togetherness forces that oppose. When one family member can finally master this, then other family members automatically take similar steps. (p. 371)

People cut off from their families of origin in order to reduce the discomfort generated by being in close contact with them. Although cutoff can reduce anxiety, people can also increase anxiety by cutting off, whereby important emotional connections and potential sources of social support may be lost. While staying away from one's family can reduce anxiety, especially when one is not under much personal stress, loss of viable emotional contact with the family of origin can also increase anxiety, particularly when one is under personal stress.

People manage emotional cutoffs in different ways. The amount of physical distance between a person and his family of origin does not equal the amount of emotional distance that exists between them. People who live several hundred miles away may be (emotionally) closer to their family of origin than persons who live only a few miles away or in the same house. In addition the number of contacts people have with their family does not indicate emotional closeness or the degree of cutoff. Contacts may be frequent but mechanistic and highly ritualized. On the other hand family contacts may be infrequent but rich and meaningful.

On the surface it would appear that the individual is in control with reference to the way he or she is handling family relationships. Unfortunately emotional cut-offs render one much more vulnerable to other intense relationships—he or she has not found a way to relate to another but has merely removed him- or herself from the emotional presence of family. Kerr and Bowen (1988) suggest that persons who run away (or isolate themselves) to achieve cutoff are more likely to become hermits. These individuals are much less able to respond effectively to problem-solving situations, especially in other interpersonal relationships. They may have been successful in removing themselves from the intense familial relationships but may go from relationship to relationship seeking the positive effects of closeness yet automatically cutting off when the intensity reaches a certain level of intolerance (Papero, 1990). Dysfunction can also manifest itself in other ways, such as superficial relationships, physical illness, depression and impulsive behaviors (Walsh, 1980).

Emotional Processes in Society

Societal regression or *emotional processes in society* is Bowen's least well developed of the eight theories defined and discussed here. In this theory Bowen extended his thinking to emotional processes operating in society and society's influence on family life. Bowen postulated that heightened anxiety in society produces greater discomfort and further anxiety in families. He reasoned that emotional processes in society influence the emotional process in families, but it is a background influence affecting all families (Kerr & Bowen, 1988). The lower the family's level of differentiation, the more susceptible a family's emotional process will be to the influence of societal emotional processes. Kerr and Bowen (1988) elaborate further:

> The concept of societal emotional process describes how a prolonged increase in societal anxiety can result in a gradual lowering of the functional level of differentiation of a society. The lower the functional level of a society, the greater the incidence of "social symptoms" such as a high crime rate, a high divorce rate, an incessant clamor for "rights," and a notable neglect of responsibilities. During the course of history, the emotional functioning of society has risen and fallen many times. Since about the mid-1960's, society has been in an emotional regression. The regression is anticipated to continue until the discomfort associated with implementing short-term solutions designed to relieve immediate anxiety becomes greater than the discomfort associated with implementing solutions that tolerate immediate anxiety and encompass a long-range view. (p. 334)

Bowen is to be applauded for his attempt to stay current in his theoretical formulations. If one were to extend his thinking with regard to emotional processes in society to today's current climate, one could extend this theory to the idea of oppression; Bowen (1978) talks about the process by which groups join together and enhance their own functioning at the expense of a third party (e.g., minority and other disadvantaged or oppressed groups). This is a key element in the construct of oppression and its deleterious impact on families—especially those families that differ from the norm in one regard or another (e.g., single-parent families, poor families, gay or lesbian families, ethnic minority families). Bowen called for societal ills (or symptoms) to be dealt with via a thoughtful approach based on principles and a degree of respect for differing viewpoints. Along this line of thought one can extend his thinking to have implications for public agencies in their relationship with families to take on more of an advocacy and empowerment approach with families in distress, especially if the source of the stress is external to the family.

GOALS OF THERAPY

The therapeutic focus of Bowen's approach is to gather data and make assessments using the eight concepts outlined above. The goals of therapy are (a) to reduce emotional reactivity in the family among its members (a reduction of anxiety is thought to reduce symptoms), (b) to increase the level of self-differentiation of family members (to improve their adaptive level of functioning), and (c) to modify the relationships in the family system by the de-triangulation of major family triangles (to form person-to-person relationships with as many members as possible in the family of origin) and by repairing cutoffs within the family (and working to resolve unfinished business with the family of origin). Symptom reduction and decreased anxiety can occur relatively quickly in Bowen therapy; however, the improvement in the basic level of differentiation is a long-term process that can take many years. (We will discuss in further detail each of these goals when we describe the *process of therapy* in Bowen family systems therapy in the next section.)

Another goal of Bowen family therapy is for the therapist to better understand himself as a person in the therapeutic system. Bowen believed in the "neutrality" of the therapist in his approach, and to this end the therapist must gain some awareness of how his own family of origin may affect his reaction to families in therapy.

For many years Bowen systematically studied his own family system, working to gain objective understanding of the system. His goal was to de-triangulate himself from major family triangles and to increase his own level of differentiation. This therapeutic move was termed *defining a self in the extended family*

(Bowen, 1978). It requires knowledge and research about the functioning of emotional systems in one's own family of origin. This process requires the therapist to begin to gain control over his or her own emotional reactivity and become a more objective observer. Bowen (1978) states:

> As the system becomes more "open" and he can begin to see the triangles and the parts in the family reaction patterns, he can begin the more complex process toward differentiating himself from the previously unrecognized myths, images, distortions, and triangles. (p. 540)

ROLE OF THE THERAPIST

The role of the "therapist" in Bowen's model of help is as coach-guide-facilitator, researcher, consultant, teacher, and expert in family systems. (We will explore, in turn, each of these therapist roles in the section of this chapter on tools and techniques.)

Bowen saw himself in more of an egalitarian role with family members. To this end therapist objectivity, as opposed to emotional reactivity, is of primary importance as the therapist enters the family system. Bowen believed it is important not to take sides with family members and to stay connected to all members of the family. Bowen felt that the more differentiation of self the therapist achieved, the less likely the therapist would be to behave in an emotionally reactive and subjective manner with the family.

Friedman (1991) warns the therapist not to get caught up in triangles with couples or become involved in the emotional processes of triangles by either over-functioning or being emotionally reactive. Friedman (1991) also points out that it is the therapist's job to be engaging without being reactive, to be stimulating without rescuing, and to teach a new way of thinking rather than use any specific behavior or therapy technique—that is the ultimate agent of change.

Bowen cautioned therapists against taking sides with family members or allowing themselves to become consumed or overwhelmed by family problems. A therapist who allows him- or herself to be fused or triangulated with family members can have a deleterious effect on family process and thus reduce his or her own effectiveness. Remaining calm, detached (but not indifferent), and objective is the goal for a successful therapeutic encounter.

Finally, the authors emphasize the importance of the therapist's awareness of his or her own family of origin issues. Not being aware of the impact of one's own family in family therapy can be an obstacle to effective family therapy. A family therapist's reaction to characteristics of the family (e.g., style of communication,

Photo 5.3 The family is an emotionally interdependent system that impacts how each family member forms attachments, manages intimacy, and deals with anxiety

Source: ©Comstock/Comstock/Thinkstock

developmental issues, structure of the family, and culture of the family) can present as obstacles to objective family therapy if this reaction is clouded by personal experiences. Objectivity in clinical work with families (in light of one's own family issues) can be largely an unconscious process. Hence it is even more imperative for the family therapist to make a conscious effort to become more aware of his or her own family issues in clinical work with families.

PROCESS OF THERAPY

The assessment process is the cornerstone of the Bowen family systems approach and hence is a major part of the actual change process. In Bowen's approach the client takes major responsibility for assessment through a tool called the *genogram* (one of the major tools of this approach to be covered separately). Via the genogram the client goes about the process of gathering and organizing intergenerational family history. The goal is to objectify the family's emotional system through a systematic study (or research) of several generations of family history.

The assessment process has two objectives. The first objective is to study the intergenerational family through time, assessing four or more generations of the family. The second objective is to uncover the nature of the *current* family emotional system.

The process of self-differentiation (from the family) is a major therapeutic goal in Bowenian therapy. Increased differentiation is obtained through the process of obtaining, organizing, and understanding family history. The family history makes clear recurrent family issues and themes that continue to impact the current generation. Studying four or five generations helps the client gather and organize the facts, clarify distortions, demystify mysteries, and clear up confusion; it also helps make clear major or nodal events in the life of the family that have sent reverberating shock waves through the family system (Bowen, 1978). Bowen (1978) explains, "Unresolved issues in past relationships are carried into new relationships and new generations until they develop into ongoing family themes around which family members polarize" (p. 492). Examples of issues include attitudes about sex, gender roles, parenting, ideals of adolescent and adult behavior, and occupational choices. These family issues, themes, myths, or rules are passed down through the generations and become highly charged issues within current generations. Reactions to such can include going along with the "party line," rebelling, or doing the exact opposite of what the parents did.

The therapeutic process includes six major steps (Walsh & McGraw, 2002):

1. Exploring the presenting problem

2. Working with the family to develop the family genogram

3. Using systematic questions to gain information about family relationships

4. Broadening the focus to larger family systems

5. Giving feedback to clients

6. Using techniques to facilitate changes

In Bowen's approach to family therapy the therapist may work with the entire family, the conjugal couple, or even just one individual from the family—or all of these configurations as therapy progresses. Bowen's theory was that change in one part of the system will effect changes in other parts of the system. For example, an adult daughter enters therapy for help with romantic relationships— she constantly finds herself in dysfunctional relationships in which she "gives all but gets nothing." An analysis of the genogram shows the daughter to be in a reversed role relationship with her mother—a multigenerational pattern, it seems. Bowen therapy would help her resolve her conflicts in her current interpersonal relationship by resolving her relationship issues with her mother. Furthermore, as the daughter begins to not allow herself to "parent" her mother, there are other shifts in the family system—most important her mother may not become nurturing but is no longer allowed to treat her daughter as if she were a girlfriend—and hence the system changes.

THE FAMILY EVALUATION INTERVIEW

The data gathered in the family evaluation interview and the assessments made relative to the eight major concepts are the basis for family diagnosis and become the therapeutic focus (Kerr & Bowen, 1988). Family evaluation interviews begin by attaining a history of the presenting problem, especially focusing on why help is sought at this point in time, how each member of the family views the problem, and what each person in the family hopes to gain from the therapy experience. Process questions (questions directed at individuals) are meant to ascertain levels of differentiation in family members, degree of emotional reactivity in the family, major family triangles, and emotional cutoffs and to explore the major theories as outlined above in this approach.

Kerr and Bowen (1988) suggest using the following questions in the initial family interview:

- Who initiated the therapy?
- What is the symptom, and which family member or family relationship is symptomatic?
- What is the immediate relationship system (this usually means the nuclear family) of the symptomatic person?
- What are the patterns of emotional functioning in the nuclear family?
- What is the intensity of the emotional process in the nuclear family?
- What influences that intensity—an overload of stressful events or a low level of adaptiveness?
- What is the nature of extended family systems, particularly in terms of their stability and availability?
- What is the degree of emotional cutoff from each extended family system?
- What is the prognosis?
- What are important directions for therapy?

The assessment process in Bowenian therapy is perhaps longer than in other models of family therapy, in that it may take several sessions to gain, organize, and analyze all pertinent information. The history of the problem (or symptom) for each individual family member must be explored—his or her reaction to the presenting problem, current level of differentiation and overall functioning, and ability to handle stress and anxiety.

The multigenerational pattern of each spouse is also to be explored in depth, especially understanding how the nuclear family is impacted by intergenerational triangles, emotional cutoffs, levels of differentiation, patterns of fusion, and projection processes. The ultimate objective of the family evaluation interview process is to objectify the family over time and develop a road map of the family's emotional system, as each spouse is thought to embody the emotional processes of preceding generations.

Bowen (1971) lists four main functions for the therapist with spouses:

1. Defining and clarifying the relationship between the spouses

2. Keeping oneself de-triangulated from the family emotional system

3. Teaching the functioning of emotional systems

4. Demonstrating differentiation by taking "I" positions during the course of therapy

TOOLS AND TECHNIQUES

Bowen family therapy is driven by the systematic exploration of the major concepts; it is not a technique-driven approach—especially relative to other models of family therapy (i.e., Satir or Minuchin). The methodology of family systems therapy is relatively simple and is determined by theoretical considerations as much as possible (Papero, 1990). The therapist does not actively attempt to *make* the family different via use of the various techniques; the clinician attempts to relate calmly and neutrally to the family. Papero (1990) clarifies this interventional process:

Interventions or some move or action taken by the therapist to impact upon the family presumably in a positive manner play little if any role. The clinician focuses on gathering information, maintaining a broad perspective, obtaining and maintaining emotional neutrality, and operating from a research perspective. (p. 71)

There are 12 commonly used techniques in Bowenian therapy, although the reader is advised that Bowenian therapists use a wide range of techniques, sometimes borrowing from other insight-oriented therapy approaches. The most widely used techniques are *the genogram, emotional neutrality or de-triangulation, the process question, relationship experiments, the "I" position, didactic teaching, role playing, journaling, letter writing, coaching,* and *the Bowenian (family) conference.* We will describe each of these techniques in turn.

The Genogram

The most central and critical technique in Bowenian therapy is the genogram. A genogram is simply a family tree that includes a visual representation of vast amounts of social data—of at least three generations of the multigenerational family. Genograms are visual maps that record genealogical relationships, major family events, achievements, occupations, marriages, divorces, illnesses, losses, family migrations and dispersals, sibling position characteristics, information about alignments, emotional cutoffs, and communication patterns. Genograms organize information about a family in a standardized manner and provide a graphic way to visualize family processes and dynamics (e.g., family projections, triangles, emotional cutoffs). Genograms offer the therapist visual representations of family social data, family processes, and family dynamics in order to investigate the presenting problem. Each partner's family background is depicted at least three generations back. Depending on the presenting problem, therapeutic focus, and level of functioning of the family, genograms can be completed both inside and outside of the therapy session (a homework assignment could be to finish a genogram began in the session; see Figures 5.1–5.3).

| Figure 5.1 | Summary of Commonly Used Genogram Symbols |

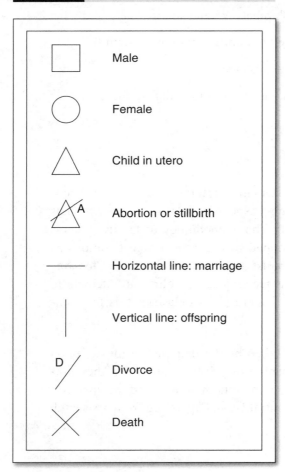

Male

Female

Child in utero

Abortion or stillbirth

Horizontal line: marriage

Vertical line: offspring

Divorce

Death

Figure 5.2 The Family Diagram

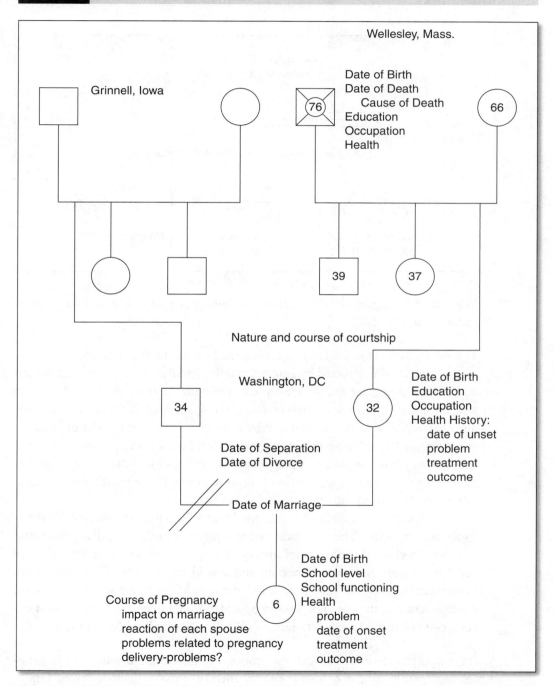

Source: Papero (1990).

Figure 5.3 Genogram Symbols to Depict Relationship Dynamics

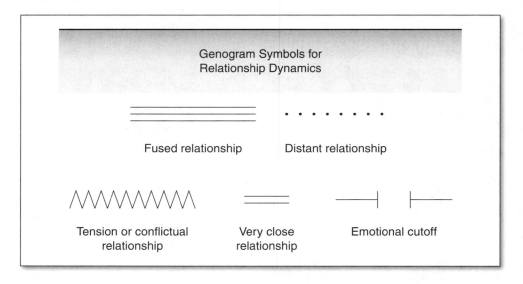

In Figure 5.2, Papero (1990) describes the *family diagram*, which is the basis of the genogram:

> The information is collected and represented on the family diagram. . . . In the diagram males are depicted by squares and the females by circles. The husband and wife of a nuclear family are represented with the male on the left and the female on the right. A solid line connects them. Each of the children they produce is connected to the marital unit by a solid line. The birth order of children is represented by placing the eldest on the left beneath the parents, and each succeeding sibling is placed to the right of the older sibling preceding it. In this manner each successive generation is represented with the most recent generation at the bottom of the diagram.
>
> As each person is added to the diagram, basic information is collected. Vital statistics are important. These include date and place of birth, date, place and cause of death, level of education, brief history of employment, and a survey of major health problems. Dates are important and should be noted for all events listed. Where health problems have been noted, the date of onset, the length and course of treatment and the outcome should be added to the diagram. In this manner a composite picture of the functioning of each family member is collected. (p. 68)

It is important to remember that the process of collecting the genogram is sometimes therapeutic in and of itself. Family members make discoveries of family patterns and themes that never before occurred to them. Family chronology and the timing of certain events help family members make important connections as to their impact on current family processes and dynamics. Engagement of the cognitive system can heighten objectivity and broaden perspective (Papero, 1990). When family members gain more objectivity about certain events or behaviors where they have previously reacted emotionally, the anxiety level is automatically lowered. When anxiety levels are lowered family members can be calmer and more objective.

Gathering family social data on the extended family is equally important to obtain, as families do not exist in a vacuum (not even nuclear families). Shifts and changes impacting the extended family (deaths, divorces, moves, illnesses, etc.) can have a major impact on the nuclear family. The authors also advise that the basic genogram and family diagram include any persons who are considered "family." Especially in the case of ethnic and ethnic minority families wherein family relationships do not always fall along biological ties, godfathers, "play uncles," and other significant "fictive kin" and family friends may have an important impact on the family.

In essence, one is never really finished with constructing the genogram; although the therapeutic focus may have moved to the analysis of the genogram, there is always more to know. The construction and study of the genogram continues throughout the therapeutic contact, which is why the genogram should be viewed as an ongoing *assessment tool* as well as a *therapeutic technique*. In fact, the analysis of the genogram continues as one incorporates other techniques, such as *de-triangulation* and *the "I" position* (to be described next in this chapter).

Emotional Neutrality/De-triangulation

Remaining objective and emotionally neutral in the therapeutic session and hence staying de-triangulated from the family system is the therapist's primary objective in order to facilitate change in the family. The therapist can best resist the emotional reactivity of the family by staying de-triangulated and not taking sides. There are many ways in which the therapist can take sides in the emotional issues of the family, sometimes without ever saying a word. Bowen (1978) suggests that therapists achieve this (emotional) neutrality through the use of modeling, nonverbal behavior, and appropriate humor. Remaining emotionally neutral is the central and most challenging task for the therapist.

The importance of staying outside of the emotional field of the family facilitates change within the family by not allowing oneself to become a mechanism by which tension (within the dyad or triad) is eased. Yet this can be a difficult task as responding emotionally (by being either charmed or angered by a family member) is a natural human response. In essence, the clinician is being asked to be aware of and to control this natural response.

The effort to remain neutral is essentially impossible if the therapist focuses on surface or content issues (sex, money, in-laws, children, etc.; Papero, 1990).

The family will inevitably attempt to involve the therapist in taking sides on the rightness or wrongness or fairness or unfairness of a given (content) issue. Taking a neutral position involves the therapist being neither too close nor too distant from the emotional processes of the family (Bowen, 1971). If the therapist responds in a calm, objective manner, he or she will be in a better position to observe and to intervene on the emotional processes of the family. Bowen (1971) suggests the therapist who is able to respond seriously or with light humor (to break the tension) is not as likely to become entangled in the emotional field of the family. The ideal is to respond to the emotionally difficult areas of the family without becoming a part of the emotional system (Papero, 1990).

The Process Question

The *process question* is a major technique used by the therapist when collecting information for the genogram and when tracking the relationship process. The process question is a way of collecting information that also serves to calm the anxiety of the family. When the anxiety level of the family is calmed, people are better able to think more clearly and possibly discover better options for managing relationships and their behaviors.

Process questions help neutralize triangles but still allow access to pertinent information ("How do you react when your wife . . . ?" or "What do you do to resolve . . . ?"). This method of questioning helps one gain information on how the parties perceive a certain situation without showing bias or intimating solutions embedded within the questioning process. By asking frequent *factual questions*, the therapist can keep the family focused on specific dynamics rather than on emotionality and reactivity; family members may also be asked to answer or speak directly to the therapist instead of each other to keep emotional reactivity and anxiety in the sessions low (Walsh & McGraw, 2002).

Relationship Experiments

Relationship experiments are therapeutic homework assignments given by the therapist to family members to further assess dysfunctional relationships (e.g., emotional cutoffs, fusion) and then geared toward altering these relationships. Process questions are used to ascertain repetitive patterns of relating and to track the direction and intensity of the relationship. When the pattern of the relationship is better understood by the therapist, then the relationship experiment or homework assignment is developed to correct the dysfunctional relationship. Family members are then told to exert as much effort as possible to accomplish the homework task and to observe their own internal emotional reaction to the experiment, as well as the impact of the relationship experiment on their behavior.

The "I" Position

In family therapy there is always pressure exerted upon the therapist to agree with or take sides with one party or another. Taking an *"I" position* entails more than achieving a state of neutrality and de-triangulation from dyads within the family. It involves the therapist taking a stance (sometimes at the risk of becoming unpopular) with involved family members. The essence of the "I" position is to be able to communicate one's position to the family without implying criticism or becoming involved in an emotional debate on a particular issue.

When the level of anxiety in the family is high there is even more pressure upon the therapist to act in a certain way. Family members often come into therapy with expectations for therapist behavior; they want the therapist to agree with their view or perception of the problem. Situations may arise in which the therapist is forced to make a statement (especially when anxiety levels are intolerable). At this point it is necessary for the therapist to take an "I" position. An "I" position can be as simple as stating, "I'm listening to your words, but I don't agree with what you're saying" (Papero, 1990).

Taking an unpopular "I" position can have a positive impact on families, especially those members who also need to define self in relation to the family. The therapist defining his or her unique self by taking the "I" position is a good way to role model for other family members who are faced with the same pressures within the family. It may encourage a family member to also take an unpopular "I" position and allow that family member to see that disagreement with a position in the family does not have to lead to dysfunction or increased family upheaval. On the contrary, making one's position known can lead to clearer communication and problem solving within a family. This may be an eye-opening experience for families in which issues of disagreement are avoided as there seems to be no middle ground to an argument—family members either remain silent or have an all-out argument. (This pattern of nonresolution could be the result of a family rule or myth: "No one disagrees with Dad, or else there will be all-out war!")

Didactic Teaching

Therapists can help family members think more clearly and more objectively about their problems and their role in the multigenerational system by teaching the family about emotional systems (the tenets of the model; Walsh & McGraw, 2002). Families can rely on their cognitive (thinking or intellectual) processes rather than emotional (or irrational) processes in their attempts to understand family problems. *Didactic teaching* can serve as a calming function that helps family members become more rational (versus emotional) in their attempts to resolve highly charged family problems.

Role Playing

Role playing is an existential technique in which members of the family are encouraged to "act out" various scenarios in the family (emotional cutoffs, fusion, triangles, etc.) and are coached (by the therapist) to explore different behaviors or reactions that may help repair the dysfunction. Role playing can help diffuse tumultuous family situations by making them less threatening and can allow family members to experience the other side of problematic family interaction and/or allow family members to experiment with different (more functional) behaviors.

Role playing (much like letter writing and journaling) can be an essential method to help an individual family member "try out" what one has been learning in therapy in preparation for an in-person confrontation (Bowenian [family] conference).

Journaling

Journaling is simply a process of the client keeping a written account of his or her internal experiences in regard to family experiences. Journaling can also be a great way for the client to log his or her reactions to therapy and to ongoing interactions within the family. To this end the journal can be shared with the therapist to facilitate the therapeutic process or can be kept private. Journaling is a good way for the client to view his or her internal or emotional progress in therapy; also, like the techniques of letter writing and role playing, it can be a good preliminary exercise for the individual family member in preparation for the Bowenian conference.

Letter Writing

Letter writing is a technique wherein family members communicate via letters written to each other. These letters can be shared, or they may remain private. Letter writing is also a helpful technique in the case of a deceased or absent family member wherein the letter is not mailed but the process of writing the letter is discussed and debriefed in therapy. Letter writing can also be used in lieu of an in-person Bowenian conference wherein either the anxiety level is too high and/or the family member to whom the letter is written is not in therapy with the client. Like the other techniques of role playing, letter writing can be a helpful technique in preparation for the in-person Bowenian conference.

Coaching

Coaching frequently occurs with only one family member in a session but can be used when others are present. The coach functions more like a teacher or consultant helping the individual family member wade through the emotional maze and work toward solutions. The therapist uses this technique to help clients prepare for letter writing and role playing. The therapist as coach helps the client anticipate clinical issues that may arise in the interaction and help him or her think through resolution for avoiding these pitfalls and roadblocks. Coaching can be supportive, instructive, and/or interpretive.

Coaching is often the main technique used with an individual in family therapy as he or she goes about the task of constructing genograms, making discoveries, and preparing for the in-person Bowenian conference. The focus is primarily on the family of origin, and the responsibility of the effort lies primarily with the individual client and not the therapist. Sessions can be held at greater intervals as the individual family member processes family issues—often in preparation for an in-person Bowenian conference.

The Bowenian Conference

The *Bowenian conference* is the culmination of the therapy process wherein an individual in therapy is prepared to have an in-person, face-to-face interaction with another family member. This is a technique wherein emotional cutoffs, fusion, and triangles are addressed. The individual family member in therapy can have a Bowenian conference with one or more individual family members. This technique is especially helpful when the other family member is not in therapy, refuses to come to therapy, lives far away so that therapy is not practical, or does not want to be in therapy with the particular family member.

An individual family member prepares for the Bowenian conference by using the above-described techniques of role playing, journaling, and letter writing. The client is coached through these preliminary exercises and then is coached in preparation for the person-to-person conference. The Bowenian conference can occur over one or more face-to-face interactions, and the individual family member is debriefed after each interaction. This debriefing process may take several sessions to accomplish, and the preparation for the Bowenian conference may take months.

The desired goal for a Bowenian conference is for the client to be able to relay to the family member his or her concerns and resolutions. This is to say that the client is not sent into a Bowenian conference dependent on or at the mercy of the other family member. Rather, the client's measure for success is merely "having his or her say" and being heard. This may include the other family member being told how his or her behavior toward that family member may change but does not entail any suggestions or prescriptions for change for that family member. However, if the Bowenian conference is well received, the result may be the family member also wanting to change some aspect of his or her behavior or wanting to enter into a few therapy sessions with the client. However, it is imperative not to make the former a goal of the interaction lest the client set him- or herself up for disappointment.

CASE ILLUSTRATION

Step 1: Exploring the presenting problem: low self-esteem.	Jenny is a 37-year-old single-parent female referred to therapy for help with what she calls a "general sense of disarray." She goes on to state that she has not been happy with her job (she is college educated with a master's degree), but due to her sense of low self-esteem she states she has a difficult time making decisions and fears that she is incompetent. She has gone for career counseling, and it was agreed that she is more prone to public relations and marketing, but she fears the heavy competition in these fields.
Job dissatisfaction but fear of venturing out.	
High level of anxiety; **adaptiveness to stress—implications for level of self-differentiation**.	Jenny also complains of having a high level of generalized anxiety. In the last 6 months she has been ill with a string of minor illnesses (severe sinus problems, repeated ear infections, and some "female problems") and is concerned over her health and mortality to the point that sometimes she "feels incapacitated."
	In the past 6 months she has had several stressors: Her 6-year-old daughter had a tonsillectomy; she had minor surgery to resolve her female problems and changed jobs—she is in customer service but still feels underemployed.
Not happy with herself or relationships—daughter, men, her mother and grandmother.	In general Jenny does not feel happy with herself and does not feel competent in any area of her life. She feels as if there is a cloud hanging over her head and "just doesn't feel happy." She is unhappy in her relationships with men and feels that these relationships have been generally superficial and short term. She is also unhappy with her relationship with her 6-year-old daughter who is always saying things to her like "You won't hug me . . . you don't love me . . . you just want another child." Jenny reports that it is hard for her to discern whether these are manipulative attempts or a genuine outcry for needed attention. She admits to feeling guilty that the father is not in their life and tries to compensate for it, but she feels like "nothing is enough, and there is not much left of Jenny."
Multigenerational conflict.	Jenny lives in a multigenerational household with her mother and maternal grandmother. Upon investigation she acknowledges not being happy with these relationships either. She states that she is always striving to gain the approval of her mother and grandmother—but to no avail. She reports that they "bump heads" on everything from child rearing to a constant disapproval of the men in her life. She has a nagging feeling that they seem happiest when she is not dating.

	Jenny states that she has spent a lot of money on self-help books and has sought counseling before, but she did not feel that her previous therapist "took her seriously."
	I asked Jenny where she wanted to begin and she stated that she would like some resolution in her relationships (with her mother, grandmother, and daughter and the men that she dates).
Step 2: Working with the family to develop the family genogram. **Construction of genogram inside session and given as homework assignment.** **Step 3: Using systematic questions to gain information about family relationships.** **Family theme and multigenerational message that govern relationships with men.**	We began by constructing a genogram that revealed some very interesting trends. It appears that Jenny is the fourth generation of single-parent females on her mother's side. It appears that her great-grandmother had a very tumultuous marriage that ended when she discovered that her husband had "another family" living nearby. From that point on it appears that the women in Jenny's family developed a strong distrust of men; they have a family saying: "Men are like buses; don't worry about 'em as there is always another one coming." (Both her mother and grandmother are single parents and have never been married.)
Naming pattern; possible multigenerational family projection processes.	In discussing the circumstances around her daughter's birth, Jenny states that her mother and grandmother began to nag her about when she was going to have children when she turned 30 years old—despite the fact that she was single and not even seriously dating anyone. When Jenny reminded her mother and grandmother of this fact they would respond by saying, "Children will be with you forever; they are the most important thing in life." Jenny says it was as if she went into a trance and (unconsciously) began a process that would result in her pregnancy with her now 6-year-old daughter—who was named for her grandmother. (Jenny was named after her great-grandmother, Jennifer.)
Multigenerational transmission process.	Jenny describes the process of becoming pregnant as a rite of passage; she states that it was almost as if she conceived as a gift to her mother and grandmother. "There wasn't a moment's hesitation for the two of them," Jenny reports, in that they were immediately joyful upon hearing the news of her pregnancy. (Jenny disclosed to me, however, that she made three appointments for an abortion. She states she knew having a baby at this point and with this person wasn't right for her.)
Emotional cutoff with daughter.	This revelation helped Jenny make a connection between her mother and grandmother's pressure on her to bear children and the unconscious resentment that she harbored toward her daughter. She began to realize that she felt that "her job was done" when she "presented" her daughter to her mother and grandmother.

(Continued)

(Continued)

Family pattern; both mother and grandmother had difficulty in this area, which may operate to reinforce family theme of "all men are no good!"—their only worth is to give children.	Jenny's genogram also revealed only one significant relationship—a man she dated for 3 years in her 20s. After that time she had a string of short-term relationships with men who seemed more interested in philandering than building a serious relationship with her. In some ways Jenny feels as if she intentionally gets involved with unavailable or undesirable men—almost like she is trying to sabotage her own romantic relationships.
Step 4: Broadening the focus to larger family systems.	
Family theme reinforced by a series of dysfunctional relationships.	Jenny's genogram also revealed that her mother and grandmother were both mostly involved with what Jenny describes as "weak and passive men, womanizers, and weekend drinkers." Both mother and grandmother had been rejected by their fathers.
Sibling position: only child.	Jenny is an only child as her two younger siblings are deceased (a miscarriage and another died at 3½ weeks old). As a result Jenny feels that all her mother and grandmother's attention—"for better or for worse"—is directed at her. Even when her mother and grandmother are not getting along she always feels in the middle of things.
Transmission of problems onto the child (Jenny). Multigenerational triangle.	As Jenny continued to reflect on the similarities in her relationships with men and her mother's and grandmother's relationships with men she became more determined to explore other generational themes and patterns that existed in her relationship with her mother and grandmother. We spent the next few sessions exploring this area.
Coaching and process questions.	I helped Jenny explore the nature of her relationship with her mother and grandmother. I needed to be careful not to show any signs of disapproval or displeasure with her mother and grandmother as I asked her questions about these relationships.
Neutral position (of the therapist).	
Nuclear family emotional process.	Jenny reflects that, growing up, every decision she made was in reference to her grandmother (including the decision to go to college and live at home). She states that it became difficult for her to make decisions without her grandmother and feels that this limits her ability to make decisions even today. Jenny reflects that she felt guilty whenever she exercised independence. (Jenny reports that her grandmother would pout and "needle" the mother if Jenny made decisions independent of their input. Jenny reports that there was a time that her grandmother would pace the floor if she stayed out even 2 hours when her daughter was first born.)
Level of differentiation is low.	
Jenny needs to take an "I" position on important matters in her life (e.g., child rearing, job changes, relationships with men).	
Interlocking triangles.	
Fusion.	

Nuclear family emotional process.	Jenny feels as though she "belongs" to her grandmother and has to be available to her to make up for the losses that the grandmother has experienced in life, almost in repayment to her mother and grandmother.
Therapist role as facilitator and consultant.	Jenny began to become more focused on what issues she wanted to work on: (a) She wanted to move to a better neighborhood with a better school system for her daughter; (b) she wanted to retool for a job that she could be more invested in; (c) she wanted to work on her self-esteem issues; (d, e, and f) she wanted to work on her relationships with her daughter, mother, and grandmother; and (g) she wanted help with her negative attitudes toward men.
Step 5: Giving feedback to clients.	I encouraged Jenny in the pursuit of all of these goals and decided that she could work independently on the first two goals; she needed no help—only encouragement from me in this regard.
Goals of therapy: (a) reduce emotional reactivity to mother and grandmother; (b) increase level of self-differentiation; (c) de-triangulate from mother and grandmother; and (d) repair emotional cutoff with daughter.	I also told Jenny that as I saw it many of her goals were intertwined with each other and that she will find that working toward one goal will undoubtedly help her make progress toward the other. I told her that I saw her self-esteem issues as being related to her relationships with her mother and grandmother as well as her negative view toward men.
Step 6: Using techniques to facilitate changes.	We agreed that we would work on her issues with her mother and grandmother, while she also worked on improving her relationship with her daughter. Then we would see where she was in terms of her attitudes toward men.
Relationship experiment technique. **Journaling.**	I began by giving her various homework assignments in reference to her relationship with her daughter, which included her planning a weekly outing with her daughter and simultaneously beginning to notice (log) when her daughter would offer complaints about the lack of attention and her own responses to her daughter's pleas.
	Jenny was seen for a total of 9 months—weekly at first and then biweekly for the last 2 months.
Bowenian family conference.	Jenny's therapy was to culminate with her moving out of the house and having a talk with her mother and grandmother about how she sees herself differently from them and the direction of her own life.

(Continued)

(Continued)

Impact of emotional triangles and family projection processes. **Differentiation of self.**	Continued exploration of multigenerational trends and family themes helped Jenny better understand several issues: • Her resentment toward her daughter, which results in lack of affection and attention toward her • Her negative attitude toward men—which is essentially her identification with her mother and grandmother • Her need to separate herself somewhat from the mother and grandmother so that she can better understand herself emotionally in terms of who she really is and what she really wants • Her difficulty making decisions and high level of generalized anxiety
Jenny participated in a series of role plays and letters written to her father to express her sorrow for him leaving the family and his feeling pushed out of the home (she chose not to mail this letter).	Jenny began her preparation for her Bowenian conference as she was feeling more confident in her ability to make progress with her relationships with her newfound knowledge and understanding.
Bowenian family conference. **Taking the "I" position with her mother and grandmother.** **Role of therapist as coach, facilitator, and expert.**	Jenny began a series of talks with her mother and grandmother, and each time we debriefed her and gave her support and encouragement and helped her with her newfound insights about the impact of her relationships with her mother and grandmother.
Repairing emotional cutoff (with daughter). **Increased self-differentiation.**	Jenny's therapy ended when she felt that she had made good progress with her daughter and held a series of "talks" with her mother and grandmother.
De-triangulation (from mother and grandmother).	She eventually moved out on her own and says that she is now more open to dating and entering a serious relationship with a man. She also is considering going back to school for another master's to pursue a marketing career.

SUMMARY

Murray Bowen is the founder of the intergenerational approach to families. Bowen's work grew out of his clinical research with schizophrenics and their families. His family systems therapy approach tracks the family through time and space. The focus of his interventions is the influence of one's family of origin on current family functioning. Bowen's work with families focused upon unresolved emotional issues within the family of origin. He believed that symptoms among family members reflect unresolved issues in the family of origin and continue to appear in later generations.

Bowen saw the family as an emotionally interdependent unit and that change in one part of the system will effect change in another part of the system. Bowen also believed that families exert pressure to conform and will pressure their members to maintain the status quo—even if that status quo is a dysfunctional state. Furthermore, these same family systems will operate to repeat dysfunctional behaviors over several generations within the family.

A key element in understanding family functioning is observing the role of anxiety in family functioning. This anxiety creates turmoil within the family; chronic anxiety is ever present within such families, and these feeling states can pass between and among family members with great speed. This anxiety can operate to override the cognitive (rational) system of the individual, and behavior can become increasingly emotional and automatic. Bowen used the term *emotional reactivity* to refer to such strong automatic responses. When anxiety pervades a family there is more of a tendency toward togetherness, and family members begin to think and act as if they are responsible for each other's happiness, comfort, and overall well-being.

Bowen offered eight interlocking concepts to explain the emotional processes of the nuclear and extended family. These concepts are triangles, nuclear family emotional process, family projection process, multigenerational transmission process, differentiation of self, sibling position, emotional cutoff, and emotional processes in society. These eight concepts represent the cornerstone of Bowen's theoretical approach to families. The first six concepts describe emotional processes that take place in the nuclear and the extended family, and the last two concepts describe emotional processes across generations in a family and in society.

The therapeutic focus of Bowen's approach is to gather data and make assessments using the eight concepts outlined above. The goals of therapy are (a) to reduce emotional reactivity in the family among its members (a reduction of anxiety is thought to reduce symptoms), (b) to increase the level of self-differentiation of family members (to improve adaptiveness), and (c) to modify the relationships in the family system by the de-triangulation of major family triangles (to form person-to-person relationships with as many members as possible in the family of origin) and by repairing cutoffs within the family (and working to resolve unfinished business with the family of origin). Another important goal of Bowen therapy is for the therapist to remain neutral in his approach and not get caught up in the emotional field of the family. The role of the Bowenian therapist is that of coach, researcher, teacher, and expert in family systems.

Assessment is actually a major part of the change process in Bowen family systems therapy, and the client takes major responsibility for assessment through a tool called the genogram. The genogram is a technique for gathering and organizing several generations of family history in order to objectify the family's emotional system. The data gathered in the genogram and in the family evaluation interview are the basis for the therapeutic focus.

The Bowen family systems approach offers a wonderful way in which to explore the impact of our family of origin on current functioning. This approach helps us understand the relationship between current behaviors and past generations. Communication patterns, attitudes, and behaviors are all impacted by multigenerational influences, and Bowen's approach to families is an efficient way to systematically study and intervene on these transgenerational processes.

RECOMMENDED READINGS

Bowen, M. (1978). *Family therapy in clinical practice.* New York, NY: Jason Aronson.

Guerin, P. J., Fogarty, T. F., Fay, L. E., & Kautto, J. G. (1996). *Working with relationship triangles: The one-two-three of psychotherapy.* New York, NY: Guilford.

Kerr, M. E., & Bowen, M. (1988). *Family evaluation: An approach based on Bowen theory.* New York, NY: Norton.

Papero, D. V. (1990). *Bowen family systems theory.* Boston, MA: Allyn & Bacon.

DISCUSSION QUESTIONS

1. What is the cornerstone of Bowen family therapy? Describe these philosophical and conceptual beliefs and how they influence this family therapy approach.

2. Why is assessment so essential to this therapy?

3. Discuss the importance of the family of origin issues of the therapist in a Bowenian approach.

REFERENCES

Bowen, M. (1966). The use of theory in clinical practice. *American Journal of Orthopsychiatry, 1*(1), 40–60.

Bowen, M. (1971). Family therapy and family group therapy. In H. Kaplan & B. Saddock (Eds.), *Comprehensive group psychotherapy* (pp. 384–421). Baltimore, MD: Williams & Wilkins.

Bowen, M. (1976). *Theory in the practice of psychotherapy.* In P. J. Guerin (Ed.), *Family therapy: Theory and practice* (pp. 42–90). New York, NY: Gardner Press.

Bowen, M. (1978). *Family therapy in clinical practice.* New York, NY: Jason Aronson.

Fogarty, T. F. (1976). *Systems concepts and dimensions of self.* In P. J. Guerin (Ed.), *Family therapy: Theory and practice.* New York, NY: Gardner Press.

Friedman, E. (1991). Bowen theory and therapy. In A. S. Gurman & D. P. Kniskern (Eds.), *Handbook of family therapy* (Vol. II). New York, NY: Brunner/Mazel.

Guerin, P. J., Fay, L., Burden, S., & Kautto, J. (1987). *The evaluation and treatment of marital conflict: A four stage approach.* New York, NY: Basic Books.

Jackson, D. D. (1957). The question of family homeostasis. *Psychiatry, Quarterly Supplement* 31, 79–90.

Kerr, M. E., & Bowen, M. (1988). *Family evaluation: An approach based on Bowen theory.* New York, NY: Norton.

Lidz, T., Cornelison, A., Fleck, S., & Terry, D. (1957). The intrafamilial environment of schizophrenic patients. *American Journal of Psychiatry, 64*(9), 241–148.

Papero, D. V. (1990). *Bowen family systems theory.* Boston, MA: Allyn & Bacon.

Papero, D. V. (1995). Bowen's family systems and marriage. In N. S. Jacobson & A. S Gurman (Eds.), *Clinical handbook of couple therapy* (pp. 11–30). New York, NY: Guilford.

Toman, W. (1961). *Family constellation: A psychological game.* New York, NY: Springer.

Walsh, W. (1980). *A primer of family therapy.* New York, NY: Springer.

Walsh, W. M., & McGraw, J. A. (2002). *Essentials of family therapy.* Denver, CO: Love.

Wylie, M. S. (1991). Family therapy's neglected prophet. *The Family Therapy Networker, 15*(2), 24–37.

Wynne, L. C., Ryckoff, I. M., & Hersch, S. I. (1958). Pseudomutuality in the family relations of schizophrenics. *Psychiatry, 21*(5), 205–220.

Chapter 6

STRUCTURAL FAMILY THERAPY

BACKGROUND AND LEADING FIGURES

Salvador Minuchin, born in Argentina, is the figure most closely identified with structural family therapy. Minuchin's family background and professional experiences greatly influenced his approach to families. Minuchin was born of European immigrant parents and reared in a huge extended family of more than 200 cousins, which gave him a great appreciation for the social context in which human beings function. Minuchin's sense of social justice was evident early on with his volunteer work with families in Israel in 1948 during the war as an army doctor for a year and a half (he was originally trained as a pediatrician). His dedication to social justice also manifested itself in his development of a therapy approach for low-income and minority families through the Wiltwyck School for Boys in New York and in his involvement with the Philadelphia Child Guidance Clinic.

Photo 6.1 Salvador Minuchin's passion for social justice was evident in his work as the director of the Philadelphia Child Guidance Clinic, which is one of the largest facilities of its kind that provide services for poor and low-income families

Source: © The Minuchin Center

Minuchin received his training as a psychiatrist in the United States under Nathan Ackerman. In 1954 Minuchin began his training as a psychoanalyst at the William Alanson White Institute and then began his work as a psychiatrist in New York at Wiltwyck, a residential school for delinquent adolescents. In 1959 Minuchin began to examine the families of low-income African American and Puerto Rican children. Minuchin discovered that these families often had multiple problems and disconnected family structures. It was then that, under the influence of Don Jackson, Minuchin began developing his theories and techniques for working with these "underorganized" families. Minuchin was especially cognizant of the influence of poverty on family functioning and began to develop special therapeutic techniques for changing the family context rather than focusing on the individual adolescent.

In 1965 Minuchin became the director of training at the Philadelphia Child Guidance Clinic, where he remained until 1981. He recruited social workers Braulio Montalvo and Jay Haley to work with him. In 1981 he founded a small group named Family Studies (now renamed the Minuchin Center for the Family) where he continued his work with poor families until his retirement in 1996. Over the years Minuchin worked with other clinicians who also influenced the development of his theories and techniques, such as Braulio Montalvo, Harry Aponte, Charles Fishman, Marianne Walters, Marion Lindblad-Goldberg, and Carter Umbarger.

Minuchin is best known for his work with and development of the Philadelphia Child Guidance Clinic as one of the largest facilities of its kind that serviced poor and low-income families. It was there that Minuchin published *Families and Family Therapy* (1974), which is an elaboration of theories for changing families through structural family therapy. However, the groundwork for structural family therapy was laid while Minuchin was at the Wiltwyck School where he developed action-oriented techniques for working with poor, disadvantaged families. Minuchin saw the need for family reorganization and for a more effective hierarchy between children and their parents, which was described in *Families of the Slums* (Minuchin,

Photo 6.2   Dr. Harry Aponte is one of the therapists that influenced the development of Structural Family Therapy. He continues his work with people of diverse ethnic, cultural, and socioeconomic backgrounds

Source: © Dr. Harry J. Aponte

Montalvo, Guerny, Rosman, & Schumer, 1967)—by far Minuchin's most impressive and groundbreaking work.

It was Minuchin's experience with diverse cultures in a variety of settings that led to his frustration with traditional psychoanalytical therapy. Minuchin saw the need for a more practical, direct, and problem-oriented family approach. In his early years at the Philadelphia Child Guidance Clinic, Minuchin began to collect research on children with psychosomatic conditions such as diabetes, asthma, and anorexia (Minuchin, Rosman, & Baker, 1978). Minuchin turned his attention to the role of family context in psychosomatic conditions. Minuchin's data began to indicate that the locus of pathology was in the context of the family, and not simply the afflicted individual. Minuchin's clinical data also indicated that psychosomatic families tend to be overprotective—stifling the child's independence and negatively impacting the confidence and competence of the child. Minuchin theorized that stress overloads the already dysfunctional family's coping mechanism and that the illness serves as a regulating function of the family system (i.e., the sick child acts as the diffuser of family conflict by diverting family attention away from family conflict). Minuchin and his colleagues developed ways to change the family context rather than directing their effort at changing the adolescent with behavioral or psychosomatic problems. It was Minuchin's success with anorexic families that drew many family therapists to the structural model wherein the structure of relationships within the family are changed.

PHILOSOPHICAL, CONCEPTUAL, AND THEORETICAL UNDERPINNINGS

Minuchin believed that an individual's symptoms are best understood in the context of the family. The family's transactional patterns must change, and that change cannot take place unless there is change in the underlying family organization or structure. Symptoms will be reduced when the therapist provides leadership in changing the structure or context in which the symptom is embedded. Minuchin postulated that once the family's structure has been changed, the positions of its members altered, it is then that each person will experience change as a result.

Minuchin saw the family as an integrated whole—a system made up of subsystems (spousal or conjugal, parental, and sibling) in which members also are a part of larger systems (community, schools, agencies) that impact its basic structure and organization. Family transactions make up the family structure and determine how each member relates to the others. A child who misbehaves in school needs *both* parents to be supportive of school efforts to remedy the situation. Structural family therapy acknowledges that the overall organization of a family can either maintain the child's acting-out behavior or operate to help reduce symptoms. The school's attempt to discipline the child will surely fail unless the family structure (both parents working with the school) is addressed. If the parents are working against each other—let's say they are too angry with each other to work in concert and the child is caught in the middle of their dispute—they fail to create an adequate boundary around their relationship. The child will suffer as they will not be able to work as a team to address the child's problem at school.

Functional and dysfunctional families are determined by the adequacy of the fit of the family's structural organization with the environmental context. A functional family is characterized by transactions that serve to meet the needs of the individuals in the family and the family unit as a whole. Typically, functional families are characterized by structures that are adaptable and well defined (Walsh & McGraw, 2002).

Dysfunctional families experience "system overload" in that the stressors associated with either environmental and/or developmental demands operate as a stressor that overloads the system in that the family's adaptive and coping mechanisms do not adequately meet the changing needs facing the family as a system. As a reaction to these (environmental and/or developmental) demands the family does not modify its structure. Rather, the family system becomes more rigid as a reaction to the stressor. The family's rigidity and inability to complete the necessary developmental task can result in dysfunction. Typically, one family member (the "identified patient") will manifest the symptom for the family and subsequently serve as a safety valve for the family by expressing system dysfunction (Friesen, 1985).

Minuchin (1974) talks about how the family has undergone changes that parallel society's changes, and he also discusses how modern urban industrial society has intruded forcefully on the family, taking over many functions that were once considered the family's duties. This has resulted in a blurring of boundaries between society and family, which once were clearly delineated. As families accommodate to society, they are changing with it. As a result, families' roles and functions are not as clear as they once were—the boundaries have moved.

Minuchin (1974) further theorizes that the family is an open system in transformation, that it constantly receives and sends inputs to and from the extrafamilial, and that it adapts to the different demands of the developmental stages it faces. As a family moves through different developmental stages it requires restructuring as a response to sociocultural transformation. The family then adapts to changed circumstances so as to maintain continuity and enhance the psychosocial growth of each member.

There are three key concepts underlying structural family therapy: *family structure*, *family subsystems*, and *boundaries*. We will discuss each of these concepts in turn.

Family Structure

Family structure is the invisible set of functional demands that organize the ways in which family members interact. A family is a system that operates through transactional patterns. Repeated transactions establish patterns of how, when, and to whom to relate, and these patterns underpin the system (Minuchin, 1974). When a mother gives a child a demand and he complies, this interaction defines who she is in relation to him and who he is in relation to her, in that context at that time. Repeated transactions of this kind constitute a transactional pattern. These transactions also regulate behavior in two ways: A power hierarchy exists, which dictates the authority and decision making in the family, and mutual expectations formed by negotiations over time are determined and fulfilled by individuals in the family (Walsh & McGraw, 2002).

Transactional patterns regulate family members' behavior and are maintained by two systems of constraint. The first of these is generic to all families and involves the universal rules governing family organization in that there must be a power hierarchy in which parents and children have different levels of authority and the parents operate interdependently as a team.

The second system of constraint is idiosyncratic and involves the mutual expectations of particular family members. These mutual expectations are derived from years of explicit and implicit negotiations among family members, often around small daily events. The nature of the original contracts is often forgotten and may have never been made explicit, but the pattern remains on automatic pilot and is a matter of mutual accommodation and functional effectiveness.

Thus there is a homeostasis—the system maintains itself. In fact the family will become resistant to change beyond a certain range and will maintain its own equilibrium as long as possible. When the family's equilibrium is upset (either due to family or individual developmental changes or through external or extrafamilial situations) alternative patterns of behavior within the family are available, but when behaviors are needed to go beyond the family's threshold of tolerance, dysfunction within the family may occur.

Minuchin (1974) theorizes that the continued existence of the family as a system depends on a sufficient range of patterns, the availability of alternative transactional patterns, and the flexibility to mobilize them when needed. In essence the family must respond to internal and external changes and be able to transform itself in new ways that meet new circumstances without losing the continuity that provides stability for its members.

Family Subsystems

The family system carries out its function through subsystems. Each individual belongs to a subsystem, and one individual may belong to two subsystems. For instance a wife is a part of the spousal/conjugal/marital subsystem or dyad, but she is also a part of the parental subsystem. Conversely a former spouse, who does not live in the household, is not a part of the conjugal dyad or subsystem but is a part of the parental subsystem—even along with the current spouse (or stepparent).

Subsystems can be formed by generation, by sex, by interest, or by function. The three main subsystems within families are the spousal or conjugal subsystem (or dyad), the parental subsystem, and the sibling subsystem. Each subsystem has different levels of power, with the parental subsystem having executive control over the children.

1. Spousal Subsystem

Sometimes termed the *conjugal* or *marital subsystem* is the component in which two adult significant others come together whose responsibility it is to rear the children and to teach them about intimacy and commitment.

The couple must develop patterns in which each spouse supports the other. The spouses must develop patterns of complementarity in which there is negotiation between the two. Both partners must yield part of their separateness and develop a mutual interdependence in a symmetrical relationship. They must learn to accommodate and meet the needs of each other.

Negotiation and accommodation are key aspects of a functional spousal subsystem. Gender rules and roles must be worked out in the early part of the relationship. Couples must decide on a division of labor that best suits their own skill sets and needs. These roles may shift and change as each individual evolves and goes through various developmental stages. Emphasis should always be placed on complementarity.

Each spouse should be supportive of the other in terms of individual interests, talents, and needs. Neither spouse should be totally accommodating, or both risk losing their own individuality. There is give and take on both sides.

2. Parental Subsystem

The parental subsystem typically consists of the parents but may also include former spouses, stepparents, and extended family (e.g., grandparents). The parental subsystem has the major responsibility of child rearing, setting rules, and enforcing regulations and discipline.

The spousal subsystem must now perform the tasks of socializing a child without losing the mutual support that should characterize the spousal subsystem. A boundary must be drawn around the spousal subsystem that allows the child access to both parents while excluding him from spousal functions.

As children grow, their developmental demands for both autonomy and guidance impose demands on the parental subsystem, which must be modified to meet them (Minuchin, 1974). The parental subsystem must adapt in order to cope with environmental stressors that present new tasks of socialization. If a child is stressed by extrafamilial situations, this can affect not only his or her relationship with his or her parents but also internal transactions of the spousal subsystem.

Our fast-paced society has imposed new challenges on the parental subsystem. The generation gap grows wider by the minute. Minuchin (1974) eloquently elaborates:

> The unquestioned authority that once characterized the patriarchal model of the parental subsystem has faded, to be replaced by a concept of flexible, rational authority. Parents are expected to understand children's developmental needs and to explain the rules they impose. Parenting is an extremely difficult process . . . no one goes through the process unscathed. (pp. 57–58)

The parenting process differs depending on the age of the child; when children are young, nurturing functions predominate—control and guidance take on more importance later in their development. As the child grows older the demands of the parents may conflict with the child's need for age-appropriate autonomy—especially during adolescence. Parenting becomes a process of mutual accommodation. Parents are faced with imposing rules that they cannot fully explain or are not fully accepted by the adolescent.

Minuchin believed that parents must protect and guide and at the same time control and restrict their children's behavior. He also believed that children cannot grow and become individuated without rejecting and attacking. In essence the process of the socialization of children is inherently conflictual. Furthermore Minuchin (1974) unequivocally states that parenting requires the use of authority and that parents cannot carry out their executive function unless they have the power to do so.

3. Sibling Subsystem

The sibling subsystem includes the children in a family. This subsystem is the first peer group for the child, wherein the child learns the process of negotiation, cooperation, competition, mutual support, and attachment (Walsh & McGraw, 2002). As children move out into the world they attempt to interact as if they were in their sibling subsystem. Eventually they learn new ways of interacting, and they bring this new knowledge back into the sibling world. However, if the child's family and social system operate on very different terms, the child may have difficulty entering other social systems; alternately these disparate worlds may collide and conflict, putting the child in a precarious position.

The significance of the sibling subsystem is seen most clearly in the case of only children. Only children learn to accommodate to the outside world very quickly. However, they may also experience difficulty in their ability to share, cooperate, and compete with others.

Boundaries

Boundaries refer to the arrangement both between subsystems and with systems outside of the family. Boundaries of a subsystem are the rules defining who participates in the subsystem and how the individuals participate. The function of boundaries is to protect the integrity (differentiation) of the subsystem in that every subsystem has different functions and makes specific demands on its members to prevent interference from other subsystems. For instance, a mother places the eldest child in charge while she goes to the store and tells the child that he is in charge *until* she gets back from the store. This message establishes the boundaries of who is in charge and when, making it clear to all that their authority is temporary and circumstantial and not a blanket invitation to become part of the parental subsystem.

Boundaries within a family can vary in their flexibility or *permeability*. The degree of flexibility or permeability impacts the nature and frequency of contact between family members. Minuchin described three types of boundaries: *clear* or *permeable*, *diffuse*, and *rigid*. We will describe each of these types of boundaries in turn.

1. Clear Boundaries

Clear boundaries promote open communication between family members. Clear boundaries are firm yet flexible wherein members of a family have open communication with one another and are supported and nurtured. Clear boundaries also allow access across subsystems to negotiate and accommodate external and developmental challenges. However, members of a family are not allowed to become members of these subsystems as they interact.

Clear boundaries also operate to increase frequency of communication between subsystems in order to facilitate change by encouraging negotiation and accommodation across subsystems. The autonomy of members and the integrity of the subsystems are not sacrificed as support is given to family members. Clear boundaries become important elements of a family system as members face developmental changes and environmental challenges, and as such the family is in a better position to make necessary structural changes.

2. Diffuse Boundaries

Families with diffuse boundaries have subsystems that are poorly defined in that the lines of authority are not clear and family members may be overinvolved with each other. There is a lack of privacy among members. Diffuse boundaries are the opposite of rigid boundaries. There is too much accommodation and negotiation. The parents are too accessible, and the necessary distinction between the subsystems is not there.

There is no clear generational boundary, and typically parents are overinvolved with their children and the children are overinvolved with their parents. Parental overinvolvement puts children at risk of becoming too dependent on parents, which may prevent them from developing the necessary skills needed in developing relationships outside of the family. In essence the parents do too much for the children and may later impair the child's judgment when it is time for the child to individuate from the family.

A child's overinvolvement with either the spousal or parental subsystem can be developmentally confusing and put the child at risk of becoming a "parentified child." That is, children who are allowed too much access to their parents often function in the role of a parent with their own siblings—to their own detriment. The developing child may experience a loss of independence and autonomy.

3. Rigid Boundaries

In families where there are rigid or inflexible boundaries there is minimal interaction and communication between the subsystems. Individual family members are isolated and often operate autonomously within and between the various subsystems. In these families, parents are slow to notice or respond to children when support is needed. As a result members in these families may learn to rely on outsiders for support and nurturance. This sense of independence may come with a price of feeling isolated and uncared for.

Families that have rigid boundaries are closed systems with minimal contact with outside systems. As a result the family system is not able to have the healthy exchange of information necessary for a family to function in the larger society. Families with rigid boundaries tend to shy away from interaction with important agencies and institutions. There is an insular characteristic to how much the family interacts with the outside world, although an individual family member—in desperation—may reach outside the family for support. This may not result in a favorable response from the family in that the family may have strict rules about being "influenced" by outsiders. Hence, the individual reaching out may exacerbate the presenting problem.

OTHER THEORIES AND CONCEPTS

Structural family therapy classifies pathology into four (overlapping) forms. The four general forms of pathology are pathology of boundaries, pathology of alliances, pathology of triads, and pathology of hierarchy. We will discuss each of these four forms of pathology in turn.

Pathology of Boundaries

Subsystem boundaries that are diffuse or too permeable (too easily and frequently crossed) are considered *enmeshed*. That is, diffuse boundaries are characterized by enmeshed relationships. In enmeshed families the boundaries are weak and poorly differentiated. There is an extreme form of proximity in which family members are overly involved with each other. There is also an intensity of interaction that may interfere with self-development. Members of an enmeshed family often possess an extreme form of family cohesiveness and loyalty. Belonging to the family can dominate all other experiences—to the detriment of its members. Enmeshment is common in psychosomatic families.

There is reverberation throughout the system, wherein an incident that impacts one member or subsystem of the family consequently impacts the rest of the family or subsystems and dyads to the same degree. For instance, if parents become worried about finances, subsequently the children are not protected and equally share in the worry over family finances; this is to say that all members of the family are equally impacted—regardless of the appropriateness of such. There is a lack of separateness between and among family members.

Subsystem boundaries that are too rigid (difficult if not impossible to cross) are considered to be *disengaged*. That is, rigid boundaries are characterized by disengaged relationships. In disengaged families there is little sense of "family," and generally very little support is offered or given. People come and go in the household as if they are separate entities. Members of a disengaged family may function autonomously but have a skewed sense of independence and lack feelings of loyalty and belonging. Minuchin (1974) eloquently illustrates this point by explaining that in an enmeshed family, parents may fret over why a child does not eat dessert; however, in a disengaged family the parents may not even be aware if the child has had dinner.

Members of disengaged families often seek support from outside the family as family members are typically too self-involved to be available to each other. Communication is very limited in disengaged families and is often strained or guarded with very little affection shown between family members. However, the family system in disengaged families is relatively isolated from its environment.

Only a high level of individual stress can reverberate strongly enough to activate the family's supportive function or cause a family to seek help from outside sources (Minuchin, 1974).

Pathology of Alliances

Healthy intrafamilial relationships can be formed based on common interests, age, or gender; these relationships are referred to as *alliances*. Whereby an alliance is a positive affinity between two family members its function is supportive and not conflict based. However, when an alliance stands in opposition to another part of the system, then it becomes a *coalition*. A coalition generally involves several family members in which there is a combative, exclusionary, or scapegoating stance toward a third party. Hence when members of different generations of a family join together against a third member, this inappropriate coalition is referred to as a *cross-generational coalition*. For example, a mother and son join together to criticize a father for his actions. The more appropriate response would be for the mother to listen to the child's complaint without comment and then privately take the issue to the father and deal with it in the spousal dyad.

Minuchin (1974) states that there must be clearly defined generational boundaries so that parents can band together for a united front, especially on key issues such as discipline. This measure is necessary to prevent children from taking over the executive function of the parenting role.

Pathology of Triads

Dysfunctional alignments are called *triads,* whereby each parent attempts to get the child to align with him or her against the other parent (Minuchin, 1974). When a parent uses a child to detour or deflect spousal conflict the boundary between parent and child will become diffuse. This unstable family arrangement is a no-win situation for the entire family, whereby regardless of whom the child sides with everyone loses. Dysfunction in the sibling subsystem will certainly occur if a member of the parental subsystem attempts to resolve subsystem conflicts outside of the parental or spousal subsystem.

Pathology of Hierarchy

When the functional decision-making hierarchy does not consist of both parents (in a two-parent household), or when a child is allowed to become part of this hierarchy, this causes a power imbalance and is referred to as an *inverted hierarchy*. As well when the children yield more power over family rules, regulations, and discipline a hierarchical imbalance ensues. Weak and ineffective hierarchies wherein the parents are not in executive control will inevitably create power struggles and cause a lack of guidance for the children, thus impairing the growth of the children in the family. Structuralists feel it is imperative that the parents maintain executive control within the family, as this is necessary for a family's stability.

STRUCTURAL MAPPING

Structural family therapists often complete family maps or family diagrams of the relationships in the family. Much like Bowen has symbols that he uses in the genogram, structuralists map out or diagram the structure of familial relationships. These symbols are used to illustrate concepts and theories discussed above, such as (closed, rigid, clear/permeable, diffuse) boundaries, alliances, coalitions, and hierarchies (see Figures 6.1–6.5).

Figure 6.1 Key Symbols for Structural Mapping

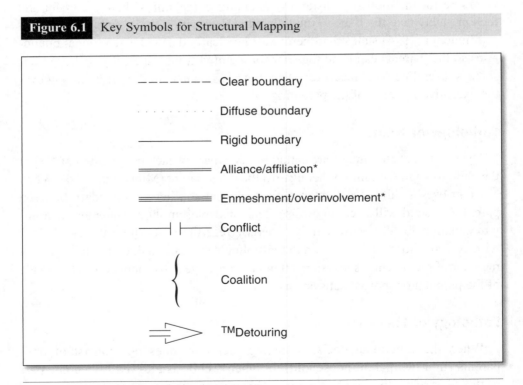

Source: Adapted from Minuchin (1974, p. 53).

| Figure 6.2 | The Map for a Healthy, Functional Two-Parent Family, With Clear Boundaries Between the Executive Subsystem and the Sibling Subsystem |

```
              M    F          (executive role)
              _____
              Children       (sibling subsystem)
```

Source: Adapted from Minuchin (1974, p. 54).

| Figure 6.3 | A Map of a Stepfamily With the Noncustodial Biological Father Still Involved in the Executive Role |

```
      M      Stepfa       F      (executive role/parental subsystem)
      _____
             Children
```

Source: Adapted from Minuchin (1974, p. 53).

| Figure 6.4 | A Map of an Enmeshed/Overinvolved Relationship Between Mother and Son, With a Cross-Generational Coalition Against the Father, With Closed Boundaries Between the Sibling Subsystem and the Parental Subsystem, With the Son also Being in the Position of Executive Control With the Mother (hierarchical imbalance) |

```
              M ≡ Son   } F
              _____
                  Siblings
```

Source: Adapted from Minuchin (1974, p. 53).

Figure 6.5	A Map of a Family with Diffuse Boundaries, Wherein Mother and Father Have a Weak Relationship, Grandmother Has an Enmeshed/Overinvolved Relationship With the Mother, and the Father is in Conflict With the Grandmother. But There Are Open Boundaries Between the Sibling Subsystem and the Parental Subsystem

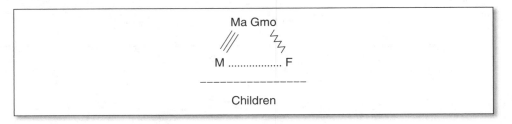

Source: Adapted from Minuchin (1974, p. 53).

GOALS OF THERAPY

Structuralists believe that family problems are maintained by dysfunctional family organization; hence the underlying family structure needs to be changed in order to solve presenting problems. A structural diagnosis of the family helps determine the smaller goals as they pertain to the specific stage of the therapeutic process (e.g., the process of "joining" in the early stages of structural family therapy—to be described later in the chapter). Attainment of the smaller goals (e.g., *boundary making* or *staging*—the process by which the therapist modifies transactional patterns to reinforce appropriate boundaries and disperse inappropriate boundaries) operates to change the underlying family structure. For instance, a "parentified child" no longer is allowed to perform as a parent in a family, boundaries are strengthened, and the child or adolescent is delegated back to the sibling subsystem.

Structural family therapists are concerned primarily with how components of the system interact, how homeostasis is obtained, how dysfunctional communication patterns develop and are sustained, and so forth. They focus particularly on transactional patterns such as the existence of alignments or coalitions, the formation of subsystems, and the permeability of their boundaries.

Structural family therapists view change occurring in a family as a process that involves three objectives: (a) to challenge the prevailing homeostatic norms; (b) to introduce crisis and flux in the system, which will position members to behave and feel differently about themselves and each other; and (c) to develop new behavioral routines or sequences that make up the new system structures that are repeated over time. The movement toward change in a structure will include periods of flux and equilibrium. The length of each phase depends on the family's ability to bear conflict and change.

The overarching goal of structural family therapy is the creation of an effective parental hierarchy. Parents are to operate in the executive role; that is, they are to be in charge of the family. Furthermore, parents are to work together in the executive role—being sure not to be relegated to the sibling subsystem. In the case of single-parent families there may be a need for the oldest child to take on parental responsibility. In these instances it is important for the single parent to make it clear under what circumstances this eldest child is to be in charge—being careful not allow this child into the parental subsystem. This can be achieved by reinforcing boundaries of the parental subsystem by not giving carte blanche to the eldest child for having authority over his or her siblings. For example, when the single parent must be absent from the home the eldest is in charge. However, when the parent returns he or she takes charge over the children with the eldest relinquishing control and being relegated back to the sibling subsystem.

In summary, the primary goal of structural family therapy is to reorganize the family structure. Specific goals are:

1. To shift members' relative position to disrupt malfunctioning patterns

2. To strengthen parental hierarchy

3. To create clear, flexible boundaries

4. To mobilize more adaptive (alternative) patterns

5. To establish the spousal subsystem as a distinct entity from the parental subsystem

ROLE OF THE THERAPIST

The primary role of the structural therapist is to facilitate change in the overall structure of the family, by altering boundaries and realigning subsystems. In structural family therapy the therapist does not assume responsibility for change. Rather the therapist operates more in the role of "director" for change, facilitating change in the underlying structure of the family by "joining" with its members to activate dormant (more functional) structures that may have been previously utilized. Hence the therapist views the family problems as a dysfunctional reaction to a crisis or simply an ineffective reaction to changing environmental circumstances or changing developmental needs, which is to say that the family therapist does not view the family as inherently flawed.

The goals of therapy operate to define the role of the therapist with different families. That is, in the case of enmeshed (overly close) families the therapist's role

Photo 6.3   Structural family therapists stress the importance of the parental subsystem having (executive) control in order to maintain hierarchical balance of the family

Source: ©iStockphoto.com/Slobo Mitic

is to strengthen boundaries around the various subsystems to allow for more differentiation between individual members. In the case of disengaged (overly distant) families, the therapist's goal is to facilitate increased interaction between family members—allowing more communication between the various subsystems. For example, parents become more accessible to (less distant from) their children.

Minuchin (1974) feels that a therapist should be able to know the developmental needs of the child and support the child's right to autonomy without minimizing the parents' rights. He further elaborates that the sibship boundaries should be protected from adult interference so that the children can experience privacy and have their own areas of interest. He also feels that it is the therapist's job to act as a translator, interpreting the children's world to the parents or vice versa (Minuchin, 1974). The overall goal is to help both subsystems (sibling and parental) develop clear but crossable boundaries with the extrafamilial.

The goals of therapy are achieved when the family structure allows for its members to interact with each other without interfering in the role and function of the various subsystems, thus redefining their relationships—even under stressful (environmental or developmental) circumstances. Rigid structures are discarded, and previously dysfunctional patterns of relating are eliminated. This may entail changes to individual members' relative positions (of distance or proximity) as well as hierarchical shifts—which may include the reinforcement of executive control in some families or increased flexibility in others. Boundaries are sufficiently clear to reflect separation yet are permeable and open enough to allow for needed interaction between various members.

In summary, therapists play many roles in structural family therapy:

- **Observer**—of family process, structure, and family interactional patterns (isomorphs)
- **Describer**—of dysfunctional sequences, helping provide descriptions of the roles that they play in the dysfunction
- **Director**—of family drama (creating an enactment—encouraging family members to re-create events that show family impasses)
- **Expert**—impressing the family with the gravity of the problem and showing knowledgeability
- **Educator**—providing simple educational instructions to correct dysfunctional behavioral sequences
- **Interpreter**—offering explanations about family problems
- **Reframer**—attending to a different facet of the multifaceted reality of any particular behavior

PROCESS OF THERAPY

Minchin viewed therapy as structural change that modifies the family's functioning so that the family can better perform in necessary tasks. As structural changes are made, these structural changes will be maintained by the family's self-regulating mechanism (Minuchin, 1974). Minuchin saw the family as a dynamic system in continual movement, with the steps in the therapeutic process overlapping and recycling in a "kaleidoscopic sequence" (Minuchin, 1974, p. 14).

There are four main strategies for establishing structural change in families (each phase is to be discussed separately in the chapter):

1. The therapist *joins* and *accommodates* the family system, taking on a leadership role—establishing trust with, showing respect for, and identifying with (understanding) the family.

2. The therapist makes a *structural diagnosis by assessing family interaction.* Family interactional patterns, family themes, and family myths are also identified.

3. The therapist challenges the symptom, the system, and the family's view of itself by *reframing* the presenting problem.

4. The therapist *makes structural changes* in the family subsystems and changes in the family's interactional patterns—thus changing various family relationships.

Joining and Accommodating

In order to effect (significant and underlying) change in the basic structure and interaction of a family the therapist must be accepted into the family system by gaining the trust of the family. This is in part achieved by identifying strengths within the family system and making these areas of competency known to the family—thus communicating respect for the family. The therapist also shows respect for how the family members operate and interact with each other by assimilating to (*accommodating*) the family's affective style. For example, with families that are more conservative and not very demonstrative the therapist accommodates the family's communicative style. Conversely, in the case of very expressive families, the therapist can be more demonstrative in his or her verbal and nonverbal communication. The therapist further adapts to the language pattern and interactive style of the family (without being condescending or phony).

The therapist further *joins* with the family by showing respect for how the family organizes itself by acknowledging coalitions and alignments between family members. The therapist also shows respect for the family hierarchy by asking the parents first their view of the presenting problem—being mindful of the most powerful member of the parental dyad—so as not to have the therapy process sabotaged and otherwise undermined.

Joining and accommodating efforts operate to build trust with the family and hence build an atmosphere that is conducive to client sharing of concerns and family vulnerabilities. When a family system feels more secure (with a given therapist) members are more likely to explore alternative ways of interacting and organizing themselves—thus potentially resolving family impasses and family problems. The goal of this stage is ultimately to create a more effective therapeutic relationship with the family.

Minuchin advocated for the therapist to bring his or her own personality into the therapeutic process to further the goals of therapy. Minuchin (1974) describes how he integrated the techniques of joining and accommodation into his own therapeutic style:

As a therapist I tend to act like a distant relative. I like to tell anecdotes about my own experiences and thinking, and to include things I have read or heard that are relevant to the particular family. I try to assimilate the family's language and to build metaphors using the family's language and myths. These methods telescope time, investing an encounter between strangers with the affect of an encounter between old acquaintances. They are accommodation techniques, which are vital to the process of joining. (p. 122)

Structural Diagnosis and Assessing Family Interaction

The therapist continues with the process of observation, hypothesis testing, and reformulations relevant to the family's structure and transactions (Walsh & McGraw, 2002). The goal in this stage is to develop a family map of the structure and interactions of the family. Structural maps (discussed previously) also illustrate pathology within boundaries, coalitions, and hierarchies. The therapist then develops a working hypothesis of the family structure based on the family map and family diagram. (The family map may also serve as an evaluative tool of the ongoing therapeutic process.) Structural diagnosis is achieved through the structural process of joining (Minuchin, 1974), in that Minuchin saw a structural diagnosis as an interactional and ongoing process. A structural diagnosis is based on data from six major areas (Walsh & McGraw, 2002):

1. The family structure, including its preferred transactional patterns and alternative patterns available.

2. The system's flexibility and its capacity for elaboration and restructuring (e.g., shifting coalitions and subsystems in response to changing circumstances).

3. The family system's resonance, reflecting its sensitivity to individual members' input. High sensitivity reflects an enmeshed system; low sensitivity reflects a disengaged system.

4. The family life context, including the sources of stress and support in the family's ecology.

5. The family's developmental stage and its performance of the tasks appropriate to that stage.

6. The identified patient's symptoms and the manner in which they are used to maintain the family's preferred transactional patterns.

Structural family therapy seeks to uncover additional information about the nature of the family's affiliations and coalitions, the nature of family conflict, and the ways in which family members typically resolve conflict. To this end, structural maps of the family are created to *highlight problem-maintaining interactions* within the family. Family members can begin to understand how their behaviors contribute to the presenting problem. The key is to achieve this without alienating the family and thus creating resistance within the family. It is important to get the family members to see that they are not the problem; rather the problem lies in the way the family tries to resolve it.

Challenging the Symptom and Reframing the Presenting Problem

Once the therapist has successfully joined with the family and established a good therapeutic relationship, the therapist challenges the symptom via a structurally focused exploration of the past. The therapist explores ways in which the symptom presents itself and pays attention to (structural and interactional) details. Structural family therapy is very action oriented, focusing on the here and now—although the discussion may be about what is going on outside of the session (Becvar & Becvar, 2000). Structural family therapists challenge the symptom by forcing the family to look at the systemic nature of the symptom. This may be achieved by a technique called *creating an enactment,* which refers to the creation of an event (family dynamics) in the therapy session by which significant transactions are highlighted. For instance, the parents may be asked to discuss their child's misbehavior in school—which may uncover interactional patterns, behavioral sequences, and/or structural obstacles to problem resolution. This technique allows the therapist to actually observe the problem firsthand. These firsthand observations may also be evident in what Minuchin called *spontaneous behavioral sequences*—firsthand observations of family transactions that occur as a natural part of family patterns. Both of these techniques allow for the therapist to make modifications in coalitions, alliances, boundary problems, and so on. The therapist may then challenge the (family) system—by rearranging seating or breaking up coalitions between members by purposefully asking a member to interact with another family member to restructure alliances. The therapist can then suggest alternative ways of relating to each other and/or alternative ways of approaching problem resolution.

Structural therapists also challenge the family's view of itself by looking at the problem from different perspectives. To this end the therapist asks the family to describe the symptom and the meaning of the symptom to the family—hoping that the symptom will be viewed in a new way that allows for problem resolution. This strategy may also entail the use of a technique called *reframing*. In reframing the therapist challenges the family's view of reality. The therapist, upon hearing the family's account of the presenting problem, then has the task of convincing the family members that reality as they have mapped it can be expanded or modified (Minuchin & Fishman, 1981). Reframing changes the meaning of the presenting problem in which other explanations are considered. The therapist helps give new meaning to the problem—meaning that allows for constructive resolution. Later in this chapter you will read in the Case Illustration about a family in which a 10-year-old African American male is about to be expelled from school for severe acting-out behavior (standing on top of desks, yelling at teachers, etc.). The family offers many hypotheses about this problem (hyperactivity, Black male racism in the school, and posttraumatic stress disorder—the boy was slapped in the face by his kindergarten teacher, and subsequently the parents pulled him out of school, home-schooling him for the next 3 years). Upon exploration of these hypotheses, the therapist decides to pose a question about how the boy feels about respect (for himself, the family, his teachers, and fellow students). You will read further in this Case Illustration how this intervention (reframing) helps the family see this problem in a different light, one that enables it to take some action toward problem resolution.

Making Structural Changes

Minuchin firmly believed that the therapist must be respectful and aware that he or she is entering a distinct system when conducting family therapy. This system is one that has established rules, roles, and self-regulating behaviors. He also warned therapists to go slowly and to attempt to become a part of that system (by joining) before attempting to change the (family) system. Once the therapist has gained entry into the family (system) Minuchin recommended that the therapist then begin to *probe for flexibility* in the system—that is, to search out areas in which the family is most amenable to change and start attempts at therapeutic change in those areas of the system.

Once the therapist has decided upon the initial area(s) to be changed in the family structure and interactional patterns—that is, once the therapist has a clear picture of what needs to be changed, what's keeping the family stuck, how it got that way, and who is willing to change (or not)—there are specific activities that the structural therapist might do in therapy:

- Realign boundaries by physically altering the proximity or distance between family subsystems. The therapist can accomplish this by meeting separately with subsystems or individuals in order to firmly establish or acknowledge boundaries.
- Help members of a disengaged family increase the frequency of contact between them.
- Help specific dyads resolve their own issues without intrusion from other members of the family—whether sibling to sibling, parent to parent, or parent to child. Such activities can be described as allowing each relationship to seek its own level.

- Teach aspects of structural theory to the family so the family can have its own cognitive way to understand better the goals and the interventions of the therapist.
- Change the way family members relate to one another so their perception of each other can change. Structural therapists believe that reality is only a perspective. The family members are acting on the validity of the perspective each has of the other. The therapist can also provide the family with other cognitive constructions.

TECHNIQUES

Some of the main techniques employed in structural family therapy are described above. Below is a brief summary of other structural family therapy techniques that are employed toward the goal of structural change.

Creating Affective Intensity

Creating affective intensity relates to the therapist's selective regulation of the degree of impact of the therapeutic message. The therapist alters his or her customary or usual affective and language style to bring more attention to the therapeutic message. This technique is used when families do not seem to be hearing the therapist's message. The therapist must make the family "hear" the therapeutic message by being more dramatic in communicating with the family and possibly gaining the family's attention to that message.

Crisis Induction

Crisis induction refers to a critical goal in structural family therapy: to introduce instability and flux in the family. The goal is to create a crisis in the family that will hopefully give the family more motivation for change. It is important to note that the therapist must give additional emotional support as the family system's homeostasis and equilibrium are threatened. This technique is especially useful as one challenges the family's prevailing homeostatic norm (e.g., the therapist gets the parents to take more control of the children).

Hierarchies

Hierarchies concern the process by which the therapist ranks dysfunctional aspects of the family system and interviews accordingly by addressing the most pressing difficulties while selectively ignoring others. This technique allows the therapist to prioritize therapeutic interventions so as not to overwhelm the family.

For instance, a therapist might elect to reinforce spousal boundaries first before electing to give attention to dysfunctional parental boundaries.

Maintenance

Maintenance refers to the selective use of therapeutic support of individuals, subsystems, or alliances to enhance their independence and strength. This technique is useful in the early stages of structural therapy by which the therapist acknowledges latent strengths within the family that may be threatened by dysfunctional and pathological boundaries, alliances, triads, and hierarchies.

Making Boundaries

The purpose of this technique is to increase healthy subsystem interactions by assisting the family in setting new boundaries, renegotiating old rules, or establishing specific functions for each subsystem—the goal of which is to increase the permeability of rigid boundaries. The therapeutic task may be to create more psychological distance between parent and child in the case of enmeshed systems or, in the case of disengaged systems, to create more emotional closeness. The therapist may also use him- or herself as a spatial boundary maker (e.g., by using arms or body to interrupt eye contact in an overinvolved dyad). Additionally, the therapist may request family members change chairs in order to signal support of a subsystem. Another example is the therapist rearranging chairs, or removing empty chairs between spouses, in order to utilize spatial metaphors to indicate the need for proximity between spouses.

Search for Strengths

The search for strengths relates to the therapist's emphasis on positive aspects of individuals and families. This is an important technique to be used in the very early stages of family therapy and is particularly useful in attempts to join with the family. Families need a sense of acceptance from the therapist despite the fact that their family system may be fraught with dysfunction and pathology. Additionally, the therapist may be able to create a positive spin on a troubling aspect of family dynamics. For instance, in the case of an overcontrolling father the therapist might gain access to the system by acknowledging how much care and concern the father shows toward his family.

Support, Education, and Guidance

The therapist gives the family alternative behavioral patterns of relating. For example, parents are instructed to give more attention to a previously neglected child.

This technique has the potential to open alternative patterns of family interaction, which may modify the structure and operate to activate dormant structural alternatives.

Task Assignments

Homework is given to various family members to facilitate change in family structure and interaction, as well as to reinforce therapeutic maneuvers being conducted within the therapy sessions. For instance, a father and daughter may be given the assignment to go on an outing together without the mother as well as without the other children in the family. This task has the structural goal of creating a stronger alliance between the two family members as well as creating some distance in an enmeshed mother-daughter relationship. These tasks may be assigned to individuals, dyads, or subsystems both within and outside of the session.

Tracking

According to Minuchin (1974), "The therapist follows the content of the family's communication and behavior and encourages them to continue. Tracking means to ask clarifying questions, to make approving remarks, or to elicit the amplification of a point. The therapist does not challenge what is being said: he positions himself as an interested party" (p. 127). The therapist deliberately adopts the symbols of the family's members' communication (e.g., significant family events, family themes, values) and amplifies these in communication with the family. This technique is considered to be affirming of the family's values and may enhance joining and accommodating efforts. Minuchin (1974) further explains tracking as being useful in exploring family structure but does not elicit the information; he leads by following or tracking the theme or family issue that is brought up by the family. Minuchin saw tracking as being useful as a restructuring strategy, much like the technique of maintenance.

Unbalancing

This is a technique that attempts to interfere with the homeostasis of the family system by attempting to change hierarchical relationships between family members by selectively supporting one member. This technique challenges and unbalances the family system, which may force the family to seek alternative transactions and solutions. For instance, the therapist may provide support for one parent to become more involved with the children, where previously this parent operated outside of the executive position—with the majority of the control lying in the hands of the other parent, almost to the exclusion of this parent. This technique provides for the rebalancing of executive control to lie within both parents, possibly moving the other parent out of the sibling position.

CASE ILLUSTRATION

IP (identified patient).	Mr. and Mrs. Lodl were referred to me by their school social worker for help with their 10-year-old son (Tony) for acting-out behaviors in the classroom. (He is in the fourth grade.) He is very disruptive in class (standing on top of the desk, shouting obscenities to his teachers, not doing his work, and disturbing others). He is about to be suspended from school for these behaviors. They are a middle-class stepfamily (second marriage for both of them) with only the mother's children residing in the home. (Mr. Lodl's children are grown and live on their own.) They are very proud of their African American heritage as evidenced by the Africentric clothing and jewelry that they typically wear, as well as their frequent references to their desire to rear a "strong Black male who will be able to contribute to society when he grows up."
	Both parents are educators (she is a fourth-grade schoolteacher, and he is a college professor). They are very politically active in their community, and it is not uncommon for them to volunteer their time and money for causes they deem important.
	There is another child in the home (a 12-year-old girl) who is not experiencing any problems. She and Tony apparently get along well together.
	It is also important to note that Tony's acting-out behavior does not occur in the home. This is Tony's first year back in school since he was in kindergarten; the parents withdrew him from school, and the mother homeschooled him after an incident where the teacher slapped Tony in the face. (The teacher was suspended and eventually fired. The Lodls decided not to press charges as they were satisfied with the school's quick response to this incident.)
Strong spousal subsystem that is an important factor in successful child rearing. **Search for strengths** important as I attempt to **join** with this family. **Accommodation and joining** with this family.	Mr. and Mrs. Lodl seem to enjoy a good relationship and state that they try hard to stay united as a couple especially as far as the children are concerned—given the fact that they are a blended family. (Mrs. Lodl did not rear her recently grown stepchildren but enjoys a good relationship with them.) I complimented them on their success as a couple and as parents of stepchildren. Both parents are very passionate and demonstrative in their language and communication—speaking very quickly. I quickly adopt this tempo and style of communication with the family.

(Continued)

(Continued)

Evidence of executive parental control and (potentially) strong hierarchy.

I am continuing with my **joining** efforts by complimenting the family's success at getting Tony to cooperate with me—**search for strengths**.

I formulate my initial **hypothesis** that Tony's acting out is related to his desire to continue to be homeschooled by the mother. I also wonder if Mrs. Lodl gets any secondary gain from her prior homeschooling and now extensive tutoring efforts (**problem-maintaining sequences**) in that both she and Tony may not want to give up their intense interaction that her extensive tutoring provides. **Possible enmeshed relationship**.

Important to get the **family's view of the problem and their hypothesis**, and I am aware that I will need to get the family members to **reframe their view of the problem** in order to come up with a possible (constructive) resolution.

I listened intently, following the content of their communication, and encouraged them to continue. **Tracking**. I did not challenge the family on its hypotheses, even though I had serious doubt as to the validity of such.

I was not surprised to find out that the pediatrician saw no evidence of hyperactivity. Additionally, Tony's behavior in my office was not indicative of a child with hyperactivity—he was able to sit extremely still throughout a 1½-hour interview. It was important that I get confirmation of my own thinking

As we begin our session I notice that Tony is very resentful of this (therapy) process and is noticeably mute and still during the initial interview where background information is taken. His answers to very simple questions like his age, favorite sport, and favorite television show are generally one-word responses—and only given upon stern admonition from the mother. I thank her for help with my interview questions and inquire if Tony is this quiet at home. They both give a resounding "no" and are very irritated at his behavior toward me.

I find it amazing that they do not experience the same misbehavior at home. They report that he does his chores when asked, gets along well with his sister, and is attentive to the mother in her tutoring efforts (which are apparently successful) to keep Tony current as he does no work in school. It is also amazing to me that Tony is current with his schoolwork. Mrs. Lodl has gone back to work after homeschooling Tony for 3½ years (she is coincidentally teaching the same grade that Tony is in).

In effect Mrs. Lodl is still homeschooling Tony even though he goes to school every day, but he doesn't really get any real instruction until the evening when his mother takes over his lesson plan. (She is in weekly contact with the teacher to obtain Tony's lesson plan so as to make sure he stays current.)

When I ask the parents why they think Tony is acting out in school and not at home, they quickly respond that there are several possible reasons for his behavior. The first is that they feel he has some sort of posttraumatic stress reaction to school as a result of being slapped by his teacher (3½ years ago). They also firmly assert that Tony is hyperactive and that coupled with his being a Black male renders him vulnerable to gendered sexism—as "the school does not really know what to do with a hyperactive Black male."

I asked when his last physical exam was, and they replied that he had just had one before the school year started. I then inquired if they had mentioned their concerns to the pediatrician and if he had noticed any hyperactivity in Tony. They replied that he did not see any evidence of hyperactivity, but they asserted that they believe he has a "touch of hyperactivity" that may be below the diagnosable level.

Toward the end of my initial interview with this family, the parents reiterated an urgency to remedy Tony's acting out, as the school was about to suspend—if not expel—him for his extreme behaviors in class.

that hyperactivity was not the reason for his acting-out behavior.

Part of my reasoning for agreeing to make a school visit with the family and school personnel is that I needed to assess for myself the "racial climate" of the school. I found this school to be located in an area where there are a number of immigrant and ethnic minority children, many of whom attended this school. I certainly didn't mean to imply or dismiss their hypothesis about Black male racism; however, I felt more at ease about the racial climate of this school—at least Tony was not the only or one of the only African American children there. Additionally, I reflected on their original hypotheses (hyperactivity, posttraumatic stress disorder, and Black male racism) and conceded to myself that there wasn't much that I could do about it (especially the possibility of Black male racism)—at least not in Tony's developmental life span. I also had my doubts about the hyperactivity and the posttraumatic stress.

Strategy 1 of SFT (structural family therapy): The therapist joins and accommodates the family system, taking on a leadership role— establishing trust with, showing respect for, and identifying (understanding) the family. (Mr. and Mrs. Lodl began to see me as their advocate, as far as the school system was concerned, after my visit to their son's school.)

Creating affective intensity. My selective regulation of the degree of impact of the therapeutic message; making sure that the family really "hears" the therapeutic message by being more dramatic.

I offered to make a visit to the school with them (in an attempt to buy Tony more time as we entered into family therapy).

In my visit with Tony's teacher and principal they agreed to "stop the clock from ticking" as it was evident that they were merely marking the days until they could suspend Tony. They seemed very pleased (and somewhat surprised) that the parents had followed through on their recommendation to get help for Tony—apparently they did not feel supported by Tony's parents. I felt this meeting had a positive impact on their working relationship with the school.

In my second interview with this family I felt as if I had gained the trust and respect of the parents and felt that they were ready to allow me to be the "expert" and make recommendations for action. I was then ready to begin my interventions.

I began this session in a very dramatic manner. I told the family that I had a chance to review Tony's school records, reflect on my visit to his school, and consider everything that the parents had told me about Tony. I told them that I was all "geared up" to start in one direction but that "it hit me right between the eyes"—I gestured with my right hand and hit my forehead with the palm of my hand as I said this—that there was another component to the problem that we had not attended to. (By then I had really peaked their curiosity about what I had to say.) I turned to Tony and said to him, "This is real important, Tony, so I need for you to really listen to what I have to say . . . because there is something that kept bugging me all the time we were talking last week. I kept feeling there was something going on that I'm not attending to."

(Continued)

(Continued)

Crisis induction. My goal was to introduce instability and flux in the family, to create a crisis in the family that will give it more motivation for change. I challenged the parents' homeostatic balance and equilibrium.

Strategy 3: The therapist challenges the symptom, the system, and the family's view of itself by *reframing* **the presenting problem.**

I told them that what had struck me right between the eyes (I repeated this expression for dramatic effect) and the thing that had stood out to me is how disrespectful Tony has been—disrespectful of himself and his own education, disrespectful to his parents, his teachers, and his fellow classmates. At that moment I saw both parents begin to stiffen and give very angry looks at Tony.

I continued to turn to Tony and asked him if he "respected himself . . . as a young man."

Tony did not answer me. I repeated the question to no avail, and then I turned to his mother and asked her if she would get Tony to respond to me. By this time she was livid and said to him with clenched teeth to "answer the lady!" By then, the stepfather chimed in and also admonished Tony to answer me.

At this point the mother rendered a speech to him on how she was "rearing him to be a strong Black male . . . a warrior for the community . . . and that I was asking him a very simple question."

He did finally answer, but Tony was so angry with having to comply that tears rolled down his cheeks. Nevertheless, I offered him tissue, continued my line of questioning, and asked him if he respected his parents. He said yes. His teachers? His fellow students? He answered yes to all of these questions.

I thanked the parents for their help and then continued with my ideas for an intervention.

Maintenance. I selectively used therapeutic support of the parental subsystem to enhance its strength and independence. This is a technique especially useful in the early stages of SFT by which the therapist acknowledges **latent strengths within the family that may be threatened by dysfunctional boundaries and hierarchies**.

Strategy 2: The therapist makes a structural diagnosis by assessing family interaction. Family themes

One of my own hypotheses is that this family was accustomed to taking up (sociopolitical) causes. And I wondered if somehow Tony had been triangled into its passion for "causes." I needed to de-triangulate him, if this was the case.

and myths are also addressed in that I had a sense that the ethnic pride of this family would not permit its members to even think that they were not rearing "a strong Black male"—**family theme**. Furthermore, I dealt with **the family myth** of hyperactivity (by my nonaction) and addressed the **family theme** of rearing a strong, successful Black male dealing with a racist society by my advocacy for the Black son in my school visit and my challenge to the parents about their son respecting himself.

Strategy 4: The therapist makes structural changes in the family. I selected the stepfather (**task assignment**) to reinforce his position in the parental hierarchy and for practical reasons (the flexibility of his schedule—being a college professor).

Unbalancing. Interfere with the homeostasis of the family system (mother-child over involvement) and attempt to change hierarchical relationship between family members (father and stepson).

I presented my ideas for an intervention, which entailed Mr. Lodl spending a day at the school sitting in on Tony's class (with the school's permission, of course; and the school was overjoyed at the prospect of getting any kind of help). I pulled Tony out for part of this intervention but informed him of our intentions. I wanted the parents to go along with me in giving Tony the impression that his stepfather might sit in on his classes day after day.

I was hoping one or two days of this maneuver would suffice. Mr. and Mrs. Lodl happily complied. I offered my assistance by phone if they needed consultation during the week. (They did not call me, and we met the next week.)

In our third session the parents happily reported that Tony had such a successful day at school that it was only necessary for Mr. Lodl to sit in on Tony's class once. They threatened to be there every day if need be. The teacher was so amazed at the drastic change in his behavior that she called me and the parents to thank us for our help. The teacher had not formerly believed that Tony was capable of such good behavior.

Mrs. Lodl was also able to drastically cut back her tutoring given that Tony was now getting his instruction in school.

I saw this family four more times. Tony only backslid once in those four weeks, and the stepfather happily returned to the classroom. At this point, we met monthly for a few months to make sure the intervention held.

SUMMARY

Minuchin is the central figure associated with structural family therapy and began to develop his theories and techniques with poor and "underorganized" families. He was especially aware of the influence of poverty on family functioning and began to develop special therapeutic techniques for changing family context rather than focusing on individuals. Minuchin believed that an individual's symptoms are best understood in the context of the family and that change cannot take place unless there is change in the underlying family organization or structure. Furthermore, Minuchin believed that once the family's structure has been changed, the positions of its members altered, it is then that each person will experience change as a result.

A key element in understanding the family is that it is an integrated whole—a system made up of subsystems (spousal, parental, and sibling) in which members are also a part of larger systems that impact its basic structure and organization. Functional and dysfunctional families are determined by the adequacy of the fit of the family's structural organization with the environmental context. Functional families are characterized by transactions that serve to meet the needs of the individual in the family and the family unit as a whole. Dysfunctional families experience "system overload" in that their adaptive and coping mechanisms do not meet the changing environmental and/or developmental demands—that is, these families do not modify their structure to meet these needs.

There are three key concepts underlying structural family therapy: family structure, family subsystems, and boundaries. Family structure is the invisible set of functional demands that organize the ways in which family members interact. A family is a system that operates through transactional patterns. These repeated patterns establish patterns of how, when, and to whom to relate, and these patterns underpin the system. The family carries out its function through subsystems. Each individual belongs to a subsystem, and one individual may belong to two subsystems (e.g., the wife is part of the spousal and the parental subsystem). Boundaries refer to the arrangement both between subsystems and with systems outside of the family. Boundaries of a subsystem are the rules defining who participates in the subsystem and how the individuals participate. (The function of boundaries is to protect the integrity [differentiation] of the subsystem in that every subsystem has different functions and makes specific demands on its members to prevent interference from other subsystems.) Minuchin described three types of boundaries: diffuse, clear, and rigid.

Structural family therapy classifies pathology into four (overlapping) forms. The four general forms of pathology are pathology of boundaries, pathology of alliances, pathology of triads, and pathology of hierarchy. Subsystem boundaries that are diffuse or too permeable are considered enmeshed. (Diffuse boundaries are characterized by enmeshed relationships where boundaries are weak and poorly differentiated.) Subsystem boundaries that are too rigid (difficult if not impossible to cross) are considered to be disengaged. (Rigid boundaries are characterized by disengaged relationships wherein there is little sense of "family," and generally very little support is offered or given.) Pathology of alliances is a coalition in which there is a combative, exclusionary, or scapegoating stance toward a third party. (When members of different generations within a family join together against a third member, this inappropriate coalition is referred to as a cross-generational coalition.) Pathology of triads is a dysfunctional alignment whereby each parent attempts to get the child to align with him or her against the other parent. Pathology of hierarchy is a weak ineffective hierarchy wherein the parents are not in executive control and there is a lack of guidance for the children. (There is a power imbalance—inverted hierarchy—when a child is allowed to become part of this hierarchy.)

Structural family therapists believe that family problems are maintained by dysfunctional family organizations; hence the underlying family structure needs to be changed in order to solve presenting problems. A structural diagnosis or family map (a diagram of the structure of family relationships) helps determine smaller goals as they pertain to the specific stage of the therapeutic process.

Structural family therapists view change occurring in a family as a process that involves three objectives: (a) to challenge the prevailing homeostatic norm; (b) to introduce crisis and flux in the system, which will position members to behave and feel differently about themselves and each other; and (c) to develop new behavioral routines or sequences that make up the new system structures that repeat over time. The length of each phase depends on the family's ability to bear conflict and change.

The primary goal of structural family therapy is to reorganize the family structure. Specific goals are:

1. To shift members' relative position to disrupt malfunctioning patterns

2. To strengthen parental hierarchy

3. To create clear, flexible boundaries

4. To mobilize more adaptive (alternative) patterns

5. To establish the spousal subsystem as a distinct entity from the parental subsystem

The primary role of the structural therapist is to facilitate change in the overall structure of the family, by altering boundaries and realigning subsystems. In the structural family approach the therapist does not assume responsibility for change. Therapists play many roles in structural family therapy: observer, describer, director, expert, educator, interpreter, and reframer.

Minchin viewed therapy as structural change that modifies the family's functioning so it can better perform in necessary tasks. There are four main strategies for establishing structural change in families:

1. The therapist *joins* and *accommodates* the family system, taking on a leadership role.

2. The therapist *makes a structural diagnosis* by assessing family interaction.

3. The therapist challenges the symptom, the system, and the family's view of itself by *reframing* the presenting problem.

4. The therapist *makes structural changes* in the family subsystems and changes in the family's interactional patterns.

There are a number of helpful and action-oriented techniques that facilitate the process of change in structural family therapy. Some of the primary techniques are joining, accommodating, reframing, making boundaries, highlighting, problem-maintaining interactions, spontaneous behavioral sequences, task assignments, and unbalancing.

Salvador Minuchin's structural family therapy is one of the most widely used approaches to family treatment. Structural family therapy offers a clear framework for understanding complex family interactions. It also offers clear guidelines for assessment and intervention. This action-oriented approach is both concrete and practical. Yet its theory is rich and inclusive.

RECOMMENDED READINGS

Gurman, A. S., & Kniskern, D. P. (Eds.). (1981). *Handbook of family therapy*. New York, NY: Brunner/Mazel.

Minuchin, S. (1974). *Families and family therapy*. Cambridge, MA: Harvard University Press.

Minuchin, S., & Fishman, H. C. (1981). *Family therapy techniques*. Cambridge, MA: Harvard University Press.

Walsh, W. M., & McGraw, J. A. (2002). *Essentials of family therapy*. Denver, CO: Love.

DISCUSSION QUESTIONS

1. What is structural family therapy's view on an individual's symptoms? Describe this process.

2. What are the three key concepts underlying structural family therapy? Define these concepts.

3. Minuchin's family therapy has a number of techniques. Identify a few of them and how each technique contributes to the overall success of this therapy approach.

REFERENCES

Becvar, D. S., & Becvar, R. J. (2000). *Family therapy: A systemic integration*. Boston, MA: Allyn & Bacon.

Friesen, J. (1985). *Structural-strategic marriage and family therapy*. New York, NY: Gardner Press.

Minuchin, S. (1974). *Families and family therapy*. Cambridge, MA: Harvard University Press.

Minuchin, S., & Fishman, H. C. (1981). *Family therapy techniques*. Cambridge, MA: Harvard University Press.

Minuchin, S., Montalvo, B., Guerny, B., Rosman, B., & Schumer, F. (1967). *Families of the slums*. New York, NY: Basic Books.

Minuchin, S., Rosman, B., & Baker, L. (1978). *Psychosomatic families: Anorexia nervosa in context*. Cambridge, MA: Harvard University Press.

Nichols, M. P. (1984). *Family therapy: Concepts and methods*. New York, NY: Gardner Press.

Walsh, W. M., & McGraw, J. A. (2002). *Essentials of family therapy*. Denver, CO: Love.

Chapter 7

STRATEGIC FAMILY THERAPY

BACKGROUND AND LEADING FIGURES

Strategic family therapy emerged from the groundwork set by the communications model of family therapy (see Chapter 4), which was then developed further by the work of Gregory Bateson and Milton Erickson in the early 1950s. The main focal point for the key developments in strategic family therapy was the Mental Research Institute (MRI) in Palo Alto, California, founded by Don Jackson in 1959. There, Bateson, Jackson, John Weakland, Jay Haley, Paul Watzlawick, Virginia Satir, Richard Fisch, and others studied communication, paradoxical communications, and human interaction. Later, Milton Erickson joined the group and brought his work in hypnotherapy. Out of these interactions came three distinct models: MRI's brief therapy, the Milan systemic model, and Haley and Madanes's strategic family therapy.

Bateson, an anthropologist by training, began his work by looking at the communication patterns in families where one member had schizophrenia. As a researcher, Bateson was more interested in observing families than in trying to get them to change. However, Erickson, in his new work on hypnotherapy, felt people could change even with brief interventions. This notion of brief intervention was taken up by Jackson and Fisch who began the Brief Therapy Project utilizing the short-term and pragmatic approach of Erickson. This project led to the development of the Palo Alto approach or, as it was soon to be called, the MRI model. The model was noted for its problem-solving focus and strategic tactics that could bring about change in a family system in a relatively brief amount of time.

Haley focused more on training and supervision after he left the MRI and joined Salvador Minuchin at the Philadelphia Child Guidance Clinic. Haley then left that program and established the Family Therapy Institute in Washington, DC, with Cloé Madanes. Madanes herself also spent time at the MRI as well as the Child Guidance Clinic, and she would become one of the most important writers on the strategic family therapy model.

By the end of the 1960s, the work of the MRI and the Brief Therapy Project was influencing another group of clinicians half a world away. Mara Selvini Palazzoli, Luigi Boscolo, Giuliana Prata, and Gianfranco Cecchin, collectively known as the Milan Group, were using the work of Bateson, Haley, and other members of the MRI in their Center for the Study of the Family in Milan, Italy. The Milan Group further developed aspects of strategic family therapy, in particular the notion of paradoxical interventions, as well as made important contributions to the family treatment of eating disorders.

The legacy of the pioneers who developed strategic family therapy is extensive. Don Jackson cofounded the influential journal, *Family Process*, with Nathan Ackerman before Jackson's untimely death in 1968 at the age of 48. Watzlawick, Weakland, and Fisch published *Change: Principles of Problem Formation and Problem Resolution* in 1974. Haley became one of the leading writers on supervision before his death in 2007. Many of the concepts of brief intervention, strategic tactics for change, and the key insights of Milton Erickson can still be seen in the current work of the brief and solution-focused family therapy models. Cloé Madanes, Peggy Papp, and Karl Tomm continued to push the development of strategic family therapy.

PHILOSOPHICAL, CONCEPTUAL, AND THEORETICAL UNDERPINNINGS

As strategic family therapy shares some theoretical connections with the communications model of family therapy, it is not surprising that one of the primary underpinnings of strategic family therapy is communication. In particular, the notion that people are always communicating was the first in a series of axioms first outlined by Watzlawick, Beavin, and Jackson (1967). Everything a person says or chooses not to say, and every action a person engages in or chooses not to engage in, is a form of communication. It is impossible, from the strategic therapy point of view, to not communicate. Once this axiom is accepted, the nature of the communication can be better understood according to its functions and messages.

The second axiom addressed by Watzlawick et al. (1967) focused on some of the functions embedded in the messages being conveyed through communication. Messages have two specific functions, report functions and command functions.

These functions are sometimes discussed in the literature as content messages and relationship messages. Report messages are the overt or explicit statements made by family members to convey information to one another. Command messages are the covert or implicit messages that imply something about the relationship between the speaker and the target listener.

For example, a husband is speaking to his wife and says, "You know, I'd really like to buy a new HDTV for the den." The wife, with arms crossed, after a deep sigh, responds, "Sure, do what you like." On the face of it, the wife's reply, taken at the overt level, tells the husband that he can get the HDTV. However, her body language (which can't be shown by the written word), for example her sighing, points to a not-so-subtle covert message that implies the wife's displeasure at the husband's idea. The husband is now left in a problematic situation. He could say, "Thanks, I'll go get one right now" as a sign that he heard the overt message. He may not understand the wife's displeasure later when he says to her, "But you told me it was OK to buy it." If the husband is tuned in to the covert message, he may say, "You don't sound too excited by the idea." Such a statement could then lead to a discussion between the two of them and a search for a solution or compromise both could live with. In either case, when overt and covert messages convey very different responses to a statement, it is contingent on the listener to decode the various messages and search for the disagreement between the messages. In clear communication, the overt and covert messages agree or support one another. In healthy relationships, the disconnect between overt and covert messages can be identified and discussed. In unhealthy relationships, the disconnect may be ignored or possibly identified but considered too difficult to discuss.

As families struggle to solve their problems and find it difficult to change their patterns of communication or behavior, strategic family therapists point to the concept of family rules as one of the forces maintaining this status quo. The family rules are implied in the command or covert messages conveyed in the family communication patterns. One of the goals of the family rules is to maintain the status quo within the family, often referred to as the *family homeostasis* (Piercy, Sprenkle, Wetchler, & Associates, 1996). For strategic family therapy, some problems within families serve a functional purpose, in that the families need the problems to be present in order to achieve some kind of balance or equilibrium within the family. (Not all family therapists agree with the idea that some families need their problems.)

The axioms taken together address the important theoretical notion of *meta-communication,* or communication about communication. From the MRI group, Bateson and his work in cybernetics established the base for strategic family therapy to look at communication in this new way. One of the key theoretical concepts to come out of cybernetics was the idea of *positive feedback loops*. For strategic family therapists, such feedback loops were the explanation for the formation of problems in families. For families, a problem is generated when the family tries to solve an initial concern but finds it difficult to solve. When the attempts to solve the problem fail, the family keeps trying and trying, often employing the same strategies, which have already failed. As attempts continue to fail and the family grows increasingly frustrated, the initial problem continues to escalate. The cycle the family has fallen into is referred to as a positive feedback loop because the end result is an increase in the problem. As noted above, some families may want the problem to stay around. For other families, it is more a function of being stuck in a cycle or loop that they feel they cannot change.

CONCEPTS

For the strategic family therapist, there are a number of concepts that emerge from the theoretical assumptions made about family functioning, family communication, and family patterns. All of the concepts discussed below work together to give rise to a family's patterns of interaction, sometimes in a healthy way that promotes family adaptation and change, and sometimes in an unhealthy way that leads to family problems.

Family Homeostasis

Family homeostasis refers to the balance or equilibrium all families seek to establish in order to function as a family. Once such an order is established within a family—that is, when a pattern of behavior, communication, and rules is set that seems to work for the family—the family as a whole is often resistant to changing that set order. The concept of homeostasis illustrates why some families find change so difficult. There is a comfort and predictability found within homeostasis, even when specific members of a family seem to be in trouble or suffering with the set order.

For a strategic family therapist, the difficulty with change brought on by homeostasis can be seen in certain kinds of family resistance to therapy. For instance, some family members during therapy may raise questions about the overall benefit of change, almost as if they are asking the therapist for a guarantee that change will be a good thing. Change implies giving up what is known and familiar for the chance to do something different, which will be unfamiliar and risky. Homeostasis speaks to the old idiom "You may not like what you have, but at least you know what it is." Even when faced with a crisis, many families will adapt momentarily to resolve the crisis but then revert to their usual set order, returning to the usual and familiar sets of behaviors, rules, and communication styles.

The strategic family therapist is put in the position of identifying the homeostatic properties within a family, making explicit the family's propensity to maintain the status quo even when faced with information that the status quo is detrimental to some members of the family and identifying the sources of resistance to change.

First-Order and Second-Order Changes

When strategic family therapists speak about change, they are usually referring to *first-order* and *second-order* changes (Watzlawick et al., 1974). A first-order change occurs when a specific *behavior* changes within the family system. A father changing his communication style in an attempt to better listen to the issues raised by his daughter so that he can be more empathetic and helpful is an example of a first-order change.

A second-order change occurs when the *rules* that govern the entire family system begin to change. For example, if the husband and wife begin working more as a team in responding to the behavior of a child, whereas that child ordinarily experienced the parents as working at cross-purposes, often to the delight of the child who could get away with more bad behavior, the unification of the parents as a team changes the rules by which the family operates—a second-order change.

For families that struggle with feeling stuck—that is, they are comfortable at some level with their homeostatic set point—second-order changes will be needed to help the family members experience a new way of interacting. In some cases, first-order changes can be worked on as a way to show the family that change is possible in order for members to develop some trust in the process and reduce their fear and resistance to other kinds of change.

Circular Causality

The strategic family therapist does not look for underlying causes or motivations as the explanation for how a pattern was established. Instead, the strategic family therapist assumes a stance that existing patterns are perpetuated by *circular causality* (Watzlawick et al., 1974). Circular causality is an outgrowth of the positive and negative feedback loops discussed above. Taken together, these two types of feedback loop lead to an iterative process in families. As a problem develops in a family, the attempts by the family to solve the problem may fail and possibly exacerbate the problem further (a positive feedback loop). Each successive interaction the family takes follows this circular pathway: The family attempts to solve the problem; the attempt fails; family anxiety and frustration grow; its next attempt is fueled by this anxiety and frustration and fails; and the cycle repeats itself.

The focus of the strategic family therapist then is not on how a problem got started in the first place—often this is unknowable—but on the circular pattern established and how to prevent the pattern from continuing. The focus is on the interactions within the family as a whole and between individual family members that allow this circular process to continue. It would seem counterintuitive to see a positive feedback loop within a family where a problem behavior is increasing as an example of *homeostasis*; however, many families adjust to such a circular process that it becomes the norm, the familiar, within that family. These families need to focus on the problem in order to function as a family based on their homeostatic needs. Again, it is by looking at the interactions within the family and identifying first-order and second-order changes that the strategic family therapist can begin to interrupt this circular process and help the family establish a new sense of homeostasis that will be more adaptable and positive.

Paradoxical Interventions

One strategy the strategic family therapist uses to interrupt the circular causality within a family is *paradoxical interventions* (Selvini Palazzoli, Boscolo, Cecchin, & Prata, 1978). These counterintuitive actions are sometimes considered controversial and have fallen out of favor over the years. However, as this model of family therapy first discussed such actions, they were designed to make explicit some of the interactions families developed to maintain their homeostatic order. After such interactions were made explicit, the family then had to struggle to either go along with the therapist and acknowledge areas of resistance or go against the therapist and begin to make first-order or second-order changes.

For example, if a teenager acts out at home by being sullen and uncommunicative, the therapist may ask the teenager to try and be more sullen and ask the parents not to try and speak to the teenager. In so doing, the parents may be relieved from continuously trying to communicate with the teen, which was constantly frustrating for them. The teen may see that being sullen is not that wonderful of an experience if he is expected to do it, even when he doesn't feel that way. Out of this process may emerge a new way for the parents to try and communicate with the teen (first-order change), and the family as a whole may no longer be so focused on the teen (second-order change and the establishment of a new homeostatic order).

Photo 7.1   The inclusion of children in family therapy provides the strategic family therapist important insight into the communication and behavioral patterns created by the family

Source: Copyright © Can Stock Photo Inc./lisafx

As these concepts show, each is intimately related to and dependent upon the others. These basic concepts flow directly from the theoretical and philosophical frameworks established by the early pioneers of strategic family therapy. Some of these concepts, especially the idea of circular causality, are now found in other models of family therapy including *solution-focused therapies* and *narrative therapies*. With these concepts in hand, the specific goals and techniques of strategic family therapy can be better understood.

GOALS OF THERAPY

Fisch (1978) stated that "as therapists, we do not regard any particular way of functioning, relating, or living as a problem if the client is not expressing discontent with it." The strategic family therapy model does not presuppose any model or notion of normality; it only considers what the client system brings to the therapy as the identified issue that has generated some "discontent." This notion of neutrality in regard to ideas about normal family functioning clearly puts this model at odds with other models of family therapy.

The primary goal of therapy, then, is the resolution of the presenting concern. The main way such a resolution is reached is by creating first- and second-order changes in the family system through the use of the techniques mentioned above. Strategic family therapy tends to work on mutually agreed-upon behavioral goals that lead to such change within the system. As such, this model shares some similarities with cognitive-behavioral family therapy. The behaviors of the family members, individually and as a system, can be identified through the process of assessment and steps taken (techniques) to move the family toward trying new behaviors to break the circular causality that has led to the escalation of the identified problem.

ROLE OF THE THERAPIST

The primary role of the therapist is to make an assessment. More will be said about the particulars of assessment below. Once a thorough assessment is conducted, the therapist can then try and discern what behavioral patterns have allowed the problem to continue and identify steps to take to begin changing the established behavioral patterns. The specific steps and techniques used within this model are discussed below. However, the key issue is that each of the techniques is geared toward changing the established pattern.

PROCESS OF THERAPY

The MRI model at its most well defined follows a six-step process for family therapy. Each step is followed in a somewhat linear fashion leading to the resolution of the identified concern. While the step-by-step process can seem overly simplified or concrete, for the strategic family therapist it presents a pragmatic process with a single goal in mind. Once the goal is achieved, therapy is over. If the family does not bring any other concerns, the therapist does not ask about other issues to work on.

1. Introduction to the Treatment Setup

The strategic family therapist begins by introducing the family to the general process of therapy and the steps to follow. There may be some general discussion about key ideas within strategic family therapy, such as homeostasis and rules, but in language the family members will understand. Also, the family therapist will reinforce the important notion of neutrality when it comes to ideas of normality. The focus of therapy is not to explore how the family is abnormal but rather to focus on an identified pattern that has developed that is causing the family some level of concern.

2. Inquiry and Definition of the Problem

The critical step in the strategic process is Step 2. The therapist and family must be able to work together to reach a clear understanding of the problem with a clear definition. As the family struggles to find the right language and words to describe its concern, the therapist can ask questions to help narrow down broad statements or clarify vague descriptions. The therapist takes time to involve all members of the family present and help each one add to the discussion of the presenting concern. The outcome of this step is a clear statement regarding the concern that the family wants to focus on in therapy.

3. Estimation of the Behavior Maintaining the Problem

Once the concern has been clearly defined, the therapist will explore with the family members steps or behaviors they have engaged in while trying to resolve the problem on their own. Such information often highlights the positive feedback loop in the cycle, those behaviors that lead to the continuation or escalation of the identified concern. This exploration may also help the therapist identify chains of behavior the family routinely engages in when faced with the identified concern. Such sequences of behavior can help the therapist identify elements of the circular causality established within the family in the face of the identified concern.

4. Setting Goals for Treatment

Based on the information generated by the family from the above steps, the strategic family therapist develops a strategy to help change the identified behavior or sequence of behaviors that maintains the problem. Historically, strategic family therapists were more directive and often set the goals for therapy with little input from the family. Over time, strategic family therapists became more collaborative, often including family members in setting specific goals to work on and the steps needed to meet the goals. This more collaborative approach helps build a stronger therapeutic relationship and can help the family see the benefits of the change process. The goals of therapy tend to be focused just on what the family has identified as the key problem behavior in the family system.

5. Selecting and Making Behavioral Interventions

The goal or goals of the therapy are then further refined into specific objectives. These objectives often include specific behavioral changes that need to be made to help the family achieve the stated goals of therapy. At this stage, the strategic family therapist can utilize the techniques outlined below. Each technique has certain strengths and weaknesses in terms of how the family may respond to the technique or the degree to which the technique can help alter the chain of behaviors identified as the problem in the family. As each family system is unique, not all techniques work equally well with all family types and situations. The strategic family therapist must use clinical judgment when deciding on the techniques to be used in the therapy.

6. Termination

Once the identified behavior is altered within the family, usually through second-order change within the family system, the therapy is concluded. As stated earlier, the strategic family therapist only works on the problems identified by the family through the first three steps outlined above of the process of therapy. If the family does not identify additional issues, the therapist does not inquire as to whether there are more issues to work on. In reality, with many families, the process of second-order change often brings to light other behavioral patterns that may interfere with such change or make sustaining such change more difficult for the family. In these cases, the strategic family therapist may repeat the process of therapy outlined above as new behavioral patterns emerge that the family wants to work on.

TOOLS AND TECHNIQUES

Assessment

Jay Haley (1976) focused much of his clinical attention on the process of assessment in strategic family therapy. For the process of strategic family therapy to go well, it had to start out well. He broke the assessment process down into four stages.

Stage 1: The Social Stage

As a first step in the process of family therapy, Haley wanted the families to have a chance to relax, get comfortable and accustomed to their new surroundings in the therapy office, and basically feel welcomed by the therapist. While this initial social interaction is occurring, the strategic family therapist is already making note of the family system and behaviors.

Stage 2: The Problem Stage

After the family is given the chance to settle in, the therapist begins to inquire from each family member his or her perspective of the problem that brought the family to therapy. The therapist may use targeted questions to get better information about the scope of the problem, how each member defines the problem, and what kinds of behavior best typify the identified problem or seem to help maintain the specified problem.

Stage 3: The Interaction Stage

Once information is gathered to help the therapist understand the identified problem, the family members are given the opportunity to discuss among themselves the identified problem and other relevant data gathered during the problem stage. Such "family member to family member" interaction provides a unique window into the family system at both a behavioral and a communication level. Often through such interactions, the therapist can begin to identify some of the concepts discussed earlier in the chapter. The therapist can use this information to better identify the kinds of techniques to use to help the family begin to work on the identified problem.

Stage 4: The Goal-Setting Stage

This stage overlaps with Step 4 of the process of therapy discussed above. The therapist discusses with the family the information gathered through the assessment process and begins to work with the family to define a specific goal for therapy and the steps needed to achieve that goal.

Directives

One of the main techniques used by strategic family therapists is directives (Haley, 1976). Directives are specific tasks assigned to the family by the therapist that the family is to carry out within some specified amount of time (usually between therapy appointments, but sometimes within a therapy session). By assigning a task, the therapist puts the family members in the position of having to interact to carry out the task or negotiate with each other how to carry out the task. Such interactions can shed light on first-order and second-order change processes within the family. In the past, strategic family therapists would come up with the tasks by utilizing their professional superiority and with little input by the family members. That has changed over time, and strategic family therapists will often collaborate with families in developing tasks based on what they may have tried to do about the problem in the past.

Ordeals

Ordeals are a specific kind of directive (Haley, 1976). Ordeals imply telling the family to engage in some unpleasant task each time the identified problem behavior occurs. The idea behind ordeals is that the family will try to not engage in the identified behavior in order to avoid engaging in the prescribed ordeal. For example, if one of the chains of behavior that maintains the specified problem is the parent yelling at the daughter when she is on the phone too long talking to her friends, the therapist may tell the parent that rather than yelling at the daughter the parent should go clean the toilets in the house. Such an ordeal may help the parent find some other way to communicate with the daughter in order to avoid cleaning the toilets.

Rituals

Rituals involve the entire family in carrying out some specified series of actions in order to highlight the patterns of interaction the family may have established that maintain the identified problem (Boscolo, Cecchin, Hoffman, & Penn, 1987). For example, the parents of a child are struggling with and constantly arguing about who gets to make decisions about the discipline of their young son and who does it better. The therapist may tell the parents that they must flip a coin to determine who is in charge and who must stay out of it. By forcing the parents to alter their pattern of behavior, they must learn to react differently to each other and change their individual behavior (first-order change) while establishing a new pattern of child rearing (second-order change).

Positive Connotations

Positive connotations were derived from the Milan model of strategic family therapy (Boscolo et al., 1987). In some sense, positive connotations are like *reframing* in therapy. The strategic family therapist might identify the problematic behavior of one family member as preserving the homeostasis within the family. For example, if a child acts out and breaks things every time he hears his parents argue, it could be construed that the child is trying to distract the parents and prevent his mother from becoming unhappy as a result of the arguing.

The child's behavior could be seen as having a positive or protective component for the mother. But with positive connotations, the strategic family therapist would look at the child's behavior and see it as serving a family system–wide need, not just the need of one family member. The strategic family therapist would identify this connection between the specific behavior and the family system need it meets and then tell the family it ought not to change this pattern. Once this chain of behavior is identified and, in a sense, prescribed to continue, the strategic family therapist can employ other techniques to help the family see the destructive nature of this pattern and begin to make first- and second-order changes.

Pretending

Pretending involves an individual family member pretending to act out identified problematic behavior and the other family members pretending to react to it in their usual fashion (Madanes, 1981). Such a technique accomplishes two things. First, it gives the family members a sense of control over the symptomatic behavior because they control the time and place of the pretending. Second, the family member who is pretending to engage in the symptomatic behavior now no longer needs to actually engage in the behavior because the pretending accomplishes the same family system goal. Once the family sees its level of control and the actual need for the behavior abates, the family is in a better position to make second-order changes within the system.

Circular Questioning

Circular questioning attempts to have family members see the relational context of their family system through the eyes of the other family members (Boscolo et al., 1987). When asked of a family member, a circular question requires the family member to answer from a relationship perspective and to try and see this relationship from an empathetic perspective. For example, the therapist might ask the father in a family, "How might your wife describe her relationship with her daughter if she were not afraid of hurting her feelings?" The father now must reflect on the relationship between mother and daughter as seen through the eyes of his wife. This kind of reflection gives family members a more holistic view of their family and a better understanding of each family member's unique perspective of the family system. As circular questioning continues, the goal of this technique is to influence family shifts from seeing the identified problem as within a family member to seeing the role and function of the entire family system in developing and maintaining the identified problem behavior.

CASE ILLUSTRATION

The presenting situation.	Mary is a 35-year-old single mother with two children, a 14-year-old son and a 12-year-old daughter. Mary has been divorced for 3 years, and her ex-husband has been out of the picture for the last 2 years. Mary sought family therapy because of concerns about her son Michael. He has been getting into trouble at school and has received detentions for acting out in the classroom, his grades have dropped over the past 6 months, and the mother is worried he may be using drugs.
	Mary says she has no problems with her daughter; Linda is an excellent student at school, has very good and supportive friends, and helps around the house as much as she can. The mother expresses some concern that Linda may be affected by Michael's bad behavior and worries that she will suffer in school or at home because of him.
	Mary wants therapy to help her figure out what to do about her son and how to help keep her daughter from being negatively affected by Michael's behavior. She feels her son has the potential to "turn things around" but seems unwilling or unable to do so.
	The family therapist makes arrangements to see all of the family the following day.
Step 1: Introduction to the treatment setup. Assessment: The social stage.	
	The therapist greets the family members and shows them into his office. He asks how the car ride over was and expresses hope that the recent snowfall didn't make things too difficult. As the family settles into the chairs, the therapist begins to note how the family members appear and how they begin to relate to one another in the office.
Early indication of metacommunication.	
	Michael presents as a quiet and reserved boy, with a slight build and longish hair that partially covers his eyes. He sits slumped in the chair and makes minimal eye contact with anyone in the room.
Eye rolling as metacommunication.	
	Linda, the daughter, presents as a somewhat typical preteen young girl. Well dressed, she seems attentive to her mother but avoidant of her brother. She glances at him periodically and rolls her eyes as if she is embarrassed by him.
Explaining the setup and introducing key elements of strategic family therapy.	

Family homeostasis.

Step 2: Inquiry and definition of the problem.

Assessment: The problem stage.

Beginning notion of circular causality and a positive feedback loop. Does Linda's ignoring her brother (her way of trying to solve the problem) lead the brother to act weird? Does the son feel "left out" when the mom and daughter hang out as a reaction to his acting out?

More details about possible circular causality and the establishment of a positive feedback loop that is maintaining Michael's behavior.

Metacommunication: Is there a disconnect between Michael's body language and voice tone and his words?

The therapist discusses a little about the process of family therapy. He says that it is important to hear from everyone in the room and that everyone's perspective is important. He says that everyone plays a role in the family and has something to contribute to making the family work well together. Families sometimes get into ruts, patterns that are hard to shake, and it takes everyone in the family to help shake things up a little to get out of the rut. He wants to hear from all members what they think are some of the reasons they are here today.

Linda jumps in and says her brother is causing a lot of stress in the home right now, that her mom frequently cries because of him, and that Linda feels like she has to make excuses for Michael to her friends for his sometimes "weird" behavior. She thinks he is just "goofing off" and could act better if he just tried to. But, she says, she doesn't know what his problem is. She wishes she liked her brother more and would like to spend time with him, but when he acts "weird" she just ends up ignoring him and hanging out with her mom.

Mary also points to her son's behavior as the principal reason they are here today. With his problems in school and problems at home, she feels there is a level of tension and stress in the home that makes everyone suffer. She is worried that Linda will begin to change as a result of this home environment.

Michael stares at the ground and speaks very quietly. He says he is sorry for causing so much concern, but he just feels like he can't do anything right. His teachers get mad at him for not doing his homework, he hates going to school because his teachers think he is a goof-off, and when he is home he doesn't want to do anything except be left alone. He crosses his arms and says kind of forcefully that it's fine that his mom and sister hang out together without him; he doesn't blame them.

The therapist asks if there are particular behaviors that happen at home that everyone agrees are of most concern.

Mary says she is most concerned about getting Michael to do his homework. She is worried that if his grades fall any further it will have a major impact on him for the rest of his life. She's worried he will get labeled as a "problem kid" and it will follow him all through high school.

(Continued)

(Continued)

	Linda says she just wants him to be in a better mood at home, like he used to be, so she can like being home and around him. She says her brother can be "kind of cool" when he wants to be. She hates seeing her mother cry over all of this and gets angry at her brother for being the cause.
Step 3: Estimation of the behavior maintaining the problem. Assessment: The interaction stage. Identifying the circular causality at work in the family and the establishment of a positive feedback loop that maintains the son's identified problematic behavior. "Family member to family member" interaction to better see how the family members act and communicate together.	Michael just nods his head in agreement but doesn't elaborate on what his mom and sister have said. He says he is sorry for being a pain but doesn't know what to do about it. Nothing seems to go right for him. The therapist states that it seems everyone agrees Michael is in a rough spot right now. When he is having difficulty it upsets the mom and daughter, and one way they cope with this is to pull together and lean on one another. Perhaps, when this happens and Michael feels excluded, it makes him more upset and he feels guilty that he is a cause of the problem. The therapist asks the family members to discuss this "take" on the presenting issue with each other to see if he, the therapist, has understood correctly what everyone has said. As the mom turns to the two kids, she asks if this is a "fair" summary of what it is like in their home right now. Linda jumps in and says yes. She looks at her mom and continues to seem to avoid making eye contact with her brother. The son says "yeah, sure" in a kind of noncommittal tone and looks at the floor. The mom asks if there is anything else the therapist should know about. Both kids just shake their head no.
Step 4: Setting goals for treatment. Assessment: The goal-setting stage. Identifying past attempts at first-order changes and how they identify positive feedback loops. In this case, punishment was a positive feedback loop as it only served to exacerbate Michael's negative behavior and the tension in the home.	The therapist indicates that there seems to be general agreement that the stress in the house caused by Michael's behavior is the key thing everyone would like to see changed. He asks if this is correct, and everyone in the room nods yes. The therapist asks what has been done in the past to try and change this pattern of behavior when it has happened before. The mom says when his grades first started to go down, she put limits on his TV watching and cell phone use. When that didn't work, she grounded him for the weekend. None of that seemed to make much of a difference and, if anything, just made the home more tense and difficult.

Collaborating with the family in establishing goals for treatment.	The mom indicated she spoke to the school counselor. The counselor, similarly, indicated that detentions were not working and that Michael seemed determined to do things that would separate him from his classmates and antagonize his teachers.
	The therapist asks if the family members have any new ideas about things they could try or other ideas about how to make things better at home for Michael and everyone else.
	Linda wonders if there is a way to spend more time with Michael rather than punish him. She laughs and says, "If we force him to be around us, maybe that will be punishment enough."
Identifying an example of problematic metacommunication in the family.	The therapist says that is kind of an interesting idea. He notes that much of what Michael does seems geared to setting him apart from others, yet he also seems, maybe, to want to be around people as well. The therapist comments that he couldn't help but notice that when Michael said he was fine with his mom and sister hanging out, he said it in kind of an angry way, like his words and feelings didn't match up.
Step 5: Selecting and making behavioral interventions.	
Identifying the underlying family homeostasis and positive feedback loop.	The therapist suggests that the family members have established a pattern that has all of them kind of trapped into doing the same thing over and over. Unfortunately, that pattern seems to also help Michael feel more isolated and gives him more reasons to feel bad about his situation. When he feels worse, he does worse.
Directives.	The therapist indicates to the family members that he will want them to try to do some things in a different way. He suggests the following:
Making first-order changes.	1. The next time Michael comes home from a bad day at school, the mom and sister will set aside time to spend with him to discuss what happened and to listen to his story.
	2. When Michael acts out at home, rather than isolate him, the mom and sister will identify a family activity that all can engage in that will distract Michael and refocus his energy into something more productive.
	The therapist wants to hear from all three what happens when these things are tried when they next meet.

SUMMARY

Strategic family therapy has its roots in the birth of family therapy. Many of the key figures in developing this model of family therapy were also key figures in the development of family therapy in general and the initial push for this mode of intervention. With the input of the clinician-researchers from the MRI and the Milan Group, this model of intervention was enthusiastically embraced by therapists and applied to many kinds of family issues. In particular, the Milan Group showed early success in treating eating disorders using this model. However, the utilization of this model peaked in the late 1980s, and newer models of family therapy have eclipsed its former influence.

Regardless of its lack of utilization in the current practice arena, the model has left a lasting impression on the field of family therapy. Key concepts such as homeostasis and circular causality are now routinely identified as essential family dynamics that other models must confront and address if they are to be successful. Also, the basic process of family therapy established by Jay Haley is still utilized in other models even if those other models use different terms to describe the process. In a sense, some of the specifics of strategic family therapy have become integrated into our fundamental understanding of families, family dynamics, and the process of change.

Another indicator of the strength and importance of this model is its direct influence on more current models of family therapy. In particular, solution-focused and narrative family therapy models show a direct link to some of the philosophical and conceptual underpinnings present in this model. The work of Jay Haley, one of the early architects of this model of family therapy, was influential in setting the groundwork for solution-focused family therapy. Some of the conceptual work on understanding communication articulated within this model can now be found in narrative family therapy. Clearly, it is a sign of how robust a model is when it provides some of the foundation for two current models of family intervention. This lasting impact is a tribute to the conceptual sophistication and technical clarity of strategic family therapy.

RECOMMENDED READINGS

Haley, J. (1976). *Problem-solving therapy.* San Francisco, CA: Jossey-Bass.

Jackson, D. (1967). *Therapy, communication and change.* Palo Alto, CA: Science and Behavior Books.

Madanes, C. (1981). *Strategic family therapy.* San Francisco, CA: Jossey-Bass.

Selvini Palazzoli, M., Boscolo, L., Cecchin, G., & Prata, G. (1978). *Paradox and counterparadox.* New York, NY: Jason Aronson.

Watzlawick, P., Beavin, J., & Jackson, D. (1967). *Pragmatics of human communication.* New York, NY: Norton.

Watzlawick, P., Weakland, J., & Fisch, R. (1974). *Change: Principles of problem formation and problem resolution.* New York, NY: Norton.

DISCUSSION QUESTIONS

1. What are the principal tenets essential to understanding strategic family therapy? Discuss.

2. Why is the concept of metacommunication critical to understanding strategic family therapy? Give some examples of metacommunication and discuss how you would understand their importance within a family relationship.

3. Strategic family therapy has a number of techniques. Identify a few of them and discuss how each technique contributes to the overall success of this therapy.

REFERENCES

Boscolo, L., Cecchin, G., Hoffman, L., & Penn, P. (1987). *Milan systemic family therapy.* New York, NY: Basic Books.

Fisch, R. (1978). Review of *Problem-Solving Therapy*, by Jay Haley. *Family Process, 17,* 107–110.

Haley, J. (1976). *Problem-solving therapy.* San Francisco, CA: Jossey-Bass.

Madanes, C. (1981). *Strategic family therapy.* San Francisco, CA: Jossey-Bass.

Marley, J. (2004). *Family involvement in treating schizophrenia: Models, essential skills, and process.* New York, NY: Haworth Press.

Piercy, F., Sprenkle, D., Wetchler, J., & Associates. (1996). *Family therapy source book* (2nd ed.). New York, NY: Guilford.

Selvini Palazzoli, M., Boscolo, L., Cecchin, G., & Prata, G. (1978). *Paradox and counterparadox.* New York, NY: Jason Aronson.

Watzlawick, P., Beavin, J., & Jackson, D. (1967). *Pragmatics of human communication.* New York, NY: Norton.

Watzlawick, P., Weakland, J., & Fisch, R. (1974). *Change: Principles of problem formation and problem resolution.* New York, NY: Norton.

Chapter 8

SOLUTION-FOCUSED FAMILY THERAPY

BACKGROUND AND LEADING FIGURES

Solution-focused family therapy is one name for a group of brief family therapy models. All of them share a common key perspective: What causes a problem is not as important as what a person or family can do right now to change the problem. The notion that the individual or family has what it takes to make changes is often referred to as a "strengths approach" to therapy. Steve de Shazer and his colleagues at the Brief Family Therapy Center (BFTC) in Milwaukee, Wisconsin, developed the model in the 1970s and 1980s.

Steve de Shazer worked in Palo Alto, California, and was heavily influenced by the Mental Research Institute (MRI) model. He brought together Bateson's work on communication and Erickson's work on brief intervention and began to develop his own ideas about the use of language in the change process. Because of his work on language and narrative, de Shazer and this model of intervention are sometimes seen as linked with the social constructivist approaches (i.e., narrative family therapy).

Along with de Shazer, his wife Insoo Kim Berg was a key figure in the development of this model. She trained clinicians all over the world in this model and was one of the more prolific authors demonstrating the usefulness of the model in various settings and with various problems. De Shazer died in 2005, and Berg died in 2007. However, many of their former coworkers and students continue to study, write, and train clinicians in this model of therapy. Eve Lipchik, Bill O'Hanlon, Michele Weiner-Davis, Scott Miller, John Walter, and Jane Peller are among the

Photo 8.1 Insoo Kim Berg and her colleagues at the Brief Family Therapy Center in Milwuakee Wisconsin helped develop the foundational principles and practices of Solution-Focused Family Therapy

Photo 8.2 Steve de Shazer was able to integrate the work of people like Jay Haley and Milton Erickson to develop the philosophical underpinnings of Solution-Focused Family Therapy

current group of therapists who continue the work of the BFTC. They have demonstrated the usefulness of this model in the areas of marital problems (Weiner-Davis, 1992), wife battering (Lipchik & Kubicki, 1996), and working with people with serious mental illness (Rowan & O'Hanlon, 1999), as well as provided key books on the basic "how to" of the model (Lipchik, 2002; Walter & Peller, 1992).

PHILOSOPHICAL, CONCEPTUAL, AND THEORETICAL UNDERPINNINGS

The primary philosophical and theoretical idea at the heart of solution-focused family therapy is that the focus must be on the present and not the past (Walter & Peller, 1992). This model makes no assumptions about nor does it inquire about the initial cause of a problem. For the solution-focused family therapist, the ultimate solution to a problem may be completely unrelated to any ideas formed by considering the initial cause of the problem.

Given de Shazer's early connection to the work of the MRI group, this model shares some similarities with strategic family therapy, yet it also makes some very important differentiations. Like strategic family therapy, the solution-focused model sees people as falling into rigid cycles of behavior that often perpetuate the problem (the positive feedback loop idea). Often, how people talk about their problems and the words they use to convey their concerns demonstrate to the solution-focused family therapist just how entrenched some of these patterns have become (de Shazer, 1991).

Unlike the strategic family therapy model, the solution-focused family therapist rejects the idea that families want their problems to persist (the notion of family homeostasis) or need their problems to function (de Shazer, 1988). The solution-focused model assumes that people and families want to change. What is needed, from the perspective of this model, is a new way of looking at and talking about the problem so that new solutions emerge that may be useful in decreasing or eliminating a problem.

Language becomes a key ingredient in the solution-focused theory. Understanding and examining how family members talk to each other about the problem and how the family talks to the therapist about the problem is crucial to this model (de Shazer, 1994). Throughout many of his writings, de Shazer focused on the role and power of words and language. He noted that the language used by the family establishes the reality of the problem as perceived and experienced by the family. Solution-focused therapists often identify the difference between "problem talk," which is negative, frustrating, and self-defeating, and "solution talk," which is more positive, future oriented, and energizing (Berg, 1994; de Shazer, 1991). This focus on the power of language links some aspects of solution-focused theory with narrative family therapy and other social constructivist approaches.

CONCEPTS

A number of concepts flow from these philosophical and theoretical positions developed by the solution-focused family therapists. In some cases, the concepts are derived from the notion of "solution talk," and in others they are derived from broad notions about language and the power of words.

Clients/Families as Experts

One of the key concepts for solution-focused family therapy is that the family is the expert of its own situation (Miller, Hubble, & Duncan, 1996). This concept is also found in other social constructivist models of family therapy. Simply put, each family has authored its own story and is the expert in relating this story to the therapist. Through the family-constructed story, the family is able to communicate how it identifies and understands its unique issues and struggles. The family is, in this perspective, the lead author of its own story. The solution-focused family therapist takes the stance of listener to the story and through the questions asked of the family helps the family flesh out the narrative in more and more detail. While the therapist may be an expert in asking questions or pulling a disjointed narrative together, the therapist does not assume to know the family based on preconceived ideas about normal family process.

The idea of the family as expert is not without its complications. First, it may seem an odd stance to encourage when people are reading a textbook on family therapy in the hopes of learning how to do family therapy. If the family is the expert, then why be trained and educated in family therapy? It can't be as simple as listening to the family tell a story and then out of that story identifying solutions to the identified problems. It is not that easy. The concept of the family as expert recognizes that the only people in the room who have lived and breathed the day-to-day existence of the family are the family members. Each family member, and the family as a whole, has a perspective to share that grounds the family issues in the uniqueness of that family.

Second, taking a stance of the family as expert may miscommunicate to families that they are under pressure to solve their own problems. Family members may say, "If we are the experts, then why are we here to see you as the family therapist?" The solution-focused family therapist needs to articulate that the "family as expert" concept is a starting point for collaboration, that it allows the uniqueness of each family member to be heard and understood by the family therapist as part of the process of family therapy.

Exceptions

For the solution-focused family therapist, an exception is a time when the identified problem did not exist or did not happen (Miller et al., 1996). Compared to other models of family therapy that may focus on when a problem occurs, how often it occurs, and attempts the family has made to correct the problem, this model turns this process completely around and asks the family to consider or reflect on times before the problem started or when the problem did not happen.

In the process of solution-focused family therapy, exceptions can be seen in two ways. First, as stated above, the therapist may work with a family to identify a time in the family before the problem existed. Such an exploration may provide important information about how the family worked together, communicated, and solved problems before the identified problem developed. Second, the therapist may talk with the family about those times when the identified problem did not occur or even those times when the conditions were right for it to occur. For example, two parents frequently argue over setting limits on their child with the mother believing the father is too strict and the father believing the mother is too permissive. In the therapy session, it comes to light that last week an issue arose about setting limits but no argument ensued. This "exception" can be explored to see how the conditions varied and may have prevented the argument. From the solution-focused perspective, many families lose sight of or don't pay attention to the "exceptions" because they are so focused on how terrible the problem has become. This will often show itself in the language the family members use to describe the problem. They may say things like "It always happens" or "We are always arguing."

This kind of global summary prevents the family members from recognizing and valuing those times when the problem did not occur.

Dominant Narrative

As with narrative family therapy, solution-focused family therapy helps the family make explicit the dominant narrative that maintains its construction of the problem (Marley, 2004). The dominant narrative is the language used by the family to create a story or explanation of the identified problem that may try to explain its origins or its persistence in the family. The narrative that the family creates often provides clues to the family therapist about how the family operates, how the family understands its issues, and what may be preventing the family from feeling capable in resolving its current problems.

A mother, father, and teenage son come to therapy. In the first meeting, the father says, "All our problems began when Tom [the son] began hanging out with kids who use drugs and smoke. Since then, nothing has gone right in the family." As the beginning articulation of a dominant narrative, this is a pretty powerful statement. Within this statement are (a) the belief that the son is to blame for the problems and (b) the belief that all problems experienced by the family are due to the son. It would be understandable if this family felt incapable of change given the overwhelming belief that the son is at fault for everything. The solution-focused family therapist would use this kind of statement as an early indicator of the narrative the family has built up over time and how that narrative impedes the family's progress or ability to change its current situation.

Language

Language, then, becomes an underlying concept that supports all of the above concepts (de Shazer, 1994; Marley, 2004). It is through the language used by the family that the therapist can discern the dominant narrative. It is through language that the family begins to exert itself as the expert of its own situation and explain its understanding of itself to the therapist. It is through language that the therapist seeks those exceptions, those brief moments in the dominant narrative when the family indicates the identified problems did not exist or did not always happen. As with other models of family therapy (e.g., narrative, strategic, communications), the power of language and how the family and the therapist utilize language becomes a key conceptual part of this model and provides the base for several of the techniques discussed below.

De Shazer's (1991, 1994) writings on language and his experience with the MRI and the development of strategic family therapy articulate a deep understanding of the power of language. There are at least three types of language in use in the family therapy situation: (a) the language of the family as it conveys its perspective to the family therapist, (b) the language of the family therapist as the therapist questions and expands on what the family is telling, and (c) the collaborative language the family and family therapist cocreate through the process of working together. For the solution-focused family therapist, it is through the understanding of the first two types of language that change can be affected in the third type, helping the family move from problem talk to solution talk and change the dominant narrative to a more adaptive and problem-solving narrative.

GOALS OF THERAPY

The overall goal of solution-focused family therapy is to help the family move from problem talk (a dominant narrative that keeps the family stuck and unable to identify solutions to its problems) to solution talk (a new dominant narrative that motivates the family to build on its strengths and capabilities to solve its own problems; O'Hanlon & Weiner-Davis, 1989). In a sense, just getting the family to change the way it talks about itself is the primary goal of this therapeutic model; it is not as necessary for the therapist and family to actually solve the problem while in therapy. For this reason, many models of solution-focused family therapy tend to add the descriptor *brief* to the model's name. Through the activity of the therapist and the use of the techniques below, it may only require a few sessions for the family to develop a new dominant narrative and begin to identify ways the family can move forward in solving problems, both the one at hand and ones that may occur in the future.

The notion that changing the way families talk is sufficient as a goal for family therapy may cause some people to hesitate about this model. Is that really all there is to it? Doesn't a family therapist have to stick around and see the family enact some changes as it grapples with the identified problem? While theoretically and conceptually, the therapist does not need to see the family work through the problem to consider the therapy a success, practically many solution-focused family therapists do indeed work with a family at least long enough to see and hear how the family puts into action some of what the members learn from therapy and how the new dominant narrative begins to drive the action of the family. One concern that is sometimes raised with this model is that the new dominant narrative that emerges could help solve current issues faced by the family, but it may also place specific family members in some disadvantaged positions within the family such that new problems are likely to emerge. Dominant narratives and the kinds of new actions, beliefs, and attitudes that are derived from this new narrative are hopefully embraced by all members of the family. However, it can be difficult to determine this unless the therapist has time with the family to see how the new narrative plays out across time and across family members.

ROLE OF THE THERAPIST

The primary role of the therapist is to (a) help elicit from the family its dominant narrative; (b) within that narrative identify exceptions; (c) based on the presence of exceptions identify for the family some alternative narratives, or at least gaps in the current dominant narrative; and (d) through this process help the family artic-ulate a new narrative that takes into account its unique strengths and weaknesses such that the family now feels capable of changing those behaviors or situations that cause difficulty for the family (Walter & Peller, 1992). As with strategic family therapy, there is no focus on the original cause of the problem. The focus is on the present situation, how the family understands it, and how to amplify the exceptions that may hold the key to the family's true ability to change what it wants changed. The solution-focused family therapist holds the belief that the family does want to change but the dominant narrative is creating a cognitive block in the family's ability to see itself as capable of change. The therapist, then, brings this hopeful, strengths-based attitude to the therapy as a way of communi-cating to the family that it is capable of change once the roadblocks are removed from considering the possibility of change.

PROCESS OF THERAPY

As with many models of therapy, the solution-focused model follows some degree of a systematic approach to what it does and how it wants to accomplish these goals. The first step in the process is usually an assessment of the family and its current situation. However, assessment can look different in this model of family therapy compared to other models. First, since the solution-focused family thera-pist holds the belief that the family is the expert of its own situation, most assess-ments do not look for any standardized intake information or the use of standardized forms to complete prior to the start of therapy. The family therapist wants to hear from each individual family member as well as from the family as a whole, in members' own words, what they feel is going on in the family. Second, because solution-focused family therapists are not interested in family dynamics or family history/family systems kind of information, the therapist will usually work with whomever shows up for therapy. There are no restrictions on who needs to be there in order for the family therapy to take place. Finally, one aspect of the assessment is to determine who in the room is a complainant, a customer, and a visitor (de Shazer, 1988). A complainant is a family member who likes to complain about the situation but expresses no motivation to change it. A customer is a family member who is motivated to change. A visitor is someone who doesn't complain and who has no motivation to change.

Part of the process of therapy is to try and get complainants and visitors to become customers. These are indications of the working relationship between the family and the therapist; they are not hard and fast differentiations. In fact, some family members may move between these three types during the course of a session or across multiple sessions.

As the early sessions of family therapy take place, the solution-focused family therapist tries to get the family members to describe or identify the concern that brought them into therapy. The problem description becomes an early attempt at understanding the dominant narrative based on how the problem is described, who does most of the talking, and how the problem is identified within the context of the family (individual blame versus a family issue). Given the strengths-based approach to this model and the need to identify and reinforce exceptions, even as the family is describing the problem, the therapist will highlight exceptions or reflect back to the family moments that happened where the family did indeed take positive steps to change the problem. In this sense, intervention with the family occurs simultaneously with the early assessment process. An intended outcome of this dual process is that it allows this model of family therapy to be effective within fewer sessions.

Finally, the goals of the family therapy are articulated and discussed. Since the family is the expert of its own situation, the goals come from the family and need to be seen as unique to that family's situation, strength, and motivation. With the goals agreed upon by all of the family members, the therapist can begin to work with the family around its abilities to change the identified problem and bring to light any cognitive blocks that prevent the family from solving the identified problem.

TOOLS AND TECHNIQUES

The tools and techniques discussed below serve several purposes. First, they can be used in either assessment or intervention processes to help elicit information and make explicit the cognitions the family holds (individually by family member or as a whole family) that may either impede its ability to solve problems or indicate strengths the family could capitalize on to solve problems. Second, the techniques can model problem-solving skills that the family can incorporate into its own repertoire and use in the future to solve problems. Finally, the techniques can be used to help move complainants and visitors into being customers by creating a motivation to change among those who feel negative or helpless about the whole process.

Questions

As with narrative family therapy, the art and science of questions play a pivotal role in the process of family therapy (Miller et al., 1996). Perhaps one of the most lasting contributions this model of family therapy may leave to the field of family therapy is the development and refinement of several types of questions that are designed to move the family forward in changing its dominant narrative and creating more motivation to change. The following examples show a range of specific types of questions that can be utilized in family therapy at almost any point in the process.

Miracle questions are often phrased as follows: "Suppose one night while you were sleeping, a miracle happened and you awoke and your problem was gone. What would you notice as being different? How would you know the problem was gone?" This kind of question provides the family member or members with the chance to identify concrete things in the environment or within themselves that would indicate the problem is gone. The specific things that would be different can then be used as goals or guides for the family therapy process. For example, after discussing with the family each member's feedback to the above question, the therapist might be able to say, "Well, since all of you indicated that X would be a good indication of the problem being gone, let's see what needs to happen to make X a reality in your family." Another advantage of such questions is that they require the family to think about a positive outcome (strengths-based approach) and move the family further along in looking at solution talk rather than problem talk.

Scaling questions help give the family some anchors in how it defines the scope and nature of the problem. A therapist may ask, "On a scale of 1 to 10, with 1 being no problem at all and 10 being the worst problem you can imagine, how would you rate X as it impacts your family?" This question can be put to each family member individually or can be used to get the family members to discuss among themselves the scope of the identified problem. This type of question provides a couple of key outcomes for the therapy. First, a scaling question requires the family to develop some kind of perspective to its identified problem. For a family that may come in and communicate that it is in crisis and facing the worst problem ever, a scaling question may force it to change its appraisal of the problem. Is it really the worst ever? If it is not a 10, then what keeps it from being the worst? Such feedback to the family members can help them reflect on the true scope of the problem and begin to identify things that are going well or right that prevent the problem from truly being a 10. Second, scaling questions can generate discussions among family members as each struggles to justify why he or she rated an issue as more of a problem or less of a problem compared to other members of the family. If the children in the family rate a problem lower than the parents, or the mother rates it lower than the father, why might that be? What are people noticing within the family (strengths? positives?) that led them to rate it lower than other members of the family? Again, the reflection back to the family and the ensuing discussion can focus on strengths of the family and move members forward toward more solution talk.

Exception questions are explicit attempts by the therapist to have the family articulate times when the identified problem did not occur or was not present. Some families may come into therapy and say, "We always fight." Such a global appraisal can be overwhelming for a family since it implies the problem is always present no matter what. The family therapist may follow up with an exception question such as "Is there ever a time when you notice you are not fighting?" A family member might respond, "Nope, we always fight." The therapist can then say, "Really? What about when you are asleep? Do you fight then? What about when you are at work?" A family member may respond, "Well, no, we don't fight then." The solution-focused family therapist has just accomplished several things. First, the information now shows that the dominant narrative ("We always fight") is incorrect. A new narrative will be needed that allows for the fact that the problem does not always occur. Second, exceptions have been identified that indicate the problem doesn't occur under certain circumstances. Finally, the exceptions may provide an opportunity to explore other times, places, and situations where the problem does not occur, thus identifying strengths within the family that can be noted and expanded.

Coping questions reinforce family strengths and help the family identify specific strengths it is drawing on to deal with its problems. Questions such as "How are you managing so well under such difficult circumstances?" or "What keeps you going when you are struggling with this problem?" both reinforce the family's basic ability to cope and generate information about coping skills and resources the family is drawing on to help it cope. As these coping resources are articulated, the family and therapist can begin to discuss ways of expanding or building on these naturally utilized coping resources and reinforce ways for the family to continue to use them.

Compliments

Compliments are just that, compliments given to the family as the session proceeds (Marley, 2004). The therapist might compliment a family member for a creative response, for coming up with a good idea in the session, for identifying a particular family strength, or for pointing out something the therapist missed in someone's comment. Compliments help accomplish several goals. First, compliments may help reduce the anxiety family members feel about being in therapy and their concern that they aren't doing the "right thing" or don't know what to do. Second, compliments bring in a more conversational tone to the therapy session and indicate a level of collaboration between the family and the therapist. Finally, compliments reinforce the strengths-based approach of this model, that positive, constructive, solution-focused contributions are noted and reinforced for the family.

Formula First Session Task

A formula first session task (de Shazer, 1985) has become a standard technique within solution-focused family therapy. Usually at the end of the first session, the therapist will ask the family members to observe and describe what happens in their family between the sessions that they would like to see continue. The task is meant to get the family members focused on the positives they experience in different aspects of their life (marriage, family, other relationships, etc.) and to allow them to describe these positives through careful observation. The task is a strengths-based approach and gets the family to pay attention to positive factors as opposed to being fixated on the problem, thus moving the family from problem talk to solution talk.

Breaks and feedback sessions help families reflect on what has transpired during the session and help the therapist develop a coherent message or plan to bring back to the family. In many places, solution-focused family therapy is done in a team approach with one therapist working with the family while additional therapists may be watching the therapy behind a mirror. When a break occurs, usually near the end of the session, the therapist may ask the family to spend 5 or 10 minutes discussing its views on what has transpired. While the family engages in this task, the therapist may consult with the observing colleagues and discuss perspectives and hear ideas about what to take back to the family in terms of feedback. In future sessions, the therapist may want to engage in a feedback session or use part of a session for a feedback process. In this case, the therapist invites the family members to reflect on and discuss how the therapy is progressing, whether it is meeting people's needs, and the extent to which the family wants the process to continue. Feedback sessions help support the collaborative nature of this model.

CASE ILLUSTRATION

	Bill and Sarah, a married couple in their early 30s, sought couples counseling to work on some problems that have emerged in their marriage. This is the first marriage for both of them. Two years ago, Sarah gave birth to their only child, a girl named Susan. Susan is a healthy toddler now.
Presenting problem from the wife's perspective.	According to Sarah, ever since the birth of their daughter, she and Bill have been having problems. Bill runs his own business and is often tired and stressed when he gets home late in the evening. Sarah, who stays at home to take care of Susan, is also very tired and stressed after being home all day. She says she and Bill rarely talk much and seem to be just "roommates" who share the same house right now. As both are tired, they easily get on each other's nerves, snap at each other all the time, and go to bed angry more often than not. Their sex life is pretty much nonexistent and has been that way for several months. The therapist recommends that Bill and Sarah come in for a session and see what can be worked on.
First session and the beginnings of the assessment process.	Bill and Sarah arrive on time for their first couple's session. The therapist greets them and tries to put them at ease as the session gets under way. The therapist says, "Since you both have been living this marriage every day, and not me, I'd like to hear from you both what has been going well and what has not been going well. That way we can get a good idea of your relationship together."
Beginning to reinforce the idea that the couple is the expert of its own situation and that both good things and problems are to be discussed.	Sarah states that they have been having problems since the birth of their daughter. Both she and Bill are tired and stressed out, get angry easily, and don't seem to get along very well right now.
	The therapist says, "When you say 'right now,' that would mean there was a time or there are times when you do get along well. When was the last time you both felt that way?"
Expanding on a possible exception to the problem. Getting the couple to identify and describe a positive time.	Bill says that last weekend, when their child slept better, he thought they had a good Sunday morning together; they had time to talk and watch a favorite morning show together. But such times rarely happen, he says, as both seem so tired all the time.
	Sarah says she remembers that morning and feels bad that more times like that don't ever seem to happen; they just happen by chance.

Pointing out an element of the dominant narrative and how it prevents the couple from appreciating positive experiences.	The therapist says both Bill and Sarah identify a good time or situation, but both seem to rush to discount it as only "rarely" happening or happening by chance. However it happens, it does happen, so the couple needs to find ways to make more of those good things and times happen.
How to build on exceptions.	The therapist asks what is the main reason each thought it was important to come to therapy and work together on the relationship.
Strengths-based approach, showing an example of how the couple made a good decision to work together.	Bill says it is the tension, how he is so tired when he gets home some nights he wants some comfort, companionship, or something to take his mind off of work, but Sarah is too tired from caring for Susan to be helpful to him.
Continued assessment and problem identification.	Sarah says she is very tired and just doesn't have anything left for Bill some nights when he comes home. They just do their own thing to de-stress after Susan is in bed; then both of them fall into bed and sleep.
	Bill says he wishes it was like before Susan was born, when they had lots of time together and a good sex life, talked together, and did things together. Sarah says she feels even more stressed out and upset when Bill talks like that, like he blames Susan for their problems.
	The therapist says that Susan isn't the issue, that most toddlers aren't that powerful to make or break relationships. However, something between the two of them changed after their daughter was born, but both must care about each other enough to make the effort to work on it and come to therapy.
Challenging the dominant narrative.	The therapist says both have identified being tired in the evening and having a difficult time finding time to spend together. The therapist wonders which one is the best place to start first.
Compliment and showing them working together on the issue.	Bill chuckles and says being tired just seems to come with the territory of running your own business and raising a child. It seems unrealistic to think therapy will help them get more rest. Sarah smiles at her husband and agrees.
	The therapist says, "The way you two looked at each other right now clearly shows me you care about each other and agree on some things. That's really good to see. So maybe we can begin on the issue of finding time to spend together. Does that sound fair?"

(Continued)

(Continued)

Problem identification.	Both Sarah and Bill nod and agree. Sarah says that if they could spend some nice time together, it would be easier to tolerate the tiredness.
	The therapist asks, "If you both went to sleep tonight and woke up tomorrow and your problem was gone, the problem of not spending time together, what would be different tomorrow? How would you know the problem was gone?"
Miracle question. Information gathered will help identify criteria both see as important to resolving the identified problem.	Bill says it would be easy; they would talk more together. Sarah says she agrees. It wouldn't even matter what they talked about; just spending time together talking with each other about anything would be nice.
	The therapist says, "You mentioned last Sunday was good but that it happened by chance. Tell me about the last time you planned to spend time together and how that worked."
Looking for more exceptions.	Sarah says about 2 weeks ago they thought if they scheduled time together every night, and stuck to the schedule, they would get to spend time together. But when the time came to do it, both were so tired, they didn't have anything to talk about and then got upset that the time they tried to set aside failed.
Information on an attempt to solve the identified problem.	The therapist says, "I applaud your attempt. I don't know if I would say it failed. Your goal was to spend time together, which you accomplished. It seems maybe you had more expectations for what that time would be like when you were together and both felt let down that it wasn't exactly what you wanted. But let's build from that attempt and see what you all can do the next time. When each of you is 'doing your own thing' to de-stress, what is it you are each doing?"
Compliment and reinforcing the positive aspect of their attempt to solve their problem.	Sarah says she usually reads a book or looks at some magazines for a while. Bill says he likes to do crossword puzzles or read the newspaper for a while to get his mind off of work.
Reinforcing the couple's attempt to solve its own problem. A coping question.	The therapist says, "OK, here's a plan to get things going that both of you have helped me see as possible. I like that you decided to try and schedule time to spend together and that both of you followed through and did get together. But here's my suggestion to build off of that solution. Stick to the schedule; make the time each night to spend at least 30 minutes together. But here's the new twist. Rather than worry about

Couple as expert of its own situation, also a compliment and indicating the plan builds on strengths already identified by the couple.	what you both will talk about, bring in what you usually do anyway. Bill, find an item in the paper that you think Sarah might be interested in and tell her about it. And Sarah, find something in one of your magazines or a passage in your book that you want to bring to Bill's attention. Now, there is only one rule: just to eliminate any stress or worry about this; if you are bored or uninterested in what the other brings to your attention, you are not allowed to say so. The goal is to spend time together and begin to get in the habit of talking with each other without the pressure to make it successful every time. So whatever the other brings to your attention, you need to be open and receptive to it and ask at least one question about it. That's it. What do you think?"
The plan builds off of the couple's coping strategies but now applies it to the identified problem.	Both Sarah and Bill agree that it sounds like something they could try and do.
	The therapist says, "I want you both to do this, especially since you both do these things already. Between now and the next time we meet, I want you to keep track of what works well over the next week, and pay attention to those times when things seem to be going well between the two of you. Then when we meet next time, we can use that information and see what the two of you can do to make sure more of the good stuff happens."
Formula first session task. Such a task both orients the couple to focus on the positive events so that the feedback can be used in making future plans and helps challenge the dominant narrative.	Bill and Sarah agree to the schedule and the assigned task and say they will report back what happens over the week.

SUMMARY

Solution-focused family therapy, as one of the constructive or constructionist therapies, continues to enjoy wide use and development. Its pragmatic approach, the clear connection between its theoretical underpinnings and techniques, and its strengths-based perspective make this model very attractive to clinicians new to family therapy or to agencies wishing to develop a family intervention component. However, some of these aspects that make it attractive have also created some of the key criticisms of the model.

The strengths-based perspective and the constant focus on positive family experiences have raised some concerns that families may not experience much empathy or understanding of their pain and concern about their identified problems. Will families feel heard and understood if they get the message that they really shouldn't talk too much about the negative experiences they are having as a family?

The pragmatic nature of the model and its development of a range of questions have led some to express concern that the model comes across as too simplistic and may not recognize the uniqueness of each family. In a sense, the concern is that the model can come across as a manualized, cookie-cutter approach to families and that the therapists may lose sight of the unique issues and concerns of the family in front of them.

Finally, the focus on technique can detract from the importance of the therapeutic relationship. If one of the goals of this therapy is to get people motivated to change, the family members need to feel connected to the therapist in a collaborative and respectful relationship. The quality of the therapeutic relationship will determine how the family responds to the tools and techniques of the model. Without a good relationship, none of the tools and techniques are likely to be effective.

Even with these potential criticisms, the model is a very active and attractive model of family therapy. It provides a pragmatic view of change within families and encourages families to see themselves as experts and ultimate authors of their own narratives. The empowerment families may experience through this process can be very powerful.

RECOMMENDED READINGS

de Shazer, S. (1988). *Clues: Investigating solutions in brief therapy.* New York, NY: Norton.
de Shazer, S. (1991). *Putting difference to work.* New York, NY: Norton
de Shazer, S. (1994). *Words were originally magic.* New York, NY: Norton.
Miller, S., Hubble, M., & Duncan, B. (1996). *Handbook of solution-focused brief therapy.* San Francisco, CA: Jossey-Bass.
Walter, J., & Peller, J. (1992). *Becoming solution-focused in brief therapy.* New York, NY: Brunner/Mazel.

DISCUSSION QUESTIONS

1. What is solution-focused family therapy's view of an individual's symptoms? Describe this process.

2. Solution-focused family therapy has a number of techniques. Identify a few of the key ones and describe how they contribute to the overall success of this therapy.

3. Identify a "dominant narrative" you may be familiar with and discuss how this narrative may influence how people understand their problems and the kinds of behaviors that may ensue. How might this model address this narrative?

REFERENCES

Berg, I. (1994). *Family-based services: A solution-focused approach.* New York, NY: Norton.

de Shazer, S. (1985). *Keys to solution in brief therapy.* New York, NY: Norton.

de Shazer, S. (1988). *Clues: Investigating solutions in brief therapy.* New York, NY: Norton.

de Shazer, S. (1991). *Putting difference to work.* New York, NY: Norton.

de Shazer, S. (1994). *Words were originally magic.* New York, NY: Norton.

Lipchik, E. (2002). *Beyond technique in solution-focused therapy.* New York, NY: Guilford.

Lipchik, E., & Kubicki, A. (1996). Solution-focused domestic violence views: Bridges toward a new reality in couples therapy. In S. Miller, M. Hubble, & B. Duncan (Eds.), *Handbook of solution-focused brief therapy.* San Francisco, CA: Jossey-Bass.

Marley, J. (2004). *Family involvement in treating schizophrenia: Models, essential skills, and process.* New York, NY: Haworth Press.

Miller, S., Hubble, M., & Duncan, B. (1996). *Handbook of solution-focused brief therapy.* San Francisco, CA: Jossey-Bass.

O'Hanlon, W., & Weiner-Davis, M. (1989). *In search of solutions: A new direction in psychotherapy.* New York, NY: Norton.

Rowan, T., & O'Hanlon, B. (1999). *Solution-focused therapy for chronic and severe mental illness.* New York, NY: Wiley.

Walter, J., & Peller, J. (1992). *Becoming solution-focused in brief therapy.* New York, NY: Brunner/Mazel.

Weiner-Davis, M. (1992). *Divorce-busting.* New York, NY: Summit Books.

Chapter 9

COGNITIVE-BEHAVIORAL FAMILY THERAPY

BACKGROUND AND LEADING FIGURES

Cognitive-behavioral family therapy has its origins in the theory of classical conditioning developed by Ivan Pavlov and later advanced by John Watson in the 1920s, as well as in the theory of operant conditioning developed by B. F. Skinner. Both sets of theories looked at specific behaviors and how such behaviors could be developed, changed, or extinguished.

Building on the classical conditioning work of Pavlov and Watson, Joseph Wolpe introduced one of the first widely utilized behavioral intervention techniques, systematic desensitization, in the late 1940s. His work led him to develop models of intervention for the treatment of anxiety, phobias, and sexual dysfunction. However, it was the operant conditioning work of Skinner in the 1950s that allowed behavioral family therapy to come into its own. Operant conditioning focuses on the consequences of behaviors. The nature of the consequence will determine whether the behavior is likely to be repeated (positively reinforced) or extinguished (punished or negatively reinforced). The thorough understanding of the sequence of behavior and consequence allowed the clinician to develop a functional analysis of the specific behavior and determine how the behavior could be reinforced or extinguished. For parents, such a model provided specific techniques that could help them ignore, and therefore extinguish, bad behavior in children and reward, and therefore encourage to happen again, positive behavior.

It was with the work of Albert Ellis (1962) and Aaron Beck (1976) in the 1960s and 1970s that the cognitive component became part of the model. Both researchers understood that one of the weaknesses of the behavioral models was the lack of change in the thoughts and attitudes of the individual attempting to change his or her behavior. The development of learning theory and rational emotive therapy (RET) provided individuals and families with techniques to identify and change thoughts and attitudes that might otherwise get in the way of the behavioral changes. The combination of cognitive focus and behavior focus has proven to be a strong theoretical as well as practical model for interventions. Cognitive-behavioral family therapy is now one of the most widely utilized and widely researched models in use today across many settings, family types, and presenting family problems.

While the pioneers in the development of cognitive-behavioral therapy models have all died, many clinicians and researchers carry on this work and expand the range of issues the model can address. In particular, the work of Falloon (1988), Jacobson and Margolin (1979), Mueser and Glynn (1999), Patterson (1971), and Stuart (1971) has increased the visibility and utility of cognitive-behavioral models of interventions.

PHILOSOPHICAL, CONCEPTUAL, AND THEORETICAL UNDERPINNINGS

Three key theoretical components work in concert to form the base for the cognitive-behavioral family therapy model: (a) social exchange theory, (b) operant conditioning, and (c) cognition.

Social exchange theory, first outlined by Thibaut and Kelley (1959), indicates that in relationships, individuals try to maximize the rewards they receive and minimize the costs they incur through their interactions. The outcomes of interactions become the focal point, for only in reflecting on the outcome of an interaction will the individual know whether it is likely going to be rewarded or punished. A good relationship, then, is one in which each member feels there are more positive rewards than costs in the exchanges. Cognitive-behavioral family therapy tries to help families develop more positive exchanges and diminish perceived costs. This is usually accomplished by helping the family develop modes of acting and communicating that encourage more positive responses amongst the members.

Operant conditioning provides a major theoretical underpinning for most current models of cognitive-behavioral family therapy. Developed by B. F. Skinner (1953), operant conditioning focuses on voluntary responses. Skinner showed that with the modulation of consequences (positive or negative reinforcement), such voluntary responses could be shaped, increased, or extinguished. For cognitive-behavioral family therapists, the focus is on identifying the consequences that emerge in families in response to behaviors.

Within families, however, there may be a lack of understanding that a reaction to a behavior is a type of consequence. Therefore, the family may not understand why the problem behavior continues or gets worse. For example, a child whines constantly at the grocery store for a piece of candy. Feeling harried and frustrated, the parent responds to the whining by letting the child pick out a piece of candy. In this case, the parent has just positively reinforced the child's behavior and has set the stage for the behavior to continue or get worse. The child, even unconsciously, now associates sufficient whining with getting the desired outcome. The parent, however, may not associate the response given as a reinforcer of the behavior. It may simply be seen as a pragmatic response to a difficult situation, one that let the parent get on with the chore at hand with a quieter child. When the child repeats this behavior in future trips to the grocery store, the parent may become frustrated at the child's behavior and now feel locked in a cycle of behavior and response that quiets the child but also reinforces the continuation of the problem behavior.

The cognitive component of cognitive-behavioral therapy addresses the notion of learned behavior and how cognition plays a part in the development and maintenance of behaviors (Bandura, 1969). As certain behaviors are reinforced by certain consequences, the person's thinking now makes room for this connection (behavior-consequence) and comes to anticipate this cycle, even if the anticipation is not at the conscious level. The person may begin to act in subtle ways, or set the stage through choices in behavior, that encourage the behavior and consequence to repeat themselves.

For the cognitive-behavioral therapist, the family may often report feeling that the problem behavior just happens—it "comes out of the blue" for no apparent reason. However, after careful analysis, it is more likely that the family has not recognized the link between behavior and consequence and the way the family sets the stage for the repeating of the cycle. The language the family members use to describe the problem can be an indication of how strong their belief system is about the cycle. When they say in response to questions about a child's acting-out behavior, "He is always bad, always doing bad things," they now give voice to their cognitions that identify whatever the child does as bad and that they expect what the child does to be bad. Such cognitions then make it unlikely that the family members will be able to identify ways of breaking the cycle of behavior-consequence because their thinking does not allow for such a change in the cycle.

CONCEPTS

A number of key concepts help translate these theoretical positions into the techniques used by cognitive-behavioral family therapists. Among some of the key concepts are learned responses, consequences, shaping, and schemas.

Learned Responses

Similar to the solution-focused and narrative models, the cognitive-behavioral model is not that interested in underlying motives or root causes of a problem (Dattilio & Reinecke, 1996). The model sees problems as symptoms of a learned response to a specific behavior-consequence cycle. The learned response is a set of behaviors and/or cognitions that develop in response to some situation the person is in and that are then reinforced by the environment that surrounds the person and the situation. For example, a father may yell at his son when the son begins to cry. If the child stops crying because he is startled by the sound of the yelling, the father may take that as a sign that yelling works—the yelling has been reinforced by the change in behavior of the child. The next time the child begins to cry, the father may then try to use the learned response to the crying, yelling, and if it works again it will add to the reinforcement of the learned response. The focus of therapy is to identify the problematic learned response and the consequences and cognitions that allow the response to continue (the reinforcers). If the learned response doesn't change, the family can become entrenched in a cycle of perpetually utilizing learned responses even when the situation or environment calls for a new kind of response or even when the learned response ceases to work but the family has no other response available to use. Since all families encounter problems at one time or another, the goal of this model is to help families develop the behavioral and cognitive skills needed to address problems when they arise before such an entrenched cycle can become established.

Consequences

Consequences are the reinforcers that determine whether a behavior is likely to be repeated more or less often (Sanders & Dadds, 1993). Consequences that help a behavior continue or escalate can be either positive or negative. Punishments are consequences designed to decrease or extinguish a behavior. For example, a young boy of 8 routinely misses his bedtime because he moves slowly at night, gets distracted by various irrelevant tasks (e.g., petting the cat, playing with his model cars), and is always needing to be prodded to stay on relevant tasks (e.g., brushing his teeth). The parents grow frustrated each night and find themselves following the boy around, constantly talking with him and trying to help him stay focused so he can get to bed on time. In this case, the parents' choice of action is a form of negative reinforcement. By engaging the child, conversing with him, they are giving him what he probably wanted in the first place and are therefore likely reinforcing his behavior and encouraging it to repeat itself on other nights. The child has learned a behavior, and the parents' learned response to this behavior causes the behavior to continue.

In order for this cycle to be interrupted, the parents will need to find an alternative way of responding to the boy's behavior in such a way that it decreases the likelihood of the behavior continuing. For example, one parent could say, "I will read you a bedtime story but only if you get your teeth brushed and you are in bed in the next 10 minutes." This kind of positive reinforcer encourages the boy to stay on task and provides a reward for good behavior that is positive for both the boy and his parents. However, it will be imperative for the parents to stick to this statement, for if the boy takes more than 10 minutes and the parents still read the bedtime story, the boy has now learned that such consequences stated by his parents are not enforced.

Shaping

Shaping refers to the use of reinforcers as rewards in the process of helping an individual change a problem behavior (Falloon, 1988). By the selective use of rewards, an individual can take small steps in changing the problem behavior, be rewarded for these small changes, and in the process begin moving toward a completely new and more positive behavior. In a sense, shaping reinforces attempts at new behaviors by breaking new behaviors down into small and manageable steps and rewarding each small step taken.

A related concept is modeling. In modeling, an individual observes a person engaging in a more positive behavior and receiving a reward for the positive behavior. The individual will be encouraged to then copy or match the positive behavior in the hope of getting the observed reward. The process of shaping provides a more immediate reward for the individual and is more connected to the actual behavior of the individual. Shaping also has the benefit of breaking down complex positive behaviors into manageable steps, something that is sometimes missing when observing others who are already competent in the positive behavior.

In a family setting, a mother and father are trying to work with their two children who constantly argue and fight over their toys, use of the TV, and use of the computer to play games. The fights occur almost daily, and while they are mostly verbal, on occasion one child may push at the other or grab an arm to pull the other child away from the toy. To expect this behavior to change and disappear overnight would be unrealistic. The parents can work together to develop a plan to begin to shape the children's behavior. First, the parents might praise each child if there have been no arguments or fights on one particular night. Second, if the children do argue, a parent may intervene and give examples of the kinds of words or expressions a person can use to express frustration or to make his or her feelings known. The next time there is an argument and one or both children use these more appropriate words, the parent can praise the children for handling their disagreement better. For each step in the process, the parents are gradually shaping the children's behavior into more appropriate expressions of feeling states and better ways of handling disagreements.

Schemas

Schemas are cognitive frameworks all people possess that help people make sense of their world (Marley, 2004). While other terms are sometimes used to describe schemas, the concept is present in many types of family therapy, including psychoanalytic, strategic, and narrative therapies. These cognitive frameworks are established through life experiences and affect how people interpret the world around them and how they then respond to the world. While schemas are ubiquitous across all people, life experiences vary and some experiences can lead people to develop schemas that function as blinders to important information or perspectives that may influence them, or some schemas may become distorted and lead individuals to misinterpret the world around them.

For cognitive-behavioral family therapists, a key issue is understanding the schemas present in the individuals in the family. This information can help the clinician better identify the cognitions that may interfere with the family's ability to change its behavior. Such distortions or faulty thinking, sometimes referred to as thinking errors, can increase the likelihood that a family will become entrenched in a problematic behavior-consequence cycle. Dattilio (1998) outlined a number of types of distortions that can be present in these cognitive frameworks. Some of the common distortions mentioned include overgeneralization, personalization, dichotomous thinking, and mind reading. Overgeneralization occurs when isolated negative experiences are taken as an indication of a general or global problem. For instance, a wife may get upset when her husband fails to pay a bill on time. While the husband may argue that this was just a mistake, the wife may interpret this mistake as a general failing of the husband to take care of their money issues. Personalization occurs when arbitrary events are interpreted as a statement about oneself. For example, a husband expects a call from his wife while she is away at a professional conference. If the wife fails to make the call, the husband may interpret this to mean she doesn't want to talk with him. Dichotomous thinking occurs when events or experiences are interpreted as all good or all bad. For example, a family taking a trip together has the experience of a child getting carsick on the way to the grandparents' house. While this only causes a momentary delay, upon arrival at the grandparents' house the husband says it was the worst trip ever and fails to acknowledge the positive interactions that occurred before and after the child got sick. Mind reading occurs when people don't see the need to communicate because they assume other people know what they are thinking. For example, a father gets angry at his son when the son does not clean up his bedroom. The father may say, "You knew I wanted this cleaned up hours ago" even though nothing was directly said between the father and son about this task.

Such cognitive distortions are one of the main roadblocks to the successful implementation of cognitive-behavioral therapy. Until the family members can identify and reflect upon these types of thinking errors present in their schemas, they often will be unable either to understand the tasks given to them by the cognitive-behavioral clinician or to implement the behaviors needed to carry out the tasks. What some clinicians identify as "sabotage," the experience of a family consciously or unconsciously undermining the clinical process, may in fact be a failure on the part of the clinician to address the distortions present in the family members' schemas.

Taken together, these concepts provide a strong foundation for the current practice of cognitive-behavioral family therapy. While some modern models of family therapy discount the mechanistic feel of the cognitive-behavioral model or fault it for being heavy with techniques but light on theory, it is clear that this model does have a theoretical history that still provides a rich foundation for the further development of intervention techniques. The concepts below help flesh out some of the particulars of this model in more detail.

GOALS OF THERAPY

The overall goal of cognitive-behavioral family therapy is the discontinuation of the identified problematic behavior and/or cognition (Falloon, 1988). As mentioned above, the cognitive-behavioral family therapist is not concerned with what caused the problematic behavior and/or cognition to begin; the focus is only on the reinforcers that allow it to continue or escalate. The goal of family therapy then is to identify the problematic behavior and/or cognition, understand the sequence of events that evoke the problematic behavior and/or cognition, identify the specific positive or negative reinforcers that occur as a consequence of the behavior and/or cognition occurring, and then work with the family to identify specific actions the family can take to extinguish the problematic behavior and/or cognition or identify and enact new behaviors and/or cognitions the family members can engage in that will be more adaptive and constructive in helping the family cope with difficult situations.

ROLE OF THE THERAPIST

The therapist in cognitive-behavioral family therapy takes a fairly active and direct role in the therapy. The therapist is an active participant in the assessment of the family situation, asking questions to better understand the sequence of events that include triggering events, evoking the problematic behavior and/or cognition, and the consequences and reinforcers generated by the problematic behavior and/or cognition. In addition, the family therapist will be very active in working with the family in developing a plan of action with the focus on changing the sequence of

Photo 9.1 Cognitive Behavioral Family Therapy addresses not only the negative behavioral patterns families engage in at home, but also those negative behaviors in the family therapy sessions

Source: Copyright © Can Stock Photo Inc./lisafx

actions that have become entrenched as a learned response within the family. While the therapist may collaborate with the family members in identifying possible courses of action designed to change this pattern of learned response, the therapist will usually play an active role in helping the family members write up the identified plan and work with them in making the plan very specific and something all can understand and agree on.

Compared to some other types of family therapy, the cognitive-behavioral family therapist is a very active and verbal part of the therapeutic process. Through the assessment and treatment planning process, the therapist will ask lots of questions, clarify sequences of action, and elicit from family members their assessment of the identified behaviors and/or cognitions. For some family therapists, this level of activity by the therapist may be construed as intrusive or as possibly undermining the family's role as "expert" of its own situation. However, this level of activity is needed, according to the theoretical and conceptual underpinning of this model, to get the data needed to understand the family schema, learned responses, and problematic sequences that have become entrenched in the family.

PROCESS OF THERAPY

The process of cognitive-behavioral family therapy is fairly straightforward. As with many models of family therapy, the first step in the process is a thorough assessment. Unlike many models of family therapy, however, the cognitive-behavioral assessment is very detailed and may take place over the first several sessions of meeting with a family.

The assessment stage of family therapy usually includes the following: (a) working with the family to identify the specific problematic behaviors and/or cognitions that brought the family into therapy in the first place; (b) careful and detailed questions designed to better understand the specifics of the identified behaviors and/or cognitions, which may include questions about the frequency of the identified problematic behavior, the duration of the problematic behavior when it occurs, the intensity of the problematic behavior when it occurs, antecedent events that may be triggers that evoke the problematic behavior, consequences that occur following the problematic behavior, or reinforcers that may encourage the continued use of the problematic behavior or discourage the use of competing behaviors, which may be more adaptive; and (c) the identification of possible reinforcers that could be used to help extinguish or change the problematic behavior.

As part of the assessment, the cognitive-behavioral family therapist may assign homework to the family to monitor, observe, and "measure" the problematic behavior in the naturally occurring family environment. Such homework may include having family members keep logs or diaries where they can record their assessment of the problematic behavior as it occurs, or they may be asked to fill out structured assessment tools during the time between meetings with the family therapist. The use of such homework, while primarily providing the family therapist with critical data needed to help the family, is also useful in (a) gauging differences between family members in their individual assessments of the identified problematic behavior and (b) determining the degree to which the family is engaged in the process of therapy by completing the homework and providing useful data. In some cases, when family members fail to complete homework assignments during the assessment process or do so in a haphazard manner that provides little useful information, such actions may indicate that they are not yet on board with the process of family therapy or may not understand the connection between the homework and the process of trying to change the problematic behavior.

Following the assessment process, the family therapist will then help the family draw up a specific treatment plan or behavioral analysis of the problematic behavior. Such a plan or analysis will often summarize the data collected to date, indicate the sequence of behaviors that have led to the entrenched learned responses experienced by the family, and indicate the kinds of reinforcers currently utilized that impede the changing of the identified problematic behavior. The assessment or analysis will then identify specific steps the family will need to take to begin to change the problematic behaviors. These steps will be built around the tools and techniques discussed below. The written plan will also identify target goals for assessing whether the interventions are working, a time frame within which to evaluate whether the interventions are working, who the responsible parties are for each step specified in the plan, and at what stage the overall plan will be reassessed to determine if it is working or in need of adjustment.

TOOLS AND TECHNIQUES

The following tools and techniques can be used in different combinations based on the nature of the family and the nature of the identified problem behavior and/or cognition. Some of the techniques, such as homework, are fairly common whereas something like coaching may be more likely to apply in only certain types of family situations.

Contracts

Contracts (Sanders & Dadds, 1993) can be one of several different types. In its most general sense, a contract is the written behavioral plan that specifies each family member's role and responsibility in the intervention process. Such contracts need to be as specific as possible and contain observable or measurable goals and activities so the family member has something by which to gauge whether the identified problematic behavior is changing or whether the family member is doing what he or she is supposed to do to try and make the identified problematic behavior change.

In a more specific case, a contract may be developed around a specific behavior as it relates to a specific family member. For example, the overall contract may spell out the plan to intervene in helping parents better set limits on their teenage son. However, the family therapist may want to add a specific contract with the son indicating that the son is not to drink alcohol as he is underage and risks serious consequences from his school if he is caught drinking. This kind of specific contract can also identify other problematic behaviors that influence the identified family-level problematic behavior or that might make difficult the implementation of some of the intervention plans. In the case situation above, the son needs to be sober and not in trouble with the school in order for the family as a whole to work on changing its family-level problematic behavior.

Finally, contracts can be ad hoc plans developed and implemented at any point in the process of therapy based on the identification of new behaviors that emerge within the family or within an individual in response to the overall family process of change. Sometimes, as the family as a whole attempts to change its learned response pattern and adopt new and more adaptive behaviors, some members of the family may resist or react negatively to these changes. If such reactions create new concerns for the family, the therapist can develop a contract for that specific new behavior and work on an intervention plan to address it.

Coaching

Coaching can be seen as a type of modeling and can be used in the process of shaping the development of new behaviors. Often, the cognitive-behavioral family therapist becomes the coach and tries to actively support attempts by family members to try out new behaviors or responses to behavior. Such support can range from simple verbal encouragement to more direct suggestions about things to try. For instance, in a family therapy session where a daughter is trying to communicate with her father without getting hostile or condescending, the therapist might praise the daughter when she uses more feeling-neutral words in the session as she tries to engage her father in a discussion. The therapist might also make specific suggestions to the daughter, such as "Maybe you want to try saying that

Photo 9.2   A key component of Cognitive Behavioral Family Therapy is a thorough assessment that involves hearing from all members of the family

Source: © Bruce Ayres/Getty Images

again; only this time try using these words and see how that works." Coaching is an opportunity for the family therapist to directly relate to and shape the family's behavior at a collective or individual level.

Functional Assessment

A functional assessment is the detailed assessment needed to best understand the identified problematic behavior (Falloon, 1988). This tool comes from operant conditioning and provides a structure for looking at the specific identified problematic behavior, the antecedents to the behavior (potential triggers), and the reinforcers of the behavior (the consequences that ensue and how they help maintain the problematic behavior). In such an assessment, the family may play a role in completing such an assessment by observing and recording data at home or wherever the problematic behavior occurs. In some cases, the problematic behavior may occur in the family therapy session, in which case the family therapist can play a role in assessing the antecedents, behavior, and reinforcers.

Homework

Homework is a general term used to denote any assignment, task, or activity the family therapist asks the family members to accomplish between sessions. The homework may involve the entire family, or different family members may have different homework assignments. Homework assignments work best when several criteria are met: (a) The homework is specific enough that all involved can clearly understand what is expected of them, (b) the homework is clearly connected to one of the goals of the behavioral intervention plan or analysis, and (c) the homework can be phrased in such a way as to be experienced by the family as a low-risk/high-gain experience that encourages completion of the homework.

For example, a therapist who is working with a mother, a father, and two young children may ask that the parents meet together without the children present for at least 15 minutes each day to discuss any child care issues that have come up and that may come up the next day. If the behavioral intervention plan identifies parental communication and child care planning as a problem in this family, then such a homework assignment would clearly be tied to the intervention goal of increasing parental communication and planning for child care issues as proactively and as a team rather than at the last minute with much frustration and anger generated by the parents' inability to plan ahead. The homework is specific enough to understand (meet for 15 minutes without the children present; discuss what has occurred and what may occur as it relates to child care issues) and presents a low-risk (it is fairly easy to chat for 15 minutes) and high-gain (immediate parental communication) situation.

Contingency Management

Contingency management (Schwitzgebel, 1967) refers to the giving of rewards or punishments (reinforcers) based on the behavior exhibited. While often discussed in behavioral therapy with children, the technique applies to any plan in which specific rewards or punishments are the expected response to a specific behavior with the goal to either (a) increase the likelihood of an appropriate behavior or (b) decrease the likelihood of a problematic behavior. As part of the behavioral plan or analysis, contingency management tries to shape differential response based on the behavior that is engaged in by the family or a family member. If, for example, when a child cries the father yells at that child and that behavior is reinforced by the child ceasing to cry, contingency management would be part of the plan to reward the father for responding differently the next time his child cries. Such a reward would need to motivate the father to engage in the more appropriate behavior more often as he begins to shape his behavior and unlearn a learned response cycle.

Contingency Contracting

Contingency contracting (Stuart, 1971) is part of the overall behavioral assessment and intervention plan in which the plan specifies the types of rewards and punishments to be given out based on the behavior exhibited. This contract spells out the conditions within which the person or persons in the family will get the reward or punishment and how such contingencies are tied to the overall behavioral assessment and intervention plan. As with other types of behavioral contracts, the contingency contract needs to be specific as to the nature of the reward or punishment, and it needs to be specific about the criteria that must be met to merit the reward or the punishment. Often, one of the more complicated aspects of contingency management is the identification of specific rewards or punishments that will be seen as relevant or motivating by the family member or members such that the contingencies will actually shape behavior. Following the thorough assessment process, as the behavioral intervention plan is being drafted, the therapist will need to discuss with the family what might be relevant contingencies that could be utilized in the plan. While a child may love to get a cookie each time the child exhibits an appropriate behavior, in the long run this might not be the best or healthiest contingency.

Premack Principle

The Premack principle (Premack, 1965) states that enjoyable high-probability behavior can be used to help reinforce low-probability behavior that is less enjoyable. For instance, if a mother is having difficulty getting her child to behave appropriately in a store, she may try to reinforce the child's compliance by promising to get the child a candy bar at the checkout line. However, the mother may find that this reinforcer does not work consistently. In discussion with the family therapist, the child identifies several other choices of behavior he would like to engage in while in the store, for example helping the mother push the cart and gather items off the shelf. When the mother goes to the store the next time, she lets the child push the cart as long as the child is behaving himself in the store. This new response (reinforcer) to the child's attempts to exhibit more appropriate behavior serves as a stronger and more enjoyable reinforcer than the promised candy bar.

In a sense, the Premack principle opens up many more possibilities as to what constitutes a relevant reinforcer. Through a careful assessment process and behavioral analysis, the family therapist needs to evaluate what each family member would consider an enjoyable behavior that could serve as a strong reinforcer to encourage the development or increased exhibition of a desired positive behavior.

Token Economies

Token economies (Falloon, 1988) are a subset of reinforcers that use the acquisition of tokens or points or some other tangible reward that can then be exchanged for some desired reward. Token economies can be used to shape behaviors by providing some kind of immediate reward for approximate behaviors or the provision of different amounts of the reinforcer based on how well someone exhibits the desired behavior. For example, a parent may work with a young child around keeping the child's room clean. If the child puts away his clothes, the child may get 10 points. If the child not only puts clothes away but also makes the bed, the child gets 15 points. In each case, the child gets an immediate and tangible reward for approximating or exhibiting the desired behavior. For a token economy to work, the acquired tokens or points must be then exchanged for some larger and pleasurable reward (the Premack principle). In the above scenario with the child, once the child amasses 100 points, for example, the child can exchange those 100 points for something the child finds as a powerful reinforcer to encourage the continued behavior of keeping the bedroom clean. Such an exchange not only provides another level of reinforcer for the development of the desired behavior; it also promotes delayed gratification. The child has to take time to amass the desired 100 points to get the even greater reward waiting when the 100 points can be exchanged. However, the immediate reward of getting the points by putting away clothes or making a bed encourages the continuation of the positive behavior on the way to the desired reward.

Token economies have been used successfully in many parents' situations, educational settings, child and adolescent treatment programs for significant behavioral problems, and the work world of adults. The regular reinforcement of desired behavior with the understanding that a larger and pleasurable reward awaits at the end of the process is a very powerful motivator for the development and maintenance of desired behaviors.

CASE ILLUSTRATION

Presenting problem.	Michael is a 35-year-old Caucasian male who has a primary diagnosis of schizophrenia. He lives with his mother (Susan, age 65) and father (Robert, age 67) in a two-bedroom apartment. Michael is the youngest of three children; the older two (Tom, age 39, and Sharon, age 43) live out of state but stay in regular contact with the family by phone. They frequently visit on the holidays as well.
	The parents have sought family therapy saying that Michael is causing more problems at home. He frequently yells loudly for no apparent reason, and this has caused stress with the apartment neighbors. Also, Michael has been lax in his personal hygiene to the point where the parents are reluctant to let people visit the apartment because of the smell. These behaviors have been going on for about 6 months and have gotten steadily worse over the last 3 months. The parents have expressed some concern about being able to keep Michael at the apartment if his behavior doesn't change and have discussed this issue with Michael's case manager at the outpatient clinic where Michael gets his medications. All three are willing to come in for therapy and see if something can be done to help Michael change his behavior.
First-session observations.	When the family arrives for the first session, all seem quiet and a little nervous. Michael is dressed appropriately but has a slight odor about him. The parents seem tired.
	After making introductions and discussing some of the parameters of the therapy, the therapist asks the family to talk more about the concerns previously expressed.
	The father states for the last 6 months or so Michael has been acting out by yelling and not bathing or doing his laundry. The father says he and his wife have tried to get him to be quieter, but they never know when he will start yelling. As for his hygiene, they have tried to convince him of the importance of staying clean, but nothing seems to motivate Michael to do better.
Beginning of a functional assessment and gathering data about the behavioral sequence (trigger, behavior, consequence).	The therapist asks the parents to pick one of the last times Michael started yelling and to think about what was happening in the apartment right before, during, and after the yelling. The mother says it happened just yesterday. The father was out of the apartment getting some groceries when Michael began yelling loudly. The mother went to Michael's room, knocked on the door, and asked what was wrong.

(Continued)

	Michael replied that everything was wrong, that he was stuck in his room and wanted people to know where he was. After about 10 minutes of yelling, Michael seemed to calm down. He came out of his room and sat down with his mother to have lunch. The mother says he seemed fine after the outburst, but she did what she usually does after such an outburst; she tried to cater to him by getting him food, getting him his favorite book, or letting him put on his favorite TV show.
"Usually does" may indicate a learned response cycle as well as the consequences experienced by Michael that help maintain the negative behavior.	The therapist asks if there are other instances when the yelling occurs. The father says it happens a few times a week and often when one parent or the other is out of the apartment.
A potential trigger that sets the behavioral cycle in action.	The therapist asks the parents to describe in more detail the yelling. How often does it occur? Is it always the same? Is it louder or softer or better or worse on some days?
Gathering more details about the behavior, its degree, its frequency, and its intensity.	Michael says he doesn't yell all the time; he yells only when he feels stuck in his room. The parents say he is always encouraged to go out of the apartment; he knows the neighborhood well and often walks to the agency to see his case manager and psychiatrist. They don't know why he feels stuck.
Michael and his sense of being stuck could be an early indicator of Michael's schema about his illness and his family.	The therapist asks Michael when the yelling began. Michael says he doesn't remember when. Maybe last winter. The therapist asks Michael if the yelling makes him feel better after he has done it. Michael says no; he knows it makes his parents upset and bothers the neighbors. He feels bad but doesn't know what else to do when he feels like yelling.
	The therapist asks the parents how they usually respond while Michael is yelling and after he stops. The mom says she usually leaves him alone when he starts yelling in his room. She might check to make sure he is OK, but then she leaves him alone. Afterward, she tries to calm him down by letting him do what he likes, making him his favorite food, that kind of thing. The dad says he kind of does the same thing, checks on him but then leaves him alone. Afterward, he encourages Michael to do things he likes and tries to help Michael calm down.
Further exploration of possible consequences and reinforcers of the behavior.	The parents are more worried about the yelling and the hygiene because their other children want to visit but are reluctant because of Michael's current behavior. They also say they are losing patience with Michael but try to stay supportive. They are just getting tired and wonder if his living with them is the best arrangement.

	The therapist asks Michael what are some of the things he likes to do that help him feel better. Michael says he likes to take walks and watch TV. He used to play a lot of card games but doesn't much anymore.
Begin exploring possible rewards. Identify more pleasurable activities (Premack principle).	The father chuckles and says he forgot about the card playing. He says Michael was an excellent card player, seemed to know hundreds of card games, and was always carrying around a deck or two of cards. The father says Michael taught the family how to play Bridge many years ago.
	The therapist asks if or when the rest of the family is going to visit next. The mom says that she and her husband are going to celebrate their 45th wedding anniversary in 4 months and the family is planning to get together then.
	The therapist says to the family that it seems Michael's yelling and poor hygiene are causing some stress in the family. Rather than think about moving Michael out, the therapist asks the family members if they are willing to look at changing some things in the family aimed at helping Michael change some of his behavior. The parents say yes, and Michael says he is sorry for being such a pain but that he will try.
Assessing motivation to change.	The therapist says that there may be many reasons or frustrations that trigger Michael's yelling or that make him not care as much about his hygiene. But it seems when he yells, he often gets left alone and then afterward gets focused on by the parents. The therapist worries that when Michael is left alone when yelling it might add to his frustration and fuel more yelling. But when he is done, he gets a lot of time and attention, which might be what he wanted in the first place. While the parents' attention is understandable as it helps calm Michael down, it may also be encouraging him to yell so he can get what he wants.
Making explicit the learned response cycle based on information gathered so far. This is critical so that the family can understand any homework or change strategies proposed.	The therapist proposes that the family members agree to a plan to make some specific changes in how they all work together and see if these changes start to change some of Michael's behavior. The therapist suggests that the family do the following between now and the next session and report how it worked.
	First, the therapist suggests that the next time Michael starts yelling, rather than leave him alone, the parent who is home should go into Michael's room and begin to talk with him

(Continued)

Introduction of a contract for behavioral change. Specific homework assignment. Changing the usually learned response cycle.	about any topic that comes to mind as long as it is not about the yelling or why he is yelling. If Michael stops yelling, the parent and Michael should leave the bedroom and continue the conversation for at least 15 minutes. Second, for each day Michael goes without yelling, he gets an hour of time with his mom and/or dad to do an activity of his choosing (taking a walk, playing a game, etc.). Third, if Michael showers at least three times during the week, he gets an hour of time with his mom and/or dad to do an activity of his choosing.
Contingency management, using the Premack principle to let Michael choose the more pleasurable activity that will be a motivator for him.	Finally, the therapist suggests that the parents encourage Michael to find structured time to revisit his love of card playing. The family should put together a plan that sets aside time for Michael to practice his card games and that sets aside 30 minutes each night for Michael and the parents to play a brief card game. The therapist asks if this initial plan is clear to everyone. The family says yes; all three members understand it. The therapist takes a few minutes to write it down while the family discusses the plan and how it might work.
A coaching opportunity can be used to shape the parents' behavior.	The parents ask what to do if, when Michael is yelling, he doesn't respond to their attempts to talk with him. The therapist says, "Suppose Michael is yelling right now. Let me see what you might do." The father says, "Hey Michael, I just read in the paper that the library has a great free movie coming next week. I thought it was one you might like to see." The therapist says, "That's a good start. Now what would you do if Michael was still yelling?" The father says, in a slightly louder voice, "Michael, you remember, you mentioned that movie, you said you really liked that actor in it." The therapist says, "Really good, just keep at it. Try not to raise your voice if he keeps yelling. Sometimes when you speak quieter, the person yelling has to quiet down to hear you." The therapist hands them the written plan and encourages them to try it for a week and to observe what happens. In the next session, they can discuss what worked well, what didn't, or any new ideas any of them have that they could try.
Encouraging the family, building a sense of collaboration and a sense that the behavioral contract may need to be adjusted once it gets put into action and the results are observed by the family.	

SUMMARY

Cognitive-behavioral family therapy has remained one of the stronger models of family intervention since its inception. Its focus on specific, measurable behaviors as well as its use of concrete techniques makes it one of the easier models of family therapy to study and research. From treating sexual dysfunction and managing bipolar disorder issues in families to maintaining people with schizophrenia in their family home, cognitive-behavioral family therapy has shown itself to be very effective in shaping appropriate behavior and eliminating problematic behavior.

As a consequence of the specificity and measurability of this model of family therapy, it tends to be a favored model within the evidence-based practice arena. The model lends itself well to clinical evaluation under both controlled and natural family settings. In a review of research on family therapy and evidence-based practice, cognitive-behavioral family therapy and specific programs utilizing the basic principles of this model tend to dominate the research literature. It is a well-utilized, well-researched model that continues to be refined to address specific family issues and identified problems.

RECOMMENDED READINGS

Dattilio, F. (1998). *Case studies in couple and family therapy: Systemic and cognitive approaches*. New York, NY: Guilford.

Dattilio, F., & Reinecke, M. (1996). *Casebook of cognitive-behavior therapy with children and adolescents*. New York, NY: Guilford.

Ellis, A. (1962). *Reason and emotion in psychotherapy*. New York, NY: Lyle Stuart.

Falloon, I. (1988). *Handbook of behavioral family therapy*. New York, NY: Guilford.

Jacobson, N., & Margolin, G. (1979). *Marital therapy: Strategies based on social learning and behavioral exchange principles*. New York, NY: Brunner/Mazel.

Mueser, K., & Glynn, S. (1999). *Behavioral family therapy for psychiatric disorders* (2nd ed.). Oakland, CA: New Harbinger.

Sanders, M., & Dadds, M. (1993). *Behavioral family intervention*. Needham Heights, MA: Allyn & Bacon.

DISCUSSION QUESTIONS

1. Locate a family therapy case study. From a cognitive-behavioral perspective, identify the learned response cycle that includes the antecedent triggers, the learned response, and the subsequent consequences or reinforcers that help maintain the problematic behavior.

2. Cognitive-behavioral family therapy has a number of specific techniques and tools for use with families. Select two or three of them and discuss how you would apply them to different family situations. Are some more useful or readily applicable than others? If so, why?

3. Cognitive-behavioral family therapy states explicitly that it does not address the underlying cause of the identified family problem. What are your opinions about this theoretical principle? Discuss what you might see as some of the strengths and weaknesses of this principle.

REFERENCES

Bandura, A. (1969). *Principles of behavior modification.* New York, NY: Holt, Rinehart & Winston.

Beck, A. (1976). *Cognitive therapy and the emotional disorders.* New York, NY: International Universities Press.

Dattilio, F. (1998). *Case studies in couple and family therapy: Systemic and cognitive approaches.* New York, NY: Guilford.

Dattilio, F., & Reinecke, M. (1996). *Casebook of cognitive-behavior therapy with children and adolescents.* New York, NY: Guilford.

Ellis, A. (1962). *Reason and emotion in psychotherapy.* New York, NY: Lyle Stuart.

Falloon, I. (1988). *Handbook of behavioral family therapy.* New York, NY: Guilford.

Jacobson, N., & Margolin, G. (1979). *Marital therapy: Strategies based on social learning and behavioral exchange principles.* New York, NY: Brunner/Mazel.

Marley, J. (2004). *Family involvement in treating schizophrenia: Models, essential skills, and process.* New York, NY: Haworth Press.

Mueser, K., & Glynn, S. (1999). *Behavioral family therapy for psychiatric disorders* (2nd ed.). Oakland, CA: New Harbinger.

Patterson, G. (1971). *Families: Application of social learning theory to family life.* Champaign, IL: Research Press.

Premack, D. (1965). Reinforcement theory. In D. Levine (Ed.), *Nebraska symposium on motivation.* Lincoln: University of Nebraska Press.

Sanders, M., & Dadds, M. (1993). *Behavioral family intervention.* Needham Heights, MA: Allyn & Bacon.

Schwitzgebel, R. (1967). Short-term operant conditioning of adolescent offenders on socially relevant variables. *Journal of Abnormal Psychology, 72,* 134–142.

Skinner, B. (1953). *Science and human behavior.* New York, NY: Macmillan.

Stuart, R. (1971). Behavioral contracting within the families of delinquents. *Journal of Behavior Therapy and Experimental Psychiatry, 2,* 1–11.

Thibaut, J., & Kelley, H. (1959). *The social psychology of groups.* New York, NY: Wiley.

Chapter 10

NARRATIVE FAMILY THERAPY

BACKGROUND AND LEADING FIGURES

The main architect of narrative family therapy was Michael White, who in the 1970s developed this model through his work in Australia. Through his interest in Gregory Bateson, Michel Foucault, and Erving Goffman, White developed a sophisticated theoretical approach to understanding how people develop narratives that construct their sense of reality and the role problems play in shaping these narratives. This "social constructivist" approach to family therapy was seen as the antithesis to the mechanistic approaches of cognitive-behavioral therapies or the illness-focused approaches from the psychoanalytical schools.

Along with White, the other primary force in the early development of narrative family therapy was David Epston, a family therapist working in New Zealand. It was Epston who keyed in on the narrative metaphor and the power of storytelling. Together, White and Epston wrote *Narrative Means to Therapeutic Ends* (1990), the first extensive exploration of narrative theory and

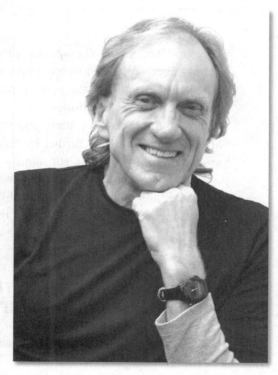

Photo 10.1 Michael White built on the philosophical works of Michel Foucault and others in his development of Narrative Family Therapy

Source: © Jill Freedman

Photo 10.2 David Epston's important work contributed to translating the philosophical concepts of narrative family therapy into a popular practice model with well-delineated techniques

Source: © Maggie Carey

narrative therapy. This was followed in 1992 by Epston and White's *Experience, Contradiction, Narrative, and Imagination: Selected Papers of David Epston and Michael White, 1989–1991.*

The work of White and Epston found a receptive audience in the United States. Jill Freedman and Gene Combs working in Evanston, Illinois, left their strategic family orientation and found the narrative perspective more in keeping with their political activism. Their work (Freedman & Combs, 1996) became an excellent and practical guide to narrative therapy and was useful in translating some of the more philosophical components of White and Epston into a more pragmatic and accessible therapeutic process. Similarly, Jeffrey Zimmerman and Vicki Dickerson (1996) wrote a very user-friendly text on narrative therapy and helped further develop the general process of therapy and provided a clear discussion of various techniques.

Throughout the 1990s, these and various other clinicians pushed the model of narrative family therapy further by refining techniques and applying the model to various client populations and family issues. While some of the political underpinnings of Foucault's initial work were lost or minimized in the push to refine techniques and translate complex philosophical perspectives into a more pragmatic model for practice, the core of the model has stayed focused on several key concepts that have their origins in the work of Foucault and others.

PHILOSOPHICAL, CONCEPTUAL, AND THEORETICAL UNDERPINNINGS

Narrative family therapy has at its cornerstone the philosophy of Michel Foucault, a French philosopher writing in the 1950s through the 1970s. Foucault (2006; Chambon, Irving, & Epstein, 1999) developed what he referred to as the "archeology of knowledge" and applied this type of exploration to the history of institutions and various populations. Through this exploration, Foucault argued that social discourse creates a power imbalance that then marginalizes different populations or allows these populations to be treated poorly by the institutions entrusted with their care. For Foucault, those who are in power create social discourse that allows them to stay in power often by marginalizing other groups who are then seen to be incapable of being in power or who need the paternalistic care from those who are in power. Truth, for Foucault, was socially constructed by this social discourse. The narratives that are created by those in power, the stories they tell or allow to be told, shape how others understand what is truthful and acceptable. For example, a social discourse might reinforce the inherent pathology of a group of people and therefore that group becomes an "other" (Gilman, 1985), a group marginalized by a community of members who believe the "truth" of those in power and allow the "other" to be treated differently or poorly. Only by digging deep and understanding where these original narratives emerged (the archeological process per Foucault) could the core narrative be exposed, reexamined, and better understood as a mechanism for maintaining the power imbalance. For Foucault, the political aspect of this perspective was to challenge the "truth" of these core narratives and the power differential they help maintain. The reexamination process (deconstruction) could then lead to the construction of a new narrative that would eliminate the power differential.

Jerome Bruner (1986) built on some of Foucault's ideas and explored further the process by which narratives can in fact shape someone's perceptions of reality. By understanding the process of storytelling and looking at how and why children gravitate to storytelling, even at a young age, Bruner showed that human beings use storytelling as an organizing framework to understand the complex world around them. When stories get repeated, they take on a unique power and help the developing mind sort and order its perceptions of the world. Stories can emphasize what is important to a given community and how relationships are understood and utilized. Stories, then, can help lay down the internal map of the individual and shape how that person responds to and acts upon the social context. For Bruner, and those who based their writings on his work, in order to understand why a person acts the way he or she does within a specific social context, one has to understand the stories that form the base of the person's understanding of the "truths" within that social context.

The narrative model of family therapy, building on these philosophical beliefs, brought in a level of political awareness not usually associated with other models of family therapy. The narrative family therapist could examine family discourse and identify how language and stories might reinforce a power differential within a specific family leading to the marginalization of one or more family members. By making explicit the power of language, how language can shape the "truth" as the family comes to understand it, narrative family therapy became one of the key social constructionist models of practice. The concepts discussed below highlight some of the ways this model of practice builds on its social constructionist roots.

CONCEPTS

The concepts discussed below help make the transition between the philosophical perspective of Foucault and the applied nature of a model for family therapy. While Foucault and Bruner never specifically wrote about family therapy, it is clear from the work of White, Epston, and others that the philosophy of social constructionism provided a strong guide to a model of family therapy.

Dominant Beliefs

One of the key concepts of narrative family therapy is the concept of dominant beliefs (White, 1995; White & Epston, 1990). Similar to solution-focused family therapy, the dominant belief is the core narrative, the key story the family tells about itself or its members that helps the family make sense of its situation and functioning. Dominant beliefs become the lens through which a family looks at itself and looks at the world it exists within.

Given that each family is made up of individual members, each member may have a slightly different take on the overall family dominant belief. Each family member has a unique place in the family system, unique experiences within the family, and unique experiences outside of the family. Narrative family therapy recognizes and embraces the idea of multiple realities at work within a family due to the above unique situation each family member has within the family. The issue is not which narrative reality is "true" but how the multiple realities within the family work together or work at odds with each other to facilitate or impede family functioning.

For example, a family may have a dominant family narrative that says it is a family that copes with adversity. The individual family members may be quick to relate stories about how the family overcame one crisis after another and pulled together to cope with very challenging events. But within that dominant narrative may reside some individual narratives about personal sacrifice, about whose issues or needs took precedence over others in order for the family as a whole to cope and survive. Such individual narratives may highlight an issue within the family that, in order for the family as a whole to survive and cope, a particular family member's individual needs have to be overlooked or ignored. If the same family member experiences such marginalization time and time again, he or she may experience the family as inherently unfair but feel uncomfortable about expressing this view since from all outward signs the family has coped well in the face of adversity. The individual's dominant belief is then at odds with the family's dominant belief. The struggle between dominant beliefs is often a sign of how power and control are distributed within a family. Those who have the power and control, via Foucault, are more apt to create dominant beliefs that support the status quo.

Discourse

Discourse for the narrative family therapist exists at two levels (Marley, 2004). First, each family exists in a social-cultural context and is therefore shaped by the social-cultural discourse that surrounds the family. For example, if the newspapers are full of stories about the plight of single mothers, same-sex couples trying to adopt children, or the influence of divorce on child development, such stories will have an impact on families that resemble the group being discussed in the social-cultural context.

A common clinical example is the family with parents seeking family therapy because their teenage son has been acting out at home by failing to follow limits set by the parents on such things as curfew and cell phone usage. The parents may say, "Well, everyone always said teenage rebellion was common; I guess we just have to put up with it until he grows out of it." The idea of teenage rebellion is a common social-cultural discourse that gets reinforced many times over in how teens are presented in the media. However, multiple research studies have found that the vast majority of teens in fact don't outwardly rebel during their teen years. The parents in the above scenario, then, ought not to just wait it out while feeling miserable; they can and should take action to address the problem in the family. But first, they need to understand how their acceptance of the social-cultural discourse is shaping their current behavior and decision making.

Second, discourse exists within each family. If the social-cultural discourse is the macro influencing factor, the family-level discourse is the micro influencing factor. The words and stories a family uses within itself, how family members are portrayed, what stories are repeated as exemplars of individual family functioning— all of these can begin to shape the perceptions each family member has of the others and of the family as a whole.

For example, in a family the younger son might be discussed using terms like *brilliant* and *star athlete* and *golden child* while the older son might be described as *a troublemaker* and *a stress to his parents* and *just barely making it in school*. To reinforce these descriptors, stories will be related that give examples of each son living out the term being described. For the sons listening to this or participating in the description of events, they will begin to see themselves as playing particular roles within the family based on the discourse used that reinforces their place in the family. For the son who is described in the more negative terms, to what extent will he feel able to offer up an alternative point of view if he senses the family does not see any alternative views? He may find it easier to "go along" with the family-level discourse even if there are times when he acts in ways that counter his negative descriptors.

Externalization

If dominant beliefs and discourse become the forces that shape a family's perception of itself and its individual members, externalization becomes a key concept that allows the family to begin to work against these narratives (White & Epston, 1990; Zimmerman & Dickerson, 1996). As described above, dominant beliefs and discourse can become internalized within a family or family member and begin to shape how the family perceives its issues and the range of ways it can act to resolve family issues. For the narrative family therapist, one of the first tasks is to help the family begin to separate itself from the power and influence of these narratives. Externalization is a process by which the family comes to talk about its issues as being outside of the family or outside of the individual family member. In a sense, externalization begins to put the onus of responsibility for some of the family's issues on the external discourse and dominant beliefs and away from the family or an individual family member. A family is helped to talk about its issues and how these problems influence the family, not how the family influences the problems. This is a key difference between narrative family therapy and many other models of family therapy. Externalization is one of the political elements developed by Foucault (2006; Chambon et al., 1999), who felt that the problems many people experienced were due not to who they were but to how society talked about who they were.

For example, in a family therapy situation where a couple has sought help for its child who is acting out in school, the therapist may try and get the family to articulate its dominant beliefs and discourse about the child. The parents may use terms like *problem child* or *he's just being terrible at school*. The narrative family therapist will work with this family to change its discourse through externalization and to see that rather than saying its "child is bad" it might begin to say he or she "is behaving in problematic ways." This is the first step toward externalization. Next, the therapist will work with the family to see the problem as the problem behavior—the problem is not the family or the child. In some cases, a narrative family therapist might discuss the problem as "visiting the family" and explain that the family now needs to respond differently to this unwelcome visitor. Such externalization helps free the family and the identified patient from being seen as the keeper of the problem and begins to move the family toward a different kind of discourse about the individual, the family, and possible courses of action to make the visitor go away. A change in the micro discourse often leads to a change in the more macro dominant beliefs held by the family.

Problem-Saturated Stories

Problem-saturated stories are a type of discourse that reinforces the kinds of discourse used in a family and often are part of establishing a pattern in a family that perpetuates a problem (Epston & White, 1992). These stories tend to cause the family to only see and discuss problems, prevent the family from noticing or utilizing alternative experiences that challenge the problem-saturated stories, and often reinforce behaviors that consistently reinforce the "truth" of a problem-saturated story.

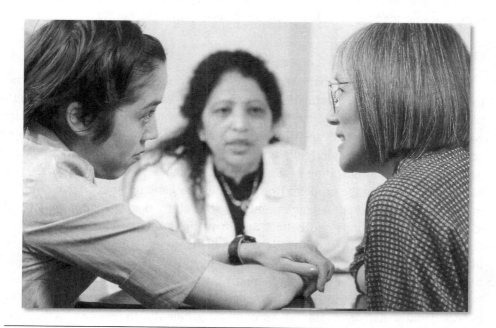

Photo 10.3   The family therapist attempts to get all members of the family to share their own narratives to better understand how these stories shape the family's understanding of its situation

Source: © Alvis Upitis/Brand X Pictures/Getty Images

For example, in the family mentioned above whose teenage son is acting out by breaking curfew and misusing his cell phone, the problem-saturated story would focus exclusively on those instances where the son acted in accordance with the dominant beliefs and discourse within the family. Each time the son did break curfew or misuse the cell phone, the family would make note of that and use it to confirm the "truth" of its perceptions of the problem. If the son did in fact keep to his curfew some of the time, or even often, those instances might not be recognized or might be minimized so that the dominant belief and discourse are not counteracted. The teen son is in a no-win situation; even attempts to do better are not seen as such. This kind of pattern, then, keeps the family stuck in its perception of the problem, consistently reinforces to the son his role as the keeper of the problem, and consistently reinforces that any attempts to change the problem must be ineffective since the dominant belief and discourse never change. This kind of "blinders on" functioning within a family is not that unusual. While the narrative family therapist may be curious about why such blinders need to exist and who benefits from the blinders, the first task will be to help the family identify that the blinders exist and that these problem-saturated stories are preventing the family members from working together to actually create change within the family.

Deconstruction

Deconstruction is the final concept that is key to the basic workings of narrative family therapy. The term *deconstruction* was well developed by Foucault (2006) as part of his "archeology of knowledge." Deconstruction is the process by which the dominant beliefs and discourse are articulated within the family therapy setting such that their underlying assumptions can be challenged and discussed. The process of externalization is one way in which the deconstruction process can begin. By separating the problem from the individual and the family, the family is provided with a different vantage point from which to examine the problem and identify the assumptions and beliefs that drive the problem. Part of the goal of deconstruction, then, is to dismantle the problematic assumptions and discourse that perpetuate the problem and reconstruct a new narrative that allows the family to challenge the problem in new and creative ways.

Following the scenario of the teenager acting out, the family connects the expected and socially and culturally reinforced notion of teen rebellion to the existence of the teen's acting out. Given that the son is a teen and rebellion is a "truth," by definition the problem must lie within the teen. He is a teen; therefore he is rebellious. Such a dominant belief will be reinforced by the discourse used within the family (our son is the problem; he's acting out) and will be reinforced by a problem-saturated story (he always breaks curfew; he always misuses his cell phone). In order to deconstruct this belief, the therapist might start with having the family articulate the dominant belief (all teens are rebellious) and identify any exceptions to this belief. For instance, do family members know other teens who seem to act differently? When the parents were teens did they act rebellious? Does their son really always act rebellious? Such "exception seeking" is similar to the process identified in solution-focused family therapy. For the narrative family therapist, an exception provides a counterargument to the "truth" of the dominant belief and family discourse. Once the basic premise of the dominant belief is challenged, the deconstruction process has begun. The family will ultimately have to develop (reconstruct) a new dominant belief that allows for the fact that not all teens are rebellious and that its teen in particular is not always rebellious. Such a reconstruction gives the family a new vantage point from which to address the specifics of its family situation without the problem-saturated blinders on limiting its perceptions and possible actions.

GOALS OF THERAPY

The principal goal of narrative family therapy is to assist the family in developing a new narrative about itself and its individual members (Freedman & Combs, 1996; Zimmerman & Dickerson, 1996). The new narrative creates new dominant beliefs and new discourse within the family such that members can cope and respond to current and future issues in a more adaptive way. Dominant beliefs drive family discourse, and family discourse leads to patterns of behavior (problem-saturated stories) that get reinforced. By helping the family articulate the underlying premises that drive its self-perception and actions, the therapist can help the family deconstruct and then reconstruct a more useful narrative.

One of the challenges of this kind of family therapy is the issue of articulating the basic dominant beliefs that shape the family's perception of itself and its individual members. In a sense, there is a fork in the road at this point in the model that speaks to the overall goals of the therapy. If the goal is to change the dominant narrative and help the family move forward in the here and now, narrative family therapy shares some goals with solution-focused family therapy in that the origin of the dominant narrative is not as important; the past is not explicitly examined for an explanation of the "why" of the dominant beliefs. However, if the "why" is to be explored and examined, this would be in keeping with Foucault's sense of the political forces in the process, in which case narrative family therapy shares some similarities with other depth-psychology models that do address the "why" of the origins of the dominant narrative. Given the social constructivist paradigm that narrative family therapy grows out of, getting at the "why" of the dominant narrative may be elusive as there are always multiple socially constructed truths at play in any perception.

ROLE OF THE THERAPIST

In narrative family therapy, the role of the therapist is one of active listening and questioning. The therapist tries to facilitate the family's ability to tell its story and through the storytelling process begin to identify the dominant beliefs and discourse the family utilizes to make sense of its current situation. The questions the therapist uses, then, help the family begin to externalize its problems, seek exceptions to its problem-saturated stories, find other situations that challenge its tendency to identify problems as being within a family member, and move toward the first step of deconstructing its current narrative. Such a therapeutic process communicates to the family members that they are the experts about their own

Photo 10.4   The dominant narrative that is created within families can shape perceptions about family member roles, responsibilities, and attitudes toward one another

Source: © Jupiterimages/Brand X Pictures/Getty Images

situation; they are the authors of their narrative, and each family narrative is a unique entity. The therapist can communicate with the family a hopeful perspective that through the externalization process the family members can come to see their concerns in a new light. This strengths-based and empowering approach can generate a positive attitude in families and provide them with motivation to master their current situation.

PROCESS OF THERAPY

The process of narrative family therapy tends to follow a more circular process. Usually, a narrative family therapist does not engage in a standard assessment process but begins by having the family articulate its story. As the family begins to tell its story, the therapist may quickly begin to reflect back to the family aspects of the story that sound like dominant beliefs or reframe statements to reflect the move toward externalizing the problem. As the story further unfolds, the therapist may look for exceptions to the problem-saturated stories the family seems to gloss over, and may begin to identify who in the family seems more in control of the dominant beliefs and discourse and who seems to be more marginalized through the process. One difference between narrative family therapy and other models of family therapy is that the narrative family therapist doesn't make judgments about what is normal or who in the family fits what diagnostic or assessment category. The narrative family therapist eschews those kinds of judgments all together and looks more at how the power distribution in the family privileges some and marginalizes others. This can be important information as the therapist begins to form a plan about how to help the family deconstruct its current narrative. As Foucault (2006; Chambon et al., 1999) pointed out, those who control the narrative often are reluctant to give up that narrative if it serves some purpose by which they benefit.

Through this circular process of storytelling, responding to questions, and reframing to push the family toward externalization and deconstruction, the construction of a new narrative can be articulated by the family that hopefully will be more adaptive both for the current situation and for future issues the family may confront. The techniques discussed below can be used at any point in this circular process of information gathering, reflection and reframing, and intervention.

TOOLS AND TECHNIQUES

The techniques described below show the emphasis placed by the narrative family therapist on helping the family articulate its unique story and begin to use its language in different ways to gain a new vantage point from which to understand the presenting issue. The model often is described as being very "conversational" and relies heavily on the family's ability to be articulate about its situation.

Externalizing Conversations

Externalizing conversations are reframing techniques that help the family begin to use different language and perceptions to discuss its presenting issues (White, 1995; White & Epston, 1990). For example, when the family with the teenager who has been acting rebellious says, "Our son is very rebellious," the therapist might turn around and say, "When this rebelliousness takes ahold of your son, what kinds of things does this rebelliousness make him do?" By reinforcing the idea that rebelliousness is the issue, not the son, the family can begin to talk about the problem in a different way, a way that hopefully decreases the extent to which the son feels marginalized or pathologized by the usual discourse he encounters within the family. If a family comes in complaining of mounting stress in the family, the therapist may say, "You all have had to cope with a lot. What happens when this stress visits your family? What does it cause to happen?" Again, the problem is externalized from the family, and the language of externalization can be reinforced as the family continues to discuss the issues that brought it in for therapy in the first place.

Questions

Similar to solution-focused family therapy, narrative family therapy has cultivated a series of specific kinds of questions. Each kind of question is tied to the process of either deconstruction or reconstruction.

Relative Influence Questions

During the therapeutic process, the therapist will ask the family many questions trying to understand how the problem has influenced the family in different ways and the extent the family has tried to take control of the problem (Epston & White, 1992). These kinds of questions are relative influence questions. They help the family gain some perspective on the overall influence of the problem on the family's functioning as well as begin to identify times or situations where the family coped better with the problem. For example, in the above scenario with the rebellious teen, the therapist might ask, "The last time rebelliousness seemed to take control of Tom [the son], how did that affect everyone in the family, including Tom?" The therapist might follow up that discussion with a further question such as "When rebelliousness convinces Tom to break curfew, do your responses to the rebelliousness help it go away or encourage it to stick around?" As you can see, even with these types of questions, the language of externalization continues to be used and reinforced for the family.

Strengths Questions

Strengths questions are designed to get the family members to examine alternative information to challenge the problem-saturated stories they often present with (Marley, 1999). Such questions can be phrased as "What is going well in the family right now?" or "What are some things that you like about the family that you wish you could see more of?" It is surprising how some families react to such questions since many families hope to focus on their problem-saturated stories and assume therapy is always focused on the negatives. A subset of strengths questions comprises the unique outcome questions. These questions help the family focus on exceptions to the problem-saturated stories. The therapist may ask the family, "Was there a time when rebelliousness tried to influence the family but you defeated it? How did the family manage that?" or "Are there times when Tom resists the rebelliousness? How does he manage to do that?" These exceptions provide information and examples of how the family prevents or exerts control over the problem at least sometimes, data that require the family to rethink its dominant beliefs and discourse.

Discourse Questions

Discourse questions address directly the dominant beliefs and discourse at work in the family that shape its perception of itself and its ability to change (Marley, 1999). The therapist might ask, "How does this belief of yours in teenage rebellion influence the family?" or "When you say all teens are rebellious, how does that belief influence your response to Tom when rebelliousness takes hold of him?" The responses to such questions help bring to light the influence of the discourse and dominant beliefs and provide an opportunity for the therapist and family to see how such beliefs often constrain the choices families have in responding more effectively to challenges when they occur. Again, the language of externalization is used in these questions to further the process of deconstruction.

Change Questions

Change questions ask the family to address directly how beliefs shape its ability to change (Marley, 1999). The therapist might ask a family, "What does this family need to believe if it plans on getting a handle on this rebelliousness?" or "If the desire of the family is to send rebelliousness packing, what beliefs will help make that so?" Often the discussions that ensue from these kinds of questions are the first steps in the reconstruction process. The family is now asked to identify alternative beliefs that will form the basis for a new narrative and discourse.

Storytelling

The conversation is created and maintained between the family and the therapist. By asking questions and eliciting more detailed responses, the therapist encourages the family to tell its own unique story. It is through the storytelling process that the full measure of the dominant beliefs, discourse, and problem-saturated stories can be articulated and made public and open for deconstruction (Epston & White, 1992). Building on Bruner's (1986) ideas about the power of stories to shape perceptions or reality, the therapist must support the family's work in articulating, often for the first time, its own unique story.

While this sounds very clear and pragmatic, it can be a difficult task for two reasons. First, many families that come to therapy are looking for answers to specific questions. For the scenario above about the rebellious teen, the parents may ask such concrete questions as "How can we make our son stick to his curfew better?" or perhaps "How can we get him to follow the house rules about cell phone use?" These are perfectly legitimate questions most parents in similar situations would probably want to ask a family therapist. To turn around and ask the family to "tell me the story of your family" will come across as odd at best to many families and might be seen as avoiding the main point (from the parents' perspective) of being in family therapy in the first place.

Second, even for families that are nurtured and supported to tell their family story, such a process may seem like it puts the onus of responsibility on the family to do all the talking and not seem very collaborative with the therapist. While it is true that storytelling is an inherently language-dominated process, the therapist must work with each family to develop a trusting and collaborative working relationship so the family feels like it can engage in the storytelling regardless of its language capabilities.

Reauthoring

As the dominant beliefs, discourse, and problem-saturated stories are articulated through the storytelling process and the exceptions and alternatives are given voice to challenge their maintenance, the deconstruction process now becomes a reconstruction process. The family is encouraged to build on these exceptions and alternative viewpoints to author a new story about itself, one that now helps it deal more effectively with problems or challenges that arise (Zimmerman & Dickerson, 1996). The therapist can reinforce this process by continuing to help the family use the language of externalization and critically examine the beliefs behind ideas about how to change. Ideally, the process of reauthoring is the construction of a new dominant belief that will support a new discourse within the family that will allow the family as a whole and each family member to experience a new set of beliefs about the family's potential and adaptability in the face of challenges.

Letters

Epston (Epston & White, 1992) pioneered the use of letters in his work with families. The therapist would write a letter to the family members congratulating them on their hard work and reinforcing the progress the family made in the last session, reiterating elements of the new narrative that the family was developing, reminding the family members of exceptions or alternatives they themselves identified in the session, and reinforcing the goals the family identified. Letters are a pragmatic way to use the power of language to reinforce the work the family is doing and allow the family to hold on to a record of its work in a concrete way as opposed to having to remember what was said in the session. Through the language used in the letter, the therapist can reinforce the language of externalization and help the family stay on course in its attempts to develop a new narrative.

Cultural Assumptions

Questions and discussions that focus on the macro discourse that surrounds a family and shapes its micro discourse often target cultural assumptions that influence the family. For instance, in the case of the rebellious teenager, the parents might be asked how they came to believe the idea that all teens are rebellious. Such questions and discussions move the direction of inquiry outward, away from the family and into the social-cultural realm. These kinds of discussions support Foucault's (2006) notion of the politics of power and control and how broader institutions can influence the perception of reality within individuals and families. For some families, understanding how they came to believe certain things about ethnicity, gender, sexuality, adolescent development, and/or other key aspects of their unique experience will be important in the deconstruction process. The power of cultural assumptions that fuel a family's dominant beliefs may be very strong and be a good indicator for why a family has difficulty imagining exceptions or alternative viewpoints.

CASE ILLUSTRATION

IP (identified patient).	Fernando Rosa is a 15-year-old Mexican American male who was named after his father, Fernando Rosa, Sr.) Fernando, Jr., was referred by the school counselor to his family physician as teachers described his behavior as "lethargic." The family physician then recommended that Fernando, Jr., see a counselor, as he had ruled out clinical depression as the cause for his lethargic behavior.
	The family was referred to the local family counseling center. The first interview consisted of Fernando, Jr., his mother, and his stepfather.
Background information (not assessment as this conveys the connotation of "absolute knowledge").	Both his father, Fernando Rosa, Sr., and his mother, Mrs. Juanita Montiel (she has taken her second husband's name), are from Mexico. They both immigrated to the United States as children, and Fernando, Jr., was born in the United States. Fernando Rosa, Sr., and Mrs. Montiel divorced several years ago when Fernando, Jr., was 6 years old.
	Antonio Montiel (Fernando, Jr.'s stepfather) is from Cuba. They are a middle-class/working-class family (the stepfather is an electrician, and the mother works inside the home). In interviewing Fernando, Jr.'s mother and stepfather they both appear to be quite acculturated.
	There are three other children in the home: Fernando, Jr.'s brother (age 10) from his mother's marriage with his father and two other siblings (ages 4 and 6) from his mother's second marriage to Mr. Montiel.
Fernando, Jr.'s school and neighborhood not having many Hispanic or ethnic minority children may perpetuate **negative and stereotypical (societal) images of Mexican and Mexican American males**.	Fernando, Jr.'s school is not very integrated, and there are not many "children of color" in his school, as his mother and stepfather live in a predominantly White neighborhood.
Both Fernando, Jr., and Fernando, Sr., may be challenged with the task of having to build healthy (cultural) **self-narratives** in the face of the **dominant discourse of politicized societal "knowledge" of Mexican American males**.	His father (Fernando Rosa, Sr.) lives nearby, and his neighborhood is what you would call the "working poor" (most individuals and their families work for minimum wage). Mr. Rosa works in a garage and takes on odd jobs as he never finished high school and does not have a trade. However, Mr. Rosa has always been diligent in providing child support (although, given his income, it is often very meager). In later interviews with Mr. Rosa, it appears that he is very "ethnically immersed" and enjoys many aspects of the Mexican culture (e.g., dress, food, entertainment).

Recognize that **stories are coproduced** and attempt to engender conditions in which **individuals become their own privileged authors**.	Fernando, Jr.'s mother is very angry with her son's biological father. It is clear from their recounting family conversations that both she and the stepfather berate Mr. Rosa in front of Fernando, Jr. and the other children.
Dominant theme (Mr. Rosa being an inept and inappropriate father figure).	
Problem-saturated stories.	In the first session it was clear that Mr. Montiel did not approve of Fernando, Jr.'s father—his occupation, his lifestyle, and (it felt like at times) his Mexican background and culture. When his stepfather offered comments (which were largely negative) Fernando, Jr., would cast his eyes downward and look around the room (seemingly in an attempt to remove himself from the conversation). Fernando, Jr.'s mother also constantly complained about Mr. Rosa's shortcomings—being very unaware of her son's reaction to the nature and tone of her opinions of his father.
Exploration of the presenting problem.	In this initial interview I asked the family members their opinion as to why they were referred to the center. The stepfather answered first and offered that they were there because of Fernando, Jr. His mother added that she was concerned that Fernando, Jr., didn't seem happy. When asked why she thought this happens, she replied that she didn't know. Fernando, Jr., also offered no opinion. (In the first session I interviewed Fernando, Jr., alone in addition to seeing all the family members together; the younger children did not attend this or any other sessions.)
Exceptions to the presenting problem.	This line of questioning went on for a while, and I asked if there were any times that Fernando, Jr., seemed to be happy. Initially they shook their heads as to indicate that they didn't know. The stepfather then answered, "Yeah, when he comes back from visiting that knucklehead father of his." (Fernando, Jr., had a blank stare on his face as if not to have heard this comment.)
Negative self narrative influenced by environmental conditions. **Be concerned with the particulars of experience rather than with the abstractions and theories** (his exposure to negative depictions of his father by his mother and his stepfather).	In this first session and in subsequent sessions where I interviewed Fernando, Jr., it became evident that he had a poor self-image. He spoke in a very low tone to the point that at times it was hard to hear him. It was apparent that Fernando, Jr., was ambivalent about his stepfather but would become quite animated when asked about his father, Fernando, Sr. Fernando, Jr.'s reply when asked about his stepfather was sparse and vague: "I don't know; he's OK I guess." However, his tone changed dramatically when asked about his father and what they did when he visited with him. He described his father as "a lot of fun" and said he teaches him about working on cars. His demeanor changed when he added that when he returned home both his mother and his stepfather would complain that his clothes had become heavily soiled. He responded, "That's what happens to mechanics; they get dirty."

(Continued)

(Continued)

Language is a powerful tool, and how one "languages" a situation or phenomenon impacts the "realities" of the family's socially constructed meaning (e.g., Fernando, Jr., is the problem).	At the end of my first session with Fernando, Jr., his mother, and his stepfather, Mr. Montiel announced that he would not be returning as he felt this was a waste of time—and that Fernando, Jr., was "just trying to get attention as he is jealous of his younger siblings and the attention that they get." I was, however, able to get his mother to commit to returning.
Asking therapeutic questions. **Exception questions** (that focus on situations of successful outcomes that **do not fit with the dominant problem-filled story**—about Mr. Rosa as a father). **Opening space for possibilities** (e.g., interventions including Mr. Rosa, which might prove to be very helpful).	In the sessions with Fernando, Jr., and his mother I asked many gentle, curious, and respectful questions. I asked both Fernando, Jr., and his mother what they thought they could do to help Fernando, Jr., have "more energy" (her new description of the initial "presenting problem"). I continued with this line of questioning, and the mother reluctantly offered that he did seem to "have more energy" after he visited his father (which had become quite infrequent over the years). She stated that she would allow Fernando, Jr., to spend some time with his father over the weekend.
Dominant story.	After four sessions with Fernando, Jr., and his mother, I asked the mother's permission to allow Mr. Rosa to attend therapy sessions with Fernando, Jr. In spite of the mother's criticism of this intervention, she agreed—but only after she volunteered negative information in an attempt to thwart my interest in wanting to work with the father-son dyad (she pointed out that the father's living quarters were unsuitable and lacked everyday conveniences, etc.). This was a very important therapeutic move for Fernando, Jr.
Exceptions to the dominant theme (Mr. Rosa as a poor father).	In the initial interview with father and son, I saw a very healthy, affectionate, and close emotional relationship between them. I had never seen Fernando, Jr., so happy, carefree, and elated. (In my prior sessions with the mother I asked her to consider allowing Fernando, Jr., to spend occasional weekends with his father—she had agreed, although ambivalently, as the father lived above the garage.)
Healthy "self-narrative" (especially in the face of difficult conditions).	I admired that Mr. Rosa, who showed up in the initial interview with heavily soiled clothes and disheveled hair, stated that he would not apologize for his appearance or his speech—he spoke very broken English as opposed to the mother who spoke English without an accent.
Storytelling (of Mr. Rosa's earlier experience as a father).	I asked Mr. Rosa to describe his experience as a father to Fernando, Jr. He started to tell me about his "postdivorce" days; however, I encouraged him to help me have a better understanding by starting from the beginning, Fernando, Jr.'s birth. A quiet calm came over his face as he recounted what a beautiful baby Fernando, Jr., was and how Fernando, Jr., seemed to understand and respond to him and his warm

Invite a self-reflective attitude.

Scaffolding (the unraveling of stories is set in motion, and people have the opportunity to discover past clues to support the notion of current competence—which becomes **the foundation for the reauthoring of the father and son's narrative about Mr. Rosa as a father**).

I encouraged Mr. Rosa to elaborate and amplify this situation (in which he performed his duties as a father in an outstanding manner by making due with his humble means).

Need to **deconstruct negative internalized images** of self as Mr. Rosa's son; and need to **reauthor his own (cultural) self-narrative** that **challenges dominant beliefs** about Mexican males.

Restorying/reauthoring.

Exception, survival, and possibility questions in order to amplify the father's strengths (as a parent).

Looking toward the future.

Significance questions (questions that search for and reveal the meaning, significance, and importance of events).

feelings toward him. He continued to recall days when he and Fernando, Jr., played ball and such.

Both he and Fernando, Jr., seemed almost "surprised" at his father's recollections of their past together as father and son. Mr. Rosa then ended by stating that he and Fernando, Jr., need to work at being together more to "get back to how we used to be."

Neither of them attempted to pretend that the father's living situation was anything less than ideal. They both unapologetically explained how they worked things out to get their basic needs met (e.g., they used a hot plate and a crock pot to cook). Mr. Rosa lived a very marginal economic existence, especially in comparison to his son's mother and stepfather.

Family therapy sessions with father and son spanned a period of 2 months. Within these 2 months several other issues were explored:

- We talked about Fernando, Jr.'s school and neighborhood not being very integrated and explored with him what it meant to him to be Mexican American (I only used this term as Mr. Rosa opened up this topic by emphasizing that he felt one of his roles as a father was to make sure that Fernando, Jr., stayed in touch with his Mexican roots). Fernando, Jr., gleefully chimed in by saying that his father cooks Mexican food "and stuff."
- We talked about misconceptions that Fernando, Jr., had about why he had not spent more time with his father, again being very careful not to set up his mother and stepfather as "villains."
- We discussed their plans to spend more time together and what they would do.

As family therapy with Fernando, Jr., and his father ended I received a call from his mother. She informed me that Fernando, Jr., seems to be happier than he was a couple of months ago and that she does not feel that Fernando, Jr., needs any more therapy. I asked his mother to what she attributes this "lighter mood" (as she described it). She responded that seeing his father more does seem to help and that she would "watch what she said" about his father in the future, if that would help Fernando, Jr., continue to feel better.

SUMMARY

Narrative family therapy, as well as other therapies that have emerged from the social constructivist paradigm, continues to be a very popular model. The strengths-based and empowerment perspectives inherent in this model make it attractive to family therapy professionals who are looking for an alternative approach to the more pathologizing models of family therapy. Further, given the inherent ability to tell stories that many people of all ages have, or how people gravitate to the act of storytelling, this model is easy to translate to families with little or no prior exposure to therapy. Everyone can tell a story. The development of specific types of questions and the use of externalizing language provide very pragmatic tools for novice family therapists to hold on to as they learn the skill and art of family therapy.

However, the model is not without its detractors. The focus on externalizing problems may come across as unsympathetic or an avoidance of a deeper issue. For example, with the rebellious teenager, it is one thing to ask, "How can the family respond better when rebelliousness takes hold of Tom?" It is another thing to ask Tom directly, "Why are you rebellious?" The issue of why—why someone is angry, why someone is depressed—is rarely addressed in most versions of narrative family therapy. In addition, by externalizing some strong emotions such as anger and depression, narrative family therapy may be communicating that such emotions are always in need of externalization. Is it OK for someone to sometimes feel angry or depressed without having to externalize the experience? Another criticism leveled at the model is that by focusing on externalizing the problem and making the problem the issue, the family as a unit with a specific structure and function can get overlooked. While social constructivists would see this as an invalid criticism since it runs contrary to their underlying philosophical beliefs, for many families there is a sense that families have structures, family members have roles, and sometimes the distribution of power and control will be unjust or unequal for legitimate reasons. For instance, a young adolescent may be very unhappy that the parents put limits on certain behaviors and become angry at feeling mistreated, but the need to establish limits is, in the long run, a good thing even if not experienced as such by the adolescent.

Those criticisms aside, narrative family therapy is a very active model and continues to be utilized with many family types and situations. The similarities, at some conceptual levels, between solution-focused family therapy and this model have led some to move forward with models that combine the key elements of each into a single coherent model (Marley, 1999).

RECOMMENDED READINGS

Bruner, J. (1986). *Actual minds, possible worlds.* Cambridge, MA: Harvard University Press.

Bruner, J. (2002). *Making stories: Law, literature, life.* New York, NY: Farrar, Straus and Giroux.

Chambon, A., Irving, A., & Epstein, L. (Eds.). (1999). *Reading Foucault for social work.* New York, NY: Columbia University Press.

Freedman, J., & Combs, G. (1996). *Narrative therapy: The social construction of preferred realities.* New York, NY: Norton.

White, M. (1995). *Re-authoring lives: Interviews and essays.* Adelaide, Western Australia: Dulwich Centre Publications.

White, M., & Epston, D. (1990). *Narrative means to therapeutic ends.* New York, NY: Norton.

Zimmerman, J., & Dickerson, V. (1996). *If problems talked: Adventures in narrative therapy.* New York, NY: Guilford.

DISCUSSION QUESTIONS

1. What are the principal tenets essential to understanding narrative family therapy? Discuss.

2. Narrative family therapy has a number of techniques. Identify a few of them and discuss how each technique contributes to the overall success of this therapy.

3. Identify a cultural assumption about a group of people and discuss how at the family level this cultural assumption might influence the family's behavior. What might a narrative family therapist do to identify the influence of this cultural assumption?

REFERENCES

Bruner, J. (1986). *Actual minds, possible worlds.* Cambridge, MA: Harvard University Press.

Chambon, A., Irving, A., & Epstein, L. (Eds.). (1999). *Reading Foucault for social work.* New York, NY: Columbia University Press.

Epston, D., & White, M. (1992). *Experience, contradiction, narrative, and imagination: Selected papers of David Epston and Michael White, 1989–1991.* Adelaide, Australia: Dulwich Centre Publications.

Foucault, M. (2006). *History of madness.* New York, NY: Routledge.

Freedman, J., & Combs, G. (1996). *Narrative therapy: The social construction of preferred realities*. New York, NY: Norton.

Gilman, S. (1985). *Difference and pathology: Stereotypes of sexuality, race, and madness*. Ithaca, NY: Cornell University Press.

Marley, J. (1999). Family therapy and schizophrenia: A developing model for practice. *Journal of Family Psychotherapy, 10*, 1–14.

Marley, J. (2004). *Family involvement in treating schizophrenia: Models, essential skills, and process*. New York, NY: Haworth Press.

White, M. (1995). *Re-authoring lives: Interviews and essays*. Adelaide, Western Australia: Dulwich Centre Publications.

White, M., & Epston, D. (1990). *Narrative means to therapeutic ends*. New York: Norton.

Zimmerman, J., & Dickerson, V. (1996). *If problems talked: Adventures in narrative therapy*. New York, NY: Guilford.

Part III

CLINICAL ISSUES IN FAMILY THERAPY

Chapter 11

PHASES OF FAMILY THERAPY

The major models of family therapy have been identified, as have the skills and techniques of each model. However, there are other clinical skills and techniques that the therapist needs in family practice that are unique to family therapy. These elements are common across models of family therapy and are outlined in this chapter to assist the family therapist in managing the complexities of family interaction and intervention.

The beginning phase of family therapy is an important time in that it sets the stage for the therapeutic relationship and interventive process. The initial stage of family therapy is also important in that this is when the therapist will be faced with managing the family's fears, anxieties, and apprehensions about family therapy. Additionally it is important for the family therapist to prepare and organize in order to sort through the myriad of family therapy concepts and theories available for understanding family dynamics and interaction.

If goal setting and contracting have been successful in the initial phase of family therapy, then deciding which problem is to be worked on first as well as which problem will be addressed first has already been determined and agreed upon. However, there are additional basic skills in the middle phase of family therapy (intervention implementation) that are needed to conduct therapy regardless of whether the family therapist begins the intervention with a target of perceptual change or behavioral change and regardless of which model of family therapy is to be utilized. In addition, as the therapist gets to know the family better and the family members begin to relax and reveal even more information about complex family dynamics, then interventions and their order may need to be refined and/or changed in the middle phase of therapy.

In the end phase of family therapy termination is the main task. The end phase of family therapy is also a unique and complex process in that the therapist has the task of deciding on termination tasks that are needed for a family system. This phase is complicated by the fact of having more than one person to deal with (e.g., having to decide when and how to terminate as the progress of family members may be uneven).

This chapter will outline and describe the basic skills that exist within the beginning, middle, and end phases of family therapy that are unique to the process of family therapy.

INITIAL PHASE ISSUES

Presession Planning

The Referral Process and Intake Information

Information on family dynamics and interaction can be gathered in the referral and intake processes. The family therapist can obtain valuable information from the referral and/or intake that may later help in engagement and assessment stages. For instance, it may be apparent that the family's motivation may be low if the referral is from an agency or a school rather than the family itself.

The intake process (for agencies) either on the phone or in person can be a valuable resource in developing presession hypotheses about family functioning. For this reason it is important for the family therapist to acknowledge that the assessment stage really begins in the initial phase of family therapy with information gained in the referral and intake processes.

The referral process is the entry point for family therapy. It is the point at which someone decides that the family needs therapy. In cases wherein a nonfamily member such as an agency staff member refers the family, there are many questions that are important to ask the referral source:

- Does the family know that it has been referred for therapy?
- Whose idea was it to seek help and why?
- What was the family's reaction to this referral? Do the family members agree or disagree with the referral person's view of the problem?
- Has the family received therapy in the past? By whom? And what were the results? It is also important for a new therapist to find out if he or she will be able to have direct contact with the previous counselor or family therapist.
- Is this a voluntary or court-ordered (i.e., institutional—e.g., school-ordered) referral? Is the family's future in some way contingent upon its following

through on the referral? If so, the family's motivational level becomes a central therapeutic issue in the initial phase of family therapy. (Unique to family therapy is the possibility that some members' motivation may be higher than others'; in this case one needs to be aware of the possibility of sabotage attempts initiated by resistant family members. More on this topic is given later in the chapter.)

- What will be the referral source's role in future interventions? For instance, will the referral source act as the case manager or provide individual therapy for a member of the family?

Once the above questions have been answered it is important to establish how or if information is to be shared, and to work out the practical aspects of sharing or receiving family information (in the case of third-person or nonagency personnel) so as to protect the confidentiality of the family. Finally, it is also important to establish if progress reports are desired (or required) by the referral source—and what information is to be shared. Obviously, it is essential to get the family's approval of the sharing of any therapy information.

Intake processes will vary quite a bit depending on agency policy or if the referral is to a private practice. Intake information may be in the form of a telephone interview by persons with varying levels of family therapy knowledge and expertise (which may include the agency's clerical staff who are merely answering the phone). Or intake information may be the result of (brief or extended) in-person encounters with other family therapists. Regardless of the point of origin of the intake, it provides an opportunity for the therapist to gather information about the presenting problem and to get a sense of the family. Intake information is also an opportunity to develop presession hypotheses (to be discussed momentarily) that will be helpful in sorting through and deciding upon (at least initially) a theoretical and conceptual framework for family assessment.

The Initial Telephone Call and Setting the First Appointment

It is important to get a concise statement of the problem from the intake process—if at all possible. If intake information is conducted in the initial telephone call, then basic demographic information on the family should be taken. Other information that should be gathered in the telephone call includes information about the presenting problem, prior interventions, whether or not all family members know about the call being made for family therapy, third-party referrals versus being self-referred, who is to be included in the initial appointment, and the therapist's fee structure and cancellation policy.

It is important to note that the authors believe that lengthy assessment information should be avoided in the telephone interview, as it is best to gather this information in the initial interview so that all family members have a chance to give their input. Otherwise, the therapist may be getting a one-sided view of the presenting problem. Additionally, there are implications for the therapeutic alliance in that the family therapist must be careful not to develop (or even appear to develop) a closer alliance with one family member over another.

Planning for the Initial Interview and Presession Hypotheses

The assessment process begins even before the initial interview, with information gathered in the intake form and in the telephone call to make the initial appointment (Brown & Brown, 2002). The information obtained in the intake and telephone interview helps set the stage for getting started in the initial interview. The therapist can develop (initial) presession hypotheses about the family.[1] A presession hypothesis is the initial thoughts that the therapist has about the family. It is the therapist's way of organizing his or her initial impressions about the family's functioning, dynamics, and interaction. Presession hypotheses assist the therapist in mentally scanning through what might be initial questions to pose to the family, as well as provide the therapist with an idea of those family concepts and theories that might be useful in the assessment process. The presession hypothesis is not meant to be a "theoretical straitjacket" for the family therapist. Rather, it is a way of organizing one's thoughts and giving the therapist an initial place to begin questioning. The presession hypothesis is also not meant to be doggedly adhered to; it is merely a way of helping the family therapist not be so overwhelmed with all that typically goes on in family therapy (multiple interactions to assess and multiple persons with whom to develop a therapeutic alliance, etc.). Approaching the initial session with an array of questions generated by one's presession hypotheses provides the therapist with some structure for the interview, while allowing these hypotheses to remain tentative enough to allow for the uniqueness of the family to emerge (Brown & Brown, 2002) in order to formulate intersession (within-session) hypotheses.

One of the advantages of family therapy is the vast number of models and proliferating theories and techniques available to the therapist that assist in understanding and in intervening in family processes. However, it is important in hypothesizing not to become so theory-specific that the ability to see other possibilities is limited (Hanna & Brown, 1995). The therapist should be flexible in formulating his or her hypotheses. It is important to test out each hypothesis with actual data gathered in the assessment stage. In other words the therapist should search out new information, identify connecting patterns, and move toward a systemic formulation of the family's behavior (Campbell, Draper, & Crutchley, 1991).

Getting Started: The Initial Interview

The beginning stage of family therapy is a dynamic, complex, and active interaction. The task of the first session is twofold: to connect with all family members present and to begin to gather information to assess the family and make treatment recommendations. All family members should be greeted individually so as to facilitate therapeutic alliances with each member. This interview should begin with answering any questions that the family may have about the referral, the intake process, the therapist, and the agency. In this interview it is also important for the therapist to identify the needs of each family member, aid family members in communicating more clearly with one another, and begin the process of establishing goals (to be addressed separately in this chapter; Hull & Mather, 2006).

Photo 11.1 Engagement is an important part of the initial stage of family therapy. Greeting all family members individually can facilitate the therapeutic alliance with each member of the family

Source: ©Jupiterimages/Comstock/Thinkstock

In the first interview the therapist completes the intake information gathered in the initial telephone call and/or the initial intake process. The therapist should share with the entire family what he or she has learned about the presenting problem so that family members can join in and give their interpretation of the problem. In exploring how the family came to seek therapy it is important to determine why the family is following through on recommendations now. The reason for wanting answers to this question is to help determine what the motivation is for therapy and who in the family is the most motivated for change. It is also important to note who speaks first, as this may be an indication of where the power in the family lies.

In presenting initial questions to the family, the therapist should be prepared to deal with negative reactions and resistance from family members and may need to balance the interview between *joining* techniques and getting information on which to build an intervention plan (Brown & Brown, 2002). The process of joining includes making the family members feel comfortable, assuring them that their concerns are valid, showing respect for each family member, and demonstrating attentiveness and responsiveness (we will discuss issues of resistance and building successful therapeutic alliances later in this chapter).

Client expectations are an important part of the therapy process and can easily impact the effectiveness of the interventions as well as influence therapeutic relationships. Families may enter with unrealistic expectations (e.g., they hope for very short-term cures for long-standing problems), and sometimes families enter therapy with hidden agendas (e.g., to get certain family members to do what they want to be done). In addition, families may come to therapy expecting only certain members to attend the therapy session (e.g., they drop off a child for a therapy session). These issues may need to become the initial focus of therapy before other interventions can be implemented.

In building a good relationship with the family, the therapist should focus on the strengths of the family. Knowing family strengths will help the therapist better understand how the family copes with problems and will assist the therapist in developing a strengths-based approach to family therapy. Pointing out the strengths of a family helps the therapist show respect for the family as well as create an atmosphere of trust and hope that family problems can be resolved. This also helps highlight what (internal and external) resources lie dormant so as to further inform the intervention plan (Brown & Christensen, 1999).

If the family has previously been in therapy, the therapist should ask questions about its prior experience and whether it is related to the current presenting problem (Brown & Brown, 2002). In any case the therapist needs to know how the family feels about therapy, its preconceived notions and expectations of therapy, what the family found helpful (or not) in its prior therapy experience, why it did not return to the previous therapist, and why it decided to seek therapy again (Brown & Brown, 2002).

In getting a statement of the presenting problem, possible questions as outlined above should be pursued with all family members. In addition there is information that should be obtained in the initial interview: previous marriages, recent deaths and illnesses, perception of the problem and expectations, history of the problem, prior attempts to resolve the problem, why the family is seeking help now, social support systems available to the family, unmet basic needs (food, shelter, health care, etc.), and whether any of these unmet needs influence or exacerbate the presenting problem.

Hypothesizing provides a way to screen data and a starting point for investigation. It is verification of prior information and provides guidelines for selecting information. Hypothesizing can be a confirming or disconfirming parallel process; it is reciprocal and cyclic in nature and has a coevolving quality. Good evidence is cumulative and prompts changes in hypotheses.

An intersession hypothesis is a series of statements or beliefs about family dynamics and interaction that assist in the assessment of the family. These statements are compared to the actual data that evolve from family therapy sessions until the therapist arrives at a clearer understanding of the family system. This is an effective way to manage all that is going on in the session, helping the therapist stay focused—pursuing relevant questions that will assist in goal setting and intervention planning.

Engagement

Worden (2003) defines *engagement* as "the forming of a therapeutic, trusting alliance between the therapist and the family that permits them to explore together the inner workings of the family relationship" (p. 17). Bordin (1982) refers to the relationship between the therapist and the client as a "working alliance" made up of three parts:

1. A consensus between therapist and client on the goals of therapy.

2. An agreement and collaboration on the relevance and implementation of various therapy tasks.

3. A strong positive affective bond between therapist and client.

Developing a successful therapeutic alliance allows the family therapist entry into the family system for assessment and intervention. The engagement phase begins in the initial interview (and sometimes in the telephone intake process). Engagement is also the beginning effort to define the issues, problems, challenges, and barriers confronting the family (Hull & Mather, 2006). Furthermore the engagement process is viewed as consisting of infusing energy, bringing a sense of hope to the situation, providing the family with a sounding board so all members know they are being heard, demonstrating support, and utilizing "use of self" in the process of understanding family members' concerns (we will explore the concept of "use of self" further in this section; Hull & Mather, 2006). Building a strong therapeutic relationship with all members of the family is an ongoing process that is crucial in family therapy. This process may be complicated by the fact that there are different levels of resistance among family members. In order for a family therapist to be effective he or she must develop a successful relationship with all members of the family, which can sometimes be tricky because family members may be saying contradictory things (Brown & Brown, 2002).

Photo 11.2   Termination of family therapy may provoke anxiety as the family maybe unsure of if they can maintain the changes made once therapy ends. It is important for therapists to have a clear plan of termination; one that allows for support of the family, but without the family continuing to be dependent on the therapist

Source: ©iStockphoto.com/eliandric

As the interview progresses, the family therapist attempts to develop a relationship—joining with the family by adjusting to the family's interactional style and pace and trying to identify strengths and resources to establish a relationship (Brown & Brown, 2002).

Therapist's Use of Self

Worden (2003) defines the therapist's *use of self* as "the ways the practitioner employs all aspects of his or her personality" (p. 66). The therapist needs to consider (before the initial interview) how he or she feels about issues of self-disclosure. To some degree these therapeutic boundaries are determined by various theoretical models—however, these boundaries are certainly mitigated by the therapist's own style, personality, and comfort level. For example, structural family therapy supports a more active and directive style than, say, the Bowenian approach. On the other hand Satir's approach emphasizes the use of verbal and nonverbal actions to communicate warmth and acceptance to the family.

There are two major issues in regard to the therapist's use of self: the use of self-disclosure and the use of personal reactions (Worden, 2003). Therapists' use of self-disclosure asks the questions "How much do I share?" "How do I answer the family's personal questions?" and "Where do I draw the boundaries on the family's questions?"

In terms of the therapist's reaction to the family and its dynamics and interactions, Worden (2003) suggests that "the therapist's sharing of personal reactions is most beneficial when (1) the treatment process has reached an impasse, (2) the family asks for feedback, (3) the therapist assumes a defensive position, or (4) therapy is about to end" (p. 68). Certainly each therapist must answer these questions for him- or herself—with the therapy model giving only a general guide as to suggestions for use of self and the role of the therapist.

Use of self is a process of "being with the client" through listening, facilitating, providing feedback, responding honestly, and using some degree of self-disclosure (Hull & Mather, 2006). Furthermore the therapist can facilitate the engagement process by a use of self by showing empathy through empathetic responding and engaging in active listening.

There is a lot of debate on what constitutes important characteristics of the therapist and one's use of self. However, there is agreement that personal characteristics do profoundly impact the therapy process (Figley & Nelson, 1989) in that the personality of the therapist influences how various models of therapy are applied—emphasizing some aspects of the model over others. The therapist must employ skills and techniques that fit with his or her personality. That is, the therapist must use his or her own personality (strengths) in building an alliance with the family (ability to be warm and empathic, use of humor, etc.).

Figley and Nelson (1989) assert that important characteristics of the therapist include being nonjudgmental, being respectful of differences of others, meeting clients where they are, and understanding that one reality does not work for every family (Lankton, Lankton, & Matthews, 1991). In addition, building a successful therapeutic relationship in family therapy can be further complicated if the therapist disagrees with the values, biases, or behaviors of a particular family member(s). Family therapists need to examine their role in client resistance (a client's lack of cooperation or lack of progress in therapy) as they may be unwittingly eliciting resistant behavior.

Family therapy is by nature an emotionally charged process in that issues discussed are likely to be issues that the therapist has struggled with in the past or is struggling with in the present. In this regard it is important to be aware of one's own ongoing issues (getting divorced, rearing adolescent children, death in the family, etc.) as well as to be aware of and understand one's own family of origin issues and how they may be interfacing with issues of the family.

It becomes particularly important to explore how one's subcultural background (e.g., race or racial identity, gender, sexual orientation, religion, or even personal appearance) may impact the therapeutic relationship. This is to say that similarities as well as differences between therapist and client may evoke negative reactions (such as resistance) or overidentification of the therapist to one or more family members.

Therapists are cautioned not to allow their own issues to influence nor to allow their own needs to be met in the therapy process. Therapists always need to ask themselves whether their reaction to the client is emanating from their own issues and/or needs or whether their reaction is truly a result of responding to clinical issues set forth by the client. When family therapists can see their own contributions to therapeutic impasses, they have more options for correcting the situation.

Assessment and Data Gathering

Assessment is a complex process that involves a bio-psycho-social focus. This includes physiological, psychological, life cycle, and social/environmental factors influencing family function and dynamics. It is important to assess both individual and family functioning. In addition the therapist needs to take into account environmental circumstances such as systems of social support, economic factors, and issues of cultural diversity (to be addressed specifically in the next chapter). That is, the therapist needs to give attention to the broader context of the symptom bearer (e.g., other social systems that may be involved).

Beginning family therapists should note that the assessment phase of family therapy is an ongoing process that continues throughout the intervention stage of family therapy. Initial data gathered by the therapist may not immediately prove to be useful; however, as the therapist gets to know the family better this information may become significant in intervention planning and implementation.

The assessment, particularly of a family (system), is an elongated process. That is, one should expect to devote at least two to three sessions to the initial assessment and intervention planning. The beginning phase of therapy sets the tone for later interventions and creates an atmosphere for change. For this reason therapists are advised not to rush into goal setting and intervention planning, at least until the family feels comfortable with the idea of therapy, as well as comfortable with the idea of a stranger "meddling in family affairs."

In assessing the family's presenting problem it is important to understand the views of all family members. It is also important to validate each family member's view of the problem. After each family member has had a chance to state his or her concerns and view of the presenting problem(s) the therapist should offer his or her understanding of the problem. The therapist will know when the initial phase ends and when the middle phase of family therapy begins when the family accepts the therapist's reframing of the presenting problem in terms of family dysfunction and interaction.

It is not uncommon for families to come in with vague and global complaints. "My parents don't understand me," for example, or "We have poor communication." In these cases it is important to help the family clarify what is meant by the presenting complaint. Oftentimes the family is unable to give any immediate examples or to narrow down the complaint (Brown & Brown, 2002). The definition of the problem must include all family members' views of the presenting problem. An important aspect of assessment is to help the family narrow down and be more specific as to what is meant by the presenting complaint. Hanna and Brown (1999, pp. 148–149) suggest that the therapist use the below questions to help clarify the presenting problem:

- What do you mean by _____?
- Give me some examples of _____.
- Describe a situation when you _____.

If the family presents several problems, then the therapist needs feedback from the family as to what issues need to be addressed first and in what order. This is a tricky feat as family members may differ in their views of the urgency of various problems. It is up to the therapist to consider several factors: who holds the power in the family (i.e., who has the ability to sabotage treatment), implications for the therapeutic relationships among various family members, and the therapist's own clinical impressions as to the most effective course of action.

In assessing the problem for planning the intervention the therapist needs to be able to describe and assess the relationships and family interactional patterns, observe an enactment of the problem behavior(s), and decide whether couple's and/or individual therapy is necessary.

There are many aspects to consider in assessing family relationships and interactional patterns—for instance, who sits next to whom, who speaks for the family, which family members interact and which do not, who speaks to whom, who answers for whom, and whether positive communication is present in the family's interactional patterns. As the therapist begins to get a better handle on family relationships and interaction, he or she should begin to connect specific interactional patterns to the presenting problem. In assessing family communication the therapist should also assess family roles, family rules, family myths, family secrets, and family rituals (see Chapter 4 on Satir's family therapy model of communication).

Salvador Minuchin (1974) suggests the technique of creating an enactment to better understand family dynamics and interaction. An enactment occurs when the family is directed to actually re-create an interaction involving a problem. Furthermore, there are questions that the family therapist should ask him- or herself as he or she observes family interaction that will further facilitate understanding of family relationships and interactions. These questions are related to the structure and organization of the family (Hanna & Brown, 1999; Hull & Mather, 2006).

There are instances in which individual and/or couples therapy is indicated in addition to family therapy. Karpel (1994) recommends individual therapy for a family member when an individualized symptom requires specialized treatment such as domestic violence situations and substance abuse. Such symptoms are a risk to other family members and should be alleviated before family or couples therapy is considered. Other symptoms that require specialized treatment are anxiety disorders and clinical depression (especially if the therapist feels that there is a suicide risk)—these symptoms require individual therapy. The decision of when to see a couple outside of family therapy sessions can be made if the relationship issues of the couple either are too pressing to ignore and/or profoundly influence family process.

By the end of the assessment period the therapist will have a definition of the problem. It is important to develop a problem definition that encompasses diverse theories and concepts using an integrative approach to family therapy, as the definition of the problem sets the stage for goal setting and selection of interventive methods.

Goal Setting With the Family and Planning for the Intervention

After the initial sessions are held in which a successful therapeutic alliance has been built (e.g., initial resistance to therapy has been resolved and the family is ready to work on the problem), the family has accepted a reframing of the presenting problem from an individual concern to that of a family systems issue, and the therapist has refined and developed working hypotheses of family dysfunction, the practitioner is now in a position to develop goals toward an intervention plan.

The therapist is faced with a multitude of decisions and tasks: which family therapy models to select; which theories, concepts, and techniques of those models best serve the family therapy process; which goals to pursue and in what order; and formulating a contract with the family. This section will address the major issues common to this phase of family therapy: goal setting and contracting.

Goal Setting

Family therapy can be a very unsettling process for the family. It is a time when families are challenged to change enduring patterns of family interaction. The uncertainty of the outcome, the newness of having a stranger involved in family affairs, and the unfamiliarity of the therapy process all make for heightened anxiety for family members. Knowing when the end (of the therapy) is to come may help alleviate some of the family distress and anxiety about this process. For these reasons it is important for the family to be involved in the determination of (short-term and long-term) therapy goals—as well as to have a voice as to the length of the process. (The mean duration of family therapy is 10 sessions per family; Walsh & McGraw, 2002).

In essence, goal setting is meant to be a collaborative process between the therapist and the family. Having the family involved in goal setting—giving the family power over its (therapeutic) fate—is also an empowering process. Involving the family in goal setting may also serve to decrease the amount of resistance in families—in that having a voice in the specific goals and the length of therapy gives the family more of a sense of ownership of the therapy process.

Establishing and differentiating short-term goals from long-term goals is also an important aspect of goal setting. It helps break down goals into more manageable tasks. It also helps the family envision what needs to be changed first in order to resolve the presenting problem. It can also help the therapist not feel so overwhelmed when families present with multiple problems.

Partializing goals (i.e., being more specific) helps further operationalize presenting problems, which facilitates therapeutic success. Being more specific in goal setting may help decrease the anxiety of the family in that specific goals help make the problem feel more manageable and solvable. Subgoals and -objectives can be used to measure the family's progress in therapy.

Goal setting should evolve from behaviors that the family wishes to change in order to resolve the presenting problem. The therapist must help the family select goals that are achievable and that address the family's definition of the problem. Intervention plans should be tailored to fit the unique "culture" of the family. The family's developmental level should also be considered in planning interventions. Goals should be developed from assessment data to fit the characteristics and requests of the family. For example, the therapist should consider whether the family is seeking insight into the problem and/or solutions to the problem.

This brings us to the issue of developing goals that are "process" oriented versus goals that are more "content" focused. Most families focus on the content of their problems (e.g., a child who is acting out). However, it is also important to bring into the family's awareness how family members *interact* when the problem occurs—the process. This distinction is important in goal planning as the relational process is an important part of resolving the content of the presenting problem. The therapist can further refine his or her hypotheses and thus develop interventions that both address the content of the problem and track the interactional behavioral sequences (processes) that operate to maintain the problem.

Goals need to be concrete and specific enough so that family members know when the goals have been achieved. For instance, a presenting complaint such as lack of respect should be behaviorally specified to establish what the child should be doing to become better behaved or to show respect. Hanna (2007) suggests that the therapist ask each family member to describe changes (goals) in more observable terms and how he or she would like things to be different—being specific about what he or she wants changed.

In summary goal setting gives structure and direction to the therapy process. Goal setting is an ongoing and continuous process. Goal setting should highlight the importance of reciprocal goals by noting that the behavior of one family member directly affects the actions of other members and should also recognize that family problems are, in fact, problems of interaction and not the result of individual pathology (Gurman & Knudson, 1978).

Planning the Intervention

All families have strengths regardless of the severity of the presenting problem or level of functioning. It is important that intervention plans be based on family strengths. Overcoming obstacles to change may be made easier if the intervention builds upon what is functional and adaptive within the family system. These strengths may include formal (availability of resources in the community) and informal (extended family, friends, and neighbors) support systems, coping mechanisms, and caring and commitment among members—all of which may be dormant in the life space of the family.

Solution-focused therapists typically start with probing for areas in which the family has experienced successes. Searching for strengths within the family communicates respect for the family and may provide useful information for the family therapist. This line of questioning may give families a new perspective on the presenting problem as well as give the families new hope that their problem is not insurmountable. When a therapist focuses on strengths it provides a good starting place for therapy and affirms that the family has assets that may help increase motivation for change and decrease anxiety (about the therapy).

Various family members may be at different levels of motivation for change—which has implications for which interventions are to be utilized as well as the goals to be pursued. It is noted that families may be more receptive to change when they are in crisis—which may end once the initial few sessions have been held and the initial crisis has been resolved (Hull & Mather, 2006). This has implications for interventive planning in that intervention plans set up early in the therapy process may need to be changed (or can be accelerated) once the family is no longer in crisis. Gehart and Tuttle (2003) state that "plans often need to be modified because of outside factors, unanticipated events, or unrealistic expectations" (p. 2).

Another obstacle to planning an intervention is when family members cannot agree upon goals to be pursued and/or in what order. One of the challenges in planning the intervention is that individual family members may have different notions about how to proceed in therapy as well as what goals will be established and in what order. This may in part be due to resistance or level of motivation, and it may in part be due to personal preferences or individual agendas. It is up to the therapist to skillfully mediate these differences of opinion in a way that preserves the therapeutic alliance with all members of the family. One resolution could be to pursue goals simultaneously whereas it is preferable to get the family members to compromise so that interventions can begin.

In more complicated cases it is more imperative for the family therapist to meet the basic and most pressing needs of the family (e.g., the need for more adequate shelter, health care, clothing, or food) before beginning the formal process of family therapy. It is important for the family therapist to understand the value of casework services to the family and to the therapeutic process. Furthermore the family therapist may need to serve in a variety of roles (advocate, educator, broker, cultural consultant, etc.).

In developing interventions it is important to understand the history and nature of the problem. Hanna (1997) categorizes problems according to their historical nature. That is, *situational* problems are new conflicts with no presenting history. *Transitional* problems are those related to normative life stages or non-normative changes in families that have had successes in earlier stages but that have been unable to make the current adaptation. *Chronic* problems are those that can be traced to difficulties that may have started as situational in an earlier time frame but have persisted through a transitional time period and now have such an extensive history that they have become an organizing influence on additional emerging problems. By understanding the nature of the problem in its historical context practitioners can begin to select the appropriate intervention. That is, the more chronic the problem, the more direct the intervention should be (Hanna, 2007).

Formulating the Contract

Once goal setting has been achieved it is time to obtain a commitment from the family. Generally, a contract will describe and outline activities for the planned intervention phase, list goals and tasks to be accomplished, and identify who will do what. The therapist then gets all members of the family to cooperate during sessions and to follow through on instructions—both inside and outside of the session. This is the time when the therapist begins to summarize the assessments that he or she has formulated and links these assessments to planned interventions. The therapist should then also connect the established and agreed-upon goals with specific interventions planned. Now it is time to develop a contract with the family.

The contract is the family's formal commitment to change. Contracts can be verbal and/or written. (It is common practice to develop written contracts with couples and with adolescents.) Contracting is an important part of the interventive process in that it clearly specifies what is expected of the family.

Contracts have several advantages (Hull & Mather, 2006). First they reduce the possibility of misunderstanding between the family and the therapist. Second they help document individual responsibilities. Third, contracts, especially written ones, emphasize the equality of responsibility between the family and the therapist. This can be empowering for some families. Fourth, contracts help make clear that the family must take action rather than expecting the therapist to create the change. Fifth, contracts are especially helpful for underorganized families as they add structure to the lives of these families. Sixth, contracts can reduce the stress and anxiety experienced by the family in that it becomes much clearer what needs to be done to resolve the problem. And finally seventh, contracts can be used to monitor, record, and evaluate change.

Contracts often need to be evaluated and renegotiated especially when new information becomes available or when the family's needs change. There are other circumstances that necessitate contract changes—for example when families fail to reach their goals in a reasonable length of time, when families make excuses for not fulfilling the contract, and when families complain about the condition of the contract (Brown & Brown, 2002). Renegotiating a contract can be an empowering experience in that families will "know that they are able to change the conditions of the contract if they so desire" (Brown & Brown, 2002, p. 108).

MIDDLE PHASE OF THERAPY

Implementation of the Intervention

The start of the intervention phase of family therapy varies depending on the specific model. For instance, Bowen's assessment phase, which includes the construction of the genogram, serves as an assessment tool and an intervention strategy and can facilitate the evaluation of therapy. Likewise therapists following the Satir approach begin their intervention in the initial phase of therapy as they affirm the self-worth of each family member by greeting each one by name; they also teach good communication skills in the early phase of therapy by modeling good communication to the family. Therapists following the Minuchin approach may physically move family members around and begin to alter boundaries via Minuchin's interviewing strategies in the assessment phase of family therapy.

Even though the working contract between therapist and family has been agreed upon there are still some clinical decisions and general guidelines that must be decided upon by the therapist. The first of these (given a particular problem area) is to decide on whether the content of the problem (the symptom of the presenting complaint) or the process of the problem (how a family interacts when the problem occurs) will be addressed. As described and discussed in the previous chapter, most families expect to focus on the symptom of the presenting problem.

The therapist may elect to focus on process over content (or vice versa) or decide to alternate between the two so that the family can feel as if "its problem" is being addressed. Level of client resistance, client expectations of what is to happen in the therapy process (task-/problem-focused or growth/insight), and theoretical framework selected for assessment and/or intervention will operate to help make this decision.

The second clinical decision and guideline that needs to be taken into account is for the therapist to remain firm in his or her selection of theory and technique(s) to be used so as to avoid moving around from problem area to problem area. It is tempting to jump from theory to theory, from technique to technique—given the rich array of therapy models that exist in family therapy. It is equally tempting to move from problem area to problem area—especially if one meets resistance and/or progress does not occur immediately. In essence, it is important to be patient with the theory, technique, and problem area selected, and to give them time to work.

Roles of the Therapist

As a successful therapeutic alliance has been established with all family members and initial resistance issues have been resolved, it is now time to consider one's role with the family in the interventive implementation stage of therapy. Certainly many of the roles that the therapist takes on are theoretically determined by family therapy model; however, there are additional roles that should be considered by the therapist that are useful across models of therapy and that transcend theory-specific therapist roles. Collins, Jordan, and Coleman (2007) provide a description of these roles:

1. The *empathic supporter* is one who identifies and reinforces family strengths while recognizing family limitations and lack of resources. The previous chapter discussed at length the importance of building interventions upon family strengths.

2. The *teacher/trainer* cultivates areas where the family is deficient or lacking in skills or knowledge. Skill areas may include deficits in communication, parenting skills, problem solving, anger management, conflict resolution, values clarification, money management, and skills of daily living.

3. The *consultant* is an advisor to the family for specific problems that arise. The therapist can provide ongoing feedback to parents and children who may be isolated or otherwise lack mechanisms to obtain specific knowledge.

4. The *enabler* expands opportunities (in the family's environment) that might not otherwise be accessible. For instance, the therapist may help a family identify and/or navigate complex agencies and organizations that are essential to their functioning (e.g., connecting an immigrant family to special services for new immigrants).

5. The *mobilizer* is knowledgeable about helping systems and community support networks and assists the family in coordinating activities and establishing better communication.

6. The *mediator* addresses stress and conflict between individuals and systems. The therapist can help mediate solutions between the family and the community when the family is in conflict or has an antagonistic relationship with an outside system.

7. The *advocate* demonstrates activism on behalf of families. Family problems may be rooted in conditions within the broader societal context. Consequently, community activism and political action give the family therapist the means to work for social and legislative reform.

Ecological Practice and Use of Collaterals

Building upon the roles described above there are times when the family therapist must intervene in the family's environment. That is, the environment becomes a central focus for intervention as the therapist helps the family solve the problem of a lack of resources or an inability to access resources in the community. Housing, health care, employment, and transportation issues are some of the many challenges that families, especially low-income families, face. Hepworth and Larsen (1993) present a range of ecological interventions for families:

- Supplementing resources in the home environment
- Developing and enhancing support systems
- Moving clients to a new environment
- Increasing the responsiveness of organizations to people's needs
- Enhancing interactions between organizations and institutions
- Improving institutional environments
- Enhancing agency environments
- Developing new resources

Ecological practice can be an empowering experience as it is important for the therapist to teach the family about the existence of and/or how to access systems of social support. The ultimate goal is to get families to learn how to get their own needs met—with the therapist operating more in the role of advocate, facilitator, and/or mediator (Collins et al., 2007).

Family therapists must not limit their collaboration to other clinicians or case managers. Working with schools, social service agencies, mental and physical health agencies, governmental agencies and institutions, and criminal justice systems and making home visits are a part of ecological practice. It can also be important to work with informal support systems such as extended family, friends, neighbors, and indigenous folk healers. Developing a good relationship with these formal and informal systems of social support toward developing a collaborative team can facilitate the family therapy process as environmental issues are resolved—helping the family focus on issues within the family that are impacting its functioning.

In working with these systems it is important for the family therapist to remain neutral (Hanna, 2007). Becoming too closely identified with the outside system may cause the therapist to side with collaborative team members resulting in coalitions against the family. In the use of collaterals the family therapist must also guard against usurping the role of the parents in their executive position—making sure that the larger system does not take over the function of the parents. Brown and Vaccaro (1991, p. 268) have developed a set of guidelines for working with the collaborative teams:

1. Establish a positive climate for change by acknowledging each person's good intentions, contribution, and significance.

2. Summarize the purpose of the meeting.

3. Ask each participant to tell how he or she sees the problem.

4. Discuss the strengths of the child or adolescent.

5. Suggest that participants tell what results they hope to see.

6. Decide how this can be accomplished. Who will do what? When?

7. Decide if other people need to be involved in the interventions.

8. Discuss obstacles to the intervention (e.g., lack of transportation, schedule conflicts).

9. Define how the participants will know if the intervention has been successful.

10. Determine if a follow-up meeting needs to be scheduled. If so, when?

Ecological interventions may provide a vehicle for developmental, preventive, or rehabilitative services (Hartman & Laird, 1983). The family is still the center of attention while attention is being paid to those social policies and organizational arrangements that underpin family practice. In short, an ecological systems perspective is an important adjunct to family therapy and can be used in a wide range of practice settings and social problem areas with any size client system.

Basic Skills and Techniques

The main task of the family therapist in this stage of implementation of the intervention is to help the family gain new insights and practice new behaviors and to reinforce more functional patterns of interaction. This section of the chapter will describe techniques designed to produce change in families. In reviewing the various techniques it is important to consider that the technique must fit the needs of the family and the goals selected for intervention in order to be successful (Walsh & McGraw, 2002).

The techniques described below do not represent or advocate for one model of family therapy over another; however, there will be some techniques that are derived from some of the models presented in this text. In any event, the techniques listed below were selected based on their utility in supplementing the techniques outlined in major models of therapy. The following are examples of interventive skills and techniques that promote new behaviors and patterns of interaction.

- *Tracking:* Tracking refers to the technique of giving the client immediate, positive, verbal, and nonverbal feedback that conveys the sense that the therapist is following what the client is saying and is really listening. The idea is to give the client a sense of empowerment through validation or confirmation of his or her feelings.

- *Enactment:* Enactment is an attempt to bring family conflict from outside the therapy into the session. A problematic scenario is actively created during an interview. Family members demonstrate how they deal with issues while the therapist observes and assesses the interaction (Collins et al., 2007, p. 282). The therapist instructs family members to reenact a specific interaction in order to assist the therapist in generating alternative solutions and interactions. The therapist may either be nondirective or actively manipulate a situation depending on the family's capacities and the theoretical orientation of the therapist.

- *Confrontation:* This technique may be used to help family members communicate more accurately and effectively with one another. The therapist encourages all family members to openly and directly discuss their perceptions of and reactions to situations. An atmosphere of trust and honesty develops, reducing the threat of reprisal or retribution.

- *Communication checks:* Communication checks ensure accurate perception on the part of all family members. The therapist establishes a pattern of continually checking his or her perceptions of what has been communicated and encourages family members to do the same. Through this technique, assumptions and inaccurate perceptions can be quickly identified and corrected.

- *Roles of the family:* Working together, the therapist and family define specific roles and expectations for each family member. The therapist encourages all family members to identify both specific expectations they have for one another and specific tasks that are part of each person's role. Consequences may have to be established for the noncompletion of tasks.

- *Rules of the family:* The therapist helps the family set general rules and specific rules that govern the family members' daily lives. Family members decide how they want to organize their daily living patterns.

- *Family meetings:* The therapist encourages clients to hold regular family meetings to supplement the therapeutic contacts. Initially, meetings can be used to practice and reinforce new behaviors learned in therapy. Eventually, meetings can take place instead of therapy (Walsh & McGraw, 2002, pp. 155–156).

- *Homework assignments:* This technique helps extend the work of therapy to the home environment. Homework assignments are very specific and detail precise behaviors to be performed. Homework assignments admittedly have a strong behavioral orientation. However, these assignments if consistent with therapeutic goals can represent a natural outgrowth of the therapy process (Worden, 2003, p. 161).

- *Focusing:* Families are notorious for attempting to resolve two or three problems at once. The therapist helps direct the discussion back to the central issue being discussed. Focusing also helps families not to go off on tangents. This is often the case when very threatening or painful issues are discussed. It is incumbent on the therapist to make a determination if the pace of therapy is moving too fast for the family to handle.

- *Use of examples:* Examples help the family therapist describe or teach a concept to a family. Examples should be compatible with the experiences of the family's life. They offer reassurance that others have faced the same challenges. Examples can illustrate alternative ways of dealing with a difficult situation and are excellent teaching aids.

- *Emphasizing strengths:* The therapist can emphasize the strengths that a family possesses by pointing out the things that the family does well. Family members should also be encouraged to talk about the ways they have coped successfully with this and other problems. Strengthening encourages a family to use its own resources to create change (Hanna & Brown, 1995).

- *Role playing:* This technique allows family members to deal with issues within the safety of the family session. In role playing a person takes on either his or her own persona or that of another person. The family member can then begin to understand what the other person is feeling (Hull & Mather, 2006).

Managing Conflict

There are times when the family cannot seem to resolve a problem or issue, and this lack of resolution creates conflict among family members. In these cases it is important to get a consensus as to what the problem is, determine whether the problem is solvable, and discuss several solutions until the family chooses one solution over the other (Brown & Brown, 2002; Hanna & Brown, 1995).

If the therapist suspects domestic violence, then the therapist is obligated to pursue and determine if this is indeed the case and alert the proper authorities (in the case of violence against children). In the case of violence between couples it is important to separate the couple and refer the batterer for individual counseling. If the domestic violence is current, the batterer may not be allowed to remain in family therapy until he or she gets help and the battering ceases.

Hanna and Brown (1995) suggest that conflict resolution has two distinct phases: problem definition and problem resolution. They further suggest that the emphasis should be on behavior change rather than insight and that solutions should be kept simple—since complex plans often fail. The therapist can help families choose a solution that is acceptable to all family members, decide how the solution will be implemented, and evaluate the proposed solution and renegotiate the contract, if necessary.

Teaching Problem-Solving and Communication Skills

Preparing the family to become independent of the therapist requires that the family possess good problem-solving and communication skills, in that the goal of family therapy is to help the family function independently of the therapist. First we need to define these two concepts and differentiate between the two.

Problem solving teaches family members to negotiate solutions to their problems on their own that are acceptable to all (Collins et al., 2007). Problem solving not only helps families deal with present difficulties but also prepares them to resolve future problems that may arise. Hence, the therapist is preparing the family for life after therapy and empowering the family to become independent. Families are encouraged to take a more active role in practicing problem-solving skills and are expected to identify their own needs and recurring issues (Collins et al., 2007). Therapists are encouraged to take on the roles of facilitator, teacher, and consultant.

Problem-solving skills are practiced in the therapy session and outside the therapy session as a homework assignment. The therapist directs the family to select an area of reoccurring conflict that it frequently experiences. (It is important for the therapist not to select an issue that has been central to the presenting problem; it is also important not to begin this process until major progress has been made in therapy.) Once the family has selected an issue, it is instructed to actually try to resolve that issue. The therapist only intervenes when he or she feels that the family has gotten off track and detoured into other areas (e.g., trying to resolve two problems at once) or when the family seems to have hit an impasse in their problem-solving attempts. In the therapist's intervention he or she may instruct or model for the family new problem-solving skills. As the therapist sees progress in family members' problem-solving skills it may be time to give the family a homework assignment addressing another issue of concern.

How a family interacts while attempting to resolve a problem is a communication skill. That is, the *process* of the interaction is the focus of communication skills training. Both verbal and nonverbal skills are addressed so that the family will learn good communication skills. Good communication skills include communication that is clear, direct, open, and honest (Satir, 1967). Families are also taught to recognize underlying or hidden messages. In other words, families are taught to identify the metacommunication of the message ("the message about the message"; Satir, 1967).

Teaching good communication skills can begin in the early phase of intervention via the role modeling of the therapist. Good communication skills can be reinforced or taught as the therapist asks family members to clarify their message so that it becomes more direct and clear. This process may take the form of instruction, modeling, and/or role playing. The therapist may also repeat the message sent by asking the family member to paraphrase what he or she heard so as to improve the listening skills of the family member (Collins et al., 2007). Family members are also advised to avoid the use of generalizations (Kinney, Haapala, & Booth, 1991).

When a family enters therapy it is not uncommon for it to have tried many different solutions to its problems. Some of these solutions have been successful, some have not, and some solutions have made things worse. It is important to determine if the family has been diligent enough in its pursuit of a resolution that the therapist's task is merely to encourage the family to keep trying. In essence, good problem-solving skills and good communication skills are the building blocks of functional families and can help families become independent of the therapist.

Resistance in Families

Resistance can occur in the beginning stage of therapy and is likely to reappear in the middle phase of therapy as well. In these initial stages of family therapy some family members may fail to see why they are involved in therapy if they are not the symptomatic member and hence may not be as motivated to change.

Resistance in families may take many forms: missed appointments, silence, helplessness, hostility among members or toward the therapist, a refusal to see progress in therapy, detouring or distracting behaviors (e.g., the manufacturing of family or individual crises that need attention in order to avoid working on ongoing issues in therapy), one family member out-talking others, failure to share relevant information, inability to understand the therapist's comments, challenging the therapist's comments, noncompliance, and the refusal to do assigned (homework) tasks. It is important for the therapist not to personalize resistance or become angry or frustrated. Communicating fear, anger, or frustration to the family may negatively impact the development of a successful therapeutic alliance.

Anderson and Stewart (1983) in their attempt to incorporate diverse views of resistance are operationally defined by different models of therapy. They define resistance as all those aspects of the therapeutic system (therapist, family members, organizations) that interact to prevent the therapeutic system (therapist + family) from achieving the family's goals for therapy. That is, families come to therapy to make changes in behaviors that they do not like or that do not work for them (Worden, 2003).

Therapeutic impasses occur because therapists are challenging the family norms in that resistance may emanate from the family's fear of change as a threat to its homeostatic balance and steady state. Hence resistance represents the family's difficulty in making those changes. In essence the family may feel threatened by change.

Some therapists view resistance as being distinguished from a lack of interest in forming a relationship with the therapist and instead define resistance as an obstruction that evolves in the process of therapy (Mishne, 1986). Other therapists see resistance as a lack of desperation in that the initial anxiety level of the family has lessened and hence the family's motivation for change has decreased (Whitaker & Keith, 1981).

Family therapists see resistance differently than psychotherapists (e.g., as a client's lack of cooperation with the therapist or a lack of progress in treatment). Hanna (2007) reports that, "in family therapy, there is a strong bias toward the notion of resistance as an interactional event characterized by the professional's lack of understanding about what is important to the family" (p. 96). Hence, it is the therapist's responsibility to understand the unique perceptual patterns that significantly influence behavioral patterns (Hanna, 2007).

Resistance is distinguished from a lack of interest in forming a relationship with the therapist and is instead defined as an obstruction that evolves in the process of therapy (Mishne, 1986). Family therapy is not a simple matter of telling family members what they need to do to resolve their problems (Worden, 2003). Resistance comprises those impasses and blocks that occur in therapy as a result of difficulty in changing family dynamics and family interactions. In essence the family may feel threatened by change. It is paradoxical that anxiety may be the motivator for family change as well as an obstacle to that same change.

Different family therapy models address the issue of resistance differently. Behaviorists minimize the importance of resistance but deal with issues of resistance implicitly by suggesting strategies that will minimize the likelihood that resistance will occur. Some behaviorists attempt to avoid resistance altogether by screening out couples and families in the assessment phase—giving the family time to learn about the therapy process before committing to it. Structuralists attempt to win the family over by employing the techniques of joining and accommodating and probe for flexibility in the family system as a starting point for interventions. Strategic family therapists attempt to overcome resistance by changing the perceived reality of family members through the use of relabeling and reframing techniques. Satir's communication approach affirms the importance of family members by using her techniques of physical touch and the sharing of self. Bowen's family of origin family therapy advises the therapist to remain calm, neutral, and objective—staying de-triangulated from family conflict.

It is important for the therapist not to personalize resistance or become angry or frustrated. Communicating fear, anger, or frustration to the family may negatively impact the development of a successful therapeutic alliance. Rather, the therapist should seek to understand the function of the resistance (e.g., moving too fast or starting therapy in a place that is too threatening for the family system) and modify interventions accordingly. Suggestions for dealing with therapeutic impasses are to explore interface issues with oneself or one's supervisor, to invite a consultant to the session, and/or to add a cotherapist.

Working With Involuntary Families

There are times when therapists are faced with working with involuntary clients. Families may present as being hostile or just ambivalent. In addition, many of these families come with problems that are long-standing. Hence it is essential that the therapist get a thorough history of the presenting problem(s).

Families that are court ordered because there is substance abuse, sexual abuse, and other domestic violence may be understandably frightened, anxious, and even ashamed. With these families it is imperative that the perpetrator or substance abuser receive individual services; often it is necessary to refer elsewhere. The therapist should expect not to begin the actual change process right away, as building the therapeutic relationship and getting a thorough family history will be the focus of the early phases of family therapy.

In cases where there is domestic violence and/or substance abuse it is also important for family members not to blame themselves for the actions of the perpetrator; this may take a long time to accomplish. Once the therapist has begun to make progress in this regard the next focus of therapy should be to explore how the violence and/or substance abuse has impacted family dynamics. This will become the focus of therapy for the middle phase of interventions.

In work with involuntary clients there is often an expectation to provide a progress report of the therapy. In these cases it is imperative that the family be consulted and give full consent as to the content of such reports—this may become a therapeutic goal unto itself.

There may be cases in which one family member is insisting on therapy and another family member does not feel that he or she needs to be involved. There may be one or more members who fail to see the purpose of therapy. Care needs to be taken in developing even therapeutic alliances with all family members—being especially careful not to ally or overidentify with the family member making the referral. One should not expect all members to make similar progress toward therapeutic goals or even agree on therapy goals. It will be important to "start where the client is."

With the involuntary client (be it mandated by an agency or institution or court ordered) part of the task in goal setting will be to make it clear what choices the family has. The family should be an active participant in deciding on therapy goals; but don't expect all members to agree—it's OK to have multiple goals that accommodate all family members.

To this end, it will be important to start the therapy on common ground so as to minimize resistance. In working with involuntary clients it is essential to search for flexibility in the system. This technique of structural family therapy advocates that the therapist start where the family is most agreeable to a particular intervention.

END PHASE ISSUES

The therapist will recognize when therapy is about to end (e.g., missed appointments, numerous cancellations, client-initiated review of therapy progress, or simply that many of the therapy goals have been met). One of the most difficult tasks for the therapist is to recognize that termination is near and/or to accept that termination is imminent—that is, in cases wherein all the therapy goals have not been met. This section of the chapter will address and explore the issues involved in the termination phase of family therapy.

Termination

There are two types of termination—planned and unplanned. In the case of a planned termination the question is very straightforward: Have the goals of therapy been met? Have the chief complaints been resolved? Is the family satisfied with its progress?

Planning for Termination

Collins et al. (2007) suggest that "the process of therapy parallels the end of each family meeting" (p. 352). They suggest that at the end of each family therapy session at least 10 minutes be reserved to summarize unfinished business, summarize the session, identify the strengths of the family, and review progress that has been made thus far.

The decision to terminate is ideally a decision made by both the therapist and the family. It is recommended that the therapist begin to space out therapy appointments toward the end of family therapy. (Four-week intervals are suggested during this stage.) This move helps the family feel more confident about the changes it has made and what life after therapy might be like. Spacing out interviews toward the end of therapy also gives the family a chance to practice new behaviors learned in therapy.

Worden (2003) outlines several steps that therapists may take toward the final (formal) termination that will consolidate the gains made in therapy and leave the door open for future contact:

1. *Take inventory:* Each family member is asked what has changed, and then he or she is asked to comment on what others have said.

2. *Provide explanations:* The therapist shares with the family his or her own impressions of the changes that have taken place and may offer a conceptual understanding of the changes that have occurred in the family.

3. *Speculate on the future:* The therapist outlines future pitfalls (family vulnerability) facing the family.

4. *Elicit feedback:* The therapist elicits feedback from the family to learn what has and has not worked with the family. This feedback may help the therapist with future cases.

5. *Leave the door open for future contacts:* The therapist develops a follow-up plan (to be discussed in more detail below). This plan helps maintain and reinforce progress made in therapy.

Unplanned Termination

In many cases therapy is ended prematurely. The research shows that, for families that have attended an average of 6 to 10 sessions, the dropout rate for family therapy is about 40% (Worden, 1994). For these and other reasons the therapist should not personalize this unscheduled termination. It may mean that the family has made all the progress it desires or that the family does not feel that it can handle any more change. However, unplanned termination may also mean that the family is dissatisfied with the services, angry with the therapist, or unwilling to make changes toward therapy goals.

The issue of termination should be addressed as early in the therapy process as possible, in order to help prevent unplanned or premature termination.

Hanna and Brown (1999) suggest the following guidelines to help prevent premature termination:

1. *Plan for termination in advance:* The therapy contract should include the estimated number of sessions for the length of therapy. The use of a contract specifying a fixed number of sessions facilitates a periodic review of therapy (Barker, 1981). In addition setting a specific time for termination helps the family and therapist plan for change.

2. *Plan to gradually withdraw therapy:* This step should be taken especially in cases in which the family is unsure that it can maintain the change. This measure can be very empowering to a family in that it can take credit for and feel more responsible for the change.

3. *Summarize the major themes:* In terminating, the therapist should summarize the major themes of therapy and observe closely to see whether the family agrees or disagrees with the summary statement. If the family disagrees, the therapist should note this and give family members the opportunity to discuss their views. On some occasions, the therapist may ask the family to summarize therapy.

4. *Ask the family to decide what needs to happen for it to return to therapy:* It is important for the therapist to help the family decide when it can no longer manage the problem and need to return to therapy. The therapist might say, "What would be the first sign that you can no longer handle this problem?" This question should help family members understand the specific changes they have made in therapy. The therapist should help the family understand that returning to therapy does not mean that the family has failed. Instead, a follow-up session can be framed as a booster shot (as additional sessions are

likely to be brief) to help the family maintain desired changes. Then if further services are sought, the therapist can reiterate that this is not an indicator of failure.

5. *Reassure the family that it has the strength and resources to deal with future problems:* In some cases, a family presents a new problem at the time of termination. If the problem is not serious, the therapist must reassure the family that it has the skills to deal with this situation on its own. Sometimes the therapist might have difficulty letting go of the family. Supervision and/or consulting with a colleague may help address this issue.

In the case of premature termination, if the therapist cannot get the family to come in one more time for a formal termination interview, then termination will have to transpire over the phone. This assumes that the therapist recognizes that the family is ready for termination and is not coming back—which also implies that the therapist is willing to accept the family's decision to terminate. In an ideal situation both parents are available by phone to briefly discuss the family's next steps. It is important to remember to keep this conversation brief, out of respect for the client who has elected not to go through a formal termination interview.

Recognizing Termination

In other cases wherein either the therapist recognizes that the family is ready for termination or the goals of therapy have been met and it is time to begin the termination process, at least two interviews are suggested to address life after therapy and the therapist's role (if any) after therapy has formally ended.

Walsh and McGraw (2002, p. 154) suggest that termination is indicated when a family displays the following behaviors:

- Present-day conflicts are resolved in mutually satisfying ways.
- Members begin to express optimism about future plans.
- The family sets realistic goals for the unit and for each individual member.
- Each member has internalized the new behaviors, attitudes, and feelings.
- The therapist reviews the family's entire therapy process and specifically reinforces the new behaviors and interactional patterns.
- The therapist checks each individual's feelings and attitudes toward the changes that have occurred to ensure that each member has personalized and internalized the changes.
- The therapist presents written and/or verbal feedback to the family concerning his or her perception of its therapeutic process.

The Therapist's Reaction to Termination

Although there are different types of termination (planned; unplanned; therapist initiated—because the therapist either is leaving the agency or feels that sufficient progress is not being made; client initiated; or mutually agreed upon), there are common factors involved in any type of termination. These common factors are the client's reaction to termination. Hellenbrand (1987) suggests that the client's emotional reaction to termination is related to the duration of contact, the intensity of the relationship, whether termination was part of a planned or unplanned process, the client's strengths and support, whether the client accomplished goals, and whether the client will continue receiving services from another worker. There is a range of emotions—both positive and negative—that can include anger, resentment, rejection, sadness, fear, relief, and/or pride (Hull & Mather, 2006). Negative emotions can arise from issues of separation and/or abandonment experienced earlier in the client's life or due to how the case was handled (e.g., the family became too dependent on the therapist or new problems arose that the family felt it could not handle alone; Hull & Mather, 2006).

The therapist may experience positive and negative feelings as well—pride and accomplishment, relief, sadness, loss, guilt (especially if goals have not been met), anger, and abandonment (Hull & Mather, 2006). Supervision and/or consultation with colleagues is recommended in cases wherein the negative feelings linger.

Collins et al. (2007) suggest that there are positive aspects of therapy, whereas much of the literature has focused on the negative aspects of termination. They assert that "termination is essentially positive because it is often used to focus upon accomplishments" (p. 362). Further, this experience may increase family members' self-esteem and self-confidence as therapeutic gains are reflected upon.

Relapse Prevention and the Follow-up Plan

Relapse prevention is an important issue in termination; however, the therapy contract should address this issue by building in certain safeguards. To this end homework assignments as discussed previously may help prevent relapse as well as reinforce new behaviors. The development of a follow-up plan can help prevent relapse. Follow-up can take the form of short-term (1 month after the last session) and/or long-term (6 months after the last session) follow-up. A follow-up plan helps the therapist check on the progress of the family to see if new problems have arisen and gives the family an opportunity to discuss what is working and what still needs to be changed (a follow-up plan can take the form of a telephone call or an in-person interview; Brown & Brown, 2002).

SUMMARY

This chapter addresses the issues and challenges of the phases of family therapy that are unique to the practice of family therapy. These issues are considered to be another layer of the process of family therapy.

Understanding the practical aspects of family therapy is an important part of the process, in that specific skills are required in clinical work with families. In preparing for the stages of family therapy different family therapy models may not address practical skills and clinical issues relevant to the various phases of family therapy. Being able to anticipate certain basic interactions with the family strengthens the nature of the process of family therapy.

The authors assert that the major models of family therapy focus on theory and technique while paying minimum attention to clinical issues unique to various phases in family therapy. This overview of the phases of family therapy is intended to review key processes that are not emphasized in models of family therapy. Understanding key issues in the phases of family therapy is an important factor related to overall success in the practice of family therapy.

Unfortunately, there are times when it is apparent that therapy is not progressing—despite valiant efforts on the part of both the therapist and the family. In cases wherein the family is not initiating termination, it is incumbent on the family therapist to terminate. Supervision and consultation with colleagues can be helpful in making interventive decisions as well as help in deciding whether to terminate or not. The authors believe that the therapist is ethically bound to consider termination when it is apparent that the family will make very little progress if therapy continues.

NOTE

1. The term *hypothesizing* was first used by the Milan Group as a formal part of its strategic technique. Hypothesizing is the process by which conclusions are formulated about the data gathered; it includes what people think about what is going on and also the assumptions that they bring to therapy.

RECOMMENDED READINGS

Brown, J. H., & Brown, C. S. (2002). *Marital therapy: Concepts and skill for effective practice.* Pacific Grove, CA: Brooks/Cole.

Collins, D., Jordan, C. & Coleman, H. (1999). *An introduction to family social work.* Itasca, IL: Peacock.

Collins, D., Jordan, C., & Coleman, H. (2007). *An introduction to family social work* (2nd ed.). Itasca, IL: Peacock.

Figley, C., & Nelson, T. (1989). Basic family therapy skills: I. Conceptualization and findings. *Journal of Marital and Family Therapy, 4*(14), 349–366.

Hanna, S. M. (2007). *The practice of family therapy: Key elements across models* (4th ed.). Belmont, CA: Thomson Brooks/Cole.

Hull, G. H., & Mather, J. (2006). *Understanding generalist practice with families.* Belmont, CA: Thomson Brooks/Cole.

DISCUSSION QUESTIONS

1. What makes family therapy unique, as opposed to work with individuals, in that there are clinical issues especially relevant to this type of therapy?

2. Select and discuss major issues in each phase of family therapy.

3. Collaboration and resistance are particularly challenging issues in family therapy. Describe this clinical process, and identify various issues and how to resolve them.

REFERENCES

Anderson, C. M., & Stewart, S. (1983). *Mastering resistance: A practical guide for family therapy.* New York, NY: Guilford.

Barker, P. (1981). *Basic family therapy.* Baltimore, MD: University Press.

Berg, I. K. (1994*). Family-based services.* New York, NY: Haworth Press.

Bordin, E. S. (1982). A working alliance based model of supervision. *The Counseling Psychologist, 11*, 35–42.

Brown, J. H., & Brown, C. S. (2002). *Marital therapy: Concepts and skill for effective practice.* Pacific Grove, CA: Brooks/Cole.

Brown, J. H., & Christensen, D. N. (1999). *Family therapy: Theory and practice.* Pacific Grove, CA: Brooks/Cole.

Brown, J. H., & Vaccaro, A. (1991). *A manual for resource and youth services coordinators.* Louisville, KY: University of Louisville and Cities in Schools.

Campbell, D., Draper, R., & Crutchley, E. (1991). The Milan systemic approach to family therapy. In A. S. Gurman & D. P. Kniskern (Eds.), *Handbook of family therapy* (Vol. 2, pp. 324–362). New York, NY: Brunner/Mazel.

Collins, D., Jordan, C., & Coleman, H. (1999). *An introduction to family social work.* Itasca, IL: Peacock.

Collins, D., Jordan, C., & Coleman, H. (2007). *An introduction to family social work* (2nd ed.). Itasca, IL: Peacock.

Figley, C., & Nelson, T. (1989). Basic family therapy skills: I. Conceptualization and findings. *Journal of Marital and Family Therapy, 4*(14), 349–366.

Gehart, D. R., & Tuttle, A. R. (2003). *Theory-based treatment planning for marriage and family therapists.* Pacific Grove, CA: Brooks/Cole.

Gurman, A. S., & Knudson, R. M. (1978). Behavioral marriage therapy: A psychodynamic systems analysis and critique. *Family Process, 17,* 121–138.

Hanna, S. M. (1997). A developmental-interactional model. In T. D. Hargrave & S. M. Hanna (Eds.), *The aging family: New visions in theory, practice and reality* (pp. 101–130). New York, NY: Brunner.

Hanna, S. M. (2007). *The practice of family therapy: Key elements across models* (4th ed.). Belmont, CA: Thomson Brooks/Cole.

Hanna, S. M., & Brown, J. H. (1995). *The practice of family therapy: Key elements across models.* Pacific Grove, CA: Brooks/Cole.

Hanna, S. M., & Brown, J. H. (1999). *The practice of family therapy: Key elements across models* (2nd ed.). Belmont, CA: Wadsworth.

Hanna, S. M. & Brown, J. H. (2004). *The practice of family therapy: Key elements across models* (3rd ed.). Belmont, CA: Wadsworth.

Hartman, A., & Laird, J. (1983). *Family-centered social work practice.* New York, NY: Free Press.

Hellenbrand, S. (1987). Termination in direct practice. In *Encyclopedia of social work* (18th ed., Vol. 2, pp. 765–770). Silver Springs, MD: National Association of Social Workers.

Hepworth, D., & Larsen, J. (1993). *Direct social work practice.* Chicago, IL: Dorsey Press.

Hull, G. H. & Mather, J. (2006). *Understanding generalist practice with families.* Belmont, CA: Thomson Brooks/Cole.

Karpel, M. A. (1994). *Evaluating couples: A handbook for practitioners.* New York, NY: Norton.

Kinney, J., Haapala, D., & Booth, C. (1991). *Keeping families together: The homebuilders model.* Hawthorne, NY: Aldine de Gruyter.

Lankton, S., Lankton, C., & Matthews, W. (1991). Ericksonian family therapy. In A. S. Gurman & D. P. Kniskern (Eds.), *Handbook of family therapy* (Vol. 2, pp. 324–362). New York, NY: Brunner/Mazel.

Minuchin, S. (1974). *Families and family therapy.* Cambridge, MA: Harvard University Press.

Mishne, J. M. (1986). *Clinical work with adolescents.* New York, NY: Free Press.

O'Hanson, W. H. (1991). *Acknowledgement and possibility.* Paper presented at the Family and Children's Agency, Louisville, KY.

Satir, V. (1967). *Conjoint family therapy.* Palo Alto, CA: Science and Behavior Books.

Walsh, F. (1980). *Lecture.* The University of Chicago School of Social Service Administration.

Walsh, W. M. (1991). *Case studies in family therapy.* Needham Heights, MA: Allyn & Bacon.

Walsh, W. M., & McGraw, J. A. (2002). *Essentials of family therapy.* Denver, CO: Love.

Whitaker, C. A., & Keith, D. V. (1981). *Symbolic-experiential family therapy approach.* New York, NY: Brunner/Mazel.

Worden, M. (1994). *Family therapy basics.* Pacific Grove, CA: Brooks/Cole.

Worden, M. (2003). *Family therapy basics* (3rd ed.). Pacific Grove, CA: Brooks/Cole.

Chapter 12

FAMILIES IN TRANSITION
Alternative Family Patterns

The traditional nuclear family consisting of a married heterosexual couple with biological children does not reflect the various family arrangements found in contemporary family life. As we survey the social landscape to obtain a picture of the complexities of family structures we see single-parent families, stepfamilies, blended families, gay and lesbian families, adoptive families, biracial families, fictive kinship families, and extended kinship families. These alternative family patterns, once seen as deviations from the traditional family structure, are now accepted in contemporary society as different ways in which individuals choose to organize their family relationships. These once "deviant" family forms are now viewed as "alternative" family patterns.

The diversity of family structures not only represents alternative patterns of family life but also reflects changing ideas about marriage. Marital relationships have undergone significant changes since the beginning of the 20th century (Lambie, 2008). In the early 20th century, marriage was seen as an institution, and the commitment to marriage was a commitment to the *institution of marriage.* Since the mid-20th-century period marriage has undergone a process of deinstitutionalization (Cherlin, 2004) with marriage being understood as providing *companionship* for the partners. Cherlin (2004) describes the nature of the couple relationship in this form of marriage:

> They were supposed to be each other's companions, friends, lovers, to the extent not imaged by the spouses in the institutional marriages of the previous era. . . . The emotional satisfaction of the spouses became an important criterion for marital success. (p. 851)

Lambie (2008) speaks to a second shift in marital relationships, which can be described as the *individualized* marriage. Because of the changing division of labor in families due to two-income households, there was less stigma associated with childbearing outside marriage, cohabitation, same-sex committed relationships, higher median age of marriage, and rising divorce rates. Couples were permitted to develop personalized agreement for marriage and divorce. The consequence of such deinstitutionalization is that the marital relationship no longer has normative expectations that specify roles and behaviors. Individualized marriages are characterized by choice and alternatives regarding whether to marry, the sequence leading to marriage, and alternative forms of relational commitment. The goal of relationships is to facilitate personal growth and intimacy through open interaction and honest sharing of feelings between partners. If personal growth and fulfillment are not achieved, then a commitment to a companionship marriage may be questioned.

Marriage can now be viewed in contemporary society as traditional, or it can take on other forms, such as voluntary marriages with the commitment to have the marriage vows periodically renewed. Trial marriages are "marriage-like relationships" that are experienced as a prelude to a formal marriage. Cohabitation describes relationships with couples who plan never to marry and same-sex couples (Anderson & Sabatelli, 2003; Blumstein & Schwartz, 1983). As we examine current census data about the diversity of family structures it is apparent that the traditional nuclear family can no longer claim to be the dominant family structure (see Table 12.1). In

Table 12.1   The Changing Family Structure

- Between 1970 and 2005 the proportion of children living with two married parents dropped from 85% to 68% (U.S. Census Bureau, 2006).
- Forty percent of first marriages, 60% of second marriages, and 73% of third marriages ended in divorce (U.S. Census Bureau, 2006).
- Seventy five percent of those who divorce will eventually remarry (U.S. Census Bureau, 2006).
- Single-parent families rose to an all-time high in 2005 to 37% of families (U.S. Census Bureau, 2006).
- Approximately 43% of all marriages are remarriages for at least one of the adults. About 65% of remarriages involve children from a prior marriage and thus form stepfamilies (U.S. Census Bureau, 1998).
- The number of cohabiting couples has increased 800% since 1960 when fewer than 500,000 couples were cohabiting. In 2005 5.5 million couples were cohabiting (U.S. Census Bureau, 2006).
- The U.S. Census Bureau in 2000 counted 601,209 same-sex unmarried partner households in the United States. This figure represents a 314% increase from 1990. One of the problems with these figures is that when same-sex couples described themselves as married in 1990 the Census Bureau reclassified the gender of the spouse and the couple was considered as heterosexual. Thus the 1990 data may represent an undercount. There is still acknowledgement of an increase in the number of same-sex unmarried partner households (Smith & Gates, 2001).

fact one might question whether this family form can only be found on the margins of family life in contemporary society.

What is revealing about these data is that these various configurations of family life represent not only alternative family structures but also major transitions in the lives of families. For example, the increased number of single parents can in part be attributed to an increase in divorce rates. Divorced individuals must cope with an array of issues resulting from multiple transitions including the transition from marriage to divorce and then to single-hood or possibly single-parenthood and from that status to possible remarriage. Some divorced individuals may opt to enter into a cohabitation relationship or move into a committed same-sex relationship.

From a family system perspective these transitions involve changes in role status, changes in and reorganization of the family structure, and changes in the interactional patterns between family members (Anderson & Sabatelli, 2003). These changes, often unanticipated, can have a reverberating and multigenerational effect on the life trajectory of families and family members. These transitions, often stressful and traumatic, can seriously tax the adaptive capacity of families and family members to handle change. While marriage, as a transition, is seen as a time of joy and of expanding one's relationship and family constellation, these transitions, beginning with the termination of marriage through divorce or separation, symbolize grieving, loss, alteration, readjustment, and organization of one's personal and family life.

This chapter will examine the transitions that families and family members experience as they attempt to cope with the impact of divorce, single parenting, and creating step- and blended families. We will also examine cohabitation relationships and the function they serve as an alternative to marriage or as a retreat from the institution of marriage. Finally we will discuss gay and lesbian families and their parenting concerns. This family structure is included in this chapter for the following reasons. There is a greater sense of openness about same-gender loving relationships that later form family units. As we looked at our earlier definition of families, gay and lesbian couples form committed relationships that reflect an intentional commitment to bond and form family structures in the same fashion as heterosexual families. There is the same level of commitment, shared child caring responsibility, and the desire, in spite of the public reaction to gay marriages, to form families (at the time of this writing there is intense legal debate and legislative action denying committed gay and lesbian partners the same legal status and recognition as heterosexual marriage couples). With the decrease of homophobia along with the continued struggle for gay rights, and as domestic partners gain more rights, there is an apparent increase in gay and lesbian families with children. As we will further discuss in this chapter, the issue of being gay or lesbian can also impact family of origin relationships. When the gay or lesbian family member "comes out" or is "discovered" by his or her family of origin, the "out" family member may have to cope with the generally societal attitudes toward gays and lesbians within the emotional and intimate relationship network of the family. Issues such as betrayal, guilt, and rejection may bring about a disruption in family of origin relationships.

The issue of accepting committed gay and lesbian relationships as equivalent to the "traditional" family structure has become one of the major battles in the cultural war being fought over the questions "What is a family?" and "What constitutes 'family values,' and who has the right to define 'what is a family'?" These questions are not easily answered in contemporary society, and perhaps we will have to live with this complexity until there is greater societal acceptance of the diversity of family forms and family structures.

FORMING THE FAMILY: THE COUPLE SYSTEM

The family life cycle begins when two individuals come together to form a committed couple relationship. Whether they view marriage as an institution, as a companionship relationship, or as a path toward personal growth or fulfillment, it is at this point that individuals make a commitment to include another person in their lives in order to form a unique relationship system. Making the decision to live together in a committed relationship is a major life decision for a couple. It is an existential decision to live one's life not as an autonomous "I" but as a relational "We." If this is the first such committed relationship, the individuals may face having to realign their prior and existing relationships with their family of origin, friends, and others in their broader social network to now include their "significant other."

Selecting a Partner

Given the culture of romance, which highly values physical attributes as the basis for initial attraction to another person, physical attractiveness is much more nuanced as a factor drawing people together. Sternberg's (1987) research on the components of what creates attraction identifies six different components:

1. *Physical attractiveness:* People look for partners whose level of physical attractiveness matches their own with men tending to place more value on a woman's physical attractiveness than women put on a man's.

2. *Arousal:* An individual is more likely to be attracted to another if he or she experiences some physical arousal.

3. *Proximity:* This may be the most important factor in that individuals are likely to meet potential partners who are in close proximity to them.

4. *Reciprocity:* People tend to be attracted to those who think like they do.

5. *Similarity:* The more similar one person is to another, the more likely the two will be attracted to each other.

6. *Barriers:* A person who is "hard to get" and a challenge may engender more attractions and intensify more passion.

Whereas they might initially draw a couple together, these factors alone might not lead to long-term marriage fulfillment, much less sustain a marriage. Larson and Hickman (1994) along with Larson and Holman (1994) identify other factors that contribute to the quality of a marital relationship. These factors are sociocultural contextual factors including individual traits and behaviors and a couple's interaction with each other. Being similar in race, socioeconomic status, religion, intelligence, and/or age is a social and cultural factor that positively affects new marriages. Individual factors such as physical and emotional health, lack of neurotic traits, and level of self-esteem also contribute positively to couple relationships.

For some couples the decision to commit to the couple relationship includes a period of courtship and/or engagement. It is during this time that the individuals are examining and coming to terms with their images of the ideal mate and the ideal couple relationship. A comparison between the "ideal" and the "real" is made with an evaluation as to whether this particular partner is the "right" one. What may be considered as "right" may be based not solely on an aura of romantic excitement and physical compatibility but on other factors including personality, social and cultural expectations, family history, and economic factors (Collins, Jordan, & Coleman, 2007).

As couples come together they will bring to the relationship differing perspectives regarding the management of couple relationships. These perspectives will reflect their family of origin experiences or their prior relationship experiences. In this new relationship the couple begins to create a new and unique couple narrative. The partners will be involved in negotiating such issues as how to manage finances, combining the nuances of lifestyle differences, the allocation of household duties, developing relationships with in-laws, if no prior sexual relationships adjusting in the areas of sexuality and sexual intimacy, and decisions about when or if to have children. Here the new couple is engaged in formulating new roles and rules to govern the family system while making compromises and negotiating around each partner's individual concrete and personal needs.

As individuals come together to form a couple relationships they may also bring to the marriage particular myths and narratives about marriage that may later lay the foundation for difficulties in marital relationships. Glick, Berman, Clarkin, and Rait (2000) have identified the following marital myths that may impact the sustainability of a particular marriage (see Table 12.2). This list of myths, derived from the work of

Table 12.2   Marital Myths

1. If life has not worked out well for a person as an individual, getting married will make everything better.

2. Marital and family life should be totally happy, and either all or most of one's happiness and personal gratifications come from the marriage or from the family.

3. Being in proximity to each other or jointly carrying out all activities as a couple will lead to individual satisfaction.

4. Marital partners should be completely honest with each other at all times.

5. A happy marriage is one in which there are no disagreements, and when couples argue it means they hate each other.

6. Marital partners should see eye to eye on every issue, and they should work toward an identical outlook as much as possible.

7. Marital partners should be as unselfish as possible and give up thinking about their own individual needs.

8. In a marital argument one partner is right and the other wrong, and the goal of such fights should be for the partners to see who can score the most points.

9. Good sexual relationships will inevitably lead to a good marriage.

10. Because marital partners increasingly understand each other's verbal and nonverbal communications there is little need to check things out with each other.

11. In marital systems positive feedback is not as necessary as negative feedback.

12. Any spouse can and should be reformed and remolded into the shape desired by the partner.

13. A stable marriage is one in which things do not change and in which there are no problems.

14. Everyone knows what a husband should be like and what a wife should be like.

15. If a marriage is not working properly, having children will rescue it.

16. No matter how bad the marriage is, it should be kept together for the sake of the children.

17. If the marriage does not work, an extramarital affair or a new marriage will cure the situation.

18. Separation and divorce represent a failure of the marriage and the individuals involved.

Ferreira (1963), Papp (1980), and Riess (1981), is quite extensive. What is important for this discussion is that individuals whose marital behaviors are informed by one of these myths may encounter some difficulties in their marital relationship.

It is important to note that not all couples come to the relationship with the level of unrealistic expectations as reflected in these marital myths. These myths along with other factors contribute to the vulnerability and termination of approximately half of all first marriages. While couples come together with the intent of creating a stable, long-term relationship, many factors including unrealistic expectations make couple relationships more vulnerable than other family relationships.

Characteristics of Successful Couple Relationships

In spite of these vulnerabilities, successful marriages do exist. Successful marriages require constant revitalization along with stability. Marriages require a delicate balance between fulfilling individual needs and fulfilling couple needs. Without compromising the integrity of the marriage, marriages that are successful allow the individuals the space and opportunity to seek some personal gratification and fulfillment outside the couple relationship. Thus the marriage is not burdened and strained with having to meet *all* the individual's needs. Finally, successful couple relationships allow for the honest expression of feelings (including negative ones). Such honest and open expressions can paradoxically moderate the expression of destructive and hostile feelings, thus allowing the couple to approach relationship issues with greater care and compassion.

Positive couple interaction is grounded in having good communication and conflict resolution skills (Balswick & Balswick, 2007). Carlson and Dinkmeyer (2003) have identified a set of relationship skills that in many respects are an antidote to the toxic impact of those marital myths listed earlier:

- Couples individually accept responsibility for their behavior and self-esteem.
- Couples can identify and align their personal and marital goals.
- Couples choose to encourage each other.
- Couples communicate their feelings with honesty and openness.
- Couples listen empathically when feelings are expressed.
- Couples seek to understand the factors that influence their relationship.
- Couples demonstrate that they accept and value each other.
- Couples choose thoughts, words, and actions that support the positive goals of their marriage.
- Couples solve marital conflicts together.
- Couples commit themselves to the ongoing process of maintaining an equal marriage.

These factors and relational skills may contribute to marital happiness especially if a couple through the exchange of mutual support and a positive attitude can build up a marital bank account of good feelings (Hetherington & Kelly, 2002). Deposits into this account can make the marriage more divorce proof. In these marriages there is the negotiated balance between the "I" and the "We." The couple relationship system strikes a balance between individual growth issues and a sense of cohesiveness.

Detecting Relationships in Trouble

There are relational dynamics that can severely deplete the marital bank account. Continued displays of contempt, hostile criticism, and disengagement can cause irreplaceable withdrawals from that account. Such marriages, depleted of emotional resources that might sustain the marriage, will find it difficult to maintain a sense of viability. Gottman's (1994, 1999) research on the interactions of unhealthy couples identifies four characteristics of couple interactions that predict such relational difficulties. Described as the "Four Horsemen of the Apocalypse" these characteristics are criticisms, contempt, defensiveness, and stonewalling. *Criticisms* are broad sweeping character attacks that usually include the word *always* or *never*. *Contempt* as the next horseman is more corrosive than criticism as it adds a sense of hostility and disrespect through verbal and/or nonverbal behaviors. The display of contempt generally provokes a defensive reaction or retaliation. Thus any possibility of problem solving, de-escalation, or reconciliation is thwarted by the defensive reaction. The next horseman is the *defensiveness* that is a response to criticism and contempt. A defensive response is a protective response. Defensiveness creates a stalemate in the relationship. As such, a defensive response can lead to more retaliation and an escalation of the conflict. The last horseman is *stonewalling*. Here one member of the relationship simply withdraws from almost all interaction with the partner. Being either overwhelmed or emotionally flooded, one partner must shut the other partner out for self-protection. Gottman (1994) predicts that when all the horsemen are present, he can determine with over 90% accuracy which couples will get divorced.

While Gottman gives attention to overly toxic interactional patterns between couples, Hetherington and Kelly (2002) identify five types of marriages that are distinguished by the way couples solve problems, express emotions, communicate, and deal with family tasks. These classifications reflect certain enduring and somewhat intractable relationship patterns between married couples. The first three types tend to be more divorce prone, whereas the last two tend to endure in spite of possible relational difficulties.

- *The pursuer-distancer marriage* tends to reflect what can be considered as traditional and perhaps stereotypical gender socialization patterns. Women are generally socialized to value intimacy and interpersonal communication whereas men are socialized to be emotionally reticent and controlled. When anxiety-laden conflict emerges demanding the couple to communicate and engage in problem-solving behaviors, these socialization patterns become evident. The wife may attempt to solve a problem by getting close and talking about and processing feelings. On the other hand the husband may handle this same content by going within himself to process the feelings. If the situation becomes emotionally overwhelming, then he might withdraw from the interaction. In other words in this recursive interaction the more the wife seeks closeness, the more the husband seeks distance.

- *The overfunctioning-underfunctioning marriage* involves the couple managing the energy, stress, and activity level within a relationship by having one person rise to the occasion to manage the anxiety, stress, or problem. The other partner displays inadequacy or incompetence in addressing the stress-laden issues. This relationship pattern can be appropriate depending on the problem, or it can be inappropriate depending on whether this is a fixed pattern of relationship. If it is a fixed relationship pattern, then the couple may have difficulties in sustaining a healthy marriage relationship. Though this relationship pattern may systemically maintain a connection between the marital partners, the ensuing resentment and frustration may over time erode the marital relationship.

- *The drifting couple marriage* represents those marital relationships in which the couple fears to address emotional issues or to negotiate those conflicts or differences that may impact the sustainability of the relationship. Failure to address these issues may cause the couple to eventually drift apart.

- *The disengaged marriage* is the couple relationship in which the individual's pursuit of self-sufficiency and personal growth is the priority. Along with this individualist stance is the personal position that there is really no the need for the other partner. It is a marriage of convenience without the sense of mutually shared values or interests.

- *The conflictual couple* involves a couple with partners who continually bicker to mediate and manage closeness, which becomes uncomfortable. This couple may sustain the relationship though it appears to be highly conflictual.

Though there are interactional patterns that are signals of a troubled marriage, these patterns are not the singular cause for divorce. The reasons that a couple may have for terminating a relationship may be multiple and complex. As many of these interactional patterns are present in troubled marriages, they generally reflect some core issues in the marital relationship. These core issues may include sexual incompatibilities, anxiety over making and/or maintaining a long-term relationship, and conflict over money, in-laws, or children. There are other issues that can further disrupt a marriage. Such issues as infidelity, drug and alcohol abuse, and physical abuse can impact feelings of trust and safety in a relationship. Finally as families move though the life cycle, difficulties in responding to changing role demands such as those brought about by the birth of a child or the return to paid work by a partner may negatively impact a marriage leading to divorce. In low-income and minority communities there are a multitude of factors that may contribute to divorce including financial stressors, chronic underemployment, and racism. Couples who have ineffective and underdeveloped communication and problem-solving skills in addressing these issues may have difficulties in sustaining a functioning marital relationship (Goldenberg & Goldenberg, 2002).

Some individuals in troubled marriages may come to a point of considering whether they can endure the dissatisfaction and stress in the relationship by staying in the relationship. With a great deal of reluctance and ambivalence they may come to the conclusion that they will gain more satisfaction by leaving the relationship. The dissatisfaction may also depend on gender. For example, Levinger (1965) noted that husbands and wives do not give the same reasons for their dissatisfaction or for terminating the relationship. Wives cite physical abuse, financial problems, mental cruelty, and neglect of home and children as reasons for terminating the relationship. Husbands on the other hand may talk about sexual incompatibility, followed by neglect of home and children, infidelity, in-law troubles, and mental cruelty, as their reasons. Though individuals may cite specific reasons Little (1982) questioned whether actual behaviors were the primary factor that led to divorce or whether the issues stemmed from a disparity between an ideal image of the spouse and the actual person. Based on Little's question the reasons individuals give for terminating a marriage may be based on disillusionment rather than dissatisfaction.

COUPLES WHO DIVORCE

One of the major unanticipated transitions in family life is divorce. Given that approximately 50% of all marriages end in divorce it can be said that a significant number of families experience the impact of divorce. Ranked at the top of the list of stressful events for individuals and families (Ahrons, 1999), divorce is also the precursor to subsequent family transitions and the emergence of alternative family structures such as single parenthood, remarriage, and step- and blended families. As we shall see in the following discussion, the phenomena of divorce do not represent a societal indictment or rejection of the institution of marriage. Marriage still remains as a choice for those individuals who desire to enter into a new committed relationship even after experiencing and terminating a troubled one. Yet divorce may be the initial event that creates possibilities for other forms of intimate relationships. As Hetherington and Kelly (2002) report in their study of nearly 1,400 families,

> I realized that the divorce revolution begun in the 1960's had created entirely new patterns of intimate relationships, with less stability, and fewer certainties but more options. People were not just marrying and staying with the same partner, the traditional pattern for married life. Half of this new generation was divorcing, and they were taking diverse pathways from marital breakups. Some were opting to cohabit or remain single or have multiple romantic partners. Others were forming relationships with partners of the same sex. Others again were remarrying, often several times. (p. 4)

What is not addressed in this statement is that the stress resulting from terminating a marriage can also significantly impact one's subsequent experiences as a single person, a single parent, or a stepparent, as well as one's experiences in other forms of committed relationships.

Divorce, which was traditionally seen as a blight on the institution of marriage and a sign of family disintegration, is an undeniable social reality. Given that 40% of first marriages end in divorce (50%–67% in some studies) and that 60% of second marriages fail, divorce is generally accepted as an unavoidable yet major experience that many marriages go through. Ahrons (1999) describes divorce as an unscheduled life transition that alters the developmental life course of a large number of families. Divorce affects the entire family unit. For example, Amato and Booth (1991) point out that children raised by a divorced single parent are significantly more likely than average to have problems in school, run away from home, develop drug dependency, become school dropouts or unemployed juvenile delinquents, or experience other serious behavioral problems. Divorce can also have multigenerational impact in that experiences with divorce in one generation can impact subsequent generations' experiences such as mate selection and myths and expectations about intimate relationships and marriage.

Divorce as a Process

While there is a tendency to focus solely on the legal event bringing about the termination of a marriage, generally there is a process that begins long before any legal action is taken. The growing dissatisfaction with a marriage may last for years prior to a decision to end the marriage. According to Paul Bohannan (1970) the divorce process consists of several overlapping stages or experiences: (a) the emotional divorce, (b) the legal divorce, (c) the economic divorce, (d) the coparent divorce, (e) the community divorce, and (f) the psychic divorce. Kaslow (2000) added the religious or spiritual divorce. What is significant about these stages is that they represent stress points for the couple as it navigates its way through the termination of the marriage. It is also at these stress points that the partners as a couple or as individuals may seek psychotherapeutic intervention.

The Emotional Divorce

In the midst of a troubled marriage individuals may come to a point in which they contemplate the termination of the marriage. These feelings may mark the initial stages of the *emotional divorce* process. One or both of the partners become disillusioned due to the discrepancy between their notion of the "ideal marriage" and what they are currently experiencing in their marriage. The disillusionment may be further fueled by the incongruity between the actual marriage and the unrealistic expectations embedded in the earlier described marital myths. As a result there is an increasing erosion of feelings toward the partner with a growing sense of dissatisfaction and disillusionment. The partner's weaknesses and deficiencies become ever so great and are seen as the cause of the deteriorating relationship. For many couples the stated reasons given for considering ending the marriage may include sexual incompatibility, in-law problems, disagreements over money, disagreements over child rearing, lifestyle differences, and religious differences. While one of the partners may cite these issues Kaslow (2000) points out that the deeper issue may be about power and control, who will get his or her way, or who will establish dominance in the relationship.

In the early stages of dissatisfaction few individuals will immediately take action toward termination of the relationship as there may be much ambivalence about whether this is the course of action one should take. The troubled person at this point may consider some ways of managing proximity to the partner by emotionally disengaging from the relationship or minimizing opportunities for physical interactions with the partner. These actions may represent the beginning process of disengaging or distancing from the emotional tension of the relationship.

This period may be a time of great emotional distress, confusion, mourning the loss of one's dream of the ideal marriage, and questioning one's self in the process. The emotional intensity experienced by both partners in this stage of the divorce, though different, can be equally debilitating (Pam, 1998). In this stage of the divorce process those contemplating divorce may find themselves struggling with feelings of anger, betrayal, loss, bitterness, ambivalence, tremendous stress, and often failure. The reality is that many of the partners who want to get the divorce may be more willing to consider this as an option than the other partners. In such cases the rejected partner feels hurt and wounded. In the meantime the partner who wants to terminate the marriage is not available to be emotionally responsive to the rejected partner and consequently not available to engage in reconciliation efforts.

In this emotional divorce stage partners are attempting to come to terms with the seemingly irreparable marital relationship. With some grief and mourning the partners begin to consider whether it is worth it to remain in the marriage and which option would be healthier for all involved. There is consideration of what life may be like as a single person. In fact the partners may begin to engage in fantasies about their postdivorce life (Goldenberg & Goldenberg, 2002). Some couples may attempt to engage in reconciliation efforts prior to making the actual decision to divorce. It is at this point that the partners may decide to enter marital or couples counseling to explore whether reconciliation is possible. Yet at this point the partner who is considering leaving the relationship may not be invested in reconciliation. This partner's intent in the counseling session may be to present justification for his or her decision and/or to convince the therapist that the only solution or resolution to the conflict is to terminate the marriage. The stance of the rejected partner may be to use the therapy process as a means to win back the affection of the partner.

The Legal Divorce

If the decision to divorce is made, then one or both of the partners initiate the *legal divorce,* which involves contacting the attorney and beginning the legal process for terminating the marriage. The initiation of legal divorce proceedings indicates that the hope for reconciliation is over and that the termination of the marriage is inevitable. As the legal process is initiated one or both of the partners may have feelings of dread regarding the pending loneliness as well as apprehension about the future. The entire legal process may take 3 months in some states with an uncontested divorce to several years depending on the state laws and the amount of anger that exists between the partners. This possible prolonged time period, too, can be very tense if the legal proceeding has taken on a decidedly adversarial nature. If the couple is able to engage in a divorce mediation process, the amount of emotional reactivity can be de-escalated. The de-escalation is critically important for couples with children, as they must find ways to remain connected as parents while separating as partners.

Though a legal divorce is initiated there still may be a degree of ambivalence present and perhaps increased bitterness, which may erupt as the legal process determines the distribution of property, assets, child support payments, alimony payments, custody, and visitation. As the legal process may exacerbate an acrimonious and adversarial climate with its litigated win-loss approach, divorce mediation can create a collaborative, win-win climate that can positively impact the postdivorce relationship. The mediation process as described by Kaslow (1988) is based on the following principles:

- Negotiating in good faith
- Full disclosure of assets
- Empowering both parties to speak on their own behalf
- Belief in clients' ability to know their own and their children's best interest and to make wise decisions on their own behalf
- Seeking a win-win collaborative and equitable agreement
- Sharing the cost of the mediator's services
- Giving real attention to the interest of the child
- That either partner or the mediator can terminate the process if he or she does not believe it is progressing in a positive and fair direction

The mediator, who is an objective and neutral third party, can provide an option for couples that can enable them to focus on what is in the best interest of all involved. When going through the legal divorce process one or both partners may feel a loss of control in advocating for what is in their best interest. These feelings may more readily occur if the divorce process becomes more adversarial. In this event the mediation process may help one feel more in control and less devastated by possible outcomes.

The Economic Divorce

The legal divorce, which by decree determines property settlement, child support, and spousal support, represents obvious changes in economic resources for both partners. In the *economic divorce* there may also be a major shift in financial burdens assumed by one or both of the now divorced parents. These changes and financial burdens are generally experienced by the custodial parent, namely the mother. About 5 in every 6 custodial parents are mothers (84%), and 1 in 6 is a father. These proportions have remained steady for the last 10 years. As their household income decreases, even with awarded child and/or spousal support, many mothers may be forced to enter the labor market and/or take on more hours at work. This increased responsibility is assumed while managing time with children, developing skills at financial management, and learning how to function independently. For women and children, the experience of divorce can be overwhelming, stressful, traumatic, and quite difficult to recover from both emotionally and financially. Even as child support may be decreed to assist the mother financially, as many as 7 million people, mostly men, are not supporting their children through support payments (Reynolds, 2005). These statistics reveal the clear likelihood of financial, and quite possibly emotional, burdens on divorced mothers and children.

The Coparent Divorce

The *coparent divorce* involves agreements on such issues as custody, visitation rights, and negotiating shared parenting responsibilities. One parent now has the status of single parent, while still having to negotiate a relationship with the now ex-spouse. As the single parent has to take the major child-rearing tasks, the non-custodial parent now has to manage having less time with the children. One of the consequences for the noncustodial parent is that he or she may feel out of touch with the children's lives. As the children move between households in joint custody arrangements or between custodial and noncustodial families they are negotiating and engaged in a binuclear family arrangement (Ahrons & Rodgers, 1987; Ganong & Coleman, 1999). The children may be a part of two households, the custodial parent's household and, through visitation, the noncustodial parent's household. This arrangement may have a profound impact on the children.

During the early stage of the divorce process, children may experience diminished parenting because of the parents' preoccupation with the troubled marriage. They no doubt witnessed and were exposed to the troubled and deteriorating relationship that precipitated the divorce. Children may find themselves struggling with loyalty to both parents even as their parents unconsciously may attempt to recruit the children to see the marriage problems from their perspective, thus indicting the spouse or ex-spouse as the problem. As parents negotiate the coparenting relationship they have to be extremely sensitive to the impact that divorce has on their children. In discussing the impact of divorce on children, Collins et al. (2007) make reference to the work of Thompson, Rudolph, and Henderson (2003), who propose the following task that children of divorce must successfully accomplish in order to move on with their lives. The parents must assist their children in handling the following issues resulting from the divorce:

- *Feelings of anxiety, abandonment, and denial:* Children of divorce need the support of parents to help them overcome these feelings. In supporting the children the parents must explain what has happened without blaming the other partner.

- *Disengaging from parental conflict and distress and resuming regular activities:* The divorce should not be allowed to encroach on routine activities in which the children have been involved.
- *Resolution of loss:* Children must grieve not only loss of a significant parent in their lives but loss of familiar surroundings such as neighborhood and community.
- *Resolving anger and self-blame:* Children may feel responsible for the breakup or blame one parent for the divorce.
- *Accepting the permanence of the divorce:* Children may not consider divorce as final and may hold on to the fantasy that their parents will reconcile. The children may scheme or develop problems to get parents back together.
- *Developing realistic hopes regarding relationships:* Children must recognize that though their parents have divorced positive marital relationships are still possible.

The Community Divorce

Following the legal divorce the former marital partners are now in two separate households and are engaged in rebuilding their lives as individuals. They are now presented to the community as no longer together and are now establishing new lifestyles and renegotiating friendship networks. Following a divorce the former partners are faced with reorganizing their life structure, dealing with coparenting issues, financial planning concerns, reorganizing family relationships with both family of origin and former in-laws, changed community status, and possible residual legal issues especially those concerning child support and visitation. Divorced individuals may find themselves taking on new roles and responsibilities including assuming new roles for child care, income production, managing finances, and making decisions without input of a spouse. They may find themselves having to form different relationships with others in the extended family including a change in status with in-laws, grandparents, and mutual friends. One of the problems that divorced couples encounter is that divorce may mean losing relationships in their former social network that are too painful to maintain or losing connections with people who were close to the other spouse.

There is also the recognition of the stigma that is still associated with divorce. To the extent that the couple's religious or ethnic community holds traditional notions of marriage, the act of divorce may be seen and/or experienced as an act of failure. Finally, divorce means establishing a different relationship and adjusting relationships between ex-spouses. This transition involves overcoming hurt, anger, and other feelings associated with the divorce process. This readjusted relationship with the ex-spouse is critically important and necessary if both are to have a relationship especially as it relates to coparenting.

The Psychic Divorce

The psychic divorce begins as the individual increasingly accepts the dissolution of the marriage and begins to "move on." The now divorced person begins the journey of redefining him- or herself as a single and unattached person. He or she becomes actively engaged in seeking new relationships, while recuperating from the trauma of the divorce. The person may engage in more reflection about the previous marriage, which might impact his or her decisions about remarriage while considering new relationships.

Ahrons (1999) addressed the issue of how both custodial and noncustodial families must reorganize to benefit the children and advised that several factors must be in place to contribute to the healthy adjustment of children in the binuclear family situation. First of all children need to have their basic economic and psychological needs met in spite of the traumatic experiences their parents have gone through. They also need the support for maintaining familial relationships in their lives that were important and meaningful for them prior to the divorce. In spite of the disruptive impact of the divorce the negative effects can be minimized if both ex-spouses integrate the divorce into their lives in a healthy way and if both maintain a supportive relationship with their children. To be avoided are postdivorce conflicts, which may become a venue for possible revenge or punishment and/or a confusing way to stay connected even after respect is gone.

The Religious or Spiritual Divorce

Kaslow (2000) describes this stage as significant for those couples who believe that their marriage was consecrated within the belief framework of a community of faith. Thus terminating the marriage may evoke concerns about having violated certain religious or spiritual tenets. There may be concerns about seeking God's displeasure or having failed in a profound and significant way and needing some assurance that they are still worthy and acceptable. The now divorced individual may be further concerned about obtaining the approval of his or her faith community. For those couples and families that are a part of a faith community and/or those who were married within a faith community there may be concerns about the stigma or acceptability of the divorce within that community. If they attended the same house of worship, then the issue of their joint presence, even though they are divorced, may have concerns for them. As a part of the community divorce process they may find themselves seeking new places of worship or distinctly different faith communities.

Therapeutic Concerns in Divorce

Divorce can be a devastating experience that impacts both partners. Regardless of whether one feels that there is no alternative to a problem marriage other than to leave the relationship or whether one finds him- or herself being rejected, the actual divorce can be emotionally devastating. There are a range of emotions and feelings that occur during this period including a sense of uncertainty, confusion, depression, rage, fear of abandonment, and ambivalence. As individuals go into marriage with a sense of what they consider will be the ideal marriage, they may begin to experience a sense of loss or the death of that dream of living "happily ever after." One of the aftereffects of divorce may be the grieving process, which may vary in its duration. If there are children, the partners may also be equally concerned about the impact of the divorce on them. At any point during the divorce process, the couple or one of the individual partners may seek individual, couples, or family counseling.

Salts (1985) identifies three stages in counseling divorcing couples: (a) the predivorce decision-making stage, (b) the restructuring stage, and (c) the postdivorce recovery stage. These stages can be well integrated with the stages of divorce as presented by Bohannan (1970) and modified by Kaslow (2000) as seen in the following chart.

Salts: Stages of Divorce Counseling	Bohannan: Stages of Divorce
Stage 1: Predivorce Decision Making	Stage 1: Emotional Divorce
Stage 2: Restructuring	Stage 2: Legal Divorce Stage 3: Economic Divorce Stage 4: Coparent Divorce
Stage 3: Postdivorce Recovery	Stage 5: Community Divorce Stage 6: Psychic Divorce Stage 7: Religious/Spiritual Divorce (Kaslow, 2000)

The Predivorce Decision-Making Phase

The emotional divorce phase marks the beginning of the divorce process. This is the point at which there is a chain of events and feelings that are precursors to the legal divorce. The person is dealing with feelings of emotional distress, disillusionment, ambivalence, anger, and rejection and is wondering if the marriage is salvable. It is at this pending moment of crisis when one or both partners may seek individual or couples counseling. The counseling at this point may be crisis oriented, time limited, and extremely stressful for clients. One of the goals of intervention is helping the couple recognize what caused the troubled marriage. The other goal is to help the couple determine whether its needs can be met within the marriage or whether alternative solutions might be considered (including divorce).

While the therapist should consider and respect the client's decision about divorce, it is his or her responsibility to help the client understand the family problem causing the unresolved marital stress. The therapist must be nonjudgmental about the client's decision as making the decision to terminate the relationship is a difficult one, and it is not unlikely that clients will be highly ambivalent and may vacillate in making that decision (Goldenberg & Goldenberg, 2002). The impact of the decision is also related to the developmental stage of the marriage relationship and the developmental stage of the individual partners. For example, a couple in the early stage of marriage might not have built up the same level of commitment as an older couple. A couple that has built a life together and has children might find it more difficult to consider a decision to terminate the marriage. On the other hand a couple in a long-term marriage over time might have experienced gradual estrangement. For this couple the decision to terminate the marriage may not be fraught with emotional turmoil. In each of these couple scenarios, the amount of ambivalence and vacillation may differ. The therapist's role is to provide the therapeutic space for the couple to consider all the possible options without suggesting or subtly maneuvering the clients to consider one option or the other as this is the time of indecisive behaviors. One of the outcomes of this process is the preparation of the clients for the next stage of possible legal divorce.

The Restructuring Phase

If the decision is made to divorce, then the couple embarks upon a journey through the legal process of obtaining a divorce. In addition there is consideration of preparation for life after divorce. This involves going through the economic and codivorce phase. The major issues revolve around rearranging the economic division of money and property and negotiating parenting responsibilities following the divorce. Whereas counseling may be appropriate at this time the couple may consider divorce mediation. The factor that a counselor has to address is that it is generally the wife who has custody of the children, and as such she is often confronted with economic survival. After divorce, the mother must often do extra work outside the home and will have less time to spend with the children. The oldest child in the sibling group can easily be co-opted into assuming the parental-child role. While empathizing with the mother's need to assign more responsibilities to the children and in many cases the oldest child, the therapist also needs to point out to the mother the developmental needs of all children, including the eldest child. In other words the child or children may not be developmentally ready to assume roles that are more appropriate for an adult.

As the parent prepares for his or her postdivorce life, a therapist may focus on helping the divorced individual feel less anxious about the divorce and postdivorce life. Therapy at this point might enable the client to manage his or her feelings, fantasies, and thoughts about life after divorce. Therapy can help minimize the emotional impact of the adversarial nature of the divorce. Interventions can also minimize and circumvent the acrimony between now divorced couples as they implement the decreed custody arrangements and the ongoing parenting plans.

Restructuring their life involves a host of issues including significant role changes for the now divorced couples. Postdivorce activities involve the ex-spouses establishing separate domiciles, which may impact children. The custodial parent is now faced with single parenthood. The noncustodial parent is challenged with developing a different relationship with his or her children. The counseling at this point should focus on supporting the individual's efforts in embracing his or her new roles as well as different relationships within his or her social networks. As a therapist undertakes working with a divorced person there must be the recognition that the client might still be working through some unresolved issues stemming from the divorce.

The Postdivorce Recovery Stage

This is the point at which the family therapist or family-centered therapist works with the client to develop a postdivorce identity. At this point a person may be cautious about entering into new relationships, as there may be an increased sense of vulnerability. A term that is often used to describe a person in the postdivorce stage is the *walking wounded*, which may make social involvement a bit more difficult due to the feeling of vulnerability. It is not uncommon for therapists to hear from clients that they have been out of the dating scene for so long they feel quite uncomfortable and rather inept in going through the dating process.

The outcome of this postdivorce recovery counseling is to establish the psychic divorce, which involves the therapist working with the client to realign his or her life without looking for support from the ex-partner. This can be a time for the divorced person to reflect on his or her personal assets and weaknesses. Such reflection can be preparatory for establishing a greater sense of independence in dealing with future life experiences and future relationships. A therapist can provide the therapeutic context in which a person can better understand oneself, relationships, why one married, and why one divorced, in order to help the person move into the next, possibly married relationship.

Sprenkle (1990) provides a further framework for postdivorce counseling indicating that the partners need to be helped with the following:

1. Accepting the end of the marriage

2. Achieving a functional postdivorce relationship with the ex-spouse

3. Achieving a reasonable emotional adjustment

4. Developing an understanding of their own contributions to the dysfunctional behavior that led to the failure of the marriage

5. Finding sources of emotional support

6. Feeling competent and comfortable with postdivorce parenting

7. Helping their children adjust to the loss without triangulating them or nourishing unrealistic expectations

8. Using the "crisis" of divorce as an opportunity for learning and personal growth

9. Negotiating the legal process in a way both feel is reasonably equitable

10. Developing physical, healthy, and personal habits consistent with adjustment for everyone

THE SINGLE-PARENT FAMILY

One of the obvious consequences of divorce involving children is the creation of the single-parent family. Whether the term *single parent* is an adequate description of postdivorce families is questioned by such authors as Ahrons and Perlmutter, 1982; Ahrons and Rodgers, 1987; and Kaslow and Schwartz, 1987 Gottman, 1993. For example Ahrons and Perlmutter describe a postdivorce family in which both parents continue to be involved in parenting as a "one-parent" household. Correspondingly a "single-parent" family is when only one of the parents is involved in parenting. These distinctions are important in understanding the significant relationships outside of the singular family unit. It is easy to ignore the existing and potential resources within the ecological network of a particular single-parent family unit (Everett & Volgy Everett, 2000).

Photo 12.1   Though divorced, the other biological parent may be available to share parenting

Source: ©iStockphoto.com/rarpia

As the percentage of divorces hovers around 50% of first marriages, single parenting has become a common family structure. According to the 2006 U.S. Census Bureau report *America's Families and Living Arrangements*, the percentage of households headed by single parents is about 9%, up from 5% in 1970. There were 12.9 million single-parent families in 2006—10.4 million single-mother families and 2.5 million single-father families. While a significant percentage of single-parent families result from divorce it is important to note that single parenthood can result from death, separation, desertion, out-of-wedlock birth, and single-parent adoption. Most single-parent households are headed by divorced women or women (teenage or adult) who have never married. Widowed and divorced women with custody of their children were about equally numerous in 1960, but by 1983 divorced mothers outnumbered widowed mothers by 5 to 1 (Glick, 1984). In addition, out-of-wedlock births have doubled the proportion of single-parent-led families in the last 25 years. What is important to note is that single parenthood is not necessarily a permanent status. Though women head about 90% of single-parent families, one third of those who are single parents through divorce remarry, thus making single parenthood a transition to remarriage. Single parenthood is viewed as a temporary condition since 80% of men and 75% women remarry (Hetherington, 1989).

Though there are many avenues to single parenthood our focus in this chapter will be on the divorced single parent. The single-parent family system that originates from divorce must deal with residual stresses and turmoil from the divorce. As we discussed the stages of divorce earlier it is clear that the single custodial parent is engaged in major life and family transitions. As the single parent moves from marriage to divorce he or she is challenged to reestablish a family system without the presence of the former spouse. Interestingly single parenthood that results from the death of a spouse may engender more community support and more public sympathy. This is especially true if the marriage was functionally satisfying. What may occur in this instance is that the deceased parent may be immortalized with efforts to keep the memory of the deceased parent alive. Interestingly the children can be recruited in this effort, which may impact the family's ability to fully grieve the loss of the parent and/or spouse (Janzen & Harris, 1997) as well as reorganize the family without the presence of the deceased spouse.

Another factor that does contribute to some of the difficulties that single-parent families encounter is public perception and social acceptance. Labeled as "broken families," single-parent families often evoke negative and powerful images, thus making it difficult for single parents to develop a positive view of themselves. As a family structure, the single-parent family is not valued as highly as the intact two-parent family as it is a family structure that is more likely to be economically dependent on public and institutional resources and support. These images may further cause children from single-parent families to feel different from children who have two parents.

The Challenges for Single Parents

As we discussed the stages of divorce, one of the common elements is stress, and the single parent is challenged with attempting to maintain a family system in the face of reduction of resources, finances, time, energy, and social support (Anderson, 1999). Divorce brings about a disruption in the family system in many areas. The single parent is no longer a part of a marital or parental subsystem involving another person. The single parent has the major if not the sole responsibility for family decisions. This shift in role functioning can also cause role overload as the single parent is now engaged in multiple roles including organizing the household; producing income, which may involve returning to work; caring for children; and adapting to and helping his or her children adapt to possible new living arrangements, which may involve different schools and different communities. As single parents are involved in rebuilding their lives they may begin to move out into a broader social network, which may involve dating and sexual relation. When this occurs a new person may be introduced into the family system, and this may change the interactional dynamics of the family system and have an impact on defining the family boundaries. In other words the issue becomes "who is in" and "who is out" of the newly emerging single-parent family household. This issue of family boundaries may even be significant as the single custodial parent deals with the broader issues of custody and visitation. The single parent has to be concerned as the children are introduced to new friends or lovers. As visitation calls for some form of continued relationship with the former spouse, the issue for the children may be one of loyalty as the children are introduced to a parent's new relationships.

As single parents move into the status of single parenthood they have to cope with the residual effects of having to make the transition from marriage to single parenthood. In that transition they will no doubt encounter a myriad of problems, some of which are psychological and some of which indicate a change in the family structure. Psychologically there will be the grief, self-blame, loss of self-esteem, and depression, which still may be present following the divorce. This may reflect the continued impact of the loss related to the end of the marriage, but single parents must also cope with the social sigma and disapproval from family and friends resulting from the divorce. It is not uncommon for the divorced couple to have to deal with loss of friends who were acquired during the marriage and to develop new friends and move into new social arenas. This social isolation has its impact in terms of an available and adequate social support network that can provide support for the single parent as he or she goes through these transitions.

Child Care Responsibilities

As pointed out earlier, in 90% of single-parent families the sole or almost sole responsibility for child rearing belongs to the mother. In this role the mother has to deal with the demands by small children for her continuous physical presence as the sole parent. If the children are young the single parent will find herself giving much attention to child care issues, especially if she has to return to work. There is the need to be more flexible in her work schedule, especially in the case of illness of the child or parent. Some single parents cope with these new demands by enlisting the extended family members in assisting in child care arrangement. For example, grandparents may be asked for assistance. In some families bringing the grandparents into the child care system can reactivate some of the original unresolved family of origin issues between the single parent and her parent.

Though divorced, the other biological parent may be available to share parenting concerns in those instances that fall outside of the agreed-upon custody arrangement such as illness of the custodial parent. Even with this arrangement the single parent has to be wary of (a) unresolved issues with the ex-spouse and (b) different and possibly conflicting parenting styles. These differences may have the impact of continuing the predivorce discord, which may have a profoundly adverse impact on the adjustment of the children. One of the concerns that some single parents may have is the impact that the absent parent has on providing a role model or appropriate gender identification for the child. For example, single mothers with male children may raise concerns about assuming both the mother and father roles. There are instances in which this concern is not only about assuming both parenting roles, but the male child's gender identity may be negatively impacted without the presence of a male role model. The custodial parent may take initiative to engage other surrogate role model images for the child. What is important for the single parent is that in coping with all the demands of single parenting (a) anger is not directed toward the child and (b) both parents continue to respond to the child's developmental needs. As both the custodial and noncustodial parents are engaged in parenting, they must recognize that their children's family frame of reference includes two family systems. In this binuclear family arrangement both parents must attend to the fact the children need support for maintaining familial relationships in their lives that were important and meaningful to them before the divorce. In addition both parents should attempt to move toward a supportive and cooperative relationship as they carry out their coparenting responsibilities. With these factors in place the chance that the children will survive the divorce without long-term psychological damage is increased.

Economic Challenges

Dealing with economic hardships is especially apparent with the female head of the family. As divorce brings about changes in the economic status of the single-parent mother, she may face economic hardship, as the single mother's income drops 30%–70% after divorce whereas the single father's income remains stable or possibly rises. The mother now has to manage the family household with limited financial resources. Mothers with no financial support may have to work full-time to attempt to carry on an adult social life, which may decrease their time with the children. There is less opportunity for a single parent to discuss pros and cons of financial decisions and to get support and feedback when decisions are made. Though financial concerns might have been one of the contributing factors that precipitated the divorce, having the sole responsibility for household financial management becomes a major undertaking. This can be especially problematic if both parents contributed to family financial responsibilities prior to the divorce.

The Noncustodial Parent

The noncustodial parent is not without some adjustment issues. Goldenberg and Goldenberg (2002) outline some of the issues that noncustodial parents cope with. What noncustodial parents encounter is in many ways similar to the issues faced by the custodial ex-spouse. The major though significant difference is the ongoing relationship with the children. Noncustodial parents may be concerned about a diminished relationship with their children in not being with them on a day-to-day basis. Further they may feel that they have lost a sense of importance in their children's lives. They have to find different ways to maintain significant contact with their children in such a way that does not activate conflict between them and the former spouse.

Aside from having to start over with rebuilding one's life; dealing with blame, grief, and depression; and establishing new social networks, the noncustodial parent may experience a change in economic status as well as a lowered living standard due to contributing to the support of two homes. This may cause conflict between the noncustodial parent and his or her new spouse if remarried. As a portion of the remarried household income is encumbered by divorce decree, there may be concern additional money may be requested by the custodial parent for child care. If the custodial parent requests that support payments be reviewed by the courts for purposes of adjustment, then tensions in the noncustodial parent household may ensue.

As both ex-spouses move through the stages of divorce they may find themselves in an array of what they might consider awkward situations such as attending an event that parents in intact families go to together (school open house, graduation, wedding, funeral), especially when one's former partner has a new mate. Here the noncustodial parent may have concern over children meeting the new lover, especially if that person has children.

Changes in Boundaries and Roles in Single-Parent Families

One of the key family system concerns for single-parent families is the issue of boundaries and roles. Given the vulnerability of many single-parent families, including minority families, there may be greater reliance on the ecological system outside of the family as they struggle to reorganize to meet the tasks of family living. The family's sense of self and identity is disrupted following a divorce, and the family theme becomes reorganized in terms of "who we are as a family." As a result the single-parent family may organize itself in several different ways. The single-parent family system may close its boundaries by forming a coalition between and hence a boundary around the single parent and child to exclude the noncustodial parent. In such a reorganization of the family system children may feel triangulated between parents as they move from the custodial household to the noncustodial household per visitation decree.

Another form of reorganization occurs when the single-parent family system becomes more rigid and cut off from the outside world. This is manifested in the family's refusal to trust, or its difficulty accepting, health or school-related interventions.

For some single-parent families as the single parent attempts to manage multiple tasks resulting in role overload a child (the oldest) may be "recruited" to become an adult substitute with the role of emotionally supporting the parent. When this occurs the generational boundaries have been blurred. A variation of this systemic role reorganization is when a child assumes parental functioning with the siblings. The existence of the parentified child results in diffused generational boundaries between the parental system and the parental child. The parental child becomes overloaded with inappropriate responsibilities or may be caught in a double bind due to lack of clarity regarding the limits of his or her responsibility. Also the parental child may be blocking the custodial parent's access to other siblings and vice versa.

If the extended family is present in the life space of the single parent, one has to be particularly attuned to the role played by the extended family, especially grandparents. The grandparent(s) may assume the executive role in the single-parent family, which leads the custodial parent to become inappropriately involved with the children. This would cause the generational boundaries between sibling subsystem and mother to become enmeshed. The custodial parent may then form a coalition with the children against the grandparent. The grandparent may double-bind the mother by expecting the mother to exercise her parent role and authority while criticizing and undermining her function. And the children may be put in a loyalty bind between mother and grandparent.

In those situations where the custodial parent becomes emotionally involved with another person the issue may be how the person gets recruited into the parental role or the role left vacant by the ex-spouse. In the case of a single-parent mother, the boyfriend may be kept out of the parental role altogether. Or the mother may put the boyfriend in a double bind by expecting him to assume a parenting role, while at the same time undermining his efforts. Another possible scenario

Photo 12.2   In their efforts to manage multiple family responsibilities, single parents often have to enlist the support from their extended family

Source: ©Creatas Images/Creatas/Thinkstock

is that the boyfriend may inappropriately exert parental power, pushing the mother and children to form a coalition against him. Finally the mother may relegate the boyfriend to the sibling subsystem.

Clinical Interventions With Single Parents

Following the trauma of divorce, single parents are faced with the task of securing financial resources and support, maintaining a household, developing social and emotional relationships, and relating to children in a way that supports their satisfactory adjustment in various settings. Single parents in the initial stages have to cope with a variety of issues that make the single-parent family system quite fragile. This fragility is due to four common postdivorce dynamics (Everett & Volgy Everett, 2000):

1. Ongoing animosity and adversarial issues resulting from prior or continuing divorce litigation

2. Individual parental adjustment conflicts and stress

3. A child's difficulty with personal adjustment, sibling or stepsibling conflicts, and/or school and peer problems

4. The former spouse's intrusion into the single-parent family system

Understanding these dynamics is critical in understanding how to plan clinical family-centered interventions with a single-parent family as each of these dynamics represents a stressor and crisis point for the single-parent family. The focus of intervention may be in part determined by which of these dynamics are salient and/or critical in the life of the single parent. The clinical decisions that guide intervention strategies are reflected in how the single-parent family system reacts to the various postdivorce dynamics. Special attention must be given to the initial emotional reactions, anger, confusion, and anxiety, that erupt as the parent and children cope with changes. The "postdivorce recovery stage" should give attention to helping the family engage in reordering its priorities as it copes with new economic realities and managing new environments, new situations, and change in access to children by parents. As the family begins to move through the postdivorce stage clinical attention should be directed toward enabling the single parent to accept the end of the marriage and work toward achieving a functional postdivorce relationship with the ex-spouse. If this can be achieved both parents can better move toward achieving a reasonable state of emotional adjustment for themselves and their children. They will be able to reach out for sources of emotional support that can facilitate a feeling of increased competence and comfort with postdivorce parenting.

The extended family can be a significant source of support and self-esteem for a single parent. The extended family is especially critical in providing emotional and instrumental assistance and can reduce feelings of loneliness and isolation. The family of origin network can be a significant resource in providing the single-parent family with child care, finances, household chores, and emotional support. Geographical barriers or unresolved family of origin issues may deny many single parents access to this valuable resource. In such cases, other extended network resources should be identified through new friendship ties, especially other single mothers, women's support groups, and social activity groups that can help the single-parent family adjust to this transitional period.

When the father is absent from the family, a key male figure, or spouse equivalent, may be present in the single-parent household. This individual may or may not live with the mother in the single-parent household, yet he may have a great deal of influence in the daily transactions of this single parent and her children. Whether a single parent utilizes such a conjugal relationship depends on the personality, and value orientation, of the single mother. The therapist's task is to explore with the single parent the value and need of having such a relationship.

If the therapist is aware of the conjugal partner, he or she can introduce the option of involving this individual in matters that concern the welfare of the children or child-rearing practices of the single parent. Rasheed and Rasheed (1999) reported that lower-class African American males contribute to the welfare of the single-mother family more than is commonly acknowledged and play an important role as a substitute father to her children.

Restructuring the Family

The absence of the noncustodial biological parent from the family requires renegotiation and a restructuring of the family system boundary. Robert Weiss (1979) noted two major changes that can occur in the transformation from a two-parent to a single-parent family. First, the "echelon structure" within the family collapses, with children being promoted to junior partner status and becoming more involved in making family decisions. Second, changes in the authority structure in a single-parent family increase communication among family members. As a result of these structural changes, enmeshment between the single parent and the children can occur resulting in parent-child conflict or idiosyncratic symptoms. The concept of enmeshment should be addressed only if it relates to the immediate problem to be solved. For example, in the case of parent-child conflict involving a single mother's unwillingness to allow her teenage son to have peer relations, enmeshment should be explored. New structural arrangements need to be developed to maintain the closeness of the parent-child relationship without emotionally suffocating the parent and child, in the case of enmeshment.

Given the range of issues that single parents encounter a variety of family therapeutic approaches can be used. Goldenberg and Goldenberg (2002) suggest brief strategic family counseling, structural family therapy, and skill-building psycho-educational programs for single-parent families. The focus should be on helping the single parent perform his or her executive role as family head as he or she makes the transition from one family structure to another. With these approaches and because of financial resource issues the focus should be on a brief, limited, short-term intervention. These approaches can help the single parent reframe his or her issues in a more constructive and positive manner. Another approach is the use of psycho-educational groups. In these groups the single parent can be exposed to different skills in effectively raising children alone while getting support from a group.

BECOMING A STEPFAMILY

As stated earlier, single parenthood may be a transition to remarriage. Data support that people will be married more than once in their lives (Ihinger-Tallman &

Pasley, 1997), making remarriage the most dominant family configuration. One fifth of married couples raising children include a stepparent, and about one fourth of all children born in the 1980s live in a stepfamily (Berger, 2000). Approximately one third of all weddings in America today form stepfamilies. About 75% of those who divorce will eventually remarry (U.S. Census Bureau, 2006). People remarry quickly. On average people remarry within 4 years of the divorce, and 30% remarry within a year. In addition since two thirds of couples cohabit before remarriage, the time between divorce cohabitation and remarriage is short (Ganong & Coleman, 2004). Forty of every 100 marriages today are a remarriage for one or both partners. Of the remarriages, 24 are a remarriage for both persons. About 65% of remarriages involve children from the prior marriage and thus form stepfamilies in America. An estimated one third of children will live in a stepparent home before the age of 18 (Parke, 2007), and 50% will have a stepparent at some point in their lives (Stewart, 2007).

Given these data it is clear that divorce and single parenting do not represent an intractable status of existence but a transitional state in preparation for remarriage. In fact according to Jones (2003) the proliferating increase in stepfamily arrangement may represent the felt need of divorced individuals to attempt to "get it right" in the subsequent marriage. With 60% of second marriages and 73% of third marriages ending in divorce, remarriages may be even more vulnerable than first marriages. Perhaps part of the reason for unsuccessful remarriages is that the stepfamily has an added degree of complexity not found in a first-time intact nuclear family. Another reason may be the level of unrealistic expectations that people entering into a remarriage situation may have. All those who remarry have the strong desire to make "this" marriage work. Yet there may be some unrealistic expectations in joining two distinct families and family histories:

- There will be instant love between all family members.
- Everything will quickly fall into place; adjustments will be easy.
- The children will be happy about the remarriage and the new family that they are now a part of.
- The stepchildren want a relationship and will be easy to get along with.

The task of stepparenting challenges these myths in a significant way.

Variety of Stepfamily Configurations

The stepfamily is an extremely complex family structure that can have many variations. Gillespie (2004) speaks to this complexity and the unique challenges faced by these various structures when she describes the five portraits of a stepfamily.

The first portrait of a stepfamily is a divorced husband with children who marries the never-married woman with no children. A never-married woman who marries a divorced man with children may be faced with the expectation that she is to assume a similar role as the former wife and mother. This woman may find herself filling the role of a first-time mother, a new experience for her, with children that she has no history with. The mother may feel frustrated in this experience along with the children, and this can create a conflict between them.

The next stepfamily profile is the woman with children from a previous marriage who marries a man who has never been married and has no children. This woman has been in the role of custodial parent with primary if not sole responsibility for child rearing and household management. This mother may feel a profound sense of relief in having someone to share her responsibilities. She may then shift many responsibilities to her new husband, causing the children to rebel especially if this husband is recruited into the fathering role. This creates a sense of conflict with the children especially as they attempt to maintain loyalty to the biological father.

The third form of stepfamily can be called the blended family. This family has many difficulties that present a unique challenge to both parents and children. It is a family in which two divorced parents with children marry. This family structure brings two distinct family cultures together with two distinct histories. Children with close ties to their biological parents may feel that they have to share their parents with other children, with their access to the biological parents being more limited. The sibling subsystem is altered with the existence of stepsibling. There may be a greater sense of a forced sharing of physical space and resources. This family form may also indicate to the siblings that the possibility of their biological parents getting back together is over.

There are those stepfamilies in which one of the partners who remarries is a widow or widower with children. Depending on the extent to which the family has dealt with the issue of mourning or grieving the death of the biological parent, the stepparent may find him- or herself being compared to the deceased biological parent due to insufficient mourning. The final form of stepfamily is the divorced or widowed parent of adult children. Even though these children have left the nest there may be limited interaction between the stepparent and the adult children, and intimacy and bonding may be difficult.

Impact of Past Experiences

While the structure of stepfamilies may vary there are some unique characteristics of stepfamilies that cut across all stepfamilies. One of the common themes is loss. Visher and Visher (1994) describe the stepfamily experience as "born of loss," and Doherty (2004) sees loss as the plotline in the lives of stepfamilies. This is loss of a spouse due either to divorce or to death. It is not only the adults who have experienced the loss but the children as well. Children of divorce may have the possible fear of further abandonment that takes expression in the form of emotional withdrawal or behavioral difficulties.

This sense of loss can have a profound and significant long-term impact on the subsequent family systems. Transitioning into a remarriage and a stepfamily arrangement involves first of all a continued resolution of the issues stemming from the previous marriage, anticipating the changes of the single-parent household structure while planning for the remarried household structure. The challenges that emerge in this process involve the ongoing mourning of the former nuclear family, the former partner, and the old neighborhood and friends and way of life. This period of mourning prepares the way to accept and to grow with the new reality of the stepfamily.

Another common characteristic is the spouse and children come to the new family configuration with a prior history in a previous marriage relationship. Based on the nature of the prior marriage there may be what is called "baggage" that may come with one's history. Related to the theme of loss there is a biological parent who is not present in the current stepparent relationship, and the child's relationship with that absent biological parent essentially predates the new stepparent relationship. So there must be a recognition of the change in the binuclear structure of the child's experiences as the membership in two households is changed in even more dramatic ways. The children may find themselves dealing with issues of divided loyalty or "invisible loyalties" that may impact their overall adjustment to the new stepfamily arrangement. Becoming a stepfamily involves the restructuring of family boundaries to include the new person (stepparent), realignment of relationship systems to include new subsystems (stepsiblings), and making room to incorporate other extended family members (stepgrandparents, noncustodial stepparents, biological and nonbiological siblings).

Family Structure

Remarriages are not easily entered into and involve ongoing efforts to consolidate the remarried family as a new family. Such efforts involve clarification of family roles and the consolidation of parental authority in the new family system in order to establish effective coparenting. Navigating the structural changes in stepfamilies is a challenge. In addition, with the entrance of a new adult figure and, in the case of blended families, new "siblings," the relationship dynamics of a stepfamily are complex in many and varied ways. The combination of two different cultures of family systems forms a new culture. Given the initial ambiguous subsystem boundaries around roles (stepparenting relationships), rules (combining the rule structure from the previous family), and differences in allocation of power and authority based on the previous experience in the prior family system, there may be a constant yet evolving shift and renegotiation of family roles and family rules.

A stepfamily must develop strategies and tasks to maintain the viability of this new family system. Members will have to work toward developing a new family identity and establish how they desire to be seen in terms of this unique constellation as a stepfamily. In this effort they are defining themselves anew in their social network, and they have to redefine themselves not from the perspective of their original nuclear family but from the perspective of a new formation of the stepfamily. In this sense they are a reconstituted family using the materials from their previous family of origin.

A stepfamily has to renew its efforts at socialization as the former nuclear family may have different styles and different rules around issues of gender, personal qualities, and how to view and relate to others in the family as well as how to develop those skills to present the self and the family to a broader environment. Within the domain of a particular family, there may be multigenerational support that can be mobilized in this effort as well.

A stepfamily may find itself shifting and changing its boundaries according to the developmental needs of the family. As a stepfamily is involved in attending to the health and welfare of the family members, as with a biological family the stepfamily must establish priorities regarding resource allocation to ensure the health and well-being of family members. The stepfamily must develop a climate within the family that allows the family members to work cooperatively to develop the family's newly established and evolving common goals. As conflict within families is inevitable, stepfamilies must have the means to manage conflict.

Parenting Concerns

Remarried couples have a strong desire to make the new marriage work. Despite the best of intentions, 60% of such couples divorce (Hetherington & Stanley-Hagan, 2000). Moreover the divorce is likely to come sooner rather than later especially when stepchildren are involved. According to Tzeng and Mare (1995) divorce rates for families with stepchildren are 50% higher than those where there are no stepchildren. These figures suggest that for at least some stepfamilies, multiple transitions will confront them and exacerbate the already problematic nature of stepparenting.

One of the most frequently reported problems in the remarried family is the relationship between stepparents and stepchildren (Coleman, Ganong, & Fine,

2000; Hobart, 1991; Pasley, Koch, & Ihinger-Tallman, 1993). This is especially evident in stepmother-stepdaughter relationships (Coleman & Ganong, 1990). Problems in stepparent-stepchild relationships also have been found to be a critical factor in the level of marital satisfaction reported between remarried husbands and wives (Brown & Booth, 1996; Coleman & Ganong, 1990), and many of the marital difficulties that remarried couples report are related to tensions between stepparents and stepchildren.

The child-rearing issue is important in that stepparents may have difficulty accepting the reality that children may neither initially like nor love their stepparent. The challenge for couples is to establish a stepparenting relationship that does not try to force the child and stepparent relationship in a particular direction. Both the biological parent and the stepparent must help children deal with and minimize the continuation and exacerbation of loyalty conflicts between the two biological parents and between each biological parent and the corresponding stepparent. The stepparent must ensure a secure place for the children's development and to maximize the potential within both family systems. The biological parent(s) and stepparent must be attuned to the developmental concerns of the children at their appropriate developmental level. They must work toward accepting and integrating the children's need for individuation from both families.

As the child experiences different rules and expectations the biological parent(s) and stepparent must be sensitive to the different rules and expectations as the children try to navigate and exist in the two homes. In areas of authority and discipline stepparents have very little authority in the family initially, and discipline issues should be handled by biological parents. One of the issues that stepparents may initially encounter in a stepfamily is that they have less influence in the area of parenting as an absent yet influential parent is elsewhere or in the memory of the stepchild. The stepparent is the outsider who walks into the family with the intent of forming a new family. How the stepparent is "invited" may indicate the ongoing acceptance by the stepchildren. If the stepparent attempts to replace the parent, then the children, especially the older child, may resist. Stepparents will have to be clear about their role in terms of whether they are disciplinarian, friend, or affectionate confidante. How they will be addressed—by first name or a name depicting their unique role in the family system—will be a critical point that facilitates their acceptance by the stepchildren. It may be easier for younger children to adjust to the stepparent, whereas older children may be more resistant and adolescents even more so.

Counseling Issues With Stepfamilies

Living in a stepfamily can be extremely challenging. The major challenge for stepfamilies is making the transition from either single parenthood or single status to this new configuration called a stepfamily, reconstituted family, or blended family. We identified different types of remarried families with some indication of the different dynamics of each. Within these families there is diversity in allocation of parental roles and a wide range of feelings and relationships among members as they build new role relationships and negotiate to build new rituals and new identities. The difference in types of remarried families speaks to different relationship dynamics.

The overall tasks in this transition to a stepfamily address two key themes, adjustment and integration: the adjustment to new roles, new tasks, and new responsibilities, and the integration of two family systems into one. For example, the role of a parent is much more clearly defined in a biological family. The role of a stepparent in a particular family may not be as clear. The organizational structure and family subsystem configuration and boundaries may be more clearly demarcated in a biological family. In a blended stepfamily the integration of two distinct sibling subsystems into a newly constructed stepfamily system is fraught with many challenges. As we described the unique characteristics of a stepfamily we have seen that there are many potential problem areas that are unique to a stepfamily. Goldenberg and Goldenberg (2002) have identified the following problem areas that may call for counseling intervention:

- Mourning for losses
- Living with differences
- Resolving loyalty issues
- Acknowledging an absent parent
- Developing a family identity
- Children living simultaneously in two households
- Overcoming boundary problems within the family system
- Learning coparenting
- Impact of prior marriage relationship with former spouse
- Impact of financial obligations to children from prior marriage

One of the major considerations that a therapist must have is to not view the stepfamily with the same lens as a biological family. Yet it is important for the therapist to enable the parents and children to view themselves as a family system and as an interdependent group of individuals with mutual and reciprocal influences (Pasley, 1996). Browning (1994), Papernow, 1993), and Visher and Visher (1983) suggest that therapists who work with stepfamilies should not see all family members simultaneously. As stepfamilies who seek therapy are already at risk, working with the entire family may increase the fragility of a fragile system (Pasley, 1996). The stepparent-stepchild relationship lacks the history of the marital relationship, and thus the therapist should work with the couple rather than the entire family. Once the couple is stable, group therapy and/or stepparent support groups may be helpful. Yet once the couple relationship is stabilized, family therapy may be helpful (Pasley, 1996).

While all the models of family therapy previously discussed may be applicable in working with the problems presented by stepfamilies, Berger (2000) suggests that narrative and solution-focused approaches may be especially helpful with this population. Such approaches enable these families to generate their own solutions and new possibilities appropriate to their unique configuration as a stepfamily and as they construct their new family system. As stepfamilies have no template in which to organize and make sense of their experiences, the therapist works with the family to normalize its experiences and validate its feelings. This may help the family think about itself in new ways, enhance self-esteem, and create a new a family narrative (Pasley, 1996). Some of the more specific issues that a family therapist may address should focus on working with the couple in developing a marital relationship while attending to the parental relationship with the biological children and/or stepchildren. This would involve working with the stepparents in defining their stepparent role. This focus will address issues of the ambiguity of role relationship and role status.

COHABITATION

Rather than remarry many divorced individuals choose cohabitation as an alternative or substitute intimate relationship. Cohabitation or living together before marriage is viewed as a much more acceptable couple arrangement in contemporary society. According to the U.S. Census Bureau (2000), 60%–75% of first marriages and 80%–85% of second marriages are preceded by cohabitation. The increase in cohabitation may be attributed to one of the following:

1. Delaying the first marriage until one is older with the median age 25 years for women and 27 for men (U.S. Census Bureau, 2000)

2. A decline in Americans who choose to marry—more than one third for 1970–1996 (U.S. Census Bureau, 2000)

3. The reduction of the stigma attached to cohabitation, due to the portrayal of cohabitation in the entertainment industry and media (Olson & Olson-Sigg, 2007)

4. The high rate of divorce, which has led couples to seek a weaker form of union with less commitment than lifelong marriage (National Marriage Project, 2000)

In Olson and Olson-Sigg's (2007) overview of cohabitation research they found that couples give several reasons for cohabiting. One reason that couples report is that there is an economic advantage in living together and sharing living expenses. Another reason speaks to being able to spend more time together by living together rather than dating and having to schedule time with each other. Through being able to spend more time with each other there is the benefit of increased emotional and sexual intimacy without the legal responsibilities involved in marriage. Thus there is less complicated dissolution of the relationship if it does not work out. For those couples who are possibly considering marriage as a possibility, cohabitation allows for the couple to enter into a form of "trial marriage" in anticipation of actual marriage. These couples may explain their decision to cohabit as an opportunity for them examine their compatibility by living together and getting to learn about each other's habits and character.

Olson and Olson-Sigg (2007) also discovered that the research findings on cohabitation revealed other significant characteristics of these couples. Many of these characteristics clearly distinguished these couples from marriage couples. Summarizing these findings, Olson and Olson-Sigg (2007) reported the following:

1. Cohabitating couples have lower levels of personal happiness and higher rates of depression than married couples (Waite & Gallagher, 2000).

2. Cohabiters value independence more than married partners and have more individual freedom (Waite & Gallagher, 2000).

3. Cohabiters have more negative attitudes about marriage than noncohabiters (Axinn & Barber, 1997).

4. Couples living together have the lowest level of premarital satisfaction when compared to other living arrangements (Olson, 2000; Stewart & Olson, 1990).

5. Marriages preceded by cohabitation are more likely to end in divorce (Popenoe & Whitehead, 1999).

6. Married couples who cohabitated prior to marriage have poorer communication skills in discussing problems than couples who did not cohabit (Cohan & Kleinbaum, 2002).

7. Cohabiting couples are less sexually committed or trustworthy (Waite & Gallagher, 2000).

8. Cohabiting males are less involved in housework and child rearing (Waite & Gallagher, 2000).

9. Cohabiting increases the risk of couple abuse and, if there are children, child abuse (Thompson, Hanson, & McLanahan, 1994).

This research overview does suggest the negative effects of cohabitation on long-term couple relationships. Yet couples increasingly choose this form of intimate relationship as an alternative to marriage. There are possible explanations for this phenomenon, which are reflected in the reasons couples give for cohabitation. Olson and Olson-Sigg (2007) conclude that cohabiting couples are more oriented toward high individual autonomy and low commitment patterns of relating. Cohabitation also reflects uncertainty and ambivalence about making the decision to marry. Goldenberg and Goldenberg (2002) describe other reasons for cohabitation as being that one or both of the partners are immature and not ready for the responsibility of a long-term committed relationship. They may want to keep their options open, not wanting to be alone, but do not wish to have or don't feel secure in an intimate partnership. There are also those situations in which one partner wants to marry and the other does not.

In Olson and Olson-Sigg's (2007) review they noted that while the research suggested that living together did not contribute to a healthy marriage or a way to avoid divorce, cohabitation that begins within 3–6 months of marriage is different from cohabitation as an alternative to marriage. With such cohabitation a few months before the wedding, if each partner has no prior cohabitation experience and no children, then adverse effects on the marriage are not strongly supported in the research (Popenoe & Whitehead, 1999).

Given these characteristics of cohabiting couples, they may not be prone to seek couples or family counseling. Exceptions may occur when one of the partners is "pushing" for marriage and the other partner is reluctant. Napier's (2000) approach in this situation is to focus on working with the committed partner to be more empowered and autonomous, which may motivate the uncommitted partner to demonstrate a converted interest in maintaining the relationship. If the uncommitted partner does not respond, then the relationship may not survive. An unplanned pregnancy can further complicate the relationship, especially if the woman hopes that the pregnancy will cause the partner to commit to marriage. In this instance the partner may feel manipulated and withdraw from the relationship. If the couple does commit to marriage, it may feel to the partners that the decision was made out of necessity or obligation because of the pregnancy. Such a decision may later cause the couple to question whether there is really a sincere commitment to each other. In the case of pregnancy the therapist may be involved in helping the clients sort through the array of options and seek the best alternative. As Napier (2000) suggests, "In this intimate decision-making territory, we [therapists] should be wary of our own prejudices, lest we bias the couple (or one individual) toward an alternative with which we are more comfortable" (p. 158).

Counseling issues may not only arise between cohabitating couples. Cohabitation can also have an impact on noncohabiting ex-spouses. In issues of custody and/or visitation, the noncustodial parent may raise issues about the custodial parent in a cohabitation relationship. This may cause a reactivation of unresolved postdivorce conflict. The therapist will have to intervene and work with divorced partners in their efforts to deal with these unresolved issues.

GAY AND LESBIAN FAMILIES

Though the number of unmarried couples has increased it is difficult to determine the number of homosexual couples. According to the Human Rights Campaign (HRC, 2001), a gay, lesbian, and bisexual advocacy group, based on 2000 U.S. Census Bureau data there has been a 314% increase in gay and lesbian families since 1990. Even with this increase it is estimated that this number is undercounted by 62%. The reason for this suspected undercount is based on the fact that the U.S. Census does not inquire about sexual orientation. Furthermore in the 1990 U.S. Census those same-sex couples who marked *married* were thrown out or the gender of the spouse was reclassified and the couple was considered as heterosexual. Thus the 1990 data may represent an undercount. There is still acknowledgement of an increase in the number of same-sex unmarried partner households. No doubt this action was due in part to the existing societal prejudice and discrimination toward gays and lesbians. It is this same discrimination that may have prevented gay and lesbians living in a family relationship from filling out the forms (HRC, 2001).

The fact is that a number of gays and lesbians do participate in and create families contrary to the perception that the gay and lesbian lifestyle is anti-family. Given the traditional understanding of what constitutes a family, a gay or lesbian couple would not fit a broader understanding of a family. Following the distinction made by Franklin and Jordan (1999) between childless gay couples and couples with children we will focus on "gay or lesbian headed families" rather than "gay or lesbian couples" (Casper, Schultz, & Wickens, 1992). These families like heterosexual families may have a variety of structures including single parenting, blended parenting, and parallel parenting by ex-mates (Franklin & Jordan, 1999). The children in these families may be from a previous heterosexual marriage, adoption, or artificial insemination. As same-sex partnerships are not legally recognized some couples are able to co-adopt though it may be more difficult in some states than others.

The major factor that differentiates a gay and lesbian family from other families is that the same-sex couple has to additionally cope with homophobic environments and institutionalized discrimination, which may include violence.

According to Franklin and Jordan (1999) there are a host of other issues that gay and lesbian families have to cope with:

1. Lesbian mothers are vulnerable to having their children taken away by their ex-husband or family of origin.

2. Gay and lesbian families have few culturally idealized models and traditions for appropriate functioning.

3. Traditional gender roles that are complementary in heterosexual relationships may provide little direction for couples with same gender role socialization. This results in gay and lesbian families being more flexible, egalitarian, and pragmatic in assignment of roles; they will do what is pragmatic rather than assign roles.

As we speak to the issue of gay and lesbian families there are several concerns that reflect society's homophobic reactions, and they are in the area of parenting. The fear is that homosexual parents are unable to provide proper parenting or that children raised by homosexual parents will have an impaired gender identity. These concerns are based on traditional family norms based on heterosexual parenting (Say & Kowalewski, 1998). Collins et al. (2007) address this issue when they summarize the research done by Lambert (2005) on gay and lesbian parenting. This research is summarized in Table 12.3.

Table 12.3   Overview of Research on Gay and Lesbian Parenting

1. Divorced lesbian mothers score "at least as high" as divorced heterosexual mothers on measures of psychological functioning.

2. There are no differences in parental sexual role behavior, interest in child rearing, responses to child behavior, or ratings of warmth toward children.

3. Divorced lesbian mothers are more fearful about losing children in custody disputes.

4. Lesbian mothers are more likely to provide children with toys relating to both genders.

5. Divorced lesbian mothers are more likely than heterosexual mothers to be living with a romantic partner.

6. The extent to which mothers are "out" and involved with feminist activism has a positive relationship with children's psychological health.

(Continued)

Table 12.3   (Continued)

7. Less information exists on gay custodial fathers. Gay fathers report higher incomes and are more likely to encourage children to play with gender-specific toys than are lesbian mothers.

8. There are no significant differences in sexual orientation, gender identification, or gender role behavior in young adults from lesbian relationships.

9. Children of lesbian relationships are more likely to consider the possibility of having lesbian or gay relationships. This might be due to the acceptance in which they lived.

10. Most children of gay and lesbian relationships identify themselves as heterosexual.

11. Children of gay and lesbian relationships have normal peer relationships.

12. Children of gay and lesbian relationships report more teasing and bullying about their parents' sexuality.

13. Early studies of lesbian mothers report that their children are more likely to have contact with fathers than are children of heterosexual mothers.

14. Children of gay and lesbian families experience more stress in their daily lives.

15. Gay and lesbian families maintain an egalitarian division of labor.

These family structures, though not legally sanctioned through marriage, nonetheless reflect many of the same emotional and relational dynamics as legally constituted families.

Counseling Issues for Gay and Lesbian Families

One of the major issues for gay and lesbian parents is "coming out" after divorce or separation from a heterosexual relationship. Coming out and disclosing one's sexual orientation to the ex-spouse, children, and family of origin can be quite traumatic and fraught with fears of rejection. Disclosure to children may be particularly difficult due to fear of losing the love and respect of one's children. These parents may request assistance from a therapist and support groups and seek guidelines on how to share their sexual orientation with their families. These individuals may have lived a life either in denial or unaware of their sexual orientation. If or when they do come out, they may identify as being bisexual rather than accept their homosexuality. If this parent comes to therapy, the task of therapy is working through the disclosure issues as one comes out to others. Support groups might be another venue to address these issues. Part of the task is to work with this parent as he or she attempts to establish a positive identity as a gay father or lesbian mother. This process can be facilitated through the process of "integrative sanctioning" (Bozett, 1987a, 1987b) in which the gay or lesbian client is able to disclose to heterosexuals who validate the homosexual aspects of the person's self-identity and to other gay men and lesbian women who validate the parental aspects of the client's self-identity.

The concerns of gay and lesbian families tend to resemble the concerns of heterosexual stepfamilies. Some of these similar concerns are coping with the experience of divorce, custody, and other transitional issues such as accepting the new adult in the family system. What makes this situation unique for gay and lesbian families is the broader social reaction and the lack of legitimization of such a family structure in the broader community. Gay and lesbian parents may not have the community support and clearly no legal sanction for their relationship. These parents are under the constant threat of being exposed. The gay male stepparent may be faced with more overt discrimination than a lesbian parent. This is in part due to a stronger reaction to gay male parenting relationships than to lesbian mothers. As with stepfamilies the clinical focus should be on the couple, and once that relationship is strengthened the entire family can be involved in treatment. As with working with stepfamilies the target concerns should address such issues as forming new family rules, rituals, boundaries, and coparenting.

Families With Gay and Lesbian Children

Another area that impacts family relationships is the disclosure of a child that he or she is gay, lesbian, or transgendered. Such disclosure of a child can create a family crisis, which can lead to cutoff. The parents may be in a state of confusion along with having misinformation about the gay lifestyle. Parents must deal with shock, guilt, anger, and embarrassment, and some may feel that their child's homosexuality is due to their inadequate parenting. The parents may attempt to engage in an array of behaviors that they hope will either shame their child into change or motivate their child to change. For example, the parents may ignore the child's partners and not invite them to special events or holidays or may try to set the child up with a member of the opposite sex in an attempt to change the child's sexual orientation, driving a wedge between them. There are situations in which an extreme reaction can even lead to violence.

INTEGRATIVE FAMILY THERAPY

This chapter acknowledges the clinical issues challenging diverse family structures. (Chapter 13 will explore an array of problems and issues that challenge families in crisis.) In light of the complexity of a myriad of clinical issues, there is a need to meet these challenges by integrating different family therapy models. The validity and efficiency of an integrative family therapy model have been tested primarily on the basis of the experience of therapists and the reports of change by families (Walsh, 1991). The utility of an integrative approach to family therapy is that the therapist has a wide range of options as far as the selection of concepts, theories, and techniques to choose from that best serve the family in its therapy process. While many schools of family therapy have goals that are theory specific, an integrated set of goals will usually involve behavior change, perceptual change, or a combination of the two (O'Hanlon, 1991).

It is important to remember that theories are the tools the therapist uses to understand family process and give direction for interventive change. Theories also help therapists organize their thoughts about the family so that a coherent assessment and interventive plan can be developed. Certainly the skill level of a therapist in applying these tools is a factor; however, we can only be as good as the tools that are available to us. This is an essential notion to keep in mind that may help prevent therapist "burnout"—that is, being aware of the limitations of our craft.

Family therapy theories and concepts should also be viewed as merely the vocabulary that the therapist uses to describe what he or she is doing with the family (Gehart & Tuttle, 2003), in that these theories evolve from the clinical practice of the theorist to explain what happened in the therapy process. This is to say that theories, concepts, and techniques are derived from the clinical practice of the architects of the various family therapy models. It is the vocabulary that the theorist uses to explain what happened (with therapists and their clients) in the therapy process.

There are so many useful theories, concepts, and techniques that it may be overwhelming at first, especially for beginning therapists. It is recommended for beginning family therapists to master a couple of major models of family therapy and slowly branch out from there. What will eventually happen is that the therapist will begin to systematically and intuitively apply concepts, theories, and techniques that he or she consistently finds useful in his or her clinical practice with families. This systematic application will eventually become the therapist's unique integrative approach to families.

The authors define integrative family therapy as a blend of the various family therapy models (concepts, issues, theories, and techniques) that the therapist systematically applies to his or her work with families. Any well-accepted technique from any of the major models of family therapy may be used in integrative family therapy (Walsh & McGraw, 2002). The family therapist is not restricted to any set of theories and techniques to be used in the therapy process even if only one or two major models of family therapy are used. That is, one is free to select any theory or technique from any model that best fits the interventive goal. However, integration of various family therapy models must include guiding principles that will help organize goals, observations, interactions, and, ultimately, the process of facilitating change (Hanna & Brown, 1995).

An important distinction to make at this point is that there is a difference between being *eclectic* and being integrative in one's clinical practice. This is to say that being eclectic is more akin to a "cafeteria approach" to clinical practice, in that the practitioner haphazardly and unsystematically selects models of therapy, perhaps depending on his or her own interests and/or mood—that is, choosing interventions not based on client information or client need. An integrative approach to clinical practice in contrast is based on one's epistemology as one considers the integration of models of therapy. "One's epistemology provides a 'lens' through which one interprets the theories one integrates" (Gehart & Tuttle, 2003, p. 16). Gehart and Tuttle (2003) go on to state "that many therapists are not as effective as they could be because they are not clear about their epistemological stance as they try to integrate concepts and methods form therapies based on vastly different epistemologies" (p. 16). They encourage therapists to carefully consider the epistemological underpinnings (theory base and assumptions) of various approaches before integrating them into their clinical practice.

Froma Walsh (1980) recommends an interesting integrative approach that takes into account both the epistemology of the model and the family's characteristics and needs. First she considers whether a growth- or insight-oriented approach is needed and/or requested by the family—such as Satir's communication approach, Ackerman's psychodynamic approach, or Bowen's family of origin approach—for a given presenting problem. Or, rather, if a task-oriented or problem-solving approach would be more effective, then Haley's strategic approach, Minuchin's structural approach, or the behavioral/social learning approach to family therapy may be needed. Next she takes into account the nature of the presenting problem—whether the nature of the problem can be classified as organizational or structural, behavioral and/or communicative, or intergenerational, psychodynamic, life cycle, and/or developmental. These dimensions allow one to consider the underlying assumptions and theory base (epistemology) of the approach, the family needs and requests, and the nature of the presenting problem. The final result is a systematic theory-driven integrative approach that considers important elements in interventive planning.

SUMMARY

The theme of this chapter is transition. This chapter discusses the variety of structures families move through. In discussing these structures there is an implicit acknowledgment of the life cycle of families as they move from marriage through separation, single parenthood, and remarriage. We further reflected on the phenomena of cohabitation and gay and lesbian heads of families. This discussion is not grounded on an ideology that critiques these various alternative family patterns. Nor do we suggest that these alternative family structures are harbingers of the demise of the family.

We can see that there is a thematic thread here, and that is the idea of the search for the committed intimate relationship. Though we find there may be historical, cultural, and social factors that contribute to the various permutations of family, and though these permutations may be birth in the crucible of loss, rejection, and pain, nonetheless we as humans seek to connect with each other however long the connection might last.

These transitions do impact family life in profound ways. Family roles, rules, and relationships change. The question "What is a family?" is asked with no definitive answer. These transitions in many ways cause us to redefine parenthood as it assumes different meanings within a particular alternative family structure. For a family therapist the task is to understand these various family patterns for themselves and not view them as some form of deviation from what is called the traditional family. For therapists, the task is to help these various family structures find their voice, tap the source of their resilience, and hoist their sails and chart their course toward their future as they are propelled by the winds of hope.

RECOMMENDED READINGS

Cherlin, A. (2004). The deinstitutionalization of American marriage. *Journal of Marriage and the Family, 66*, 848–861.

Cohan, C. L. & Kleinbaum, S. (2002). Toward a greater understanding of the cohabitation effect: Premarital cohabitation and marital communication. *Journal of Marriage and Family, 64*, 180–192.

Ganong, L., & Coleman, M. (2004). *Stepfamily relationships: Development, dynamics and interventions.* New York, NY: Kluwer Academic/Plenum.

Olson, D. H. (2000). Circumplex model of marital and family systems. *Journal of Family Therapy, 22*, 144–167.

Parke, M. (2007). *Are married parents really better for children? What research says about the effects of family structure on child well-being.* Couples and married research and policy brief: Center for Law and Social Policy (May).

Stewart, S. (2007). *Brave new stepfamilies: Diverse paths toward stepfamily living.* Thousand Oaks, CA: Sage.

Waite, L., & Gallagher, M. (2000). *The case for marriage: Why married people are happier, healthier, and better off financially.* New York, NY: Doubleday.

DISCUSSION QUESTIONS

1. Cherlin (2004) and Lambie (2008) speak to the changes in society's view of marriage beginning in the 20th century. In what ways have these changing views of the institution of marriage contributed to the current complexities of family structures?

2. Discuss how certain "marital myths" have contributed to the stability and/or vulnerability of couples' relationships.

3. This chapter gives attention to the variety of structures families move through. In discussing these structures there is an implicit acknowledgment of the life cycle of families as they move from marriage through separation, single parenthood, and remarriage. We further reflected on the phenomena of cohabitation and gay and lesbian families. For a family therapist what are some of the important assessment and intervention considerations for each of these family structures?

REFERENCES

Ahrons, C. (1999). Divorce: An unscheduled family transition. In B. Carter & M. McGoldrick (Eds.), *The expanded life cycle: Individual, family and social perspectives* (pp. 381–397). Needham Heights, MA: Allyn & Bacon.

Ahrons, C., & Perlmutter, M. S. (1982). The relationship between former spouses: A fundamental subsystem in the remarriage family. In L. Messinger (Ed.), *Therapy with remarriage families* (pp. 31–46). Rockville, MD: Aspen.

Ahrons, C., & Rodgers, R. (1987). *Divorced families.* New York, NY: Norton.

Amato, P. R., & Booth, A. (1991). The consequences of divorce for attitudes toward divorce and gender roles. *Journal of Family Issues, 12*(3), 306–322.

Anderson, C. M. (1999). Single-parent families: Strengths, vulnerabilities and interventions. In B. Carter & M. McGoldrick (Eds.), *The expanded life cycle: Individual, family and social perspectives* (pp. 319–416). Boston, MA: Allyn & Bacon.

Anderson, S. A., & Sabatelli, R. M. (2003). *Family interaction: A multigenerational developmental perspective* (3rd ed.). Boston, MA: Pearson Education.

Axinn, W. G., & Barber, J. S. (1997). Living arrangement and family formation attitudes in early childhood. *Journal of Marriage and the Family, 59*, 595–611.

Balswick, J. O., & Balswick, J. D. (2007). *The family.* Grand Rapids, MI: Baker Academic.

Berger, R. (2000). Stepfamilies in a cultural context. *Journal of Divorce and Remarriage, 33*, 111–130.

Blumstein, P., & Schwartz, P. W. (1983). *American couples.* New York, NY: William Morrow.

Bohannan, P. (1970). *Divorce and after.* Garden City, NY: Doubleday.

Bozett, F. W. (1987a). Children of gay fathers. In F. W. Bozett (Ed.), *Gay and lesbian parents* (pp. 39–58). New York, NY: Praeger.

Bozett, F. W. (1987b). Gay fathers. In F. W. Bozett (Ed.), *Gay and lesbian parents* (pp. 2–23). New York, NY: Praeger.

Brown, S., & Booth, A. (1996). Cohabitation versus marriage: A comparison of relationship quality. *Journal of Marriage and the Family, 58,* 668–678.

Browning, S. (1994). Treating stepfamilies: Alternatives to traditional family therapy. In K. Parsley & M. Ihinger-Tallman (Eds.), *Stepparenting: Issues in theory, research, and practice* (pp. 175–198). Westport: CT: Greenwood.

Carlson, J., & Dinkmeyer, D. (2003). *TIME for a better marriage.* Atascadero, CA: Impact.

Casper, V., Schultz, S., & Wickens, E. (1992). Breaking the silences: Lesbian and gay parents and the schools. *Teachers College Record, 94*(1), 109–137.

Cherlin, A. (2004). The deinstitutionalization of American marriage. *Journal of Marriage and the Family, 66,* 848–861.

Cohan, C. L., & Kleinbaum, S. (2002). Toward a greater understanding of the cohabitation effect: Premarital cohabitation and marital communication. *Journal of Marriage and Family, 64,* 180–192.

Coleman, M., & Ganong, L. H. (1990). Remarriage and stepfamily research in the 1980's: Increased interest in old family forms. *Journal of Marriage and the Family, 52*(4), 925–940.

Coleman, M., Ganong, L. H., & Fine, M. A. (2000). Reinvestigating marriage: Another decade of progress. *Journal of Marriage and the Family, 62*(4), 1288–1307.

Collins, D., Jordan, C., & Coleman, H. (2007). *An introduction to family social work* (2nd ed.). Belmont, CA: Thomson.

Doherty, W. J. (2004). The citizen therapist: Finding the right lever. *Psychotherapy Networker, 28*(6), 50–51, 68.

Everett, C. A., & Volgy Everett, S. S. (2000). Single-parent families: Dynamic and treatment issues. In W. C. Nichols, M. A. Pace-Nichols, D. S. Becvar, & A. Y. Napier (Eds.), *Handbook of family development and intervention* (pp. 323–340). New York, NY: Wiley.

Ferreira, A. J. (1963). Family myths and homeostasis. *Archives of General Psychiatry, 12,* 64–71.

Franklin, C., & Jordan, C. (1999). *Family practice: Brief systems methods for social work.* Pacific Grove, CA: Brooks/Cole.

Ganong, L., & Coleman, M. (1999). *Changing families, changing responsibilities.* Mahwah, NJ: Erlbaum.

Ganong, L., & Coleman, M. (2004). *Stepfamily relationships: Development, dynamics and interventions.* New York, NY: Kluwer Academic/Plenum.

Gehart, D. R., & Tuttle, A. R. (2003). *Theory-based treatment planning for marriage and family therapists.* Pacific Grove, CA: Brooks/Cole.

Gillespie, N. N. (2004). *Portraits of a stepfamily.* Retrieved from http://www.troubled with.com/Relationships/A000000841.cfm?topic=relationships%3a%2

Glick, I. D., Berman, E. M., Clarkin, J. F., & Rait, D. S. (2000). *Marital and family therapy.* Washington, DC: American Psychiatric Press.

Glick, P. C. (1984). American household structure in transition. *Family Planning Perspectives, 16,* 205–211.

Goldenberg, H., & Goldenberg, I. (2002). *Counseling today's families.* Pacific Grove, CA: Brooks/Cole.

Gottman, J. M. (1993). *Why marriages succeed or fail.* New York, NY: Simon & Schuster.

Gottman, J. M. (1994). *What predicts divorce? The relationship between marital processes and marital outcome.* Hillsdale, NJ: Erlbaum.

Gottman, J. M. (1999). *The marriage clinic.* New York, NY: Norton.

Hanna, S. M., & Brown, J. H. (1995). *The practice of family therapy: Key elements across models.* Pacific Grove, CA: Brooks/Cole.

Hetherington, E. M. (1989). Coping with family transition: Winners, losers and survivors. *Child Development, 60,* 1–14.

Hetherington, E. M., & Kelly, J. (2002). *For better or for worse.* New York, NY: Norton.

Hetherington, E. M., & Stanley-Hagan, M. M. (2000). Diversity among stepfamilies. In D. H. Demo, M. A. Fine, & K. R. Allen (Eds.), *Handbook of family diversity* (pp. 173–197). New York, NY: Oxford University Press.

Hobart, C. (1991). Conflict in remarriages. *Journal of Divorce and Remarriage, 15,* 69–86.

Human Rights Campaign. (2001, August 22). *Gay and lesbian families in the United States: Same-sex unmarried partner households.* Retrieved from http://www.urban.org/UploadedPDF/1000491_gl_partner_households.pdf

Ihinger-Tallman, M., & Pasley, K. (1997). Stepfamilies in 1984 and today: A scholarly perspective. *Marriage and Family Review, 26*(1/2), 19–40.

Janzen, C., & Harris, O. (1997). *Family treatment in social work practice* (3rd ed.). Itasca, IL: Peacock.

Jones, A. C. (2003). Restructuring the stepfamily: Old myths, new stories. *Social Work, 48*(2), 228–236.

Kaslow, F. W. (1988). The psychological dimensions of divorce mediation. In J. Folberg & A. Milne (Eds.), *Divorce mediation: Theory and practice* (pp. 83–103). New York, NY: Guilford.

Kaslow, F. W. (2000). (Ed.). *Handbook of couple and family forensics.* New York, NY: Wiley.

Kaslow, F. W., & Schwartz, L. L. (1987). *The dynamics of divorce: A life cycle perspective.* New York, NY: Brunner/Mazel.

Lambert, S. (2005). Gay and lesbian families: What we know and where to go from here. *The Family Journal, 13*(1), 43–51.

Lambie, R. L. (2008). *Family systems within educational and community context.* Denver, CO: Love.

Larson, J., & Hickman, R. (2004). Are college marriage textbooks teaching students the premarital predictors of marital quality? *Family Relations, 53,* 385–392.

Larson, J., & Holman, T. B. (1994). Premarital predictors of marital quality and stability. *Family Relations, 43,* 228–237.

Levinger, G. (1965). Marital cohesiveness and dissolution: An integrative review. *Journal of Marriage and the Family, 27*(1), 19–28.

Little, M. (1982). *Family breakup.* San Francisco, CA: Jossey-Bass.

Napier, A. Y. (2000). Making a marriage. In W. C. Nichols, M. A. Pace-Nichols, D. S. Becvar, & A. Napier (Eds.), *Handbook of family development and intervention* (pp. 145–170). New York, NY: Wiley.

National Marriage Project. (2000, June). *The State of Our Union*. New Brunswick, NJ: Rutgers University Press.

O'Hanlon, W. H. (1991). *Acknowledgement and possibility*. Paper presented at the Family and Children's Agency, Louisville, KY.

Olson, D. H. (2000). Circumplex model of marital and family systems. *Journal of Family Therapy, 22*, 144–167.

Olson, D. H., & Olson-Sigg, A. (2007). *Overview of cohabitation research: For use with PREPARE-Enrich*. Life Innovations.

Pam, A. (1998). *Splitting up: Enmeshment and estrangement in the process of divorce*. New York, NY: Guilford.

Papernow, P. (1993). *Becoming a stepfamily: Patterns of development in remarried families*. San Francisco, CA: Jossey-Bass.

Papp, P. (1980). The Greek course and other techniques of paradoxical therapy. *Family Process*, 19, 45–57.

Parke, M. (2007). *Are married parents really better for children? What research says about the effects of family structure on child well-being*. Couples and married research and policy brief: Center for Law and Social Policy (May).

Pasley, K. (1996). Successful stepfamily therapy: Clients' perspectives. *Journal of Marital and Family Therapy*. Retrieved from http://findarticles.com/p/articles/mi_qa3658/is_199607/ai_n8741292/print?tag=artBody;coll

Pasley, K., Koch, M., & Ihinger-Tallman, M. (1993). Problems in remarriage: An exploratory study of intact and terminated remarriages. *Journal of Divorce and Remarriage, 20*, 63–83.

Popenoe, D., & Whitehead, B. (1999). *Should we live together? What young adults need to know about cohabitation before marriage*. New Brunswick, NJ: The National Marriage Project.

Rasheed, J. M., & Rasheed, M. N. (1999). *Social work practice with African American men: The invisible presence*. Thousand Oaks, CA: Sage.

Reynolds, J. (2005). In the face of conflict: Work-life conflict and desired work hour adjustment. *Journal of Marriage and Family, 68*, 109–124.

Riess, D. (1981). *The family's construction of reality*. Cambridge, MA: Harvard University Press.

Salts, C. J. (1985). Divorce stage theory and therapy: Therapeutic implication through the divorcing process. In D. H. Sprenkle (Ed.), *Divorce therapy*. New York, NY: Haworth Press.

Say, E., & Kowalewski, M. R. (1998). *Gay, lesbian and family values*. Cleveland, OH: Pilgrim Press.

Smith, D. M., & Gates, G. (2001, August 22). *Gay and lesbian families in the United States: Same-sex unmarried partner households*. Retrieved from http://www.urban.org/publications/1000491.html

Sprenkle, D. H. (1990). Continuity and change. *Journal of Marital and Family Therapy, 16*, 337–340.

Sternberg, R. (1987). *The triangle of love: Intimacy, passion, commitment*. New York, NY: Basic Books.

Stewart, K. L., & Olson, D. H. (1990). *Predicting premarital satisfaction on PREPARE using background factors*. Unpublished manuscript, PREPARE/ENRICH Inc., Minneapolis, MN.

Stewart, S. (2007). *Brave new stepfamilies: Diverse paths toward stepfamily living.* Thousand Oaks, CA: Sage.

Thompson, C., Rudolph, L., & Henderson, D. (2003). *Counseling children* (6th ed.). Pacific Grove, CA: Wadsworth.

Thompson, E., Hanson, T. L., & McLanahan, S. S. (1994). Family structure and child well-being: Economic resources versus parental behaviors. *Social Forces, 73,* 221–242.

Tzeng, J. M., & Mare, R. D. (1995). Labor market and socioeconomic effects on marital stability. *Social Science Research, 24,* 329–351.

U.S. Census Bureau. (2000). American family and living arrangement. In *Current population reports* (Series P20-537). Washington, DC: U.S. Government Printing Office.

U.S. Census Bureau. (1998). Marital status and living arrangements. In *Current population reports* (Series P20-514). Washington, DC: U.S. Government Printing Office.

U.S. Census Bureau. (2006). *America's families and living arrangements: 2006.* Retrieved from http://www.census.gov/population/www/socdemo/hh-fam/cps2006.html

Visher, E. B., & Visher, J. S. (1983). Stepparenting: Blending families. In H. I. McCubbin & C. R. Figley (Eds.), *Stress and the family: Vol I. Coping with normative transitions* (pp. 133–146). New York, NY: Brunner/Mazel.

Visher, E. B., & Visher, J. S. (1994). Avoiding the mind field of stepfamily therapy. In D. K. Huntley (Ed.), *Understanding stepfamilies: Implication for assessment and treatment* (pp. 25–34). Alexandria, VA: American Counseling Association.

Waite, L., & Gallagher, M. (2000). *The case for marriage: Why married people are happier, healthier, and better off financially.* New York, NY: Doubleday.

Walsh, F. (1980). *An integrative approach to family therapy.* Lecture given at The University of Chicago School of Social Service Administration, Chicago, IL.

Walsh, W. M. (1991). *Case studies in family therapy.* Needham Heights, MA: Allyn & Bacon.

Walsh, W. M., & McGraw, J. A. (2002). *Essentials of family therapy.* Denver, CO: Love.

Weiss, R. S. (1979). *Going it alone: The family life and social situation of the single parent.* New York, NY: Basic Books.

Chapter 13

FAMILY STRESS, CRISIS, AND TRAUMA
Building Family Resilience

In this chapter we will examine the impact of stress, crisis, and trauma on families. We will also give attention to how family-focused and strength-based clinical interventions can assist families in drawing upon their reservoir of untapped strengths as they cope with stressful and traumatic life events. Stress, strain, and tension are an inevitable part of family life. As families move through the life cycle they experience major developmental transitions such as births, deaths, marriages, family members leaving home, and the formation of new households. Though many of these life cycle events are often predictable and anticipated, these events may also be accompanied by varying degrees of family strain, as the family adjusts and adapts to these changes in its own unique way. Families handle the transitions and changes in different ways; some families experience difficulties in coping with change, while other families seem to adapt more easily. For example, the birth of the first child may be the cause of celebration and excitement. Though the family (including extended family members) and the couple may prepare for the birth of the first child, the challenges of parenting may be accompanied by an initial period of strain and tension as they adapt and adjust to their new roles and responsibilities. The birth of a child not only changes the physical composition of the family; the couple must now renegotiate its relationship to include parenting responsibilities without impairing the preexisting relationship. Some couples are able to make this role transition with little difficulty. Other couples, depending on the nature of their couple relationship, may find the transition to parenthood a bit challenging.

The family, as a system of interacting relationships, is also impacted by the maturational milestones of each family member. As children move through their developmental life cycle, and as the parents experience their own life cycle challenges, the family system may be impacted in significant ways. One of the impacts of change is in the domain of roles and relationships. Given the example of a couple transitioning into the role of parenthood there are other role changes as well. For example, family role assignments such as providing resources, offering nurturing and emotional support, and ensuring the maintenance and management of the family system may be impacted by the birth of a child. During times of developmental transitions within a family system, individual roles and relationships may have to be redefined and reassigned to cope with and manage change. Having roles redefined and reassigned may create stress, strain, and tension within the family.

Stress, strain, and tension are an unavoidable and integral part of family life. The stress generated by the family life cycle can cause stress for individual family members, and the developmental changes experienced by individual family members

Photo 13.1 Though many life cycle events are predictable and anticipated, they may be accompanied by varying degrees of family strain

Source: ©iStockphoto.com/Larisa Lofitskaya

can introduce tension into the family system. Though family stress is a normal part of family life, there are those changes within families that only minimally upset the regular routine of a family. These changes do not produce a significant level of stress or tension, and the family is able to address these changes through its available resources and its existing repertoire of coping and problem-solving strategies.

However, there are unexpected and unplanned changes that emerge within a family and/or those unplanned external events that intrude into the life of a family. Both internal and external events can create unanticipated stress. The nature, duration, and intensity of the stress associated with these changes can propel a family into a state of crisis, which may result in a period of family disorganization. One such family hardship is experiencing the death of a family member. Experiencing the sudden death of a family member (let's say through violence or war) should not minimize the experience of the death of a loved one as a result of a prolonged and/or terminal illness. However, experiencing the sudden loss of a loved one may generate greater family stress than the death of a family member from a prolonged illness.

An external event that may also create unanticipated stress and hardship is the sudden job loss of a family member. The loss of a job not only impacts the financial status of the family; it may also impact the family member's self-respect (and/or the respect he or she receives from the other members of the family). Such a loss may result in anger and/or depression. The source of these stressor events (whether internal and/or external) may call for the family to mobilize existing new internal and/or external resources to help cope with these stressful events.

Finally, there are those external traumatic events as well as events or conditions within a family that because of their prolonged, overwhelming, and unpredictable nature can profoundly disrupt family life. These traumatic experiences can leave family members with high levels of fear and helplessness and a sense of a loss of control in the face of these traumatic events. These calamities are described in the *Diagnostic and Statistical Manual of Mental Disorders* (DSM-IV-TR) as those events that "involve actual or threaten death or serious injury, or other threat to one's physical integrity; or witnessing an event that involves death, injury, or threat to the physical integrity of another person; or learning about unexpected or violent death, serious fear of the threat of death or injury experienced by a family member or other close associate. The person's response to the event must involve intense fear, and/or horror (in children, the response must involve disorganized or agitated behavior)" (American Psychiatric Association [APA], 2000, p. 463). These events can include natural disasters, mass interpersonal violence, rape and sexual assault, domestic violence, war, physical assault, and child physical and sexual abuse. The term *trauma*, which derives from the Latin word *wound*, speaks to the psychological and systemic wounds such events can inflict upon the life of the family. As the wounds caused by the traumatic events can be deep and massive, the recovery and healing process may be protracted requiring even more specialized interventions.

Families are challenged to develop coping capacities and skills to protect the family and members of the family from major disruption during these times of change, stress, crisis, and trauma. What is being suggested is that the stress that emerges from family transitions as well as from unanticipated and possibly traumatic events can impact a family on a very fundamental level. These stressors may call for the family members to bond together emotionally and to be flexible in their role assignments, relationship rules, and communication patterns in order to adapt to new developmental and situational challenges. Some families due to their resilience are able to cope with these events and bounce back from adverse situations whereas other families become overwhelmed by such events due to their vulnerability.

Though change is a part of the fabric of family life, families may differ in their capacity and ability to manage these changes. They may not have the inner resources, strengths, and problem-solving capabilities to both ensure the development of individual family members and protect the family unit from major disruptions (McCubbin & McCubbin, 1993). For example, divorce in families is a disruptive event and one of the major challenges for the family system to adjust to. The family's capacity to adjust and adapt to change is an indication of the family's resilience. In the case of divorced families, their capacity to change is revealed as they move through single parenthood and possibly remarriage, which may result in a blended or reconstituted family arrangement.

Stress, crisis, and trauma can reverberate throughout a family system and can shape the experiences of families over generations. Parental history of trauma, mental illness, and/or substance abuse in one generation appears to be strongly implicated in creating substantial risk for children in the next generation. Families do endure hardships over time and encounter a range of stressors, some of which are difficult and some of which are not. There are also those families that encounter a multitude of stressors simultaneously or concurrently. These multistressed families are so overwhelmed by the prolonged, constant, and insidious nature of multiple stressors that the overall family functioning is seriously impaired.

What is important for our discussion is that stressor events require modification in the family system and family dynamics. When stress goes beyond a critical threshold, the family may experience difficulty in adaptation. Functional and resilient families find it easy to adapt as they reorganize their meaning and belief system, relationship system, and communication system. These families are flexible and are able to change their subsystems. Dysfunctional or nonresilient families find it difficult to make these adaptations. It is these nonresilient families that often seek therapeutic intervention to assist them in managing the impact of stress, crisis, and/or trauma to build their capacity to cope with future stressful events.

UNDERSTANDING STRESS

The term *stress* is applicable in describing the range of feelings and emotions that are part of a person's everyday experience. In the course of a person's life one is likely to experience some worry and anxiety over such issues as finances, family discord, social interactions (such as giving a speech, changing and interviewing for new jobs), making life-altering decisions, illness, and disease. These events in life represent a demand that creates a form of tension, strain, or stress within the person. Selye (1974) describes this form of tension as a "nonspecific response of the body to any demand made upon it" (p. 27). As a physiological response to these demands, stress can cause health problems like headaches, high blood pressure, insomnia, and even depression. Lazarus (1966) states, "From the homeostatic point of view, stress is some stimulus condition that results in disequilibrium in the system that produces a dynamic kind of strain . . . against which mechanisms of equilibrium are activated" (p. 12). With this specific understanding of stress there is a clear interaction between the stressor event and the psychological response to the event. The goal of the response is to bring the system or organism back into a state of homeostasis. The nature of the response to the stress is reflective of the magnitude and the duration of the stressor along with the person's coping capacity. Table 13.1 describes the adaptive and maladaptive response to stressor events. Note that the capacity to adapt to a stressor event or situation is determined by the duration and magnitude of the stress.

Table 13.1   Stages of Maladaptive Response to Stressors

Stage I. Alarm

- When the stressor event increases, the person increases his or her efforts to strive and to maintain a level of aspiration and effective performance (*fight*). If the objectives are achieved, then the problem is solved. If not, then inner conflict occurs, which can lead to the next stage.

Stage II. Resistance

- The person feels increased demands from the stressor events with more energy exerted to manage stress. After a while the person gives up mentally and becomes detached. The person may appear to be involved but merely goes by the book with no enthusiasm (*flight*).

Stage III. Exhaustion

- If the state of resistance continues, there is a breakdown in the person's ability to cope and manage job-related stress. There is resulting severe anxiety and perhaps a "breakdown" or "burnout."

Individual Strategies to Decrease Stress and Burnout

Burnout is a reaction to high and unmanageable stress. Managing burnout requires that the individual undertake an array of approaches or strategies to cope and manage his or her stress "exhaustion." Some of the approaches may involve some of the following activities:

- Goal setting and time management
- Challenging thoughts that produce burnout
- Relaxation techniques
- Exercise/hobbies
- Pleasurable goodies
- Humor
- Getting expectations in line with reality
- Retreats
- Group therapy/support groups

The primary issue for managing stress in one's life is to recognize stressful situations and confront them with the intent to either cope with or improve them. To the extent one does not take some form of action, personal stress can become debilitating on a physiological, psychological, and social level. A maladaptive response to stress impairs one's ability to maintain psychosocial balance. What is particularly significant about stress and burnout is that they reflect a pattern of commitment to a task that does not yield the desired outcomes. As a result of continued effort with no positive or validating feedback, the person enters into a state of physical and emotional fatigue. The above strategies offer a means to address the fatigue as well as to inoculate oneself from further stress.

FAMILY STRESS ADAPTATION THEORIES

The theme that has been reiterated several times in this chapter is that family life is stressful. As stress is a fact of family life the study of the impact of stress on the family can be traced back to the Depression era of the 1930s. It was during this period that many families were overwhelmed by the impact of massive unemployment. Research conducted by Angell (1936) and Cavan and Ranck (1938) sought to examine how families were coping with stress resulting from unemployment and the loss of family income. They discovered that the family's reaction was based on two factors: integration and adaptability. Integration reflected how close family members felt toward each other, their sense of family unity, and how economically interdependent they were. Adaptability reflected how flexible family members were in talking about the problem and their willingness to make decisions as a family unit. These studies revealed that families that both were integrated and could easily adapt their family roles to meet the needs of the situation were more capable in dealing with the stress of job and income loss.

ABC-X Model of Family Stress

As the Depression profoundly impacted families, World War II was another period in which families found themselves having to cope with an array of stressful events. In the aftermath of World War II, Reuben Hill (1949) conducted an extensive study on the impact of stress on family life. As Hill sought to understand the impact of stress on families he viewed stress not as inherent in the stressor event itself but as the response of the family to the stressor event. A stressor is an event that changes some aspect of the family system. In addition to changing the family system Hill proposed that family stress results from the interaction of three factors: (a) the stressful event itself, (b) the resources or strengths the family possesses at the time of the stressor event, and (c) the family's perception of the event. This understanding of family stress formed the framework for Hill's *ABC-X* model of family stress, which remains as the foundation of contemporary family stress theories including the *Double ABC-X Model* (McCubbin & Patterson, 1982) and the *Mundane Extreme Environmental Stress Model* (MEES) (Peters & Massey, 1983). The *Family Resilience Model* developed by Walsh (2006) derives much of its core ideas from Hill's early formulations. These models, especially the *Family and Community Resilience Framework*, will inform our later discussion on family-based interventions with families experiencing stress and trauma.

Photo 13.2   Froma Walsh's *Family and Community Resilience Framework (2006),* describes clinical interventions that strengthen vulnerable and multi-stressed families recovering from trauma

In the ABC-X model, *A* represents the provoking or stressor event, *B* is the family's resources or strengths, *C* is the definition or meaning attached to the event by the family, and *X* is the actual stress or crisis. We will focus more specifically on the elements of this model.

The stressor event (A): A stressor event is a demand encountered by the family that causes the family to mobilize its resources to meet the demand. It is important to note that some events, though stressful, are also celebratory. An example is a marriage ceremony. Though there may be much stress in preparation for the actual wedding, the outcome of having two individuals join in matrimony is a cause for celebration. There are also those stressful events that can have a more devastating impact on the family such as a divorce. One event represents addition, growth, and expansion of a family; the other event represents a loss. It is often a loss that is at the core of a stress-inducing experience. Stressor events and persistent stresses affect the entire family and all its members, posing risks not only for individual dysfunction but also for relational conflict and family breakdown.

In a study of experiences that disrupt family life Holmes and Rahe (1967) ranked 43 stress-producing events with a score of 100 representing the greatest amount of stress. Of the 12 most stressful events, 8 involved the family (see Table 13.2). From this study it is apparent that one of the major sources of stress for individuals is the family.

Table 13.2   Stressful Events

Stressor Event	*Level of Stress*
1. Death of a spouse	100
2. Divorce	73
3. Marital separation	65
4. Detention in jail or other institution	63
5. Death of a close family member	63
6. Major personal injury or illness	53
7. Marriage	50
8. Being fired	47
9. Marital reconciliation	45
10. Retirement	45
11. Major change in the health or behavior of a family member	44
12. Pregnancy	40

Even as the above stressor events impact family life, stressful events may have a differential impact on families depending on a variety of factors. For example, Lipman-Blumen (1975) has identified several indicators regarding the impact of various stressor events on families. Some of these indicators are as follows:

1. The first indicator is whether the stress is internal or external. Some stress is based on decisions made by family members that can bring about stressful changes in the family. For example, a decision to relocate based on expanded job opportunities has a different impact on the emotional life of a family than a decision to relocate due to the sudden loss of the current job.

2. The number of family members impacted by the stressor is another indicator. If one member of a family is in a stressful job situation, though it might impact the emotional climate of the family, it is not as stressful as both spouses losing their job. In the latter situation the emotional and economic impact is much greater.

3. Is the stressor sudden, or was there a gradual onset? Staying with the employment example, the sudden loss of a job due to the unanticipated and unexpected layoff has a more profound impact on the person than the loss of a job after a series of poor evaluations and prior disciplinary actions. In the latter situation there might be some anticipation of the stressor event (i.e., job loss).

4. The severity of a stressor is another indicator of the possible impact. For example, is the person dealing with the death of a child or the purchase of a new home? These two events differ significantly in their magnitude and impact on family life.

5. The length of time family members have to cope with the stressor is another indicator of the degree to which a stressor might impact a family. Caring for a family member with a debilitating and degenerative disease such as ALS (Lou Gehrig's disease) is intensely more stressful than dealing with a child with the flu.

6. Whether the stressor is expected or not makes a difference in terms of impact. As families move through the family life cycle, family members can anticipate what are considered as normative stressor events such as the birth of children. There are those unanticipated stressor events such as the sudden death of a family member that can have a more profound and devastating impact on the family.

In summary not all stressor events are equal in magnitude and impact. Additionally the extent to which a family is able to cope with stress is influenced by those resources that can be mobilized to assist in its coping strategies.

Photo 13.3   As children move through their developmental life cycle, and as the parents experience their own life cycle challenges, the family may undergo significant stress
Source: ©Creatas Images/Creatas/Thinkstock

Resources (B): A family's ability to mediate the impact of the stressor event on the family is determined by its ability to access potential resources to assist it in coping with the stressor. Some of these resources reside within members of the family. These resources could include factors such as family income, education, job history, physical and emotional health, and problem-solving skills. Referring to the cited studies of Angell (1936) and Cavan and Ranck (1938) the family's ability to integrate and adapt in stressful situations is an internal resource. External resources would include the family's support network including friends, neighbors, coworkers, members of the family's faith community, community groups, and human service organizations. It is these resources that a family can draw upon in times of stress. These resources can enable a family to both adapt to and cope with the stressor event(s), as well as have a buffer against the possible devastating effect of the stressor events. Some families have many resources to draw upon. Yet, depending on the magnitude of the stressor events, these resources may be quickly depleted. The "resource poor" families along with the families that are bereft of resources will find themselves quite vulnerable to the impact of stressor events.

Definition and meaning of the event (C): The impact of the stressor event on a family is also mediated by the definition or meaning the family gives to the event. When encountering stressor events a family's idiosyncratic "family theme," or those attitudes, beliefs, and values that consciously or unconsciously organize the life of a particular family, will act as an interpretive framework for making sense of the events. Some families may interpret a stressor event as more challenging than threatening or insurmountable. Such a stance may motivate a family to mobilize and utilize its resources in a more effective manner than a family that feels that the effects of the stressor event are insurmountable.

A family's interpretive frame will also be reflective in its problem-solving strategies. In discussing elements of family problem solving, Balswick and Balswick (2007) refer to the five stages of family problem solving described by Tallman and Gray (1987). These are the stages that families may go through to cope with and manage stressor events:

1. The greater the threat to a family's perceived welfare, the more the situation will be perceived as a problem. As Tallman and Gray (1987) state, "The most salient problems for the family as a unit will be either external threats to its ability to care for and protect its members or internal threats to its viability and functioning" (p. 13). In addition the more immediate a situation is, the more likely it is to be perceived as a problem. An example given by Balswick and Balswick (2007) is that spousal abuse, which is a serious threat to the family system, may temporarily have lower priority when a family has to deal with a more immediate problem such as a burst pipe in the bathroom.

2. A family decision to solve a problem is more likely to be made if the family members believe that they can do something about the problem. If there is confidence, then there is motivation to act. Families are also less likely to act on problems when the stress is either very low or very high. Families experiencing very high stress may engage in defensive avoidance rather than constructive problem solving. Defensive avoidance may include selective inattention, forgetfulness, distortion of the meaning of warning messages, wishful rationalization, and minimization of the severity of the problem. Families are further less likely to engage in actions that may prevent stress and are more likely to engage in activities to correct a negative situation after it has occurred.

3. Families will consider which options are most effective based on the information gathered. They will tend to look not for the best solution but for the most satisfactory means to solve the problem. "Satisfactory" means are those that entail the least inconvenience in terms of time, money, energy, and

resources. Once a solution is reached, the family may abandon the pursuit of perhaps more sustainable solutions.

4. Families may struggle with sustaining the implementation of their chosen solution to a problem. Though a more optimal strategy of family problem solving is to implement a problem-solving strategy and then evaluate its effectiveness, families may lack the patience to wait for the problem-solving strategy to work. As the magnitude of a stressor may initially heighten following the deployment of a problem-solving strategy, families may react by not following through with the solution.

5. The final stage of family problem solving involves evaluating the effectiveness of the solution. A flexible family will make the needed adjustment and discard what is not working and try something new.

As we look at the problem-solving strategy employed by a family, we can see that the effectiveness in coping is determined by the interaction between the *A*, *B*, and *C* components of Hill's (1949) family stress model.

Actual stress or crisis (X): The degree to which a family will experience stress is determined by the above components of this model. A family will enter into a crisis when it is unable to maintain a state of homeostasis because of the stressor event. Not all stressors will lead to a crisis (or an acute stress reaction). Nor does a crisis permanently disrupt a family. In fact many families experience enhanced functioning after navigating through a crisis event. This enhanced functioning reflects the family's ability to not only bounce back but also flourish. This is a mark of the family's resilience.

The Double ABC-X Model

It is often not just one single event that propels a family into stress or an acute stress reaction. The crisis state may result from an accumulation of events that essentially "pile up" on a family, thus causing the acute stress reaction. Taking this observation into consideration, McCubbin and Patterson (1982) developed the *Double ABC-X Model.* Beginning with the traditional ABC-X model, McCubbin and Patterson observed that first there are three components to the *A* or stress factor that need to be considered in understanding the full impact of stress on the family. There is not only the initial stressor, but there are present: (a) unresolved aspects of the initial stressor event, (b) changes and events that go on within the family regardless of stressor, and (c) the consequences of the family's effort to cope with the stressor event. An example of a *double A* stressor is provided by Ingoldsby,

Smith, and Miller (2004) in their example of a father who has lost his job, which is the initial stressor event. There may be other events transpiring within the family; through not directly related to the stressor event they may be compounded by the event. An example of compounded stress is this family having to pay increased school tuition for the children. The family is now faced with a job loss along with increased financial responsibilities. Given that the father has lost his job and is now at home, there is a role change with the wife being the only parent working and the family having to accommodate the father being at home. The father now finds himself assuming some child care responsibilities while looking for a job. In this scenario it is evident that families may experience multiple stressors at one time. These multiple stressors, which now extend beyond the initial stress event (job loss), create even more significant changes within the family system.

The *double B resource* factor refers to the observation that families may deplete their available resources to cope with stressor events. In doing so they must acquire and draw upon new resources, learn new skills, or strengthen old skills. The *double C* factor, or the family's perception of the stressor, speaks not only to the family's perception and interpretation of the initial stressor but also to how the family interprets its response to the stressor. For example, families faced with the sudden death of a loved one will not only respond to the experience itself but will also assess their ability to cope over the long term with that event. Family members might consider how the family can really "move on" in the face of loss. Finally the *double X* factor is the only reaction to the crisis event or the anticipated adjustment to the event. The *double X* factor represents the actual postcrisis adaptation to the stressor event. Here the consideration is how the family actually functions over the long term following the crisis event. Long-term adaptation is of course contingent on how the family has interpreted the stress and the resources it can access to cope with the stress.

Mundane Extreme Environmental Stress Model

The Mundane Extreme Environmental Stress Model (MEES) is a particular model of stress that takes into account the impact of oppression, racism, and discrimination on the daily lives of individuals and families of color (Peters & Massey, 1983). Racism and oppression are viewed not as an additional stressor but as one that is woven into the very fabric of the everyday experiences of people of color and impoverished families. Poor families and families of color encounter frequent crises and stress that severely impact their functions. These are multistressed and vulnerable families that are at high risk for extensive family conflict, health and mental health issues, and substance abuse. These are the families that have been variously labeled as dysfunctional or multiproblem families. Though they appear inundated and overloaded with a multitude of stressors, such pejorative labels as *multiproblem* or *dysfunctional* may ignore critical and salient ecological and systemic factors that contribute to their social and economic marginalization. Furthermore such labels may cause one not to consider the inherent though hidden strength for coping with change that may reside within the family or within one's ecological space. Within these families the stress of racism and oppression is an additional element of the *A* factor in the ABC-X model. Peters and Massey (1983) also suggest that an additional *D* factor be added to represent the pervasive environmental stress associated with being a minority.

FROM FAMILY STRESS TO FAMILY CRISIS

Determining the distinction between stress and crisis is often difficult especially in light of the increasing use of the term *acute stress reaction* to replace the term *crisis* (Brett, 1996). One of the distinctions made between the two constructs is that stress is viewed as a continuous variable or as varying in the amount experienced and crisis is a categorical variable—that is, a person is either experiencing a crisis or is not (Boss, 1987; McKenry & Price, 1994). Hill (1949) defines *crisis* as a "situation in which the usual behavior patterns are found to be unrewarding and new ones are called for immediately" (p. 51). Families in crisis are those that are experiencing a period of disorganization as their previous strategies in coping with stressor events are inadequate, inoperable, or blocked (Boss, 1987). The family remains in this stage of disorganization until the point at which it is able to reorganize and adjust to the stressor event. Hill's (1949) "roller-coaster profile of adjustment to crisis," depicted in Figure 13.1, describes the process of responding to crisis events.

| Figure 13.1 | Roller-Coaster Model of Adjustment to Crisis |

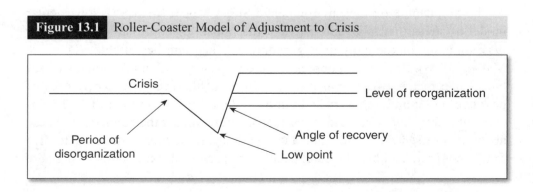

As a family moves through its own unique life cycle, it may encounter several crisis events that threaten to disrupt the family's equilibrium. At the point of crisis the family may experience a period of disorganization. The acuteness of the angle in the above figure represents the level of disorganization of the family following its inability to cope with a crisis event. The severity of the disorganization may be reflected in the severity of the reactions of the family or family members. Families that reach the "low point" or hit bottom may display some extreme behavioral reactions such as suicide. The phase that follows hitting bottom is the period of recovery. The length of time it takes between family disorganization and recovery is identified in Figure 13.1 as the angle of recovery. The narrower the angle of the recovery period, the shorter the adjustment period will be. This reorganization or adjustment phase may bring the family back to its precrisis level of functioning or to a higher level of reorganization. Depending on the magnitude and traumatic nature of the event, the family may not be able to recover and may remain at a level of functioning lower than its precrisis state.

THE "FACE" OF TRAUMA

Thus far our discussion has focused on the characteristics of family stress and crisis. There is another phenomenon that has captured the attention of mental health professionals, and that is the psychological effects of trauma. Though the experience of traumatic events has been a part of the collective human experience, the psychological effects of trauma were only recognized as a diagnostic category in the third edition of the *Diagnostic and Statistical Manual of Mental Disorders* (DSM-III; APA, 1980). The classification of *posttraumatic stress disorder* (PTSD) was an effort to capture and describe the symptoms experienced by individual victims of traumatic events. Though the classification of PTSD was formulated in 1980, the psychological impact of traumatic events on individuals was clearly a part of the experiences of many individuals and of soldiers in combat. While some of the early work on family stress was based on the experience of families during the Depression, Hill (1949) examined the impact returning World War II veterans had on their families. Many veterans experienced difficulty in reintegrating into society and their families. They also had difficulties integrating their wartime experiences into a postwar world. The soldiers who experienced combat reported experiencing emotional breakdown, nightmares, uncontrollable crying, and memory loss during and following their combat experience. Herman (1997) described that the emotional stress due to prolonged exposure to violent death, such as what is experienced in combat,

Photo 13.4   Family members must have the level of mutual support that allows them to maintain a sense of relational connectedness in the face of trauma

Source: ©iStockphoto.com/Wouter van Caspel

produces a neurotic syndrome resembling hysteria in men. Following the Vietnam War there was greater attention given to the impact of combat and the resulting psychological trauma experienced by veterans. In the early 1980s the Veterans Administration began to develop PTSD treatment programs for veterans as there was greater recognition that many of the emotional issues that Vietnam veterans displayed were in fact symptoms of PTSD.

Given the greater awareness of the impact of violent events on individuals, the understanding of trauma expanded beyond the experiences of those in military combat. The *Diagnostic and Statistical Manual of Mental Disorders* (DSM-IV; APA, 1994) described traumatic events to include "violent personal assault (sexual assault physical attack, robbery, mugging), being kidnapped, being taken hostage, terrorist attack, torture, incarceration as a prisoner of war or in a concentration camp, natural or manmade disasters, severe automobile accidents, or being diagnosed with a life-threatening illness" (p. 424).

PTSD is defined in the DSM-IV (APA, 1994) as "the development of characteristic symptoms following exposure to an extreme stressor" (p. 424), "in which the person's response involved intense fear, helplessness or horror" (p. 428). The specific symptoms of PTSD include the following:

1. Recurrent and intrusive distressing recollection of the event

2. Recurrent distressing dreams of the event

3. Acting or feeling as if the traumatic event is recurring (e.g., having flashbacks)

4. Intense psychological distress at exposure to internal or external cues that symbolize or resemble an aspect of the traumatic event

5. Physiological reactivity on exposure to internal or external cues that symbolize or resemble an aspect of the traumatic event

6. Efforts to avoid thoughts, feelings, or conversations associated with the trauma

7. Efforts to avoid activities, places, or people that arouse recollections of the trauma

8. Inability to recall an important aspect of the trauma

9. Markedly diminished interest or participation in significant activities

10. Feeling of detachment or estrangement from others

11. Restricted range of affect

12. Sense of foreshortened future

13. Difficulty falling or staying asleep

14. Irritability or outburst of anger

15. Difficulty concentrating

16. Hyper-vigilance

17. Exaggerated startle response (APA, 1994)

Distinguishing trauma from stress and crisis is significant in that while some stressor events may lead to a family crisis, there are those events that have a more profound traumatic impact on individuals and families. In addition to the impact of the event, there are other factors that differentiate "normative" stressors from more traumatic events. For example, if one can anticipate a potential stressful event and engage in appropriate preparations for that event, the likelihood of that event having a traumatic impact on the individual is lessened. The impact of stress can also be lessened if one has had previous experience with a particular stressor or has someone within his or her life space that has experienced or is currently experiencing that same or a similar stress event. Such factors as having previous experiences and having the opportunity to share those experiences either retrospectively or in the moment can protect individuals from experiencing the full impact of the stressor event. Normative stressors are often shared experiences or anticipated aspects of the common human experience. One the other hand, traumatic events are characterized by unanticipated stressors, which rob a person of any sense of control over the intensity or duration of the event (see Table 13.3).

Table 13.3	General Differences Between Normative and Traumatic Stressors	

Characteristic	Normative Stressor	Traumatic Stressor
Time to prepare	Some	Little to none
Degree of anticipation	Great	None
Previous experience	Some	None
Source of guidance	Many	Few, if any
Experienced by others	Universally	Infrequently
Time in "crisis"	None to little	Little to much
Sense of control	Moderate to high	Little to none

Source: Adapted from Figley & Barnes (2005).

Trauma-Informed Clinical Interventions

Given the increased recognition of the pervasive impact that trauma has on the lives of individuals, there have been increased efforts to develop trauma-informed clinical interventions. One such approach was proposed in Herman's (1997) model of trauma recovery. In this model she has developed three stages of intervention that can promote the recovery from traumatic experiences.

Stage 1: The initial stage requires the establishment of a safe therapeutic environment. Given the impact of trauma, a traumatized individual does not feel safe in his or her body. There are further issues of being out of control with one's emotions and thinking. Because of not feeling safe and in control, traumatized individuals may initiate hyper-vigilant and control mechanisms to feel more in control. A safe therapeutic environment enables victims to feel comfortable in remembering and experiencing their traumatic experiences with the goal of helping them view their reactions and feelings as a posttraumatic stress response to horrifying experiences. Here the victim is assisted in being able to understand these events in a more realistic manner with a more realistic appraisal of the nature of the event. The therapist can work with the client to gain control of those feelings that have emerged from these experiences so that the victim can reengage with his or her social support system.

Stage 2: The therapist and the victim involved are in a process of remembering and mourning the cognitions, emotions, and losses associated with the traumatic event. In this stage the victim is encouraged to recount the traumatic experience with the therapist "bearing witness" to the client's narrative. In this process the client is encouraged to reconnect with his or her pretrauma life. In summary, in this stage the client is in a process of reconstructing the event in the retellings along with experiencing a transformative reconstruction of his or her posttrauma life.

Stage 3: In this stage, the traumatized person begins to reconnect to his or her social world in an effort to build a new life. This new existence will be reflective of the insights gained from the previous experiences.

Herman's (1997) model, along with others (Briere & Scott, 2006; Saakvitne, Pearlman, & the Staff of the Traumatic Stress Institute, 1996; Wise, 2005), primarily focuses on the impact of trauma on individuals. Family therapists who work with families that have experienced trauma are called to assess the impact of trauma not only on individual family members but on the family system as well. Barnes, Todal, and Barnes (2002) note that trauma can have a long-lasting impact on families. Figley and Barnes (2005) state, "This wound [trauma] to the family may affect much more than the family's life routine and may be observable through disruptions in the family members' stable patterns associated with communication, discipline, and emotional support. Failure on the part of the family to deal with these disruptions in family interactional patterns may ultimately result in increased arguments, resentments, and attention-seeking interactions between family members" (p. 392).

THE IMPACT OF TRAUMA ON RELATIONSHIPS AND FAMILY LIFE

Implicit in the description of trauma is the impact that trauma has on one's network of relationships. The impact of trauma extends beyond the life of the individual survivor. The survivor's family, personal, and work relationships are affected as well. Trauma involves symptoms that interfere with trust, emotional closeness, communication, reasonable assertiveness, and effective problem solving. Some of the symptoms noted in those diagnosed with PTSD include the following:

- A loss of interest in social and sexual activities. The survivor may feel distant from others and experience feelings of emotional numbness.
- Significant others feeling hurt, alienated, angry, distant, and discouraged due to the survivor's inability to overcome the effects of trauma.
- The survivor feeling irritable, guarded, easily startled, worried, or anxious, thus impairing his or her ability to relax, socialize, or be intimate without being tense or demanding.

- Difficulties in falling or staying asleep and severe nightmares that may create difficulties for the survivor and his or her partner to sleep together.
- The survivor experiencing trauma memories, reminders, and flashbacks. Attempts to avoid such memories can create difficulties in maintaining a relationship.
- The partner experiencing secondary or vicarious traumatization.

Survivors of childhood sexual abuse, physical abuse, rape, and domestic violence often report feeling a lasting sense of terror, horror, vulnerability, and betrayal that interferes with significant relationships. For example:

- For survivors who are in close relationships and who begin to trust, there is the sense of not wanting to let their guard down. There may be the feeling of both closeness and possible danger.
- Survivors may struggle with suppressing their intense anger resulting from the traumatic experience, and thus they may avoid closeness with significant others or create distance through expressions of criticism or dissatisfaction with their significant others.
- Intimate relationships with survivors may be marked by episodes of verbal and physical violence.
- Alcohol and substance abuse or addiction resulting from an attempt of the survivor to cope with trauma can impair relationships.

Remember from our previous discussion there are those stressors that emerge from transitional and developmental changes within a family. For those events there may be a period of anticipation and preparation. With traumatic events there is little time to prepare, as these events burst into the lives of families with no preparation. In addition to the suddenness of these events the family may have no experience to draw upon to help it cope with the traumatic experience. There may be no one to help or support the family, in that the traumatic events may not have been experienced by others in its resource and support network. Furthermore the family may have little or no control over the event such as a natural disaster. The sudden onset of the event without warning can immediately thrust a family into a state of helplessness and despair. In these instances, the individual and family members may not have the language to describe the impact of these events on their lives. They may have no one in their support network to "bear witness" to their trauma narratives. It is not uncommon for combat veterans to experience difficulties in talking about their combat experiences with others. As one combat veteran of the Iraq War shared with one of the authors, "I only tell people that I shot at people and they shot at me—that is all I can talk about." In another situation involving a World War II veteran, he shared with his family that he spent his time in Europe in a noncombatant position. Upon his death they found his combat metal signifying that he had indeed been in combat. Exposure to a traumatic event can be significant beyond measure. Traumatic events may cause a person to keep at bay the intense emotional experiences associated with the trauma. The significance of families for trauma victims is that they may serve as a support or resource in the victim's recovery. The family may also become a "trauma-organized system" (Banyard, Englund, & Rozelle, 2001) in that the traumatic experience is manifested on a family system level. In this situation the family becomes an obstacle to the traumatized member's recovery.

The Impact of Trauma on the Family

The question for consideration at this point is "What is the impact of trauma on families?" Catherall (2004) in his work on trauma and the family refers to Figley's (1989) description of the four ways in which family systems can be traumatized:

1. *Simultaneous effects:* All members of the family are directly affected by the traumatic event such as a natural disaster or an auto accident.

2. *Vicarious effects:* Other members are traumatized vicariously when they learn that one or more family members have experienced an emotionally traumatic event.

3. *Secondary traumatic stress:* Other family members are traumatized by being exposed to the experience of the traumatized member. Kishur (1985) originally labeled this as chiasmal effects, but the modern term is *secondary traumatic stress disorder* (Figley, 1995).

4. *Intrafamily trauma:* Family members are traumatized by other family members, as in cases of abuse.

This classification raises many interesting features about trauma. Whereas attention is generally focused on the individual trauma victim, the impact of trauma within the family is not always direct. Through the process of secondary trauma, family members can indirectly experience trauma by learning about the primary traumatic experience of a loved one either through indirect or through frequent interactions with the trauma victim. The reactions to or symptoms of primary and secondary trauma can appear to be similar as both the victim and family members attempt to make sense of the trauma experience.

Family members of primary trauma victims often display the same emotional, cognitive, and behavioral symptoms as those reported by the victim. Those with secondary trauma report intrusive thoughts, nightmares, flashbacks, feelings of detachment and estrangement from others, restrictive affect, avoidance of activities that remind them of the event, sleep disturbances, hyper-vigilance, and fatigue (Barnes, 2005). In these situations the mental health professional not only must be attuned to the symptoms displayed by the trauma victim but also must be aware of those secondary symptoms displayed by family members.

Traumatic events also impact the family's worldview. Traumatic events can cause the family to be concerned about safety issues leading to a hyper-vigilant stance toward the world. Janoff-Bulman (1992) describes this phenomenon as a state of "shattered assumptions" in which one believes that the world is safe and meaningful, thus supporting a sense of personal invulnerability that is altered by the traumatic event. The world is no longer safe; nor is the person invulnerable to tragedy. Trauma may cause the family to be overly concerned about protecting the safety of the family. Such families may develop closed and/or rigid boundaries. Depending on the traumatic event, especially one impacting children, both parents and children may develop an intense level of emotional bonding that represents a movement from emotional closeness and supportiveness to a more emotionally enmeshed parent-child relationship in the effort to protect the children from further harm (Newby, Brown, Pawletko, Gold, & Whitt, 2000). Families may experience a range of other reactions following traumatic events:

- Anticipation of the possibility of other distressing experiences
- Anger at those considered to be the cause of the traumatic event, which can be displaced on family members
- The feeling of a lack of control or the feeling of insecurity
- Feeling unable to process the feelings with each other along with each family member trying to make sense of the event
- Fear of not being able to handle the feelings through discussion, thus avoiding discussion
- Impatience, misunderstandings, arguments over small things, and withdrawal from each other (e.g., parents who divorce after the death of a child)

Complex Trauma and the Family

Many families have also been victims of complex trauma. These are families that have had a protracted and sustained exposure to the various forms of trauma as described by Figley (1989). For those families in which intrafamily trauma occurs there is often this sustained exposure to trauma. In these instances there is the resulting feeling of a lack of control, along with the perceived inability to escape from the situation. The victims feel there is no option but to stay in a particular trauma-laden family environment. In these families one will find family members victimized by and/or exposed to child physical, sexual, and emotional abuse; domestic violence; and drug and alcohol abuse. These repeated and sustained traumatic experiences result in family members experiencing multiple violations of personal boundaries. (Note: Families that experience prolonged community violence as well as racism and oppression could also be seen as experiencing protracted exposure to trauma.)

Though not yet a diagnostic category in the *DSM,* the classification of *complex trauma* speaks to the pervasive negative impact of trauma within a family. Much like PTSD, the sustained exposure to trauma can cause an array of emotional and psychological difficulties. Sustained exposure to trauma can result in a loss of a sense of safety, trust, and self-worth due to being in a situation of continued revictimization. Adults with complex trauma no doubt experienced prolonged interpersonal traumatization during their childhood, which in turn may impact their family relationships and their role performance as adults. They carry their unhealed, wounded sense of self from childhood into their adult roles. They find the "ghost" from the past haunting the present.

The impact of trauma on a family can influence a family over several generations. Parental history of trauma along with mental illness and/or substance abuse in one generation appears to strongly implicate a substantial risk for the experience of intrafamily trauma in the next generation. For example, a mother with a history of child sexual abuse along with a family history of substance abuse may experience difficulties in caring for and nurturing her child (see Table 13.4).

Table 13.4　The Generational Impact of Trauma

- Women who experienced any form of abuse as children are more likely to report drug dependence as adults, while women who have experienced both physical and sexual abuse double their risk for substance abuse compared with women who have experienced only one type of abuse (Najavits, Weiss, & Shaw, 1997).
- According to the Child Welfare League of America (2003), 70% of child maltreatment cases involve substance abuse, and a child whose parents have problems with alcohol or other drugs are 3 to 4 times more likely to be abused and/or neglected than those children whose parents do not.
- Cash and Wilke (2003) found that having been sexually abused prior to the age of 15, having an alcoholic parent, or having an extended family history of substance abuse significantly predicts the odds of a mother neglecting her children later in life.
- Children exposed to violence are associated with psychological, interpersonal, and sexual difficulties that persist into adulthood (Davis & Petretic-Jackson, 2000; Harris, 1996; Ouimette & Brown, 2003; van der Kolk, McFarlane, & Weisaeth, 1996).

Source: Adapted from Tracy & Johnson (2006).

Another factor that has a reverberating and multigenerational impact results from a child's exposure to intrafamilial violence. Such early exposure to violence can contribute to a range of adulthood difficulties including one's ability to parent.

A combination of childhood exposure to complex trauma in the form of family violence, substance abuse, and impaired parenting in one generation impacts future generations. This factor of course raises concerns for family-focused mental health practitioners in the area of child welfare. Children are affected when parents are traumatized. As parents are overwhelmed by their own traumatic experiences they are unable to fully address the task of parenting (Sternberg et al., 1993)). Parents who have suffered from trauma may in fact traumatize their children.

These parents may demonstrate an array of affective and behavioral responses to their early trauma, which in turn may have a potential effect on their parenting. For example, some of the typically observed affective responses to trauma include the following:

- Anger/irritability
- Anxiety/nervousness
- Depression
- Shame
- Hopelessness
- Sense of isolation, loneliness
- Emotional numbing
- Feeling different from others

Such affective responses can impact the parents' capacity to feel close or connected to their child. This possible withdrawal from the child can result in a lack of sensitivity to the child's age-appropriate needs and behaviors. Such difficulties in being able to empathically and emotionally connect with the child may be observed in the parents' low tolerance for the child's age-appropriate "acting out" (Tracy & Johnson, 2006). Trauma also impacts behavior in a variety of ways. Some of the typically observed behavioral responses to trauma include aggressive behaviors; a high tolerance for inappropriate behavior; a low tolerance for chaotic, busy, or complex environments/situations; and an avoidance (often unconscious) of triggering trauma-related situations. These behavioral responses can increase the risk of child maltreatment, the parents' difficulty in setting appropriate boundaries and limits, difficulties in distinguishing between discipline and punishment, and the parents becoming easily overwhelmed with everyday demands of parenting (Tracy & Johnson, 2006).

INTRAFAMILY TRAUMA:
FAMILY VIOLENCE AND ALCOHOLISM

Whereas the impact of trauma on a family can take place in the domains as described above by Figley (1989), the focus of the following discussion will be on the area of intrafamily trauma. Intrafamily trauma is defined as a family member experiencing complex trauma. In the domain of intrafamily trauma, family violence and alcoholism are intricately related. In the prior discussion on the impact of PTSD, both alcoholism and violence emerged as symptomatic of an inability to cope with the experience of trauma. Based on these observations many theorists and clinicians have examined the relationship between family violence, alcoholism, and trauma. Tian Dayton (2000) views unresolved and untreated childhood trauma as the cause of addiction. From her perspective it is the presence of alcoholism that negatively impacts the homeostasis of the family system. Other theorists conclude that women involved in domestic violence either as victims or perpetrators are likely to abuse and/or neglect their children (Jones, Gross, & Becker, 2002; Tracy & Johnson, 2006). According to the National Clearinghouse on Child Abuse and Neglect Information (2002), the overlap between child maltreatment and domestic violence ranges from 30% to 60% of all cases that involve either experience. According to Sedlak and Broadhurst (1996), intimate partner violence perpetration and child maltreatment are highly correlated with substance abuse and addiction. The Child Welfare League of America (2003) found that 70% of child maltreatment cases involve substance abuse. A child whose parents have problems with alcohol and/or other drugs are 3 to 4 times more likely to be abused and or neglected than those children whose parents are not (Tracy & Johnson, 2006). These studies indicate that there is a correlation among childhood trauma, substance abuse, and family violence.

Recent work in the area of trauma and violence has addressed the impact that family violence, especially in the form of child abuse, has on the neurophysiology and neurobiology of the infant. The experience of violence impacts parts of the brain, especially the orbitofrontal region, which influences the ability to form attachment relationships. The experience of trauma in childhood can also impact the child's ability to regulate the intensity, frequency, and duration of negative emotions such as rage, anger, and shame (Karr-Morse & Wiley, 1997). Impaired attachment development in childhood impacts the adult's ability to form secure attachments in the array of adult relationships—both within and outside the family. Attachment issues are clearly implicated in the disruptive family attachments manifested in incidents of family violence. Potter-Efron (2005) describes the significance of attachment when he defines attachment as an enduring emotional bond that involves a tendency to seek closeness to another person especially in stressful situations. Attachment is a mutual regulatory system that provides safety, protection, and a sense of security for the infant. When that attachment is disrupted through impaired parenting, a heightened sense of insecurity and lack of protection is incorporated into a person's sense of self and consequently one's sense of self in relationships.

Family Violence

Thomas (2007) raises the issue that our approach to family violence tends to be splinted, in that we tend to focus on abuse in two different areas with their own theories, trained professionals, and research and governmental agencies. These areas are child abuse (both physical and sexual abuse) and domestic violence. Remember from our previous discussion of family violence research that there is an interrelationship between domestic violence and child abuse. In a domestic violence assessment the clinician should also be sensitive to the presence of child abuse. Thomas (2007) proposes that the studies and research in attachment theory might be applicable as an integrating framework to respond to the broader issue of family violence. Thomas believes that the role of the therapist is to help people improve the quality of their attachments. In our earlier discussion, we indicated that attachment may be impaired by earlier childhood experiences, which in turn can cause a degree of emotional and behavioral dysregulation in stressful family situations. Within the domain of environmental and family instability insecure attachment factors may contribute to an eruption of various types of family violence.

Families are challenged to respond to the different developmental and sometimes competing needs and interests of family members. Research is beginning to indicate the central role of stress in family violence (Margolin & Gordis, 2003; Salzinger et al., 2002). If there is intense stress, which can lead to intense conflict (often family violence), it is postulated that individual family members will have severe insecure attachment issues, poor impulse control, and insufficient problem-solving skills.

The systemic impact of family violence is profound. Not only is there physical harm inflicted upon vulnerable family members, but the fact that a family member is committing the violent act creates psychological harm for all family members. One of the functions of a family is to provide primary emotional and physical support in an environment of safety and trust; hence an act of violence perpetrated by a family member is an act of betrayal of that trust. The concept of *betrayal trauma* (Freyd, 1996) has been designated as another form of trauma that virtually intensifies the reality of the trauma at the hands of a family member. In order to maintain attachment to the abuser, the victim must on some level deny the psychic pain associated with the abuse yet still exist in a relationship of abuse and violation. This state of "beingness" creates a sense of confusion about what to think and feel about the perpetrator. The impact of violence not only has its physical impact, but as Perry (1997) states the "most destructive violence does not break bones, it breaks minds" and "emotional violence does not result in the death of the body, it results in the death of the soul" (p. 3).

Family violence can take on many forms and is quite complex. The various types of family violence are described by Appel and Holden (1998):

1. *Single perpetrator:* One parent abuses the other parent and the children.

2. *Sequential perpetrator:* One parent abuses the other parent, who in turn abuses the children.

3. *Dual perpetrator:* One parent abuses the other parent, and both parents abuse the children.

4. *Marital violence:* The parents mutually abuse each other and the children.

5. *Family dysfunction:* Both parents abuse each other, and the children abuse one or both of the parents and each other.

The nature of the violent act may be complex in regard to the actual act committed and the lethality of the act. For example, children may be emotionally, physically, and sexually abused by parents; parents can be assaulted and murdered by children; siblings can attack each other (both physically and sexually); families may engage in elder abuse. In each of these scenarios it is often the most vulnerable, the most dependent, and those with the least power to protect themselves who become victims. As a result, women and children are most often the victims of family violence and should be the primary target for clinical interventions.

We recognize the profound impact that domestic violence has on a child within a family. However, in cases of child abuse and neglect it is important for family therapists to coordinate their services within the domain of public and private child welfare institutions and the criminal and civil court systems. Whereas selected family therapy interventions are appropriate in this area, family-based child welfare interventions are also critical in cases of child abuse and neglect. To this end we have chosen to focus primarily on the area of partner domestic violence.

Domestic Violence

The traditional understanding of family violence, especially domestic violence, is that it is grounded in a patriarchal cultural worldview. The fact is that the cultural practices in many societies support this traditional understanding of one of the causes of family violence. Yet it is a mistake to assume that family violence is solely perpetrated on women by men. Men can be victims of spousal abuse. Current research indicates that abuse may be multiple and that family violence can include both men and women as victims and perpetrators (Hamel, 2007a, 2007b). While the causes of abuse are varied in terms of the nature of the violent act, both men and women are physically and emotionally impacted by abuse. This stance is not meant to ignore that women do suffer the greater share of abuse; due to a man's size and physical strength, there is a greater degree of lethality associated with men battering women.

When domestic violence occurs the family atmosphere becomes charged with a sense of hyper-vigilance due to the abuse, the threats, and the anticipation of further abuse. In the proverbial sense, family members "walk on pins and needles" hoping not to provoke the abuser. It is not uncommon that following the abuse, the abuser attempts (through promises and bribes) to reengage the victim(s) into the relationship, and members may tend to actively ignore or dismiss the problems in an attempt to keep the tension low. Walker (1979) describes this cycle in the following manner:

- *Build-up phase:* This time is characterized by increasing tension between the partners.
- *Stand-over phase:* The offender uses aggression and violence to frighten and control his partner. Following the assault the offender moves into the remorse phase.
- *Remorse phase:* The offender feels ashamed of his behavior, tries to minimize it, and blames it on the survivor (e.g., "She knows I get mad when she does that," or "It was only a bit of a shove"). The spouse may go along with her partner because to do otherwise could mean acknowledging the terror and the danger with which she is living.
- *Pursuit phase:* The offender attempts to convince his partner that she needs him. If the buyback attempts seem not to be working, he is likely to resort to threats and violence. This can be a life-threatening time, for many women are murdered in this phase.
- *Honeymoon phase:* There is a high degree of intimacy, as couples cling to each other after the near separation. Eventually and sometimes very quickly, the cycle resumes itself.

This mode of adaptation as reflected in this cycle is used by the perpetrator (and victim) to control tension within the family, and this inhibits effective problem solving in the family. Minor problems are brushed aside and ignored, and this avoidance increases intrafamily tensions. As Ragg (2006) states, "The male's lack of assertiveness, dependency and tendency to overreact to perceived slights also inhibits entry into problem solving exchanges" (p. 401). Consequently all family members learn to avoid problem solving. As a result, the victim may stay in the relationship for a variety of reasons:

1. Fear of the partner's action and reaction to leaving

2. Inability to cope with the effects of abuse in terms of self-esteem

3. Unwillingness to cope with the sense of aloneness and isolation from family and possibly children

4. Economic dependency and the fear of not being able to support oneself

These reasons point to the fact that the victim is psychologically, physically, and emotionally restrained in her decision-making process and capacity to leave (Seanger, 2000). Some victims may also have some religious reasons for not leaving. The point for consideration is that all victims are under severe and often prolonged stress, causing some to turn to alcoholism and drugs to find relief. The prolonged exposure to domestic violence can create a state of complex trauma for these victims, in that they are also dealing with multiple stressors that include the reasons for not leaving the perpetrator.

Clinical Issues in Treating Family Violence

One of the primary concerns in providing family and couples therapy in situations of domestic violence is that therapy may put the victim at further risk. Evocative materials may come up in a session that may cause the violence to escalate after the session is over. The perpetrator may use materials to rationalize the abusive behavior, so the issue of a safety plan is quite important. Thus a family-based intervention in domestic violence raises serious concerns about the safety of the victim. What is being suggested is that any family-based interventions must take safety issues into consideration. Family therapy is only appropriate when the certain conditions exist. Based on the premise of providing safety for the victim, Hamel (2007a) prescribes the following basic conditions for engaging a family with a history of violence in therapy:

1. Victims and perpetrator want this type of treatment.

2. The victim is aware of potential dangers and has a safety plan.

3. An adult must accept the responsibility in cases of child abuse.

4. There are no custody issues if the parents are going through a divorce.

5. Results of a lethality evaluation indicate low probability of danger.

6. Perpetrator does not have obsessional thoughts about the victim.

7. The therapists have been trained in both domestic violence and family therapy.

8. None of the clients are using drugs or alcohol.

9. Treatment is mandated in cases of substance abuse.

10. Neither of the partners exhibit psychotic behavior.

In the event that there is concern that violence cannot be controlled due to the relationship dynamics of the couple or individual pathology, then the perpetrator or the dominant aggressor should be treated separately or in a group format. If the perpetrator is involved in the treatment process, the goals of intervention should be working with the family to do the following:

1. Better cope with stress.

2. Challenge the dysfunctional, irrational beliefs that cause and exacerbate violent behavior (including societal messages about violence).

3. Learn prosocial anger management.

4. Learn conflict resolution skills and heal from childhood trauma and emotional disorders family members may have suffered.

The therapist should further work toward making the distinction between primary problems, which are the initial or precipitating cause of the conflict, and secondary problems, which result from the ineffective attempts to resolve those issues. From a cognitive-behavioral perspective the therapist should move toward helping the family learn that as individual family members they have control only over their own behavior, emotions, and thoughts. In other words the therapist challenges the assumption that one family member can control the inner state of another family member.

Hamel (2007a) describes an intervention strategy that involves three phases (see Table 13.5). The first phase focuses on behavioral changes that involve the elimination of physical aggression along with developing conflict management and conflict containment skills. The second phase moves toward a focus on relationship issues with the development of communication and problem-solving skills. In this second phase the focus is clearly on understanding and managing self in relationships. The treatment approach in the third phase utilizes a more insight-oriented approach. In this phase there is more in-depth

| **Table 13.5** | Phases of Treatment for Family Violence |

Phase I. *Psycho-educational*	*Phase II.* *Psycho-educational/cognitive*	*Phase III.* *Cognitive/insight-oriented*
<u>Type of change sought</u> First-order, behavioral	<u>Type of change sought</u> First-order, behavioral, internal	<u>Type of change sought</u> Second-order, systems-level, (deeper) internal
<u>Goals</u> • Eliminate physical aggression • Avoid secondary problems • Minimum ventilation of affect • Build confidence and trust • Learn role of stress, conflict, escalation dynamics, impact of control tactics, and importance of equalitarian decision making • Acquire basic management, communication, and conflict containment skills	<u>Goals</u> • Reduce verbal/psychological aggression • Address lesser primary problems • More ventilation of affect • Continue trust and confidence building • Limited discussion of process • Identify and challenge "self-talk" • Expand communication skills, and learn conflict resolution and problem-solving techniques • Assertiveness training	<u>Goals</u> • Eliminate verbal/psychological aggression • Address core issues • Full expression of affect encouraged • Greater attention to process • Identify belief systems underlying distorted self-talk • Begin working through family of origin issues

Source: Adapted from Hamel (2007a, 2007b).

exploration of one's inner world, cognitive distortions, and family of origin issues. In a rather simplistic description of this treatment approach, the first phase involves the perpetrator stopping the violent behaviors; the second phase calls for supporting the perpetrator's ability to manage, understand, and build relationships; and the third phase is enhancing the perpetrator's capacity for self-understanding and self-awareness. What is important is that all phases of these treatment interventions are conducted within the context of safety and accountability. In this context of safety, the perpetrator is held accountable for his or her actions.

Conducting therapy with families in which violence and abuse are major presenting problems is quite challenging for a therapist. There is constant concern about safety issues and the possible eruption of violence on whatever level. In addressing these concerns, Thomas (2007) suggests not so much techniques to work with these families but a stance the therapist should take in working with this population:

- To expect family members to respect each other and not resort to violence, the therapist must model this by respecting the client and creating a climate of therapeutic safety. This involves separating therapy from control functions.
- Look for family strengths and exceptions to violent patterns of interaction. This solution-focused, strength-based approach allows the therapist to identify and reinforce exceptions.
- Take a stance of "respectful inquiry" to understand why the client behaves a certain way. This provides a space for more openness rather than guardedness and defensiveness.
- Be aware of one's own anxiety and anger in working with this client population as such may get in the way of being clinically effective.
- If therapy is not working, widen the system to include a broader support network of family and friends.

Alcoholism, Substance Abuse, and Family Trauma

Alcoholism and other forms of substance abuse can have such a profound effect on families that family interactions can become organized around the presence of abuse within the family. According to Steinglass, Bennett, Wolin, and Reiss (1987), alcoholic families are behavioral systems in which alcoholism and alcoholic-related behaviors have become central organizing principles around which family life is structured. Furthermore:

1. The introduction of alcoholism into family life has the potential to profoundly alter the balance that exists between growth and regulation within the family. The family will no doubt focus energy on short-term stability at the expense of long-term growth.

2. The impact of alcoholism and alcohol-related behaviors on family functioning is most clearly seen in the types of changes that occur in regulatory behaviors as the family accommodates family life to the demands of alcoholism.

3. The types of alterations that occur in regulatory behaviors can in turn be seen to profoundly influence the overall shape of family growth and developmental changes that are labeled as "developmental distortions" (Steinglass et al., 1987, pp. 47–48).

Pattison (1982) points out that there are major themes that describe the interaction of alcoholic members with their families. First and foremost the alcoholic member places significant stress on the family system. Other members may have to adopt roles to cope with the alcoholic member that are not in their own best interest. For instance, a young son may have to assume a parental role and care for an infant sibling because his mother is frequently drunk. Conflict in the marriage or with children may precipitate excessive drinking and may in turn maintain the drinking pattern. Thus alcoholism may serve as (a) a symptom of family dysfunction; (b) a method of coping with family stress; (c) a consequence of dysfunctional family rules, roles, and structure; and/or (d) a combination of these functions. The pain of addiction causes people to separate from one another as it can fracture the family's relationship system. Since the family is not able to emotionally support members due to the presence of alcoholism or other forms of substance abuse, the members try to develop coping mechanisms to fill the void. The alcoholic family member may tend to use a similar pattern, which is based on an illusion. The substance-abusing family member holds the illusion that he or she can escape the pain of the family by using a substance or addictive behaviors. The partner of a substance abuser depends on the illusion that he or she can escape the pain if he or she can get the addict to stop acting out—if he or she can control the other. And control comes in a variety of forms—from overt control and dominance to wheedling, manipulating, seductive, or even compliant behavior designed to control the addict. So the cycle of addiction spirals into the next generation.

Alcoholism is a family disease. Addiction is a relationship issue, and it may be transmitted from one generation to the next. If one generation has an alcoholic family member, the chances increase that the next generation also will have an alcoholic member. Nonalcoholic sons or daughters of alcoholic individuals frequently marry an alcoholic person and keep the intergeneration cycle functioning. Parental substance abuse also strains the marriage, causing a shift in responsibilities; that is, the nonabusing parent is forced to take on other responsibilities.

What is often unique about family members in a substance-abusing family is that they are taught not to betray the family. In other words there is a contract to keep the secret of alcoholism in the family. The family "secret" is enforced by not having friends over or allowing children to go to their friends' house. In being taught to lie, children experience internal conflict. A part of them knows the truth, but to survive they must deny their healthy intuition and response to dysfunctional behavior. They also develop certain coping skills that keep people at a distance. This behavior creates a split of self: public versus private self.

Alcoholic families are in many ways abusive families. As an addictive system an alcoholic family is, by necessity, an abusive system because it handicaps family members in the development of healthy coping skills, self-esteem, and a sense of what is normal or real. The needs of the addictive person always come before the needs of other family members. As with such abuse in alcoholic families, there is intentional abuse—when one person intentionally hurts others. Intentional abuse can be physical, emotional, psychological, or sexual. The abuse can also be unintentional by causing collateral emotional damage to members of the family and sometimes economic damage to the entire family.

Treatment Issues

Though alcoholism and other forms of substance abuse clearly impact the family, traditional system-oriented family therapy is not the generally prescribed intervention, except in a long-term residential treatment program where the client's family involvement is a part of the therapeutic plan. Furthermore treatment of alcohol and substance abuse can be complex as the alcoholic or chemically dependent person may have a range of mental health issues and other psychosocial problems such as vocational impairment.

When families in which alcoholism is present do come to therapy, they rarely identify alcoholism as being the presenting problem. If the clinician does not assess for alcoholism or substance abuse, the issue may go unnoticed and not be identified as an issue (at least for a while). Clinical wisdom supports the observation that when alcoholism is present and not treated, there can be no real movement in addressing the other issues. It is advised that alcohol or substance abuse issues be addressed before the other issues are addressed (Fenell & Weinhold, 2003).

There have been some concerns as to whether alcoholism can be treated through family therapy interventions. The issue revolves around whether intervening in the family system can impact the drinking cycle. It is generally accepted practice that a combination of approaches, including family therapy and self-help approaches such as Alcoholics Anonymous groups, can address both the drinking cycle and family patterns that emerged in response to the drinking cycle. Family therapy can help the addicted person and his or her family deal with the stress of withdrawal, as well as assist in relapse prevention. Here the goal of the therapist is helping the family understand how alcoholism affects the family as well as identify what leads to the onset of or relapse in drinking.

One area in which a family therapy approach has demonstrated some effectiveness is in the treatment of adolescent substance abusers. One treatment approach, multidimensional family therapy (MDFT), has demonstrated effectiveness in addressing issues of substance abuse and conduct disorders. This approach, developed by Liddle, Dakof, Parker, Diamond, and Tejeda (2001), addresses multiple areas of an adolescent's life: emotional and cognitive functioning, family and peer relationships, and social behaviors. This approach also works with parents, encouraging them to build more positive relationships with their children. This particular therapeutic model has yielded some significant results that indicate that a carefully designed family-based and multisystemic approach to chemical dependency has merit. The MDFT model also suggests that the effectiveness of an intervention may be determined by who is the target, their developmental stages, and their position in the family system—which in this case is the adolescent.

FAMILY ADAPTATION AND RESILIENCE

This chapter has focused on the impact of stress, crisis, and trauma on families. The primary focus has been on those families that have not been able to adapt to stress. We can conclude that a maladaptive response to stress heightens vulnerability and risks for individual and relationship distress. Because of their maladaptation to stress, many families have displayed some of the following difficulties:

- Denying the existence of stress-related problems
- Using drugs, alcohol, or addictive substances to deal with the stress
- Isolating from one's support network
- Avoiding the stress-induced family problems through acts of family violence
- Projecting anger and frustration onto others both within and outside the family

There are those families that appear to cope with the stressor through positive mechanisms. These families may use such mechanisms as the following:

- Coping with the stress or crisis through directly addressing its impact on the family
- Seeking help for substance abuse problems or domestic issues
- Turning to support networks such as neighbors, community, friends, and faith communities
- A solutions-oriented problem-solving style
- A high tolerance for and patience with all family members during highly stressful times
- A clear and direct expression of commitment and affection

- An open and effective communication
- High family cohesion and pride
- Flexible family roles shared by more than one member
- Efficient resource utilization or finding strength and support from friends and relatives from outside the family unit
- An absence of violence
- An infrequency of substance abuse

The above families demonstrate what can be called *resilience.* When we speak of resiliency we are describing families that survive and thrive in the face of an adversity that normally would predict negative outcomes for families (Kitano & Lewis, 2005). Resiliency is the power to bounce back after experiencing some personal or life event (Rak & Patterson, 1996). According to Condly (2006) a family's capacity to be resilient is based on three characteristics: (a) the intelligence and temperament of individual family members, (b) the systemic elements of the family, and (c) the degree of social support. Characteristics of healthy and resilient families are further described in the Circumplex Model of Family Functioning (Olson, Sprenkle, & Russell, 1983). This model identifies three characteristics central to resilience and healthy families: (a) cohesion, which facilitates togetherness and individuality; (b) adaptability, balance, flexibility, and stability; and (c) clear, open, consistent communication. McCubbin and McCubbin (1993) describe family health in terms of family resiliency and the family's "ability to respond to and eventually adapt to the situations and crisis encountered over the family life cycle" (p. 6). In resilient families, the family is able to mediate the impact of stress for all members and relationships within the family and can influence the course of many crisis events.

These families have certain characteristics, known as protective factors, that act as an antidote to stress, crisis, and adversity. These protective factors are "those internal and external resources that promote positive developmental outcomes and help children prevail over adversity. As in risk factors, protective factors include dispositional, familial and extra familial characteristics. In aggregate they are the positive forces that contribute to adaptive outcome in the presences of risk" (Garmezy, 1993, as quoted in Fraser, 2004, p. 5). Some of these characteristics are parental resilience, social connections, concrete support in times of need, age-appropriate social and emotional behavior, and communicative competence of family members. Strong families help build resilient behaviors in children as they teach problem-solving skills and provide positive and supportive care of children. Families that have the capacity to respond to family system needs as well as the ability to meet individual needs (while coping with the challenges of living) are the most resilient to stress, crisis, and trauma.

Interventions Supporting Resiliency

In spite of how families have been impacted by stress, crisis, and trauma, a strength-based perspective would acknowledge that all individuals and families have the potential for greater resilience. The question becomes one of how we can maximize that potential.

Walsh (2006) provides some answers to this question in referring to Rutter's (1987) four general protective mechanisms, which promote resilience in vulnerable families:

1. Decrease risk factors.

   - Anticipate and prepare for threatening circumstances.
   - Reduce exposure or overload of stress.
   - Provide information; alter catastrophic beliefs.

2. Reduce negative chain reactions that heighten risk for sustained impact and further stress.

   - Buffer stress effects; overcome obstacles.
   - Alter maladaptive coping strategies.
   - Withstand aftershocks and prolonged strains; rebound from setbacks.

3. Strengthen protective family process and reduce vulnerabilities.

   - Enhance family strengths; increase opportunities and abilities for success.
   - Mobilize and shore up resources toward recovery and mastery.
   - Rebuild, reorganize, and reorient in aftermath.
   - Anticipate and prepare for both likely and unforeseen new challenges.

4. Bolster family and individual pride and efficacy through successful problem mastery.

   - Gain competence, confidence, and connectedness through collaborative efforts.
   - Manage challenges over time for sustained competence under duress. (Walsh, 2006, p. 141)

These protective mechanisms are incorporated into Walsh's (2006) *Family and Community Resilience Framework*. Walsh's work provides a clear framework for developing clinical interventions to strengthen vulnerable multistressed families and families recovering from trauma. For families to become resilient, they must take action to decrease risk factors, as well as develop effective strategies for absorbing stress. This can be accomplished through strengthening the family system, as a buttress against stress, and enhancing a sense of agency and competence in being able to handle future stressors.

In our previous discussion these precepts are congruent with family stress adaptation models. In these models the central theme guiding an understanding of the impact of stress is that stress in and of itself is neutral. It is the combination of three factors—how the event is perceived and the meanings attributed to that event, the adaptive capacity to proactively respond to the stressor event, and the resources that can be drawn upon to cope with the stressor event—that influences the overall impact of the stressor event on the family and the family's reaction to the event. Resilience is the ability to withstand and rebound from the challenges these events pose for families. Family resilience includes family traits and processes that allow the family to be resistant to disruption during change, adapt in times of crisis, and emerge more resourceful after a stressful event. It is this understanding of stress and resilience that forms the foundation of Walsh's (2006) resilience approach with families.

Walsh's (2006) framework for family-based interventions should be grounded in strengths and resiliency-based orientations. As such these interventions should have the following characteristics:

1. They should be resource based and not deficit based.

2. They should be family centered rather than individually based.

3. They should come from a holistic perspective rather than a fragmented approach.

4. They should be prevention oriented rather than crisis reactive.

While her focus is on traumatic loss Walsh (2006) expands our understanding of loss beyond physical loss or the loss of a loved one. Losing a state of psychological wholeness, important roles, significant relationships, an intact family unit, important affiliations, and connections with a sense of community may result in symptoms such as depression and anxiety, substance abuse, and relational conflicts. Walsh's resiliency model provides one framework that can assist families in their efforts to cope with these losses.

As we saw in the ABC-X model, the *B* component speaks to how an event is perceived and the meaning given to the belief. For Walsh (2006), a family's belief system is the "heart and soul" of family resilience. As the family is able to understand and interpret the event from the perspective of challenge and hopefulness (rather than from a perspective of defeat and hopelessness), members are able to engage in problem-solving activities that allow them to navigate through adverse situations, bounce back, and possibly be transformed by the experience. A family's belief system can provide its members with hope, confidence, and a sense of agency in coping with stressful events. This allows the family to manage and master the situation while being able to realistically appraise what can or cannot be done in a given stress-laden situation. Families with resilient belief systems may also have the capacity to draw upon larger spiritual and transcendent frameworks of meaning. These frameworks can provide the family with the strength, faith, courage, and perseverance to not only endure the stress, crisis, or trauma but to come through the "storm" at perhaps a higher level of functioning.

Though a family's belief system is important in seeing options and possibilities, the family must have a family structure that while under stress is flexible enough to rebound and reorganize after its encounter with stressful events without becoming disorganized or dysfunctional. The family's organizational structure becomes the "shock absorber for stress." Such families must have the type of leadership structure that can provide a sense of support and protection for vulnerable family members. Respect, support, boundary maintenance—all are critical elements in resilient families. These families must also have the requisite array of resources, including social, economic, and institutional, to enable them to maintain their organizational and structural integrity. The family must have and maintain its structural intactness while allowing appropriate and necessary support to assist it in coping with crisis events. As described in the early theories of family stress adaptation, the family must have those integrative and adaptive qualities to maintain its integrity in the face of stress and trauma.

Finally the family must have the level of mutual support that allows the family to communicate and maintain a sense of relational connectedness in the face of stress. Such connectedness facilitates family communication, family problem solving, and emotional sharing. The ability to maintain open communication among family members, as the family is coping with stress, allows the family to honor its individual members while encouraging and supporting collaborative problem-solving efforts.

These three keys, belief system, organizational patterns, and communication (Walsh, 2006), are all necessary elements in building family resilience (see Table 13.6). No single construct of the model is sufficient enough to build family resiliency. All three provide the protective factors, as well as provide a framework for clinical interventions that support the building of resilient families.

Table 13.6   Keys to Family Resilience

Belief System The Heart and Soul of Resilience	*Organizational Patterns* Family Shock Absorbers	*Communications* Facilitating Mutual Support and Problem Solving

1. Making Meaning Out of Crisis and Adversity
  • Viewing vulnerability as human: distress as understandable
  • Viewing crisis as shared experience
  • Viewing crisis as a challenge, comprehensible, manageable
 	
2. Developing a Positive Outlook
  • Hope and confidence in overcoming odds/barriers
  • Affirming strengths and building on potential
  • Seizing opportunities: active initiation and perseverance
  • Mastering the possible and accepting what cannot be changed
  • Courage
 	
3. Transcendence and Sense of Spirituality
  • Larger values and purpose
  • Spirituality: faith practices and rituals
  • Transformation through learning, reassessing self, and potential for growth out of adverse situations
  • Understanding that crisis is both a threat and an opportunity
	1. Flexibility
	  • Rebounding, reorganizing, adapting to fit new challenges
	  • Stability through disruptions
	  • Strong leadership that can nurture, guide, and protect children and vulnerable members
	
	2. Connectedness
	  • Mutual trust, support, collaboration, and commitment
	  • Respecting individual needs, differences, and boundaries
	  • Seeking reconnection and reconciliation with wounded relationships
	
	3. Social, Economic, and Institutional Resources
	  • Mobilizing extended kin and social supports
	  • Recruiting mentoring relationships
	  • Building financial security; balancing work and family strains
	  • Engaging larger institutional/structural supports
		1. Clarifying Situation and Options
		  • Clear consistent messages (words and actions)
		  • Clarifying ambiguous information and expectations
		  • Truth seeking/truth speaking
		
		2. Open Emotional Sharing
		  • Sharing range of feelings
		  • Mutual empathy with toleration for differences
		  • Assuming responsibilities for own feelings, behaviors; avoiding blaming others
		  • Pleasurable interactions
		
		3. Collaborative Problem Solving
		  • Identifying problems, stressors, constraints, options
		  • Creative brainstorming and resourcefulness
		  • Shared decision making: negotiation, fairness, reciprocity
		  • Managing conflicts; repairing hurts and misunderstandings
		  • Focusing on goals: take concrete steps
		  • Building on success: learning from mistakes
		  • Being proactive: taking preventive steps to avert crisis and prepare for future challenges and devise "Plan B"

Source: Adapted from Walsh (2006).

Walsh (2006) defines resilience as "the capacity to rebound from adversity strengthened and more resourceful. It is an active process of endurance, self-righting, and growth in response to crisis and challenge. . . . Resilience entails more the merely surviving, getting through or escaping. . . . The qualities of resilience enable people to heal from painful wounds, take charge of their lives and go on to live fully and love well" (p. 4). Resilience is functioning if not at the same level then at a higher level. Again utilizing Hill's (1949) "roller-coaster profile of adjustment to crisis" we can see in Figure 13.2 that crisis can be transformative in that it can raise a family to a higher level of functioning. In other words, this higher level of functioning moves a family beyond the level of reorganizing to precrisis levels.

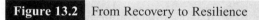

Figure 13.2   From Recovery to Resilience

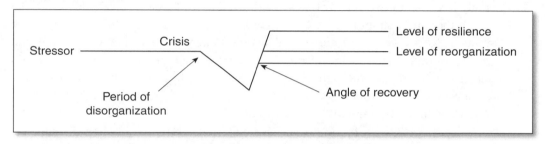

Source: Adapted from Walsh (2006).

For practitioners who work with traumatized families, Walsh (2006) suggests the following practice guidelines to strengthen family resilience:

1. Convey conviction in potential to overcome adversity through shared efforts.

2. Use respectful language and framing to humanize and contextualize distress.
   - View distress as understandable and common in adverse situations (normal response to abnormal situations).
   - Decrease shame, blame, and pathologizing.

3. Provide a safe haven for sharing pain, fears, and challenges.
   - Show compassion for suffering and struggle.
   - Build communication, empathy, and support of members.

4. Identify and affirm strengths and courage alongside vulnerabilities and constraints.

5. Tap into kin, community, and spiritual resources to deal with challenges.

6. View crisis as an opportunity for learning, change, and growth.

7. Shift focus from problems to possibilities.
   - Gain mastery, healing, and transformation out of adversity.
   - Rekindle and reorient future hopes and dreams.

8. Integrate adverse experience into the fabric of individual and relational lives.

SUMMARY

Though Walsh's framework is being presented as a clinical approach to building family resiliency we must offer a cautionary note. Bussey (2007) suggests that some therapists should be careful in applying the idea of resilience after severe trauma. Recovery from trauma that involves interpersonal violence, assault and multiple traumas that occur in rapid succession, may take longer. Bussey (2007) states, "It is more useful to think of resilience in the face of trauma as a process or a journey available to all, and the absence of resilience in the face of adversity as reflecting an early stage of that journey" (p. 307).

Clinical work with families that have experienced trauma is often difficult yet rewarding. Wise (2005) issues another caution for the clinician. Clinicians working with these families are not immune to secondary stress and trauma. As we bear witness to the trauma of others we need to be cognizant of our own needs and strengths, lest we become potential victims of burnout.

RECOMMENDED READINGS

Banyard, V. L., Englund, D. W. & Rozelle, D. (2001). Parenting the traumatized child: Attending to the needs of nonoffending caregivers of traumatized children. *Psychotherapy, 38*, 74–87.

Barnes, M. F. (2005). When a child is traumatized or physically injured: The secondary trauma of parents. In D. R. Catherall (Ed.), *Specific stressors: Interventions with couples and families* (pp. 73–90). New York, NY: Brunner-Routledge.

Briere, J., & Scott, C. (2006). *Principles of trauma therapy: A guide to symptoms, evaluation and treatment.* Thousand Oaks, CA: Sage.

Bussey, M. (2007). Trauma transformed through empowerment and resilience. In M. Bussey & J. B. Wise (Ed.), *Trauma transformed: An empowerment response* (pp. 300–309). New York, NY: Columbia University Press.

Figley, C. R. (1995). *Compassion fatigue: Secondary traumatic stress disorders from treating the traumatized.* New York, NY: Brunner/Mazel.

Figley, C. R., & Barnes, M. (2005). External trauma and families. In P. C. McKenry & S. J. Price (Eds.), *Families and change* (3rd ed.). Los Angeles, CA: Sage.

Hamel, J. (2007a). Domestic violence: A gender-inclusive conception. In J. Hamel & T. Nicholls (Eds.), *Family approaches to domestic violence: A guide to gender-inclusive research and treatment* (pp. 3–27). New York, NY: Springer.

Hamel, J. (2007b). Gender-inclusive family interventions in domestic violence: An overview. In J. Hamel & T. Nicholls (Eds.), *Family approaches to domestic violence: A guide to gender-inclusive research and treatment* (pp. 247–274). New York, NY: Springer.

Herman, J. L. (1997). *Trauma and recovery.* New York, NY: Basic Books.

Margolin, G., & Gordis, E. (2003). Co-occurrence between marital aggression and parents' child abuse potential: The impact of cumulative stress. *Violence and Victims, 18*(3), 243–258.

Ouimette, P., & Brown, P. J. (Eds.). (2003). *Trauma and substance abuse: Causes, consequences, and treatment of comorbid disorders.* Washington, DC: American Psychological Association.

Walsh, F. (2006). *Strengthening family resilience.* New York, NY: Guilford.

Wise, J. B. (2005). *Empowerment practice with families in distress.* New York, NY: Columbia University Press.

DISCUSSION QUESTIONS

1. What is the impact of the various forms of trauma on the family system?

2. How can family-focused and strength-based clinical interventions assist families in coping with stressful and traumatic life events?

3. Thomas (2007) proposes that the studies and research in attachment theory might be applicable as an integrating framework to respond to the broader issue of family violence. How might attachment theory enable the family therapist to gain a broader understanding of family violence?

4. What is the significance of the concepts *resiliency* and *protective factors* in understanding how families cope with trauma and adversity? How are these concepts incorporated into Walsh's (2006) *Family and Community Resilience Framework*?

REFERENCES

American Psychiatric Association. (1980). *Diagnostic and statistical manual of mental disorders* (3rd ed.). Washington, DC: Author.

American Psychiatric Association. (1994). *Diagnostic and statistical manual of mental disorders* (4th ed.). Washington, DC: Author.

American Psychiatric Association. (2000). *Diagnostic and statistical manual of mental disorders* (4th ed., text rev.) Washington, DC: Author.

Angell, R. C. (1936). *The family encounters the depression.* New York, NY: Scribner.

Appel, A. E., & Holden, G. W. (1998). The co-occurrence of spouse and physical child abuse: A review and appraisal. *Journal of Family Psychology, 12*(4), 578–599.

Balswick, J. O., & Balswick, J. K. (2007). *The family.* Grand Rapids, MI: Baker Academic.

Banyard, V. L., Englund, D. W., & Rozelle, D. (2001). Parenting the traumatized child: Attending to the needs of nonoffending caregivers of traumatized children. *Psychotherapy, 38*, 74–87.

Barnes, M. F. (2005). When a child is traumatized or physically injured: The secondary trauma of parents. In D. R. Catherall (Ed.), *Specific stressors: Interventions with couples and families* (pp. 73–90). New York, NY: Brunner-Routledge.

Barnes, M. F., Todal, J. L., & Barnes, A. (2002). Family secondary trauma on the pediatric critical care unit. *Journal of Trauma Practice, 1*, 5–29.

Boss, P. (1987). Family stress. In M. Sussman & S. Steinmetz (Eds.), *Handbook of marriage and the family* (pp. 695–723). New York, NY: Plenum.

Brett, E. A. (1996). The classification of posttraumatic stress disorder. In B. A. van der Kolk, A. C. MacFarlane, & L. Weisaeth (Ed.), *Traumatic stress: The effects of overwhelming experience of mind, body, and society* (pp. 117–128). New York, NY: Guilford.

Briere, J., & Scott, C. (2006). *Principles of trauma therapy: A guide to symptoms, evaluation and treatment.* Thousand Oaks, CA: Sage.

Bussey, M. (2007). Trauma transformed through empowerment and resilience. In M. Bussey & J. B. Wise (Ed.), *Trauma transformed: An empowerment response* (pp. 300–309). New York, NY: Columbia University Press.

Cash, S. J., & Wilke, D. J. (2003). An ecological model of maternal substance abuse and child neglect: Issues analyses and recommendations. *American Journal of Orthopsychiatry, 73*(4), 392–404.

Catherall, D. (2004). *Handbook of stress, trauma, and the family.* Hove, East Sussex, England: Brunner-Routledge.

Cavan, R. S., & Ranck, K. H. (1938). *The family and the depression.* Chicago, IL: University of Chicago Press.

Child Welfare League of America. (2003). *National fact sheet 2003: Making children a national priority.* Retrieved from www.cwla.org/advocacy/nationalfactsheet03.htm

Condly, S. J. (2006). Resilience in children: A review of the literature with implications for education. *Urban Education, 41*(3), 211–236.

Davis, J. L., & Petretic-Jackson, P. A. (2000). The impact of child sexual abuse on adult interpersonal functioning: A review and synthesis of the empirical literature. *Aggression and Violent Behavior, 5*(3), 291–328.

Dayton, T. (2000). *Trauma and addiction: Ending the cycle of pain through emotional literacy.* Deerfield Beach, FL: Health Communications.

Fenell, D. L., & Weinhold, B. K. (2003). *Counseling families: An introduction to marriage and family therapy.* Denver, CO: Love.

Figley, C. R. (1989). *Helping traumatized families.* San Francisco, CA: Jossey-Bass.

Figley, C. R. (1995). *Compassion fatigue: Secondary traumatic stress disorders from treating the traumatized.* New York, NY: Brunner/Mazel.

Figley, C. R., & Barnes, M. (2005). External trauma and families. In P. C. McKenry & S. J. Price (Eds.), *Families and change* (3rd ed.). Los Angeles, CA: Sage.

Fraser, M. W. (Ed). (2004). *Risk and resilience in childhood: An ecological perspective* (2nd ed.). Washington, DC: NASW Press.

Freyd, J. J. (1996). *Betrayal trauma: The logic of forgetting childhood abuse.* Cambridge, MA: Harvard University Press.

Garmezy, N. (1993). Children in poverty: Resilience despite risk. *Psychiatry, 56*, 127–136.

Hamel, J. (2007a). Domestic violence: A gender-inclusive conception. In J. Hamel & T. Nicholls (Eds.), *Family approaches to domestic violence: A guide to gender-inclusive research and treatment* (pp. 3–27). New York, NY: Springer.

Hamel, J. (2007b). Gender-inclusive family interventions in domestic violence: An overview. In J. Hamel & T. Nicholls (Eds.), *Family approaches to domestic violence: A guide to gender-inclusive research and treatment* (pp. 247–274). New York, NY: Springer.

Harris, M. (1996). Treating sexual abuse trauma with dually diagnosed women. *Community Mental Health Journal, 32*(4), 371–385.

Herman, J. L. (1997). *Trauma and recovery.* New York, NY: Basic Books.

Hill, R. (1949). *Families under stress: Adjustment to the crisis of war separation and reunion.* New York, NY: Harper and Brothers.

Holmes, T., & Rahe, R. (1967). The social readjustment rating scale. *Journal of Psychosomatic Research, 2*, 213–218.

Ingoldsby, B. B., Smith, S. R., & Miller, J. E. (2004). *Exploring family theories.* Los Angeles, CA: Roxbury.

Janoff-Bulman, R. (1992). *Shattered assumptions: Toward a new psychology of trauma.* Toronto, ON, Canada: Free Press.

Jones, L. P., Gross, E., & Becker, I. (2002). The characteristics of domestic violence victims in child protective service caseloads. *Families in Society: The Journal of Contemporary Human Services, 83*(4), 405–415.

Karr-Morse, R., & Wiley, M. S. (1997). *Ghost from the nursery: Tracing the roots of violence.* New York, NY: Atlantic Monthly Press.

Kishur, G. R. (1985). *Chiasmal effects of traumatic stressors: The emotional cost of support.* Master's thesis, Purdue University, West Lafayette, IN.

Kitano, M. K., & Lewis, R. B. (2005). Resilience and coping: Implications for gifted children and youth at risk. *Roeper Review, 27*(4), 200–205.

Lazarus, R. S. (1966). *Psychological stress and the coping process.* New York, NY: McGraw-Hill.

Liddle, H. A., Dakof, G. A., Parker, K., Diamond, G. S., & Tejeda, M. (2001). Multidimensional family therapy for adolescent drug abuse: Results of a randomized clinical trial. *American Journal of Drug and Alcohol Abuse, 27*(4), 651.

Lipman-Blumen, J. (1975). A crisis framework applied to macrosociological family changes: Marriage, divorce and occupational trends associated with World War II. *Journal of Marriage and the Family, 42*, 889–902.

Margolin, G., & Gordis, E. (2003). Co-occurrence between marital aggression and parents' child abuse potential: The impact of cumulative stress. *Violence and Victims, 18*(3), 243–258.

McCubbin, H. I., & Patterson, J. M. (1982). Family adaptation to crisis. In H. I. McCubbin, A. E. Cauble, & J. M. Patterson (Eds.), *Family stress, coping, and social support* (pp. 26–47). Springfield, IL: Charles C Thomas.

McCubbin, M. A., & McCubbin, H. I. (1993). Families coping with illness: The resiliency model of family stress, adjustment and adaptation. In C. B. Danielson, B. Hamel-Bissel, & P. Winstead-Fry (Eds.), *Families health & illness: Perspectives on coping and intervention* (pp. 21–63). St. Louis, MO: Mosby.

McKenry, P. C., & Price, S. J. (1994). Families coping with problems and change: A conceptual overview. In P. C. McKenry & S. J. Price (Eds.), *Families and change: Coping with stressful events* (pp. 1–18). Thousand Oaks, CA: Sage.

Najavits, L. M., Weiss, R. D., & Shaw, S. R. (1997). The link between substance and post-traumatic stress disorders in women: A research review. *American Journal on Addictions, 6,* 273–286.

National Clearinghouse on Child Abuse and Neglect Information. (2002). *In harm's way: Domestic violence and child maltreatment.* Retrieved from http://library.adoption .com/articles/in-harms-way-domestic-violence-and-child-maltreatment.html

Newby, W. L., Brown, R. T., Pawletko, T. M., Gold, S. H., & Whitt, J. K. (2000). Social skills and psychological adjustment of child and adolescent cancer survivors. *Psycho-Oncology, 9,* 113–126.

Olson, D. H., Sprenkle, D. H., & Russell, C. S. (1983). Circumplex model of marital and family systems: VI. Theoretical update. *Family Process, 22,* 69–83.

Ouimette, P., & Brown, P. J. (Eds.). (2003). *Trauma and substance abuse: Causes, consequences, and treatment of comorbid disorders.* Washington, DC: American Psychological Association.

Pattison, E. M. (1982). Family dynamic and intervention in alcoholism. In A. S. Gurman (Ed.), *Questions and answers in the practice of family therapy* (Vol. 2). New York, NY: Brunner/Mazel.

Perry, B. D. (1997). Incubated in terror: Neurodevelopmental factors in the "cycle of violence." In J. D. Osofsky (Ed.), *Children in a violent society* (pp. 124–149). New York, NY: Guilford.

Peters, M. F., & Massey, G. (1983). Chronic vs. mundane stress in family stress theories: The case of Black families in White America. *Marriage and Family Review, 6,* 193–218.

Potter-Efron, R. T. (2005). *Handbook of anger management: Individual, couple, family, and group approaches.* New York, NY: Haworth Clinical Practice Press.

Ragg, M. D. (2006). *Building family practice skills: Methods, strategies, and tools.* Belmont CA: Thomson.

Rak, C. F., & Patterson, L. W. (1996). Promoting resilience in at-risk children. *Journal of Counseling and Development, 74*(4), 368–373.

Rutter, M. (1987). Psychological resilience and protective mechanism. *American Journal of Orthopsychiatry, 57,* 316–331.

Saakvitne, K. W., Pearlman, L. A., & the Staff of the Traumatic Stress Institute. (1996). *Transforming the pain: A workbook on vicarious traumatization.* New York, NY: Norton.

Salzinger, S., Feldman, R., Ing-mak, D., Majica, E., Stockhammer, T., & Rosario, M. (2002). Effects of partner violence and physical child abuse on child behavior: A study of abused and comparison children. *Journal of Family Violence, 17*(1), 23–52.

Seanger, S. A. (2000). *Family violence: A review of the dysfunctional behavior patterns.* Retrieved from http://www.mincava.umn.edu/documents/familyviolence/family violence.html

Sedlak, A. J., & Broadhurst, D. D. (1996). *Executive summary of the third national incidence study of child abuse and neglect.* Retrieved from http://www.childwelfare.gov/pubs/statsinfo/nis3.cfm

Selye, H. (1974). *Stress without distress.* Philadelphia, PA: Lippincott.

Steinglass, P., Bennett, L., Wolin, S., & Reiss, D. (1987). *The alcoholic family.* New York, NY: Basic Books.

Sternberg, K. J., Lamb, M. E., Greenbaum, C., Cicchett, D., Dawud, R. M., Krispin, O., et al. (1993). Effects of domestic violence on children's behavior problems and depression. *Developmental Psychology, 29*(1), 44–52.

Tallman, I., & Gray, L. (1987). *A theory of problem solving applied to families.* Paper presented at the Theory-Methodological Workshop, National Council on Family Relations, Atlanta, GA.

Thomas, M. (2007). Treatment of family violence: A systemic perspective. In J. Hamel & T. Nicholls (Eds.), *Family approaches to domestic violence: A guide to gender-inclusive research and treatment* (pp. 417–436). New York, NY: Springer.

Tracy, E. M., & Johnson, P. J. (2006). The intergenerational transmission of family violence. In N. Boyd Webb (Ed.), *Working with traumatized youth in child welfare* (pp. 113–133). New York, NY: Guilford.

van der Kolk, B. A., McFarlane, A. C., & Weisaeth, L. (Eds). (1996). *Traumatic stress: The effects of overwhelming experience on mind, body, and society,* New York, NY: Guilford.

Walker, L. E. A. (1979). *Battered women.* New York, NY: Harper & Row.

Walsh, F. (2006). *Strengthening family resilience.* New York, NY: Guilford.

Wise, J. B. (2005). *Empowerment practice with families in distress.* New York, NY: Columbia University Press.

Chapter 14

FAMILY THERAPY RESEARCH

Implications for the Practicing Family Therapist

OVERVIEW/HISTORY OF FAMILY THERAPY RESEARCH

The historical development of family therapy as a model of practice was at least initially interwoven with the process of research. Many of the early pioneers in family therapy were well-trained clinical researchers who saw no differentiation between the research process and clinical practice. Researcher-clinicians such as Lyman Wynne, Nathan Ackerman, Don Jackson, and others moved easily between providing clinical services to families and researching the process as they went along. In addition, many of these early pioneers began their clinical-research activity with families that had a family member with schizophrenia. People such as Murray Bowen, Carl Whitaker, and Gregory Bateson all focused on schizophrenia and its impact on families. By focusing on the development and process of schizophrenia within the family context, these early researchers began to focus on specific family processes and structures that seemed to help families cope and those that impeded the ability to cope. The importance of family communication, roles within families, and family structures such as triangulation and hierarchies, concepts that became critical in the development of some family therapy models, was originally identified and discussed within the context of these early clinical-research projects.

The focus of much of the early family therapy research was on outcome studies. Such studies tried to identify whether people did better when they received family therapy as opposed to individual therapy or some other kind of intervention. Given that the therapeutic landscape of the 1950s and 1960s was dominated by psychodynamic-oriented individual therapy models, it was critical for the new field of family therapy to establish its legitimacy through outcome studies. However, as is often the case when researching a new entity, the studies often were not well designed and their support for family therapy often was weak or ambiguous. The 1970s and 1980s saw the development of new models of family therapy, including cognitive-behavioral–based interventions. These newer models were more amenable to rigorous research designs and the use of newer technology (e.g., videotapes) to better evaluate the outcomes of family interventions. Videotapes also opened the door to more rigorous studies focused on the process of family therapy, the actions that went on during the provision of family therapy, and how different processes affected the outcome of therapy. In the 1990s, the research of John Gottman and his colleagues on couples therapy moved research to a new level. By placing couples in a replica of an apartment; assigning them tasks to perform; hooking the individuals up to monitors to measure heart rate, blood pressure, and other physiological processes; and videotaping the whole process, his research lab was able to identify key aspects of healthy relationships that increase the likelihood that the couple will stay together.

The 1990s and the new millennium saw the rise of evidence-based practice and the focus on rigorous research studies and meta-analyses. The push was to provide clinicians with data that could be used to help them select the type of family intervention best suited to the family and the family issue. Evidence-based practice was not meant to be a substitute for the clinical assessment process or the collaborative process of building a relationship with the family and using many sources of information in the intervention planning process. Rather, evidence-based practice was meant to supplement this clinical process by providing the therapist with another source of information about family therapy models and their demonstrated effectiveness.

As models of family therapy continue to proliferate, they often build their legitimacy through anecdotal case studies that show the effectiveness of the model when applied to a specific kind of family issue. Once the case studies encourage others to adopt the model, there is a push to better study the model and its utility across family types and issues. However, research on family therapy is not without its conceptual, methodological, and ethical issues. Some of these issues are discussed below followed by a review of some key studies that point out some of the trends within family therapy research.

ISSUES IN FAMILY THERAPY RESEARCH

Conceptual Issues

The primary conceptual issue facing researchers on family therapy is the confusion that arises by not understanding the difference between paradigm, theory, model, technique, and action (Marley, 2004). The hierarchy is as follows:

Paradigm (most abstract): Overarching belief system about the way the world works.

↓

Theory: Set of explanatory and/or predictive propositions derived from the paradigm.

↓

Model: A set of concepts that translate the propositions derived from the theory into a guide for action for the therapist.

↓

Technique: An action or task the therapist can take that makes explicit one of the concepts within the model.

↓

Action (least abstract): The specific language or behavior utilized to make the technique explicit in the therapy setting.

Problems in family therapy research can become evident in a couple of different ways. First, each of these terms describes a different level of abstraction from the most abstract (*paradigm*) to the least (*action*). Yet when some researchers attempt to study family therapy, it is not clear which level of abstraction they are trying to understand within a model of family therapy or to compare between types of family therapy. In some cases, researchers use the terms *model* and *theory* interchangeably even though they address a different set of issues and exist at different levels of abstraction.

Second, many types of family therapy emerge from the same or similar paradigms or share similar theoretical constructs. Systems theory forms the basis for Bowenian family therapy, systemic family therapy, strategic family therapy, communications family therapy, the Milan version of strategic family therapy, and structural family therapy. It can be almost impossible to research the differences between these models of family therapy because they all share similar theoretical constructs. While these models overlap theoretically, they do differ in how they translate the theory and the kinds of techniques derived from them. Therefore, it would be possible to study these models at the level of technique and action and discern differences between them. Comparing structural family therapy and, for example, cognitive-behavioral family therapy is clearer since both have very divergent theoretical constructs that come from very different paradigms about how the world works.

Finally, while the arrows in the diagram flow downward from most abstract to least abstract, the reverse process can be very telling as it relates to the coherence of a proposed model of family therapy. A person should be able to take a specific technique, for example the use of a family genogram, and trace its connection upward to higher levels of abstraction. Does the action needed in therapy make sense given the technique proposed? Does the technique seem rationally derived from the model? And on up the diagram. Techniques or actions that seem unconnected to or not clearly derived from a model may undermine the coherence of the model and its theoretical constructs.

Clinicians who are reading family therapy research or contemplating conducting research on some aspect of family therapy need to be clear about (a) what level of abstraction is the focus of the research; (b) if comparing models of family therapy, whether there is sufficient differentiation between theoretical constructs such that the models can be clearly differentiated; and (c) if evaluating a specific model of family therapy, whether there is a clear connection between the actions and techniques being evaluated and the higher levels of abstraction that form the basis of the model. The ability to address these conceptual issues will help produce more useful and coherent research on family therapy models.

Methodological Issues

Sprenkle and Moon (1996) discussed that the field of family therapy research has undergone two distinct shifts in its brief history. First, the field primarily supported and advocated for more quantitative and experimental approaches to research. Several assumptions were behind this initial push in research. Quantitative research provided the new field of family therapy with some scientific credibility and helped it be seen as more legitimate within the practice arena. Also, quantitative studies forced some models of family therapy to take a closer look at some of their beliefs and theories as such concepts were often vaguely defined and not easily translated into the research process. In the process of translating them for the purposes of research, it became clear that some models were on conceptually shaky ground.

Following the push for scientific legitimacy through quantitative research, the field of family therapy shifted again "from a strict adherence to quantitative methods to incorporation and gradual acceptance of alternative methodologies, especially qualitative ones" (Sprenkle & Moon, 1996, p. 4). This second shift was in part supported by the growth of postmodern and constructivist theories and their influence on family therapy practice. These constructivist perspectives questioned the idea of an objective truth that could be identified and measured by quantitative methods. Studies by Beitin (2008); Deacon and Piercy (2000); Faulkner, Klock, and Gale (2002); Gehart, Ratliff, and Lyle (2001); and Piercy and Thomas (1998) demonstrated the importance of the qualitative perspective in the development of family therapy. As with many professions and clinical practices, family therapy research soon divided along two lines, those who supported quantitative methodologies and those who supported qualitative methodologies. The two "camps" that evolved from this split, while battling over preferred methodologies, never addressed the main point: Which model of family therapy is the most effective, and what components of family therapy make it as useful if not more useful in addressing issues facing many families?

The objectivist (quantitative) and constructivist (qualitative) methodologies emerge from different paradigms, and each has its own strengths and weaknesses in terms of the kinds of questions it can address and the kinds of findings it generates that can be translated into clinical practice guidelines. However, Sprenkle and Moon (1996) primarily advocate for a pluralistic approach to family therapy research, the appropriate use of both methodologies, that gives family therapy research its best opportunity to study and discern the strengths, utility, and limitations of family therapy models and techniques. Sometimes referred to in the literature as "mixed methodology" research, it can provide the researcher with a depth and breadth of study where each methodology supports the other.

Ethical Issues

Several ethical issues arise when contemplating family therapy research. While some of the ethical issues are common in any type of research, some are unique to the process of family therapy research.

Recruitment of Research Participants and Protection From Harm

How to get families involved in research and then how to protect them from harm during the research process are two fundamental ethical issues that must be addressed early on in the process (Israel & Hay, 2006). Many families may be desperate for help and will agree to anything in order to access services. Consequently, clinicians and researchers who are interested in conducting research on family therapy must inform and screen potential families for involvement in research. Triage, the concept of identifying families most in need of services based on the severity of their situation, can be important in this process. Families most in need of services may be good candidates for some research studies, especially if researching the effectiveness of an already developed intervention. However, if studying a new intervention with an as yet unknown level of effectiveness, families most in need may be inappropriate for such studies.

Families need to be carefully informed about the nature of the research study as part of the screening process. It is important for clinicians not to "oversell" the possible benefits of the study or to "underrepresent" the possible risks of the study. One way to protect families from the potential harms of the study is to make sure the family knows what those harms are and how they may be applicable to the family's specific situation. Harm can take the form of emotional stress, psychological discomfort, and embarrassment brought on by the nature of the questions asked or other methodologies used (e.g., videotapes of sessions that will be reviewed and coded by others). For family therapy research, it is also important to remember that different family members may have different levels of appreciation for the risks of the research or have different thresholds for emotional or psychological stress. What is tolerable for a parent may be intolerable for an adolescent. Family therapy research is unique in this sense in that it must take into account various perspectives of risks and benefits as experienced by each member of the family involved.

Informed Consent

The process and documentation of informed consent is critical in all ethical research processes (Israel & Hay, 2006). Informed consent provides the family with the necessary information about the study, what is expected of the family members and their participation, what they will specifically be asked to do to fulfill the needs of the research process, and how the information gathered through the methodologies used will be collected, stored, protected, and potentially disseminated. The informed consent process is the main way for a family to understand the possible risks and benefits of the research process and how the researchers plan to minimize or respond to any of the potential risks.

For family therapy research, the informed consent process has some unique features. First, who can consent for the research? In many families with children at different ages, the consent process must allow for each individual family member to consent in order for the research process to be approved and used. In families with very young children, parental consent may be sufficient. One question that arises, then, is what if only some members of the family agree and others do not?

The simple answer is that the research cannot happen. Given the increased use of mixed methodology, it may be the case that some family members consent to some parts of the research process (e.g., filling out forms) but don't consent to other parts of the research (e.g., videotaping of sessions). The researcher will need to be prepared for these variations and have a plan in place on how to respond to the differential perceptions of each family member and what needs to be consented to in order for the research to be carried out.

Confidentiality and Mandated Reporting

Much of family therapy research is based on the gathering of information about how families react to and respond to the problems they face. The research requires family members to be forthcoming about the kinds of activities that go on within the family, activities that may be embarrassing or distressing to the family that has sought out help. The family needs to know and understand that most clinical researchers are mandated reporters by law, that these professionals must report suspected instances of child abuse or elder abuse if the family discloses information about such possible abuse. The family members will need to reflect on what their issues are, what the research will ask of them, and how the information they reveal through the research process will be used. The researcher will need to have a protocol in place in order to respond appropriately to information that may indicate potential abuse and to inform families that such a breach of confidentiality will occur if indications of abuse are identified during the research process.

Families From Diverse Ethnic/Cultural Communities

Research ethics in the United States has its foundation in Western European cultural assumptions about consent, confidentiality, protection, and harm. As family therapy has reached out to culturally and ethnically diverse families both in the United States and abroad, it is clear that many of these research ethics assumptions do not match the assumptions held by these families (Trimble & Fisher, 2006). What defines a family? Who has the ability to consent to research? What are possible risks and benefits to the research process? Such fundamental questions can be answered in a myriad of ways when including diverse families in the research process. The researcher will need to understand the particular cultural and ethnic characteristics of diverse families and how the research process may need to be adjusted to support such families' unique perspectives and needs.

The conceptual, methodological, and ethical issues discussed above reflect the complexity of conducting research on families. However, even given these complexities, the use of research to better understand the process and outcome of family therapy interventions is very strong and more widespread. Utilizing mixed methods, meta-analyses, and in many cases sophisticated analytic tools, family therapy research has provided the practice of family therapy with a firm base from which to build. Through the research, some models show more support and utility than others, some techniques are more useful to more types of families than others, and many questions about the process and outcome of family therapy still remain unanswered.

FAMILY THERAPY PROCESS RESEARCH

Family therapy process research attempts to answer the basic question of what makes family therapy effective (Pinsof, 1981). What transpires in the provision of family therapy that actually helps families change or resolve their issues? This is a simple question but one that is actually very hard to answer. The studies discussed below have used both quantitative and qualitative approaches in trying to answer this important question.

Gurman, Kniskern, and Pinsof (1986), in reviewing the literature on family therapy process research, noted that to better understand the process of change in family therapy, researchers should focus on "chunks" of family therapy (several sessions) and the role of the therapeutic alliance. The authors also recommend using instruments that are designed specifically to document change across time during family therapy sessions. Such an instrument was developed by Friedlander et al. (2006). These authors reported on the development of the System for Observing Family Therapy Alliances (SOFTA). The instrument looks at two dimensions that are common across therapy modalities, emotional connection to the therapist and engagement in the therapeutic process. The SOFTA also has two additional dimensions that look at the unique issues of conjoint treatment, safety within the therapeutic system, and shared sense of purpose within the family. The psychometric properties of the SOFTA support its use in research studies focused on family therapy process.

Friedlander, Wildman, Heatherington, and Skowron (1994) examined the process of change in family therapy. They identified 36 studies dating from 1963 that could be examined for information about what is known about the change process. The authors identified three hierarchically ordered levels of in-session processes that promote change: speech acts, important incidents or change episodes, and lastly the therapeutic relationship.

Christensen, Russell, Miller, and Peterson (1998) used a qualitative investigation to identify key elements within family therapy that promoted change within couples therapy. The study identified three dimensions of change that played a role in the change process: affect, communication, and cognition. Further, the study identified five commonalities for change in the therapeutic relationship that promoted change: safety, fairness, normalization, hope, and pacing. The authors noted that the process of change in couples therapy is a gradual process.

Helmke and Sprenkle (2000) looked at the experience of pivotal moments in family therapy as a catalyst for change. The authors collected qualitative data before and after each therapy session, at the end of the therapy relationship, and approximately 2 weeks following the end of therapy. The clients interviewed identified key pivotal moments that occurred in the process of the therapy that they equated with change. The moments identified tended to be very individualized and not necessarily shared by the spouse or therapist. The pivotal moments were more likely to occur while discussing the presenting problem that brought the couple to therapy.

Photo 14.1   Research on the effectiveness of family therapy begins with a thorough assessment of the family using valid and reliable assessment tools

Source: ©iStockphoto.com/Alina555

The studies discussed above highlight some of the important trends in process research on family and marital therapy. Many of the studies focus on the importance of the therapeutic relationship and the degree of engagement in therapy experienced by the family or couple. More still remains to be known about the process of family therapy, those key steps or experiences that happen, sometimes by chance, that families feel are critical to their ability to change. More refined assessment tools and other types of research methodologies may help better identify these experiences and how different models can promote the process of change.

FAMILY THERAPY OUTCOME RESEARCH

Family therapy outcome research attempts to answer the question of how families fair after the provision of family therapy. Do some models of family therapy lead to better short-term and long-term outcomes? Do certain things need to happen in the family therapy, regardless of model, to ensure good short-term and long-term outcomes? These are important questions that often are complicated to answer.

Since the mid-1980s, there have been a number of meta-analyses and integrative reviews that looked at the published research studies on family therapy and tried to identify those models or elements that lead to good short-term and long-term outcomes. Hazelrigg, Cooper, and Borduin (1987) looked at a number of published studies and reviewed their effectiveness. After integrating the various types of statistical analyses present in the different studies, the authors concluded that family therapy had a positive impact when compared to both no treatment and alternative treatment conditions. The follow-up data showed that family therapy continued to have a positive effect on families over time, but the effects diminished over time.

Markus, Lange, and Petigrew (1990) followed up with a meta-analysis of previously published research studies. The authors examined 19 studies published between 1967 and 1987. The authors found that at the end of treatment, the patients who received family therapy were better off than 76% of the patients who received some alternative treatment, a minimal treatment, or no treatment. Their meta-analysis showed that the effects of family therapy were still pronounced 1 year after the end of treatment but began to diminish after 18 months. They concluded that more studies should be conducted that used longer-term follow-up to better assess long-term outcomes.

Piercy and Sprenkle (1990) also conducted a review of the published research literature to discern some of the outcome data. The authors focused primarily on systems-based family therapy models, specifically strategic and Milan systemic therapies. The authors found a lack of good control studies and general weaknesses in the methodology of many of the published research studies. As such, the authors cautioned drawing any conclusions from the published research until the research included more rigorous designs and analysis.

Shadish et al. (1993) conducted a meta-analysis of 163 trials of family therapy with a focus on family and marital therapies. The meta-analysis found that those patients who received family or marital therapy showed more improved outcomes than those patients in the control groups. The authors indicated that behavioral models were usually more effective in producing positive outcomes than systemic, humanistic, psychodynamic, or eclectic approaches.

Dunn and Scwebel (1995) focused on marital therapy in their meta-analysis of outcome research. They examined 15 studies they felt were rigorous in research design. The models examined in these studies included behavioral marital therapy, cognitive-behavioral marital therapy, and insight-oriented marital therapy. All three models were found to be more effective in creating change in the relationships when compared to control groups. The insight-oriented model was most effective in bringing change in spouses' general relationship assessment. The cognitive-behavioral model was most effective in showing significant change in the spouses' posttherapy relationship-related cognitions.

Several outcome studies have focused on specific family-based problems in their assessment of outcome data. Stanton and Shadish (1997) looked at family-couple treatment in treating drug abuse in their meta-analysis. The authors examined 15 published studies on drug abuse outcomes. They found evidence that family therapy was more effective when compared to individual counseling, peer group therapy, or family psycho-education. The authors proposed that family therapy may enhance and improve the overall effectiveness when used in conjunction with these other treatment modalities. Further, family therapy helped maintain high rates of engagement and retention in services when compared to the other treatment modalities.

Baucom, Mueser, Shoham, and Daiuto (1998) examined empirically supported family interventions for treatment of marital distress and adult mental health issues. The authors identified behavioral marital therapy and emotion-focused therapy as the most effective for treating marital distress. Insight-oriented marital therapy, cognitive-behavioral marital therapy, couples cognitive therapy, and couples systemic therapy were all identified as possibly effective. All of the models examined were more effective than control or wait list conditions.

Carr (2000) looked at systemic consultation in the treatment of child-based problems. Most of the studies examined by the author supported the use of cognitive-behavioral and psycho-educational approaches for the best outcomes when treating childhood problems such as abuse and neglect, conduct problems, emotional problems, and psychosomatic problems.

Photo 14.2   Alan Gurman helped advance the use of rigorous research methodology in the study of family therapy models

Source: © Alan S. Gurman

Most recently, Asen (2002) reviewed published family therapy studies focusing on systemic-based family therapy models. These models included structural, strategic, Milan, social constructivist, narrative, brief solution-focused, psycho-educational, and behavioral family/couples therapy. The author identified research studies that supported the use of such models in the treatment of adolescent anorexia nervosa, schizophrenia, and mood disorders.

The published outcome studies on family therapy provide a beginning to understanding the impact some models of family therapy have on families and the families' long-term progress. The studies discussed above show that some models of family therapy tend to have better outcomes than other models. As Gurman et al. (1986) pointed out, 66%–75% of cases improve with the use of family therapy. However, the studies in general show that providing family therapy, regardless of model, is better than providing no services or an alternative service. There is also some support for the idea that adding family therapy services to other services may boost the effectiveness of those other services. Clearly, there are still issues with the rigorousness of the methodology used in the studies that make up the published meta-analyses, and further outcome studies need to be conducted that follow families for longer periods of time. However, the outcome research to date clearly supports the use of family therapy in many settings and with many types of family issues.

FAMILY THERAPY ASSESSMENT TOOLS FOR RESEARCH

The ability to assess family therapy processes and outcomes often relies on reliable and valid assessment and evaluation tools. The development and refinement of standardized evaluation tools has been an important trend in family therapy research. While the SOFTA was discussed above, several other types of such tools exist and may be useful for those considering family therapy research.

The McMaster Family Assessment Device (Aksiter & Stevenson-Hinde, 1991) is a 60-item self-report questionnaire that collects information on seven dimensions of family functioning: problem solving, communication, roles, attractive responsiveness, affect involvement, behavior control, and general functioning. The assessment tool has been used with different populations and presenting problems. The authors support its use as an efficient and cost-effective screening tool to assess family functioning.

The Family Assessment Measure (FAM) was developed based on the process model of family functioning (Skinner, Steinhauer, & Sitarenios, 2000). The FAM collects data on seven dimensions across three family levels. The seven dimensions are task accomplishment, role performance, communication, affective expression, involvement, control, and values and norms. The three levels are the whole family, various dyadic relationships, and individual functioning. The FAM has been used in a variety of clinical and nonclinical settings, and its psychometric properties are very strong. Comments from clinicians who use the FAM indicate the measure provides a rich source of data on family functioning.

The North Carolina Family Assessment Scale (NCFAS) was designed to support family preservation services (Reed-Ashcraft, Kirk, & Fraser, 2001). The scale has been refined and contains 25 items that collect data on four dimensions: overall environment, overall child well-being, overall family interactions, and overall family safety. The psychometric properties support this as a valid instrument to use when assessing families along the stated dimensions.

These are just a handful of the various tools and scales available to clinicians and researchers who are interested in family therapy research. A number of measures also exist that focus on particular presenting problems (e.g., child behavior issues) or broader family concerns (e.g., adult mental illness). Such tools can be used for general clinical assessment and treatment planning as well as form the basis of a research study.

EVIDENCE-BASED PRACTICE AND FAMILY THERAPY

Over the past decade, the emphasis in the research literature has been on evidence-based practice (EBP). The focus on EBP has been to provide a source of information for clinicians and families to consider when selecting an appropriate intervention for the presenting problem. EBP tries to systematize and synthesize the research literature, identify those studies that show a particular intervention modality is valid and effective, and then make that model of

Photo 14.3   Research on the process of family therapy requires gathering good information about what actually transpires between the therapist and the family during therapy sessions

Source: ©iStockphoto.com/gary milner

intervention more widely known by the clinicians who can then implement the valid and effective intervention. EBP is one step or response to bridging the gap between the research area of family therapy and the practice arm (Pinsof & Wynne, 2000).

One of the issues that has arisen within the field of family therapy in response to EBP is the concern that EBP supports or privileges some models of family therapy over other models. While there is not 100% consensus within EBP advocates, the general sense is that the research studies that can support an intervention need to meet rigorous research standards. As it happens, some models of family therapy are more easily able to meet these criteria than other models. For instance, rigorous research requires a well-defined family therapy variable that can be well measured, and change in that variable can be well measured through the use of a well-defined intervention technique. One model of family therapy, cognitive-behavioral family therapy, based on its theoretical and conceptual basis, lends itself well to such clear definitions. Other models of family therapy, for instance Bowenian family therapy, may have a harder time meeting such rigorous standards for clear and measurable definitions. There is some validity to this concern. But in the process of responding to the demands of EBP, practitioners and advocates of many models of family therapy have revisited some of the underlying assumptions and concepts of their models and attempted to better define and refine these sometimes vague concepts. Such "updating" of any family therapy model is a welcome development and ensures the models do not become stagnant entities.

A number of studies in recent years have attempted to provide the kind of rigorous research to help move family therapy into the EBP arena. Studies by Barkley, Guevremont, Anastopoulos, and Fletcher (1992) and Henggeler, Meton, and Smith (1992) were early attempts to identify specific intervention strategies targeted to specific types of family issues and problems. More recently, studies by Cottrell and Boston (2002); Gaynor et al. (2003); Hogue, Dauber, Samuolis, and Liddle (2006); and Robbins et al. (2008) have furthered the presence and strength of family therapy in the EBP field.

Clearly, more research on specific family models, family types, and family issues needs to be done to better discern what it is about family therapy that makes it effective in creating both short-term change and long-term change as well as gains for families. However, in the last several decades, family therapy has come a long way from relying on compelling case studies to relying on rigorous research. Clinicians now have more data to consider when identifying possible courses of action to take with families when addressing their needs and concerns. Families, as well, have more information available to them to help them make informed decisions about the kinds of services they can advocate for to get their needs met.

SUMMARY

Family therapy research is a very active field of study. As the many studies cited above demonstrate, different research methodologies are utilized, different kinds of questions are being asked, and the fundamental utility of family therapy models and techniques is being carefully examined. While some models of family therapy have held up well under the scrutiny of research, others have not faired as well or have had to be refined to address weaknesses identified through research.

The future push for EBP and the stance family therapy practitioners take toward EBP will be critical in the coming years. There is nothing inherent in EBP that diminishes the role of the clinician in evaluating and engaging with families in the treatment planning process. Nor is there anything in EBP that prevents clinicians and families from utilizing any of the models of family therapy discussed in this text. The pressure may come from funding sources, third-party reimbursers who may see EBP as a means to contain costs. Such insurers could, for instance, reimburse only for family intervention models and techniques that meet the criteria for an EBP. This may leave some practitioners who prefer other models of family therapy in a difficult position.

RECOMMENDED READINGS

Israel, M., & Hay, I. (2006). *Research ethics for social scientists*. Thousand Oaks, CA: Sage.

Marley, J. (2004). *Family involvement in treating schizophrenia: Models, essential skills, and process*. New York, NY: Haworth Press.

Sales, B., & Folkman, S. (Eds.). (2000). *Ethics in research with human participants*. Washington, DC: American Psychological Association.

Sprenkle, D., & Moon, S. (Eds.). (1996). *Research methods in family therapy*. New York, NY: Guilford.

Trimble, J., & Fisher, C. (Eds.). (2006). *The handbook of ethical research with ethnocultural populations and communities*. Thousand Oaks, CA: Sage.

DISCUSSION QUESTIONS

1. Locate and read in depth one of the research studies cited in this chapter. Discuss some of the strengths and weaknesses of the research study, its methodology, and its report of findings. How might the findings of this specific research study inform your practice with families?

2. Select a model of family therapy discussed in this book. What are some of the key propositions, concepts, and techniques of this model? How would you go about trying to study the overall effectiveness of this model of family therapy? Discuss and support your research plan.

3. Identify some of the barriers that exist, if any, between the process of family therapy research and translating those findings into useable information for family therapy practitioners. What are some ways those barriers could be overcome?

REFERENCES

Aksiter, J., & Stevenson-Hinde, J. (1991). Identifying families at risk: Exploring the potential of the McMaster Family Assessment Device. *Journal of Family Therapy, 13*, 411–421.

Asen, E. (2002). Outcome research in family therapy. *Advances in Psychiatric Treatment, 8*, 230–238.

Barkley, R. A., Guevremont, D. C., Anastopoulos, A. D., & Fletcher, K. E. (1992). A comparison of three family therapy programs for treating family conflicts in adolescents with attention-deficit hyperactivity disorder. *Journal of Consulting and Clinical Psychology, 60*, 450–462.

Baucom, D., Mueser, K., Shoham, V., & Daiuto, A. (1998). Empirically supported couple and family interventions for marital distress and adult mental health problems. *Journal of Counseling and Clinical Psychology, 66*, 53–88.

Beitin, B. K. (2008). Qualitative research in marriage and family therapy: Who is in the interview? *Contemporary Family Therapy, 30*, 48–58.

Carr, A. (2000). Evidence-based practice in family therapy and systemic consultation: I. Child-focused problems. *Journal of Family Therapy, 22*, 29–60.

Christensen, L. I., Russell, C. S., Miller, R. B., & Peterson, C. M. (1998). The process of change in couples therapy: A qualitative investigation. *Journal of Marital and Family Therapy, 24*, 177–188.

Cottrell, D., & Boston, P. (2002). Practitioner review: The effectiveness of systemic therapy for children and adolescents. *Journal of Child Psychology and Psychiatry, 43*, 573–586.

Deacon, S., & Piercy, F. (2000). Qualitative evaluation of family therapy programs: A participatory approach. *Journal of Marital and Family Therapy, 26*, 39–45.

Dunn, R. L., & Scwebel, A. I. (1995). Meta-analytic review of marital therapy outcome research. *Journal of Family Psychology, 9*, 58–68.

Faulkner, R. A., Klock, K., & Gale, J. E. (2002). Qualitative research trends in family therapy: Publication trends from 1980–1999. *Journal of Marital and Family Therapy, 28*, 69–74.

Friedlander, M. L., Esudero, V., Horvath, A. O., Heatherington, L., Cabero, A., Martens, M. P. (2006). System of observing family therapy alliances: a tool for research and practice. *Journal of Counseling Psychology, 53*, 214–224.

Friedlander, M. L., Wildman, J., Heatherington, L., & Skowron, E. A. (1994). What we do and don't know about the process of family therapy. *Journal of Family Psychology, 8*, 390–416.

Gaynor, S. C., Weersing, V. R., Kolko, D. J., Birmaher, B., Heo, J., & Brent, D. (2003). The prevalence and impact of large sudden improvements during adolescent therapy for depression: A comparison across cognitive-behavioral, family, and supportive therapy. *Journal of Consulting and Clinical Psychology, 71*, 386–393.

Gehart, D. R., Ratliff, D. A., & Lyle, R. R. (2001). Qualitative research in family therapy: A substantive and methodological review. *Journal of Marital and Family Therapy, 27*, 261–274.

Gurman, A., Kniskern, D., & Pinsof, W. (1986). Research on the process and outcome of marital and family therapy. In S. Garfield & A. Bergin (Eds.), *Handbook of psychotherapy and behavior change* (pp. 565–624). New York, NY: Wiley.

Hazelrigg, M. D., Cooper, H. M., & Borduin, C. M. (1987). Evaluating the effectiveness of family therapies: An integrative review and analysis. *Psychological Bulletin, 101*, 428–442.

Helmke, K. B., & Sprenkle, D. H. (2000). Clients perceptions of pivotal moments in couples therapy: A qualitative study of change in therapy. *Journal of Marital and Family Therapy, 26*, 469–483.

Henggeler, S. W., Meton, G. B., & Smith, L. A. (1992). Family preservation using multisystemic therapy: An effective alternative to incarcerating serious juvenile offenders. *Journal of Consulting and Clinical Psychology, 60*, 953–961.

Hogue, A., Dauber, S., Samuolis, J., & Liddle, H. (2006). Treatment techniques and outcomes in Multidimensional Family Therapy for adolescent behavior problems. *Journal of Family Psychology, 20*, 535–543.

Israel, M., & Hay, I. (2006). Research ethics for social scientists. Thousand Oaks, CA: Sage.

Markus, E., Lange, A., & Petigrew, T. F. (1990). Effectiveness of family therapy: A meta-analysis. *Journal of Family Therapy, 12*, 205–221.

Marley, J. (2004). *Family involvement in treating schizophrenia: Models, essential skills, and process.* New York, NY: Haworth Press.

Piercy, F., & Sprenkle, D. (1990). Marriage and family therapy: A decade review. *Journal of Marriage and the Family, 52*, 1116–1126.

Piercy, F. P., & Thomas, V. (1998). Participatory evaluation research: An introduction for family therapists. *Journal of Marital and Family Therapy, 24*(2), 165–176.

Pinsof, W. (1981). Family therapy process research. In A. Gurman & D. Kniskern (Eds.), *Handbook of family therapy* (pp. 699–741). New York, NY: Brunner/Mazel.

Pinsof, W. M., & Wynne, L. C. (2000). Toward progress research: Closing the gap between family therapy practice and research. *Journal of Marital and Family Therapy, 26*, 1–8.

Reed-Ashcraft, K., Kirk, R., & Fraser, M. (2001). The reliability and validity of the North Carolina family assessment measure. *Research on Social Work Practice, 11*, 503–520.

Robbins, M. S., Szapocznik, J., Turner, C. W., Dillon, F., Mitrani, V. B., & Feaster, D. J. (2008). The efficacy of structural ecosystems therapy with drug-abusing, dependent African-American and Hispanic American adolescents. *Journal of Family Psychology, 22*, 51–61.

Shadish, W. R., Montgomery, L. M., Wilson, P., Wilson, M. R., Bright, I., & Okwumabua, T. (1993). Effects of family and marital psychotherapies: A meta-analysis. *Journal of Consulting and Clinical Psychology, 61*, 992–1002.

Skinner, H., Steinhauer, P., & Sitarenios, G. (2000). Family assessment measure (FAM) and process model of family functioning. *Journal of Family Therapy, 22*, 190–210.

Sprenkle, D., & Moon, S. (Eds.). (1996). *Research methods in family therapy*. New York, NY: Guilford.

Stanton, M., & Shadish, W. (1997). Outcome, attrition, and family-couples treatment for drug abuse: A meta-analysis and review controlled, comparative studies. *Psychological Bulletin, 122*, 170–191.

Trimble, J., & Fisher, C. (Eds.). (2006). *The handbook of ethical research with ethnocultural populations and communities*. Thousand Oaks, CA: Sage.

Turner, W. L., Wieling, E., & Allen, W. D. (2004, July). Developing culturally effective family-based research programs: Implications for family therapists. *Journal of Marital and Family Therapy*, 257–270.

AAMFT CODE OF ETHICS

AAMFT Code of Ethics

PREAMBLE

The Board of Directors of the American Association for Marriage and Family Therapy (AAMFT) hereby promulgates, pursuant to Article 2, Section 2.013 of the Association's Bylaws, the Revised AAMFT Code of Ethics, effective July 1, 2001.

The AAMFT strives to honor the public trust in marriage and family therapists by setting standards for ethical practice as described in this Code. The ethical standards define professional expectations and are enforced by the AAMFT Ethics Committee. The absence of an explicit reference to a specific behavior or situation in the Code does not mean that the behavior is ethical or unethical. The standards are not exhaustive. Marriage and family therapists who are uncertain about the ethics of a particular course of action are encouraged to seek counsel from consultants, attorneys, supervisors, colleagues, or other appropriate authorities.

Both law and ethics govern the practice of marriage and family therapy. When making decisions regarding professional behavior, marriage and family therapists must consider the AAMFT Code of Ethics and applicable laws and regulations. If the AAMFT Code of Ethics prescribes a standard higher than that required by law, marriage and family therapists must meet the higher standard of the AAMFT Code of Ethics. Marriage and family therapists comply with the mandates of law, but make known their commitment to the AAMFT Code of Ethics and take steps to resolve the conflict in a responsible manner. The AAMFT supports legal mandates for reporting of alleged unethical conduct.

The AAMFT Code of Ethics is binding on Members of AAMFT in all membership categories, AAMFT-Approved Supervisors, and applicants for membership and the Approved Supervisor designation (hereafter, AAMFT Member). AAMFT Members have an obligation to be familiar with the AAMFT Code of

Ethics and its application to their professional services. Lack of awareness or misunderstanding of an ethical standard is not a defense to a charge of unethical conduct.

The process for filing, investigating, and resolving complaints of unethical conduct is described in the current Procedures for Handling Ethical Matters of the AAMFT Ethics Committee. Persons accused are considered innocent by the Ethics Committee until proven guilty, except as otherwise provided, and are entitled to due process. If an AAMFT Member resigns in anticipation of, or during the course of, an ethics investigation, the Ethics Committee will complete its investigation. Any publication of action taken by the Association will include the fact that the Member attempted to resign during the investigation.

Contents

1. Responsibility to clients

2. Confidentiality

3. Professional competence and integrity

4. Responsibility to students and supervisees

5. Responsibility to research participants

6. Responsibility to the profession

7. Financial arrangements

8. Advertising

PRINCIPLE I

RESPONSIBILITY TO CLIENTS

Marriage and family therapists advance the welfare of families and individuals. They respect the rights of those persons seeking their assistance, and make reasonable efforts to ensure that their services are used appropriately.

1.1 Marriage and family therapists provide professional assistance to persons without discrimination on the basis of race, age, ethnicity, socioeconomic status, disability, gender, health status, religion, national origin, or sexual orientation.

1.2 Marriage and family therapists obtain appropriate informed consent to therapy or related procedures as early as feasible in the therapeutic relationship, and use language that is reasonably understandable to clients. The content of informed consent may vary depending upon the client and treatment plan; however, informed consent generally necessitates that the client: (a) has the capacity to consent; (b) has been adequately informed of significant information concerning treatment processes and procedures; (c) has been adequately informed of potential risks and benefits of treatments for which generally recognized standards do not yet exist; (d) has freely and without undue influence expressed consent; and (e) has provided consent that is appropriately documented. When persons, due to age or mental status, are legally incapable of giving informed consent, marriage and family therapists obtain informed permission from a legally authorized person, if such substitute consent is legally permissible.

1.3 Marriage and family therapists are aware of their influential positions with respect to clients, and they avoid exploiting the trust and dependency of such persons. Therapists, therefore, make every effort to avoid conditions and multiple relationships with clients that could impair professional judgment or increase the risk of exploitation. Such relationships include, but are not limited to, business or close personal relationships with a client or the client's immediate family. When the risk of impairment or exploitation exists due to conditions or multiple roles, therapists take appropriate precautions.

1.4 Sexual intimacy with clients is prohibited.

1.5 Sexual intimacy with former clients is likely to be harmful and is therefore prohibited for two years following the termination of therapy or last professional contact. In an effort to avoid exploiting the trust and dependency of clients, marriage and family therapists should not engage in sexual intimacy with former clients after the two years following termination or last professional contact. Should therapists engage in sexual intimacy with former clients following two years after termination or last professional contact, the burden shifts to the therapist to demonstrate that there has been no exploitation or injury to the former client or to the client's immediate family.

1.6 Marriage and family therapists comply with applicable laws regarding the reporting of alleged unethical conduct.

1.7 Marriage and family therapists do not use their professional relationships with clients to further their own interests.

1.8 Marriage and family therapists respect the rights of clients to make decisions and help them to understand the consequences of these decisions. Therapists clearly advise the clients that they have the responsibility to make decisions regarding relationships such as cohabitation, marriage, divorce, separation, reconciliation, custody, and visitation.

1.9 Marriage and family therapists continue therapeutic relationships only so long as it is reasonably clear that clients are benefiting from the relationship.

1.10 Marriage and family therapists assist persons in obtaining other therapeutic services if the therapist is unable or unwilling, for appropriate reasons, to provide professional help.

1.11 Marriage and family therapists do not abandon or neglect clients in treatment without making reasonable arrangements for the continuation of such treatment.

1.12 Marriage and family therapists obtain written informed consent from clients before videotaping, audio recording, or permitting third-party observation.

1.13 Marriage and family therapists, upon agreeing to provide services to a person or entity at the request of a third party, clarify, to the extent feasible and at the outset of the service, the nature of the relationship with each party and the limits of confidentiality.

PRINCIPLE II

CONFIDENTIALITY

Marriage and family therapists have unique confidentiality concerns because the client in a therapeutic relationship may be more than one person. Therapists respect and guard the confidences of each individual client.

2.1 Marriage and family therapists disclose to clients and other interested parties, as early as feasible in their professional contacts, the nature of confidentiality and possible limitations of the clients' right to confidentiality. Therapists review with clients the circumstances where confidential information may be requested and where disclosure of confidential information may be legally required. Circumstances may necessitate repeated disclosures.

2.2 Marriage and family therapists do not disclose client confidences except by written authorization or waiver, or where mandated or permitted by law. Verbal authorization will not be sufficient except in emergency situations, unless prohibited by law. When providing couple, family, or group treatment, the therapist does not disclose information outside the treatment context without a written authorization from each individual competent to execute a waiver. In the context of couple, family or group treatment, the therapist may not reveal any individual's confidences to others in the client unit without the prior written permission of that individual.

2.3 Marriage and family therapists use client and/or clinical materials in teaching, writing, consulting, research, and public presentations only if a written waiver has been obtained in accordance with Subprinciple 2.2, or when appropriate steps have been taken to protect client identity and confidentiality.

2.4 Marriage and family therapists store, safeguard, and dispose of client records in ways that maintain confidentiality and in accord with applicable laws and professional standards.

2.5 Subsequent to the therapist moving from the area, [subsequent to the therapist] closing the practice, or upon the death of the therapist, a marriage and family therapist arranges for the storage, transfer, or disposal of client records in ways that maintain confidentiality and safeguard the welfare of clients.

2.6 Marriage and family therapists, when consulting with colleagues or referral sources, do not share confidential information that could reasonably lead to the identification of a client, research participant, supervisee, or other person with whom they have a confidential relationship unless they have obtained the prior written consent of the client, research participant, supervisee, or other person with whom they have a confidential relationship. Information may be shared only to the extent necessary to achieve the purposes of the consultation.

PRINCIPLE III

PROFESSIONAL COMPETENCE AND INTEGRITY

Marriage and family therapists maintain high standards of professional competence and integrity.

3.1 Marriage and family therapists pursue knowledge of new developments and maintain competence in marriage and family therapy through education, training, or supervised experience.

3.2 Marriage and family therapists maintain adequate knowledge of and adhere to applicable laws, ethics, and professional standards.

3.3 Marriage and family therapists seek appropriate professional assistance for their personal problems or conflicts that may impair work performance or clinical judgment.

3.4 Marriage and family therapists do not provide services that create a conflict of interest that may impair work performance or clinical judgment.

3.5 Marriage and family therapists, as presenters, teachers, supervisors, consultants and researchers, are dedicated to high standards of scholarship, present accurate information, and disclose potential conflicts of interest.

3.6 Marriage and family therapists maintain accurate and adequate clinical and financial records.

3.7 While developing new skills in specialty areas, marriage and family therapists take steps to ensure the competence of their work and to protect clients from possible harm. Marriage and family therapists practice in specialty areas new to them only after appropriate education, training, or supervised experience.

3.8 Marriage and family therapists do not engage in sexual or other forms of harassment of clients, students, trainees, supervisees, employees, colleagues, or research subjects.

3.9 Marriage and family therapists do not engage in the exploitation of clients, students, trainees, supervisees, employees, colleagues, or research subjects.

3.10 Marriage and family therapists do not give to or receive from clients (a) gifts of substantial value or (b) gifts that impair the integrity or efficacy of the therapeutic relationship.

3.11 Marriage and family therapists do not diagnose, treat, or advise on problems outside the recognized boundaries of their competencies.

3.12 Marriage and family therapists make efforts to prevent the distortion or misuse of their clinical and research findings.

3.13 Marriage and family therapists, because of their ability to influence and alter the lives of others, exercise special care when making public their professional recommendations and opinions through testimony or other public statements.

3.14 To avoid a conflict of interests, marriage and family therapists who treat minors or adults involved in custody or visitation actions may not also perform forensic evaluations for custody, residence, or visitation of the minor. The marriage and family therapist who treats the minor may provide the court or mental health professional performing the evaluation with information about the minor from the marriage and family therapist's perspective as a treating marriage and family therapist, so long as the marriage and family therapist does not violate confidentiality.

3.15 Marriage and family therapists are in violation of this Code and subject to termination of membership or other appropriate action if they: (a) are convicted of any felony; (b) are convicted of a misdemeanor related to their qualifications or functions; (c) engage in conduct which could lead to conviction of a felony, or a misdemeanor related to their qualifications or functions; (d) are expelled from or disciplined by other professional organizations; (e) have their licenses or certificates suspended or revoked or are otherwise disciplined by regulatory bodies; (f) continue to practice marriage and family therapy while no longer competent to do so because they are impaired by physical or mental causes or the abuse of alcohol or other substances; or (g) fail to cooperate with the Association at any point from the inception of an ethical complaint through the completion of all proceedings regarding that complaint.

PRINCIPLE IV

RESPONSIBILITY TO STUDENTS AND SUPERVISEES

Marriage and family therapists do not exploit the trust and dependency of students and supervisees.

4.1 Marriage and family therapists are aware of their influential positions with respect to students and supervisees, and they avoid exploiting the trust and dependency of such persons. Therapists, therefore, make every effort to avoid conditions and multiple relationships that could impair professional objectivity or increase the risk of exploitation. When the risk of impairment or exploitation exists due to conditions or multiple roles, therapists take appropriate precautions.

4.2 Marriage and family therapists do not provide therapy to current students or supervisees.

4.3 Marriage and family therapists do not engage in sexual intimacy with students or supervisees during the evaluative or training relationship between the therapist and student or supervisee. Should a supervisor engage in sexual activity with a former supervisee, the burden of proof shifts to the supervisor to demonstrate that there has been no exploitation or injury to the supervisee.

4.4 Marriage and family therapists do not permit students or supervisees to perform or to hold themselves out as competent to perform professional services beyond their training, level of experience, and competence.

4.5 Marriage and family therapists take reasonable measures to ensure that services provided by supervisees are professional.

4.6 Marriage and family therapists avoid accepting as supervisees or students those individuals with whom a prior or existing relationship could compromise the therapist's objectivity. When such situations cannot be avoided, therapists take appropriate precautions to maintain objectivity. Examples of such relationships include, but are not limited to, those individuals with whom the therapist has a current or prior sexual, close personal, immediate familial, or therapeutic relationship.

4.7 Marriage and family therapists do not disclose supervisee confidences except by written authorization or waiver, or when mandated or permitted by law. In educational or training settings where there are multiple supervisors, disclosures are permitted only to other professional colleagues, administrators, or employers who share responsibility for training of the supervisee. Verbal authorization will not be sufficient except in emergency situations, unless prohibited by law.

PRINCIPLE V

RESPONSIBILITY TO RESEARCH PARTICIPANTS

Investigators respect the dignity and protect the welfare of research participants, and are aware of applicable laws and regulations and professional standards governing the conduct of research.

5.1 Investigators are responsible for making careful examinations of ethical acceptability in planning studies. To the extent that services to research participants may be compromised by participation in research, investigators seek the ethical advice of qualified professionals not directly involved in the investigation and observe safeguards to protect the rights of research participants.

5.2 Investigators requesting participant involvement in research inform participants of the aspects of the research that might reasonably be expected to influence willingness to participate. Investigators are especially sensitive to the possibility of diminished consent when participants are also receiving clinical services, or have impairments which limit understanding and/or communication, or when participants are children.

5.3 Investigators respect each participant's freedom to decline participation in or to withdraw from a research study at any time. This obligation requires special thought and consideration when investigators or other members of the research team are in positions of authority or influence over participants. Marriage and family therapists, therefore, make every effort to avoid multiple relationships with research participants that could impair professional judgment or increase the risk of exploitation.

5.4 Information obtained about a research participant during the course of an investigation is confidential unless there is a waiver previously obtained in writing. When the possibility exists that others, including family members, may obtain access to such information, this possibility, together with the plan for protecting confidentiality, is explained as part of the procedure for obtaining informed consent.

PRINCIPLE VI

RESPONSIBILITY TO THE PROFESSION

Marriage and family therapists respect the rights and responsibilities of professional colleagues and participate in activities that advance the goals of the profession.

6.1 Marriage and family therapists remain accountable to the standards of the profession when acting as members or employees of organizations. If the mandates of an organization with which a marriage and family therapist is affiliated, through employment, contract or otherwise, conflict with the AAMFT Code of Ethics, marriage and family therapists make known to the organization their commitment to the AAMFT Code of Ethics and attempt to resolve the conflict in a way that allows the fullest adherence to the Code of Ethics.

6.2 Marriage and family therapists assign publication credit to those who have contributed to a publication in proportion to their contributions and in accordance with customary professional publication practices.

6.3 Marriage and family therapists do not accept or require authorship credit for a publication based on research from a student's program, unless the therapist made a substantial contribution beyond being a faculty advisor or research committee member. Coauthorship on a student thesis, dissertation, or project should be determined in accordance with principles of fairness and justice.

6.4 Marriage and family therapists who are the authors of books or other materials that are published or distributed do not plagiarize or fail to cite persons to whom credit for original ideas or work is due.

6.5 Marriage and family therapists who are the authors of books or other materials published or distributed by an organization take reasonable precautions to ensure that the organization promotes and advertises the materials accurately and factually.

6.6 Marriage and family therapists participate in activities that contribute to a better community and society, including devoting a portion of their professional activity to services for which there is little or no financial return.

6.7 Marriage and family therapists are concerned with developing laws and regulations pertaining to marriage and family therapy that serve the public interest, and with altering such laws and regulations that are not in the public interest.

6.8 Marriage and family therapists encourage public participation in the design and delivery of professional services and in the regulation of practitioners.

PRINCIPLE VII

FINANCIAL ARRANGEMENTS

Marriage and family therapists make financial arrangements with clients, third-party payors, and supervisees that are reasonably understandable and conform to accepted professional practices.

7.1 Marriage and family therapists do not offer or accept kickbacks, rebates, bonuses, or other remuneration for referrals; fee-for-service arrangements are not prohibited.

7.2 Prior to entering into the therapeutic or supervisory relationship, marriage and family therapists clearly disclose and explain to clients and supervisees: (a) all financial arrangements and fees related to professional services, including charges for canceled or missed appointments; (b) the use of collection agencies or legal measures for nonpayment; and (c) the procedure for obtaining payment from the client, to the extent allowed by law, if payment is denied by the third-party payor. Once services have begun, therapists provide reasonable notice of any changes in fees or other charges.

7.3 Marriage and family therapists give reasonable notice to clients with unpaid balances of their intent to seek collection by agency or legal recourse. When such action is taken, therapists will not disclose clinical information.

7.4 Marriage and family therapists represent facts truthfully to clients, third-party payors, and supervisees regarding services rendered.

7.5 Marriage and family therapists ordinarily refrain from accepting goods and services from clients in return for services rendered. Bartering for professional services may be conducted only if: (a) the supervisee or client requests it, (b) the relationship is not exploitative, (c) the professional relationship is not distorted, and (d) a clear written contract is established.

7.6 Marriage and family therapists may not withhold records under their immediate control that are requested and needed for a client's treatment solely because payment has not been received for past services, except as otherwise provided by law.

PRINCIPLE VIII

ADVERTISING

Marriage and family therapists engage in appropriate informational activities, including those that enable the public, referral sources, or others to choose professional services on an informed basis.

8.1 Marriage and family therapists accurately represent their competencies, education, training, and experience relevant to their practice of marriage and family therapy.

8.2 Marriage and family therapists ensure that advertisements and publications in any media (such as directories, announcements, business cards, newspapers, radio, television, Internet, and facsimiles) convey information that is necessary for the public to make an appropriate selection of professional services. Information could include: (a) office information, such as name, address, telephone number, credit card acceptability, fees, languages spoken, and office hours; (b) qualifying clinical degree (see Subprinciple 8.5); (c) other earned degrees (see Subprinciple 8.5) and state or provincial licensures and/or certifications; (d) AAMFT clinical member status; and (e) description of practice.

8.3 Marriage and family therapists do not use names that could mislead the public concerning the identity, responsibility, source, and status of those practicing under that name, and do not hold themselves out as being partners or associates of a firm if they are not.

8.4 Marriage and family therapists do not use any professional identification (such as a business card, office sign, letterhead, Internet, or telephone or association directory listing) if it includes a statement or claim that is false, fraudulent, misleading, or deceptive.

8.5 In representing their educational qualifications, marriage and family therapists list and claim as evidence only those earned degrees: (a) from institutions accredited by regional accreditation sources recognized by the United States Department of Education, (b) from institutions recognized by states or provinces that license or certify marriage and family therapists, or (c) from equivalent foreign institutions.

8.6 Marriage and family therapists correct, wherever possible, false, misleading, or inaccurate information and representations made by others concerning the therapist's qualifications, services, or products.

8.7 Marriage and family therapists make certain that the qualifications of their employees or supervisees are represented in a manner that is not false, misleading, or deceptive.

8.8 Marriage and family therapists do not represent themselves as providing specialized services unless they have the appropriate education, training, or supervised experience.

This Code is published by:

American Association for Marriage and Family Therapy
112 South Alfred Street
Alexandria, VA 22314
Phone: (703) 838-9808
Fax: (703) 838-9805
www.aamft.org

Violations of this Code should be brought in writing to the attention of:

AAMFT Ethics Committee
112 South Alfred Street
Alexandria, VA 22314
Phone: (703) 838-9808
Fax: (703) 838-9805
e-mail: ethics@aamft.org

INDEX

ABOUT THE AUTHORS

Janice M. Rasheed is a professor of social work and the director of the Institute for Innovations in Practice, Research, and Training at Loyola University Chicago's School of Social Work. Dr. Rasheed received her master's degree in social work from the University of Michigan at Ann Arbor and her doctorate in social welfare from Columbia University in New York. She was the coprincipal investigator for a multiyear research grant funded by the John D. and Catherine T. MacArthur Foundation. She has published articles in many professional journals and is the author of chapters in books dealing with the subjects of research, program planning, African American family life, and family therapy. Dr. Rasheed published an entry on "Family Practice Interventions" in the *Encyclopedia of Social Work* (National Association of Social Workers, Oxford University Press, 2008). She is the coauthor of two books: *Social Work Practice with African American Men: The Invisible Presence* (Sage, 1999) and *Family Therapy with Ethnic Minorities* (Sage, 2004). She has taught courses in family and couples therapy, courses in cross-cultural practice, and research courses in the undergraduate, master's, and doctoral programs. Dr. Rasheed also conducts workshops and training in these areas of clinical practice. She is a licensed clinical social worker in Illinois and has maintained a private practice since 1979, specializing in couples and family therapy. She has served as an "Approved Supervisor" (in training) at the Northwestern University Family Institute.

Mikal N. Rasheed is an associate professor and the director of the graduate social work program at Chicago State University. He received his master's degree in social work from the University of Chicago School of Social Service Administration and his doctorate from Loyola University Chicago's School of Social Work. He has published in the area of aging, as well as an entry on "Family Practice Interventions" in the *Encyclopedia of Social Work* (National Association of Social

Workers, Oxford University Press, 2008). He is the coauthor of two books: *Social Work Practice with African American Men: The Invisible Presence* (Sage, 1999) and *Family Therapy with Ethnic Minorities* (Sage, 2004). He has taught courses on men's issues in social work practice, cross-cultural practice, family and couples therapy, and ethics in both graduate and undergraduate programs. Dr. Rasheed conducts workshops and training in the area of diversity and ethics. He is a licensed clinical social worker in Illinois and has maintained a private practice in which he specializes in men's issues, practice with people of color, and couples and family therapy.

James A. Marley is the associate dean, an associate professor, and the director of the PhD program at Loyola University Chicago's School of Social Work. He received his bachelor's degree in social work from the University of Illinois at Urbana-Champaign and his master's degree in social work and his doctorate from the University of Illinois at Chicago. He teaches courses on research ethics, professional ethics, and practice with people with serious mental illness. His research and writing focus on family therapy with people with severe mental illness, social work ethics, research ethics, the intersection of ethics with social work practice with people with severe mental illness, and the social-environmental influences on people with severe mental illness. He is the author of several articles related to his work with people with severe mental illness and a book on family therapy in the treatment of schizophrenia. He is currently editing a book on social work ethics and coauthoring a book on social work practice with people with severe mental illness. Dr. Marley serves on the editorial board of *Clinical Social Work Journal* and is a Fellow of the American Orthopsychiatric Association, a member of the Commission on Global Social Work Education for the Council on Social Work Education, and the monitor for the National Association of Social Workers Illinois Chapter Committee on Ethics. He frequently serves as an expert witness for the Illinois Department of Professional Regulation, the Illinois Attorney General's Office, and private attorneys on cases related to social work ethics, social work malpractice and incompetence, assessment and diagnosis of mental health disorders, and wrongful death allegations.